Organizational Behavior

Third Edition

Chris Neck dedicates this book to his wife, Jennifer, and his children, Bryton and GiGe, for helping him realize what is truly important in life.

Jeff Houghton dedicates this book to his wife, Loree, and sons, Pierce and Sloan, and thanks them for all their support, encouragement, and love.

Emma Murray dedicates this book to her husband Sam, and daughters, Ava and Anya.

Sara Miller McCune founded SAGE Publishing in 1965 to support the dissemination of usable knowledge and educate a global community. SAGE publishes more than 1000 journals and over 800 new books each year, spanning a wide range of subject areas. Our growing selection of library products includes archives, data, case studies and video. SAGE remains majority owned by our founder and after her lifetime will become owned by a charitable trust that secures the company's continued independence.

Los Angeles | London | New Delhi | Singapore | Washington DC | Melbourne

Organizational Behavior

A Skill-Building Approach

Third Edition

Christopher P. Neck
Arizona State University

Jeffery D. Houghton
West Virginia University

Emma L. Murray

SAGE

Los Angeles | London | New Delhi
Singapore | Washington DC | Melbourne

SAGE

FOR INFORMATION:

SAGE Publications, Inc.
2455 Teller Road
Thousand Oaks, California 91320
E-mail: order@sagepub.com

SAGE Publications Ltd.
1 Oliver's Yard
55 City Road
London EC1Y 1SP
United Kingdom

SAGE Publications India Pvt. Ltd.
Unit No. 323-333, Third Floor, F-Block
International Trade Tower
Nehru Place, New Delhi 110 019
India

SAGE Publications Asia-Pacific Pte. Ltd
18 Cross Street #10-10/11/12
China Square Central
Singapore 048423

ISBN 978-1-0719-1582-0

This book is printed on acid-free paper.

23 24 25 26 27 10 9 8 7 6 5 4 3 2 1

Acquisitions Editor: Lauren Gobell

Content Development Editor: Cassie Carey

Production Editor: Rebecca Lee

Copy Editor: Rachel Keith

Typesetter: diacriTech

Cover Designer: Candice Harman

Product Marketer: Jennifer Haldeman

BRIEF CONTENTS

DETAILED CONTENTS

PREFACE

Nikos Kazantzakis once wrote:

> Ideal teachers are those who use themselves as bridges over which they invite their students to cross; then having facilitated their crossing, joyfully collapse, encouraging them to create bridges of their own.

Our goal as an author team was to write an organizational behavior (OB) textbook that really engaged students—not one that involved memorizing its content for the sole purpose of passing exams and then quickly forgetting whatever they had learned. We wanted to write a textbook that students could use well after the semester was over to help them actively learn and think critically in order to understand how people behave as they pursue their career goals. In other words, we wanted to help students "build bridges" to their goals and dreams. We hope we have achieved our goal in *Organizational Behavior: A Skill-Building Approach* 3e for students in organizational behavior classes across the world.

In our 21st-century business world, organizational behavior has taken on a new significance. In a business world characterized by fierce competition as well as vast changes due to the COVID-19 pandemic, it is people who act as differentiators in the workplace. In every aspect of business, people are the cornerstone of success. This is why it is so important to understand human behavior.

The following quote from Curt Coffman and Gabriela Gonzalez-Molina in *Follow This Path: How the World's Greatest Organizations Drive Growth by Unleashing Human Potential* (2002) reinforces the importance of understanding human behavior in organizations:

> The success of your organization doesn't depend on your understanding of economics, or organizational development, or marketing. It depends, quite simply, on your understanding of human psychology: how each individual employee connects with your company and how each individual employee connects with your customers. (xii)

One of the earliest studies of organizational behavior was carried out at AT&T's Western Electric Hawthorne plant by Harvard's Elton Mayo in 1927. The principal findings of this study showed that when workers are given the opportunity to contribute their thinking and learning to workplace issues, their job performance improves. This finding is still relevant today. Studies in organizational behavior add to our understanding of the individuals working within all types of businesses, from corporate to entrepreneurial. *Organizational Behavior: A Skill-Building Approach* attempts to capture the body of knowledge that encompasses the organizational behavioral research into a book that is fun to read, captures the reader's attention, and imparts the organizational behavioral knowledge in a way that promotes critical thinking.

OUR VISION

Organizational Behavior: A Skill-Building Approach is a textbook for college-level undergraduate students seeking insight into individual behavior, group behavior, organizational structure, and organizational processes through the lens of critical thinking.

Organizational behavior courses are defined by the following trends: larger course sizes, the need for continually changing content to stay relevant, and instructors working to make vast online resources meaningful to the student experience. The cumulative effect of these trends on instructors is a much more demanding environment for teaching and learning. In a quickly changing business environment, many books need a complete rewrite to be fully up to date. Even better, though, this is a new book—written from today's perspective, with an eye to the near future. Our goal in writing this book is to bring to the classroom a fresh view of human behavior in organizations.

What Makes Our Book Unique

Skill-building approach. Students are provided with opportunities to develop motivational, leadership, and teamwork skills that will help them to analyze behavioral patterns and take appropriate actions to help shape and influence those behaviors in positive ways. Supporting students in building and developing the skills and abilities that will allow them to make decisions and take actions that result in expected and desirable behaviors and related outcomes is the primary objective of our textbook.

Practical applications, self-assessments, experiential exercises, and additional pedagogical features make OB come to life and encourage students to engage with OB concepts in meaningful ways.

A Skill-Building Approach

We believe that in today's business world, organizational behavior is more important than ever. Companies are looking for employees and managers who have strong organizational behavior skills. Leadership, teamwork, motivational capabilities, decision-making, communication, ethics, and creativity are valuable and essential people skills needed in organizations.

Our text provides a comprehensive overview of OB theories and processes with a strong emphasis on skill-building applications in order to equip students with the information and skills they need to thrive in organizations today.

Why Critical Thinking Matters in OB

Critical thinking is an essential skill; managers use critical thinking to understand, explain, predict, and influence behavior in the workplace. A critical thinker uses their intelligence, knowledge, and skills to question and carefully explore situations and to arrive at thoughtful conclusions based on evidence and reason. Someone thinking critically is able to get past biases and view situations from different perspectives to ultimately improve their understanding of the world.

Business leaders use critical thinking when making decisions, solving problems, gathering information, and asking questions. Time and again, research has shown the effectiveness of critical thinking in the workplace. In an article published in the journal *Current Directions in Psychological Science,* the authors report that cognitive ability tests, including critical-thinking tests, "are among the strongest and most consistent predictors of performance across academic and work settings."[1]

In *Organizational Behavior: A Skill-Building Approach,* we use the components and core skills of critical thinking to teach the many facets of organizational behavior to students. Adding critical thinking to these behaviors further enhances students' abilities to strategically think as well as analyze and solve problems. By seeking first to understand the dynamics of human behavior, then sharing the knowledge learned, they will be able to build more successful relationships within their personal and professional lives.

How Our Book Incorporates Critical Thinking

A lot of OB books claim to help students to develop their critical-thinking skills. What makes our book different? Our book incorporates critical thinking on every page. Instead of passively reading through each chapter, the student is asked to pause, reflect, and engage more critically with the content.

Chapter 1 explains the central role critical thinking plays in OB and introduces a five-step **critical-thinking framework** that students can apply to challenging scenarios, problems, decisions, and other issues.

Critical-Thinking questions at the end of each case study are designed to challenge students to think critically and achieve higher levels of learning.

Examining the Evidence boxes highlight a recent seminal OB study from high-quality OB journals and discuss its practical applications in the business world. Critical-thinking questions at the end of each box allow students to see how research in academe applies to real-life settings.

These critical-thinking elements are perfect for assignments or class discussions and lively debate.

NEW TO THIS EDITION

In addition to updating 80% of the chapter references, we have added two new end of chapter exercises and one online exercise for use in online and hybrid classes to each chapter. We wrote 15 new case studies on real-world companies, including Hilton, Caribou, and Hubspot. We included up-to-date coverage of the lasting effects of the COVID-19 pandemic, diversity, equity, and inclusion, and virtual work. Lastly, we added a new chapter on diversity, equity, and inclusion, and made personality and individual differences its own chapter.

Please read the section below to see the chapter-specific changes that have been made.

CHAPTER-BY-CHAPTER CHANGES

Chapter 1: Why Organizational Behavior Matters

- New opening case: Hilton
- More detailed explanation of the impact of the COVID-19 pandemic on the four functions of management
- Updated research on the effectiveness of critical thinking in the workplace
- Additional discussion on the skills required for employees and how they relate to organizational behavior
- Updated case: CVS Health

Chapter 2: Diversity, Equity, Inclusion (DEI) NEW CHAPTER

- New opening case: Dolby Laboratories
- New Examining the Evidence feature: Can Diversity and Meritocracy Both Be Encouraged?
- Explains the importance of DEI in OB
- Discusses workplace diversity and different types of diversity
- Describes cross-cultural diversity in virtual collaboration
- Outlines the impact of equity and equality in the workplace
- Illustrates the power of inclusion in a working environment
- Identifies the different ways businesses can promote a DEI culture
- New case: CBRE Group

Chapter 3: Personality and Individual Differences NEW CHAPTER

- New opening case: The Peak Fleet
- Discusses why individual differences are important
- Contrasts the nature and nurture explanations of personality development
- Distinguishes among the trait theories of personality
- Describes the approaches to assessing and interpreting character strengths
- Differentiates among the most common personality attributes
- New Examining the Evidence feature: The Role of Grit and Psychological Capital in Academic Performance
- New case: Adobe

Chapter 4: Perception and Learning

- Updated case: Twitter
- Discusses how the COVID-19 pandemic has impacted the perception of the workplace
- More detailed explanation of the components of the perception process supported by recent research

- Updated Examining the Evidence feature: Snakes, Self-Efficacy, and Task Performance: Too Much of a Good Thing?
- Further discussion of the different types of perceptual distortions supported by the latest studies and research
- Discusses behavioral theory using current research and media examples
- New case: Catch & Release

Chapter 5: Emotions, Attitudes, and Stress

- Updated case: Under Armour
- Expanded discussion of the role of emotions in the workplace supported by current research
- Describes the importance of considering cultural variations in emotional expression
- Enhanced discussion of emotional intelligence using current research and real-world examples
- New Examining the Evidence feature: Psychological Capital, Coping Style, and Perceived Stress
- Updated information and real-world examples on employee engagement and new section added on the drivers of engagement
- Greater coverage of stress in the workplace including updated information regarding the causes of stress, different ways to manage stress, and the impact of stress on job satisfaction
- New section on employee well-being including the seven pillars of well-being, illustrated by new research and real-world examples
- New case: Zoom Video Communications

Chapter 6: Motivation: Concepts and Theoretical Perspectives

- Updated case: AriZona Iced Tea
- Greater depth added to McClelland's Acquired Needs Theory
- Enhanced discussion, research, and examples on money as a motivator
- Updated Examining the Evidence feature: Money as a Motivator
- Current research and real-world examples added to support equity theory discussion
- New case: Caribou

Chapter 7: Motivation: Practices and Applications

- New opening case: Spotify
- Expanded discussion of intrinsic motivation
- New Examining the Evidence feature: Gamification as a Motivator in the Workplace
- New section illustrating the impact of the COVID-19 pandemic on worker motivation
- Enhanced discussion of motivation through job design
- Further explores psychological empowerment through current research and real-world examples
- New case: Sephora

Chapter 8: Teams

- Updated opening case: Thomas Jefferson University Hospital
- More current information added to the section on building effective teams
- Enhanced discussion of cyberloafing supported by current research
- Further discussion on virtual teams using current research, including information on managing virtual teams
- Updated team decision-making with the latest research
- New section on digital brainstorming
- New case: PepsiCo

Chapter 9: Decision-Making, Creativity, and Innovation

- Updated opening case: ASU
- Explains the impact of the COVID-19 pandemic on programmed decisions

- Enriched discussion on heuristics, biases, and errors using current research and real-world examples
- New research and examples to illustrate the factors that inspire creativity
- New Examining the Evidence feature: Are Advanced Technologies Destroying Collaborative Creativity?
- New research and examples added to the innovation process and types of innovation
- Updated case: McDonald's

Chapter 10: Ethics and Social Responsibility

- Updated case: IBM
- New discussion on the impact of the COVID-19 pandemic on ethical behavior
- New section on ethical corporate scandals
- New section on ethics and artificial intelligence (AI)
- New information added on the concept of "moral blindness"
- Current research and studies added to support sections on leadership in relation to power, privilege, and consistency
- New information demonstrating the ways in which leaders can build trust
- New research and real-world examples added support the ethical challenges of followers
- New section explaining Carroll's Pyramid of Corporate Social Responsibility
- New section discussing ethical learning as a lifelong process
- Updated case: JetBlue

Chapter 11: Effective Communication

- Updated opening case: Uber
- Enhanced discussion of communication channels supported by current research and real-world examples
- New information describing some tips for video conferencing etiquette
- Enriched explanation of the barriers to communication using current research
- New case: Stagecoach Group

Chapter 12: Trust, Conflict and Negotiation

- Updated opening case: NFL
- Expanded introduction discussing the impact of the COVID-19 pandemic on trust
- New section explaining the three core drivers of trust, illustrated by The Trust Triangle
- Current research and real-world examples added to enhance the discussion on conflict
- New case: Allied Grape Growers

Chapter 13: Leadership Perspectives

- Updated opening case: Proctor and Gamble
- Enriched introduction discussing the effect of the COVID-19 pandemic on leadership
- Updated real-world examples and research added to the leader emergence discussion
- Real-world examples and current research added to describe the different types of leaders
- Real-world examples, studies, and current research added to empowering leadership section
- New Examining the Evidence feature: Empowering Leadership: The Paradox of Simultaneously Maintaining and Letting Go of Control
- Enriched discussion of cross-cultural leadership
- Expanded discussion on leadership and gender using current research and real-world examples
- Updated case: Chobani Yogurt

Chapter 14: Influence, Power, and Politics

- Enhanced discussion of the various sources of power illustrated by real-world examples
- Real-world examples and current research added to describe the tactics for influencing others

- New discussion of "political skill" supported by current studies
- New information discussing the four types of political players
- New content describing politics in relation to visibility and remote working
- New case: Starbucks

Chapter 15: Organizations and Culture

- Updated opening case: REI
- Revised opening introduction including research on the impact of the COVID-19 pandemic on organizational culture
- New media examples to highlight strong and weak cultures
- New Examining the Evidence feature: Linking Organizational Culture and Performance
- New case: Hubspot

Chapter 16: Organizational Change and Structure

- Updated case: Google
- New Examining the Evidence feature: Formalization and Centralization: Can Organizational Structure Substitute for Leadership?
- New introduction profiling major corporate changes that took place during the COVID-19 pandemic
- Current research added to support the impact of the 2017 #MeToo movement
- New media examples and research illustrating the topic of internal and external forces for change
- New examples demonstrating the different types of organizational structures
- Updated case: General Electric

END-OF-CHAPTER FEATURES

In each chapter, we include traditional chapter review materials to help students check their comprehension and prepare for quizzes and exams.

In Review is organized by learning objective, summarizes key chapter information.

Up for Debate challenges students to think critically and develop and discuss their own viewpoints across a wide range of issues, including diversity, emotional well-being, and ethics.

Short exercises, experiential exercises, and online exercises are designed to help students build valuable experience and increase their skills through decision-oriented and hands-on exercises.

Self-assessments *(online only)* allow students to apply chapter content to their own lives and better understand their own behaviors, skills, and strengths.

Case studies profile real-world companies and people and illustrate how OB concepts function in the real world, providing students with engaging case examples and opportunities to apply OB concepts to the case studies.

CONTENT AND ORGANIZATION

Each chapter is introduced by an OB model that provides students with a big-picture overview of how all the chapters and parts fit together.

Chapter 1, "Why Organizational Behavior Matters," explains the concept of OB and its significance in today's organizations, demonstrates the value of critical thinking in OB, and describes the major challenges and opportunities in the field of OB.

Chapter 2, "Diversity, Equity, and Inclusion (DEI)," discusses the importance of DEI in OB, describes different types of diversity, outlines the benefits of an inclusive working environment, and identifies positive ways for managers to promote a DEI culture.

Chapter 3, "Personality and Individual Differences," describes the similarities and differences between people, and explores personality development, trait theories of personality, and common personality attributes.

Chapter 4, "Perception and Learning," illustrates the factors that influence and distort our perception, and applies attribution theory, reinforcement theory, and social cognitive theory to learning and behavior.

Chapter 5, "Emotion, Attitudes, and Stress," explores how the influence of emotions on behavior, identifies the importance of workplace attitudes, and discusses the outcomes of stress in the workplace and the benefits of employee well-being.

Chapter 6, "Motivation: Concepts and Theoretical Perspectives," explains the motivation process and explores the different theories of motivation and how they influence behavior in the workforce.

Chapter 7, "Motivation: Practices and Applications," explores intrinsic and extrinsic motivation, outlines the various aspects of job design, and discusses psychological empowerment as a form of motivation.

Chapter 8, "Teams," emphasizes the critical role of teams and teamwork, explores the different types of teams, and analyzes the components that make up an effective team.

Chapter 9, "Decision-Making, Creativity, and Innovation," emphasizes decision-making as a key aspect of OB, identifies how we make decisions in the real world, and highlights the critical role of creativity and innovation in today's organizations.

Chapter 10, "Ethics and Social Responsibility in Organizations," describes the importance of ethics in organizations and discusses ethical dilemmas, assesses the challenges of ethical leaders and followers, and explores different approaches to building ethical and socially responsible organizations.

Chapter 11, "Effective Communication," describes the different types of communication channels, explores the key barriers to effective communication, and emphasizes the critical nature of cross-cultural communication.

Chapter 12, "Trust, Conflict, and Negotiation," describes the core drivers of trust in organizations, explains the different types of conflict and conflict management, and outlines the steps of the negotiation process.

Chapter 13, "Leadership Perspectives," discusses different types of leaders and leadership theories, discusses leadership across cultures, and identifies gender issues in leadership.

Chapter 14, "Influence, Power, and Politics," describes different types of influence tactics and their outcomes, discusses the concept of power and its relationship to leadership, and explores the different causes and forms of organizational politics.

Chapter 15, "Organizations and Culture," explores the facets and functions of organizational culture, illustrates they ways in which organizations adapt their practices across cultures, and outlines several approaches used by organizations to shape culture.

Chapter 16, "Organizational Change and Structure," describes the forces for change in organizations, discusses resistance to change and ways to minimize it, and explains how organizational development (OD) is used to cope with internal and external changes.

LIST OF CASE STUDIES

Chapter-Opening Case Studies

1. Hilton
2. Dolby Laboratories, Inc.
3. The Peak Fleet
4. Twitter's Adaptability
5. Kevin Plank, Founder of Under Armour
6. AriZona Iced Tea: Organizational Motivation

7. Spotify
8. The Team at Thomas Jefferson University Hospital Emergency Department
9. Creativity and Innovation, Arizona State University
10. IBM's Ethical Supply Chains
11. Uber's Organizational Communication
12. Distrust in the National Football League (NFL)
13. Procter and Gamble's Leadership Training Program
14. Managerial Power at NextEra Energy Inc.
15. Recreational Equipment Incorporated's (REI) Organizational Culture
16. Google's Organizational Development and Change

End-of-Chapter Case Studies

1. CVS Health
2. CBRE Group, Inc.
3. Adobe Inc.
4. Catch&Release
5. Eric Yuan and Zoom Video Communications, Inc.
6. Caribou
7. Sephora
8. PepsiCo
9. McDonald's Decision-Making and Innovation
10. JetBlue's Ethical Response to a Crisis
11. Stagecoach Group
12. Allied Grape Growers
13. Leadership Perspective at Chobani
14. Starbucks
15. HubSpot's Organizational Culture
16. Organizational Change and Structure at General Electric (GE)

ACKNOWLEDGMENTS

While the authors get their names on the front cover, it takes a community to write a textbook. The authors would like to thank all those people who have supported our efforts in writing this book. There are a plethora of people who contributed to making this text a reality. First, we thank all the students who over the years have encouraged us to leave our teaching comfort zone to explore new and innovative ways of teaching. It was through these experiences that we obtained the courage to attempt to write such a book as the third edition of *Organizational Behavior: A Skill-Building Approach*. We also thank our respective deans Ohad Kadan at Arizona State (W. P. Carey School of Business) and Joshua Hall at West Virginia University's John Chambers College of Business & Economics for their support for this project. We thank our department heads (Wei Shen, Arizona State, and Abhishek Srivastava, West Virginia University) for their encouragement as well. Chris Neck thanks Joanna Grabski (Dean of the College of Integrative Sciences and Arts at Arizona State University) for her steadfast support and encouragement to excel in the classroom.

For their thoughtful and helpful comments and ideas on our manuscript, we sincerely thank the following reviewers. Our book is a better product because of their insightful suggestions.

REVIEWER ACKNOWLEDGMENTS

Keanon Alderson, California Baptists University
Michael J. Alleruzzo, Saint Joseph's University
Angela Balog, Saint Francis University
Dave Beaudry, Ph.D., Keene State College
Curt Beck, Concordia University
David J. Biemer, Texas State University
Frederick R. Brodzinski, The City College of New York
Deborah S. Butler, Georgia State University
Min Carter, Southern Illinois University
Adriana Machado Casali, Conestoga College
Vallari Chandna, University of Wisconsin, Green Bay
Steven D. Charlier, Georgia Southern University
Alex Chen, University of Central Arkansas
Huaizhong Chen, West Virginia University
Yi-Yu Chen, New Jersey City University
Muntakim Choudhury, Stockton University
Amanda L. Christensen, University of Cincinnati
Todd A. Conkright, Creighton University
Dr. Patrick Coyle, Lycoming College
Christine R. Day, Eastern Michigan University
Eric B. Dent, Fayetteville State University
Summer Zwanziger Elsinger, University of Wisconsin, Platteville
Janice S. Gates, Western Illinois University
Katrina Graham, Suffolk University
Jennifer Griffith, University of New Hampshire
Robert D. Gulbro, Florida Institute of Technology
Linda Hefferin, Columbia College of Missouri
Laura Yu Hickerson, James Madison University

Nathan Himelstein, Essex County College
David Hofstetter, Clark University
Kristin Holmberg-Wright, University of Wisconsin, Parkside
Samira B. Hussein, Johnson County Community College
Jason Jackson, Kaplan University
Avan Jassawalla, SUNY Geneseo
Desiree Keever, State University of New York, Delhi
Susan Knapp, Kaplan University
Stephanie A. Kodatt, Ph.D., Texas A&M University
Egbert Johannes Kollaard, Wright State University
Monica Law, Ph.D., Marywood University
Kevin G. Love, Ph.D., Central Michigan University
Marla Lowenthal, University of San Francisco
Daniel S. Marrone, Farmingdale State College
Warren Matthews, LeTourneau University
Jacqueline Mayfield, Texas A&M International University
Milton Mayfield, Texas A&M International University
Colleen A. McLaughlin, Liberty University
Maria Minor, Kaplan University
Tommy Nichols, Texas Wesleyan University
Lisa M. Nieman, Indiana Wesleyan University
Kathleen Novak, University of Denver
Audrey M. Parajon, Wilmington University
Jeffrey B. Paul, The University of Tulsa
Tracy H. Porter, Cleveland State University
Alicia J. Revely, Miami University
Harriet L. Rojas, Indiana Wesleyan University
Annette B. Roter, Viterbo University
Mike Shaner, Saint Louis University
Joseph Simon, Casper College
Andrea E. Smith-Hunter, Siena College
Ann Snell, Tulane University
Kristin Sotak, State University of New York at Oswego
Howard Stanger, Canisius College
Chad Stevens, Keystone College
Palaniappan Thiagarajan, Jackson State University
Marjolijn van der Velde, Devenport University
Dr. Richard J. Vaughan, University of St. Francis
Maria D. Vitale, Brandman University, Chaffey College, and UCLA Extension
Bob Waris, University of Missouri-Kansas City
Michael L. Woodward, Shorter University
Guorong Zhu, Salem State University

As mentioned previously, it takes a team to write a textbook, and we thank those behind-the-scenes individuals who assisted in the research, development, or editing of various parts of this third edition. Specifically, Chris Neck would like to thank Sam Markel and Sachitha Bhat for their above-and-beyond help. This textbook was made better by their talents and contributions.

In addition, we thank the fine folks at SAGE for bringing this book to fruition. Our dream of creating an innovative OB textbook and ancillary package has become a reality because of our amazing, energetic, and encouraging acquisitions editor, Lauren Gobell. She has been a champion for this book and our ideas (and there were many!) every step of the way. We can't thank her enough for her dedication and support. Adeline Grout, our talented developmental editor, pushed us to explore new ideas and kept us on track to write the best book possible. Rebecca Lee, our production editor, made sure that everything that needed to happen did indeed happen and kept all of us on track. We appreciate all of their hard work, creativity, and attention to detail. We are also grateful to Ashlee Blunk and Mark Achenbach from SAGE, who planted the seeds for this book many years ago. We are grateful to Harriet Rojas (Indiana Wesleyan University), Milton R. Mayfield (Texas A&M International University), Jacqueline R. Mayfield (Texas A&M International University), and Steven Stovall (Southeast Missouri State University) for contributing valuable, hands-on experiential exercises. Designer Candice Harman came up with an elegant and contemporary look for this book that visually brings to life our ideas more than we could have ever imagined. Cassie Carey took care of a myriad of tasks during the development of the manuscript with an energy and enthusiasm that was inspiring. Jennifer Haldeman, our product marketer, did a great job coordinating the promotion of our book, from organizing focus groups to overseeing all of the professor outreach efforts. And we thank our families for "living without us" as we worked diligently on completing this textbook.

ABOUT THE AUTHORS

Dr. Christopher P. Neck is currently an associate professor of management at Arizona State University, where he held the title University Master Teacher. From 1994 to 2009, he was part of the Pamplin College of Business faculty at Virginia Tech. He received his PhD in management from Arizona State University and his MBA from Louisiana State University. Neck is author or coauthor of 22 books including *Self-Leadership: The Definitive Guide to Personal Excellence* (2017, SAGE; 2nd ed. , 2019, SAGE); *Get a Kick Out of Life: Expect the Best of Your Body, Mind, and Soul at Any Age* (2017, Clovercroft); *Fit To Lead: The Proven 8-week Solution for Shaping Up Your Body, Your Mind, and Your Career* (2004, St. Martin's Press; 2012, Carpenter's Sons); *Mastering Self-Leadership: Empowering Yourself for Personal Excellence* (6th ed., 2013, Pearson); *The Wisdom of Solomon at Work* (2001, Berrett-Koehler); *For Team Members Only: Making Your Workplace Team Productive and Hassle-Free* (1997, Amacom Books); and *Medicine for the Mind: Healing Words to Help You Soar* (4thed. , 2012, Wiley). Neck is also the coauthor of the principles of management textbook, *Management: A Balanced Approach to the 21st Century* (2013, Wiley; 2nd ed., 2017; Wiley, 3rd ed., 2021, SAGE); an introductory to entrepreneurship textbook, *Entrepreneurship* (2017, SAGE; 2nd ed. , 2020, SAGE); and an introductory to organizational behavior textbook, *Organizational Behavior* (2017, SAGE; 2nd ed. , 2019, SAGE; 3rd ed. , 2023, SAGE).

Dr. Neck's research specialties include employee/executive fitness, self-leadership, leadership, group decision-making processes, and self-managing teams. He has over 150 publications in the form of books, chapters, and articles in various journals. Some of the outlets in which Neck's work has appeared include *Organizational Behavior and Human Decision Processes, The Journal of Organizational Behavior, The Academy of Management Executive, Journal of Applied Behavioral Science, The Journal of Managerial Psychology, Executive Excellence, Human Relations, Human Resource Development Quarterly, Journal of Leadership Studies, Educational Leadership*, and *The Commercial Law Journal*.

Neck is the deputy editor of *The Journal of Leadership and Management*. Due to Neck's expertise in management, he has been cited in numerous national publications including *The Washington Post, The Wall Street Journal, The Los Angeles Times, The Houston Chronicle*, and *TheChicago Tribune*.

Dr. Neck was recently voted as a semi-finalist (out of 140 nominations) for the prestigious international 2020 Baylor University Cherry Award for Great Teaching. He finished in the top six of all nominations. Neck was also the recipient of the 2007 Business Week Favorite Professor Award. He is featured on www.businessweek.com as one of the approximately 20 professors from across the world receiving this award.

Dr. Neck has taught over 60,000 students during his career in higher education. Neck currently teaches a mega section of Management Principles to approximately 1000 students at Arizona State University.

Neck was the recipient of the 2020 John W. Teets Outstanding Undergraduate Teaching Award (voted by W. P. Carey students). Neck also received the Order of Omega Outstanding Teaching Award for 2012. This award is awarded to one professor at Arizona State by the Alpha Lambda chapter of this leadership fraternity. His class sizes at Virginia Tech filled rooms up to 2500 students. He received numerous teaching awards during his tenure at Virginia Tech, including the 2002 Wine Award for Teaching Excellence. Also, Neck was the 10-time winner (1996, 1998, 2000, 2002, 2004, 2005, 2006, 2007, 2008, and 2009) of the Students' Choice Teacher of The Year Award (voted by the students for the best teacher of the year within the entire university). Also, some of the organizations who have participated in Neck's management development training include GE/Toshiba, Busch Gardens, Clark Construction, the United States Army, Crestar, American Family Insurance, Sales and Marketing Executives International, American Airlines, American Electric Power, W. L. Gore & Associates, Dillard's Department Stores, and Prudential Life Insurance. Neck is also an avid runner. He has completed 12 marathons, including the Boston Marathon, New York City Marathon, and the San Diego Marathon. In fact, his personal record for a single long-distance run—is a 48-mile run.

Dr. Jeffery D. Houghton completed his PhD in management at Virginia Polytechnic Institute and State University (Virginia Tech) and is currently a professor of management at West Virginia University (WVU). Dr. Houghton has taught college-level business courses at Virginia Tech, Abilene Christian University (Texas), Lipscomb University (Tennessee), the International University (Vienna, Austria), and for the U.S. Justice Department-Federal Bureau of Prisons. Prior to pursuing a full-time career in academics, he worked in the banking industry as a loan officer and branch manager.

A member of the Honor Society of Phi Kappa Phi, Dr. Houghton's research specialties include human behavior, motivation, personality, leadership, and self-leadership. He has published more than 70 peer-reviewed journal articles, book chapters, and books, and his work has been cited more than 7,000 times in academic journals. He has coauthored several books: *Self-Leadership: The Definitive Guide to Personal Excellence* (2017, SAGE; 2nd ed., 2019, SAGE), *Management: A Balanced Approach to the 21st Century* (2013, Wiley; 2nd ed., 2017, Wiley; 3rd ed., 2021, SAGE), and *Organizational Behavior* (2017, SAGE; 2nd ed., 2019, SAGE; 3rd ed., 2023, SAGE). He currently teaches undergraduate-, master's-, and doctoral-level courses in management, organizational behavior, and leadership. Dr. Houghton was named the 2013 Beta Gamma Sigma Professor of the Year for the WVU College of Business and Economics, awarded annually to one faculty member within the college as selected by a vote of the student members of Beta Gamma Sigma; and he received the 2008 Outstanding Teaching Award for the WVU College of Business and Economics, awarded annually to one faculty member for outstanding teaching.

In addition to his research and teaching activities, Dr. Houghton has consulted and conducted training seminars for companies including the Federal Bureau of Investigations, Pfizer Pharmaceuticals, and the Bruce Hardwood Floors Company. In his spare time, Dr. Houghton enjoys traveling, classic mystery novels, mountain biking, and snow skiing. Finally, Dr. Houghton has trained for and completed two marathons, the Marine Corps Marathon in Washington, D.C., and the Dallas White Rock Marathon in Dallas, Texas.

Emma L. Murray completed a bachelor of arts degree in English and Spanish at University College Dublin (UCD) in County Dublin, Ireland, followed by a Higher Diploma (Hdip) in business studies and information technology at the Michael Smurfit Graduate School of Business in County Dublin, Ireland. Following her studies, Emma spent nearly a decade in investment banking before becoming a full-time writer and author.

Emma has worked on numerous texts, including business and economics, self-help, and psychology. Emma is the coauthor of the principles of management textbook, *Management: A Balanced Approach to the 21st Century* (2013, Wiley; 2nd ed., 2017, Wiley; 3rd ed., 2021, SAGE); an introductory to entrepreneurship textbook, *Entrepreneurship,* (2017, SAGE; 2nd ed. , 2020, SAGE); and an introductory to organizational behavior textbook, *Organizational Behavior* (2017, SAGE; 2nd ed., 2019, SAGE; 3rd ed., 2023). She lives in London, U. K. with her husband and two children.

PART I

INTRODUCTION

BalkansCat

1 WHY ORGANIZATIONAL BEHAVIOR MATTERS

LEARNING OBJECTIVES

By the end of this chapter, you will be able to:

1.1 Explain the basic concept of organizational behavior and its value in organizations

1.2 Describe the key role of managing human capital in creating a sustainable competitive advantage for organizations

1.3 Identify the major behavioral science disciplines that contribute to OB

1.4 Demonstrate the value of critical thinking in the context of OB

1.5 Identify the major challenges and opportunities in the field of OB

1.6 Differentiate the three basic levels of analysis at which OB may be examined

Case Study: Hilton

Hilton Worldwide is one of the world's largest and fastest-growing hospitality companies. As of 2022, Hilton's 18-brand portfolio includes nearly 7,000 owned, managed, or franchised properties that span 122 countries and territories across the globe.[1] In 2019, Hilton was named *Fortune Magazine*'s Best Company to Work For in the U.S., the first hospitality company to ever earn this prestigious ranking as well as the only employer outside the tech sector to receive the award since 2004.[2]

The Hilton Effect

Prior to the company's 100th anniversary in 2019, Hilton commissioned Stanford Graduate School of Business professor Chip Heath and business author Karla Starr to write about Hilton's impact over more than a century in hospitality. The duo examined the company's historical successes and interviewed present and former Hilton employees to grasp what has made the organization so effective for so long. They prepared a 65-page white paper, titled "The Hilton Effect," on how the company has impacted travelers, the travel industry, and the communities it serves around the world.[3]

Unsurprisingly, what Heath and Starr found makes Hilton so effective is neither its properties nor its iconic brand, but its people and how the organization nurtures their skills. "Empowering and engaging employees is in Hilton's DNA," the paper reads. "Conrad Hilton was never known as a 'look-over-your-shoulder' manager." From the beginning, Hilton advocated autonomy over strict guidelines and standards, engaging employees' intrinsic motivation to grow and develop themselves to elevate the entire organization. A common saying at Hilton is "The reward for good work is more work." Team members interviewed for the white paper explained that the phrase doesn't simply mean more work; it means more *challenging* work. "Hilton employees benefit from a kind of promise: your colleagues will challenge you to stretch your skills. If you've mastered the small-town hotel, it's time to hit the center city."

Don't Just Talk the Talk, Walk the Walk

Sometimes the more challenging work is to move from the center city back to the small-town hotel. Feedback from employees on the ground can help corporate leadership identify and address unmet needs, but some challenges are difficult to capture in surveys from on high. One of Hilton's most successful strategies for listening to team members is an official program that works much like the reality television series *Undercover Boss*: the Hilton Senior Leadership Business Immersion program.

Hilton's chief human resources officer, Matthew Schuyler, says the program is "an experience that connects senior leaders to the most fundamental aspect of the business—hotel operations. The three-day program entails working back of house, or what we refer to as 'Heart of House,' in departments including Housekeeping, Food & Beverage, Banqueting, and Engineering."

Mike Gathright, Hilton's senior vice president, took part in an immersion at two Hilton properties in Seattle, Washington. Gathright was struck by the reactions the senior leadership team received: "I still remember one of the housekeeper's excitement as I worked alongside her cleaning rooms. She asked if she could take a picture!"

Management consultant Dana Brownlee wrote for Forbes, "When staff see executive leaders working beside them carrying luggage and serving drinks, it sends a strong message of solidarity and shows that leaders are serious about understanding the challenges of running a 24/7/365 business that literally never closes."[4]

Some immersion experiences yield benefits even more tangible than boosted morale. Participating executives in one program noticed frontline team members wearing uncomfortable and impractical clothing for their duties. When they returned to their corporate offices, the execs created the "Hilton Under Armour Wardrobe Program," which supplies comfortable, breathable clothing for all Hilton team members around the world.[5]

COVID-19 and Hilton's Response

No survey, executive immersion program, or organizational behavior managerial technique could predict or prepare Hilton for the COVID-19 pandemic, however. "Never in Hilton's 101-year history has our industry faced a global crisis that brings travel to a virtual standstill," Hilton's president and CEO, Chris Nassetta, said in 2020. "I am devastated that to protect our business, we have been forced to take actions that directly impact our Team Members." Many hotels completely suspended operations, and those that remained open did so at diminished capacity. Hundreds of thousands of team members were furloughed in the early days of the COVID-19 pandemic. At the corporate level, Hilton cut 2,100 jobs globally—nearly a quarter of its total corporate workforce. Nassetta's salary was paused in late March, and executive committee pay was reduced by 50% for the duration of the crisis.[6] Despite tremendous setbacks, Hilton met the greatest challenge in the company's history with steadfast dedication to its team members.

Hilton employees continued to receive health benefits and were eligible to apply for unemployment benefits while furloughed. The company activated its Team Member Assistance program and gave financial aid to workers and workers' families who were directly impacted by the virus. The creation of Hilton's Alumni Talent Network offered access to permanent full-time opportunities at dozens of partner organizations and provided outplacement assistance services to many staff. Determined to emerge stronger on the other side of the crisis, the company's response was not simply to relinquish all of its talented workers to other firms. Hilton committed to notify alumni first when there were new jobs at the company, accelerate their recruitment process, and developed an audacious plan to support its displaced workforce until it was time to rebuild.[7]

Hilton partnered with Albertsons, Amazon, CVS, Sunrise Senior Living, Walgreens, and other companies to collectively fill more than 200,000 temporary essential worker positions that saw increased demand during the pandemic. Hilton shifted its recruitment engine into reverse to give furloughed team members direct access to these positions and expedited hiring processes through the Hilton Workforce Resource Center. "The recognized quality of our team members, including their hospitality and service culture training, make them ideal candidates to quickly step in and assist organizations in these temporary assignments," Nigel Glennie, vice president of corporate communications, told *USA Today*. Glennie continued, "We plan to welcome these team members back when travel resumes. Our partners need workers and our team members need to work right now, so this is an initiative we put together with the sole intent of helping our people, even though we can't be the ones to employ them right now."[8]

Hilton's investment in its team members paid off. Innovations in contactless check-in and payment options for guests, widespread vaccination availability, relaxed travel restrictions, and pent-up demand enabled Hilton to quickly bounce back as the crisis began to subside. The company restored most of its furloughed workforce to their previous positions and recently eclipsed the 1,000,000-room milestone across all their properties worldwide.

"The Hilton Effect for me is the positive impact that we've had on the world, the opportunities that Team Members have had to contribute to the environment of the people around them," Chris Nassetta says in the afterword to the white paper. "I think the world is a better place because Hilton was born into it 100 years ago. And if we continue to do our job, the world will be a better place because Hilton is in it for the next 100 years."

Critical-Thinking Questions

1. Hilton management was so keen on explaining the company's organizational behavior that they commissioned consultants to write "The Hilton Effect." How do you think the publication serves to predict and influence organizational behavior at Hilton?

2. Describe how Hilton's management of human capital gives them a competitive advantage in the hospitality industry. Do you think their workforce's strengths are rareness, value, inimitability, or a combination of all three?

3. This case study examined Hilton's OB on the individual and organizational levels. How do you think "The Hilton Effect" and the company's responses to the COVID-19 pandemic affect OB on a team level?

WHAT IS ORGANIZATIONAL BEHAVIOR AND WHY IS IT IMPORTANT?

Today's continually changing, uncertain world needs managers who can address the challenges of an altered working environment and work hard to understand, anticipate, and direct people in a way that fosters connectivity, belonging, and fairness. In the past, technology was the biggest disruption to work, but today the COVID-19 pandemic has turned the world of work upside down, leaving managers to face the challenge of communicating with a remote workforce, equipping employees with new digital skills, and supporting people in navigating this period of unprecedented change. However, fast-paced organizations like Hilton need the right people with the right skills to achieve success. This is why organizational behavior has taken on a new level of importance; people with organizational behavior skills are now regarded as a valuable and essential commodity. In an environment in which competition is fiercer than ever, people will differentiate your business from anyone else's. No matter what area of business you work in, people are the cornerstone of success.

We define **organizational behavior** (OB) as a field of study focused on understanding, explaining, and improving attitudes of individuals and groups in organizations.[9] An **organization** is a structured arrangement of people working together to accomplish specific goals. In short, OB focuses on figuring out how and why individual employees and groups of employees behave the way they do within an organizational setting. Researchers carry out studies in OB, and managers or consultants establish whether this research can be applied in a real-world organization. This research has uncovered some surprising results. One study found that 88% of American employees expect flexible options in their working hours and location, 86% would prefer to work in a diverse team, and 86% would like to redesign their own careers by refining their current skills or acquiring new ones. But all of these desires have a good chance of being met only when employees have good managers.[10]

This is certainly the case at Hilton, where employees are motivated and empowered by managers who provide them with challenging opportunities and take the time to listen to their concerns. Being treated well, respected, and rewarded for excellent service is often considered more important than money. There is a common expression: "Employees don't quit jobs, they quit managers." The point is that managers who lack OB skills lose good employees. This is why it's important to learn OB skills if your goal is to become a manager who people will listen to and respect.

How Studying Organizational Behavior Benefits You in the Workplace

Understanding the ways people act and interact within organizations provides three key advantages:

1. You can *explain* behavior. You can explain why your manager, coworkers, or subordinates are doing what they're doing.

2. You can *predict* behavior. You can anticipate what your manager, coworkers, or subordinates will do in certain circumstances and situations.

3. You can *influence* behavior. You can shape the actions of your subordinates, as well as those of your manager and coworkers, to help them accomplish their goals and achieve organizational objectives.

Although explaining and predicting behavior are undoubtedly useful skills, *influencing* behavior is probably of greatest interest to a practicing manager. Once you're equipped with knowledge about your employees' work behaviors, you can use it to optimize performance by providing effective direction and guidance. This explains why managing organizational behavior (i.e., focusing on the behavior and actions of employees and how they apply their knowledge and skills to achieve organizational objectives) is so important in today's organizations. There is a common belief that OB is just common sense, but this isn't the case. We can't rely on common sense alone to truly understand the behaviors of others; if we did, we would be in danger of using inaccurate generalizations, incorrect suppositions, and common misconceptions to justify or define other people's behaviors. OB provides a systematic approach, based on scientific evidence, to further our understanding of behavior that goes far beyond common sense.

Put simply, OB is for everyone. It applies to everyday situations where you find yourself interacting with people, from the workplace to home life to the basketball court. Explaining and predicting behavior is useful to both formal managers in organizations and all employees, given that we all have the ability to influence coworkers. Throughout this book, we'll show how OB concepts can relate to all employees at all levels of a company.

With the understanding that OB can benefit all employees and all levels in an organization, let's take a closer look at formal managers and what a manager actually does in the workplace.

The Four Functions of Management

Let's remind ourselves what a manager actually does in the workplace. Typically, managers carry out four main functions: planning, organizing, leading, and controlling (see Figure 1.1).[11]

In *planning*, a manager evaluates an organization's current position and where it wants to be in the future, then sets goals, designs strategies, and identifies actions and resources needed to achieve success. *Organizing* means arranging resources such as people and functions to implement the strategy made during the planning stage. Managers ensure goals are achieved by *leading* teams and individuals effectively, which means motivating and communicating with people to achieve goals. The *controlling* function allows managers to monitor employee performance, ensure milestones are being reached, and take corrective or preventative action where necessary.

OB is an integral part of these four functions, as each function involves people "behaving" in certain ways to achieve specific tasks and duties. Successful planning, organizing, leading, and controlling would not be possible without managers following some fundamental OB principles. Table 1.1 outlines

FIGURE 1.1 ■ The Four Functions of Managers

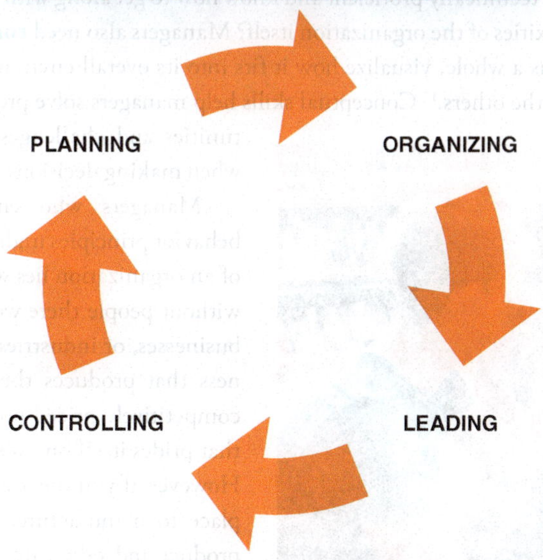

Source: Carpenter, M., Bauer, T., & Erdogan, B. (2012). Chapter 15: The essentials of control. In *Management principles*. https://2012books.lardbucket.org/books/management-principles-v1.1/s19-the-essentials-of-control.html

TABLE 1.1 ■ Impact of COVID-19 on the Four Functions of Management

Planning	**Some participants did not have a crisis plan before COVID-19. Those that did said the plan was dated and inadequate for pandemic circumstances.**
Organizing	Most agreed that the pandemic forced them to organize work differently, through delegation where appropriate.
Leading	Respondents believed in leading by example and showing support for the team.
Controlling	Managers used formal and informal check-ins to encourage communication between senior management and staff and between the team members themselves.

the impact of COVID-19 on the four functions in relation to internal communication within organizations (government and private institutions), as researched by graduate students at the University of Ottawa in 2021.[12]

Organizational members need to be equipped with specific skills to carry out their roles effectively.[13] First, they must have technical skills. A **technical skill** is an aptitude for performing and applying specialized tasks.[14] Today's members need to be proficient in using the latest technologies, including databases, artificial intelligence (for some roles), spreadsheets, email, and social networking tools.

Although technical skills are important, they can be learned on the job; to be really effective, managers need to possess **human skills**, or the ability to relate to other people.[15] People with effective human skills take the feelings of others into account and are adept at dealing with conflict. These skills are essential for managing relationships not only with peers and employees but also with competitors, partners, suppliers, and stakeholders. Managers with human skills also realize the importance of communicating and sharing information across the organization in order to achieve goals. Hilton is a good example of an organization that uses human skills to boost morale; for instance, members of the executive team work beside employees, helping them to carry luggage, clean rooms, and serve drinks. This shows workers that senior management understands the challenges of their different roles and how committed they are to ensuring every employee is heard and acknowledged.

A key facet of human skills is **emotional intelligence** (EI), which is an awareness of how your actions and emotions affect those around you and the ability to understand and empathize with the feelings of others (see Chapter 5).[16]

Managers need to be technically proficient and know how to get along with people, but what about dealing with the complexities of the organization itself? Managers also need **conceptual skills** in order to see the organization as a whole, visualize how it fits into its overall environment, and understand how each part relates to the others.[17] Conceptual skills help managers solve problems, identify opportunities and challenges, and think creatively when making decisions.

Studying organizational behavior can help you to understand how and why individuals and groups interact.

Managers who embrace organizational behavior principles understand that the success of an organization lies with its people and that without people there would be no companies, businesses, or industries. You may have a business that produces the highest-quality, most competitively priced product in the market or that prides itself on excellent customer service. However, if you don't have the right people in place to manufacture, market, and sell your product and take care of your customers, the business will suffer. Similarly, if some of your coworkers lose motivation and provide lower levels of customer service, the company will lose business, and perhaps even its reputation. Either of these problems can bring about decreases in profits, reduced employee wages and bonuses, staff layoffs, and in extreme cases, bankruptcy.

How do managers achieve the best outcomes for their organizations? A **strategic OB approach** is based on the idea that people are the key to productivity, competitive edge, and financial success. This means that managers must place a high value on **human capital**, which is the sum of people's skills, knowledge, experience, and general attributes.[18] Let's take a closer look at where human capital fits into organizations and how it is managed.

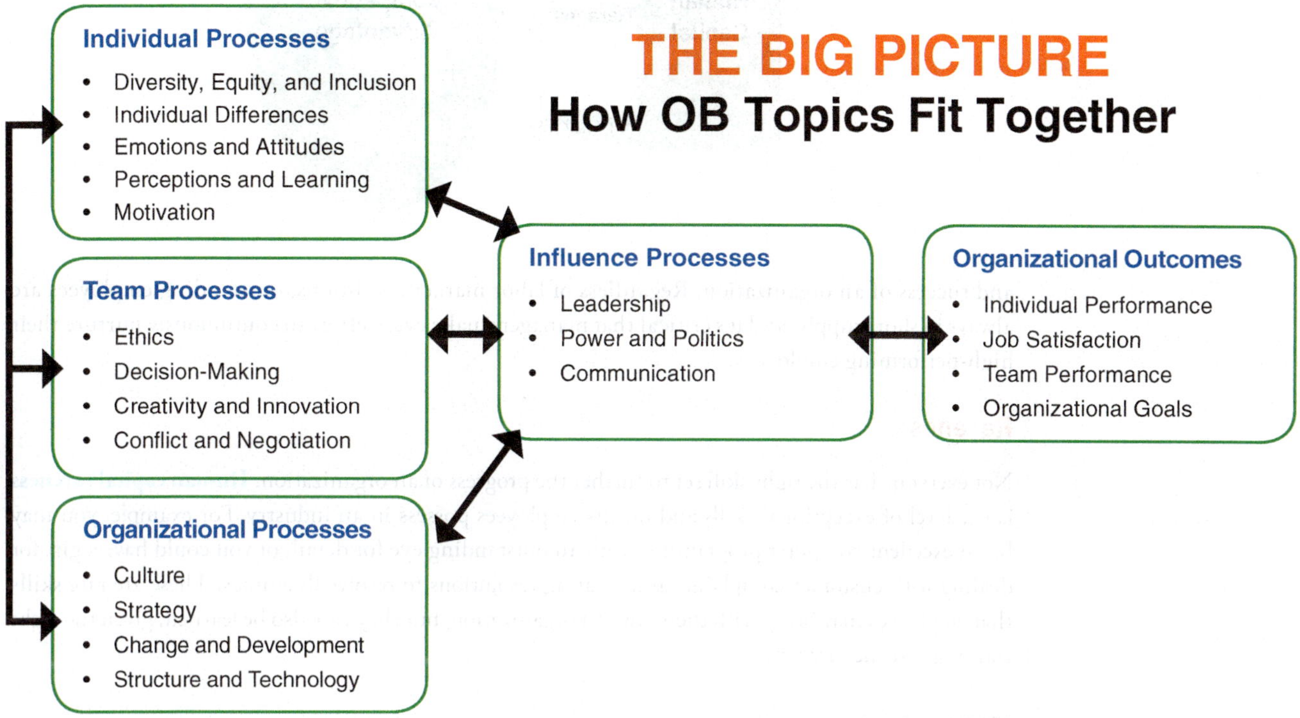

MANAGING HUMAN CAPITAL

Organizations have two kinds of resources: tangible and intangible. Physical assets such as equipment, property, and inventory are examples of *tangible* resources. *Intangible* resources include an organization's reputation and culture, its relationships with customers, and the trust between managers and coworkers. Although it's difficult to measure intangible resources because of their subtle nature, they remain crucial for organizations competing in a global economy.

Human capital falls into the category of critical intangible resources. Today's managers focus on enriching their human capital by nurturing and enhancing their employees' knowledge and skills. The possibilities of building on human capital are endless—empowered, satisfied, knowledgeable employees can achieve so much for the organization and its customers. Human capital is essential for gaining **competitive advantage**, the edge that gives organizations a more beneficial position than their competitors and allows them to generate more profits and retain more customers (see Figure 1.2).[19] Hilton stands out among its competitors because of its commitment to nurturing its human capital. Three main aspects of human capital enhance true competitive advantage: value, rareness, and inimitability.[20]

Value

Employees can add value in many different ways, but there's a difference between merely fulfilling the requirements of your job and working with an eye on company strategy. **Human capital value** accumulates when employees work toward the strategic goals of an organization to achieve competitive advantage. Although it's essential that employees have the skills and abilities to execute a company strategy, they must also have a genuine willingness to contribute to the performance

FIGURE 1.2 ■ How Human Capital Enhances Competitive Advantage

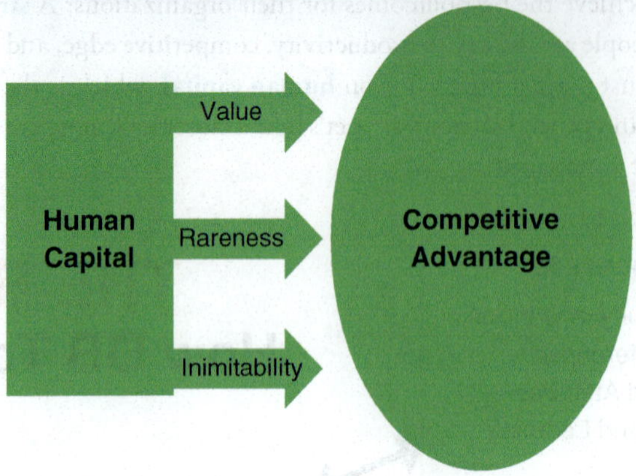

and success of an organization. Regardless of labor market conditions, outstanding employees are always in short supply, and it's critical that managers make every effort to continuously nurture their high-performing employees.

Rareness

Not everyone has the right skill set to further the progress of an organization. **Human capital rareness** is the level of exceptional skills and talents employees possess in an industry. For example, you may be an excellent computer programmer with an outstanding eye for detail, or you could have a gift for dealing with customer complaints and creating resolutions to resolve dilemmas. These are rare skills that employees may bring with them into an organization, but they can also be learned, given the right training and encouragement.

Inimitability

Employees may be able to add real value and possess rare and important skills, but these attributes must be inimitable (i.e., unique and difficult to copy or replicate) for an organization to achieve success. **Human capital inimitability** is the degree to which the skills and talents of employees can be emulated by other organizations. The higher the level of inimitability, the more competitive an organization will be. For example, what's to prevent an excellent computer programmer from going to a competitor that offers the same services and opportunities? Successful organizations ensure that their talented employees possess skills and talents that are difficult to imitate. This means employees have a degree of *tacit knowledge*: they have a feel or an instinct for a method or a process but can't easily articulate it; they just know it's right. An organization's culture or values are also difficult to imitate and often determine why employees choose to work for one company over another that offers similar products and services. Usually, this comes down to the organization's shared values, attitudes, and culture.

BEHAVIORAL SCIENCE DISCIPLINES THAT CONTRIBUTE TO OB

In the early days of management theory, studies focused on how workers could perform manual labor more efficiently (on a factory assembly line, for example) and how physical working conditions could be improved for better employee performance. There was little focus on the human element (i.e., how individual characteristics, communication, and interpersonal relationships affect organizations). Over the past hundred years, however, researchers have carried out a host of studies on the practice and application of OB, taking full advantage of its strong links to five main behavioral science disciplines: psychology, sociology, social psychology, political science, and anthropology (see Figure 1.3).

FIGURE 1.3 ■ Disciplines Contributing to the Field of Organizational Behavior

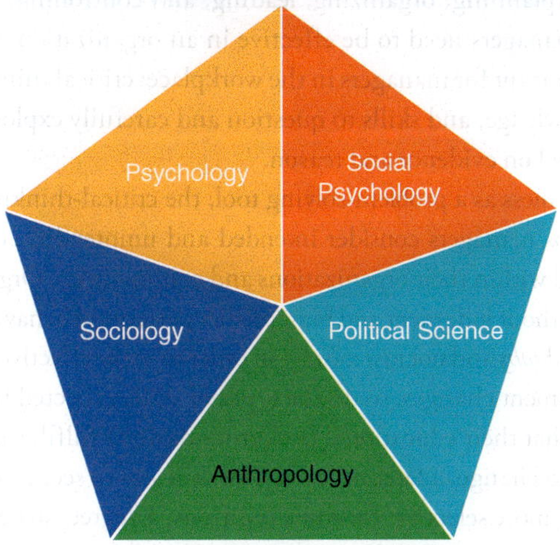

Psychology

Psychology is the scientific study of the human mind that seeks to measure and explain behavioral characteristics. Early organizational psychological research and theory focused on the factors affecting work performance and efficiency, such as lethargy and boredom. More recently, psychologists have focused on the mental health and well-being of employees in relationship to their work performance and created methods to help employees deal with challenges such as job stress. Psychologists have also helped design performance appraisals, decision-making processes, recruitment techniques, and training programs.

Sociology

While psychology focuses on the individual, **sociology** looks at the way groups behave and how they communicate and exchange information in a social setting. Sociologists have made valuable contributions to OB within areas such as group dynamics, communication, power, organizational culture, and conflict.

Social Psychology

Social psychology mixes concepts from sociology and psychology and focuses on the way people influence each other in a social setting. Social psychologists look at behaviors, feelings, actions, beliefs, and intentions and how they are constructed and influenced by others. They have made significant contributions to reducing the level of prejudice, discrimination, and stereotyping by designing processes to change attitudes, build communication, and improve the way groups work together.

Political Science

Political science studies the behavior of individuals and groups within a political environment. Political scientists focus particularly on how conflict is managed and structured, how power is distributed, and how power is abused or manipulated for the purposes of self-interest. Their studies have helped improve our understanding of how different interests, motivations, and preferences can lead to conflict and power struggles between individuals and groups.

Anthropology

Anthropology is the study of people and their activities in relation to societal, environmental, and cultural influences. In a global organizational environment, anthropological research has become even more significant because it increases our understanding of other cultures and the types of values and attitudes held by others from other countries and organizations.

A CRITICAL-THINKING APPROACH TO OB

In the section "What Is Organizational Behavior and Why Is It Important?" we outlined the four main functions of management (planning, organizing, leading, and controlling) and the skills (technical, human, and conceptual) managers need to be effective in an organization. However, another skill is becoming increasingly important for managers in the workplace: critical thinking. **Critical thinking** is the use of intelligence, knowledge, and skills to question and carefully explore situations and arrive at thoughtful conclusions based on evidence and reason.[21]

Increasingly used in business as a problem-solving tool, the critical-thinking approach is a powerful analytical method that helps managers consider intended and unintended consequences of individual behaviors on their teams and within their organizations and communities. Organizations need managers who think independently without judgment and bias, predict patterns of behaviors and processes, and ask the right questions—*how* and *why* and not just *what*—in order to make effective and thoughtful decisions.

As the business environment changes, so do the types of skills expected from employees. New and recent graduates may find that their educational backgrounds don't fulfill the requirements of organizations and may be forced to change, adapt, or learn new skill sets to secure a job. Furthermore, many organizations are becoming more selective; for some positions, a degree isn't enough.

Your ability to think critically will differentiate you from other job applicants. In an interview situation, critical thinkers take the time to think carefully about the questions they're asked, base their responses on facts or experience rather than emotion or bias, consider different viewpoints or perspectives equally, and compare their responses with similar examples that have occurred in the past. Once hired, critical thinkers are more likely to succeed. After all, most companies don't employ graduates to simply go through the motions or to be a mere cog in the wheel. They expect their employees to play a pivotal role in helping the company achieve its organizational goals. And when a company does well, everyone benefits. You don't need to be an expert in critical thinking to get a job. Many of these skills can be learned in the workplace. However, employers look for candidates who have a questioning mind, a willingness to embrace change, and a keen desire to learn.

Indeed, as research shows, businesses are desperate to attract employees with critical- thinking skills.[22] Why? Because organizations are undergoing such rapid change that they need their employees to consistently introduce new, fresh ideas to stay ahead of the competition.

Business leaders use critical thinking when making decisions, solving problems, gathering information, and asking questions. Time and again, research has shown the effectiveness of critical thinking in the workplace:

1. According to a 2016 survey of nearly 64,000 managers and more than 14,000 recent graduates, 60% of managers believe critical thinking to be the number-one soft skill lacking in new graduates.[23]
2. In 2017, research found that critical thinking is more influential than intelligence in predicting good or bad decision-making.[24]
3. In 2020, a survey conducted by the American Enterprise Institute found that 70% of STEM (science, technology, engineering, and math) workers considered critical thinking an essential skill in that field.[25]
4. The PwC 23rd CEO Survey released in 2020 found that 74% of CEOs are worried about finding employees who possess critical-thinking skills such as creativity, problem-solving, and the ability to navigate digital technology.[26]
5. In 2021, the World Economic Forum reported that critical thinking will be at the top of the list of skills employers seek over the next five years.[27]

Rachel Lyubovitzky, cofounder of New Jersey–based technology company EverythingBenefits, said, "The ability to think critically will be crucial as we chart the course toward a post-COVID world. Businesses will continue to face challenges that will require teams to be innovative in their problem-solving and communicating frequently."[28] Table 1.2 shows other skills that employers considered to be important for job applicants.

TABLE 1.2 ■ The Top 10 Skills Employers Are Looking For in 2021[29]

1.	Growth mindset: the belief that skills can be gained through hard work and perseverance.
2.	Continuous learning: the ability to continuously build and learn new skills.
3.	Critical thinking: the process of arriving at thoughtful conclusions based on evidence and reason.
4.	Survival skills: the drive to adapt and succeed despite obstacles and downfalls.
5.	Resilience, curiosity: the capability to be curious about the world and adjust easily in times of change.
6.	Flexibility: the capacity to cope with change and ambiguity.
7.	Dedication: the power to show up to work and fully commit.
8.	Coaching mindset: the ability to collaborate with others and support teams through listening and empathy.
9.	Comfort with ambiguity: the capability to navigate a changing landscape and understand the purpose of the company.
10.	Thriving in a virtual environment: the capacity to stay visible when working remotely through collaboration, responsiveness, and promoting team success.

The Five Steps of Critical Thinking

The process of critical thinking provides you with the tools to make better decisions as a manager and help you to predict the effects and consequences of those decisions. Most important, you will be better able to manage the complexities of human behavior and initiate behavioral changes by following the critical-thinking process. There are five steps to applying critical thinking in order to manage and change behavior (Figure 1.4): *observe* (recognize the behavior), *interpret* (understand the cause and effects of behavior), *analyze* (investigate the causes and effects of behavior), *evaluate* (assess the consequences of changing behavior), and *explain* (justify a change to behavior).

Let's use an example to illustrate the five steps of critical-thinking methodology. Suppose you're the manager of a restaurant owned by a local businesswoman. Samir, one of your waitstaff, has failed to show up for several shifts without giving any meaningful reason. Since Samir is usually reliable, you are puzzled by this absenteeism. Because you don't have all the facts, you decide to use critical-thinking skills to investigate the real source of the problem.

FIGURE 1.4 ■ Five-Step Critical-Thinking Framework for Managing and Changing Behavior

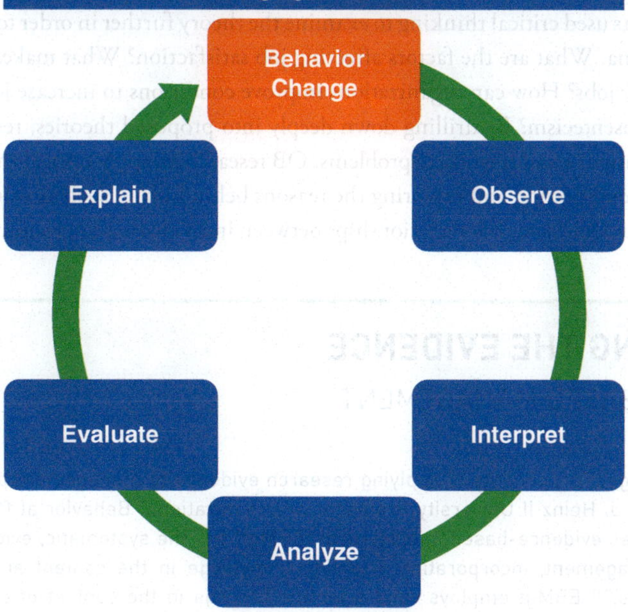

Source: Neck, C. P., Houghton, J. D., & Murray, E. L. (2014). *Management*, p. 5. Wiley.

The next time Samir comes to work, you *observe* the situation objectively, suspending all bias and judgment. You notice that Samir is abrupt with customers, doesn't attempt to communicate with fellow colleagues, and walks across the restaurant with a heavy gait. This helps you to *interpret* the situation better, giving you enough evidence to deduce that your employee is not happy. You might *analyze* these effects and think of a way to deal with the behavior.

What should you do? You decide to *evaluate* the situation and assess the consequences of trying to change Samir's behavior. Based on Samir's performance, Jessica, the restaurant owner, tells you to fire Samir, but you *explain* to Jessica why you believe an attempt to change their behavior might be justified, and Jessica agrees to give Samir another chance.

You set up a meeting with Samir to discover the reasons behind the unexplained absences and unmotivated behavior at work. Samir apologizes and tells you they have become dissatisfied with the job and would much rather work on the front desk of the restaurant, greeting customers and taking reservations. Following a trial period at the front desk, Samir demonstrates a *behavior change* by becoming more motivated.

Of course, there could be many ways to handle this dilemma, but it's clear that critical thinking can help to find the best solution for each situation when dealing with the complexities of real-life challenges.

In the next section, we explore how managers use OB research findings to enhance their critical-thinking skills.

Research in OB

Researchers use the scientific method to conduct research that managers can use to understand their employees and enhance critical thinking in OB. Researchers often begin with a **theory**, a set of principles intended to explain behavioral phenomena in organizations.[30] OB researchers may also use **models**, simplified snapshots of reality, to summarize and illustrate the reasons behind certain behaviors such as absenteeism or employee turnover. Connecting the elements of these models are **independent variables**, which are factors that remain unchanged, and **dependent variables**, factors affected by independent variables. Researchers then write a prediction called a **hypothesis**, a statement that specifies the relationships between the two variables. For example, much OB research has been carried out on the **correlation**, or the reciprocal relationship, between job satisfaction (independent variable) and absenteeism (dependent variable).

Researchers discovered that employees who were more satisfied in their jobs had higher attendance at work than those who had lower levels of job satisfaction. At first glance, this seems pretty reasonable—you may feel more inclined to call in sick when you dislike your job. But it doesn't end there. OB researchers used critical thinking to examine the theory further in order to provide a solution to this work dilemma. What are the factors affecting job satisfaction? What makes employees happy or miserable in their jobs? How can organizations improve conditions to increase job satisfaction and decrease levels of absenteeism? By drilling down deeply into proposed theories, researchers have created practical resolutions to address these problems. OB researchers apply critical thinking to facets of an organization by questioning and exploring the reasons behind issues such as work stress, unethical behavior, lack of team cohesion, poor relationships between individuals and groups, and many more.

EXAMINING THE EVIDENCE

EVIDENCE-BASED MANAGEMENT

One of the strongest proponents of applying research evidence to management practice, Denise M. Rousseau, H. J. Heinz II University Professor of Organizational Behavior at Carnegie Mellon University, defines evidence-based management (EBMgt) as "the systematic, evidence-informed practice of management, incorporating scientific knowledge in the content and processes of making decisions."[31] EBMgt employs valid scientific findings in the context of critical thinking, decision-making, and judgment to help managers obtain and use the best and most reliable information available to increase managerial and organizational effectiveness.

But why is it important for managers to think critically about and incorporate current research findings into their management practices and decision-making? A good parallel comes from the field of medicine. You may naturally assume that medical doctors and health care practitioners use the latest and best research evidence available in the field of medicine to make their decisions. Yet despite the thousands of studies conducted and published in the field of medicine each year, studies suggest that only about 15% of doctors make evidence-based decisions. Instead, most rely on obsolete information they learned in school, unproven traditions, personal experiences, and information provided by vendors selling medical products and services. During the past two decades, however, evidence-based medicine has begun to revolutionize the way medical practitioners make decisions and prescribe treatments.

Stanford professors Jeffrey Pfeffer and Robert I. Sutton argue that managers should take a similar evidence-based approach in making decisions, taking actions, and prescribing cures for organizational ills: "Managers are actually much more ignorant than doctors about which prescriptions are reliable—and they're less eager to find out. If doctors practiced medicine like many companies practice management, there would be more unnecessarily sick or dead patients and many more doctors in jail or suffering other penalties for malpractice."[32]

Professor Rousseau suggests that EBMgt consists of four basic activities: (1) obtaining the best scientific information available, (2) systematically assessing organizational facts, (3) using critical thinking and reflective judgment to apply the research evidence, and (4) considering key ethical issues.[33] Throughout the remainder of the text, you will be presented with current research evidence from the field of OB and asked to think critically about how you might apply these findings in your current or future career as a management practitioner.

Critical-Thinking Questions

1. What are some of the primary advantages of evidence-based management practices?
2. What makes it difficult for managers to be evidence based in their actions and decision-making?

We could apply the same critical-thinking method to the issue of work/life balance (independent variable) and its relationship to stress (dependent variable), which is one of the main issues facing today's organizations. Employees who sacrifice their personal lives for too many hours in the office may be subject to higher levels of stress. Conversely, workers who achieve a balance between their personal and working lives may have lower levels of stress. We may conclude from this that an acceptable work/life balance leads to higher levels of job satisfaction. Using critical thinking, managers explore how they can help their employees achieve a balance between work and play.

Yet, for all the research that exists on OB and the debates it continues to inspire, it's still universally agreed that there's no one best way of managing people. In fact, there's a theory for that too. It's called **contingency thinking**, and it states that our actions must be dependent on the nature of the situation. In other words, one size does not fit all. Every single circumstance brings about a whole new set of questions and solutions—this is where critical thinking comes into play. By asking the right questions to fit each scenario, managers have a better chance of resolving problems. Related to contingency thinking is **evidence-based management**, which relies on a variety of sources of evidence to make decisions.[34] Successful OB managers use this wealth of research findings as a basis for understanding different situations.

Open Systems Theory

A key OB research finding that has had a significant impact on managers' use of critical thinking is called **open systems theory**. According to this theory, organizations are systems that interact with (are *open* to) their environments and use their environments to obtain resources, or inputs, and transform those inputs into outputs that are returned to the environment for consumption.[35] Open systems theory maintains that all organizations are unique and subject to internal and external environmental influences that can affect their efficiency. To ensure the smooth running of an organization, a defined structure should be in place that can accommodate problems and opportunities as they arise. Let's take a look at how a car manufacturing company might operate, according to this theory (see Figure 1.5).

FIGURE 1.5 ■ Open Systems Theory: Inputs and Outputs

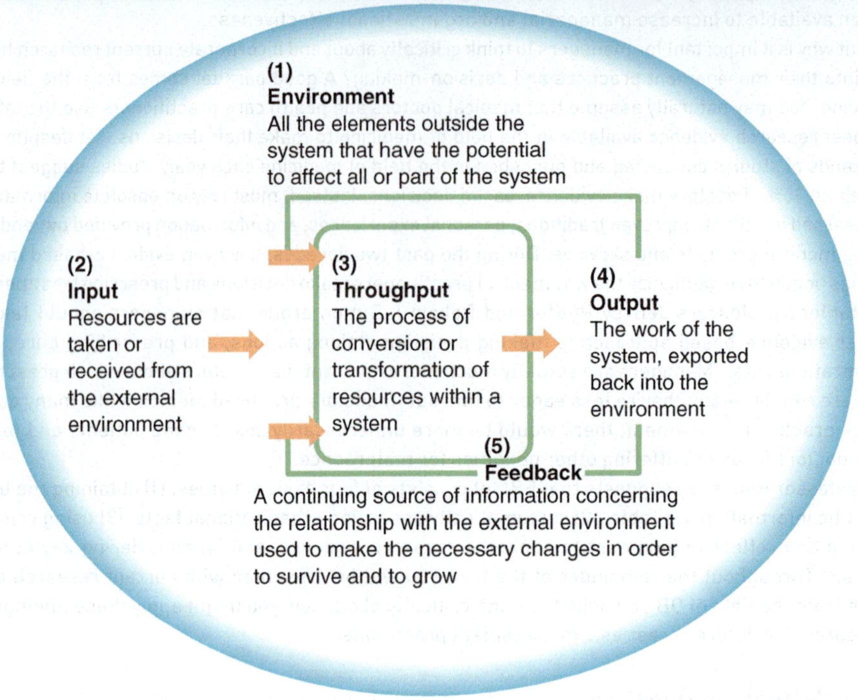

Source: CSAP Institute for Partnership Development. (n.d.). *File:Basic open system model.gif* [Diagram]. U.S. Department of Health and Human Services. https://commons.wikimedia.org/wiki/File:Basic_Open_System_Model.gif

In this example, a car manufacturing company takes inputs from suppliers of certain goods or materials and then uses these resources to manufacture cars within the organization itself ("throughput" in the figure) before exporting them back into the environment as outputs. Put into a general context, this means organizations use input from their resources, such as technology, people, money, raw materials, information, and processes, and transform them into the finished product or output, which they sell.

When open systems work well, they create a **value chain**, the sequence of activities carried out by organizations to deliver valued goods and services to consumers.[36] In the car example, if every link in the chain is working efficiently, suppliers are satisfied with the way they have been treated by the car company and continue to meet its specifications, employees are productive and manufacture the car in good time and within budget, and consumers are gratified with their new purchase. However, a poorly managed value chain can have disastrous consequences. Suppliers that go out of business, high employee turnover, and a dissatisfied consumer base can all lead to the decline of an organization.

Open systems strive to find a balance between themselves and their environment and to remain harmonious, especially in the face of environmental changes. A strong open system can be crucial to organizational survival, especially in today's organizations that are continually adjusting to meet the demands of global challenges and opportunities.

OB CHALLENGES AND OPPORTUNITIES

Organizations are in a continual state of flux and transformation. The resulting uncertainty has immeasurably influenced the behavior of people and organizations. So what can you expect when you enter the workforce? Next, we discuss some of the main challenges and opportunities facing organizations today (see Figure 1.6).

FIGURE 1.6 ■ Challenges and Opportunities Facing Today's Organizations

Globalization

Globalization is a process by which the world has become increasingly interconnected through trade, culture, technology, and politics. It has had a huge influence on OB. Many organizations now have offices all over the world, and you are very likely to be working with people from abroad or from cultures different from yours. It is essential to be able to work well with others regardless of their location or background. Communicating effectively across time zones and via the latest technological methods is important.

Economic Factors

Economic events have had a significant effect on the workplace. The COVID-19 pandemic caused a massive recession as businesses were shut down, leading to reduced customer spending and investment, reduced wages, unemployment, bankruptcy, and poverty.[37] Organizations are continuously strategizing to overcome economic stumbling blocks by seeking out talent and focusing on the skill set of their workforce to find innovative ways to differentiate themselves from the competition. To flourish in a work environment that is continually in flux, you will need to be agile, adaptable, and open to learning new skills.

In an increasingly global economy with more companies expanding internationally, having a strong grasp of organizational behavior can help individuals to relate to and respect their colleagues.

Workforce Diversity

The demographic profile of the United States is changing, and the resulting diversity in the workforce is encouraging organizations to foster inclusive working environments that don't discriminate against employees regardless of gender, race, ethnicity, age, sexual orientation, or disability.[38] In most large organizations, employees are educated about diversity and taught the importance of respecting individual differences. Forming and building good working relationships is central to achieving professional success. You'll need to respect others and accept people without prejudice if you want to get ahead in the workplace.

Customer Service

Organizations are creating customer-responsive cultures to meet the increasing needs and changing demands of their customer bases. Companies are striving to understand the customers' needs first and then tailor the product to customer requirements. In most businesses, you will carry out some level of customer service, whether you're dealing with external clients (customers) or internal ones (coworkers). In doing so, you'll need to develop a customer-focused attitude and think creatively about how to satisfy customers' needs.

People Skills

Managers and employees must have excellent people skills, such as the ability to communicate and interact with others, in order to work harmoniously with their colleagues. Being able to relate to other people has just as much impact on success as your technical skills, especially when you're leading and managing teams.

Innovation and Change

Organizations need to stimulate innovation and change by becoming faster and more agile than the competition. Tangible resources such as physical equipment are no longer the mainstays of an organization. The organization's most important assets are its people and their ability to continuously create, strategize, innovate, and convert their ideas into quality products and processes. Critical thinking is imperative in innovation; you will need to question, analyze, and create to come up with new, original ideas that will appeal to your customers to secure a competitive advantage.

Sustainability

Many organizations are striving to build a more sustainable and responsible global marketplace by taking environmental factors into consideration during decision-making and goal setting. Whatever role you play, you will need to take into account the effects your decisions and the decisions of others may have on the environment, your community, and the organization itself.

Throughout this book, we explore these and other factors that influence OB, including leadership, and the effects of a new generation of workers on the workplace. In the next section, we analyze one of the most important elements of global OB: ethical behavior in organizations.

THREE LEVELS OF ANALYSIS IN OB

There are three main levels of analysis within the OB model: individuals, teams, and organizations (see Figure 1.7).[39] Each level builds on the previous one. For example, individuals working well together lay the foundation for effective teams, which in turn work together to achieve organizational goals.

Individuals

Individuals are the foundation of organizations, and the way they work and behave makes or breaks a business. The role of managers is to integrate individuals into the organization, nurture their skills and attributes, and balance their needs and expectations accordingly. When managers do this successfully, individuals will achieve high levels of job satisfaction, motivating them to work toward attaining organizational goals. For instance, Dimple Thakkar, founder of the social media and online marketing agency Synhergy Marketing, based in California, believes that the key to business success is to nurture happy, productive, engaged employees, which is why Synhergy's remote work program is specifically designed to provide employees with a better work/life balance.[40]

FIGURE 1.7 ■ The Three Main Levels of Analysis

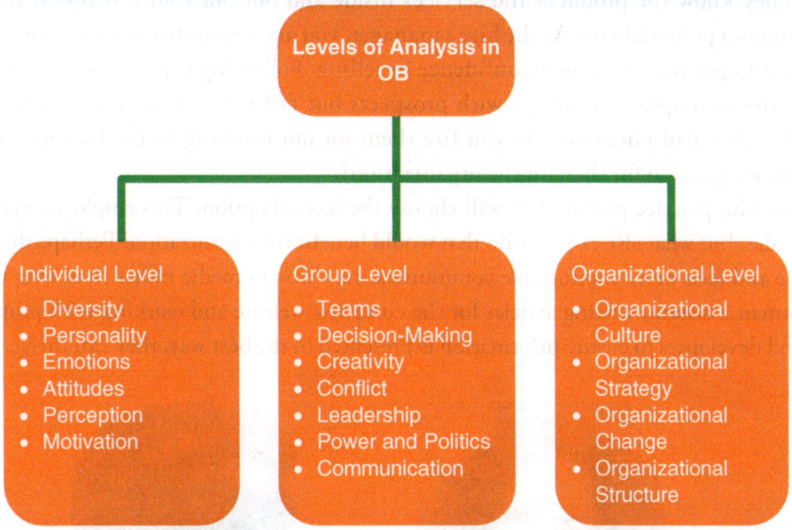

Teams

Teams or groups exist in all organizations, large or small, and their effective functioning is essential to the success of any organization. Teams are complex because they consist of many different personalities and attitudes. Managers who understand the dynamics of a team and the way it's structured also better understand the underlying behaviors of individuals within the group. A good example is the manager of Manchester United Football Club, Sir Alex Ferguson, who helped to grow the team into a world-famous brand. Ferguson was well known for listening to the younger members and hearing their thoughts, believing them to be "the people most in touch with the realities of today and the prospects for tomorrow."[41]

Organizations

Organizations provide individuals and groups with the tools and systems they need to achieve objectives and goals. The attitudes and behavior of employees are influenced by the way organizations are structured. For instance, a recent survey reported that employees derive job satisfaction from a flexible working structure that provides them the freedom to set their own goals and standards.[42]

With organizations continually juggling market changes and customer demands, the success of a business depends on its workforce as never before. But how do managers get the best from individuals, teams, and the organization itself? Let's explore the impact of positive OB and high-involvement management.

Positive OB and High-Involvement Management

Drawing from a range of organizational research and theories, scholarship on **positive organizational behavior** focuses on the strengths, virtues, vitality, and resilience of individuals and organizations.[43] The idea is that nurturing the strengths of individuals rather than attempting to "fix" their weaknesses is far more beneficial to achieving organizational goals. Employees will gain more self-confidence and feel more positive about their skills and abilities, leading to better performance. Research shows that employees working for companies that value positive organizational behavior experience less stress, exhibit greater concern for others, and gain more enjoyment from work, leading to higher degrees of motivation.[44] Managers who practice positive OB value human capital as their most important resource.

Say you're the manager of a sales and marketing department. You need your sales team to reach a specific sales target by the end of each month. However, one of your new hires, a recent business graduate, is regularly failing to meet objectives, bringing down the department's sales total. When you arrange a one-to-one meeting, the hire admits finding the role tougher than they thought it would be. They know the products and services inside and out but find it difficult to persuade people to discuss a potential sale. As the hire's manager, you arrange additional training to improve their sales technique and build their confidence in selling. Following extensive training, they succeed in securing a couple of meetings with prospects but fail to sell anything. When you hired them, you felt they had potential. Do you fire them for not bringing in the business, or do you consider another position for them in the organization?

Managers who practice positive OB will choose the second option. This employee may not be a good fit for sales, but what else can they do that would benefit the organization? Perhaps the employee loves to write and feels more comfortable communicating through media rather than over the phone. As a web content assistant, writing articles for the company website and working with project teams, designers, and developers to ensure information is presented in the best way, they can thrive.

Managers who practice positive OB will communicate with their employees and learn their strengths to discover the position best suited to their skills.

© iStockphoto.com/pixelfit

This is just one example of how managers get the best from (and for) their employees using positive behavior. Most people are hired for a reason, but it's entirely possible that some may not be the best fit in the role they were hired for. In such a case, managers who value their human capital should make every effort to match employees' skill sets with a more appropriate position. Otherwise, organizations could face the dilemmas of low job satisfaction and reduced productivity, leading to an increase in absenteeism and high turnover.

High Involvement Management

Positive OB places the highest priority on the well-being of employees. This style of management is closely linked with **high-involvement management**, a strategy in which managers empower employees to make decisions, provide them with extensive training and opportunities to increase their knowledge base, share important information, and provide incentive compensation.[45] Increasing employee involvement in this way is a very democratic approach to management, giving all employees, including those who carry out basic duties, a say in how the work is conducted. They are then more likely to work hard and be more willing to adapt to new processes and learn new tasks. Empowered, satisfied employees strive to achieve organizational goals.

Again, this type of approach works only when the right employees are selected to work in an organization. They must be the right cultural fit and believe in the values and mission of the company. Equally, managers must treat employees with respect, listen carefully to their ideas, and be willing to admit to themselves and their employees that they don't have all the answers. When high-involvement management is effective, it helps to build strong relationships between employees and managers, fosters trust, and increases job satisfaction and productivity.

High-involvement managers have different ways of empowering their employees. Take Anissa Jones, for instance. Jones is a chiropractor, author, business consultant, and the founder of Total Health Chiropractic and Wellness Center, based in Atlanta, and believes employees should be given the opportunity to take responsibility for tasks rather than being micromanaged. For example, employees can present agenda items at meetings and take the lead on certain tasks.[46] Would you like to work for a company like Total Health Chiropractic and Wellness Center that strongly promotes autonomy and accountability? Do you think you would fit in and buy into the ethos of this type of organization? If you're not the type of person who likes to take the lead on work tasks, then perhaps this might not be the right work culture for you. Remember, high-involvement management works best when employees are a good fit for the organization.

iStockphoto/fizkes

Throughout this text, we present a number of real-world case studies that demonstrate a critical-thinking perspective in relation to OB. We've structured this book to explore the challenges and opportunities facing OB on individual, group, and organizational levels. We explore the complexities of human behavior, including individual behaviors, emotions, and attitudes. We also examine OB in the context of leadership, motivation, teamwork, and culture.

At the heart of every job, regardless of the industry, lies the need to get along with people and to fit in with the values and culture of the organization. However, in today's organizations, fitting in does not mean agreeing with everything to maintain the status quo, nor does it mean laughing at your manager's jokes (especially when you don't think they're very funny!). Instead, applying critical thinking by asking questions, suspending bias, and providing creative solutions, all of which you'll experience in this book, form the new norm. Understanding and gaining knowledge about OB is a lifelong learning process. Your career success depends on your ability to learn from your everyday experiences and on the way you conduct your relationships with others, behave, and communicate.

In a world where the only constant is change, it's more important than ever to manage our own behavior and understand the feelings, attitudes, and behaviors of others around us so we can work harmoniously and productively and succeed in a complex working environment.

IN REVIEW

1.1 Explain the basic concept of organizational behavior and its value in organizations

Organizational behavior studies how and why individual employees and groups of employees behave the way they do within an organizational setting. The three main reasons for studying organizational behavior in your organization are to be able to *explain* it, *predict* it, and *influence* it.

1.2 Describe the key role of managing human capital in creating a sustainable competitive advantage for organizations

Human capital is essential for gaining **competitive advantage**, the edge that gives organizations a more beneficial position than their competitors and allows them to generate more profits and retain more customers. Three main aspects of human capital enhance true competitive advantage: *value, rareness*, and *inimitability.*

1.3 Identify the major behavioral science disciplines that contribute to OB

Psychology is the scientific study of the human mind that seeks to measure and explain behavioral characteristics. **Sociology** is the study of the behavior of groups and how they relate to each other in a social setting. **Social psychology** blends concepts from sociology and psychology and focuses on how people influence each other in a social setting. **Political science** studies the behavior of individuals and groups within a political environment. **Anthropology** is the study of people and their activities in relation to societal, environmental, and cultural influences.

1.4 Demonstrate the value of critical thinking in the context of OB

Critical thinking is the ability to use intelligence, knowledge, and skills to question and carefully explore situations and arrive at thoughtful conclusions based on evidence and reason. The critical-thinking approach is a powerful analytical method that helps managers consider intended and unintended consequences of behaviors on their teams, organizations, and communities.

1.5 Identify the major challenges and opportunities in the field of OB

The process of *globalization* has had a huge influence on OB. The *economy* has had a significant effect on OB. Organizations are continually strategizing to overcome economic stumbling blocks by hiring talent and focusing on the skill sets of their workforce to find new, innovative ways to differentiate themselves from the competition. *Workforce diversity* develops when organizations foster working environments that don't discriminate against others regardless of gender, race, ethnicity, age, sexual orientation, and disability. Organizations are creating *customer-responsive cultures* to meet the increasing needs and changing demands of their customer base. Managers and employees must have excellent people skills and use them on the job to work harmoniously with their colleagues. Organizations need to stimulate *innovation* and *change* by becoming faster and more agile than the competition. There is a growing commitment to fostering an *ethical culture* and improving ethical behavior in the workplace. Many organizations are striving to build a more sustainable and responsible global marketplace by taking environmental factors into consideration during decision-making and goal-setting practices.

1.6 Differentiate the three basic levels of analysis at which OB may be examined

There are three main levels of analysis within the OB model: individuals, teams, and organizations. Individuals are the foundation of organizations: the way they work and behave makes or breaks a business. The role of managers is to integrate individuals into the organization, nurture their skills and attributes, and balance their needs and expectations accordingly. Teams or groups exist in all organizations, large or small, and have a significant influence on the behavior of individual team members. **Positive organizational behavior** focuses on the strengths, virtues, vitality, and resilience of individuals and organizations.

High-involvement management occurs when managers empower employees to make decisions, provide them with extensive training and the opportunities to increase their knowledge base, share important information, and provide incentive compensation. This type of approach works only when the right employees are selected to work in an organization. When high-involvement management is effective, it helps to build strong relationships between individuals and teams, fosters trust, and increases job satisfaction and productivity.

KEY TERMS

Anthropology (p. 11)
Competitive advantage (p. 9)
Conceptual skill (p. 8)
Contingency thinking (p. 15)
Correlation (p. 14)
Critical thinking (p. 12)
Dependent variables (p. 14)
Emotional intelligence (p. 8)
Evidence-based management (p. 15)
High-involvement management (p. 20)
Human capital (p. 9)
Human capital inimitability (p. 10)
Human capital rareness (p. 10)
Human capital value (p. 9)
Human skills (p. 8)
Hypothesis (p. 14)
Independent variables (p. 14)
Model (p. 14)
Open systems theory (p. 15)
Organization (p. 6)
Organizational behavior (p. 6)
Political science (p. 11)
Positive organizational behavior (p. 22)
Psychology (p. 11)
Social psychology (p. 11)
Sociology (p. 11)
Strategic OB approach (p. 9)
Technical skill (p. 8)
Theory (p. 14)
Value chain (p. 16)

UP FOR DEBATE: HIRING CRITERIA

When hiring employees, the emotional intelligence of the potential employee is more important than their IQ. Agree or disagree?

EXERCISE 1.1: ORGANIZATIONAL BEHAVIOR IN AN INTERNATIONAL FIRM

Objective

The purpose of this exercise is to gain a greater understanding of organizational behavior as it applies to globalization.

Instructions

Globalization is a major consideration for large, diversified companies and their understanding of organizational behavior. Suppose you work for an American organization that has been operating in this country for over a hundred years. The company manufactures a variety of light bulbs but over the last 10 years has specialized in LED bulbs. As the business has grown, the leaders of the organization have begun to see opportunities to expand internationally for the first time in the firm's history. The CEO wants to begin international operations next year with a manufacturing plant in a country outside the United States.

In teams of three to six, choose a country in which to open a new division of your company. Select one you are either familiar with or can readily find information about. Next, determine what you would need to know about the country and its culture for the new facility to be successful. For example, does the country and culture you selected value individualism or teams more? Is the country one where loud, expressive communication is commonplace, or does interpersonal communication tend to be more quiet and subdued? Assume that 95% of the employees will be hired from the country you selected and only 5% will be expatriates from the United States.

Reflection Questions

1. How important is it for managers to understand both organizational behavior *and* globalization when operating an international organization?
2. What could managers do to ensure that the employees hired have a firm understanding of the accepted standards of behavior in the company?
3. How about the 5% of the employees who will be relocating from the United States? What challenges will they have in adjusting to this new country and culture? How can the company assist them in acclimating more quickly and easily to this new working environment?

Exercise contributed by Steven Stovall, Southeast Missouri State University.

EXERCISE 1.2: WHO CAN BE CEO?

Objective

The purpose of this exercise is to grasp the concept of human capital and its value to organizations.

Instructions

Human capital is described as the sum of people's skills, knowledge, experience, and general attributes. To be the president or chief executive officer (CEO) of a firm, one must be strong in all of these factors. The top leaders of organizations change over time due to the death or retirement of the CEO, the CEO moving on to a different organization voluntarily, or the board of directors asking the CEO to step down because of poor performance.

When the board of directors at a major corporation has an opening for a CEO and they want to promote someone from within the organization, they examine all the qualifications of various candidates—the human capital of those vying for the position.

The question for the class to discuss is this: Can anyone be a CEO? Does every single employee in a company have the same skill set, knowledge about the firm and the industry, experience in the field, and other general attributes to step into the role of CEO? Why or why not?

Reflection Questions

1. If you feel that anyone can be CEO, what do you base this on? And if you feel otherwise—that only certain individuals can be CEO—what would prevent others from filling that role? What is it they're missing?
2. How do companies identify human capital in their organization? What ways could a board of directors evaluate who is most qualified to be CEO?

What training and development could a company offer to prepare more candidates to be the top manager of an organization? Are all the qualifications a CEO should have able to be learned, or are they innate skills these individuals are born with?

Exercise contributed by Steven Stovall, Southeast Missouri State University.

EXERCISE 1.3: YOUR EXPERIENCE WITH OB

Objective

This exercise will help you to better *understand* organizational behavior, its concepts, and its uses by helping you to *explain* and *discuss* your organizational experiences in terms of Chapter 1 concepts.

Instructions

Step 1 (10 minutes): Think about an organization you are or have been a member of. It can be any type of organization as discussed in the first chapter of this text (e.g., social, religious, charitable). After selecting your organization, think about a problem the organization has had. Write down a brief (no more than half a page) narrative describing this problem. Be sure to explain the problem using the concept terms from Chapter 1. Also, try to identify the level at which this problem existed: individual, group, organizational, or across multiple levels.

Step 2 (10 minutes): Find a partner and read each other the problems you wrote about. Select the most interesting of the two write-ups. Together rewrite the description so that it clarifies any points that are unclear and is more concrete in its use and application of chapter concepts.

Step 3 (10 minutes): As a pair, find another pair to form a quad. Each pair should read the situation write-up selected in Step 2 to the other pair. Again, select the situation that is the most interesting, and work together as a group to improve the situation description. Clarify any misuse of terms and be sure that as much of the situation as possible is described using chapter concepts.

Step 4 (10 to 30 minutes): Select one person from the quad to read the write-up chosen by the entire quad as the most interesting to the entire class. The person who reads the situation should be someone other than the person who initially wrote about the situation, but everyone should be prepared to help clarify any points about the write-up using chapter concepts.

Reflection Questions

Think about the process of identifying organizational problems in terms of the organizational behavior concepts you're learning.

1. How did identifying the problem in this way change the way you thought about the problem?
2. How did linking the problem to the concepts help you think about methods for dealing with the problem?
3. How did thinking about the level of the problem shape the way you thought about the problem?
4. When listening to other groups, note how their descriptions used chapter concepts. Were there any usages that surprised you or you were uncertain about?

Exercise contributed by Milton R. Mayfield, Professor of Business, Texas A&M International University, and Jacqueline R. Mayfield, Professor of Business, Texas A&M International University.

ONLINE EXERCISE 1.1: UNDERSTANDING ORGANIZATIONAL CHALLENGES AND OPPORTUNITIES

Objective

The purpose of this exercise is to gain an understanding of the challenges and opportunities facing organizations today.

Instructions

This chapter identifies seven challenges and opportunities facing organizations (globalization, people skills, innovation and change, etc.). These challenges and opportunities may be either external (e.g., globalization) or internal (e.g., people skills).

In an online discussion group, choose one of the seven challenges and opportunities, then provide an example of how that is both a challenge and an opportunity for an organization. For example, if you chose globalization, an example of a challenge would be understanding different cultures in the workplace (for instance, you might be working alongside someone from Japan who tends to bow or lower their head when greeting you). An example of an opportunity would be that the company will be able to offer its products or services to an entirely new consumer overseas.

Reflection Questions

1. Are any of the seven challenges and opportunities (globalization, people skills, innovation and change, etc.) more important than the others? Explain.

2. Select one of the challenges and opportunities listed in the chapter. Think about an organization you currently work for or have worked for before. How well or how poorly does/did that organization perform with that challenge or opportunity?

3. How successful would an organization be if it ignored one or more of these challenges and opportunities? Explain.

Exercise contributed by Steven Stovall, Southeast Missouri State University.

ONLINE EXERCISE 1.2: UNDERSTANDING SKILLS

Objective

The purpose of this exercise is to gain an appreciation for technical, human, and conceptual skills.

Instructions

Technical, human, and conceptual skills are used to varying degrees by managers at all levels of an organization. For example, a forklift driver will have more technical skills, while the vice president of sales will have more conceptual skills.

Have each person on the discussion board post a job title familiar to that individual. If it's a job title peculiar to a particular industry or one that many won't readily recognize, offer a brief a description of the job. Once the job title is posted, discuss whether that job title would involve more conceptual, human, or technical skills. Discuss why you think one job title would involve more of one set of skills than another job title that has been posted.

Reflection Questions

1. What kinds of jobs have more conceptual skills? More human skills? More technical skills?
2. Are human skills important for every job title? Why or why not?
3. How effective would the president of a company be if they had strong technical skills but weak conceptual skills? What about a janitor who had excellent conceptual skills but poor technical skills?
4. In your current job or in jobs you have had in the past, which skills have been most important: technical, human, or conceptual? Explain.

Exercise contributed by Steven Stovall, Southeast Missouri State University.

CASE 1.1: CVS HEALTH

Time and time again, job satisfaction has been proven to have large effects on the bottom line; employee happiness and productiveness go hand in hand. As mentioned in this chapter, human capital, which is the sum of people's skills, knowledge, experience, and general attributes, is a key element of competitive advantage. One way to influence people and employees is from a sociological perspective, which involves managers and corporations committing to a bigger picture. The text speaks on the ways in which feelings, actions, and beliefs can influence the behavior of employees and consumers, and CVS Health has spent considerable time and resources forming a fulfilling mission.

Making Difficult Decisions

In September 2014, CVS Corporation made a landmark decision: they ceased all tobacco sales in their nearly 7,900 locations at the time. The CVS bottom line took a $2 billion annual reduction, which was a risky move for a Fortune 500 company, but the CVS mission became clear to all employees and consumers.[47] They had branded themselves as a leading provider of health services, and they could no longer square their cigarette sales with their genuine pursuits in health care. The people at CVS and the upper management team decided that a value chain must be viable in the marketplace, but it must also reside within their corporation's bigger mission.

While there may be short-term financial losses embedded in decisions like these, they give employees a reason to find more fulfillment in their work and have financially lucrative sociological side effects. For example, since CVS was the first drugstore to eliminate tobacco, many prominent figures came out in support of the effort, ranging from Bill Gates, founder of Microsoft, to then-president Barack Obama. These larger societal implications can make short-term difficulties pay off in the long run. Studies have shown that CVS's decision led to a reduction in total cigarette purchases, from any seller, of 95 million packs in eight months.[48] In addition, considering how heavy smokers are twice as likely to be hospitalized and stand a greater risk of dying from COVID-19, this short-term decision has greatly benefited society in ways that wouldn't have been expected. Overall, CVS revenues have increased from around $139.4 billion at the end of 2014 to $268.7 billion in 2020.[49]

The Value Chain

At first glance, it can be difficult to understand how a decline in sales could improve a company's value chain, described in the text as the sequence of activities carried out by organizations to deliver valued goods and services to consumers. "For now," explained executive Eileen Howard Boone, "we focused on helping our customers lead tobacco-free lives. We believe passionately that is a powerful preventive health measure that will have a positive impact on their health and quality of life. I'm so proud that we are the first national pharmacy chain to stop the sale of tobacco products. While it produced $2 billion in annual sales, we wanted to take a bold step in support of the health and well-being of our patients and customers and I truly hope [it] will continue to fuel the public health discussion."[50] CVS and their employees are committed to creating healthy lives, and they believe they can now provide that valuable service better than ever as they maintain a more fulfilling, long-term outlook on their value chain.

Aside from making waves in their industry with their decision to nix tobacco sales, the leadership members at CVS have sought to define their business on their own terms. The text describes the value of having a purpose, on the individual employee level all the way up to the corporate level, and CVS describes theirs as such: "We're reinventing pharmacy to have a more active, supportive role in each person's unique health experience and in the greater health care environment."[51] A consistent purpose like this one can play a key role in keeping a company on track in spite of financial gains and losses and the ebbs and flows of the market as a whole. CVS (NYSE: CVS) stock has seen some large fluctuations, but they have grown steadily on a long-term basis even amid the COVID-19 pandemic, and they rose all the way to number four on the Fortune 500 list in 2021.[52]

Ethics

It's no stretch to see the ethical implications of the CVS tobacco-free decision: they believe it's worth short-term pains to benefit the health of their communities. Ethics are morals that guide behavior—but they never make answers black and white, and often create ethical dilemmas. While all of CVS's best practices don't fit into a case study, the company takes a number of notable measures to ensure they promote ethical behavior. CVS ensures that all their suppliers, of which they have thousands, go through application and compliance processes to guarantee ethical sourcing. They also offer a website for customers and employees to report any ethical dilemmas and offenses they notice, as the pharmaceutical and health industries present many difficult decisions and temptations.

Conclusion

In sum, many large corporations have issues, but many also have valuable best practices, from which all managers and business owners can learn. CVS has taken meaningful strides to improve their corporate culture, management style, and society as a whole, all the while investing in the growth and improvement of their value chain.

Case Questions

1. Describe the big decision that CVS Health made. How does it relate to the text?
2. How does the text describe ethics, and how do they play a role at CVS Health?

PART II

INDIVIDUAL PROCESSES

dpa picture alliance/Alamy Stock Photo

2 DIVERSITY, EQUITY, AND INCLUSION (DEI)

LEARNING OBJECTIVES

By the end of this chapter, you will be able to:

2.1 Explain the importance of DEI in OB

2.2 Discuss diversity in the workplace

2.3 Discuss how diversity influences identity in the workplace

2.4 Describe the impact of equity and equality in the workplace

2.5 Illustrate the power of inclusion in a working environment

2.6 Identify the different ways businesses can promote a DEI culture

Case Study: Dolby Laboratories, Inc.

Dolby Laboratories, the creators of Dolby Digital, Dolby Atmos, and Dolby Vision audiovisual technologies, is an American company with offices and employees worldwide. For more than 50 years, the household name has developed standards in audio noise reduction and home and cinema surround sound, but the fact that a company's workforce spans time zones, languages, and cultures doesn't guarantee that it will be a diverse, equitable, and inclusive employer. Dolby utilized innovative hiring practices and created employee organizations to support its goals for diversity, equity, and inclusion, which quickly proved very popular.

Blind hiring, a common practice for reducing bias in recruitment, traces its beginnings to the performing arts industry. In the 1970s, less than 5% of musicians at the top North American orchestras were women. Members of the Toronto Symphony Orchestra noticed how white and male dominated their ensemble was and implemented a simple change to their audition procedure that quickly increased the diversity of the band's composition. Similar to the contemporary TV singing competition *The Voice*, where contestants perform for judges whose backs are turned to the singer, the orchestra erected a sonically transparent screen to separate symphony hopefuls from the judges, concealing their identities so they would be evaluated solely by their musical ability. The practice of "blind" auditions soon became the standard for orchestras nationwide, and by 1997 female musicians comprised 25% of the top American symphonies' performers.[1]

Outside the concert hall, however, most business recruitment relies on résumé reviews and candidate interviews; there is no audition to be blinded. Traditional blind hiring techniques merely redact applicants' names and other identifying information from their résumés. This can help job seekers avoid being overlooked by recruiters with unconscious biases, such as preference for one gender over another or names that sound a certain way, but still misses the meritocratic aspect of the blind symphony auditions.[2] This simple form of blind hiring wasn't good enough for Dolby, and they sought a more comprehensive solution.

Dolby Laboratories was one of GapJumpers' first clients, adopting the company's innovative blind audition technology in 2015.[3] Entrepreneur Petar Vujosevic had cofounded GapJumpers in 2014 as a platform where employers design challenges for prospective talent to complete when applying to their job postings. "We've essentially applied software technology to allow companies to experience the same kind of results that orchestras have achieved with blind hiring," Vujosevic says. "Right now, we are able to do blind auditions for software engineering roles, design roles, marketing roles, communication roles and allow candidates that might on paper not be a good fit, prove that they actually are."[4]

Blind hiring (and utilizing analogous tech solutions like GapJumpers) can help companies reduce bias during the talent acquisition process, but that's just one element of creating a diverse, equitable, and inclusive organization. Even a company with a multicultural and gender-inclusive workforce must take intentional steps to empower its employees and make them feel valued and visible at all levels of the organization.

As part of its Diversity, Inclusion, and Belonging strategy, Dolby has instituted 13 volunteer-led Employee Networks (ENs), communities organized around ethnicity, sexual orientation, and other social dimensions of diversity. More than 32% of the Dolby Labs workforce participates in its ENs.

Lauren Glover, senior manager of people communications and experiences, says of Dolby ENs, "Having Employee Networks be so visible in the Company's strategy is powerful. As a Black employee, as the Co-Founder of Obsidian, as a person of a certain dimension of diversity, I feel safe and empowered to say, 'This is how I want the company to reach people like me—and here's how we go and do it.'"[5]

As Dolby's website states, "Dolby's ENs include: WE focused on Women's Empowerment, Spectrum supporting LGBT+, PAX focused on the Pan-Asian Experience, Obsidian for employees who are Black or of African descent, Mundo for our Latinx/Hispanic community, DIVE—our Dolby's Indigenous Voices Elevated group, the Anti-Racism Community, Path for new and early-career employees, the Parents Network, INxS: Inclusion at Sydney for our Australian office, a regional network for EMEA, one for China (expanding across Asia in FY22), and AGAPE for Dolby's Christian community."[6]

The creation of Employee Networks has paid dividends both for employee engagement and Dolby's research and development projects. Kelsey McIntosh, senior data analyst in the Intellectual Property Protection Group and coleader of WE, summarizes the impact of the groups: "When the employee networks started, you saw a shift in Dolby's culture. People were more engaged, more friendly. Now, you get to know people from other departments and have exposure to even more diverse ideas and experiences. There's always something fun and meaningful happening, and it is all driven by the employees."[7]

Critical-Thinking Questions

1. What is blind hiring, and how can it reduce biases in the recruitment process?
2. Where do facially unbiased hiring practices fall short, and what did Dolby Laboratories do to complete the DEI triad?
3. Describe some of the day-to-day benefits of Dolby's Employee Networks. If you were at Dolby Labs, would you join any of the 13 existing ENs? Would you create your own?

DEI IN OB

Diversity, equity, and inclusion (DEI) is a term used to describe programs and policies that encourage the representation and participation of diverse groups of people, including people of different genders, races and ethnicities, abilities and disabilities, religions, cultures, ages, and sexual orientations and people with diverse backgrounds, experiences, and skills and expertise.[8] DEI has become a hot topic for organizations all over the world, even more so since the onset of the COVID-19 pandemic. Systemic racial violence and injustice, hate crimes, social activism, and stalled career growth of women in the workplace have shined the spotlight on DEI, leading large numbers of corporations to pledge their commitment by devoting more attention and resources to DEI. For example, Dolby has created a DEI organization by implementing blind audition technology into its recruitment strategies to promote fairness in its hiring processes and formed 13 volunteer-led Employee Networks focusing on ethnicity, sexual orientation, and other social dimensions of diversity.

Why is DEI so important in the workplace? Because today's workplace welcomes more people from different backgrounds and different experiences than ever before. Globalization has led to a workforce of cross-cultural work teams composed of people from diverse backgrounds who deserve to be treated fairly and equitably. As Figure 2.1 depicts, each element of DEI interacts with the others to create a culture that supports employee views, beliefs, and values.

In the business world, the benefits of supporting DEI initiatives are enormous. For example, studies have shown that companies that champion DEI are more likely to outperform their less diverse peers, earn higher revenues, attract a larger customer base, and increase their profits. Companies with higher DEI also demonstrate a rise in employee satisfaction, retention, and engagement.[9] In contrast, research shows that organizations lacking in DEI can promote stereotyping, which can lead to destructive discriminatory behaviour.[10]

Stereotyping is the tendency to believe that certain people or things share the same characteristics. Stereotypes can exist at every level of an organization and are often based on incorrect assumptions about a person's gender, culture, religion, or physical characteristics. For instance, the belief that women with blond hair aren't intelligent is a common example of a stereotype. Research shows that people who experience negative stereotyping in the workplace are more likely to have lower career confidence, fewer career aspirations, and poorer job attitudes than those who are not stereotyped.[11] Stereotyping can lead to discrimination if it is not addressed.

Discrimination is the unfair treatment of people and groups based on certain characteristics, such as race, age, gender, religion, disability, or sexual orientation.[12] While stereotyping involves prejudiced

FIGURE 2.1 ■ DEI

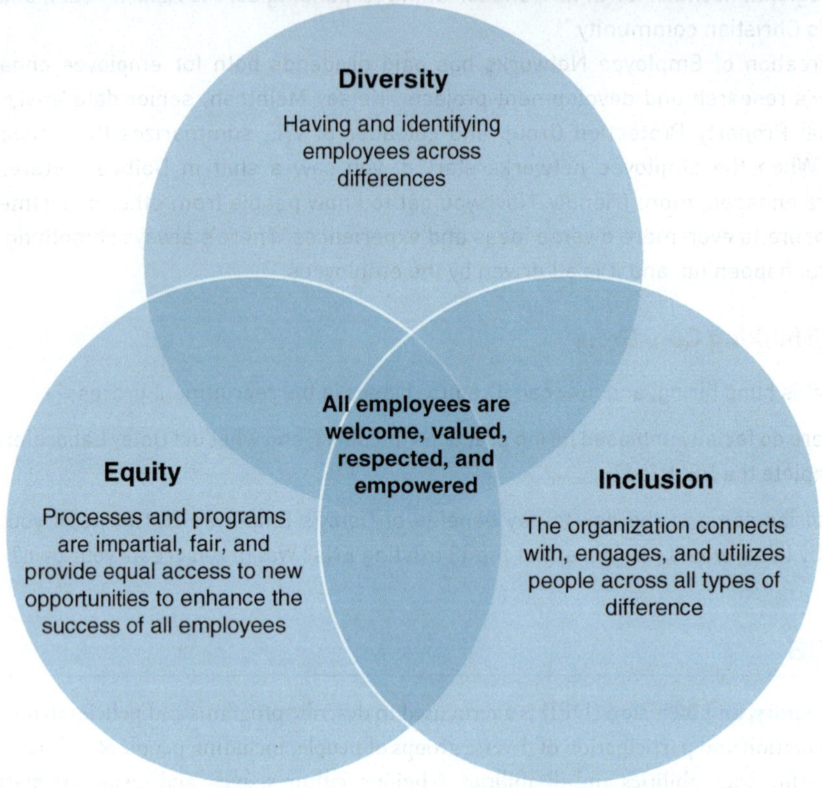

beliefs about individuals or groups, discrimination is the process of acting on those beliefs. Making derogatory comments about a person's race or color, excluding particular groups or individuals from the recruitment process, and paying unequal salaries to equally qualified employees in the same role are examples of workplace discrimination.

The following sections explore each element of DEI in greater depth.

DIVERSITY IN THE WORKPLACE

Diversity is the presence of differences within a given setting and is expressed in many forms, including race and ethnicity, gender and gender identity, sexual orientation, socioeconomic status, language, culture, national origin, religion, age, strength and ability, and political standpoints.[13]

In the past, banking heavyweights Morgan Stanley and Bank of America Merrill Lynch have paid millions settling sex discrimination and race discrimination claims. Widely publicized cases like these have encouraged organizations to care more about diversity and realize the importance of respecting individual differences in order to form and build successful professional relationships. In broader terms, **workplace diversity** refers to the degree to which an organization includes people from different cultures and backgrounds; it involves recognizing, respecting, and valuing both individual and group differences by treating people as individuals in an effort to promote an inclusive culture.[14]

As our case study shows, Dolby is a great example of a company that implements recruitment strategies targeted specifically at underrepresented groups. Dolby has an excellent reputation for fairness because of its commitment to DEI.

One of the most effective ways organizations can encourage acceptance of differences and create a harmonious workforce is through the management of diversity.

However, there are also challenges to managing a diverse workforce—diversity does not simply mean recognizing the differences between us. For diversity to succeed, managers must promote inclusiveness, tackle discrimination, and respect and value the differences between people.

In a recent survey of the "top 50 companies for diversity" run by DiversityInc, hotel giant Hilton took the number-one spot while department store chain Kohl's came last on the list.[15] McKinsey research has shown that ignoring diversity is bad for business. Companies that don't foster a diverse workforce may be negatively perceived by customers, existing employees, and potential younger candidates who value diversity as a priority in organizations.[16]

Surface-Level and Deep-Level Diversity

There are two main types of diversity: surface-level diversity and deep-level diversity (see Figure 2.2).[17] **Surface-level diversity** describes the easily perceived differences between us, such as age and generation, race and ethnicity, gender and sexual orientation, and physical and/or mental ability. This type of diversity can lead to discrimination when managers or recruiters judge or stereotype others on the basis of superficial differences. For example, if they believe performance declines with age, they will choose a younger candidate over an older candidate.

In contrast, **deep-level diversity** describes verbal and nonverbal behaviors that aren't as easily perceived because they lie below the surface. Deep-level diversity may include attitudes, values, beliefs, and personality traits. People first identify surface-level differences in others and then become aware of deep-level differences as they get to know someone. For example, initially Myra and Jorge might treat each other with caution because of dissimilarities between their cultural backgrounds or native languages. As their relationship deepens and they learn about each other's underlying attitudes, values, and beliefs, however, their surface-level perceptions of difference may subside. Myra and Jorge may begin to find common ground and recognize the similarities they share with one other.

Age/Generation Diversity

With workforce demographics shifting and the number of mature people in the workplace rising, many organizations are finding ways to leverage age diversity, which means including people of all different ages within the workplace.[18] According to a recent report from the New School's Schwartz Centre for Economic Policy Analysis, more than 3 million Americans age 50 and older have lost their jobs due to the pandemic recession. Ageism campaigner Kate Edwards said that the pandemic has "doubled down on the subtle perception that [older workers] are different. Now you are not just an intellectual liability but you are a physical liability to the company, you're old, you're vulnerable to Covid-19, you could be dead next week."[19]

FIGURE 2.2 ■ Surface-Level and Deep-Level Diversity

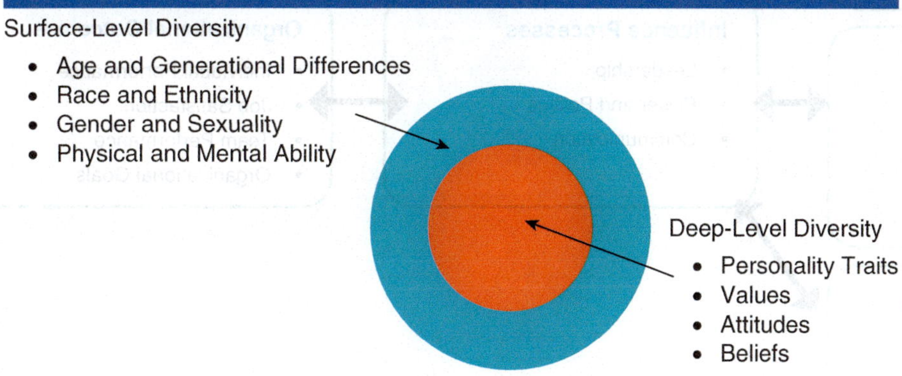

Source: Huszczo, G., & Endres, M. (2013, February). Joint effects of gender and personality on choice of happiness strategies. *Europe's Journal of Psychology, 9*(1), 136–149.

Regardless of the discrimination against older workers during the pandemic, it is no easy task managing age diversity, particularly as today's workforce spans five generations:

- Traditionalists (also known as the Silent Generation (born 1925 to 1945)
- Baby boomers (1946 to 1964)
- Generation X (1965 to 1980)
- Millennials (1981 to 2000)
- Generation Z (2001 to 2020)

Managers need to treat age-diverse workforces thoughtfully, without falling prey to stereotypes often portrayed by the popular media. For example, traditionalists and baby boomers are often described as "old-school," conservative, averse to change, and not up-to-date with the latest technology, while younger employees such as Gen Xers are considered to be independent but despondent, millennials are thought to be driven and technology savvy but entitled, and Gen Zers are regarded as progressive but disloyal. These generalizations are dangerous and problematic because they often influence opinions before the employees start their new jobs. One study found that employees subject to age-based stereotypes were less likely to commit to their role or pursue long-term professional goals.[20]

Applying these stereotypes to individuals could lead to bias and conflict among workers of different ages in an organization. Organizations dealing with a multigenerational workforce need to focus on the strengths and weaknesses of their individual employees and should be able to foster the transfer of knowledge across age groups while bridging differences and building on commonalities in order to create a cohesive, dynamic workforce.

Managers of multigenerational teams need to find ways of addressing age diversity by encouraging communication between team members, respecting the opinions of others while sharing and emphasizing organizational values, creating a collaborate environment that fosters greater learning and

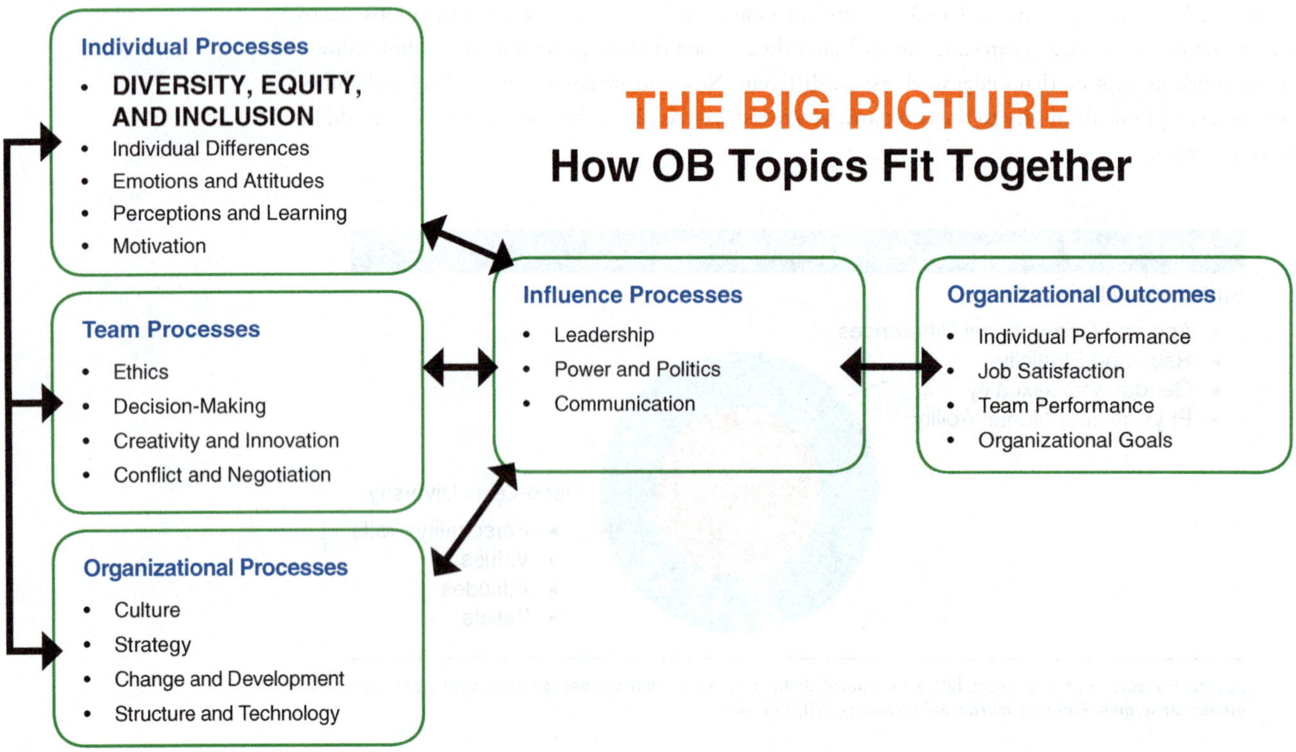

FIGURE 2.3 ■ Age Diversity. Today's workforce spans five generations, including baby boomers (media giant Oprah Winfrey), Generation X (Williams-Sonoma CEO Laura Alber), and millennials (Facebook founder Mark Zuckerberg).

Source: Images by Mike Marsland/Mike Marsland/WireImage, Getty/Bloomberg/Contributor, © iStockphoto.com/FLDphotos

knowledge sharing, and cultivating an understanding that people are all different and have the capacity to offer valuable insights regardless of their age or generation.[21]

Race and Ethnicity

Today's workplace is made up of people from different racial groups and ethnicities, yet racial and ethnic prejudice persists. Sometimes the terms *race* and *ethnicity* are used interchangeably, but **race** is related to factors of physical appearance such as skin, hair, or eye color, whereas **ethnicity** is associated with sociological factors such as nationality, culture, language, and ancestry.[22]

No one should ever feel uncomfortable because of their race or ethnicity. Racial and ethnic prejudice often stems from ignorance and stereotypes that individuals may not even be aware influence them. Racial and ethnic discrimination has played a prominent role in U.S. history, and it is only in the last few decades that significant strides have been made to overcome such discrimination. There is much more work to be done. For instance, along with women, people of color (POC) have experienced difficulties during the COVID-19 pandemic, particularly in relation to health and safety in the workplace, household responsibilities, and career prospects, compared to white people.[23] Women of color are also more likely to face discrimination at work, leading to burnout, stress, and negative feelings about their roles.[24]

Making an effort to develop a deeper sense of racial and cultural awareness by becoming familiar with the history of racial and ethnic discrimination in the United States and learning about various languages and cultural traditions goes a long way toward building group harmony in the workplace. And treating every person you work with as an individual rather than a collection of predetermined labels goes a long way toward establishing trust and understanding.

Gender Diversity

Gender diversity is the equal representation of men, women, and nonbinary people in the workplace.[25] In the United States, the treatment of women in the workplace—like the treatment of people of color—has come a long way during the past 50 years. In the past, wealthier women were often expected to take care of their children and their home rather than having a career, while women with less financial stability often did double duty caring for their own households as well as working to supplement their family's income. The jobs available to women were limited and paid less than similar jobs available

Kamala Harris is the first woman, the first Black American, and the first South Asian American to be elected vice president.

KAMIL KRZACZYNSKI/Contributor/Getty Images

to men, and most employers considered women to be physically, emotionally, and mentally inferior to men in their ability to contribute to the workplace.

Today, women occupy positions and roles in every industry, and laws and regulations have been put in place to counteract discrimination against them. However, though women have made great strides in achieving equality, differences in salary and hiring practices remain. For example, many women are still hampered by a **glass ceiling**, an invisible barrier that limits their ability to progress to more senior positions.[26] In 2021, Jane Fraser smashed the glass ceiling by becoming the first female CEO on Wall Street to take the chief leadership position at Citibank.[27] Although Fraser's ascent undoubtedly advances the progression of women to executive positions, it is worth noting that in 2020, women made up only 5% of CEOs globally and were outnumbered by men approximately 17 to 1 at the CEO level.[28]

Associated with the glass ceiling is a phenomenon known as the **glass cliff**, whereby women or ethnic minorities are given leadership positions during periods of crisis without any support.[29] Although many leadership roles give people an opportunity to prove themselves, glass cliff positions often result in stress, burnout, and career setbacks. Research shows that glass cliffs exist in a variety of industries, including corporations, politics, and sports. For example, studies have shown that white women and women of color are more likely to be promoted to CEO positions in struggling companies. Similarly, in the field of U.S. college men's basketball, researchers found that coaches from ethnic minorities were more likely than their white counterparts to be appointed as coaches of losing teams.[30]

Michelle Ryan, director of the Global Institute for Women's Leadership at the Australian National University, believes that glass cliff positions could have a negative impact on gender equality. Ryan said, "Having women in glass cliff positions can help reinforce gender stereotypes that women aren't good at leadership . . . If women are in risky and precarious positions their performance might be evaluated more negatively, and hence the cycle of inequality continues."[31]

Organizations can address the glass cliff phenomenon by acknowledging it, educating people about its destructive impact, and ensuring that all leaders are given the same support irrespective of their racial group, gender or ethnicity.

Another example of gender inequality is the gender pay gap. Although this has narrowed somewhat over the over the last few decades, it still exists. For instance, in 2020, women were paid less than men for comparable jobs and would need to work an extra 42 days to earn the same as their male peers.[32]

Finally, McKinsey surveys showed that women were among the diverse groups who experienced difficulty balancing work and home life during the pandemic. Women were more likely than men to express their concern about the increase in household responsibilities, and U.S. mothers were four to five times more likely to reduce their working hours than fathers in order to cope with childcare, homeschool, and other domestic duties. Mothers also spent an extra three hours a week on childcare and housework compared to fathers. One in four women in corporate roles had considered reducing their workload or leaving the workforce altogether because of the pressure of this "double shift."[33] Overall, 3 million women dropped out of the workforce during 2020 and the beginning of 2021.[34]

Sexual Orientation

Sexual orientation refers to a person's sexual identity and the gender(s) to which they are attracted. Types of sexual orientation include lesbian, gay, bisexual, transgender, queer, and asexual (LGBTQ+). According to a 2021 Gallup Poll based on 15,000 interviews with Americans age 18 and older, 5.6% of adults identify as LGBT, with more than 50% of those identifying as bisexual.[35]

The United States has come a long way during the past few decades in fighting discrimination against sexual and gender identities in the workplace. Same-sex marriage was legalized in all 50 states in 2015, and in 2020, the Supreme Court ruled that the 1964 Civil Rights Act, which prohibits discrimination based on sex as well as gender, race, color, national origin, and religion, should also include sexual orientation and gender identity. This means employers across the nation who fire employees based on their sexual or gender preference will be breaking civil rights laws.[36]

Although this is positive news from a legal standpoint, more needs to be done in the workplace to address LGBTQ+ needs. Reports showed that, like women, LGBTQ+ employees struggled during the COVID-19 pandemic, but for different reasons. LGBTQ+ employees were more likely to experience isolation, lack of connectivity, and fear of job loss compared with their straight and cisgender counterparts. They also reported feeling overwhelmed by workload increases and stressed out over performance reviews.[37]

Diversity of Abilities

Ability diversity is the representation of people with different levels of mental and physical abilities within an organization. More than 60 million people in the United States have a **disability**, a physical or mental impairment that substantially limits one or more of their major life activities, and just 17.9% of them are employed.[38] Unemployment has risen since the COVID-19 crisis, particularly among people with disabilities; as of August 2020, over 1 million had been dismissed from the workplace since the pandemic began. Most of the job losses have been in retail and hospitality, the argument being that people with underlying conditions are more at risk in public-facing roles.[39]

Although people with physical and mental impairments may not be able to carry out certain tasks, there is still a huge range of tasks they can excel at. Skills can be taught, and people can be trained to improve their skills; jobs may or may not require particular physical abilities, like the ability to walk unaided. Employers also must ensure that the physical work space is adapted to certain needs and foster a working culture and recruitment process that are open to people with disabilities. For example, British telecommunications company Virgin Media has partnered with disability charity Scope to make sure employment opportunities are accessible to disabled people; other large companies, such as professional services network EY and multinational technology organization Microsoft, have created hiring programs focusing on neurodiverse candidates, including those with autism.[40] Managing ability diversity begins with selecting employees with abilities that fit the role best. This in turn leads to increased productivity and job satisfaction.

Legal Framework for Diversity

Following the 1964 Civil Rights Act, successive presidents issued executive orders requiring **affirmative action**, proactive steps taken by organizations to counteract discrimination against underrepresented groups and women.[41] The Americans with Disabilities Act (ADA) addresses discrimination against people with disabilities.[42]

The U.S. Equal Employment Opportunity Commission (EEOC) is the government agency charged with "enforcing federal laws that make it illegal to discriminate against a job applicant or an employee because of the person's race, color, religion, sex (including pregnancy), national origin, age (40 or older), disability, or genetic information."[43] The EEOC reported that more than 60,000 workplace discrimination charges were filed in 2021; discriminatory acts targeting race and disability accounted for the highest numbers of charges.[44] What are the practical implications of these legislative acts for managers? Table 2.1 lists some of the issues involved.

TABLE 2.1 ■ A Legal Framework for Diversity in Practice

Job advertisements	It is illegal for an employer to publish a job advertisement that discourages someone from applying for a job because of their race, color, religion, sex (including their gender identity, sexual orientation, or pregnancy), national origin, age (40 or older), disability status, or genetic information.	For example, a help wanted ad that seeks "females" or "recent college graduates" may discourage men and people over 40 from applying and may violate the law.
Recruitment	It is illegal for an employer to recruit new employees in a way that discriminates against them because of their race, color, religion, sex (including their gender identity, sexual orientation, or pregnancy), national origin, age (40 or older), disability, or genetic information.	For example, an employer's reliance on word-of-mouth recruitment through its mostly Hispanic workforce may violate the law if the result is that almost all new hires are Hispanic.
Job referrals	It is illegal for an employer, an employment agency, or a union to take into account a person's race, color, religion, sex (including their gender identity, sexual orientation, or pregnancy), national origin, age (40 or older), disability, or genetic information when making decisions about job referrals.	For example, an employer's preference for candidates who go to a certain church may violate the law.
Job assignments and promotions	It is illegal for an employer to make decisions about job assignments and promotions based on an employee's race, color, religion, sex (including their gender identity, sexual orientation, or pregnancy), national origin, age (40 or older), disability, or genetic information.	For example, an employer violates the law when they give preference to employees of a certain race when making shift assignments or when they segregate employees of a particular national origin from other employees or from customers.
Pay and benefits	It is illegal for an employer to discriminate against an employee in the payment of wages or employee benefits on the basis of their race, color, religion, sex (including their gender identity, sexual orientation, or pregnancy), national origin, age (40 or older), disability, or genetic information. Employee benefits include sick and vacation leave, insurance, access to overtime and overtime pay, and retirement programs.	For example, an employer violates the law when they pay Hispanic workers less than African American workers because of their national origin, or when they pay men and women in the same workplace unequal pay for equal work.
Discipline and discharge	It is illegal for an employer to take into account a person's race, color, religion, sex (including their gender identity, sexual orientation, or pregnancy), national origin, age (40 or older), disability, or genetic information when making decisions about discipline or discharge.	For example, when a white employee and an Asian employee commit a similar offense, an employer violates the law by disciplining them differently.
Employment references	It is illegal for an employer to give a negative or false employment reference (or refuse to give a reference) because of a person's race, color, religion, sex (including their gender identity, sexual orientation, or pregnancy), national origin, age (40 or older), disability, or genetic information.	For example, an employer contacted to supply a reference for a female worker violates the law by citing having children or pregnancy as a negative trait.

TABLE 2.1 ■ A Legal Framework for Diversity in Practice (*Continued*)

Reasonable accommodation and disability	The law requires an employer to provide reasonable accommodation to an employee or a job applicant with a disability, unless doing so would cause significant difficulty or expense for the employer. A reasonable accommodation is any change in the workplace (or in the ways things are usually done) to help a person with a disability apply for a job, perform the duties of a job, or enjoy the benefits and privileges of employment.	Reasonable accommodation might include, for example, providing a ramp for a wheelchair user or providing a reader or an interpreter for a blind or deaf employee or applicant.
Reasonable accommodation and religion	The law requires an employer to provide reasonable accommodation for an employee's religious beliefs or practices, unless doing so would cause difficulty or expense for the employer.	Reasonable accommodation might include, for example, providing structured breaks during the day for prayer or to attend religious services.
Training and apprenticeship programs	It is illegal for a training or apprenticeship program to discriminate on the basis of an race, color, religion, sex (including gender identity, sexual orientation, or pregnancy), national origin, age (40 or older), disability, or genetic information.	For example, an employer violates the law by denying training opportunities to African American employees because of their race.
Terms and conditions of employment	It is illegal for an employer to make any employment decision on the basis of a person's race, color, religion, sex (including their gender identity, sexual orientation, or pregnancy), national origin, age (40 or older), disability, or genetic information.	An employer violates the law by discriminating when making decisions about hiring, firing, promotions, or pay, or when granting breaks, approving leave, assigning work stations, or setting any other term or condition of employment, however small.

Source: U.S. Equal Employment Opportunity Commission. (n.d.). *Prohibited employment policies/practices.* http://www1.eeoc.gov//laws/practices/index.cfm?renderforprint=1.

DIVERSITY AND IDENTITY

Diversity means embracing an individual's whole identity, but elements of a person's personality are often discriminated against.

Intersectionality is a term coined by Kimberlé Crenshaw, a professor at Columbia Law School, to describe how different types of discrimination—against race, class, gender, religion, sexual orientation, disability, or other individual characteristics—may overlap with one another, manifesting in negative outcomes.[45] In other words, people experience prejudice and discrimination in different ways. For instance, not all women share the same experiences just because they are the same gender; white women may not experience oppression or discrimination in the same way as women of color. Organizations must take race and gender into account when identifying barriers for women of color by taking the following steps:[46]

- **Separate pay data by gender and race:** Although many organizations have made moves to address the gender pay gap between men and women, very few companies focus on the disparity in pay in terms of race *and* gender. For example, PayScale reported that women of color are more likely than white women to be paid less at the beginning of their careers, a gap that widens throughout their careers. By disaggregating the pay data by gender and race, organizations can uncover the biggest pay gaps and take steps to close them.
- **Provide employee engagement surveys by race and gender:** Like pay data, employee engagement surveys tend to be analyzed by race or gender, which doesn't provide

organizations with a holistic view of every employee's experience. Analyzing the results of employee engagement surveys by race, ethnicity, and gender gives organizations a better opportunity to address any issues around employee satisfaction, well-being, and inclusion.

- **Fund and support employee resource groups (ERGs) for specific groups:** Organizations must focus on setting up ERGs for the most marginalized and underrepresented groups in the workplace in order to achieve an inclusive environment. For instance, an ERG led by white women may not appeal to women of color when they don't share the same concerns.
- **Take an intersectional approach to diversity training:** Some organizations focus solely on gender and diversity of thought, thereby avoiding racial diversity and failing to discuss the challenges faced by people of color. This can lead to a general lack of understanding of how people from different races experience discrimination and could also alienate women of color in the organization.
- **Improve gender representation and include racial representation:** Although many initiatives been put in place to improve gender representation in the workplace, particularly in visible or senior roles, data show that women of color aren't benefiting in the same way as white women. Organizations can address this issue not just by creating a target for the number of women serving on the company board but also by specifying how many of those board members will be women of color.

Research has found that organizations that don't include intersectionality in their DEI programs and initiatives tend to have greater wage inequality, fewer opportunities for professional development, increased discrimination in hiring practices, higher levels of sexual harassment (particularly among women of color), and bigger turnover rates.[47]

Microaggressions

People with intersectional identities may experience **microaggressions**: verbal, behavioral, or environmental slights or insults made against a target person or group.[48] A white person telling a person from an ethnic minority, "You're so articulate!" is an example of a verbal microaggression, as the remark suggests surprise that a person from an ethnic background would have the ability to speak well; a security guard following a person of color around a store to ensure nothing stolen is an example of a behavioral microaggression; and a student who attends a college where all the buildings on campus are named after white people is an example of an environmental microaggression.

Microaggressions may be subtle, seemingly innocuous, and sometimes even well intentioned; nevertheless, racial slights are stigmatizing and harmful and can have detrimental effects on targeted individuals and groups as well as the organization itself. For example, in 2021, Salesforce received criticism for its DEI efforts when two employees publicly resigned, citing a culture of discrimination and microaggressions.[49] Research shows that daily experiences of microaggressions can lead to low self-esteem, higher stress levels, anxiety, and depression.[50] Organizations can prevent microaggressions at work by creating a culture of psychological safety. Table 2.2 outlines several ways in which leaders can manage microaggressions at work.

Stigmatized Identities

Some people are reluctant to disclose their full identities in the workplace for fear of mistreatment or discrimination. These are called **concealable stigmatized identities** (CSIs), identities that are kept hidden because they carry negative stereotypes.[51] Examples of CSIs include sexual orientation, religion, and mental illness. Although some identities such as race, gender, and age are mostly visible to others, CSIs are not always immediately obvious. Research shows that employees with mental illness and expectant mothers tend to take a position of nondisclosure at first, preferring to weigh the pros and cons before they disclose any information.[52] Sexual orientation minorities, employees with disabilities,

TABLE 2.2 ■ How to Manage Microaggressions in the Workplace

Manage microaggressions when they happen
Leaders are responsible for how team members behave at work and must also lead by example. Calling out microaggressions as they occur encourages other employees to do the same. Identifying microaggressions also provides leaders with opportunities to raise questions about the culture, the types of microaggressions in play, why the situation happened in the first place, and what can be done to prevent it from happening in the future.
Create a listening strategy
Employees who are negatively impacted by microaggressions need a safe space where they can express their concerns to their leaders without fear of ridicule or dismissal. Leaders can create a listening strategy by making sure employees feel heard, taking the time to check in with them, sharing the actions that will be taken to address the situation, and updating them on the outcome.
Use moments of microaggression to build self-awareness
There are times leaders themselves unknowingly contribute to microaggressions through lack of awareness or understanding. Leaders must take steps to overcome unconscious biases and prejudices in order to confront microaggressions head on. Building self-awareness in this way enable leaders to educate others about the differences between people and different lived experiences.

Source: King, M. (2021, June 21). *Three ways leaders can manage microaggressions at work.* Forbes. https://www.forbes.com/sites/michelleking/2021/06/21/three-ways-leaders-can-manage-microaggressions-at-work/?sh=156272843540.

employees with mental illness, and people from a lower socioeconomic status have also been found to be more likely to conceal their identities for fear of being stigmatized by others.[53]

However, researchers have also discovered that perceptions of one's work environment play a large role in making the decision to disclose identity. For instance, people working in hostile or unsupportive work environments were less likely to be truly authentic for fear of being treated differently, being stereotyped, or losing their jobs.[54] Other studies showed that people who had been discriminated against in the past based on their mental illness or sexual orientation were less likely to disclose their identities at work.[55] With regard to mental illness, factors such as requesting time off for doctor appointments and needing workplace accommodations were reported to influence disclosure decisions.[56]

To counteract the destructive impact of CSIs, organizations need to foster a safe culture where employees feel empowered and comfortable enough to express their authentic selves at work.

Stereotype Threat

Social identities such as a person's race or gender can trigger **stereotype threat**, or a fear of confirming a negative stereotype about one's own group.[57] For example, an individual who is concerned that performing badly on an exam will confirm negative beliefs about the intelligence of their gender, race, or other social identity group is experiencing stereotype threat.

When identity is tied to negative outcomes, people tend to look for cues to confirm the threat. If the threat is confirmed, the individual will think about whether they have the ability and desire to deal with it. If the answer is no, they are more likely to perform badly.[58] In contrast, if the cues do not confirm an identity threat, performance is more likely to remain steady or improve.[59]

Stereotype threat can have a destructive impact on the individual and society as whole. The fear of confirming negative stereotypes (such as weak intellectual ability) may lead to lack of motivation, low confidence, and poor engagement.[60] For instance, some women may choose to avoid a STEM career for fear they will not live up to their male counterparts, thereby confirming the negative stereotype that men are better at STEM subjects than women.[61] At a societal level, the impact of stereotype threat can lead to a culture of self-doubt where people make little effort to succeed because they presume that failure is inevitable.[62] Stereotype threat may also discourage people from applying for jobs, putting themselves forward for promotion, or performing to their optimal level.

Organizations can reduce stereotype threat at work by analyzing the threat and taking actions to reduce it, such as challenging negative stereotypes when they arise, creating support groups for underrepresented employees, providing training to improve communication between managers and underrepresented groups, and actively working to eliminate microaggressions in the workplace.[63]

CAN DIVERSITY AND MERITOCRACY BOTH BE ENCOURAGED?

EXAMINING THE EVIDENCE

One of the challenges organizations face as they strive to enhance organizational diversity is the paradoxical tension between the values of diversity and meritocracy. A meritocracy is a system in which people are selected or advanced based on demonstrated abilities and merit. A diversity-meritocracy paradox can arise when policies aimed at benefiting and providing opportunities to marginalized groups are perceived as threatening advantaged groups and vice versa. Recently, researchers Alison M. Konrad, Orlando C. Richard, and Yang Yang explored this paradox, noting that diversity and meritocracy are interrelated such that advancing each value can enhance the other by increasing perceptions of fairness and justice.[64] They suggest that successfully managing the diversity-meritocracy paradox involves ensuring that diversity practices are perceived as having process integrity while meritocracy practices are perceived as being focused on individual competence. Balancing these two perceptions can create what these researchers call an "organizational ambidexterity" that may help organizations simultaneously respond to pressures to enhance both diversity and meritocracy.

Critical-Thinking Questions

1. What specific actions can managers take to increase the fairness perceptions of both diversity and meritocracy initiatives in organizations simultaneously?
2. Toward this end, which organizational practices should be identity blind and which should be identity conscious?

EQUITY AND EQUALITY IN THE WORKPLACE

Equity is the process of ensuring that processes and programs are impartial and fair and provide equal access to new opportunities so as to enhance the success of all employees. Organizations achieve equity when they create an inclusive, diverse, and equal working environment. Although equity is sometimes confused with equality, the two terms are very different. Whereas equity is based on individual needs, **equality** is the process of ensuring that everyone is given the same opportunities and resources regardless of individual need.[65] For instance, the decision to provide all schools with computer labs that have the same quantity of computers and are accessible during the same hours of operation is an example of equality. The provision of more computer labs with longer hours of operation in lower-income neighborhoods where many people may not have a computer at home is an example of equity.[66]

Although some companies have made great progress in cultivating a fair and equal workplace, high levels of inequity still exist, as evidenced by sexual harassment, gender-based hiring, gender pay gaps, and pay disparity between white and POC/LGBTQ+ groups (Table 2.3).

Managers can create a more equitable workplace by providing transparency for the wage range across different roles, ensuring equitable benefits for all employees, and continually assessing equity practices. In 2021, French personal care company L'Oreal became the first company worldwide to receive EDGE (Economic Dividends for Gender Equality) certification after achieving organizational gender pay equity through the use of a pay assessment tool. The tool allows companies to go beyond gender, age, disability, race, ethnicity, and sexual orientation by analyzing policies, practices, and numbers across different areas in the organization, including equal pay, recruitment and promotion, leadership training and development, flexible working, and company culture. Thanks to feedback from 3,500 of its employees, L'Oreal has a greater understanding of how to meet the needs of its staff and adapt its policies to create a more fair and equitable company.[67]

TABLE 2.3 ■ 10 Ways Inequity Exists in the Workplace
Women still earn 20% less than men
Mothers earn less than women without children
Older workers are fired more frequently during periods of rising unemployment
Workers with disabilities with higher education than their peers are paid less
Black workers earn less than three-quarters of the pay given to white workers
Asian American and Pacific Islander (AAPI) women earn less than white males
Native American women earn less than their white male peers
Latinx workers with a college degree earn less than white male peers
LGBTQ+ workers still face compensation inequities
Transgender men experience pay increases when they transition, whereas transgender women experience pay decreases

Source: Johanson, K. (2021, August 5). 10 ways inequity still very much exists in the workplace. *Newsweek*. https://www.newsweek.com/10-ways-inequity-still-very-much-exists-workplace-1616254.

INCLUSION

Although more and more organizations are dedicated to the progression of DEI, inclusion remains the most difficult element to measure across the company.

Inclusion is the practice of ensuring that people are welcomed and feel a sense of belonging in the workplace.[68] An inclusive working environment is a place where everyone feels valued and respected, where all employees are involved in decision-making processes and feel comfortable sharing their ideas, and where everyone is considered part of the team.[69] Inclusive workplaces build awareness, encourage connection with others, and nurture a culture of empathy and mutual respect.

A recent Gartner survey showed that "setting goals and tracking DEI progress through metrics" was one of the main priorities for DEI leaders in 2021.[70] Yet although some companies have the tools to assess diversity and equity, tracking inclusion isn't so straightforward. In another Gartner survey sent to almost 10,000 employees around the world, respondents were asked to rate their level of agreement with statements indicative of an inclusive environment, such as those assessing fair treatment, respect for differences of others, trust, belonging, and diversity.[71]

These responses are a useful way for organizations to measure the inclusivity in work environments and take action to address certain issues. When organizations successfully measure DEI, they are up to 20% more likely to have an inclusive culture than their peers.[72]

Coupon code site Coupon Lawn, based in Toronto, champions inclusion by celebrating cultural events, holidays, and movements such as Pride parades, Women's Day, and Martin Luther King Jr. Day together as a team as a way of showing respect to employees from various backgrounds. This initiative increases awareness and builds knowledge and understanding about events that other employees may not have been exposed to before.[73]

Inclusion and the Formerly Incarcerated

Currently, the DEI sector mostly focuses on people of color, women, people with disabilities, and people who identify as LGBTQ+. But what about the formerly incarcerated? Statistics show there are 5 million ex-prisoners living in the U.S., and just 27% of that number are employed. Only 50% with a criminal record receive a call back.[74]

Diversity and inclusion speaker and former prisoner Shelley Winner believes that companies are too afraid to hire incarcerated people, as they perceive them as violent, lazy, and a liability. Yet if companies do open up their recruitment policies to the formerly incarcerated, not only are they offering new job opportunities for people with criminal records but they are also helping to solve the issue of mass incarceration by keeping people out of prison.[75] As Michelle Cirocco, chief social responsibility officer for Televerde, a company based in Phoenix, Arizona, that focuses on preparing and training incarcerated women for release, said, "inclusion means everyone."[76]

Dave's Killer Bread, based in Milwaukee, Oregon, is a good example of a company that gives second chances to people with a criminal history. Founder Dave Dahl spent 15 years in prison before joining the family bakery, creating a unique brand of healthy, organic bread and growing the business exponentially. In 2015, Dahl sold the business to Flowers Foods, a producer and marketer of packed bakery food, for $275 million, but the principle of giving ex-convicts a second chance holds fast.[77]

PROMOTING A DEI CULTURE

Despite the commitment of many organizations to DEI, many DEI programs falter, and progress remains stagnant in some industries. At the end of 2020, only one in six diverse employees felt more supported since the beginning of the COVID-19 crisis.[78] Here are some reasons that companies are struggling to implement their DEI programs:

Failure to Reduce Bias

Many organizations attempt to implement DEI training programs to raise awareness of bias. **Bias** refers to the tendency to show prejudice against another person or group. DEI training can help reduce **implicit bias**, which is a set of positive or negative stereotypes someone may unconsciously hold toward a person or group, and break down prejudices or psychological barriers among those who struggle to accept coworkers they perceive as different.

Many organizations design DEI programs around reducing bias by giving managers a list of dos and don'ts in the hope that by following these rules, they will suspend their biases. Studies have shown that DEI programs aren't very effective, as people don't suspend their bias so easily and tend to forget everything they've learned within a few hours or days.[79]

Another study carried out by Harvard organizational sociology professor Frank Dobbin found that employees tended to react negatively to mandatory DEI programs because they felt like they were being "controlled." This can provoke a backlash; for example, managers who resent being ordered to give up their time so they can be lectured or being told what to do tend to harbor more bias as a result.[80]

How do companies reduce bias? In some studies, voluntary training has helped to reduce bias. When people make their own decision to take DEI training (rather than perceiving it as something they have been forced into), they are more likely to be more open to it.

1. **Antiquated Hiring Tests**

   DEI programs often stumble because of inadequate skills tests. A 2017 study published in the *Proceedings of the National Academy of Sciences* found that racial discrimination in hiring has remained consistently high over the last 25 years.[81] The study also discovered that candidates whose résumés bore white-sounding names were more than 20% more likely to proceed to an interview than candidates with Latinx- or Black-sounding names. The cost of discriminatory hiring can be enormous, with big companies such as Microsoft and Wells Fargo paying out millions of dollars to settle allegations of discriminatory hiring tests. Hiring tests can actually highlight bias rather than reduce it.[82]

   To make hiring fairer and more unbiased, Google, Apple and IBM have eliminated the requirement for college degrees from their job postings as part of their DEI initiative. This move opens up opportunities for everyone, not just for people with a four-year-degree.

Companies must also tailor hiring tests for the specific role rather than relying on a one-size-fits-all approach that doesn't provide accurate insight into candidates' capabilities.[83]

Despite the evidence questioning the effectiveness of DEI programs, it is vital that organizations create environments that embrace every employee, regardless of background, age, culture, ethnicity, or other differences. Here are more positive ways managers can promote DEI:

2. **Equitable Recruitment Programs**

   Implementing college recruitment programs specifically targeted at diverse colleges and universities and not just majority-white institutions motivates managers to actively involve themselves in the hiring processes. As a consequence, they become more focused on the goal itself rather than their own biases. These recruitment practices could also be monitored by a diversity task officer or a diversity task team. Dolby is a good example of a company that has made its recruitment practices more equitable through the implementation of blind hiring processes.

3. **Mentoring**

   Mentoring encourages managers to get involved with people from different races, ethnicities, and genders by coaching and sponsoring them for key projects and assignments, which again helps to reduce whatever biases they may hold. Ivy League professor and TEDx speaker Dr. Eli Joseph credited much of his success to mentors and believed they are particularly essential for enabling people of color "to identify their strengths and weaknesses, as well as their areas for growth, while preparing them to accomplish their professional goals and objectives."[84]

4. **Connecting Diverse Groups Through Storytelling**

   Increasing contact between diverse groups of people in the workplace and providing a safe space to learn from each other's experiences without judgment builds inclusion, cultivates relationships, and allows people to work together as equals. For example, when people share stories about their different experiences, they gain empathy and an expanded concept of standing in someone else's shoes. One study found that storytelling is a useful inclusion tool that may change perspectives and have a lasting impact on our ability to respond without prejudice. Companies can encourage storytelling through social forums and meetups, listening sessions, and round-robin questions in meetings.[85]

5. **Collect, Count, and Compare DEI Data**

   Organizations need to install systems to collect and count DEI data on and compare this data to the numbers at other organizations. For example, HR systems used to gather data such as workforce demographics, employee experience, and feedback from employee programs can be a powerful way for organizations to increase DEI accountability and transparency.[86]

6. **Hire for DEI at Senior Levels**

   Many companies are investing in supporting DEI by changing their policies, adding new resources, revamping the traditional approach to the working day, and ensuring that practices are fair and equitable for all. There is a huge opportunity for all companies to build DEI workplaces if they create conditions where everyone can thrive.

   DEI modeling begins at the top. DEI programs will only be successful if there are a range of senior decision-makers who represent a wide variety of different opinions, views, and perspectives.[87] A lack of diversity across senior management impacts decision-making and sends a poor message about DEI to employees.

IN REVIEW

2.1 Explain the importance of DEI in OB

Diversity, equity, and inclusion (DEI) is a term used to describe programs and policies that encourage the representation and participation of diverse groups of people, including people of different genders, races and ethnicities, abilities and disabilities, religions, cultures, ages, and sexual orientations and people with diverse backgrounds, experiences, and skills and expertise. DEI is so important in OB because today's workplace is populated with more people from different backgrounds and different experiences than ever before, and they deserve to be treated fairly and equitably. In the business world, the benefits of supporting DEI initiatives are enormous: better financial performance, a larger customer base, and significant rises in employee satisfaction, retention and engagement.

2.2 Discuss diversity in the workplace

Workplace diversity refers to the degree to which an organization includes people from different cultures and backgrounds; it involves recognizing, respecting, and valuing both individual and group differences by treating people as individuals in an effort to promote an inclusive culture. There are two main types of diversity: **Surface-level diversity** describes the easily perceived differences between us, such as age/generation, race/ethnicity, gender, sexual orientation, and ability. **Deep-level diversity** describes verbal and nonverbal behaviors that are not as easily perceived because they lie below the surface, such as differences in attitudes, values, beliefs, and personality.

2.3 Discuss how diversity influences identity in the workplace

Diversity means embracing an individual's whole identity, but elements of a person's personality are often discriminated against. **Intersectionality** describes how different types of discrimination—against race, class, gender, religion, sexual orientation, disability, or other individual characteristics—may overlap with one another, manifesting in negative outcomes. People with intersectional identities may experience **microaggressions**—verbal, behavioral, or environmental slights or insults made against a target person or group. Some people are reluctant to disclose their full identities in the workplace for fear of mistreatment or discrimination. These are called **concealable stigmatized identities** (CSIs), identities that are kept hidden because they carry negative stereotypes. Social identities such as a person's race or gender can trigger **stereotype threat**—a fear of confirming a negative stereotype about one's own group.

2.4 Describe the impact of equity and equality in the workplace

Although equity is sometimes confused with equality, the two terms are very different: **equity** is the process of ensuring that processes and programs are impartial, are fair, and provide equal access to new opportunities so as to enhance the success of all employees; **equality** is the process of ensuring that everyone is given the same opportunities and resources regardless of individual need.

Managers can create a more equitable workplace by providing transparency for the wage range across different roles, ensuring equitable benefits for all employees, and continually assessing equity practices.

2.5 Illustrate the power of inclusion in a working environment

Inclusion is the practice of ensuring that people are welcomed and feel a sense of belonging in the workplace. An inclusive working environment is a place where everyone feels valued and respected, where all employees are involved in decision-making processes and feel comfortable sharing their ideas, and where everyone is considered part of the team. The DEI sector mostly focuses on people of color, women, people with disabilities, and people who identify as LGBTQ+, but some organizations are focusing on giving opportunities and second chances to the formerly incarcerated.

2.6 Identify the different ways businesses can promote a DEI culture

Many DEI programs falter for a number of reasons: failure to reduce **bias**, which refers to the tendency to show unfair prejudice against another person or group; antiquated hiring tests; and mandatory training programs. Managers can promote DEI by implementing more equitable college recruitment programs; by reducing **implicit bias**, the set of positive or negative stereotypes someone may unconsciously hold toward a person or group; by breaking down prejudices or psychological barriers among those who struggle to accept coworkers they perceive as different; through mentoring and storytelling; by tracking DEI data to monitor DEI levels; and by hiring for DEI at organizational levels.

KEY TERMS

Ability diversity (p. 39)
Affirmative action (p. 39)
Bias (p. 46)
Concealable stigmatized identities (p. 42)
Deep-level diversity (p. 35)
Disability (p. 39)
Discrimination (p. 33)
Diversity (p. 34)
Diversity, equity, and inclusion (p. 33)
Equality (p. 44)
Equity (p. 44)
Ethnicity (p. 37)
Gender diversity (p. 37)
Glass ceiling (p. 38)
Glass cliff (p. 38)
Implicit bias (p. 46)
Inclusion (p. 45)
Intersectionality (p. 41)
Microaggressions (p. 42)
Race (p. 37)
Sexual orientation (p. 39)
Stereotype threat (p. 43)
Stereotyping (p. 33)
Surface-level diversity (p. 35)
Workplace diversity (p. 34)

UP FOR DEBATE: DEI BUSINESS INITIATIVES AS PART OF PERFORMANCE REVIEWS

An important part of a manager's performance review each year should be how well they have incorporated DEI efforts into the company. Agree or disagree?

Explain your answer.

EXERCISE 2.1: WE'RE NOT ALL THE SAME

Objective

The purpose of this exercise is to gain a greater understanding of diversity.

Instructions

This is an individual exercise. Find someone different from you—older, younger, different gender, different race, or other difference. Explain that you're studying the concept of diversity for a class and ask their permission to be interviewed. Ask questions such as, "Have you ever felt that you weren't included in an event or situation?" "Do you think you were ever passed over for a job or promotion because of biases from a manager?" and "How can we best learn from one another?"

Once you have interviewed the individual, write a memo to your professor detailing what you've learned from this experience.

Reflection Questions

1. How did you go about finding someone to talk to? Did you face any resistance to your request for an interview? Explain.
2. What was your key takeaway from this experience? What did you discover that you weren't aware of before this?
3. What if someone selected you as their person to interview because you were different from them? How would you respond?

Exercise contributed by Steven Stovall, Southeast Missouri State University.

EXERCISE 2.2: YOUR UNIVERSITY'S DEI OFFICE

Objective

The purpose of this exercise is to gain a greater understanding of diversity, equity, and inclusion (DEI) offices.

Instructions

Most institutions of higher education now have a diversity, equity, and inclusion (DEI) function or office. There are different names for these, including DEI Office, Diversity Committee, Office of Diversity, and so forth. In groups of three to six, discover whether your university has such an office or function on campus. If so, find out what services and opportunities your university's DEI efforts support. If you can't locate a DEI office or function, have your group develop a set of five goals for such an effort on your campus.

Reflection Questions

1. Why is having a DEI office or committee on your campus important?
2. How easy was it to locate information about your university's DEI efforts? What could the university do differently to support this?
3. Are your university's DEI efforts student focused or employee focused? Or is it a combination of both? What should it be? Explain.

Exercise contributed by Steven Stovall, Southeast Missouri State University.

EXERCISE 2.3: DEFINING DIVERSITY

Objective

The purpose of this exercise is to grasp the meaning of diversity.

Instructions

All of us approach diversity through our personal lens on the world. However, each of us is different from everyone else in numerous ways. Beyond demographic differences such as age, race, and gender, there are other ways we are unique. Some of us come from very poor backgrounds or rural or urban areas. Others may have been raised in a broken home or have mental or behavioral issues. Still others might consider themselves different because they don't have ready access to resources or have obstacles that prevent them from getting jobs or being among the public. Diversity, in its broadest sense, is wide ranging.

With this in mind, the instructor will capture on the board at the front of the room the class's definition of diversity. The process begins with one person providing an idea of how they think diversity should be defined. Then the next person will give their thoughts, and so on until everyone has contributed.

As a class, try to piece the information written on the board into an overarching definition of diversity.

Reflection Questions

1. How did your definition of diversity differ from those of some of your classmates?
2. What surprised you about this discussion?
3. How did the class arrive at a cohesive definition of diversity? Did everyone agree? Explain.
4. How has your definition of diversity changed after participating in this exercise?

Exercise contributed by Steven Stovall, Southeast Missouri State University.

ONLINE EXERCISE 2.1: DIVERSITY IN THE WORKPLACE

Objective

The purpose of this exercise is to gain an appreciation of organizations' diversity efforts.

Instructions

Conduct an online search for an organization that promotes diversity among employees— for example, by instituting inclusive methods of recruiting new hires or by prioritizing inclusivity on their boards or among the staff. You might also seek an organization that approaches marketing to consumers with a strong sense of diversity in mind.

Once you locate an example of an organization promoting diversity, examine the level of diversity being offered. For example, do they seem to focus on women, or do they take broader strokes of inclusivity? Write a paper for your instructor that answers the following questions.

Reflection Questions

1. When organizations promote diversity, do you feel they're doing it for reasons of true diversity, or is it to ensure customers buy more of their products or services? Explain.
2. What approaches did the organization you selected use to promote diversity? Are they outlined on their website? Did you find an article discussing their diversity efforts? Have they made diversity an integral part of their infrastructure by establishing a DEI office, strong policies and procedures, and fully transparent diversity initiatives?
3. How does seeing or reading about an organization's diversity efforts impact your perceptions of that organization?

Exercise contributed by Steven Stovall, Southeast Missouri State University.

ONLINE EXERCISE 2.2: HAVE YOU FELT EXCLUDED?

Objective

The purpose of this exercise is to understand feelings of exclusion and discrimination.

Instructions

In an online discussion group, post an experience you had where you felt excluded or discriminated against. Think about a time when you felt you weren't being included because of the color of your skin, your gender, or others' unfounded perceptions of you. Describe the situation, and then share your feelings about the experience.

Reflection Questions

1. Describe your thoughts about sharing something so personal.
2. As you read others' posts, did you feel a sense of connection with others who may have gone through something similar to you? Discuss.
3. Were you surprised that so many people had experiences of exclusion? Why or why not?

Exercise contributed by Steven Stovall, Southeast Missouri State University.

CASE 2.1: CBRE GROUP, INC.

In the early 2020s, diversity, equity, and inclusion (DEI) has been an increasing focus of conversations about organizational behavior and corporate culture as workers seek to be more visible, empowered, and represented in their industries. At the same time, consumers are increasingly considering how a brand's values compare to their own when making purchasing decisions. Many new businesses are being built from the ground up with DEI principles in mind, and established firms are learning to incorporate inclusive best practices into their organizations. Coldwell Banker Richard Ellis Group, Inc., has an over-100-year history in commercial real estate and is a leader in corporate diversity, equity, and inclusion, not just within the organization and its workforce but also in regard to its suppliers and marketplace stakeholders.

Headquartered in Dallas, Texas, CBRE Group, Inc., is the largest commercial real estate services and investment firm in the world. CBRE employs more than 100,000 people worldwide, serving clients in more than 100 countries. The company's diversity, equity, and inclusion efforts have been widely recognized by prominent publications in recent years. Forbes named CBRE one of America's Best Employers for Diversity in 2018, 2019, and 2020. The company was added to 3BL Media's 100 Best Corporate Citizens list in 2020, has been on Ethisphere's World's Most Ethical Companies list for seven years running and on Bloomberg's Gender-Equality Index twice, was honored as a Best Place to Work for LGBTQ Equality according to the Human Rights Campaign, and earned a perfect score on the Corporate Equality Index (CEI) eight years in a row. In 2021, the Disability Equality Index, a collaboration between the American Association of People With Disabilities and Disability:IN, called CBRE a "Best Place to Work for Disability Inclusion," and the *Dallas Business Journal* named CBRE an Outstanding Diversity & Inclusion Organization in 2021.[88]

The large brokerage created a brand-new chief diversity officer role in June 2020 and promoted Tim Dismond, a division president in the company's Global Workplace Solutions (GWS) Enterprise business, to be its first officeholder. While many organizations relegate DEI responsibilities to the realm of human resources, ancillary to strategic business decision-making, CBRE made diversity and inclusion coequal to the company's most important functions. As a member of CBRE's executive committee, Dismond is one of 12 global executives who set the company vision and report directly to Bob Sulentic, CEO and president of CBRE.[89]

In an interview with National Real Estate Investor, Dismond detailed CBRE's three-pronged diversity and inclusion strategy: "I'm focusing on our resources across three key areas: culture, talent and marketplace. With each, I've identified several programs and initiatives intended to create a more diverse and inclusive workplace." For culture, the company is introducing interactive inclusion-focused training for managers that addresses microaggressions and unconscious bias. Prior to Dismond's promotion, some of CBRE's talent-focused DEI policies stipulated that:

- a visibly diverse candidate should be included at the in-person interview stage for all positions at the Director level and above.
- the panel of interviewers for all positions at the Director level and above should include a visibly diverse interviewer.
- a diversity and inclusion-focused objective [should be] included in all performance appraisals for employees at the Director level and above.[90]

Since 2020, the company has launched many more holistic talent initiatives, including:

- increasing the funding of a program that targets diverse talent for Advisory and Global Workplace Solutions business segments
- implementing global policies regarding such matters as racial misconduct, employment of relatives, and diverse interview slates and panels for open positions in order to create a more equitable workplace
- introducing a new mentoring program, EMERGE, that is designed specifically for Employee Business Resource Groups

- sponsoring unconscious bias training for CBRE employees and leaders
- continuing to partner with organizations such as CREW Network, the National Black MBA Association, Disability:IN, and Reaching Out MBA
- targeting recruiting programs for Historically Black Colleges & Universities (HBCUs) to introduce the CRE industry and the different career paths to students[91]

One way CBRE is promoting DEI in the marketplace is by engaging in social-justice-focused philanthropy, having contributed $1,000,000 each to the National Urban League and the Legal Defense and Educational Fund in 2020. However, CBRE's most substantial commitment to DEI outside its own workforce is its spending on diverse suppliers.

In October 2020, CBRE pledged to spend $1 billion with diverse suppliers in 2021 and to grow that annual spending to $3 billion by 2025. If the company succeeds, it will join the Billion Dollar Roundtable (BDR), a prestigious association of 28 companies that are global leaders in supplier diversity and spend more than $1 billion with suppliers who are women, veterans, disabled, or members of POC/LGBTQ+ groups.[92] BDR members promote and share supply chain diversity best practices and encourage other corporations to increase their diverse supplier spending commitments every year.[93] Tim Dismond said of the spending pledge, "Supplier diversity allows us to make an even greater contribution to the long-term economic stability of our communities. Our commitment will directly benefit underrepresented business and in turn, those businesses will elevate the people and areas where they are located by creating sustainable jobs and tax revenue."[94] Dismond added, "I am proud to share that we are currently trending to surpass our 2021 goal and are implementing additional strategies to strengthen the relationships and opportunities we have with minority suppliers."[95]

CBRE Group has earned its many DEI accolades by demonstrating its commitment to promoting diversity, equity, and inclusion when attracting, retaining, and developing talent within their workforce and in the marketplace with their suppliers and stakeholders. In just a few years they may be one of the top spenders on diverse suppliers and thus one of the biggest voices on the future of inclusive supply chains.

Critical-Thinking Questions

1. How does CBRE Group promote diversity, equity, and inclusion in the marketplace, outside its workforce?
2. What did CBRE do differently than most organizations when creating Tim Dismond's role and establishing a diversity officer?
3. Do you know the kinds of suppliers your favorite companies use to manufacture and deliver their products and services? Research a company you admire and see how they stack up against CBRE and others with a seat at the Billion Dollar Roundtable.

iStockphoto/Morsa Images

3 PERSONALITY AND INDIVIDUAL DIFFERENCES

LEARNING OBJECTIVES

By the end of this chapter, you will be able to:

3.1 Discuss why individual differences are important

3.2 Contrast the nature and nurture explanations of personality development

3.3 Distinguish among the trait theories of personality

3.4 Describe the approaches to assessing and interpreting character strengths

3.5 Differentiate among the most common personality attributes

Case Study: The PEAK Fleet

The PEAK Fleet is a values-driven organizational development consulting firm. Founded in 2016 by Jen Coyne and Brian Stinson, the company takes its name from four core *PEAK Values®*: Persistence, Empathy, Authenticity, and Kindness. Through keynote speakerships, engaging workshops, leadership events, advisory services and more, the company's mission is to "help organizations succeed by creating an engaged workforce that thrives together."[1]

Self-Awareness and Awareness of Others

The PEAK Fleet promises to help organizations better understand their workers, help employees better understand themselves, and support all members in applying the insights they gain about their individual values and personality differences to form more effective, cohesive teams that are aligned with the company's purpose. All teams experience conflict, and workplaces with diverse teams often face more challenges than others. On the *People+Profit Show: Elevating Humanity Through Business*, a podcast presented by Conscious Capitalism Arizona, Brian, one of the PEAK Fleet's founders, shared how critical values are to teams that want to thrive:

> I believe that most, if not all, conflict is actually not about the person or the issue; it's about having different values but not knowing it. So if you can first be clear about your own values and then make them transparent to others, then you can either avoid conflict or at least navigate through conflict more easily.[2]

A magnetic set of corporate values, when clearly communicated, attracts and engages like-minded talent but can also repel individuals with the self-awareness to recognize they are not aligned with a company.

> The day you walk in and you feel like your values are not being served or you don't think there's alignment is the day you should look for a new organization or a new job.[3]

Without intentionally identifying and communicating their core values, however, individuals and companies can't enjoy the harmony that value alignment brings to an organization. PEAK Fleet cofounders Jen and Brian seek to solve this problem by using lessons they learned while working together in leadership development and information technology at Intel.

The PEAK Fleet's Beginnings

As the son of an entrepreneur, Brian Stinson believed they would follow a similar path and become a founder. But just six months before college, Brian discovered a love of math. When Stinson's precalculus teacher told the class, "If you like this, this is what engineers do" and wrote the average engineer's salary on the board, the decision was made. According to Brian, "that one moment of five minutes of exposure to engineering changed my complete trajectory." They went on to work for Intel for 21 years, managing workforce strategy for the company's 6,000-person worldwide IT organization. Despite becoming a data-driven high-tech engineer, Brian never lost their passion for people, culture, and teams.

> I finally figured out that that was my purpose, to use my engineering degree and knowledge to look at a group of people as a system and maximize for things like morale and skills and engagement.[4]

Jen Coyne, CPA and certified project management professional, met Brian in 2006 when they were assigned to the same team at Intel, working on employee experience and people strategy. Jen and Brian held on to similar job roles through multiple restructurings at Intel, and their paths kept crossing as they volunteered for organizational leadership development task forces around the globe. There they discovered their shared passions for teams and company culture. "One of my analogies is that once you've flown first class, you don't ever want to go back to coach," Brian says. "Over our careers, we've worked on great teams with great culture, with great leadership, and we've also worked on the opposite of that. Once you've experienced amazing culture where you feel like there's a clear sense of purpose, you have a connection to your coworkers, you feel like your manager has your back, you have clarity of success, it doesn't feel like work. You just want more of it, you don't want it to ever end, you want everybody to experience it."[5]

After Intel: A Benefit Corporation for Good

When Jen and Brian founded the PEAK Fleet in 2016, they intended to create a triple-bottom-line company—that is, one focused on people, planet, and profit. In addition to being a woman-owned business (Jen serves as majority owner and CEO of the PEAK Fleet), the cofounders incorporated many benefit company principles into their business model from the beginning. Thus, the PEAK Fleet was quickly certified as a BCFG (Benefit Corporation for Good) when it applied in 2019 and recertified in 2020.[6] Brian says the BCFG community and the commitment to conscious capitalism embedded in the certification process helps the company differentiate its approach with clients:

> These people get it. If it's somebody who already understands the tenets of purpose over profit, understands conscious leadership, conscious culture, stakeholder alignment, then we can get right into talking about culture and values and purpose. We can go right there. But if someone isn't as sort of aware or enlightened, then I'm going to have to talk about hard business metrics. It might be the cost of a bad hire, it might be the cost of turnover, the cost of some other business metric they're trying to move—"I'm trying to increase this process improvement," or "I'm trying to cultivate more innovative thinking"—and so I have to make the translation for them often.[7]

PEAK Values

One of the PEAK Fleet's most popular translation tools is the PEAK Values® Card Deck. The deck includes fifty-eight 3.5 × 3.5-inch cards printed with core values and definitions as well as group and personal reflection exercises for identifying and communicating those values. Thousands of people in the corporations, NGOs, governmental agencies, and educational institutions the PEAK Fleet serves have completed PEAK Values exercises. The company's four eponymous PEAK Values and their definitions are given in Table 3.1.[8]

Values: Nurture Versus Nature?

In an interview on the *Future of Work: Water Cooler Conversations* podcast, Jen and Brian weighed in on whether values stem more from nurture or nature. Both cofounders cited nurture and nature as sources of core values, but Jen highlighted the importance of the consulting firm's behavioral exercises, noting that two people may have the same values but different ideas about how to apply and implement them. For Brian, the company's founding itself is a full-circle synthesis of nurture and nature: "It's been interesting that since leaving Intel and starting the PEAK Fleet, I got to return to those entrepreneurial roots that I kind of developed 30 plus years ago."[9]

TABLE 3.1 ■ PEAK Values®

Persistence	*Continuing to try to do something even though it is difficult or opposed by other people.* *Synonyms: perseverance, grit, tenacity, endurance*
Empathy	*The instinctive ability to understand another's feelings and respond appropriately to them.* *Synonyms: appreciation, compassion, understanding*
Authenticity	*Being true to one's own character or spirit.* *Synonyms: legitimate, bona fide, genuine*
Kindness	*Being friendly or courteous.* *Synonyms: benevolence, grace, courtesy*

Critical-Thinking Questions

1. Would you have chosen the same four core values as the founders of the PEAK Fleet? Come up with two additional core values that can transcend personality differences and make an organization more effective.
2. Are you surprised by Brian's assertion that Benefit Corporations for Good are often more amenable to core values conversations? How else might you "translate" these terms the way the PEAK Values Card Deck exercises do?
3. Think of a time your core values were challenged by a coworker or a superior. Looking back, how might you both have responded differently if you better understood each other's perspectives?

THE IMPORTANCE OF INDIVIDUAL DIFFERENCES

Have you ever been teamed up with someone for a school or work project who just seemed so different from you? What made that person unique? Maybe they had opinions or beliefs different from your own, liked music you hated, or had hobbies you considered strange. How did you handle working together? Did you just focus on getting the job done, or did you make an effort to find some common ground?

In class and at work, you are surrounded by a multitude of individual personalities and behaviors and are expected to work well with others regardless of how different they seem to you. As we mentioned in Chapter 1, people are the key to ensuring competitive advantage and organizational success, and today's managers keep a close eye on team dynamics and the relationships among team members. The PEAK Fleet featured in our case has selected four core values to support organizations in engaging with their employees and helping employees to understand themselves better. Working in a harmonious organizational environment is the ultimate goal for managers, but to realize this goal, we need to understand more about the differences and similarities between us and the way they guide our behavior.

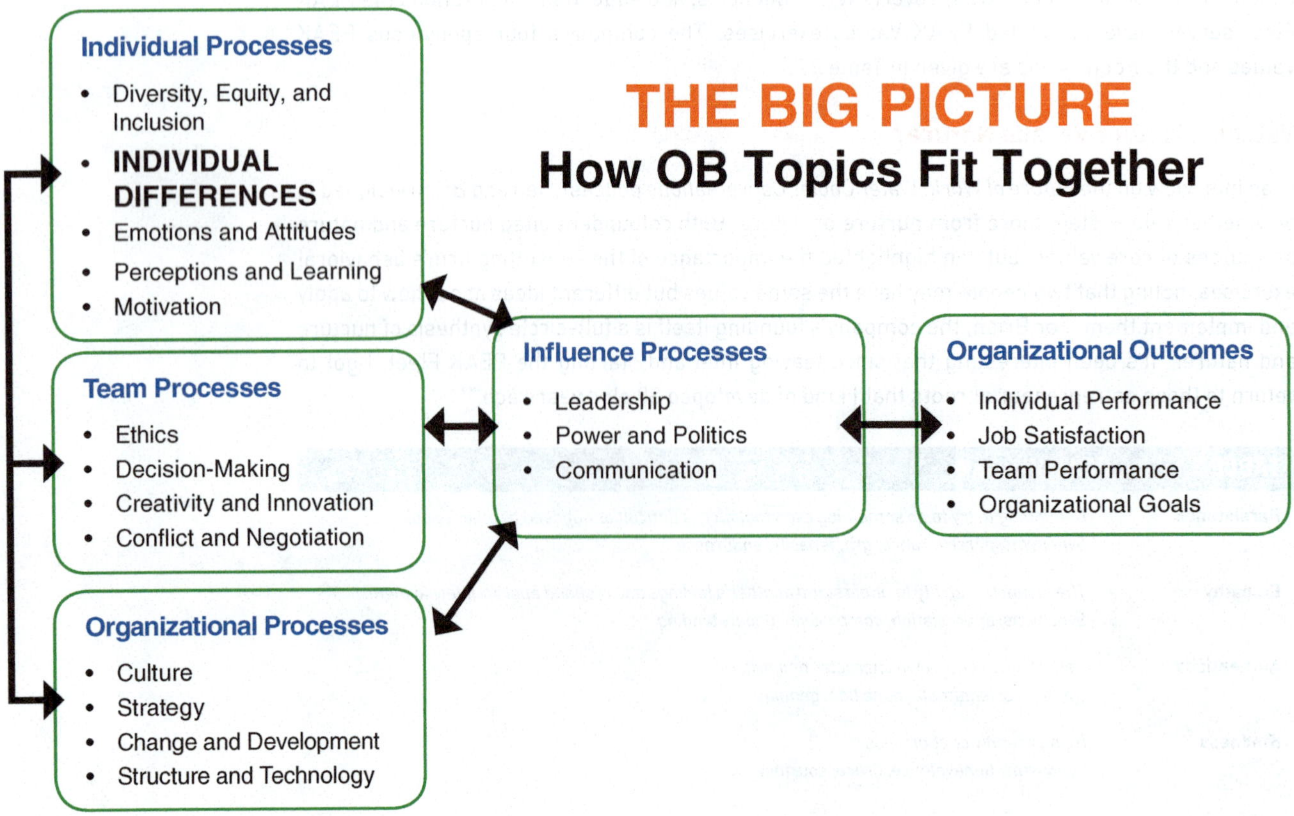

Being different from each other makes us each unique. We define **individual differences** as the behavioral and cognitive similarities and differences among people.[10] In short, we need to understand not only people who are like us (which is relatively easy) but also people who are not like us and who think, behave, and make decisions differently than we do. When you can analyze the differences and similarities among your coworkers, you will have a better idea why people act the way they do. To understand individual differences, we must also have a high degree of **self-awareness**, or awareness of our own feelings, behaviors, personalities, likes, and dislikes.[11] We must also possess an **awareness of others**, a consciousness of other people's feelings, behaviors, personalities, likes, and dislikes.[12] But how easy is it to define ourselves?

We generally have a perception of ourselves as distinct human beings. This is called our **self-concept**, the belief we have about who we are and how we feel about ourselves.[13] Social and academic influences and the culture in which we are raised play a significant role in our belief system. For example, we might be influenced by the beliefs held by our parents, friends, teachers, or coworkers.

Actress and model Emma Watson demonstrates self-esteem and self-efficacy through serving as the UN Women goodwill ambassador.

Samir Hussein/Getty Images

Our self-concept can be divided into two key components: self-esteem and self-efficacy. **Self-esteem** is the belief we have about our own worth.[14] People with high self-esteem perceive themselves to be confident, to have high self-worth, and to be capable of taking on challenges. In contrast, people with low self-esteem are full of self-doubt, have a rather low opinion of themselves, and tend to shy away from challenges.

The other part of self-concept is **self-efficacy**, our belief in our ability to succeed in a specific task or situation.[15] However, just because you have high self-esteem doesn't mean you have a strong sense of self-efficacy. For example, you may be confident about completing coursework but have a low sense of self-efficacy when taking the exams.

NATURE VERSUS NURTURE

We often regard people as having "good personalities" or "bad personalities," but what does that really mean? Is someone's personality "good" because we have something in common with that person and get along with them? Or is someone's personality "bad" because they ignore or offend us? What is personality, after all?

We define **personality** as a stable and unique pattern of traits, characteristics, and resulting behaviors that gives an individual their identity.[16] When we understand different personalities, we can better understand the behaviors and motivations of others rather than making snap judgments that are often inaccurate.

Where does personality come from? Research has proven that we inherit some physical characteristics from our parents; you may have your father's blue eyes or your mother's curly hair, for example. However, the origins of our personality traits have yet to be fully determined, and the nature-versus-nurture debate still rages. Is personality inherited (nature), or is it influenced by our environment and upbringing (nurture)? In the documentary *Three Identical Strangers*, a set of identical triplets who had no knowledge of each other came together at age 19 by pure chance.[17] Their story reignited the nature-versus-nurture debate. Although at first it appeared that nature and DNA were the chief determinants of the triplets' future, by the end of the documentary, some experts were less convinced, believing that nurture played a key role. And others believe it is impossible to judge at all. Geneticist Steve Jones of University College London said, "The trouble is that people look at the nature-nurture debate like a cake and assume you can have a slice of environment and then a slice of genetic factors. You can't. They are baked together and cannot be separated without finding some way to unbake your cake."[18]

In the next section, we explore how many organizations use assessment tools to get a better understanding of their employees' personality traits.

THE TRAIT THEORIES OF PERSONALITY

Researchers have spent decades carrying out different studies of **personality traits**, the characteristics that describe our thoughts, feelings, and behaviors.[19] But we are such complex creatures that no one theory has yet established a clear definition of personality. Still, trait theories are useful as they help to the further our understanding of personality.

Carl Jung's Trait Theory and the MBTI

In the 1920s, noted psychologist Carl Jung formulated two major orientations of personality: **introversion**, the personality trait of focusing on internal feelings rather than outside stimulation; and **extraversion** (also known as extroversion), the personality trait of obtaining gratification from outside stimulation.[20] Jung also identified four basic personality functions (thinking, feeling, sensing, and intuiting).[21] Other researchers and psychologists have since built on this theory, including Katharine Cook Briggs and their daughter Isabel Briggs Myers during World War II.[22]

The Myers-Briggs Type Indicator (MBTI) is a psychometric questionnaire used to evaluate four psychological preferences that combine to describe sixteen personality types.[23] Initially drafted as a questionnaire, the test was developed into the official MBTI in 1962. It is the most widely used personality assessment instrument in the world.[24]

Myers-Briggs Preferences

Each MBTI profile is made up of four psychological preferences, each of which is one of a pair (see Figure 3.1). According to the theory, we have a tendency to lean toward one of the characteristics within each pair, which determines our preference in each case.

FIGURE 3.1 ■ Myers-Briggs Preferences

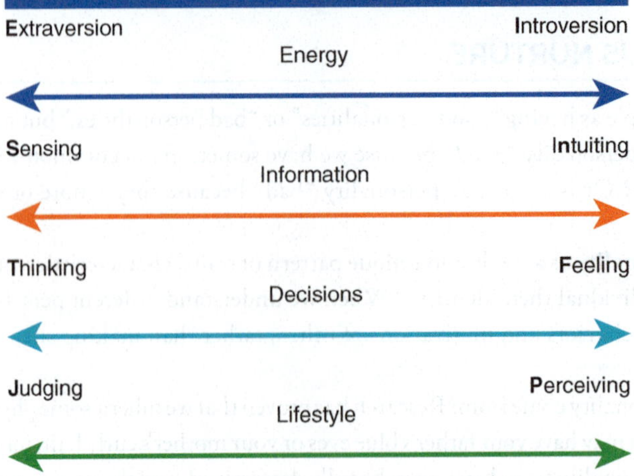

The four pairs of preferences are as follows:

- Extraversion (E) versus Introversion (I): Extraverts tend to be outgoing, talkative, and expressive; introverts tend to be reserved and like to work by themselves.
- Sensing (S) versus Intuiting (N): Sensing people prefer tangible, concrete, real-life information based on known facts; intuitive people tend to be imaginative, creative, and insightful.
- Thinking (T) versus Feeling (F): Thinking people use reason and logic to make decisions; feeling people draw from their own values when making decisions.
- Judging (J) versus Perceiving (P): Judging people prefer order, structure, plans, and rules; perceiving people are flexible and adaptable and like to keep their options open.

Psychological Preferences and "Always-On" Culture

Myers-Briggs researchers carried out a study to assess how different personalities cope with remote working and the blurring of boundaries between work and home.[25] Over the course of 2018 and 2019, over 1,000 people were surveyed about their personality type, behavior, degree of job satisfaction, and experiences of work/home conflict.

The results were mixed. More than 10% enjoyed "always-on," culture as they had greater flexibility as to when and where they worked and generally were more satisfied and engaged in their roles. Others felt differently, believing that "always-on" culture led to higher stress levels, an inability to switch off, greater distractions at work and at home, and less capacity to focus. The results helped the researchers to create strategies to cope with the stress of always being on, using the four psychological preferences featured in the Myers-Briggs Type Indicator model:

1. Switching Off: Introversion Versus Extraversion

   Introverts can disconnect by finding a quiet area at home or at work and absorbing themselves in something they're passionate about. They can also try to limit online meetings, but they need to make sure they do have some contact with other people.

   Extraverts can use exercise to switch off and can also benefit from doing something new and different, taking lots of breaks, and staying in touch with others through video, not just voice.

2. Information Overload: Sensing Versus Intuition

   To avoid becoming overwhelmed with information, sensing people need to step back, see the bigger picture, and talk to others to get their views on the issue.

   Intuitive people can become distracted by too much information, as it causes them to leap from one idea to another. They need to try one thing at a time, commit to it, and try to ground themselves in the moment.

3. Creating Boundaries: Thinking Versus Feeling

   Without face-to-face contact, thinking people can be easily misunderstood; they should read through emails and messages before they send them to ensure they don't come across as terse and impersonal.

   Feeling people can create boundaries by finding a balance between taking care of themselves and supporting others. They can do this by figuring out the type of support they need most and taking steps to find it.

4. Establishing Work/Life Balance: Judging Versus Perceiving

   Judging people can create a more suitable work/life balance by setting clear rules around the use of technology at home: switching off devices not in use, creating a designated work space and staying away from it outside working hours, and telling others when they will and won't be available will help reduce stress levels.

   Although perceiving people may enjoy the flexibility of working from home, they need to be mindful that others may not feel the same way. They also could benefit from the distraction of other activities outside the working day to break up the work routine.

The MBTI can be beneficial in understanding ourselves and increasing our self-awareness. It is also useful for identifying individual differences between us that can be a source of conflict and misunderstanding. The MBTI theory holds that by broadening our perspectives of others,2 knowing what motivates them, and understanding why they behave and communicate in the way they do, we will build better relationships.

Criticisms of the MBTI

Although countless organizations all over the world still use the MBTI, it has been heavily criticized by academics for providing a simplified, limited view of personality.[26] For instance, one important area of personality is **emotional stability**, the extent to which we can remain calm and composed. At the opposite end of the spectrum for this trait is **neuroticism**, a tendency to be tense, moody, irritable, and temperamental. The more emotionally stable you are, the lower your level of neuroticism. The MBTI tells us very little about these traits.

Early research also questions the reliability of MBTI, as it is possible for the same person to get different results once they retake the test.[27] It has also been questioned for its validity in connecting "types" outcomes to the real world—for example, how certain people classified as a certain type will perform in a particular role.[28] Furthermore, the MBTI has also been criticized for being too "black and white," as it tends to box individual personalities into two main categories: introverts and extraverts.[29] Michael Ashton, professor of psychology at Brock University in Ontario, said, "This is a shortcoming, because people don't fall neatly into two categories on any personality dimension; instead, people have many different degrees of the dimension."[30]

Finally, the MBTI has been disparaged for assessing only four aspects of personality differences when past research has determined that there are at least five or six personality dimensions.[31]

Despite these criticisms, the MBTI can be a valuable tool for increasing self-awareness, generating insights, encouraging self-exploration and self-reflection, and understanding others. It can also motivate people into taking steps to change or improve certain aspects of their own personalities. Whatever results you get after completing the questionnaire, remember they are not a definitive description of your personality type—they are merely suggestions based on psychological preferences and are open to interpretation.

Eysenck's Personality Theory

In the late 1940s, German psychologist Hans Eysenck proposed a personality theory based on traits that were believed to be largely controlled by genetic influences.[32] At first, Eysenck's theory was based on two dimensions, Introversion/Extroversion and Neuroticism/Stability, but a third dimension, Self-Control/Psychoticism,[33] was added in 1966 (see Figure 3.2).

According to Eysenck, introverts inherit a highly aroused nervous system, prefer less stimulating environments, and tend to be reserved, quiet, reliable and pessimistic, whereas extraverts inherit an under-aroused nervous system, seek more stimulating environments, and tend to be optimistic, carefree, and impulsive.

Eysenck also believed that people who inherit a highly reactive nervous system are prone to neuroticism and emotional instability, whereas people with a less reactive nervous system will remain calm, stable, and levelheaded in stressful situations.

FIGURE 3.2 ■ Eysenck's Personality Theory

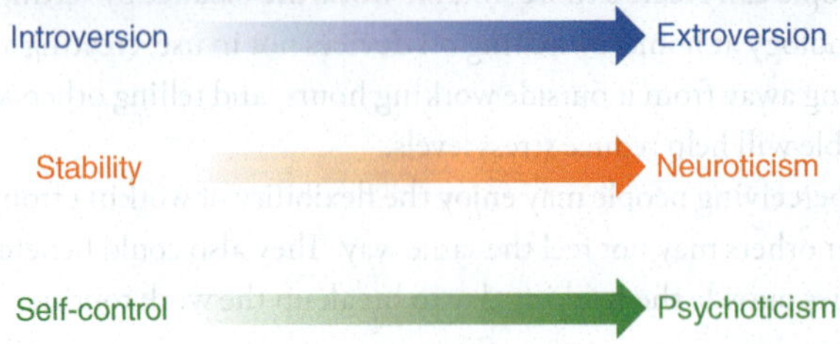

Finally, Eysenck related psychoticism (i.e., people lacking in empathy, behaving cruelly or aggressively) to high levels of testosterone, stating that people with lower levels exhibit more self-control and balanced behavior.

Although heavily based on genetic factors, Eysenck's theory argues that conditioning and socialization during childhood also play a role in shaping our personality. Therefore, the theory takes both nature and nurture into account.

Cattell's 16 Personality Factors Trait Theory

In the late 1940s, British psychologist Raymond Cattell created a model composed of 16 personality traits[34] (Table 3.2) before going on to create the 16PF Questionnaire, which is still commonly used in career counselling, in marriage counseling, and in business for employee recruitment and selection. Cattell believed we all possess each of the 16 personality traits to varying degrees—for example, whereas some people can be calm, others are more high- strung.

Both Cattell's and Eysenck's theories have been the subject of extensive research and debate.[35] Cattell's theory has received some criticism from researchers for being overly complicated and impossible to replicate, whereas Eysenck's theory is considered to lack robustness, as it focuses on too few traits. However, investigations into both Cattell's and Eysenck's methods gave rise to the Big Five Factor Model, which soon became the dominant trait theory to describe the building blocks of personality.

Big Five Factor Model

The Big Five Factor Model is based on the "lexical hypothesis," which is the idea that if there is a meaningful difference in personality, it is encoded in language—we have a word for it. One hundred years ago, researchers started compiling lists of adjectives from dictionaries: 20,000 words, 30,000 words. Then they reduced these words down to the fewest categories possible using a statistical technique called factor analysis. Over decades of research, five primary factors continued to emerge. In other words, you can't reduce the words to fewer categories, and thus these five categories represent the five basic dimensions of human personality.

TABLE 3.2 ■ Cattell's 16 Personality Factors Trait Theory
1. **Abstractedness:** Imaginative versus practical
2. **Apprehension:** Worried versus confident
3. **Dominance:** Forceful versus submissive
4. **Emotional stability:** Calm versus high-strung
5. **Liveliness:** Spontaneous versus restrained
6. **Openness to change:** Flexible versus attached to the familiar
7. **Perfectionism:** Controlled versus undisciplined
8. **Privateness:** Discreet versus open
9. **Reasoning:** Abstract versus concrete
10. **Rule-consciousness:** Conforming versus nonconforming
11. **Self-reliance:** Self-sufficient versus dependent
12. **Sensitivity:** Tenderhearted versus tough-minded
13. **Social boldness:** Uninhibited versus shy
14. **Tension:** Inpatient versus relaxed
15. **Vigilance:** Suspicious versus trusting
16. **Warmth:** Outgoing versus reserved

This model is widely accepted in academia and used more frequently in academic research. The **Big Five model**, outlined in Table 3.3, describes five basic dimensions of personality, including Extraversion, Agreeableness, Conscientiousness, Neuroticism (or Emotional Stability), and Openness to Experience and is frequently used to evaluate and assess people in the workplace.[36]

The Big Five personality test scores these personality dimensions from low to high, and a combination of these traits gives us an idea of what type of personality the individual possesses. For example, a person may score high in extraversion (very sociable) but low on conscientiousness (not very responsible). This analysis gives employers a better idea of the worker's profile and how they might fit into a certain role, and it is a useful way of assessing and predicting job performance. It also provides a more complete view of personality traits than earlier theories that saw traits as contradictory rather than as different in degree, because it allows for the many complexities of the human temperament.

The Big Five model has become the dominant trait theory of personality guiding research today. While the model has been subject to a certain amount of criticism,[37] the weight of evidence suggests that the five-factor structure remains remarkably stable over time, generalizes across cultures and languages, and shows substantial agreement across self and other rating sources.[38] This growing body of validating evidence further solidifies the Big Five model's status as the most widely accepted and influential modern trait theory of personality.

Researchers have proposed the concept of core self-evaluation (CSE), which refers to the appraisals that people make of their own abilities, self-worth, control, and capabilities.[39] For example, people who have a high core self-evaluation think of themselves in a positive way and have a high degree of confidence in their own skills and abilities, whereas people with low core self-evaluation tend to lack confidence and think negatively of themselves. CSE involves four main personality dimensions: locus of control, emotional stability, self-efficacy, and self-esteem. Research links these four traits with job satisfaction and work performance.

Earlier in the chapter, we described three of these dimensions: emotional stability, self-efficacy, and self-esteem. **Locus of control** is the extent to which people believe they have influence over events.[40] There are two types: **internal locus of control**, which allows people to believe they are responsible for influencing events; and **external locus of control**, which allows people to believe outside influences are responsible for their fate.

The HEXACO Model of Personality

Although the Big Five model of personality has become a standard framework for personality in the field of OB, in recent years a competing model of personality has emerged that adds a sixth personality dimension to the basic five factors.

The HEXACO model of personality consists of the six dimensions of Honesty-Humility (H), Emotionality (E), Extraversion (X), Agreeableness (A), Conscientiousness (C), and Openness to Experience (O).[41] Although aspects of all five factors from the Big Five Factor Model are interpreted

TABLE 3.3 ■ The Big Five Model

Openness to Experience	The dimension of being curious, creative, and receptive to new ideas
Conscientiousness	The dimension of being thoughtful, organized, responsible, and achievement oriented
Neuroticism	The dimension of being tense, moody, irritable, and temperamental
Extraversion	The dimension of being outgoing, sociable, assertive, and talkative
Agreeableness	The dimension of being trusting, good natured, tolerant, forgiving, and cooperative

Sources: Barrick, M. R., & Mount, M. K. (1991, Spring). The Big Five personality dimensions and job performance: A meta-analysis. *Personnel Psychology, 44*(1), 1–26; John, O. P., & Srivastava, S. (1999). The Big Five trait taxonomy: History, measurement, and theoretical perspectives. In L. A. Pervin & O. P. John (Eds.), *Handbook of Personality: Theory and Research* (2nd ed., pp. 102–138). Guilford Press.

somewhat differently in the HEXACO model, the addition of the Honesty-Humility dimension represents the biggest departure from the classic framework.

The Honesty-Humility factor includes trait descriptors such as honesty, sincerity, fairness, and modesty as opposed to greediness, conceitedness, deceitfulness, and pretentiousness—concepts that were traditionally elements of Agreeableness in the Big Five model.[42] Focusing on honesty-humility as a separate personality dimension may have important implications for managerial practice.

For example, the results of a recent study by Professors Jocelyn Wiltshire and Kibeom Lee of the University of Calgary and Joshua S. Bourdage of Western University suggest that employees rating low on the honesty-humility dimension may be more likely to engage in counterproductive work behaviors and impression management behaviors and to experience greater job stress and decreased job satisfaction when working in a highly political work environment,[43] while another recent study found that low levels of honesty-humility were related to the intention to commit premeditated and calculated vengeful acts.[44]

Yet the search for the most accurate personality test continues. In 2021, Ray Dalio, founder of investment firm Bridgewater Associates, collaborated with expert psychologists to develop a free online personality assessment called PrinciplesYou.[45] The test takes up to 40 minutes, and participants are required to rate statements such as "I get stressed out easily" on a seven-point scale ranging from "Agree Strongly" to "Disagree Strongly." The test is intended to help people better understand themselves and how they interact with others. Participants also have the ability to share the results with friends and family. Data gathered from the test are used only to improve the accuracy of the statements. Dalio says, "Knowing how you think and how others you interact with think is critical in getting what you want in both your personal life and in work."[46]

Person-Job Fit and Person-Organization (P-O) Fit

Person-job fit theory is the process of identifying the skills, experiences, and competencies are needed to fulfill job description requirements.[47] For example, an accounting role would require a level of accounting knowledge. Person-job fit is measured during the recruitment process through job interviews, résumés, reference checks, and preselection assessments.

Person-organization fit (or P-O fit) theory can be defined as the compatibility between an employee and an organization.[48] P-O fit occurs when a candidate's own beliefs and values correspond with the mission, values, and ethics of the organization. For example, a candidate who believes in doing good in the world and is keen on giving back to the community will be more likely to fit into an organizational culture that shares the same values. P-O fit is more difficult to measure than person-job fit, as it can't be assessed through the same testing methods. Typically, organizations focus on characteristics such as personality, attitudes, self-confidence, and interpersonal skills when considering a candidate for a role. Recent research found that the Big Five personality framework was a useful tool for measuring personality-based P-O fit in addition to being a reliable predictor of future attitudes, behavior, and overall job performance.[49] Benefits of P-O fit for the organization include:[50]

- Higher quality of work
- Increased productivity
- Improved employee retention
- Enhanced engagement, leading to higher levels of collaboration and motivation
- Greater likelihood that candidates will refer the organization to family and friends

Although some job candidates are likely to have the right skills to fulfill the requirement of a role, having the required qualifications doesn't mean the candidates will stay in the organization long-term if they feel they don't fit in there. A lack of P-O fit can lead to negative outcomes. For instance, 74% of companies reported that hiring the wrong candidate costs an average of $14,900.[51] There are also consequences for employees who don't fit well into the organizational culture or share its values, as there are for the teams who work with them. These consequences include:[52]

- Increased stress and exhaustion
- Lower job satisfaction
- Low morale within the team
- Lack of team and individual motivation
- Low productivity
- Poor-quality work
- Higher employee turnover

Our individual personalities and differences can cause challenges to working relationships and impede our ability to fit into an organization. But focusing on our character strengths can go a long way toward creating bonds and improving our interactions with others.

THE ROLE OF GRIT AND PSYCHOLOGICAL CAPITAL IN ACADEMIC PERFORMANCE

EXAMINING THE EVIDENCE

Beyond the individual difference concepts discussed elsewhere in this chapter, grit and psychological capital are two additional individual concepts that have received substantial research attention in recent years. Angela Duckworth and colleagues have developed grit as a psychological concept, defining it "as a trait-level perseverance and passion for long-term goals."[53] Grit is especially helpful in sustaining effort toward long-term goal completion. In contrast, psychological capital (PsyCap) is described as a positive psychological state resulting from having confidence in one's ability to succeed at difficult tasks (self-efficacy), having positive expectations for current and future successes (optimism), sustaining and refocusing efforts toward achieving goals (hope), and overcoming and recovering from setbacks and adversity (resilience).[54] Research evidence has connected both grit and PsyCap to important individual outcomes, including students' academic success. One recent study conducted by Kyle W. Luthan, Brett C. Luthans, and T. Daniel Chaffin found that these concepts may work together to help explain academic performance outcomes.[55] In short, their results suggest that having the trait characteristic of grittiness can result in higher levels of the positive state of PsyCap, which in turn leads to better academic performance. In other words, these findings suggest that PsyCap is the mechanism that facilitates or translates the positive effects of grit in enhancing academic performance.

Critical-Thinking Questions

1. What might students and educators do to help students apply their grittiness more effectively in the context of academic performance?
2. Could managers use similar approaches to help gritty employees perform more effectively in their jobs? Why or why not?

CHARACTER STRENGTHS

In addition to looking at personality characteristics and traits, researchers have increased their focus on **character strengths**—positive qualities that benefit ourselves and others, such as wisdom, courage, and gratitude.[56] Research has shown that recognizing and cultivating our positive personality traits and developing our character strengths enhances our own well-being, increases our happiness, leads to greater self-acceptance, improves our mental health, generates more positive experiences at work and school, and improves our relationships with others.[57]

Character strengths are an aspect of positive psychology, a field pioneered by Dr. Martin Seligman of the University of Pennsylvania that explores ways to help people recognize their positive traits or strengths—rather than their perceived weaknesses and failings—and nurture them to their full potential.[58] Research in positive psychology has made great strides over the last 15 years, especially with regard to understanding the behavioral factors associated with happiness. The following section describes three character assessments widely used in training: the VIA Survey of Character Strengths, the DiSC personal assessment tool, and the CliftonStrengths Assessment.

The Values in Action (VIA) Survey of Character Strengths

Designed by Drs. Christopher Peterson and Martin Seligman, the Values in Action (VIA) Survey of Character Strengths measures 24 character strengths divided into six categories[59] (Table 3.4). These individual character strengths are measured against a full survey, which takes 15 minutes to complete and consists of a total of 240 questions such as "I know that I will succeed with the goals I set for myself" (Hope) and "I always treat people fairly whether I like them or not" (Fairness). Responses are based on a scale of 1 to 5, where 1 equals "very much like me" and 5 equals "very much unlike me."

TABLE 3.4 ■ VIA Survey of Character Strengths

Signature Strengths	Meaning
Wisdom and Knowledge	
1. Creativity 2. Curiosity 3. Judgment 4. Love of Learning 5. Perspective	1. The ability to develop something unique and original 2. Inquisitiveness and interest to know 3. The power of rationalization and critical thinking 4. The affinity to participate in new activities to adapt to something new 5. Wisdom and perception to see the world as others see it
Courage	
1. Bravery 2. Perseverance 3. Honesty 4. Zest	1. Courage, valor, fearlessness 2. Persistence and the power to hang on during times of distress 3. Genuineness, truthfulness, and authenticity 4. The energy to live life fully and face challenges with grit and positivity
Humanity	
1. Love 2. Kindness 3. Social Intelligence	1. The power to feel and show affection to others and develop long-lasting relationships 2. Mercifulness and empathy 3. The ability to communicate effectively and form strong social bonds
Justice	
1. Teamwork 2. Fairness 3. Leadership	1. The motivation to work as part of a team and strive to achieve group goals 2. The virtue of treating everyone equally and making unbiased judgments 3. The capacity to be the face of a team, supervise effectively, and empower others
Temperance	
1. Forgiveness 2. Humility 3. Prudence 4. Self-regulation	1. The ability to accept others' shortcomings 2. Modesty and a humble nature 3. Rational thinking and the power to interpret things logically 4. Control over oneself and command over self-expression
Transcendence	
1. Appreciation 2. Gratitude 3. Hope 4. Humor 5. Spirituality	1. Praising the self and surroundings 2. Feeling and expressing thankfulness, including for the small things in life 3. Positive, future-oriented feelings and optimism 4. The ability to approach life with a playful, light attitude 5. Religious faithfulness and commitment

Source: Peterson, C., & Seligman, M. E. P. (2004). *Character strengths and virtues: A handbook and classification.* American Psychological Association.

While the VIA characters strengths assessment tool has been praised for its reliability and consistency (e.g., the questionnaire appears to produce consistent scores for the same individual over a certain time period), one study has raised some potential underlying issues with the assessment itself.[60] Overall, it is considered a psychometrically valid tool that explores and raises awareness of signature strengths.[61]

The DiSC Personal Assessment Tool

Another example of a character strengths–focused assessment tool used in the workplace is the DiSC assessment (Figure 3.3), first proposed by Dr. William Marston in 1928.[62] DiSC is used by more than 1 million people every year in the workplace to improve teamwork, communication, and productivity. The acronym DiSC stands for four main personality profiles in the model:

(D)ominance: people with dominant personalities may be confident and strong-willed

(i)nfluence: influential people may be more open and relationship focused and inclined to persuade others

(S)teadiness: people with steady personalities may be reliable and value cooperation and sincerity in others

(C)onscientiousness: conscientious people focus on quality, accuracy, expertise, and competency

The DiSC assessment consists of approximately 80 items presented on 5-point scales, where 1 equals "strongly disagree" and 5 equals "strongly agree." Examples include "Accuracy is a priority for me," "I can be pretty forceful with my opinions," and "I love meeting new people."

Studies of DiSC have concluded that like the VIA assessment tool, it gives consistent results when repeated by the same individual at a later time.[63]

The CliftonStrengths Assessment

The CliftonStrengths Assessment was developed by educational psychologist Donald Clifton in 2001.[64] Like DiSC, it is commonly used in organizational settings and supports people in identifying different strengths. The tool is made up of 34 strength themes separated into four principal domains and includes 177 paired statements, each of which must be responded to on a 5-point scale within 20 seconds (Table 3.5). For example, on one side of the scale might be "Starting conversations is an effort for me" and on the other side "I get a rush from striking up a conversation with a stranger." Participants rate the accuracy of each statement as it applies to them.

There is substantial evidence in support of the validity of the CliftonStrengths Assessment in terms of consistency of results over certain periods of time.[65]

FIGURE 3.3 ■ DiSC Personal Assessment Tool

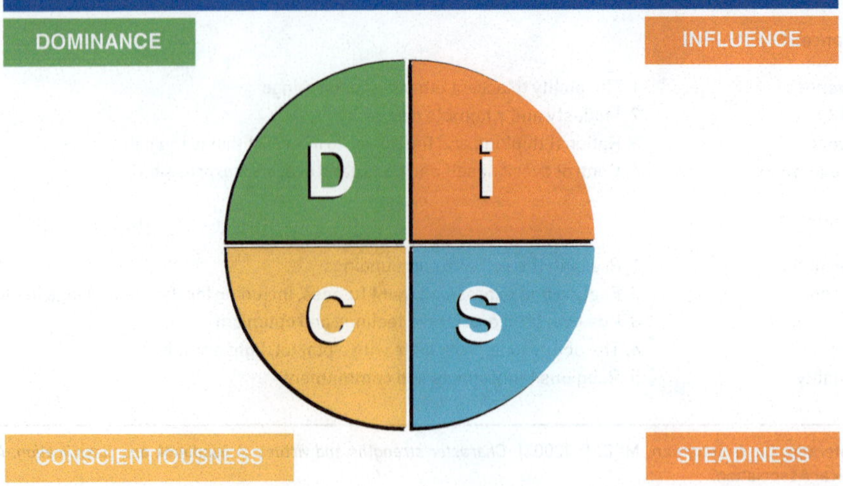

TABLE 3.5 ■ CliftonStrengths Assessment

Executing	Relationship Building	Strategic Thinking	Influencing
Achiever	Adaptability	Analytical	Activator
Arranger	Connectedness	Context	Command
Belief	Developer	Futuristic	Communication
Consistency	Empathy	Ideation	Competition
Deliberative	Harmony	Input	Maximizer
Discipline	Includer	Intellection	Self-Assurance
Focus	Individualization	Learner	Significance
Responsibility	Positivity	Strategic	Woo
Restorative	Relator		

OTHER PERSONALITY ATTRIBUTES

Personal conception is the degree to which individuals relate to and think about their social and physical environments and their personal beliefs regarding a range of issues. Our personal conception of ourselves is dependent on the personality dimensions shown in Figure 3.4.

Self-Monitoring

Self-monitoring is the degree to which people adjust their behavior to accommodate different situations.[66] High self-monitors might hold back on expressing their true feelings and behaviors if they think the situation doesn't call for it or others might not approve. In short, they match their behavior

FIGURE 3.4 ■ Dimensions of Personality

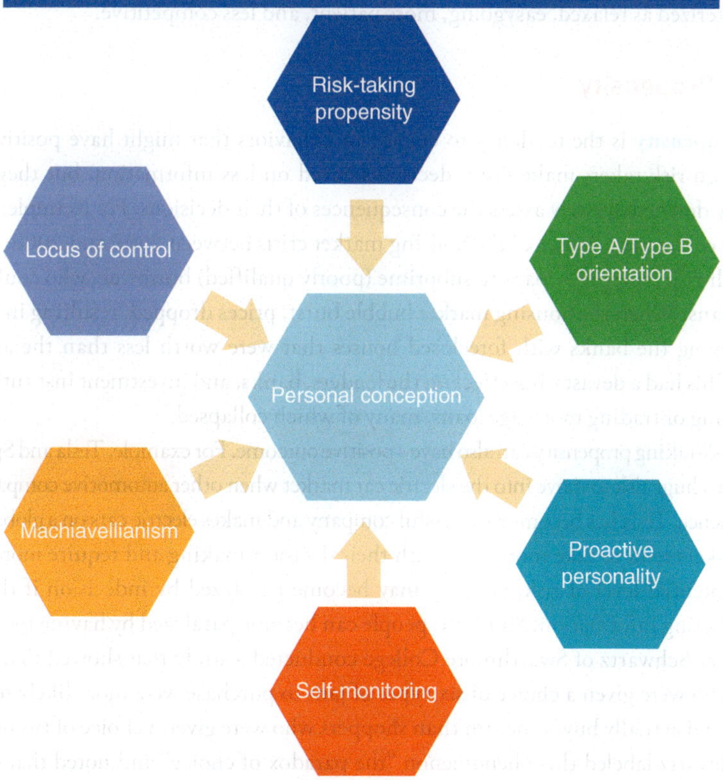

to the requirements of the situation. In contrast, low self-monitors don't disguise their behaviors, have little regard for how others perceive them, and refuse to change any aspect of themselves to accommodate any given situation. Their attitude is "What you see is what you get." Research shows that self-monitoring can be helpful in highlighting and changing certain behaviors, particularly for inactive or deskbound people and people suffering from depression. Learning how to self-monitor can draw awareness to certain issues and enable people to address them through therapy or other means.[67]

Proactive Personality

Proactive personality is the extent to which individuals take the initiative to change their circumstances.[68] Those who are high in proactive personality look for opportunities to change events and take action to ensure the desired change takes place. People who are low in proactive personality are generally more accepting of the status quo and take very little action to change the circumstances surrounding them. Today's organizations actively seek out proactive people because they are more likely to react positively to and adapt to an ever-changing work environment. Research shows that proactive people are better performers, contributors, and innovators than their less assertive colleagues. However, recent research also demonstrates that employee proactivity can go wrong if it's not channeled in the right way. In one study, researchers interviewed 25 workers across all types of industries to investigate whether employee proactivity leads to positive or negative outcomes. They discovered that proactivity has successful outcomes only when employees have enough personal and professional interest in the task; when they feel secure enough to share ideas and generate the support of others before taking the lead; and when their ideas for change align with organizational goals. Without these three factors in place, employees are more likely to burn out, alienate coworkers and managers, or waste time and resources.[69]

Type A/Type B Orientation

The way employees react to stressful situations is of particular interest to OB managers. For example, some people thrive under pressure and perceive tight deadlines as a challenge, whereas others may struggle and react negatively. Researchers have defined two main personality types to gauge how workers cope under pressure: Type A and Type B.[70] People with a **Type A orientation** are characterized as competitive, impatient, aggressive, and achievement oriented. Conversely, those with a **Type B orientation** are characterized as relaxed, easygoing, more patient, and less competitive.

Risk-Taking Propensity

Risk-taking propensity is the tendency to engage in behaviors that might have positive or negative outcomes.[71] High risk takers make faster decisions based on less information, but they risk making mistakes if they don't adequately assess the consequences of their decisions. For example, excessive risk taking was one of the main causes of the housing market crisis between 2007 and 2008, because lenders granted high-risk mortgages loans to subprime (poorly qualified) borrowers who couldn't afford to pay back the loans. When the housing market bubble burst, prices dropped, resulting in high volumes of defaults, leaving the banks with foreclosed houses that were worth less than the amount of the original loan. This had a devastating effect on the lenders, banks, and investment institutions that were involved in selling or trading mortgage loans, many of which collapsed.[72]

However, risk-taking propensity can also have a positive outcome. For example, Tesla and SpaceX founder Elon Musk took a huge risk to move into the electric car market when other automotive companies chose not to. As a consequence, Tesla has become a successful company and makes electric cars on a global scale.[73]

Low risk takers tend to take more time with their decision-making and require more information to assess the potential level of risk, yet they may become paralyzed by indecision if they spend too much time gathering information. Similarly, people can become paralyzed by having too much choice. Researcher Barry Schwartz of Swarthmore College conducted a study that showed that shoppers at a grocery store who were given a choice of six types of jam to purchase were more likely to make a purchase decision and actually buy some jam than shoppers who were given a choice of twenty-four different types.[74] Schwartz labeled this phenomenon "the paradox of choice" and noted that our cherished freedom of choice may actually lead to decision-making uncertainty and dissatisfaction with decision outcomes. In other words, having too many choices may cause people to be unhappy with their decisions or to have difficulties in making any decision at all. Decision-making can be especially difficult for "maximizers"—those individuals determined to make only the best choices.

The Dark Triad

The dark triad comprises three negative personality attributes: narcissism, psychopathy, and Machiavellianism.[75] Narcissistic people tend to be dominant, entitled, and superior and harbor grandiose ideas about themselves. A recent studyfound that CEOs displaying higher-than-average levels of narcissistic tendencies were more likely to get caught up in lawsuits.[76] CEOs such as Oracle's Larry Ellison, Tesla's Elon Musk, and Steve Jobs at Apple have all been described as narcissists because of their huge levels of self-confidence and strong commitment to winning at all costs.[77] Psychopathic leaders tend to lack empathy and interest in the well-being of others while demonstrating high levels of impulsive behaviors. Another study has found that leaders who portray both psychopathic and narcissistic tendencies have a serious impact on the likelihood of depression in employees, all of which has a destructive effect on employee and organizational performance.[78] Finally, leaders with **Machiavellian** (inspired by philosopher Niccolò Machiavelli's book *The Prince*) leanings tend to be manipulative, opportunistic, and unprincipled. In other words, Machiavellian leaders will do anything to achieve their own success.

Russian president Vladimir Putin has been compared to Machiavelli owing to his manipulation of Russian public opinion through propaganda and use of extreme measures and unethical practices in the guise of "protecting Russia" from its so-called "enemies" in the West.[79] Popular culture is also littered with Machiavellian figures such as Tony Soprano from the crime drama *The Sopranos*, Claire Underwood in the political thriller *House of Cards*, and Lord Petyr Baelish from the fantasy drama series *Game of Thrones*. Each of these figures, real or fictional, raises the classic question discussed in Machiavelli's book *The Prince*: Is it better to be feared than loved?[80]

As we have seen, despite the amount of research and theories carried out, the human personality still remains something of a mystery. However, by applying some of the research toward understanding our own differences and the differences of others, we have a better chance of building productive relationships inside and outside the workplace.

IN REVIEW

3.1 Discuss why individual differences are important

Individual differences are the behavioral and cognitive similarities and differences among people. We don't just need to understand people who are the same as us, but also those different from us in the way they think, make decisions, and behave. When we can analyze the differences and similarities among our coworkers, we have a better idea why people act the way they do.

3.2 Contrast the nature and nurture explanations of personality development

Personality is a stable and unique pattern of traits, characteristics, and resulting behaviors that gives an individual their identity. The origins of our personality traits have yet to be fully determined, and the nature-versus-nurture debate continues on. The nature side of the debate argues that personality is inherited, while the nurture side argues that personality is influenced by the environment.

3.3 Distinguish among the trait theories of personality

Personality traits are the characteristics that describe our thoughts, feelings, and behaviors. Although there is still no clear definition of personality, trait theories are useful as they help to the further our understanding of personality.

Carl Jung formulated two major orientations of personality, **introversion** and **extraversion** (also known as extroversion), which have been built on by other theorists.

The Myers-Briggs Type Indicator (MBTI) is a psychometric questionnaire used to evaluate four psychological preferences that combine to describe sixteen personality types.

Eysenck's personality theory was based on two dimensions, Introversion/Extroversion and Neuroticism/Stability, and later a third, Self-Control/Psychoticism.

Cattell's 16 Personality Factors Trait Theory holds that everyone possesses each of 16 personality traits to varying degrees.

The Big Five Factor Model describes five basic dimensions of personality: Extraversion, Agreeableness, Conscientiousness, Neuroticism (or Emotional Stability), and Openness to Experience.

The HEXACO model of personality consists of the six dimensions of Honesty-Humility (H), Emotionality (E), Extraversion (X), Agreeableness (A), Conscientiousness (C), and Openness to Experience (O).

Person-job fit theory is the process of identifying the skills, experiences, and competencies needed to fulfill job description requirements, and person-organization fit (or P-O fit) can be defined as the compatibility between an employee and an organization.

3.4 Describe the approaches to assessing and interpreting character strengths

Developing our **character strengths** enhances our own well-being, increases our happiness, leads to greater self-acceptance, improves our mental health, generates more positive experiences at work and school, and improves our relationships with others. Three character assessments are widely used in workplace training: the VIA Survey of Character Strengths, the DiSC personal assessment tool, and the CliftonStrengths Assessment.

3.5 Differentiate among the most common personality attributes

Personal conception is the degree to which individuals relate to and think about their social and physical environments and their personal beliefs regarding a range of issues. Our personal conception of ourselves is dependent on personality dimensions such as self-monitoring, degree of proactive personality, Type A versus Type B orientation, and risk-taking propensity. The dark triad comprises three negative personality attributes: narcissism, psychopathy, and Machiavellianism.

KEY TERMS

Awareness of others (p. 59)
Big Five model (p. 64)
Character strengths (p. 66)
Emotional stability (p. 62)
External locus of control (p. 64)
Extraversion (p. 60)
Individual differences (p. 59)
Internal locus of control (p. 64)
Introversion (p. 60)
Locus of control (p. 64)
Machiavellianism (p. 71)
Neuroticism (p. 62)
Personal conception (p. 69)
Personality (p. 59)
Personality traits (p. 60)
Person-job fit (p. 65)
Proactive personality (p. 70)
Risk-taking propensity (p. 70)
Self-awareness (p. 59)
Self-concept (p. 59)
Self-efficacy (p. 59)
Self-esteem (p. 59)
Self-monitoring (p. 69)
Type A orientation (p. 70)
Type B orientation (p. 70)

UP FOR DEBATE: PERSONALITY TESTING

Companies use personality tests to hire employees and to understand them better. It is estimated that approximately 75% of Fortune 500 companies use personality tests for such purposes. Do you think the use of personality testing is a good or bad thing from the employee's perspective? What about the employer's?

CASE 3.1: ADOBE INC.

Adobe Inc. is an American software company best known for its flagship Photoshop image-editing software, its Creative Cloud subscription suite, and the development of the Portable Document Format (PDF) for files. The company was founded in 1982 by Charles Geschke and John Warnock, two computer scientists who worked together at Xerox PARC in the late 1970s. Adobe Creek, the company's namesake, ran through Warnock's backyard at their home in Los Altos, California, where the duo started the company in Warnock's garage. As of 2022, Adobe employs more than 25,000 people worldwide and is a component of the S&P 500, S&P 100, and NASDAQ-100 stock market indices.[81]

Products Come and Go; Values Are Here to Stay

Adobe became a household name selling its boxed creativity software for hundreds of dollars apiece, but its transformation to cloud software and marketing services under the direction of CEO Shantanu Narayen elevated the company to one of the world's largest brands. Brad Smith, former CEO of Intuit, told *Business Insider* that it was Narayen's focus on people that led to successful innovation at Adobe. "I think what has differentiated him from many in the Valley is he is an amazing people leader and culture builder, and he can show not only the technology and product vision, but how to build a culture that's built to last," Smith said.[82] Narayen detailed their approach to *Investors' Business Daily*:

> **Adobe's values are to be genuine, exceptional, innovative, and involved**. When our mission and these values align with our employees' personal values and aspirations, then they can do their best work and the company is better for it. People can amaze you with their ingenuity. It's up to leadership to set aspirational goals, then get out of your peoples' way and remove obstacles. When we do this, I'm always amazed at what our people can accomplish.[83]

Michael Stoddart is the director of strategic business for Digital Media Enterprise at Adobe Asia Pacific. When Stoddart joined the company as an IT manager more than 25 years ago, Adobe Asia Pacific had just 10 employees. While at Adobe, Stoddart has continually had opportunities to learn and build expertise with new technologies, especially when the marketing industry was undergoing a major transformation from analog to digital tools. In an industry where three years can be a long time to remain at one organization, Stoddart is asked what keeps them at Adobe after nearly three decades. Stoddart responds that while projects have changed, the company's commitment to its employees persists: "It hasn't been the same company. What's important is to look for a digital-first, agile company that can keep pace with a fast-changing environment to help its employees build the skills and knowledge they need to stay relevant and advance in their careers."[84]

Alberto De Caro is a senior multi-solution architect for Europe, the Middle East, and Africa (EMEA) at Adobe. While De Caro was in the process of being hired as a senior consultant in the Italian market in 2014, their future manager challenged them to grow their customer-focused competency: "Alberto, you are a good professional, but you have mostly back-office experience. You've never had a major client-facing connection." Balancing technical proficiency with relational soft skills can be a career-long challenge for many professionals. Indeed, how to cultivate well-rounded teams and equip employees to be able to switch gears according to the situation is a conundrum managers face in every industry, not just tech. De Caro credits Adobe's company values for helping it develop strategic business expertise. "It was magic. I'm now working for a company with a great culture where I can really express myself. I'm supported in taking risks and expressing my leadership. And I know that everyone shares the same vision, culture, and objectives, so when I need support, I know my team will help. Similarly, my teammates can count on me—because we are all focused on taking care of our clients."[85]

Adobe for All

Adobe began its annual Adobe for All Summit in September 2018 with more than 1,200 employees in attendance at the San Jose Convention Center. Katie Juran, senior director of diversity and inclusion, kicked off the summit and outlined its three goals: "Empower attendees of all levels to own and drive their careers; inspire and equip—especially people managers—to help others be successful; and activate attendees as champions for the Adobe For All vision."[86] In its second year, the company asked event attendees to volunteer as speakers. Juran says, "I expected we may get a few dozen volunteers, but we wound up receiving more than 640! I was blown away by our employees' willingness to trust their colleagues and open up on stage this way."[87] Eight speakers were selected to inspire their colleagues with stories of their personal challenges and overcoming setbacks. The 2019 summit closed with an outline of five steps, dubbed *"Adobe for All in Action,"* that employees can take to make their teams more dynamic and inclusive (see Table 3.6).

TABLE 3.6 ■ Adobe for All in Action
Appreciate the Unique: Value the differences in others' stories and ideas.
Amplify Others: Help everyone's voice be heard.
Enhance the Team: Consider what a new addition will bring that's different.
Rethink Routine: Look to equalize meetings, assignments, and social events.
Open Up: Speak up for what you need and encourage feedback.[88]

Progressive People Policies

Great Place to Work and *Fortune magazine* have named Adobe one of the "100 Best Companies to Work For" every year since 2001. *Forbes, Fortune,* and *Glassdoor* have each listed Adobe as one of the "World's Best Workplaces," and *Comparably* has recognized the company on their lists for "Best Company Culture," "Best CEO," "Best Companies for Women," and "Best Companies for Diversity." In addition, Adobe is a leader in gender pay parity and ethnic pay parity between employees from underrepresented demographic groups (URM) and non-URM employees in the U.S.[89] Adobe puts its people first to accomplish its mission to *"Change the World Through Digital Experiences."*

Critical-Thinking Questions

1. Think of a team you were on that didn't value individual differences. Which of the *Adobe for All in Action* steps could you take to foster collaboration as a leader?
2. Do you know someone who can only "talk tech," like Alberto De Caro did prior to joining Adobe? How would you encourage them to develop their soft skills as a manager?
3. Do you think that focusing on employees as individuals the way Adobe does could be an element of corporate social responsibility (CSR) as well?

EXERCISE 3.1: USING DISC TO EVALUATE A CELEBRITY

Objective

The purpose of this exercise is to understand the DiSC personal assessment tool.

Instructions

Form groups of four to eight. As a team, think of someone famous—could be a politician, movie star, online influencer, sports figure, etc. Try to agree on someone that everyone knows. Then, once this famous individual is chosen, conduct a DiSC personal assessment on this person. Obviously, you don't have the instruments or access to the celebrity to ask them to complete them, but based on what you know (or think you know!) about this person, how do you suppose they would rate on the four personality profiles in the model? Recall from the chapter that the four profiles are Dominance (D), Influence (i), Steadiness (S), and Conscientious (C).

Reflection Questions

1. Which of the four DiSC personality profiles did your team rank the highest for this celebrity? The lowest? Explain.
2. Was it easy to agree on each of the personality profiles? Which of the four did you discuss most? Explain.
3. How accurate of an assessment of this individual do you think your team provided? How difficult is it to make such an assessment without truly knowing the person and being able to ask them specific questions?

Exercise contributed by Steven Stovall, Southeast Missouri State University.

EXERCISE 3.2: APPLYING THE BIG FIVE FACTOR MODEL

Objective

The purpose of this exercise is to understand the Big Five Factor Model.

Instructions

Find one or two people to partner with for this exercise. First, take a few moments to rate yourself as either high, medium, or low on each of the Big Five Factor Model's dimensions of personality. You may need to study the chapter to understand each of the dimensions (Openness to Experience, Conscientiousness, Neuroticism, Extraversion, and Agreeableness).

Once you have rated yourself on each of the five as either high, medium, or low, take turns sharing how you rated yourself and explain why you feel this way in your self-assessment. As your partner or partners share their ratings, ask for examples or offer support for their analysis.

Reflection Questions

1. Which of the five dimensions do you feel is your highest dimension and which is the lowest? Explain.
2. How did your self-assessment differ from the assessment of your partner(s)? Or were they similar?
3. Which dimension was the most difficult to provide an accurate self-assessment on? Why do you think that is?
4. What did you learn about yourself and others by conducting this exercise?

Exercise contributed by Steven Stovall, Southeast Missouri State University.

EXERCISE 3.3: EVALUATING THE MAJOR TRAIT THEORIES

Objective

The purpose of this exercise is to grasp the merits and drawbacks of each of the major trait theories.

Instructions

This is an exercise for the entire class. The instructor will provide one of the trait theories presented in this chapter. As a group, provide pros and cons for the theory. The instructor will write down the pros and cons for each one as the class discusses the merits or drawbacks of each. The major theories are:

- Jung's Introversion and Extraversion
- Myers-Briggs Type Indicator
- Eysenck's Personality Theory

- Cattell's 16 Personality Factors
- The Big Five Factor Model
- The HEXACO Model

Reflection Questions

1. Which of the theories did the class seem to like best? Explain.
2. Which of the theories presented makes the most sense to you? Why?
3. Which theory has the least applicability in an organization? In other words, if you were to avoid one of these theories in making an assessment of coworkers or employees, which would it be?

Exercise contributed by Steven Stovall, Southeast Missouri State University.

ONLINE EXERCISE 3.1: UNDERSTANDING PERSONAL CONCEPTION

Objective

The purpose of this exercise is to understand the concept of personal conception.

Instructions

Personal conception is the degree to which individuals relate to and think about their social and physical environments and their personal beliefs regarding a range of issues. Your conception of yourself is dependent on the personality dimensions of risk-taking propensity, Type A/B orientation, proactive personality, self-monitoring, Machiavellianism, and locus of control.

In an online discussion group, share your analysis of your personal conception. Proceed through each of the six personality dimensions, evaluating yourself. Then explain how this evaluation influences your personal conception.

Reflection Questions

1. Which of these personality dimensions do you feel is strongest for you? Weakest or least influential? Explain.
2. How difficult is it to self-assess these dimensions? For example, how did you evaluate yourself on the dimension of Machiavellianism? Which was the most difficult to self-assess and why?
3. How did your self-assessment differ from that of others who posted their self-assessments? Were any similar to yours? Discuss.

Exercise contributed by Steven Stovall, Southeast Missouri State University.

ONLINE EXERCISE 3.2: EVALUATING SELF-ESTEEM AND SELF-EFFICACY

Objective

The purpose of this exercise is to grasp the concepts of self-esteem and self-efficacy.

Instructions

Think of characters from a streaming or TV show. Find one that exhibits high self-esteem. Then find one who exhibits a strong sense of self-efficacy. You might even find one who has both! Recall that self-esteem is the beliefs we have about our own worth following the self-evaluation process and self-efficacy is the belief we have in our ability to succeed in a specific task or situation.

In your evaluation of the characters, explain why you provided the assessment you did. For example, in the show *Rick and Morty*, Rick has both high self-esteem and self-efficacy. He has an extremely high degree of self-esteem because he is constantly putting his own worth higher than that of every other living being in the universe. Additionally, he has an incredibly high sense of self-efficacy because he feels he never fails at any task he undertakes. Again, it's fine to select one character for self-esteem and another one for self-efficacy, even if they're from different shows.

Reflection Questions

1. Do you feel you have a high degree of self-esteem and self-efficacy? Why or why not?
2. What character or characters can you think of who have low self-esteem and self-efficacy?
3. Why do some people have high self-esteem but low self-efficacy?
4. Have the character or characters you chose ever exhibited low self-esteem or low self-efficacy? Explain.

Exercise contributed by Steven Stovall, Southeast Missouri State University.

Anadolu Agency/Contributor/Getty Images

4 PERCEPTION AND LEARNING

LEARNING OBJECTIVES

By the end of this chapter, you will be able to:

4.1 Describe the basic concept of perception

4.2 Explain the different types of perceptual distortions

4.3 Apply attribution theory to more effectively interpret behavior

4.4 Use reinforcement theory to understand learning and modify behavior

4.5 Apply social cognitive theory to social learning and cognitive processes

Case Study: Twitter's Adaptability

A Tech Giant

The seemingly indestructible tech giant that we know as Twitter consistently finds itself at the front of the pack alongside the other tech giants of our day. Twitter generates over $3.8 billion in revenues and employs over 5,500 people all over the world.[1] In addition, it reports over 206 million daily users.[2] What started as a tiny podcast start-up in Silicon Valley is now a 21st-century cultural phenomenon. World leaders, professional athletes, and students use Twitter as a means of making their voices heard.

Twitter is an incredibly powerful tool at the fingertips of everyone with access to the internet. In response to the ever-shifting sphere of technology and global trends, Twitter's functions are constantly changing. Through regular updates and improvements to its user interface, Twitter is always one step ahead of its competitors. If Twitter had been unable to adapt early on, it would surely have failed. Ever since Twitter's start under the name Odeo back in 2005, it has proved to be a great example of the success that comes when a company masters the ability to adapt to changing market conditions.[3]

Humble Beginnings

In 2005, Evan Williams and some friends moved to Silicon Valley and created the start-up Odeo, a podcasting platform. At the time, podcasts were all the rage. With 14 full-time employees finally rolling out their product in summer 2005, it looked as though Odeo couldn't fail. However, another company called Apple had just launched its free podcasting service, rendering Odeo's product irrelevant. CEO Evan Williams needed to pivot—and fast. Williams asked employees to collectively come up with any potential solution. After long days and nights of throwing around new business ideas, the Odeo team decided to completely shift gears from a podcasting platform to a status-updating micro-blogging platform. The idea was originally conceived by Jack Dorsey, one of Odeo's web designers.[4]

A Slow, Volatile Start

It took about six months for things to really kick off for Twitter. After the slow start, Evan Williams wrote a letter to investors urging them to pull out their money and is quoted as saying, "By the way, Twitter, which you may have read about, is one of the pieces of value that I see in Odeo, but it's much too early to tell what's there. Almost two months after launch, Twitter has less than five thousand registered users. I will continue to invest in Twitter, but it's hard to say it justifies the venture investment Odeo certainly holds—especially since that investment was for a different market altogether."[5]

The everyday tech consumer wasn't ready for the service Twitter offered. This new service came with new challenges for Twitter's employees. Employees would stay long hours researching new marketing techniques, computer engineering designs, and new ways to grow Twitter's brand. The key to Twitter's ultimate success was the team's ability to learn on the job and then quickly apply what they learned. At a conference in Austin, Twitter was introduced as a way for attendees to share their thoughts and experiences with other attendees via a "status." The platform was hugely popular at the conference, and the number of users skyrocketed. After a few short months, Twitter became one of the world's most widely visited websites, with over 1 million subscribers.[6]

Management in Action

The theme of Twitter's success is, simply, adaptability. A business is most able to adapt to new trends and technology only when it has a workforce of employees who have the ability to learn on the fly. Managers play a huge role in empowering their employees to do this, hence the corporate culture of Twitter that originated when Evan Williams turned to employees to come up with new ideas. Ever since, Twitter has maintained a corporate culture that emphasizes employee contributions, learning, and advancement. According to one employee, "the company culture here is absolutely amazing. You also get to work on meaningful projects that impact the platform and the company."[7]

Twitter's managers do many different things to maintain this perception of their corporate culture. Twitter's culture of learning and development shapes employees' perceptions in a way that encourages them to buy in to the overarching mission. There are programs in place at Twitter to help enhance employees' various skills, whether they're learning to code, aiming to get an MBA, or planning to start a business venture of their own. Twitter's empowering environment then enables employees to put what they've learned into practice. The amount of power that Twitter entrusts to its employees is huge. Workers are empowered to go explore and find data, build things, and generally choose the course of action they think will have the most impact. This has a dynamic influence on employee self-efficacy, which, as we learned in Chapter 3, is the belief one has in one's own ability to succeed in a specific task or situation. When employees believe in themselves, they won't be afraid to take risks, just like Jack Dorsey did by pushing for Twitter.[8]

A recent action by Twitter management supports the contention that Twitter empowers its employees by allowing them to work wherever they want. Due to the COVID epidemic, Twitter employees worked from home. Now, unlike other companies that are switching back to an in-person setting, Twitter has announced that their employees can continue to work from home as long as they would like.[9]

Additionally, by giving employees the power to contribute to the direction of the organization, managers consequently allow them to decide whether they want to learn more or not. Naturally, employees who don't strive to learn will perform poorly and eventually lose their job. On the other hand, employees who go out of their way to learn more naturally empower themselves to do more. They can do this by first setting goals through self-regulation, then finding learning methods that work best for them. Vicarious learning, or learning by emulating the behavior of managers, is just one of the very reliable methods that team members can employ to develop their skills in the workplace. Twitter managers are willing to help any employee seeking to grow by providing constructive criticism and giving employees an opportunity to take part in more advanced projects. Their performance is then evaluated, and various types of reinforcement are offered along with constructive criticism. This good balance makes for an ideal learning environment that pushes employees to grow while also empowering them to seek out guidance and growth on their own.[10]

Critical-Thinking Questions

1. What was valuable about Evan Williams's decision to task employees with mustering up a new business idea?
2. How are employee empowerment, adaptability, and on-the-job training related?

PERCEPTION: INTERPRETING OUR ENVIRONMENT

A number of years ago, the *Washington Post* carried out an experiment in perception by placing world-famous violinist Joshua Bell, disguised as a street musician, in a Washington Metro station.[11] Wearing a baseball cap, T-shirt, and jeans, Bell performed a 43-minute set of six classical pieces for unsuspecting commuters. Of the 1,097 who passed by, only seven stopped for just over a minute to listen to Bell's virtuoso performance before continuing their journey. By the end of the performance, Bell had made a grand total of $30 and a few cents—hardly enough to buy a ticket to one of their own sell-out concerts.

So what does this experiment tell us about perception? Was it because Bell was dressed as a street musician that the commuters didn't stop to listen? Or was it because of the setting—after all, how likely is it that a world-famous musician would perform for free in a Metro station? Whatever the reason, we can conclude that most people perceived Bell to be someone other than who they were, which caused an inability to recognize and appreciate Bell's talent as a musician.

We define **perception** as the process by which we receive and interpret information from our environment.[12] Managing perceptions in the workplace is important for nurturing a healthy organizational culture, especially when people hold different perceptions about their colleagues, how tasks are carried out, and even the organization itself.

As our case study shows, Twitter intentionally shapes employees' perceptions in a positive way by nurturing an empowering environment of learning and development that encourages them to buy in to Twitter's overarching mission. Take a look at Figure 4.1. What do you see?

You might say you see a simple pattern of wreaths, while others may see bright rays or beams emanating from the center. Although the rays are just an illusion, many of us see them because the brain "connects the dots" between certain areas in the wreaths.[13]

In this trick drawing, neither answer is the "right" one. The cartoon illustrates the fact that we often perceive things differently from one another.

Information from our environment can also affect our perception.

The COVID-19 pandemic has changed our perception of the traditional workplace, leading thousands of employees to choose companies with a more flexible working structure. Yet some organizations hold different perceptions of how the post-COVID workplace should operate. While some companies such as Dropbox and Slack have chosen to go fully remote and others such as Apple and Amazon have gone for a "hybrid" approach, some organizations, like Netflix and Goldman Sachs, perceive the situation differently, believing that the office should be the primary workplace. Netflix CEO Reed Hastings has stated views on remote working, saying, "Not being able to get together in person, particularly internationally, is a pure negative."[14]

FIGURE 4.1 ■ Optical Illusion: The Scintillating Starburst

In the new "scintillating starburst" illusion, bright rays emanate from the center of the design through concentric wreaths of star polygons. (Image credit: Courtesy of Michael Karlovich, Recursia LLC)

Source: https://www.livescience.com/scintillating-starburst-illusion.html

Components of the Perception Process

A number of factors may influence and distort perception, including the perceiver, the environment, and the focal object.

The Perceiver

Perceptions are shaped by past experiences, culture, attitude, values, upbringing, and more. This means the nature of the perceiver has a strong influence on the perceptual process. For example, say you were raised in an environment where working hard and being on time were considered very important. You might have a negative attitude toward a coworker who comes to work late or takes long work breaks. Once you have formed this perception, it might be difficult for you to change your mind about your coworker even if they perform well.

The Environment

The context or the setting also affects the perception process. For example, you may perceive danger if you hear footsteps behind you on your walk home at night, yet chances are you would barely notice the footsteps if you were walking down a busy street during the day. You're still the same person, but your perception of danger is dependent on the situation or context (i.e., nighttime versus daytime).

The Focal Object

The person, thing, or event being interpreted also affects our perception. In almost a decade of selfie-obsessed culture, the act of taking a picture of oneself has been perceived by many as narcissistic and a desperate attempt for approval. However, researchers who developed the campaign #ScientistsWhoSelfie discovered that selfies can also be an important way for people to connect and communicate with others from all over the world. During the study, researchers found that scientists who posted selfies with their work on Instagram increased positive public perception.[15] Rather than being negatively stereotyped as "nerdy" or boring, people began to see the "human side," which helped

Violinist Joshua Bell posed as a street performer in a Washington Metro station as part of an experiment by the *Washington Post*. At the end of the day, Bell had made just over $30 for performing six classical pieces.

Michael Williamson/The Washington Post/Getty Images

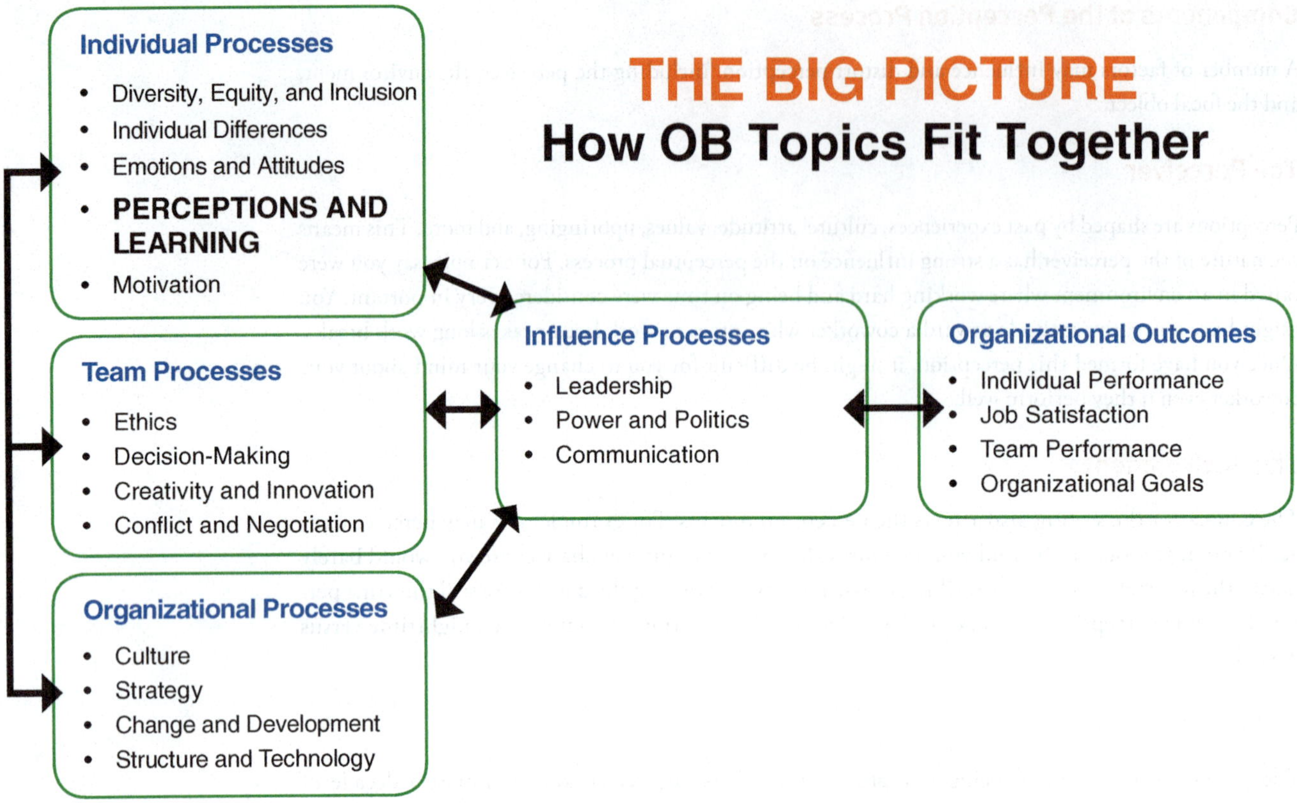

to build public trust. Paige Jarreau, the lead author on the study, believed that scientists generated such a positive response because they weren't "trying to look cute on camera" but were telling a story about science in a way that helped to build trust from their followers.[16]

Many businesspeople choose to drive expensive cars because they feel it makes a good impression on others, who they hope will perceive them as wealthy, successful, and professional. However, in today's social context, do people really perceive owners of expensive cars in this way, or do they resent them for flaunting their success?[17] We tend to perceive objects in terms of contrast. For example, we might interpret the driver of the expensive car in a different way than we view someone else, depending on their situation. Similarly, we perceive people who stand out differently from others—a work colleague who is vocal in meetings might be perceived differently from one who says very little.

Why Is Perception Important?

In 1936, psychologist Kurt Lewin observed that people act not upon the basis of reality but upon their *perceptions* of reality.[18] In other words, we tend to interpret events differently from what actually happens in our environment. Therefore, understanding perception is a critical part of understanding behavior. In the workplace, the way we're perceived and the way we perceive others are crucial for career progress and for building our relationships. For example, leaders and managers' success or failure depends on how they're perceived by employees. They could give all the speeches in the world about the future of the company, but if they're perceived as disingenuous, they're unlikely to build loyalty and trust. This is why many people in leadership roles use self-critiquing techniques, such as videoing themselves or seeking feedback from others, in order to perceive themselves as others do. Leaders who create positive relationships with their teams, demonstrate high levels of expertise and judgment, and follow through with their promises and commitments are more likely to be perceived in a favorable light (see Part IV for more on leadership).[19]

Uncritically allowing our perceptions to take control can create distorted versions of reality that can be very harmful to working relationships.

COMMON PERCEPTUAL DISTORTIONS

Each and every day, we take in and process a huge amount of complex information. Our attempts to organize and sift this information can lead to inaccuracies and cloud our perceptions of different people, situations, and events. Let's explore some common perceptual distortions.

- **Stereotypes** are an individual's fixed beliefs about the characteristics of a particular group.[20] When we have a particular feeling or attitude (often negative) toward members of a specific group, we call this *prejudice*. Stereotypes can also be found in the language we use. In a study exploring the stereotypes in MBA case studies, researchers discovered that women and people of color were often described in stereotypical language.[21] In one case, the author describes a woman leader in terms that would not be adopted for a male leader while also reinforcing stereotypes that women are family oriented and "nice."[22] Researchers suggest the authors of these cases should play close attention to the language they use, remove stereotypical descriptions, and teach students how to identify problematic language.[23]
- **Selective attention** is the tendency to selectively focus on aspects of situations that are most aligned with our own interests, values, and attitudes.[24] Two classic experiments show the power of selective attention. In the first, participants are asked to watch a short video of six people playing basketball.[25] The challenge is to count the number of passes made by the three players wearing white T-shirts. During the game, a gorilla walks into the middle of the players, thumps its chest, and leaves. Over half of the participants in the experiment missed the gorilla because their attention was focused on counting the passes. The second experiment, called "the door study," shows a man asking another man for directions.[26] At one point, people carrying a door pass between them, allowing the man who's asking directions to quickly swap places with another person. The person giving directions doesn't notice they're interacting with an entirely different person. Both these experiments reveal how much we miss around us without having any idea of what we're missing.
- **Halo effect** is a perception problem in which our impression of someone is influenced by how we think or feel about their character.[27] Sometimes our perceptions are influenced by people we consider attractive. For example, a recent study exploring the impact of beauty on the amount of tips received by servers in several restaurants in Virginia found that servers considered to be more attractive by customers received nearly $1,261 more in tips than their arguably less attractive colleagues.[28] The study also showed that beauty mattered more for female servers than male servers, thus demonstrating how the halo effect can cause unfairness and discrimination.
- **Primacy effect** is a perception problem in which an individual assesses a person quickly on the basis of the first information encountered.[29] Research conducted by Harvard Executive Fellow, executive coach, and professional matchmaker Rachel Greenwald illustrated the impact of the primacy effect in both business and romantic relationships.[30] Greenwald discovered that people tend to pass judgment too quickly on the basis of early information. In other words, first impressions count for a lot. In the online dating world, a perceived poor first impression can result in one party "ghosting" another party, while in a business environment, the interviewer could reject the candidate for making a minor mistake. Greenwald advised that people who express curiosity, actively listen, show empathy, and build self-awareness have a greater chance of making a positive first impression.
- **Recency effect** is a perception problem in which we use the most recent information available to assess a person.[31] It's the reason many of us can recall only the last few items on our shopping list and why we can remember what we had for lunch today but struggle to remember what we had to eat two weeks ago. Today's managers conducting performance reviews must be aware of the recency effect and take into account the strained circumstances (juggling work with young children, isolation, caring for elderly relatives) many employees

have been working under during the pandemic and avoid basing their reviews on their most recent performance.[32]

- **Contrast effect** takes place when people rank something higher or lower than they should as a result of exposure to recent events or situations.[33] Contrast effect occurs particularly among recruiters, who tend to look at large volumes of résumés in a row, judging each résumé on the one that came before it, or when interviewing, forming an opinion on candidates based on the candidate before them.[34] This is problematic, as recruiters should be basing their opinions on how candidates' skills and attributes fit the job rather than making comparisons with others.

- **Projecting** is a process in which people transfer their own thoughts, motivations, feelings, and desires to others.[35] For example, a person who takes a dislike to someone else may project their own feelings onto that person and convince themselves that the other person doesn't like them either.[36]

- **Self-fulfilling prophecy** occurs when a person bases behavior on preexisting expectations about another person or situation in order to create an outcome aligned with those expectations.[37] One type of self-fulfilling prophecy is the "Pygmalion effect," where high expectations are thought to improve performance in a certain area. However, research has shown that excessively high expectation can lead to work-related stress and burnout.[38] Setting realistic expectations, rewarding effort, delegating tasks, and encouraging feedback are useful ways to reduce the risk of work-related stress.

- **Impression management** (IM) is the process by which we attempt to influence the perceptions others may have of us.[39] For example, influencers tend to engage in IM on social media sites such as Facebook and Instagram to make a certain impression on their followers. Successful influencers often work with big brands on marketing campaigns, and consumers place huge trust in their endorsements. One study showed that one in three people trust an influencer's words more than the company's brand statement.[40] When influencers build an online identity, their followers expect them to uphold it, but despite practicing impression management techniques, not all influencers can keep up the facade. For example, successful vegan Instagrammar Yovana Mendoza lost thousands of followers for perceived lack of authenticity when a photograph emerged showing the influencer eating fish.[41] A facet of impression management is **ingratiation**, in which an individual attempts to influence others by becoming more attractive or likable.[42] A recent study of manufacturing companies in China found that subordinates who behave in the most ingratiating manner toward their supervisors outside the workplace have a greater chance of a higher bonus or promotion.[43]

Forming accurate perceptions of others is a complex process. Awareness of these common perceptual distortions may help you to avoid making them about others and may also allow you to combat inaccurate perceptions others may form about you. In addition to becoming familiar with perceptual distortion, it's important to understand attribution theory.

COMMON ATTRIBUTION ERRORS

When we see someone behave in a certain way, we tend to try to make sense of it or at least attach some meaning to it. **Attribution theory** holds that people look to explain the behavior of others in two ways: by making *internal attributions*, attributing behavior to personal characteristics, or by making *external attributions*, attributing behavior to situational factors.[44]

For example, say you worked with a colleague called Amahle who has a problem with absenteeism. How would you make sense of their behavior? Do you think they're lazy and indifferent? Or do you think they might be so overloaded with responsibilities that they find the prospect of coming to work overwhelming? If you choose the first option, you are ascribing Amahle's behavior to internal causes: you believe their absenteeism is a result of laziness and apathy. However, if you choose the latter option,

FIGURE 4.2 ■ Determinants of Attribution

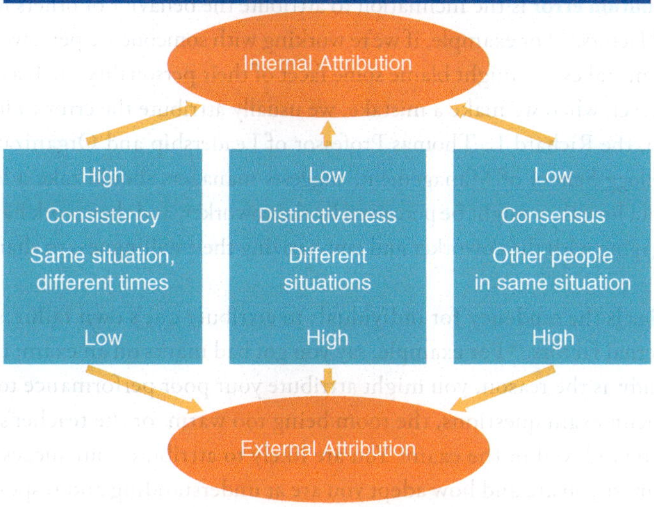

Source: Mehlman, R. C., & Snyder, C. R. (1985, October). Excuse theory: A test of the self-protective role of attributions. *Journal of Personality and Social Psychology, 49*(4), 994–1001.

you are attributing Amahle's behavior to external causes: you blame overwhelming amounts of work for their poor attendance record.

Three factors influence our internal and external attributions: consistency, distinctiveness, and consensus, as outlined in Figure 4.2.[45]

Consistency is the extent to which a person responds in the same way over a period of time. For example, if Amahle is late arriving to work every morning (high consistency in the same situation), we tend to ascribe their tardiness to internal causes and assume Amahle is just not a punctual person. If, however, Amahle is late to work only on Fridays (low consistency in the same situation), then we might assume an external cause, such as that Amahle needs to drop the children off at school.

Distinctiveness is the extent to which a person behaves consistently in similar situations. For example, if Amahle tends to be frequently late to work, late returning from lunch, and late to midmorning staff meetings (low distinctiveness across situations), we might ascribe this behavior to internal factors such as being lazy and indifferent. Conversely, if Amahle is punctual in most situations but is sometimes late returning from lunch (high distinctiveness across situations), we might ascribe their tardiness in that particular situation to the fact that Amahle sometimes visits an elderly person during lunch to help with heavy chores.

Consensus looks at how everyone else responds in the same situation. For example, if several people in the office are absent or late on the same day (high consensus with other people in the same situation), we might ascribe this behavior to an external factor such as a dust storm that has slowed the morning commute for everyone or a virus or flu that has spread through the office. Conversely, if everyone but Amahle has arrived on time and isn't absent on a given day (low consensus with other people in the same situation), we are more likely to attribute Amahle's tardiness or absence to internal factors.

It's important to try to make sense of the behaviors of others in order to form the most meaningful conclusion. However, as the following section shows, it's also easy for us to make wrong judgments.

When perceiving others, we sometimes make erroneous judgments when assessing their behaviors. Take Nike employee Amanda, for instance. Amanda traveled a lot but still wanted to stay connected to the team, so they instituted an open-door policy when they returned to the office. During a performance review, Amanda was shocked to read that some people didn't feel they were being listened to. When they investigated further, they found that what they perceived as multitasking (replying to emails, etc.) during the meetings had been perceived as rudeness. So Amanda changed around their office and made sure they gave full attention to the person they were talking to and kept their computer out of sight. In making these changes, Amanda was able to change people's erroneous judgment about their behavior.[46]

There are two common attribution errors: fundamental attribution error and self-serving bias. **Fundamental attribution error** is the inclination to attribute the behavior of others to internal factors more than external factors.[47] For example, if we're working with someone we perceive to be difficult or who keeps making mistakes, we might blame some facet of their personality, such as laziness or being disorganized. However, when we make a mistake, we usually attribute the error to forces beyond our control. Brian Uzzi, the Richard L. Thomas Professor of Leadership and Organizational Change at Northwestern's Kellogg School of Management, suggests managers should take a look at their own behavior, think about how they might be perceived by the coworker, and then work hard to improve the relationship by engaging with the coworker and emphasizing their willingness to share skills and work collaboratively.[48]

Self-serving bias is the tendency for individuals to attribute one's own failures to external factors more than internal factors.[49] For example, say you got bad marks on an exam; instead of accepting your lack of study as the reason, you might attribute your poor performance to external factors such as overly difficult exam questions, the room being too warm, or the teacher's lack of preparation. But what if you did well in the exam? You are likely to attribute your success to internal factors, such as how smart you are and how adept you are at understanding and responding well to the questions.[50]

LEARNING PROCESSES: BEHAVIORAL THEORY

Perception is shaped by **learning**, an ongoing process through which individuals adjust their behavior based on experience.[51] Understanding the way we learn is essential to OB because it has a direct influence on our work performance, our ability to relate to others, and our career progression. We all learn in different ways, and it's never too late to learn new skills. In fact, recent studies have shown that contrary to common thought, the brain has the ability to learn new skills at any age. For example, Priscilla Sitienei, a midwife from Ndalat in rural Kenya, never learned to read and write. At the age of 90, Sitienei started to attend lessons in a local school and managed to overcome a lifetime of illiteracy. Studies show that mastering a new discipline also helps to maintain our cognitive health (our ability to think clearly, learn, and remember).[52]

Learning opens up so many opportunities for us in every aspect of our daily existence.

To better understand learning behaviors, it is useful to evaluate the behavioral interpretations provided by different theorists over the past century. The behavioral view holds that behavior is shaped and learned as a result of external environmental stimuli. There are three important contributions within the behavioral perspective: classical conditioning, operant conditioning, and reinforcement theory.

Classical Conditioning

The concept of **classical conditioning** was developed by Russian physiologist Ivan Pavlov. Classical conditioning suggests that learning can be accomplished through the use of stimuli.[53] Pavlov's most famous experiment used different stimuli to elicit a behavioral response in dogs. Pavlov found that dogs began to salivate in response to the ringing of a bell—a *neutral stimulus*—before they were given food—an *unconditioned stimulus*. Eventually, the bell became a *conditioned stimulus* that caused the dogs to salivate (*conditioned response*) without the food being present. The steps are outlined in Figure 4.3.

We find evidence of classical conditioning in the workplace during fire drills. Most companies carry out fire drills to instill safety procedures in their employees in the event of a fire. When we hear the fire alarm (conditioned stimulus), we respond by leaving the building (conditioned response). However, if we saw a fire (unconditioned response) in the office without the fire alarm going off, many of us would react with the conditioned response of running away from the perceived danger. Although classical conditioning explains a great deal about why we react to certain stimuli, researchers have developed more sophisticated theories to explain why we behave the way we do.

FIGURE 4.3 ■ Classical Conditioning

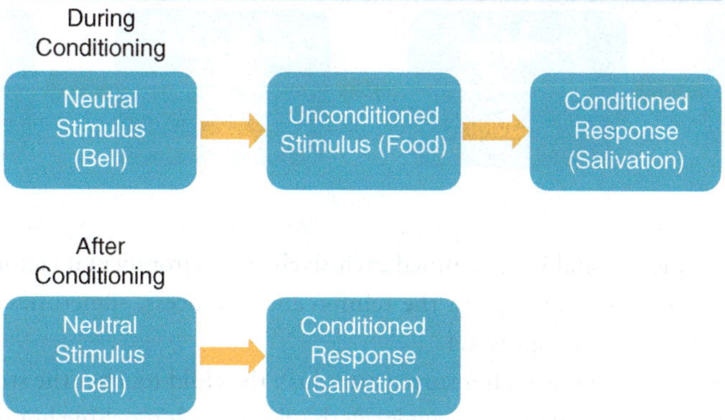

Operant Conditioning Theory

Operant conditioning is the process of forming associations between learning and behavior that occurs when the consequences of behavior are being controlled.[54] At the root of operant conditioning is the law of effect theory devised by U.S. psychologist E. L. Thorndike, which states that behavior followed by pleasant results is more likely to be repeated, whereas behavior followed by unpleasant results is not.[55] For example, if your manager praises you for taking initiative and conducting a complex task by yourself, you are more likely to repeat the behavior in the future. Theorists have since refined operant conditioning into the more comprehensive reinforcement theory.

Reinforcement Theory

Pioneered by psychologist B. F. Skinner and colleagues, reinforcement theory is the most fully developed theory of operant conditioning to date.[56] We define **reinforcement** as the application of consequences for the purpose of establishing patterns of behavior. Within **reinforcement theory**, behavior is

Operant conditioning follows the idea that a behavior followed by positive results is likely to be repeated. Rewarding employees for a job well done can encourage further positive performance.

FIGURE 4.4 ■ Reinforcement Theory

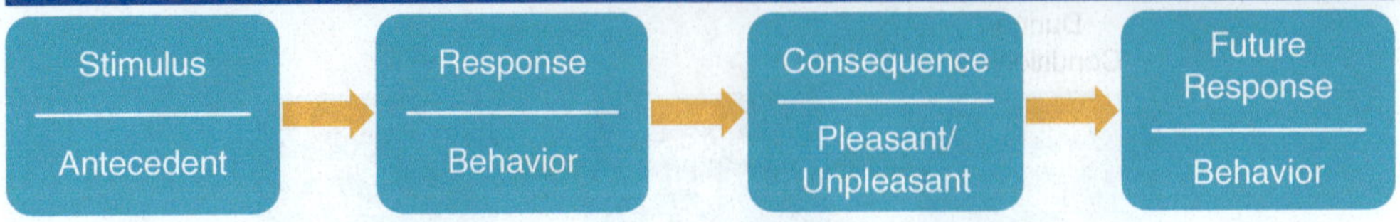

a function of its consequences and is determined exclusively by environmental factors such as external stimuli and other reinforcers. The steps in the reinforcement process, sometimes referred to as the ABCs of behavior, are outlined in Figure 4.4.

For example, a curious child sees a hot stove (stimulus); the child touches the stove (response); the child gets burned and cries out in pain (consequence); the child avoids touching hot stoves in the future (future responses).

The practical application of reinforcement in the workplace is called **organizational behavior modification**, which is the use of behavioral techniques to reinforce positive work behavior and discourage unhelpful work behavior.[57] Fast-casual health foods restaurant chain Sweetgreen headquartered in California builds a positive working environment by rewarding employees for achievements, providing emergency financial support, and offering workers opportunities to work on impact projects to support the community. These efforts help boost positivity and morale throughout the company, leading to higher work performance.[58] There are four main types of behavioral reinforcement techniques: positive reinforcement, negative reinforcement, punishment, and extinction.

Positive and Negative Reinforcement

Many managers use **positive reinforcement**, in which positive consequences are used to reinforce positive behaviors and make the employee more likely to behave in similar ways in the same or similar situations.[59] Research shows that positive reinforcement is a more powerful motivator than punishment and helps to build trust between managers and teams. Casmin Wisner, PR specialist at Utah-based cloud communications provider Jive Communications, credited their manager for supporting failures and highlighting achievements: "What makes me want to keep working harder, however, isn't the kind messages of security during my failures, which have encouraged me to fail fast" . . . "but the recognition and praise for my accomplishments."[60]

Conversely, **negative reinforcement** is the removal of a particular item or stimulus following the demonstration of a certain behavior in order to increase that behavior. For example, you leave the house early for work (the behavior) to avoid the risk of being delayed by the morning rush-hour traffic (removal of stimulus).[61]

In another example of positive and negative reinforcement, a group of university psychology students carried out a behavioral experiment on their professor. The professor had a habit of pacing back and forth and up and down the classroom during lectures, which the students found distracting and frustrating. To encourage the professor to remain in the center of the room, the students applied the positive reinforcement of behaving as if they were fully engaged and focused. However, when the professor wandered to another point in the room, the students behaved as if they weren't listening until the professor returned to the center of the room, at which time they refocused their attention, thereby providing negative reinforcement. A quarter of the way through the semester, the students noticed a change in the professor's lecturing habit: remaining in the center of the classroom from then on.[62]

Punishment

Punishment is the administration of unpleasant consequences or the removal of positive ones for the purpose of discouraging undesirable behavior.[63] There are two types of punishment: positive punishment—the administering of unpleasant consequences—and negative punishment—the removal of pleasant consequences.[64] For example, say your manager reprimands you for being late for a meeting—this is positive punishment because your manager has administered unpleasant consequences that decrease the likelihood of you being late again. Conversely, suppose that after reprimanding you, your manager begins to behave dismissively toward you. This is negative punishment because your manager has removed positively reinforcing consequences in an effort to eliminate your unappreciated behavior.

Extinction

Using punishment techniques in the workplace can be risky and demotivating, which is why many managers often choose **extinction**, the absence of any consequences, which reduces the likelihood that the behavior will be repeated in the same or similar situations.[65] In one example, an employee continually makes jokes during important meetings, resulting in disapproving frowns from some teammates and laughter from others. In this situation, the employee may be seeking attention, which both the positive and negative reactions are rewarding. The manager instructs the rest of the team to pay no attention to this person during meetings. As a result, jokes are no longer made because the reinforcing consequences of that behavior have been removed.

Schedules of Reinforcement

Schedules of reinforcement determine how often specific instances of behaviors will be reinforced. In the real world, it is unrealistic to think that every single behavior will be reinforced every time it occurs, but some organizations select a reinforcement schedule when they are trying to reinforce specific desired behaviors. There are two main types of schedules: continuous reinforcement and intermittent reinforcement.

Continuous reinforcement is a reinforcement schedule in which behavior is rewarded every time it takes place.[66] For example, some companies reward their sales teams with commissions every time they make a sale.

In **intermittent reinforcement**, behavior is not rewarded every time it occurs.[67] There are four types of intermittent schedules:

- Many companies use a *fixed interval schedule*, a reward provided only after a certain period of time has elapsed, as the most common form of reinforcement schedule.[68] For example, employees receive a monthly or annual paycheck.
- A *fixed ratio schedule* is followed when desired behaviors are rewarded after they have been exhibited a fixed number of times.[69] For example, production line workers may be rewarded with a cash incentive every time they produce a certain number of items.
- A *variable interval schedule* is designed to reinforce behavior at varying times.[70] For example, an employee may be rewarded with high praise following desirable behavior during periods of different length. However, employers need to ensure that too much time doesn't pass between reinforcements, because this might reduce the schedule's effectiveness.
- Finally, a *variable ratio schedule* rewards people after the desired behavior has occurred after a varying number of times.[71] For example, in a call center, the higher the number of calls workers make, the higher the chance of closing a sale, leading to greater financial compensation.

Behavioral theory provides a greater understanding of workplace behavior that occurs in response to external environmental stimuli. However, cognitive theorists believe the behavioral view is too limited, arguing that behavioral theorists don't take into account the mental processes behind the behavior. In the next section, we explore the cognitive view and the role it plays in shaping human behavior.

LEARNING PROCESSES: THE COGNITIVE VIEW

In **social cognitive theory**, psychologist Albert Bandura proposed that we learn by observing, imitating, and modeling the behavior of others within our social context.[72] The theory holds that our cognitive processes, which include awareness, perception, reasoning, and judgment, play important roles in how we learn new knowledge and skills.

This type of learning is particularly significant in the workplace, where employees tend to model the behavior of their managers. For example, a manager who demonstrates commitment, works late when needed, and completes projects on time is likely to lead a team with a similar work ethic. Conversely, if a manager arrives to work late, leaves early, and takes long lunch breaks, employees are likely to imitate this behavior, leading to a decrease in work productivity and performance.

There are several important aspects of social cognitive theory. The first is **self-efficacy**, which describes our personal belief in our ability to perform certain tasks or behaviors.[73] When we have a high level of self-belief, we are more likely to take risks. Google builds self-efficacy by encouraging smart risk-taking in education, inclusion, and economic development. This approach boosts employee engagement and unites workers toward achieving a common goal.[74]

The second component of social cognitive theory is **vicarious learning**, a process of learning by watching the actions or behaviors of another person. America Needs You (ANY), a New York–based nonprofit organization, supports new graduates in finding employment by fostering vicarious learning through its mentorship program.[75] Graduates engage in one-on-one mentoring to establish their career goals and learn how to boost their career development. During the pandemic, when many people were forced to work remotely, ANY embraced the merging of professional and personal life, built rapport by encouraging mentors and mentees to talk about topics outside work and academics, and reassuring mentees that any interruptions from children or pets were completely accepted. By taking a holistic mentorship approach, ANY was able to build relationships and create clarity of purpose.

EXAMINING THE EVIDENCE

SNAKES, SELF-EFFICACY, AND TASK PERFORMANCE: TOO MUCH OF A GOOD THING?

Some very interesting early classic studies examining the concept of self-efficacy focused on people with a fear of snakes.[76] Albert Bandura and colleagues set up an experiment using both an experimental group and a control group, with a pretest indicating that both groups had a strong fear of snakes and low self-efficacy for approaching and handling them. The researchers then carried out an intervention with the experimental group. They explained that the snakes weren't poisonous and wouldn't bite and described how the snakes would react when the subjects handled them. They also informed the group that the snakes weren't cold and slimy but actually dry and scaly. The researchers then measured the fear and self-efficacy levels in both groups again. Both groups still had a high fear of snakes, but the experimental group had a much higher level of self-efficacy for approaching and handling the snakes. Consequently, when members of both groups were asked to approach and handle the snakes, those from the experimental group whose level of self-efficacy had increased were able to do so at a much higher rate than those with low self-efficacy.

Although hundreds of studies have shown similar positive effects for self-efficacy on task performance, some recent studies have called this relationship into question.[77] These studies suggest that high levels of self-efficacy within an individual could cause that person to become overconfident and to allocate fewer resources and less effort to the task at hand, thereby resulting in lower levels of task performance. For example, one study of students playing an analytical game showed a negative relationship between self-efficacy and performance.[78] Self-efficacy resulted in overconfidence and the increased likelihood of making a logical error in the game. These findings suggest that too much self-efficacy could be too much of a good thing. In support of this assertion, a recent study showed that in a group of nascent entrepreneurs, entrepreneurial self-efficacy had a curvilinear relationship with entrepreneurial performance.[79] Performance increased until it reached a "tipping point" at which too much self-efficacy became a problem for the entrepreneurs, causing them to become overconfident and to "overshoot" their objectives. Much like some vitamins, self-efficacy appears to be beneficial in moderate doses but may become toxic at higher levels.

Critical-Thinking Questions

1. Given the conflicting research evidence, how can self-efficacy affect individual task performance in the workplace?
2. What can managers do to try to enhance the positive effects of self-efficacy in their employees while minimizing the possible negative effects?

Companies like Google promote vicarious learning by creating small kitchen spaces to encourage communication and learning opportunities.

Vicarious learning also influences our degree of self-efficacy.[80] For example, if you see a colleague on a similar career path successfully giving the weekly presentation during a meeting, you might be more inclined to volunteer to do the next one because you have observed this event as a positive experience, thereby increasing your self-efficacy for doing presentations. However, if you observe the same colleague stumble nervously through the presentation, it might give you second thoughts about doing one yourself, resulting in low self-efficacy for giving presentations.

The third factor of social cognitive theory is **self-regulation**, the process in which we set goals that create a discrepancy between a desired state and a current state.[81] This discrepancy creates tension, which drives us to increase effort to reduce tension and reach the goal. For example, your manager sets a goal for you to complete a complex project within two weeks; you might feel uncomfortable or nervous about your ability to achieve the goal within the allotted time frame, so you work harder in order to reduce your feelings of discomfort and to successfully complete the assignment on time. Self-regulation can also protect our well-being. In a time where constant connectivity has become the new norm, it is important to practice the willpower to switch off from our devices and set clear boundaries between work life and home life.[82]

Triadic Reciprocal Model of Behavior

Bandura also believed human functioning is shaped by three factors that are reciprocally related: reinforcement, cognitive processes, and behavior.[83] The relationship is shown graphically in the **triadic reciprocal model of behavior** (Figure 4.5).

FIGURE 4.5 ■ Triadic Reciprocal Model of Behavior

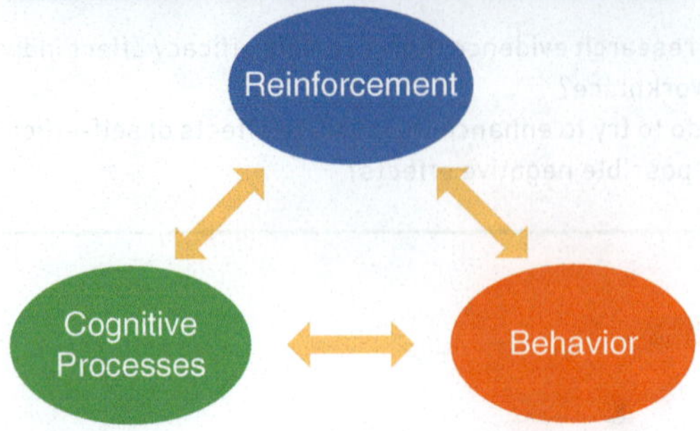

Figure 4.5 shows how cognitive processes mediate the effects of reinforcers on behavior and how behavior influences both reinforcers and cognitive processes. Consider two quarterbacks in a football game. The first throws an interception, which causes the belief that they're not an effective passer, thereby lowering self-efficacy for completing passes. Lower self-efficacy results in more mistakes and thus higher levels of incompletions and interceptions. This poor play encourages the defensive players to try even harder, which creates more negative reinforcers in the form of pressure.

In contrast, the second quarterback also throws an interception. However, unlike the first, the quarterback acknowledges the mistake and is determined to try harder; self-efficacy remains constant. An increase in efforts leads to a touchdown pass. This success further increases self-efficacy. The defensive players become tentative because of this good play, which leads to even more success for the quarterback.

In this chapter, we have focused on the nature of perception and the differing ways in which we perceive each other and ourselves. We have also explored learning and its importance to our working, personal, and professional lives. In the next chapter, we look at how motivation, attitudes, and stress impact our behavior.

IN REVIEW

4.1 Describe the basic concept of perception

Perception is the process by which we receive and interpret information from our environment. A number of factors influence and perhaps distort perception, including the perceiver, the environment, and the focal object. Perceptions are shaped by past experiences, culture, attitude, values, upbringing, and so on. This means that the nature of the *perceiver* has a strong influence on the perceptual process. The context or the setting affects the perception process as well. The person, thing, or event being interpreted also affects our perception.

4.2 Explain the different types of perceptual distortions

People process a huge amount of complex information, and their attempts to organize and sift this information can lead to inaccuracies. There are a number of common perceptual distortions. **Stereotypes** are an individual's fixed beliefs about the characteristics of a particular group. **Selective attention** is the tendency to selectively focus on aspects of situations that are most aligned with our own interests, values, and attitudes. **Halo effect** is a perception problem through which we form a positive or negative view of one aspect of an individual based on our overall impressions of that person. **Primacy effect** is a perception problem through which we assess a person quickly on the basis of the first information encountered. **Recency effect** is a perception problem through which we use the most recent information available to assess a person. **Contrast effect** takes place when people rank something higher or lower than they should as a result of exposure to recent events or situations. **Projecting** is a process through which people transfer their own thoughts, motivations, feelings, and desires to others.

Self-fulfilling prophecy occurs when a person bases their behavior on preexisting expectations about another person or situation in order to create an outcome aligned with those expectations. **Impression management** is the process by which we attempt to influence the perceptions others may have of us. A facet of impression management is **ingratiation**, by which an individual attempts to influence others by becoming more attractive or likable.

4.3 Apply attribution theory to more effectively interpret behavior

Attribution theory holds that people look to explain the behavior of others in two ways: by making *internal attributions*, attributing behavior to personal characteristics, or by making *external attributions*, attributing behavior to situational factors.

There are three types of determinants of attribution that influence our internal and external attributions: distinctiveness, consensus, and consistency. *Distinctiveness* is the extent to which a person behaves consistently in similar situations. *Consensus* involves looking at how everyone else responds in the same situation. *Consistency* is the extent to which a person responds in the same way over a period of time.

4.4 Use reinforcement theory to understand learning and modify behavior

Learning is an ongoing process through which individuals adjust their behavior based on experience. **Reinforcement** is defined as the application of consequences to establish patterns of behavior. Within reinforcement theory, behavior is determined exclusively by environmental factors such as external stimuli and other reinforcers.

The practical application of reinforcement in the workplace is called **organizational behavior modification**, which is the use of behavioral techniques to reinforce positive work behavior and discourage unhelpful work behavior.

4.5 Apply social cognitive theory to social learning and cognitive processes

The **social cognitive theory** proposes that learning takes place through observation, imitation, and the modeling of others within a social context. There are several important components to social cognitive theory. The first is self-efficacy, which describes our personal conviction in our ability to perform certain tasks or behaviors. The second component to social learning is **vicarious learning**, a process of learning that involves watching the actions or behaviors of another person. Vicarious learning influences our degree of self-efficacy. The third factor of social learning is **self-regulation**, in which people set goals that create a discrepancy between the desired state and the current state.

KEY TERMS

Attribution theory (p. 86)
Classical conditioning (p. 88)
Continuous reinforcement (p. 91)
Contrast effect (p. 86)
Extinction (p. 91)
Fundamental attribution error (p. 88)
Halo effect (p. 85)
Impression management (p. 86)
Ingratiation (p. 86)
Intermittent reinforcement (p. 91)
Learning (p. 88)
Negative reinforcement (p. 90)
Operant conditioning (p. 89)
Organizational behavior modification (p. 90)
Perception (p. 82)
Positive reinforcement (p. 90)
Primacy effect (p. 85)
Projecting (p. 86)
Punishment (p. 90)
Recency effect (p. 85)
Reinforcement theory (p. 89)
Reinforcement (p. 89)
Selective attention (p. 85)
Self-efficacy (p. 92)
Self-fulfilling prophecy (p. 86)
Self-regulation (p. 93)
Self-serving bias (p. 88)
Social cognitive theory (p. 91)
Stereotypes (p. 85)
Triadic reciprocal model of behavior (p. 93)
Vicarious learning (p. 92)

UP FOR DEBATE: FIRST IMPRESSIONS

Will Rogers said, "You never get a second chance to make a good first impression." Given what you've learned about perception in this chapter, do you agree or disagree with this quote?

EXERCISE 4.1: THE POWER OF PERCEPTION

Objective

The purpose of this exercise is to gain a greater of perceptions.

Instructions

Perception is the process by which we receive and interpret information from our environment. Given that definition, think about your perceptions of this very course. In this exercise, you'll pair up with another student and discuss your initial perceptions of this course. Discuss what you initially thought based on the professor, the syllabus, assignments, other students, and so on.

Recall the first day of the class and your very first thoughts. Whether the course is a traditional classroom-style class, an online class, or a hybrid course, try to remember how you initially felt about it.

Reflection Questions

1. What did you glean from the classroom environment on that first day that affected your perception of the course? What factors had the greatest influence? Do you still have these same perceptions about the course? Why or why not?
2. Did your partner have similar perceptions of the course? How were your and your partner's perceptions the same? Different?
3. What were your initial perceptions when you started your most recent job? How were those perceptions formed? Have your perceptions about the job changed? Why or why not?

EXERCISE 4.2: HOW ARE STEREOTYPES FORMED?

Objective

The purpose of this exercise is to grasp the concept of stereotypes.

Instructions

All kinds of stereotypes exist in business. As a class, brainstorm common business stereotypes you have heard of or you may even believe to be true. Your professor will capture the list on the board. Think in terms of every demographic—race, age, gender, social class, etc.

Once the list is complete, discuss why these stereotypes exist. Why do some continue while others aren't so common? Are any of the stereotypes true? How does this affect our interactions with one another in the workplace?

Reflection Questions

1. How are stereotypes formed? Can our ideas about stereotypes change? Why or why not?
2. What stereotypes have you personally experienced in the workplace—as the one being stereotyped or where you stereotyped another person? How do you feel now about this experience?
3. How difficult was the process of identifying stereotypes in this exercise? Did any of the stereotypes make you feel uncomfortable? If so, why?

EXERCISE 4.3: THE MAZE RAT AND POSITIVE REINFORCEMENT AND PUNISHMENT

Objective

The purpose of this exercise is to grasp the concepts of positive reinforcement and punishment.

Instructions

This exercise requires several volunteers from the class and involves creating an obstacle course that a student will complete while blindfolded. First, a volunteer is chosen to be the "maze rat." Once this person is selected, they leave the room for a moment. Then, three more volunteers come down to the front of the room and create a very simple obstacle course, consisting of tables and chairs. Again, nothing too complex—just something that keeps the "maze rat" from getting from point A to point B in a straight line. Finally, a volunteer is chosen to provide positive reinforcement.

Once the obstacle course is created, the "maze rat" is blindfolded (a scarf or jacket over their head should suffice) and brought by hand back into the classroom. The "maze rat" is placed at point A and told they must get to point B in the obstacle course without removing the blindfold.

The "maze rat" is released and must slowly and carefully make their way to point B. If the "maze rat" goes in the wrong direction, the entire class should yell their disapproval. When the "maze rat" takes a step in the right direction, the person who volunteered to provide positive reinforcement will hand the "maze rat" a piece of candy.

The "maze rat" continues through the obstacle course—receiving positive reinforcement in the form of candy when the right path is chosen and punishment in the form of yelling from the audience when the wrong path is charted.

This continues until the "maze rat" completes the obstacle course and arrives at point B.

Reflection Questions

1. How effective was the punishment and positive reinforcement in helping the "maze rat" get from point A to point B?
2. What if no punishment or positive reinforcement occurred during this exercise? Would it have taken the "maze rat" longer to arrive at point B? Why or why not?
3. In the workplace, what forms of punishment and positive reinforcement are utilized? How effective are these?

Exercise contributed by Steven Stovall, Southeast Missouri State University.

ONLINE EXERCISE 4.1: UNDERSTANDING PERCEPTIONS ABOUT WORKPLACE NORMS

Objective

The purpose of this exercise is to gain an appreciation for perceptions about workplace norms.

Instructions

On a discussion board, post a commonly accepted practice at your most recent job. For example, some companies highly regard being on time for every meeting; others value ensuring that PowerPoint presentations follow a particular format. Still others have everyone use the same workplace jargon or wear similar clothes even though no uniform is required. Try to recall a particular norm from your job and explain it on your initial post.

Comment on others' posts, asking questions like "How did that norm emerge?" and "Why is that important at your company?" Engage in a dialogue with one another as to why and how these norms occur and are perpetuated. Most importantly, ask about perceptions of these norms. Do people seem to like the norm, do they resent it, or do they simply accept it without any real thought? Have their perceptions changed since they first encountered a particular workplace norm?

Reflection Questions

1. In the workplace, who do you think usually establishes a particular norm—the top leaders of the organization or the front-line workers?
2. How has your own perceptions changed since the first day of the job you posted about? Do you still think of the norms associated with your organization as odd, or have you accepted them as quite normal at this point? Why?
3. Were you surprised by anyone else's post? Did someone post a norm to which you had an instant negative reaction? What was it, and what is your perception of your reaction? If you worked at that particular company, do you think your perception of the norm would change? Why or why not?

Exercise contributed by Steven Stovall, Southeast Missouri State University.

ONLINE EXERCISE 4.2: UNDERSTANDING LEARNING PROCESSES

Objective

The purpose of this exercise is to gain an understanding of the differences between various learning processes.

Instructions

Conduct an internet search for a company policy—attendance, quality of work, theft, etc. Try to find a policy that also includes consequences for violation of that policy. Once you have read the policy and the consequences, determine what learning process is being demonstrated by this company. Is it punishment? Positive reinforcement? Negative reinforcement? Some other learning process? Explain your conclusion.

Reflection Questions

1. When you initially conducted your internet search for an organizational policy, did you suspect you would see "punishment" as the primary learning process? Why or why not?
2. Are there any violations of a company's policy for which you would approve of "punishment" as the learning process? For example, would stealing from the organization warrant punishment, or something less? What about sexual harassment? Bringing a firearm to work?
3. What if an organization didn't have policies or learning processes in place for violations of company norms and standards of behavior? What would be the result of a work environment where there were no learning processes when employees violated those norms and standards?

Exercise contributed by Steven Stovall, Southeast Missouri State University.

CASE 4.1: CATCH&RELEASE

The Best Camera Is the One That's With You

The early 2000s saw a revolution in the production and distribution of media. The advent of inexpensive, high-quality digital recording devices and the ubiquity of Web 2.0 platforms to host user-generated content (UGC) gave rise to the era of participatory media. By May 2019, YouTube claimed that more than 500 hours of video were uploaded to the site every minute, and the platform's usage is only increasing.[84] Brands want to use amateur UGC (called "found content") for its authentic, emotionally resonant quality, but unlike traditional stock footage shot by professionals, it's not always clear where a viral social media post originated or who can claim ownership of it.

Analisa Goodin isn't your typical MBA-holding Silicon Valley start-up founder. Goodin is a practicing artist and earned an MFA in art history and theory at the California College of the Arts. While working in image research at a San Francisco ad agency, Goodin came across the perfect video snippet for a commercial the firm was producing. The agency's team had "a whole laundry list of questions," they told GingerBread Capital. "Who shot this? Can we license this for the spot? How much do they want for it? Can we set the price?" Faced with the difficulties of securing the rights to the found content, Goodin had an epiphany: "I have the opportunity to reverse-engineer an entire marketplace!"[85] In 2014 they founded Visual Catch, the creative consultancy that became Catch&Release, a venture-backed tech start-up with a mission to make the internet licensable.

"Adaptability Is Built Into Our Culture."

For its first few years, Visual Catch handled only the creative side of discovering found content for production shops and didn't focus on the legal or financial aspects of licensing it. When it became clear that Goodin's clients needed both, the firm was rebranded as Catch&Release, which was "born to do it all—content curation, clearance, licensing, indemnification—all powered by Curation Intelligence™," the company's AI.[86]

"I developed a pretty decent spidey sense about whether or not a piece of content could be licensed."[87]

Transforming Visual Catch from a service-based revenue model into Catch&Release, which focuses on its technology product, was the first test of the company's adaptability. Goodin likens the difference to farming, where as a service provider "you're tending a plot of land with seeds already planted and growing the business customer by customer," whereas when you shift into product mode, "now you're ripping out plants and buying up more acreage. We're not just optimizing by project but optimizing for an entire market. It's like going from a micro view to a macro view." The company's first iteration was not so micro, however, achieving $3 million in service revenue before seeking outside investment in 2017.

Bootstrapping a company with its own revenue has both benefits and drawbacks compared to raising outside capital from the beginning. On the *Startup Foundations* podcast, Analisa Goodin told host Greg Miaskiewicz that scaling the business without the funding to invest in engineering and marketing had been challenging but forced the company to intimately understand their early customers' needs. Establishing deep relationships with their customers and holding open conversations within the team about how to solve customer pain points paid tremendous dividends in raising funds to develop Catch&Release's technology.[88]

The company's $14 million Series A in 2021 brought its total investment to over $26 million. Catch&Release has leveraged the capital infusions to go beyond its typical customer base in the advertising production industry and create new opportunities with its technology. The company's Content Exchange serves both the supply and demand sides of the creative equation by enabling brands to discover and license found content while providing a secure marketplace for content creators to sell their work and receive fair compensation for it. Amateur UGC curated and licensed by Catch&Release has been used by many of the world's biggest brands, like Nike, Twitter, and Verizon, in addition to being featured in Super Bowl ads.[89]

According to Analisa Goodin, "found content is now a permanent part of the creative mix."[90] When Catch&Release surveyed 100 advertising professionals, 87% of respondents indicated that they anticipated their use of found content to increase in 2022. The proliferation of new streaming services and social media platforms that host user-generated content is accelerating every year. Catch&Release aims to adapt with the internet and remain brands' premier choice for discovering authentic media for engaging with consumers on these emerging venues.

"Think Big, but Start Small."

Scaling any new business venture demands continual learning and adaptation based on customer feedback. In an interview with the *San Francisco Business Times*, Goodin advises entrepreneurs that adaptability is the key to success, telling them not to wait to start until they have the perfect business plan, team, or funding. Instead, "what you need to do is just figure out the smallest little ways that you can validate that what you're doing is solving a need and just keep growing it up from there." Goodin adds, "You've got to be able to measure small increments of success and failure really early on to know that you're on the right path; so think big, but start small."[91]

Critical-Thinking Questions

1. Advertisers employ many perceptual distortions to persuade consumers to buy their products. Do you think the perceived authenticity of found content results in more honest advertising? Why or why not?
2. How did Catch&Release benefit from social learning while shifting from being a service provider to being a product-based revenue model?
3. Analisa Goodin's artistic background allowed them to cultivate a sense of self-efficacy and ability to self-regulate. How do you think these contributed to their success as a founder?

iStock photo/JHVEPhoto

5 EMOTIONS, ATTITUDES, AND STRESS

LEARNING OBJECTIVES

By the end of this chapter, you will be able to:

5.1 Describe the basic concept of emotions in the context of organizational behavior

5.2 Discuss the various roles of emotions in the workplace

5.3 Explain the ways in which attitudes influence behavior in organizations

5.4 Illustrate the ways in which stress can affect behavior in the workplace

5.5 Discuss different outcomes of stress and the benefits of nurturing employee well-being

Case Study: Kevin Plank, Founder of Under Armour

Stressful Beginnings

As a collegiate football player, Kevin Plank had a constant irritation: the undershirt always became too sweaty, to the point of annoyance. Like many other founders, Kevin began a new business called Under Armour in an effort to solve this problem. The solution? A new type of clothing, one that would stay dry and light in extreme heat—a type of revolutionized sportswear.[1]

Plank's idea has since grown into many products, which together made $4.5 billion in revenue in 2020.[2]

But the path to success hasn't been easy. Throughout the process of beginning Under Armour, Plank had to deal with varying stressful roadblocks. For example, in 1996, Kevin invested $20,000 of their savings and took on $40,000 in credit debt to begin producing and selling the product. However, sales that year amounted to only $17,000. Making so little struck a real blow to Plank's hopes of getting the business off the ground. Yet Plank was determined not to let emotion cloud good judgment.[3]

"You need to put your hands around the throat of your business, and you need to run it. There's no other way," Kevin says.[4] This shows how from the beginning, Plank has been determined to lead by facing difficulties rather than allowing them to negatively affect the business.

Operational Pressure and Emotions

Today, Under Armour still faces difficult situations at the organization's most important levels, and they require calm and effective solutions. Through a critical-thinking approach consisting of many innovative tactics, Under Armour employees constantly receive treatment that limits the potential for unhealthy levels of stress, called distress, and promotes healthy levels of stress, or eustress. A few things induce stress at Under Armour, but one primary example is its market share. Under Armour began trading as a public company in 2005, and since then its stock has seen times of extreme growth and times of extreme decline. This volatility paired with Under Armour's large sales creates constant expectations for positive financial reports, and the commentary on substandard reports can be scathing.[5]

Constant pressure from the markets is felt in all public companies, especially those with varied years of great growth like Under Armour's. Furthermore, how companies react to uncertain situations such as the COVID-19 pandemic always plays a role in valuing public companies like Under Armour, and in 2020 this was a significant issue to tackle. In the beginning of September 2020, the company laid off around 600 employees as part of a cost-cutting plan.[6] This decision saw backlash from several employees, and the company's stock price continued to decrease. Limiting stress related to this issue to a healthy level, but also to a level where employees still constantly seek to manage the company in shareholders' best interests, involves managing the office behavioral environment accordingly.

Through a couple of decades of massive growth and stressful market conditions, Under Armour maintains a relaxed atmosphere in its corporate setting. This is no accident; Under Armour strives to accommodate all levels of employees as well as possible, and as mentioned above, they must innovate in order to do so. For example, to start the day, UA workers at one office in Baltimore take a water taxi to the building. According to primary interviews, many enjoy the ride and use it as a time to relax and refocus; there's even a company-sponsored yoga class offered after work. Under Armour encourages employees to dress in a laid-back manner and offers them a 50% discount on UA products. According to employees at UA, an office space where members of the organization consistently wear its products and receive little things designed to relieve the emotional stress of a demanding business has been an important part of managing Under Armour's organizational behavior and success. Furthermore, formal suit-and-tie dress is one less thing for employees to stress about, and this assists in preventing employee anxiety from surpassing the healthy state of eustress.[7]

Additional Management Methods

CEO Kevin Plank has done more than just offer relaxing options for employees at corporate offices; many employees have shared their experiences. For example, Under Armour often treats members of the organization to big sporting events—not just so they can see their brand in action but so they can get in on the action. Plank advises the team to "stay humble" and reminds them that no one person is bigger than the Under Armour brand. Another area in the business where effective team management can be seen is in the UA "performance center." As mentioned before, employees receive generous discounts on products, like those of many organizations, but at the performance center they work out using the gear. Over a hundred Under Armour workers can be seen exercising at the same company gym on a given day.[8]

Employees also recount stories about interactions with some of the greatest UA athletes, such as basketball player Stephen Curry. One even received an autographed shoe. This company involvement is a unique and simple way to engage employees: let them partake in the outcome of their hard work. Not only does this build affinity within the brand, but a demanding workload becomes much more mentally and physically bearable when there are tangible benefits besides a paycheck.[9]

It's important, in Kevin Plank's view, to make sure that employees are comfortable, happy, and ready to succeed before putting them to work. Under Armour prides itself on having entrepreneurial team members, and this starts with their situation in the workplace. Scott Salkeld, the head of innovation at UA, describes a favorite perk as "limitless opportunities" and states that endless opportunities coupled with a healthy work environment are the key to overcoming difficult tasks.[10]

From beginning in a basement to becoming part of the soul of Baltimore, Under Armour has seen countless challenges and successes and has grown to be a useful study in organizational behavior. Today Under Armour constantly attempts to maintain four pillars of greatness, which it defines as "Make a great product, tell a great story, provide great service, and build a great team."[11] Although UA's primary concern is developing innovative sporting wear, a key piece of its successful business is building a great Under Armour team: innovative, passionate people working toward the same goal.

Making that happen is a challenge for all organizations, large or small, and takes constant efforts at reducing stress and resolving conflicts. Every day, organizations must find ways to solve problems; there is a danger that emotions will get in the way of hard work and success.

Critical-Thinking Questions

1. How can personal stress affect the process of beginning and managing an organization, and how can you confront this?
2. What types of things can management do to relieve a demanding atmosphere, and why is this important?
3. Does managing one's own stress and attitude play a role in managing those of others? Explain.

EMOTIONS IN ORGANIZATIONAL BEHAVIOR

Our Under Armour case study describes the roller coaster of stress and emotions involved in running a business. The founder of Under Armour, Kevin Plank, is determined to confront adversity head-on by creating strategies to minimize stress and negative emotions for employees. But what about the types of feelings and emotions you might feel on a daily basis? How do you deal with those? Say one morning your professor gives you an important, complex assignment and tells you it has to be completed by the end of the day. How do you feel? Are you excited at the thought of a new challenge, or fearful because the task is so complex? Do you feel angry with your professor because you have been given such a tight deadline?

People or events elicit a variety of feelings that cause us to respond in different ways. These are called **affects**, a broad term covering a wide range of feelings, including emotions and moods.[12] We may react to certain situations with sadness, anger, or elation. These responses are **emotions**, which are defined as intense feelings directed at a specific object or person.[13] Emotions are numerous and intense, but they are usually also short-lived. For example, in the scenario described, it's likely that your intense feeling of anger toward your professor will dissipate as soon as you begin to focus on the task.

But what if your professor has caught you on a day when you feel like you can't be bothered with working at all? In fact, now that you think about it, you've felt a bit down for the past few days and feel like a short deadline is the last thing you need, since you're feeling so unmotivated. In this case, you are probably experiencing a negative **mood**, which consists of less intense and more generalized feelings not directed at a specific object or person.[14] Moods last longer than emotions. Of course, moods can also be positive, and we often categorize ourselves and others as being in a "good mood" or a "bad mood."

OB researchers have identified two basic types of mood dimensions: positive affect and negative affect. **Positive affect** includes emotions such as excitement, cheerfulness, and self-assurance, while **negative affect** includes emotions such as boredom, lethargy, and depression.[15] The sources of moods and emotions are complex. Factors such as lack of sleep and exercise, the weather, and the amount of stress we're under might play a part, but there are no concrete answers to explain the underlying reasons for our feelings and moods.

Although there are clear differences between emotions and moods, they do influence each other. Emotions can turn into moods when you lose focus on what caused the feeling in the first place, and good or bad moods can trigger a stronger, more intense emotional response. For example, your feelings of anger toward your professor for giving you a complex assignment on short notice may put you in a bad mood, which distracts you from focusing on the task. Conversely, if you were already in a bad mood before you were handed the project, your angry feelings may intensify even more after you receive the last-minute assignment. While your negative feelings are justified from your perspective, what about your classmates, friends, and others around you? How does your mood affect them?

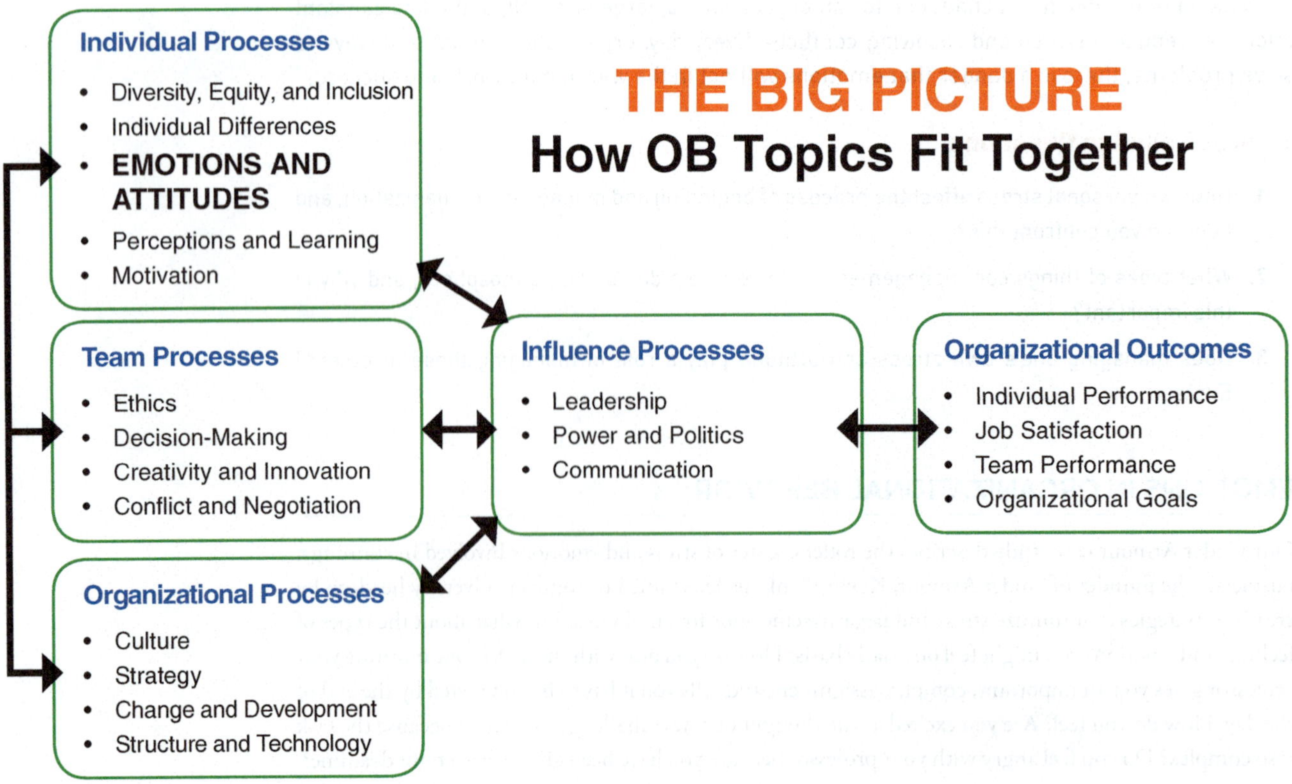

EMOTIONS IN THE WORKPLACE

Most of us experience heightened emotional states at least once in a while. When we are feeling frustrated, angry, or disappointed, we may choose to shout, storm out of a room, or curl up in a quiet place to calm down for a while. However, in the workplace, emotional outbursts could seriously damage your professional reputation and affect your work performance.

Research has found that acknowledging painful or distressing emotions is a powerful way to build trust.[16] Emotions are particularly significant because of the uncertainty of returning to work after the disruption of the pandemic. It is far more beneficial for a manager or a team leader to say something like, "You looked a bit upset when you showed up late to the meeting today. Is everything okay?" than "The meeting didn't go as well because of your late arrival. How do you think it went?" The former approach acknowledges and validates the emotion and builds trust between the manager and the employee, whereas the latter dismisses how the employee may be feeling. Overall, the worst thing is to do nothing. Employees need to feel safe enough to share their emotions to feel validated and worthy and to be able to trust the people leading them.[17]

Supporters reach for signatures and handshakes as Donald Trump greets the crowd after speaking at a campaign rally in Las Vegas, Nevada.

Jabin Botsford/The *Washington Post* via Getty Images

Emotional Contagion

Moods and emotions are contagious and have a strong influence on group behavior. **Emotional contagion** is a phenomenon in which emotions experienced by one or more individuals in a work group spread to the others.[18] Researchers have found that negative emotions tend to spread more quickly than positive emotions, which can affect morale, productivity, and motivation. Negative emotional contagion tends to occur during times of fear and uncertainty like the COVID-19 pandemic.[19] When fear is perpetuated by the people around us and amplified through social media, it's easy to be influenced by these emotions. Research has shown that although we have very little awareness of emotional contagion and how it influences our behavior, we do have the capability to do something about it.[20] Understanding how emotional contagion works helps us recognize our own negative feelings and create steps to change our behavior. For instance, cutting out social media and staying away from people and coworkers who spread fear rather than focus on the facts are just two ways we can stem our own

Waiters are expected to be friendly and approachable even when they're tired or dealing with difficult situations. This can create a burden of emotional labor for the employee.

© iStockphoto.com/LightFieldStudios

negative emotions.[21] Good mental hygiene can lead to positive emotional contagion, which creates an environment in which people work better together, experience less conflict, and experience higher levels of work performance.[22] Managers and leaders who have positive attitudes generally have the ability to inspire their employees to work well together.

Emotional Labor

The concept of **emotional labor** refers to the process of managing our feelings so that we present positive emotions even when they're contrary to our actual feelings.[23] Hotel employees, salespeople, flight attendants, wait staff, and tour operators are all examples of the types of service workers who are expected to smile and be pleasant even in the most demanding circumstances. Today's organizations are increasingly customer oriented, and many managers expect their employees to present a positive face when interacting with their external customers as well as with their internal clients and coworkers.

Researchers have discovered that employees who "put on a happy face" at work or fake positive emotions experience fewer benefits at work than those who are genuinely positive.[24] People who make real efforts to be positive tend to experience lower levels of fatigue, are more productive, receive more personal and professional support from their coworkers, and are more likely to make progress on their goals. People who fake positive emotions feel burned out, see themselves as less authentic, and receive less support from their coworkers. Overall, it is more productive to make genuine efforts to be positive when attempting to build better relationships at work and experience a happier working environment.[25]

Surface Acting versus Deep Acting

When you engage in emotional labor, you are expected to regulate your true feelings in order to achieve organizational goals. People tend to use two emotional labor techniques to control their real emotions: surface acting and deep acting.[26] **Surface acting** occurs when a person suppresses their true feelings while displaying the organizationally desirable ones. For example, you may fake a smile or use a soft tone of voice when dealing with a difficult customer even when, underneath, you are offended. In **deep acting**, you try to change your emotions to better match the emotions your employer requires in the situation. For example, rather than feeling irritated by the demanding customer, you attempt to empathize by putting yourself in the customer's position and trying to feel their frustration.

Both surface acting and deep acting through social interaction can affect the level of work strain felt by individual employees (see Figure 5.1). As shown in the figure, people who amplify positive emotions like happiness or even embarrassment through deep acting will generate a favorable response from others, which decreases work strain. Those who display high levels of anger or contempt will receive a negative response, thus increasing work strain. Similarly, those who put on a fake display of surface acting will also receive an unfavorable response from others, which again increases work strain.

Display Rules

Many organizations teach their employees **display rules**, the basic norms that govern which emotions should be displayed and which should be suppressed.[27] Different organizations have different rules that accord with their company culture. In one classic study from the eighties, researchers published an example of formal display rules discovered in an employee handbook for supermarket cashiers. Cashiers were instructed to greet customers cheerfully with a friendly smile at all times: "Smile!! Service with a smile and a friendly attitude will keep them [customers] coming back!"[28]

FIGURE 5.1 ■ Social Interaction Model

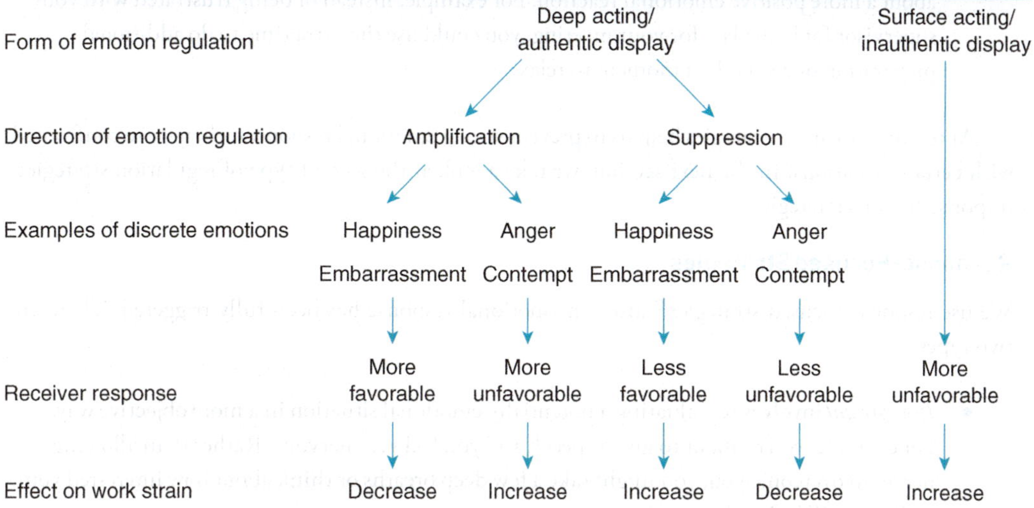

Source: Republished with permission of Academy of Management, from Côté, S. (2005, July). A social interaction model of the effects of emotion regulation on work strain. *Academy of Management Review, 30*(3), 509–530; permission conveyed through Copyright Clearance Center, Inc.

Emotional Dissonance

It is challenging to put on a happy face all the time, especially if you're experiencing emotional upheaval at home or dealing with work stress. When you feel this way, sometimes the last thing you want to do is to be cheerful and helpful to difficult customers. Under these circumstances, you might experience **emotional dissonance**, a discrepancy between the emotions you display and the emotions you actually feel.[29] For example, you may feel angry with a particularly demanding and rude customer, but you are compelled to be polite regardless of your true feelings. A recent study analyzing the impact of emotional dissonance in an Italian supermarket chain found that employees who experienced negative relationships with customers were more likely to suffer from poor health and high levels of burnout. Findings also suggested that customer training and guidance on how to manage emotions at work can help to support those in daily contact with customers.[30]

Emotional Regulation

Every day we are exposed to situations that can trigger a range of strong emotions. Most of us try to control our feelings through **emotional regulation**, a set of processes through which people influence their own emotions and the ways in which they experience and express them.[31] The two main kinds of regulation strategies are antecedent focused and response focused.

Antecedent-Focused Strategies

Antecedent-focused strategies[32] come into play before the emotional response has been fully triggered. They include the following:

- *Situation selection* lets you choose or avoid situations that have the potential to generate certain emotional responses. For example, some people might avoid engaging with an unpopular coworker.
- *Situation modification* involves altering a situation to change its emotional impact. For example, you might move physically closer to a person if you want to positively engage them in a serious discussion.
- *Attention deployment* consists of refocusing your attention to an area of a situation that results in a more positive emotional outcome. For example, if you're anxious about a looming deadline, you might distract yourself by taking a short break to recharge your energy levels and refresh your focus.

- *Cognitive change* lets you reassess an event or situation to see the bigger picture and bring about a more positive emotional reaction. For example, instead of being frustrated with your supervisor for being late for your meeting, you could use the extra time to do additional preparation or even take a moment to relax.

Antecedent-focused strategies help us to prevent strong emotional responses when we're confronted with certain situations. In the next section, we take a look at the second type of regulation strategies: response-focused strategies.

Response-Focused Strategies

We use response-focused strategies[33] after an emotional response has been fully triggered. There are two types:

- *Reappraisal* involves reevaluating a potentially emotional situation in a more objective way. For example, you're about to give a speech and you feel very nervous. Rather than allowing nerves to overcome you, you might take a few deep breaths or think about how interested your audience will be in what you have to say.
- *Suppression* occurs when we consciously mask inward emotional reactions with more positive or neutral behavioral responses. For example, you may feel inclined to laugh when a colleague mispronounces someone else's name, but you keep your emotions in check so as not to appear insensitive.

Response-focused strategies help us to prevent any outwardly perceivable expression of emotion in order to support us in coping with certain situations.

It is equally important to consider cultural variations in emotional expression. For example, in the United States it is acceptable to show enthusiasm at work when the situation is appropriate and to debate points with passion in a meeting. However, in Japan and China, this sort of emotional expression is not tolerated and may be perceived as showing off. Similarly, people in the United Kingdom can be quite reserved and understated and tend to play down their emotions in a business setting. When dealing with different cultures, it is extremely important to learn the language of emotion in order to gain a greater understanding of emotional expression. Just because a person from a different culture may not seem enthusiastic doesn't mean they aren't excited; they might just be showing their emotions in a different way.[34]

Emotional Intelligence

Imagine you're working on a complex project and one of your teammates is having such difficulty carrying out their role that they slow down the rest of the team and jeopardize the deadline. Do you complain to your manager that this employee is letting the team down? Or do you try to manage the situation by offering your support and helping your teammate learn the right skills? If you chose the latter option, you probably have high levels of emotional intelligence (EI), the ability to understand emotions in yourself and others in order to effectively manage your own behaviors and your interpersonal relationships.[35] Contrary to some assumptions, EI is not about "being nice" but rather has to do with the ability to harness your skills to build more productive relationships with others.[36]

Since the pandemic began, organizations have begun basing hiring and promoting decisions on EI more than ever. Companies need people with strong emotional intelligence to support coworkers who are struggling with the uncertainty of new working practices and to be a positive influence during work-related interactions.

Related to EI is the use of "soft skills," or competencies that rely on personality traits such as empathy, listening ability, and good communication to build work relationships. Job candidates with soft skills are in demand because they're generally better at making decisions, accepting feedback, working well with others, resolving conflicts, motivating others, and demonstrating leadership.[37]

In fact, according to the World Economic Forum's Future of Jobs Report, emotional intelligence ranked number four in the top ten most desired job skills in 2021[38] For example, telecom tech company Ciena, based in Maryland, actively seek candidates who have the ability to answer questions designed to gauge their degree of emotional intelligence.[39] For instance, instead of asking candidates standard interview questions, such as "Tell me about a project you have worked on of which you are particularly proud," interviewers ask questions structured to evoke a response based on EI: "Tell me about a moment where you needed to influence a group or a person to drive a positive outcome on a project. What did you do? How did you figure out that you needed to take that action?"

Ciena then assesses the responses to see if the candidate is right for the company.

The Aflac booth at a job fair in Southern Florida. When recruiting new employees, Aflac looks for people who display high levels of emotional intelligence in addition to technical skills.

Joe Raedle/Getty Images

The Four Dimensions of EI

There are four dimensions[40] of EI (see Figure 5.2):

1. *Self-awareness*: a good understanding of your own emotions
2. *Self-management*: the ability to control and regulate emotions and impulses
3. *Social awareness*: skills in perceiving, empathizing with, and reacting appropriately to the emotions of others
4. *Relationship management*: the ability to manage the emotions of others to build strong and healthy relationships with them

Despite the popularity of the EI concept during the past decade, some theorists question its validity, citing a lack of evidence and criticizing the ways in which EI is tested and measured and the resulting conclusions.[41] Others denounce EI as "pop psychology."[42] Despite these criticisms, EI is becoming more popular in the workplace and more valued as a desired skill among employees. For example, according to a recent survey of hiring managers, nearly 75% believed emotional intelligence to be more valuable in their employees than their intelligence quotient (IQ).[43]

FIGURE 5.2 ■ The Four Dimensions of EI

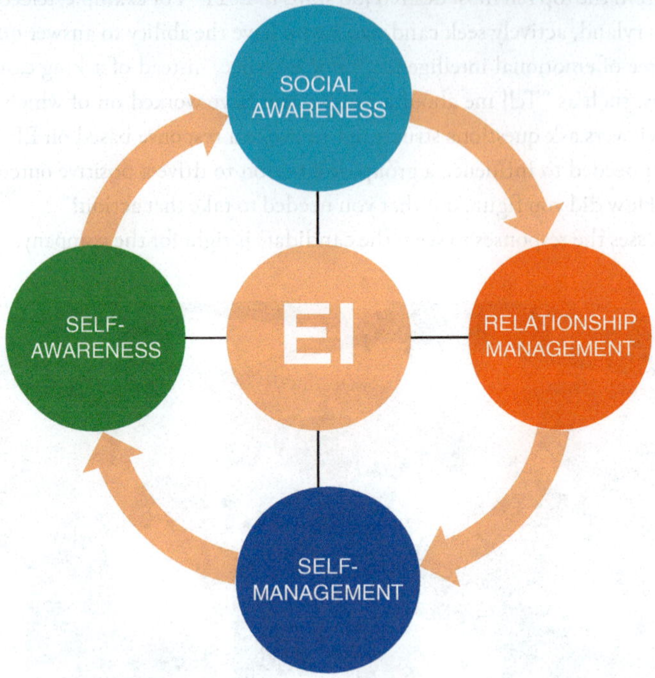

ATTITUDES AND BEHAVIOR

Research shows a correlation between emotional intelligence and work attitudes.[44] But what is attitude, and why is it so important in the workplace? We define **attitude** as a learned tendency to consistently respond positively or negatively to people or events.[45] Attitudes determine our likes and dislikes and help us to make judgments about other people or events. Our beliefs provide us with the necessary information to shape our attitudes, which in turn shape our behaviors.

How Attitudes Are Created

To truly understand attitudes, we need to understand how they are created (Figure 5.3). Three main elements form our attitudes.[46]

1. *Cognitive appraisal* reflects the sum total of a person's underlying beliefs, opinions, information, and knowledge about a specific object, person, or event. For example, "My professor is overbearing"; "My partner is smart and beautiful"; "The Steelers are the best team in the NFL."
2. *Affective evaluation* reflects a person's positive and negative feelings toward a specific object, person, or event. For example, "I don't like my professor"; "I love my partner"; "I like the Steelers."
3. *Behavioral intention* is the perceived likelihood that someone will behave in a particular way toward a specific object, person, or event. For example, "I will not take another course with my professor"; "I will kiss my partner"; "I will root for the Steelers."

While behavioral intention is the strongest predictor of actual behavior, it doesn't *necessarily* predict our behavior. **Social norms**, the informal rules that govern behavior in groups and societies, and other behavioral controls may intervene, stopping us from carrying out our intended or most desired action.[47] For example, perhaps Neda has been belittled in front of coworkers by their manager. While Neda's behavioral intention may be to defend themselves by telling their manager that their behavior is unprofessional and destructive, social norms suggest that telling off your manager is professionally inappropriate. Meanwhile, in this example, an especially relevant behavioral control is the knowledge that Neda might be fired by responding to their manager in the way that their behavioral intention demands!

FIGURE 5.3 ■ The Relationship Between Attitudes and Behaviors

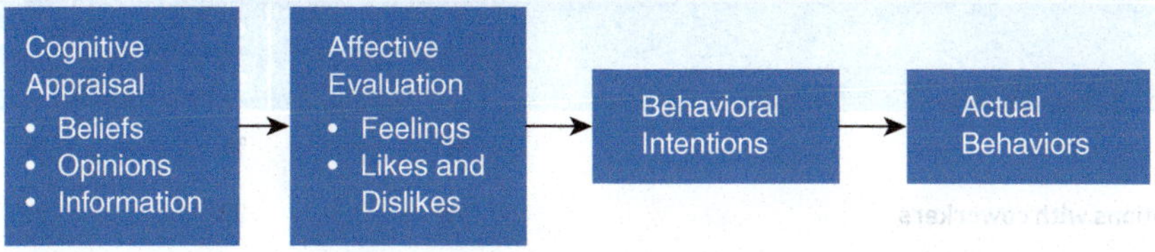

Source: Fishbein, M., & Ajzen, I. (1975). *Belief, attitude, intention, and behavior: An introduction to theory and research.* Addison-Wesley.

Cognitive Dissonance

Originally coined by psychologist Leon Festinger, **cognitive dissonance** is the stress and discomfort individuals experience when they face an inconsistency among their beliefs, attitudes, values, and behaviors.[48] Festinger observed that people prefer consistency and thus tend to alter their attitudes, beliefs, or behaviors to restore harmony.

For example, despite the evidence that smoking is detrimental to health, Prisha likes to smoke and has a positive attitude toward smoking. However, it also makes Prisha uneasy that they may be carrying out a behavior that has a negative effect on their health. To alleviate the psychological discomfort associated with their cognitive dissonance in relation to smoking, Prisha has a number of choices:

- Change the behavior (Prisha will stop smoking)
- Change the belief or attitude (Prisha doesn't believe the evidence that suggests smoking is dangerous to health)
- Rationalize the inconsistency in Prisha's knowledge that smoking is unhealthy and recognize the behavioral choice to keep smoking (Prisha believes smoking is dangerous for most people, but not for Prisha)

As this example illustrates, although we strive to quell the discomfort we feel when attitudes and behaviors contradict each other, the manner in which we try to reconcile dissonant beliefs, values, or attitudes may not be very rational.

Common Workplace Attitudes

As we have learned, attitudes play a big part in influencing our behavior at work. The attitudes we bring to the workplace are critical in three main areas: job satisfaction, employee engagement, and organizational commitment. **Job satisfaction** is the degree to which an individual feels positive or negative about a job.[49] Despite the COVID-19 crisis, the rise in unemployment, and the switch from office to remote working, job satisfaction hit a 20-year high in 2020 according to the Conference Board Job Satisfaction Survey. How is this the case when unemployment is so high in a labor market so weak? The answer is that many of the unemployed were not crowding the market by looking for a job just yet; some hoped to return to their old jobs; some were concerned about being exposed to the virus at work; and some, without benefits, did not have the childcare support.

Those still employed have benefited from the additional efforts and resources provided by some companies, such as expanded mental health support, flexible work options, sick leave, family leave, and greater senior care benefits.[50] In 2021, LA-based female-first beverage brand Bev, selling a variety of sugar-free canned wines, was listed among the best places to work in the U.S. Bev offers unlimited paid time off, provides free health care, and prioritizes inclusion, accountability, and kindness. This cat-friendly workplace even offers employees the opportunity to bring home a kitten after one year of work.[51]

Table 5.1 lists common characteristics of job satisfaction in the United States. As the table illustrates, factors such as relations with coworkers, safe working conditions, and job flexibility are correlated with job satisfaction.

TABLE 5.1 ■ Employees' Satisfaction With Various Job Factors

	Completely satisfied	Somewhat satisfied	Total satisfied
	%	%	%
Your relations with coworkers	72	23	95
The physical safety conditions of your workplace	72	20	92
Your job security	67	25	92
The flexibility of your hours	65	22	87
Your boss or immediate supervisor	63	25	88
The amount of work required of you	55	30	85
The recognition you receive for work accomplishments	52	29	81
The amount of vacation time you receive	52	26	78
The health insurance benefits your employer offers	45	22	67
Your chances for promotion	42	28	70
The amount of money you earn	38	37	75
The retirement plan your employer offers	38	29	67
The amount of on-the-job stress	32	36	68

Source: Brenan, M. (2021, September 8). *U.S. workers' satisfaction with job safety rebounds.* Gallup. https://news.gallup.com/poll/354593/workers-satisfaction-job-safety-rebounds.aspx

Employee engagement is a connection with the organization and passion for the job.[52] Job satisfaction and job performance are significantly related. According to a recent Gallup report, more than 50% of employees are disengaged in the workplace.[53] Employee disengagement costs the U.S. economy up to $550 billion every year due to lack of motivation, errors, missed deadlines, and poor customer service.[54] Research shows that engaged employees experience less burnout, stay with the organization longer, and perform at a higher level.

With another study, conducted in 2021, showing that over 55% of the workforce is intending to look for a new job in the next year, it is even more important for organizations to engage employees.

Yet there is often disparity between what organizations think their employees need and what their employees actually want. Researchers have highlighted the following important drivers of engagement:[55]

1. Connecting organizational goals with employee values

   Employees are more likely to stay longer in an organization if the mission and goals align with their own values in relation to social change. Studies have found that employees are willing to take less financial benefits to work for a company that makes a societal impact.

2. Relating work activities to the organizational purpose

   For employees to feel fully engaged, they must feel that their day-to-day work activities are aligned with the organizational purpose. One way to do this is to reframe roles. For example, hospital cleaners are vital for preventing the spread of germs and bacteria rather than being "just a cleaner."

3. Creating groups to connect with others

   People feel more bonded to an organization when they have the opportunity to share their values and goals with others. Some companies run employee resource groups (ERGs) for people with similar interests or backgrounds. For example, over half the partners at multinational accounting company KPMG belong to at least one ERG, such as the Hispano Latino Network, the Asian Pacific Islander Network, the KPMG Network of Women, or pride@kpmg.

4. Giving employees more time

   Studies have shown that the pandemic has extended the working day by an average of 48.5 minutes, which has had a negative impact on leisure activities. Extra mandatory paid time off and paid vacations are an effective way to reduce burnout and increase feelings of engagement. For example, in 2021 online dating company Bumble gave employees an extra week off to reduce the level of stress generated by the pandemic.

5. Discouraging after-hours emails

   Organizations can actively encourage more downtime by switching off email notifications after working hours. For example, car manufacturer Volkswagen turns off email routing 30 minutes before the end of the working day and turns it back on again the next day, 30 minutes before the work begins. By structuring the day in this manner, the company gives employees more opportunity to switch off and relax.

Organizational commitment is an employee's psychological connection to an organization.[56] Although it may sound similar to employee engagement, there is an important difference. Employee engagement focuses on how individuals identify with the organization and how they feel about their roles, whereas organizational commitment is the extent to which employees dedicate themselves to achieving the goals of their roles and the organization. High organizational commitment is associated with increased engagement and vice versa.

Psychologists John Meyer and Natalie Allen developed the Three-Component Model of Commitment (1991) to illustrate three different components that may have an impact on how employees feel about the organizations they work for.[57] The three components are affective commitment, continuance commitment, and normative commitment.[58]

1. **Affective commitment** refers to an employee's perceived positive emotional attachment to the organization. Affectively committed employees tend to enjoy their work, identify with organizational goals and values, and hold a strong desire to be a part of the organization. People who love their jobs are more likely to progress in their roles, think more creatively, and show a willingness to take risks.
2. **Continuance commitment** occurs when employees feel a need to remain in an organization because the perceived losses of leaving are greater than the benefits that might be gained in a new organization. Some of these losses include monetary considerations such as salary, benefits, and pension, in addition to social costs such as friendship with work colleagues. This sense of perceived losses tends to rise with age and experience and particularly affects employees in an established, successful role. However, staying in a job for these reasons could impact employees' abilities to grow and develop and discourage them from taking risks for fear of jeopardizing their long-standing reputation.
3. **Normative commitment** relates to the degree to which employees feel they should stay in the organization because of a feeling of loyalty or obligation. For instance, some employees feel they should remain in an organization because it has invested a great deal in their training or paid for their college tuition. This sense of duty may also be a result of family upbringing where loyalty was considered an essential character trait. Normative commitment is often present in organizations that regularly reward loyalty with incentives and other strategies. Employees who remain in an organization solely out of a sense of duty may lack the motivation and drive needed to fulfill the requirements of their role.

Organizational Citizenship

Organizational citizenship behavior (OCB) is discretionary and voluntary behavior that is not a part of the employee's specific role requirements and is not formally rewarded.[59] For example, Jane Malyon is the founder of the English Cream Tea Company, based in Essex in the Southeast of England, which delivers hampers of traditional clotted cream and scones in addition to offering vegan options across

High levels of workplace stress can lead to loss of productivity and even illness.

the UK. When a hamper was stuck at a hub 200 miles away from the company headquarters, Malyon and the team made a fresh one and drove it 90 minutes to the recipient, whose family had ordered the hamper as a 75th birthday gift. The result? A very happy customer and a satisfied team who had quite literally gone the extra mile.[60]

Counterproductive work behaviors (CWBs) are voluntary behaviors that purposefully disrupt or harm the organization.[61] CWBs include avoiding work or taking shortcuts, creating conflict, harassing coworkers, being physically or verbally aggressive, and stealing or sabotaging work efforts. In 2021, video game company Activision Blizzard, headquartered in Santa Monica, California, fired 20 people for several types of CWB in the workplace, including sexual misconduct and gender discrimination.[62]

STRESS IN THE WORKPLACE

Most of us know what it feels like to be stressed. We may feel under pressure about making a deadline, taking an exam, or giving a presentation in front of a large audience. **Stress** is a response that occurs when a person perceives a situation as threatening to their well-being when their resources have been taxed or exceeded.[63] Gallup's latest State of the Global Workplace report, which surveyed workers from all over the world to gauge stress levels during the pandemic, found that U.S. workers were among the most stressed out in the world. Some reasons for this stress included fears over the virus, ill health, financial concerns, changes to how we live and work, social isolation, lockdowns, and racial trauma (see Chapter 2).[64]

One million workers miss work every day due to stress. Statistics show that more than 80% of U.S. workers suffer from stress, which costs U.S. businesses $300 billion every year on medical bills and loss of productivity.[65]

Stress in the workplace can affect the behavior of people working in an organization, leading to poor health and absenteeism. Table 5.2 lists more causes of stress at work.

The symptoms resulting from stress in the workplace include back pain, fatigue, headaches, and complaint about being stressed. Additional symptoms may include anxiety, irritability, depression, apathy, poor concentration, stomach problems, and insomnia. Managers can reduce stress in the

TABLE 5.2 ■ Causes of Stress in the Workplace

- Inability to cope with work demands
- Lack of control over how one works
- Insufficient information and support
- Conflict in working relationships
- Poor understanding of one's role and responsibilities
- Lack of engagement when the organization is undergoing change

Source: Health and Safety Executive. (n.d.). *Work-related stress and how to manage it.* https://www.hse.gov.uk/stress/causes.htm

workplace by learning to identify signs of stress, talking to workers, and actively finding ways to support them.

Stressors

There are many sources of stress in the workplace. **Stressors** are environmental stimuli that place demands on individuals. There are two main types:[66]

- *Challenge stressors* are associated with workload, job demands, job complexity, and deadlines and are positively related to motivation and performance. For instance, people may work better when stressed if there is an opportunity for a pay raise or promotion. Studies have shown that while challenge stressors can have a positive effect on employees' learning at work, the act of coping with challenge stressors can also increase pressure, leading to a more stressful working environment.[67]
- *Hindrance stressors* inhibit progress toward objectives; examples are role ambiguity or conflict, hassles, red tape, and highly political environments. Research shows that while challenge stressors can improve job performance, hindrance stressors are negatively related to motivation and performance.[68]

Stress-Strain-Outcomes Model

Over time, hindrance stressors can lead to strains. **Strain** reactions include both physiological responses, such as an adrenaline rush or increased heart rate and blood pressure, and psychological reactions, such as fatigue and irritability (e.g., you may argue with a coworker).[69] While strain reactions may disappear when the cause of the stress is removed, they can persist over a long time, which may result in damage to physical health (heart problems) or psychological health (burnout).

Research shows that people who can mentally detach themselves from work (psychological detachment) during their leisure time experience high life satisfaction and fewer psychological strains at work, without losing their sense of engagement.[70] In contrast, people who remain highly involved in work and don't mentally detach themselves tend to experience high strain levels, such as low life satisfaction and burnout.

Figure 5.4 shows that unless organizations find ways to reduce stress, stressors can cause strains, which can lead to poor performance and low motivation.

However, stress doesn't have to always be negative, nor is it a permanent condition. In the next section we explore different aspects of stress and ways of managing it.

FIGURE 5.4 ■ Workplace Stressors and Outcomes

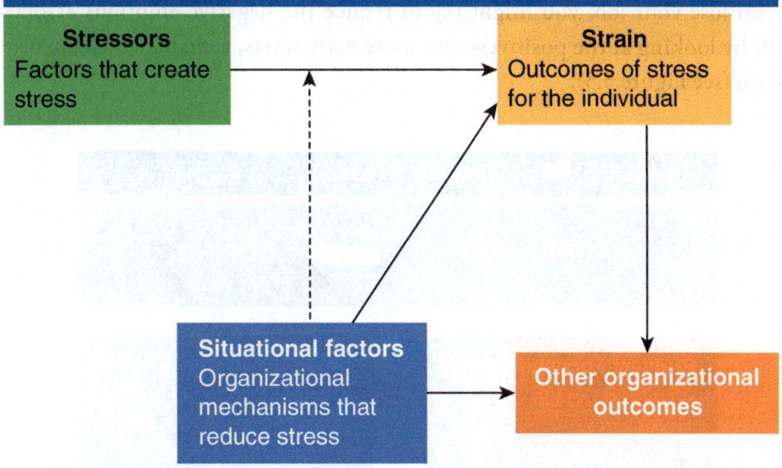

STRESS-RELATED OUTCOMES AND EMPLOYEE WELL-BEING

Although high degrees of stress can be destructive to our behaviors and harmful to our health, stress isn't always negative. **Eustress** comprises a moderate level of stressors that have constructive and positive effects on effort and performance.[71] In other words, it is a "good" type of stress that can be attained by working out, achieving deadlines, or competing in a sports event. In contrast, bad stress, also known as **distress**, comprises high levels of stressors that have destructive and negative effects on effort and performance.[72] We tend to experience this sort of stress when we're having difficulty at work or struggling with personal problems such as divorce or a death in the family. Under Armour strives to transform distress to eustress by encouraging employees to dress informally, which helps employees to feel more relaxed in a corporate setting.

There are three elements to distress:[73]

- The *physiological element* is manifested as negative physical health effects, such as insomnia or exhaustion. According to a study by the National Institutes of Health, insomnia increased during the pandemic due to changes in working routines, decreased activity caused by long periods at home during lockdown, and concerns over health and job stability.[74]
- The *psychological element* appears as negative attitudes and emotions that can lower job satisfaction, among other results. Some experts attribute negative attitudes to the U.S. political class for failing to respond appropriately to the pandemic.[75]
- *Job burnout* consists of emotional exhaustion, cynicism, and loss of interest in the job and a feeling of lack of control over work and life that can result from ongoing exposure to high levels of stressors. Some reasons for burnout include a toxic workplace culture, being micromanaged, demands to work faster, working longer hours, and coping with an increased workload. According to a recent survey of 1,500 people from 46 countries assessing levels of burnout, most were struggling with trying to cope with work and general well-being during the pandemic.[76]

Managing Stress

The good thing about stress is that it can be managed.

Coping is the effort to manage, reduce, or minimize stressors.[77] There are two types of coping:[78] **Problem-focused coping** aims to reduce or eliminate stressors through understanding the problem and seeking practical ways to resolve it. For example, if you're unhappy in your job, leaving might relieve your worry and anxiety over it. **Emotion-focused coping** is an effort to change your emotional reaction to a stressor by using positive language and distracting techniques. For example, if you lose your job, you might try to reduce the negative emotions associated with a stressful event by looking at the positives—no more early starts, a chance to create or revisit your goals, and so on (see Figure 5.5).

FIGURE 5.5 ■ Managing Stress

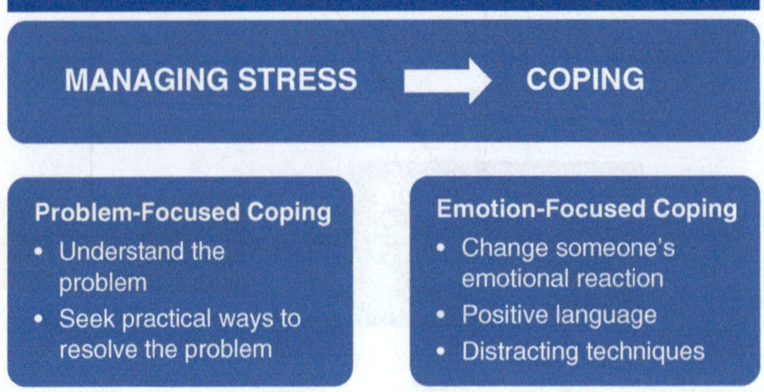

Seven Ways to Manage Stress[79]

1. Meditate

   Just a few minutes of meditating per day helps to relieve stress and quiet the mind. Find a quiet place, focus on your breathing, and allow your mind to clear. Apps like Smiling Mind, Calm, Insight Timer, and Headspace are easily accessible and useful for guided meditation.

2. Breathe deeply

   If you're feeling stressed or anxious, take five deep breaths five times a day. Deep breathing can help to cut distractions, slow your heart rate, pump more oxygen into the lowest part of your lungs, and stabilize your blood pressure.

3. Practice gratitude

   Expressing appreciation is a valuable technique for relieving stressful symptoms. Research shows that practicing gratitude distracts us from negative emotions, makes us feel happier, and puts us in a better frame of mind. A "gratitude journal" is a useful way to record and remind yourself of the things you are most grateful for.

4. Listen to music

   Music is a powerful stress reliever and healer. Studies have found that music decreases our stress hormones, strengthens our immune response, and accelerates the healing process after surgery. Neuroscientists have discovered that the song "Weightless" by Marconi Union can reduce stress by 65%.[80] Table 5.3 lists more songs that have a similarly relaxing effect.

5. Reach out

   Remember that you don't have to cope with your stressful feelings on your own. Reach out to your friends, relatives, or trusted colleagues. You can also make use of the resources provided by your company, such as counseling and other support programs. Talking to others and sharing the problem is a useful way to get some perspective on the issue.

6. Get some exercise

   You don't have to be a professional athlete to get rid of stress. Many forms of exercise, including dance, yoga, Pilates, walking, and playing sports, can make you feel good. When you're feeling stressed, go for a quick walk around the block, or do some stretching exercises like head rolls and shoulder shrugs.

7. Laugh

   It may seem impossible to consider laughter when you're stressed out, but laughter relieves and releases tension, strengthens our immune systems, improves our moods, and helps us to manage difficult situations. Chatting with friends, watching a comedy show, or looking at comical memes on social media can be effective ways to lift your mood during a difficult time.

EXAMINING THE EVIDENCE

PSYCHOLOGICAL CAPITAL, COPING STYLE, AND PERCEIVED STRESS

During the COVID-19 pandemic, many people experienced increased levels of work-related stress, especially during lockdown periods when many people were working from home. In fact, a Harris Poll conducted in April through May 2020 found that 70% of working adults identified work as a significant stressor in their lives.[81] While some people used adaptive coping strategies such as exercise or meditation to deal with the heightened stress levels, others turned to maladaptive coping strategies such as binge drinking. But what causes people to choose one coping style over another? Research suggests that individual cognitive resources may help to shape individual coping styles. Psychological Capital (PsyCap) is one such cognitive resource.

PsyCap involves having confidence in one's ability to succeed at difficult tasks (self-efficacy), having positive expectations for current and future successes (optimism), sustaining and refocusing efforts toward achieving goals (hope), and overcoming and recovering from setbacks and adversity (resilience).[82] Researchers Sherry A. Maykrantz, Brandye D. Nobiling, Richard A. Oxarart, Luke A. Langlinais, and Jeffery D. Houghton conducted a study in May 2020 in an effort to identify how PsyCap might affect individual coping styles.[83] They found a strong positive relationship between PsyCap and adaptive coping and a strong negative relationship between PsyCap and maladaptive coping. Maladaptive coping in turn was strongly positively related to perceived stress, while adaptive coping was negatively related to perceived stress. These results suggest that PsyCap may be especially useful for reducing maladaptive coping and perceived stress. Importantly, PsyCap is a resource that can be enhanced and improved through employee assistance programs and training interventions and may therefore be an important tool for helping to reduce employee work-related stress.

Critical-Thinking Questions

1. What are the primary implications of this research regarding employee coping strategies?
2. What specifically can managers do to ensure that employees are using the most appropriate coping strategies to deal with work-related stress?

Employee Well-Being

We've seen that there are different degrees and types of stress and various ways of managing it. In recognition of the implications of stress and the blurred lines between work and life, many organizations are prioritizing ways to improve employee well-being and mental health within a culture of workplace flexibility.

A **well-being program** is a holistic approach taken by organizations to provide support in the areas of physical and mental health.[84] In addition to boosting physical and mental health, nurturing employee well-being could involve addressing their emotional, financial, and social health, their sense of community, and their purpose (Figure 5.6).[85] Research shows that employees who participate in well-being programs are more engaged and experience more improvement in their physical, financial, and mental health than workers who do not.

Pillar 1: Physical Well-Being

Physical well-being includes exercise, sleep, lifestyle, and food choices. Accountancy firm PWC runs a well-being program that focuses on sleep habits, catalogs the amount of time spent standing in meetings, and tracks what food is consumed and when.[86]

TABLE 5.3 ■ Songs That Relieve Stress

1.	"Weightless" by Marconi Union
2.	"Electra" by Airstream
3.	"Mellomaniac (Chillout Mix)" by DJ Shah
4.	"Watermark" by Enya
5.	"Strawberry Swing" by Coldplay
6.	"Please Don't Go" by Barcelona
7.	"Pure Shores" by All Saints
8.	"Someone Like You" by Adele
9.	"Canzonetta Sull'aria" by Mozart
10.	"We Can Fly" by Rue du Soleil (Café Del Mar)

Source: Curtin, M. (2017, May 30). Neuroscience says listening to this song reduces anxiety by up to 65 percent. *Inc.* https://www.inc.com/melanie-curtin/neuroscience-says-listening-to-this-one-song-reduces-anxiety-by-up-to-65-percent.html

FIGURE 5.6 ■ Seven Pillars of Employee Well-being

Source: Meister, J. (2021, August 4.). *The future of work is employee well-being.* Forbes. https://www.forbes.com/sites/jeannemeister/2021/08/04/the-future-of-work-is-worker-well-being/?sh=75af5094aed0

Pillar 2: Career Well-Being

An increasing number of employees are looking for jobs that offer remote working, a better compensation plan, and more work/life balance. Well-being programs can support these requirements by providing higher compensation, enriched learning and development programs, and online coaching.[87]

Pillar 3: Financial Well-Being

Well-being programs could also provide valuable support and help relieve the increased financial stress brought on by the pandemic. Suze Orman, cofounder of start-up SecureSave, a company that helps companies set up emergency savings accounts (ESAs) for their employees, believes that all organizations should offer an ESA to employees that is deducted from their salary when an emergency arises.[88] This makes it easier for employees to save for the unexpected.

Pillar 4: Social Well-Being

Forging meaningful relationships is key to employee happiness. Loneliness was one of the biggest side effects of the pandemic. Computer hardware company HP has created community groups for remote workers and for working parents to ensure that people stay connected.[89]

Pillar 5: Community Well-Being

Organizations that offer employees opportunities to get involved with the local community boost engagement and retention. U.S. technology corporation Cisco believes in the spirit of community enrichment and sponsors its employees in volunteering for community programs.[90]

Pillar 6: Emotional Well-Being

Supporting employee mental health has become even more essential since the pandemic. Reports have shown a rise in stress-related symptoms, such as changes in sleep habits and greater alcohol consumption. Well-being programs that incorporate flexibility, inclusion, and provide a safe space for employees to discuss their mental health struggles help to destigmatize mental health.[91]

Pillar 7: Purpose-Driven Well-Being

More employees than ever prefer to work for an organization whose values match their own. Studies have reported that more than 40% of millennials and nearly 50% of Gen Zers choose companies based on their own personal ethics.[92]

Another major benefit of well-being programs is that they save organizations money by reducing absenteeism and lower the cost of providing medical insurance. The corporate well-being market is estimated to be worth $87.4 billion by 2026, which is one of the major reasons that more and more organizations are investing in well-being programs that support their employees in all aspects of their work and personal lives.[93]

Fortune 500 companies often participate in Fitbit wellness programs to help increase morale, reduce employee turnover, and cultivate a healthier, more productive workforce.

Richard Levine/Alamy Stock Photo

In this chapter we have explored the impact of emotions, attitudes, and stress on individuals and organizations. As you have seen, reducing stress and resolving conflicts requires the ability to communicate with people with different attitudes, behaviors, and personalities.

IN REVIEW

5.1 Describe the basic concept of emotions in the context of organizational behavior

Emotions are intense feelings directed at a specific object or person. They are numerous and intense but are usually fleeting. **Moods** are less intense and more generalized feelings not directed at a specific object or person; they last longer than emotions.

Emotions can turn into moods when we lose focus of what caused the feeling in the first place; both good and bad moods can trigger stronger, more intense emotional responses.

5.2 Discuss the various roles of emotions in the workplace

In the workplace, emotional outbursts could seriously damage your professional reputation as well as your work performance. **Emotional contagion** is a phenomenon in which emotions experienced by a few people in a work group are spread to the others. **Emotional labor** takes place when, in the course of the job, service industry employees must display emotions different from those they are actually feeling. **Emotional dissonance** is a discrepancy between the emotions a person displays and the emotions they actually feel. **Emotional regulation** is a set of processes through which people influence their own emotions and the ways in which they experience and express them. Emotional intelligence (EI) is the ability to understand emotions in ourselves and others in order to effectively manage our own behaviors and relationships with others. People tend to use two emotional labor techniques to control their real emotions: surface acting and deep acting. **Surface acting** occurs when a person suppresses their true feelings while displaying the organizationally desirable ones, and **deep acting** takes place when you try to change your emotions to better match the emotions your employer requires in the situation.

5.3 Explain the ways in which attitudes influence behavior in organizations

An **attitude** is a learned tendency to consistently respond positively or negatively to people or events. Our workplace attitudes are critical in three main areas: job satisfaction, employee engagement, and organizational commitment. **Job satisfaction** is the degree to which an individual feels positive or negative about a job. There is a strong relationship between job satisfaction and job performance. **Employee engagement** is a connection with the organization and passion for one's job. **Organizational commitment** is an employee's psychological connection to an organization. **Organizational citizenship behaviors** (OCBs) are discretionary and voluntary behaviors that are not a part of the employee's specific role requirements and are not formally rewarded, while **counterproductive work behaviors** (CWBs) are voluntary behaviors that purposefully disrupt or harm the organization.

5.4 Illustrate the ways in which stress can affect behavior in the workplace

Stress is a response that occurs when a situation is perceived as threatening to a person's well-being when their resources are taxed or exceeded. **Stressors** are environmental stimuli that place demands on individuals. The outcomes of stress can be either positive or negative.

5.5 Discuss different outcomes of stress and the benefits of nurturing employee well-being

Although high degrees of stress can be destructive to our behaviors and harmful to our health, stress isn't always negative. **Eustress** is a moderate level of stressors that have constructive and positive effects on effort and performance. In contrast, **distress** is characterized by high levels of stressors that have destructive and negative effects on effort and performance. **Coping** is the effort to manage, reduce, or minimize stressors. **Problem-focused coping** aims to reduce or eliminate stressors through understanding the problem and seeking practical ways to resolve it; **emotion-focused coping** is an effort to change your emotional reaction to a stressor by using positive language and distracting techniques. Many organizations offer well-being programs as a way of helping their employees manage stress. A **well-being program** is a holistic approach taken by organizations to provide support in the areas of physical and mental health.

KEY TERMS

Affective commitment (p. 113)
Affects (p. 104)
Attitude (p. 110)
Cognitive dissonance (p. 111)
Continuance commitment (p. 113)
Coping (p. 116)
Counterproductive work behaviors (p. 114)
Deep acting (p. 106)
Display rules (p. 106)
Distress (p. 116)
Emotional contagion (p. 105)
Emotional dissonance (p. 107)
Emotional labor (p. 106)
Emotional regulation (p. 107)
Emotion-focused coping (p. 116)
Emotions (p. 104)
Employee engagement (p. 112)
Eustress (p. 116)
Job satisfaction (p. 111)
Moods (p. 120)
Negative affect (p. 104)
Normative commitment (p. 113)
Organizational citizenship behavior (p. 113)
Organizational commitment (p. 113)
Positive affect (p. 104)
Problem-focused coping (p. 116)
Social norms (p. 110)
Strain (p. 115)
Stress (p. 114)
Stressors (p. 115)
Surface acting (p. 106)
Well-being program (p. 118)

UP FOR DEBATE: EMPLOYEE EMOTIONAL WELL-BEING

The workplace demands hard work and consistent job performance, and employees and managers often don't have time to worry about much else. A member of a company isn't responsible in any way for their fellow employee's emotional well-being, as this harms a professional environment. Agree or disagree? Explain your answer.

EXERCISE 5.1: COPING WITH STRESS

Objective

The purpose of this exercise is to gain a greater understanding of how others cope with stress.

Instructions

Stress is unavoidable in our lives. You have stress associated with classes but also in your social life, in the activities you're involved with, and so on. Some people have additional stress due to their health or home life. Given that there is always going to be some stress in our lives, being able to cope with it is important.

In groups of three to five, discuss the things that cause you the most stress. Is it tight deadlines or worrying about where you'll work after graduation? Is it an upcoming assignment that you haven't started yet, or is it an important conversation you need to have with a friend? Identify a stressor in your life and ask the others in the group to offer suggestions for how to cope with the stress. Take turns, permitting each person to provide their major stressor and others to offer methods for coping.

Reflection Questions

1. Were the suggestions you received helpful in alleviating your stress? Why or why not?
2. Sometimes just talking about something stressful is helpful. Did the process of revealing your stressor to the group in itself help you cope? Why or why not?
3. What coping suggestions did you receive that will help you in the workplace? Are the same coping mechanisms applicable for a work situation versus a personal situation? Why or why not?

Exercise contributed by Steven Stovall, Southeast Missouri State University.

EXERCISE 5.2: ROLE PLAY FOR RECOGNIZING EMOTIONS

Objective

The purpose of this exercise is to grasp the concept of emotions and how to recognize them in others.

Instructions

Emotions are an integral part of our lives. We exhibit some blatantly; others we try to stifle. In this exercise, a series of role plays will give you an opportunity to see if you can readily recognize emotions in others.

The professor will ask for volunteers or choose people at random for this role-play exercise. In teams of two, each pair of students will come up with a quick skit that demonstrates a particular emotion. Once the teams are formed, they will take a few moments privately to determine what the skit will consist of—it may be verbal and/or nonverbal. Remember, emotions can be either positive or negative. One team might demonstrate *anger*, another *happiness*. One might show the emotion of *betrayal*, another *pride*. After pairs are formed, determine which emotion you're going to demonstrate and act it out in front of the audience. The audience will attempt to identify which emotion is being demonstrated. There should be between eight and ten different emotions exhibited among the pairings of students.

Reflection Questions

1. How easy was it to recognize each emotion? What elements—verbal or nonverbal—caused you to realize which emotion was being demonstrated?
2. In a workplace setting, how common are the emotions demonstrated in your class? Which emotions do we tend to see most often at work?
3. If you were one of those participating in the role play, how did you decide what words or actions you would use to convey the emotion? If you were in the audience, what would you have done differently to convey that same emotion?

Exercise contributed by Steven Stovall, Southeast Missouri State University.

EXERCISE 5.3: MOURNING AT THE DECO CHOCOLATE COMPANY

Objective

In this exercise, you will develop your ability to *describe* emotions in an organizational context, *discuss* the roles these emotions play in the workplace, and *develop examples* of the effects of workplace stress.

Background

You are a manager at the Deco Chocolate Company. Deco Chocolate is a small, boutique chocolate company that specializes in high-end, custom-designed, handcrafted chocolates for special events such as large weddings and corporate banquets. The company has been highly profitable, but due to the nature of its service, it has remained relatively small, with only 118 employees.

The company is very close-knit, with all current employees having been personally selected by one of the founders, the former president (Mary Washington) or the former vice president of HR (her husband, Hank Washington). The founders would regularly invite workers at all levels to their home for dinners or parties. Reciprocally, there was rarely a wedding, birth, bar mitzvah, or other major life event that the founders were not invited to as well. In brief, Mary and Hank developed the company into a true family.

This made the car crash and subsequent death of Mary and Hank last week a truly devastating loss to everyone in the company. A strong succession plan created by Mary Washington has ensured a smooth operational transition for the company, but the emotional fallout is quite different. There have been noticeable signs of grief, depression, and a general drop in worker morale and performance. In addition, more withdrawal behaviors such as absenteeism, lateness, and even looking for external employment have occurred.

While the company has provided grief counseling for the workers, the acting president realizes that the managers need to take an active role in helping the workers process their feelings and continue to sustain the company. To facilitate this process, the acting president has called a meeting of all company managers to discuss the situation and how to best proceed.

Instructions

For the exercise, form small groups (five to seven people). In each group, one person should take the role of the acting company president. This person's task will mainly be to make sure that everyone in the group has a chance to contribute to the discussion and to encourage exploration of ideas. Everyone else will assume the role of a company manager. In the group, discuss the emotional issues that you expect company workers are experiencing as well as those you're experiencing yourselves as managers.

Discuss how the company's family atmosphere both aids and hinders workers in processing the situation. You may want to have a special discussion about the extra emotional labor that workers (especially employees who have to interact with the public as part of their jobs and managers who have to maintain smooth business processes) are encountering. Also, discuss the role of stress in the situation. Finally, be sure to ground your discussion in concrete steps that can be taken to improve affected workplace outcomes such as performance, turnover, absenteeism, loyalty, and job satisfaction.

At the end of the discussion, have one person present an overview of the group's discussion and recommended steps to the class.

Reflection Questions

1. How did using chapter terms and concepts help shape how you understood the situation and what you thought about it?
2. Did use of these concepts provide you with better insights into dealing with the situation? Also, look for differences between your group's presentation and other groups' presentations.
3. Were there any insights brought up that your group did not see?
4. Finally, while this exercise dealt with a negative situation, there are many positive situations and attendant emotions that arise at work. How could you use chapter concepts to recognize and promote such positive emotions?

Exercise contributed by Milton R. Mayfield, Professor of Business, Texas A&M International University, and Jacqueline R. Mayfield, Professor of Business, Texas A&M International University.

ONLINE EXERCISE 5.1: UNDERSTANDING ATTITUDES AND JOB SATISFACTION

Objective

The purpose of this exercise is to gain an appreciation for the relationship between attitudes and job satisfaction.

Instructions

An attitude is a learned tendency to consistently respond positively or negatively to people or events. Attitudes help shape our behaviors and whether or not we're satisfied with our jobs.

The website Glassdoor.com is an online platform that shows how satisfied employees (and former employees) are with a particular firm. Go to the website and look up companies in your town or city. Find three companies that are highly rated—above 4.0 stars. What comments tell you that this is an enjoyable place to work? Prepare a short report on all three companies, detailing why they're rated so highly. Submit this to your professor.

Reflection Questions

1. What conclusions can you draw about these three companies? Would you want to work for any of the three? Why or why not?
2. How reliable do you think the ratings and comments are for each company? How do the ratings and comments influence your opinion of the organizations? What do you think some of the attitudes of those who posted comments on the website are?
3. Why are some firms so highly rated while others have very poor ratings? What factors enable one company to have a high degree of job satisfaction while another has a low degree of job satisfaction?

Exercise contributed by Steven Stovall, Southeast Missouri State University.

ONLINE EXERCISE 5.2: UNDERSTANDING EMOTIONS

Objective

The purpose of this exercise is to gain an understanding of emotions in the workplace.

Instructions

Emotions are a natural human reaction to a stimulus. We display emotions throughout the day as we encounter others, events, and situations. Emotions are also commonplace at work. Conduct an internet search for a short video (less than five minutes) of someone showing an emotion at work. It might be someone happy, angry, sad, etc. Identify what emotion is being demonstrated in the video.

Reflection Questions

1. Write a paragraph describing what you see in the video. Be specific about tone of voice, words uttered (if there are words), and nonverbal behavior. Try to capture, in words, the essence of what is visible in the video. Does the emotion represent a positive affect or negative affect?
2. Based on what is demonstrated in the video, could emotional contagion occur? If so, how? If not, why not?
3. Assume that you work with the individual featured in the video you selected and that you are this person's supervisor. Write a memo to yourself, documenting the emotion you see exhibited by this employee.

Exercise contributed by Steven Stovall, Southeast Missouri State University.

CASE 5.1: ERIC YUAN AND ZOOM VIDEO COMMUNICATIONS, INC.

"Do you feel burnt out at work? Do you look forward to interacting with your coworkers? Are you typically excited about going to work each day?" These are just a few of the questions that workplace culture and compensation monitoring site *Comparably* asks in its anonymous Happiest Employees survey.[94] Happy, fulfilled workers are more productive and loyal to their employers, whereas workplaces defined by stress and burnout suffer from high employee turnover and can quickly earn a reputation as an undesirable place to work. Top companies are increasingly adding CXOs, or *"chief experience officers,"* to their executive teams, many of whom are tasked with promoting employee happiness with the same vigor as customer satisfaction (as well as pursuing top spots on rankings like *Comparably* and *Glassdoor*). Employees can benefit from the cultural improvements that new leadership brings, but organizational overhauls are often less effective than designing an empathetic, supportive company culture from the outset.

Eric Yuan has been in the videoconferencing business for a long time. Born and raised in Tai'an, China, Yuan immigrated to the United States in 1997 and was one of the first 20 hires as a software engineer at a small Silicon Valley firm called Webex. In 2007, Cisco Systems acquired Webex for $3.2 billion, by which time Yuan was the company's vice president of engineering. When users of Cisco Webex reported that they were unhappy with the platform, Yuan began work on a more user-friendly videoconferencing app with integrated chat features and cloud-based collaboration and presented suggestions to improve the product to Cisco management. But they responded with the tech industry mantra: "The user is not the customer."[95] Despite Yuan's 14-year history at the company, Yuan knew that leaving was the right choice to make. "Every day, when I woke up, I was not very happy. I even did not want to go to the office to work," Yuan said in an interview with *CNBC Make It*.[96] They thought about the kind of company they wanted to work for over the next 20 years and left Cisco to establish Zoom Video Communications in 2011.

The end of Yuan's tenure at Cisco was not the only time they faced repudiation. Before they settled in the United States, Yuan's visa applications were denied eight times; they were finally granted entry on the ninth attempt. Yuan drew from this experience when it came to maintaining a calm attitude and regulating their emotions upon entering the rejection-filled world of a start-up foundation. One meeting with a skeptical VC investor who told Yuan all the reasons that Zoom was destined to fail was particularly impactful: "When I got back to my office, I changed my screensaver to just three big words: 'YOU ARE WRONG,'" Yoan told Emergence Capital. "That was my screensaver for many years."[97] Yuan resolved to prove the detractors wrong and make Zoom a success, starting with employees' happiness. "Company culture is my number one priority. It's more important than the team, the product, the business model, or the investors. All of those things can be fixed and made better over time. But culture has to be established on day one. Once you have a culture problem, it's very hard to fix."

Eric Yuan is not alone among CEOs who say their employees are their number-one priority. Most agree with the imperative to make their organization an uplifting place to work, but simply declaring your company has a culture of happiness won't make it so. Zoom delivers on its promise to its employees by cultivating a caring culture that manifests itself in many ways. Employees receive competitive compensation, stock, and health care benefits, including mental health, wellness, and fertility benefits. As one might expect from the leading name in videoconferencing software, Zoom encourages its employees to work from home. "One thing we always tell our employees is, 'Every morning, when you wake up, the first question you should ask yourself is *Do I feel happy or not?*'" Yuan told *Entrepreneur magazine*. "If you feel happy, please come to the office quickly. If you do not feel happy, you can stay at home."[98] "Zoomies" (as Zoom employees call themselves) can receive reimbursements for home office equipment, exercise equipment, groceries, and even food delivery.[99] In addition to its corporate philanthropy, the company matches employee contributions to charitable organizations via the Zoom Cares program. Finally, the company promotes self-learning, reimbursing costs for books that employees buy for themselves or their family.[100] "At the end of the day, it's about the employee's happiness. Your business can't go to the next level unless all employees can get there. We all have to get better every day to succeed," Yuan said during a session on "How to Be an Empathetic Leader" at G2 Reach in 2019.[101] Through all these programs and more, Zoom exemplifies an organization that cares about its employees, earning it top spots in rankings of employee happiness and workplace satisfaction from *Glassdoor, Inc. magazine, Comparably*, and others.

Few companies were so well positioned to adapt to the challenges of the COVID-19 pandemic as Zoom, which became an instant household name among remote workers, distance learners, and families alike in 2020. But like any "overnight success," the company's good fortune had been years in the making. "Zoom's culture is: Deliver happiness. If we are happy, the customer is happy. It's a simple formula, and we lead by example."[102]

Critical-Thinking Questions

1. How did personal experience with workplace stress inform Eric Yuan's goals and leadership style when they founded Zoom?
2. Much of Zoom's "deliver happiness" culture is intended to transform distress to eustress at the company. Do you believe it's effective? Why or why not?
3. Describe how Zoom's employee wellness programs promote organizational commitment among its workforce.

Medicimage Education/Alamy Stock Photo

6 MOTIVATION: CONCEPTS AND THEORETICAL PERSPECTIVES

LEARNING OBJECTIVES

By the end of this chapter, you will be able to:

6.1 Explain the basic motivation process

6.2 Compare the various needs theories of motivation

6.3 Apply goal-setting theory in organizational contexts

6.4 Examine equity theory in the context of organizational justice and distinguish among the predictable outcomes of perceived inequity

6.5 Describe the expectancy theory of motivation and its practical implications

Case Study: AriZona Iced Tea: Organizational Motivation

In one of the most competitive industries in the world, with competitors spending more on advertising than the GDPs of entire countries, AriZona Iced Tea stands out as an innovator. In a market for drinks without alcohol, Coca-Cola and Pepsi are the obvious leaders, but they do so with billions of dollars to use in advertising and with over a century each of growth under their belts.[1] AriZona Iced Tea and its managers compete in the same space as these other beverage behemoths with a limited staff, all motivated toward the goal of cost cutting. With companies like Pepsi and Coca-Cola devoting small armies to marketing, a brand like AriZona needs an edge. Their advantage is a workforce that is fully motivated toward lowering costs and creating interest for their product without ever needing to do their own marketing.

AriZona Iced Tea broke into the market in 1992 after founders John Ferolito and Don Vultaggio saw the success of Snapple, founded in 1970. In a market for premixed tea drinks where Snapple was king, AriZona quickly shot to dominance with their larger size and lower price point of less than a dollar. Since 1992, AriZona Iced Tea has dominated their portion of the beverage market while growing their brand and keeping their price point the same.[2]

So how does a beverage company produce a drink priced cheaper than water for twenty-five years? Founder Don Vultaggio says, "It comes down to incorporating new technology into our entire process."[3] To a beverage company like AriZona, it represents a team of motivated employees continuously increasing efficiency without alienating the customer by raising the price of their product. Vultaggio understood employees and customers from the start, and AriZona Iced Tea has built their brand around pleasing their loyal fan base.

Since its early days, AriZona has found a number of areas where it can increase efficiency and lower its own costs, the first of which is aluminum usage. AriZona currently uses 40% less aluminum per can than it used in the nineties. The AriZona team identified that the easiest way to increase efficiency and avoid the price volatility of raw materials was to use less aluminum. Because AriZona uses a larger can with thinner walls, their prices aren't affected by the volatile market for aluminum cans.[4]

Another way that the AriZona team keeps prices down through efficient technology lies in their packaging methods. AriZona Iced Tea beverages are now packaged twice as fast as they were in the early stages of the company. This means that supply will always be at or above the level of demand, allowing them to sell more cans to more people and further hold down costs.[5]

Most beverage companies have relatively centralized packaging operations that require all of their product to be distributed over long distances using a somewhat complicated supply chain. AriZona, on the other hand, has at least 40 canning centers located across the United States that allow for shorter transport distances and lower fuel costs. This, paired with the policy of transporting AriZona beverages only at night to avoid traffic, greatly reduces transportation costs.[6]

All of these efficient uses of resources have allowed AriZona to keep their cost per can at 99 cents, but the greatest advantage AriZona has in price leadership is their team's advertising strategy. Founder Don Vultaggio decided early on in AriZona's history that the best way to have a cheap product in the beverage industry was to not advertise anywhere but on the can. Vultaggio says, "We feel like it's more important to spend money on something that our customer really cares about, instead of buying billboards or putting our cans in the hands of some celebrity for a few minutes."[7]

AriZona and its employees decided at their inception that they needed to be different from other beverage companies in their advertising practices or they would get pushed out of the market. They decided that their team motivations needed to be a little different from those of the current top dogs in their market. AriZona needed to make it their motivation to cut costs anywhere they could and market their beverage by making it the best and cheapest product they could. This is ultimately what made AriZona the brand they are today, because without the huge advertising costs, they were able to undercut larger beverage companies and create a following of loyal customers.[8]

Customers are loyal to AriZona for the quirkiness of the brand and the taste and consistency of the product. One thing that is inseparable from loyalty to the brand is the always-low price of 99 cents. It has been one of AriZona's most challenging goals so far to keep it at that price point for three decades, but it has quite possibly been the main aspect of their product that has kept them relevant. The goal of 99 cents has been the rallying point for the AriZona team and has motivated employees toward something.[9]

As a result, AriZona has always kept the suggested retail price right on the can to keep merchants from marking it up and muddling their brand for the sake of higher profits. Vultaggio thinks it's fair to think of this suggested retail price as an agreement that the merchant accepts when choosing to sell their product. If AriZona is going to be motivated to keep to that 99-cent price point, the outcome can't be higher profits on the merchant's end. Vultaggio says, "We definitely try to protect that suggested retail price because, again, the price is part of us. That being said, it's hard to police that, nationwide."[10] Their price is intertwined with their brand as a whole, so changing it would mean tweaking the ethos of the entire company.

A team that is motivated to keep their price low has generated a loyalty to the brand, which has in turn allowed AriZona to maintain itself as a staple of convenience stores across the nation. Of course, there's a reason many merchants don't mind raising the price of the can above the recommended retail price. Due to AriZona being the least expensive beverage in convenience stores, the margin these stores make off of AriZona cans is smaller than what they get for most other products. On the whole, if convenience stores had a choice, they would carry a product with higher profit margins in place of AriZona Iced Tea. However, AriZona has gained a fair amount of market power due to the demand and consistency of its customer following. AriZona Iced Tea always sells, and if a convenience store doesn't sell it, many customers will go somewhere else to get it. This leaves merchants little choice but to carry a product that makes less per square foot than many other products.[11]

The AriZona Iced Tea team has established itself as an effective cost leader in its segment of the beverage industry since its founding in 1992. Through innovation, lean thinking on the part of employees, and a creative advertising strategy, it has been able to keep its prices the same since 1992. In return for the low price, AriZona Iced Tea has a loyal fan base that will keep the beverage in stores for years to come.

Critical-Thinking Questions

1. What was the beverage market like in 1992 when AriZona entered it?
2. How did AriZona Iced Tea differentiate itself from competitors and maintain dominance in its segment?
3. Why have merchants kept AriZona products in their stores despite low margins per can?

THE MOTIVATION PROCESS

Have you ever successfully completed a goal, such as passing an exam or getting a job, and wondered how you did it? Think about the behaviors you exhibited to achieve your objectives. To pass the exam, you probably studied hard for long periods of time, and to get the job, you likely prepared for the interview by researching the company and practicing responses to potential interview questions. Whatever your intended goal, you wouldn't have achieved it without motivation. Take the AriZona Iced Tea employees featured in our case study. The individual goal for each employee was to boost efficiency and keep costs down, which has allowed the company to meet the organizational goal of selling its product at 99 cents without any investment in marketing. Highly motivated employees tend to be happier and more engaged in their roles, provide innovative ideas, build better relationships with customers, and be more productive.[12] We define **motivation** as forces from within individuals that stimulate and drive them to achieve goals.[13] These forces help us to persist with our efforts to achieve specific objectives at work or in our daily life.

FIGURE 6.1 ■ The Motivation Process

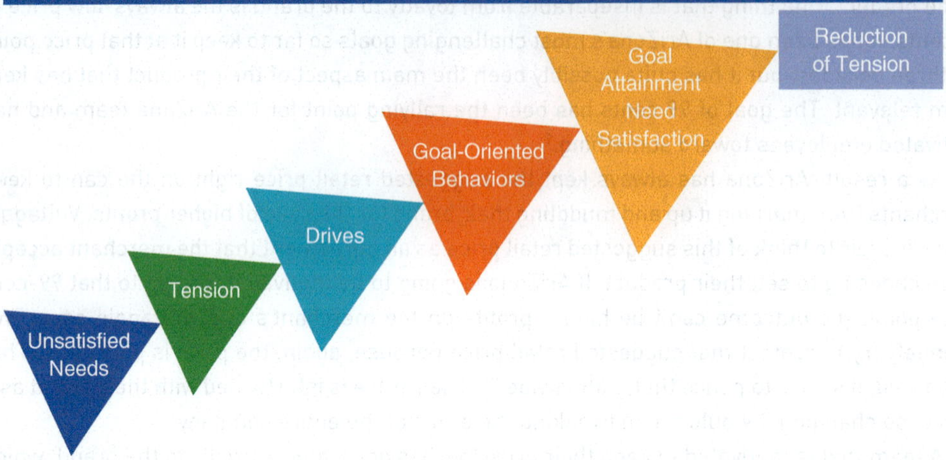

But how does motivation affect the way we behave? Motivation is a process by which behavior is *energized*, meaning we have the strength to keep going even when things aren't going our way; *directed*, meaning the efforts we invest in our work also benefit our employer; and *maintained*, meaning we keep our intention to work over some period of time to achieve our objectives.[14]

The motivation process is shaped by unsatisfied needs and the resulting tension, as shown in detail in Figure 6.1. For example, you may have an unsatisfied goal to achieve a high grade in an exam, which creates tension. The demand to satisfy this need and relieve the discomfort drives you to study hard, which helps you to attain your goal, thus reducing tension. Similarly, the AriZona Iced Tea team has a motivational goal to keep the price on the can at 99 cents. Any change to this would lead to customer dissatisfaction. It is this discomfort that motivates employees to reduce costs to ensure the price point stays the same.

The motivation process is best understood through several motivation theories, most of which we discuss in the next section.

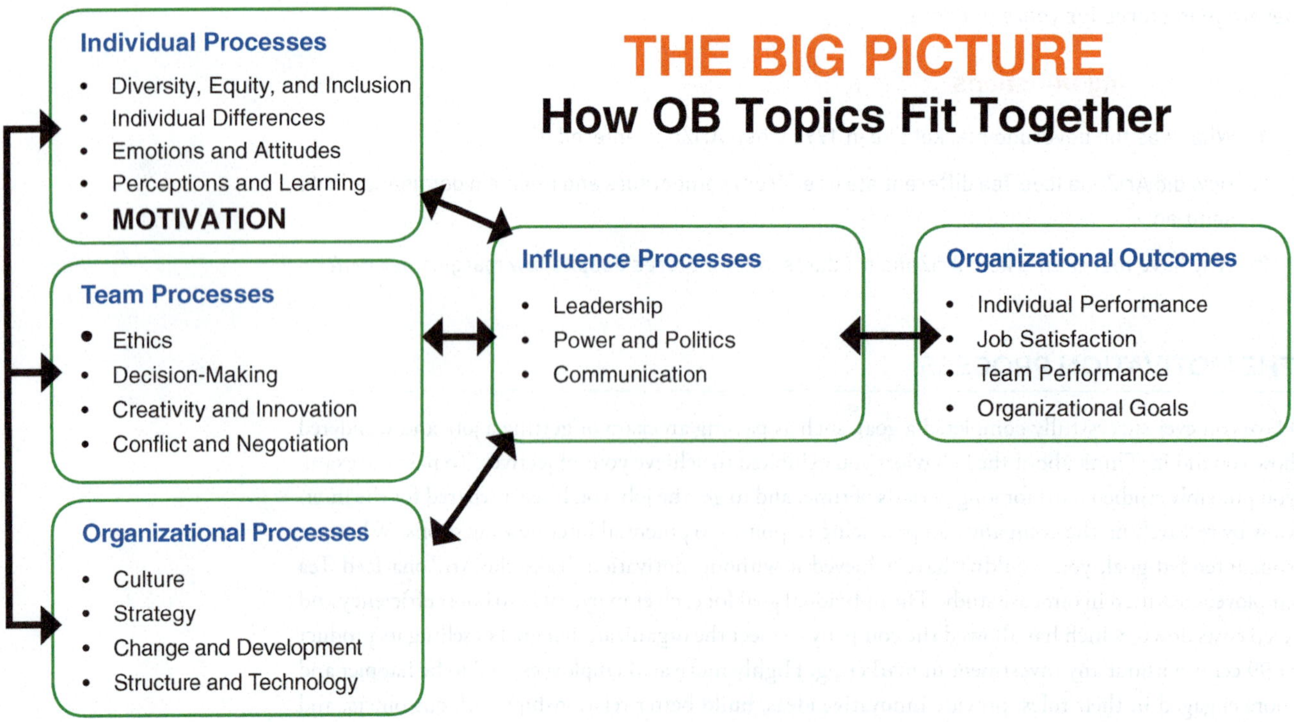

NEEDS THEORIES

There are many theories about motivation, but most focus on the idea that motivation is based on different needs and the behavioral outcomes of those needs.

Researchers have spent decades attempting to identify the underlying factors that motivate people. Needs motivation theories are generally divided into two categories: content theories and process theories.[15] **Content theories** explain why people have different needs at different times and how these needs motivate behavior. In other words, what are the types of factors that motivate people? There are four main content theories: Maslow's hierarchy of needs, Alderfer's ERG theory, McClelland's need theory, and Herzberg's two-factor theory. While content theories focus on what motivates us, **process theories** describe the cognitive processes through which needs are translated into behavior. Simply put, process theories look at how our needs drive, influence, and sustain our behavior. The process theories we investigate in this chapter are equity theory, goal-setting theory, and expectancy theory.

In this section we'll explore several needs theories of motivation: Maslow's hierarchy of needs, Alderfer's ERG theory, Herzberg's two-factor theory, McClelland's acquired needs theory, and money as a motivator.

Maslow's Hierarchy of Needs

Psychologist Abraham Maslow developed one of the most popular needs theories, referred to as the **hierarchy of needs theory**,[16] which is visually depicted as a pyramid of five levels of individual needs with physiological needs at the bottom and self-actualization needs at the top (Figure 6.2). Maslow's theory teaches that each need must be satisfied before we can move up the pyramid to satisfy the need above it. For example, at the base of the pyramid, we need to satisfy the physiological need to eat food and drink water in order to survive before we can satisfy our safety needs, such as looking after our families or getting a job. Maslow's hierarchy is based on the belief that successfully accomplishing

FIGURE 6.2 ■ Maslow's Hierarchy of Needs

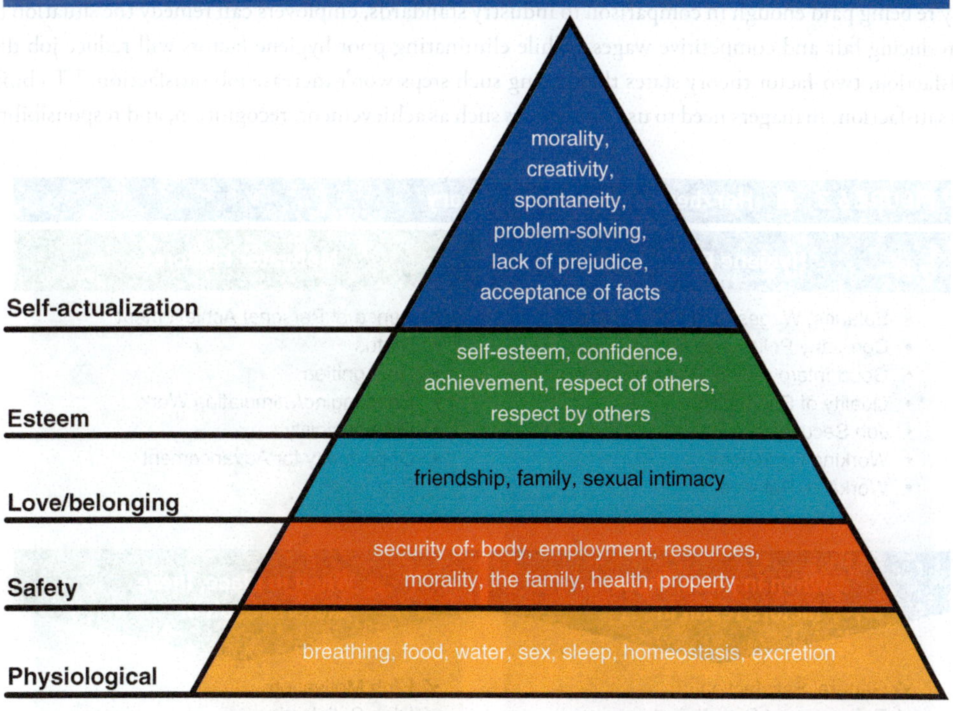

Source: Factoryjoe (Mazlow's Hierarchy of Needs.svg) [CC BY-SA 3.0 (http://creativecommons.org/licenses/by-sa/3.0)], via Wikimedia Commons.

the lower-level needs leads to the achievement of higher-level needs, such as gaining confidence, self-esteem, and finally self-actualization.

Though Maslow's theory is useful for identifying categories of needs, there has been much debate about its implication that each need loses its importance as soon as it has been satisfied.[17] For example, according to the hierarchy, people who reach self-actualization won't be as concerned with gaining the respect of others. Researchers have also argued against the step-by-step sequence of Maslow's hierarchy, proposing that people may be motivated to satisfy these needs in a number of different ways or even simultaneously.[18]

ERG Theory

Developed by psychologist Clayton Alderfer, **ERG theory** also suggests that people are motivated by categories of needs arranged in the form of a hierarchy.[19] Instead of Maslow's five need categories, however, Alderfer includes only three: existence needs (E), relatedness needs (R), and growth needs (G). *Existence needs* are similar to Maslow's physiological and safety needs, *relatedness needs* are comparable to Maslow's love/belonging needs, and *growth needs* bear similarities to Maslow's esteem needs and self-actualization needs. Alderfer proposed that instead of satisfying needs one step at a time, we can satisfy different levels in any order or even at the same time, depending on the circumstances. ERG theory has received more support from researchers than Maslow's hierarchy of needs, but further research needs to be carried out to fully test the validity of Alderfer's model.

Herzberg's Two-Factor Theory

A third theory of motivation, developed by psychologist Frederick Herzberg, is called **two-factor theory** (or *motivation-hygiene theory* or *dual theory*). It explores the impact of motivational influences on job satisfaction.[20] Herzberg conducted interviews with hundreds of workers before identifying two main factors influencing employee behavior: hygiene factors and motivators (Figure 6.3). **Hygiene factors** are sources of job satisfaction such as salary, status, and security. Herzberg found that the first step to employee satisfaction is to eliminate poor hygiene factors. For example, if employees don't feel they're being paid enough in comparison to industry standards, employers can remedy the situation by introducing fair and competitive wages. While eliminating poor hygiene factors will reduce job dissatisfaction, two-factor theory states that taking such steps won't increase job satisfaction.[21] To build job satisfaction, managers need to use **motivators** such as achievement, recognition, and responsibility.

FIGURE 6.3 ■ Herzberg's Two-Factor Theory

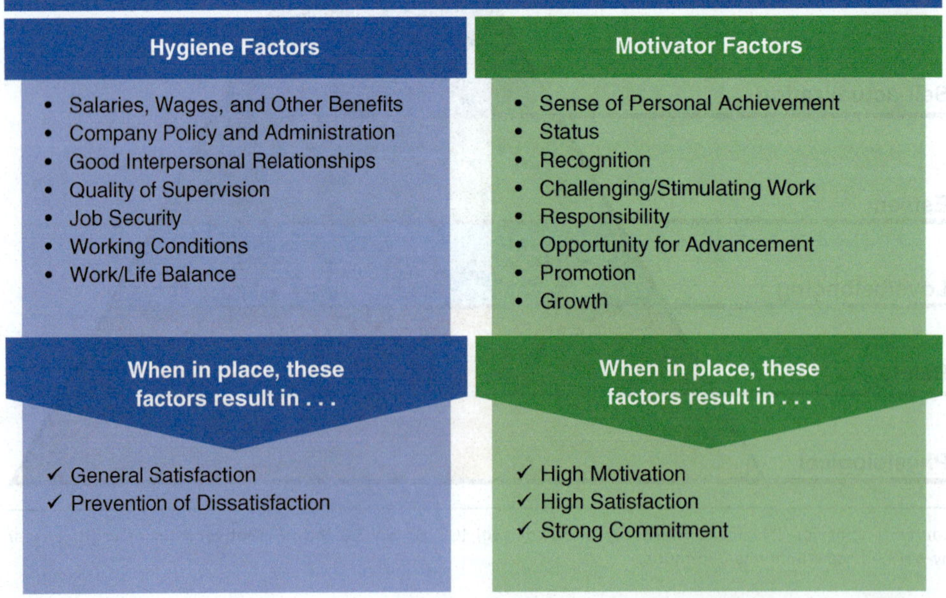

Sources: Herzberg, F., Mausner, B., & Snyderman, B. B. (1959). *The motivation to work* (2nd ed.). Wiley; Herzberg, F. (2003, January). One more time: How do you motivate employees? *Harvard Business Review, 81*(1), 87–96.

According to Herzberg, effective motivators lead to a highly stimulated, motivated workforce, whereas in the absence of motivators, employees can become ambivalent or apathetic toward their roles. Over the years, Herzberg's two-factor theory has received a number of criticisms for being too narrow in scope. Some theorists have questioned Herzberg's assumption that satisfied employees are more productive. Others have argued that what motivates one person might not necessarily motivate another. The theory has also been criticized for not accounting for individual differences, meaning that some individuals may respond differently to hygiene or motivator factors.[22]

Despite these criticisms, Herzberg's two-factor theory has been an important influence on the motivational techniques employed by managers with their workforce in the areas of job security, job enrichment, and job satisfaction.[23]

McClelland's Acquired Needs Theory

Developed by psychological theorist David McClelland, **acquired needs theory** holds that our needs are shaped over time and formed by our experiences and cultural background. McClelland classified needs into three main categories: need for achievement, need for affiliation, and need for power.[24] According to the theory, one of these needs is the dominant motivator, but all three, in particular the need for achievement, can be learned through training.

- **Need for achievement** is the desire to excel. People who are achievement oriented are generally positive in nature, tend to set their own goals, thrive on feedback, and take ownership of their work. High achievers do well in challenging environments but may lose motivation in routine roles. Ashley Rouse, founder and CEO of North Carolina–based small-batch jam company Trade Street Jam Co., is a good example of a person with a desire to excel. When the pandemic put a stop to in-person events, Rouse moved the majority of the business online. Rouse believes that honesty, humbleness, and transparency in business are key to creating a successful company because they invite the loyalty of staff and customers.[25]
- **Need for affiliation** is the desire to belong to a group and to be liked. Generally, people who possess this need as a dominant motivator like to maintain the status quo, prefer collaborating rather than competing, and feel a strong desire for others' approval. They tend not to make

Sara Blakely, creator of Spanx.

Moses Robinson/Contributor/Getty Images

good managers because they don't like to make unpopular decisions or give orders for fear of falling out of favor with their colleagues. Without daily contact with others, people with strong affiliation needs might lose motivation, which may lead to job dissatisfaction.

- **Need for power** is the desire to control and influence the behavior of others. There are two types of power. *Institutional power* is the power an individual exerts for the good of the organization and its employees, and *personal power* is power focused on controlling and manipulating others for personal gain. North Korean president Kim Jong-un, Russian president Vladimir Putin, and United Arab Emirates president Sheikh Khalifa Nahyan are examples of dictators who use their power to coerce and control their followers.

Each of the content theorists—Maslow, Alderfer, Herzberg, and McClelland—focused on our human needs and what motivates us to satisfy those needs (Figure 6.4). Yet in many organizations, money is used as a prime motivator for employees.

Money as a Motivator

Money is one of the primary mechanisms managers used for motivating people in the workplace, and employees are often expected to hit financial targets to receive a monetary reward or bonus. Some companies used money as motivator to tackle burnout (see Chapter 5) in the aftermath of the COVID-19 pandemic. For example, global investment bank Credit Suisse based in Switzerland announced that it was giving a one-time bonus of $20,000 to junior investment bankers as a reward for all the long hours and hard work they'd put in during the pandemic.[26] While many companies may believe in the benefits of money as an incentive, how does this idea fit in with the content theories? Generally, money sits with lower-level needs: safety and physiological requirements in Maslow's hierarchy of needs, existence in Alderfer's ERG theory, and hygiene factors in Herzberg's two-factor theory. Money provides us with food, housing, clothing, and all the necessities of life. If money is so important, why did the theorists not consider it a high-level need?

Most people who live in modern societies and work in contemporary organizations receive a paycheck that affords them a certain standard of living. This means their lower-level needs are already being satisfied. Instead, people focus on higher-level needs such as belongingness, esteem, and self-actualization per Maslow; relatedness and growth per Alderfer; and motivator factors per Herzberg. Money isn't as important here, according to these theorists.

Money can sometimes become a status symbol or an indication of success, and some people are paid far more than others. For example, in 2021, Tesla and SpaceX founder Elon Musk had a net worth of more than $150 billion and became the second-wealthiest person (Amazon founder Jeff Bezos takes the top spot) in the world. However, appealing as it might be to earn millions, money generally doesn't relate directly to the needs people are trying to satisfy in the workplace. This isn't to say that money

FIGURE 6.4 ■ Comparison of the Four Content Theories of Motivation

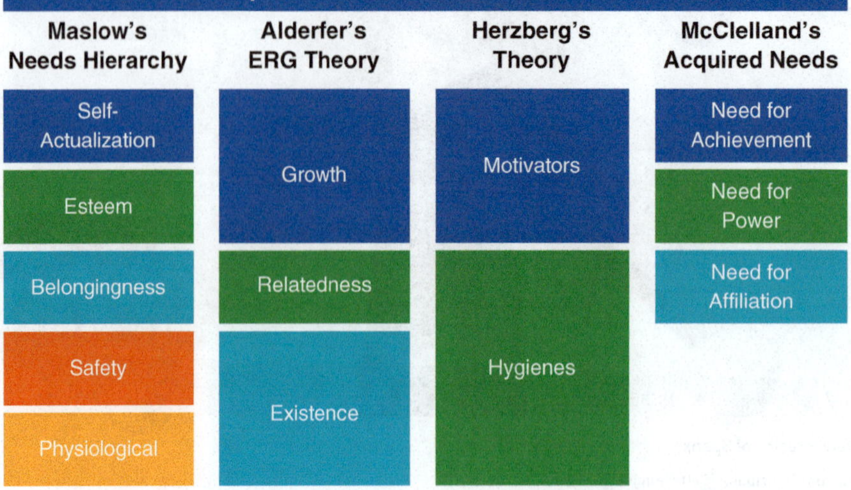

is unimportant, but rather that it may not be the most important or most effective motivator. For example, promising an employee a 10-cent-per-hour raise or a $300 year-end bonus may not necessarily increase motivation. Instead, these theories suggest, people are motivated by their affiliation with others and the opportunity to achieve, grow, and be recognized for their accomplishments.

Research also shows that using cash as an incentive doesn't always work. In one study, more than 80% of U.S. employees stated that they don't feel recognized or rewarded despite the salaries they're being paid. Harvard Business School assistant professor Ashley V. Whillans believes that showing appreciation for employees is a powerful motivator: "Cash matters in people's lives, but it's not all that matters" . . . "What really matters in the workplace is helping employees feel appreciated."[27]

There are many simple ways in which companies can show their appreciation for employees. For example, online software service Typeform, based in Barcelona, Spain, encourages its employees to recognize hard work by celebrating with a spontaneous round of applause; clothing and shoe retailer Zappos runs a "Monthly Hero" program where the winner receives a gift card, a monthly parking spot, and a cape; and social networking platform Dribbble recognizes achievements by using the personalized-videos app Cameo to give celebrity shout-outs to their high performers (singer Rebecca Black and rapper Flava Flav are among the Cameo stars who have sent messages to Dribble employees).[28] These companies have managed to create a committed and loyal workforce through their application of innovative motivators in lieu of high salaries and cash bonuses. Yet regardless of the amount of cash incentives or creative perks, work will never get done without the existence of clear work-related goals.

EXAMINING THE EVIDENCE MONEY AS A MOTIVATOR

Few behavioral researchers would argue that money has no motivational effect on employees. Indeed, a number of studies suggest that financial incentives can increase certain types of work performance.[29] However, in the best-selling book *Drive: The Surprising Truth About What Motivates Us*, author Daniel Pink explains that a growing body of scientific evidence suggests that higher pay and/or bonus incentives tend to result in increased performance only for very basic tasks involving mechanical skills.[30] In contrast, if a task requires greater cognitive skills, creativity, or critical thinking, higher pay could lead to lower performance. For example, one group of researchers conducted a series of experiments in which subjects completed basic tasks under different financial reward conditions ranging from relatively small to moderate to very large and across different types of tasks involving motor skills, creativity, and memory respectively.[31] The researchers observed, "One cannot assume that introducing or raising incentives will always improve performance." In short, these findings suggest that financial incentives—especially very large ones—could increase task motivation to a higher-than-optimal level, leading to "choking" under pressure and reduced performance. In contrast, small to moderate financial inducements may work best, especially when used to motivate the performance of noncognitive tasks that don't require employees to learn or develop specialized skills or work collaboratively with others. The researchers concluded, "Perhaps there is good reason why so many workers continue to be paid on a straight salary basis."

Critical-Thinking Questions

1. Many companies offer large financial incentives for tasks that require creativity, problem-solving, and memory. Based on the research findings described here, what is a possible limitation to this approach?
2. How can managers most effectively use nonfinancial incentives to increase employee performance?

GOAL-SETTING THEORY

What motivates us to go to work or even bother having a job at all? The answer is goals. Having goals to work toward gives us a sense of purpose and is the primary reason we get out of bed and go to work. One of the most important theories in practice in organizations today is goal-setting theory. **Goal-setting**

theory was developed by Edwin Locke and Gary Latham in the 1960s and suggests that human performance is directed by conscious goals and intentions.[32] Studies of the effects of goal-setting in the workplace have shown that employees are motivated by clear goals accompanied by appropriate feedback.[33] In other words, employees benefit from goals as they provide direction and the motivation to meet those goals.

Goals can have both direct and indirect effects. *Direct effects* motivate and energize us, helping us to achieve objectives, and *indirect* effects encourage us to use cognitive skills such as planning and strategizing to attain our goals. For example, the direct effect of buying a house involves ownership of the house, but it also has the indirect effect of prompting us to work out how to pay the mortgage.

Specific Goals

Research has shown that people respond more to clear, well-defined goals and produce better results than vague or "Do your best" goals.[34] Managers can set specific goals by making them clear and easy to understand, ensure they're challenging but attainable, make them measurable, and set them within a distinct time frame. For example, a sales team might set a goal for each member to acquire 10 new customers or sell 200 products a month. Because of the specificity of the goal, each team member knows exactly what to do to meet the challenge. Many organizations use the acronym S.M.A.R.T. to guide their goal-setting (see Figure 6.5).

Difficult Goals

Similarly, researchers have found that goals set at a high but not unreasonable level of difficulty produce better results than less challenging or easier goals.[35] Business coach Lattice Hudson believes that setting goals outside our comfort zone and "get[ting] comfortable with the uncomfortable" allows us to push through our boundaries toward success.[36]

Goal Acceptance and Commitment

In general, employees who accept and commit to goals set by or developed in participation with their managers have higher levels of performance and are more motivated to achieve their objectives.[37] Companies with committed employees tend to have low turnover. The employees featured in the AriZona Iced Tea case study unite to meet the company's overriding goal: to work as efficiently as possible to maintain the beverage's long-standing price point.

Andres Pira, founder and CEO of real estate company Blue Horizon Developments based in Phuket, Thailand, believes in celebrating goal achievement by going on outings with the whole team. For example, one year when the team reached a significant sales target, Pira organized a four-day climbing trip to the top of one of Southeast Asia's most active volcanos. Pira credited this trip with bonding the team together and for their care and support of each other in the workplace from then on, which led to greater commitment and even higher goal achievement.[38]

FIGURE 6.5 ■ S.M.A.R.T. Goals

S.M.A.R.T. GOALS

SPECIFIC → WHAT EXACTLY DO YOU WANT TO ACHIEVE?

MEANINGFUL → HOW FAR AWAY ARE YOU FROM COMPLETING YOUR GOAL?

ACHIEVABLE → HOW REALISTIC AND ATTAINABLE IS YOUR GOAL?

RELEVANT → IS YOUR GOAL IN LINE WITH THE COMPANY'S MISSION, VALUES, AND VISION?

TIME-BOUND → WHAT IS YOUR TARGET TO COMPLETE THE GOAL?

The Goldilocks Rule

Have you ever wondered why you may achieve some goals but not others? Or why you start out so determined to reach a goal one week only to give up the next? This may be because your goal is either too hard or too easy. The Goldilocks theory states that goals should fall somewhere in the middle in terms of difficulty (just right) in order to be achievable.[39] For example, say you're playing tennis with a friend. If you're pretty good at tennis and your friend is just a beginner, you will mostly likely win easily, but you may also lose motivation because the game isn't challenging enough.

In contrast, say you're playing against a professional tennis player—the game is far more challenging, but you might still lose motivation because the game is too tough and you're not good enough to win, let alone score many points. However, if you play against someone who is pretty equal to you in terms of skill, then the game becomes more engaging. Sure, you might lose a few points, but you will also win a few. You will be more motivated to finish the game because victory is possible. The point is that the most achievable goals are the ones that are at "just manageable levels of difficulty"—ones that are within our reach if we persevere enough.

How do you stay motivated to achieve your desired goals? Remember the Goldilocks rule and work toward goals that fall within the margins of difficulty rather than extremes. Next, make sure to measure your progress and ask for feedback wherever possible so you know how far away you are from achieving your goal.

Feedback

Goals that are accompanied by regular feedback are more likely to motivate employees.[40] Natalie McVeigh, managing director of New York–based accounting firm EisnerAmper, believes that giving and receiving feedback is essential for development as long it's accompanied by some sort of action. McVeigh says, "The most important step in this process is making sure something happens with the feedback you are given."[41]

Goals are often arranged in hierarchies in order to assess which ones take priority.[42] For example, **behavioral goals**, which are short-term goals that provide employees with frequent feedback about their performance, are positioned farther up the hierarchy than **performance goals**, which are long-term goals set into the future. Setting goals too far into the future can be demotivating for employees. But out-of-range goals aren't the only thing that demotivates employees. Motivation can also be determined by our perception of fairness in relation to our own roles in an organization.

EQUITY THEORY

The concept of **equity theory**, introduced by psychologist J. Stacey Adams, holds that motivation is based on our perception of how fairly we're being treated in comparison with others.[43] In other words, people may be motivated when they perceive their treatment as fair but demotivated if they consider their treatment to be unfair. According to this theory, our perception of what's fair depends on the ratio O/I, where O equals outcomes like the recognition, pay, and status we enjoy and I equals inputs like our effort, experience, and ability (Figure 6.6).

FIGURE 6.6 ■ Equity Theory

Person | **Referent Other**

$$\frac{\text{Outcomes}}{\text{Inputs}} = \frac{\text{Outcomes}}{\text{Inputs}}$$

People tend to compare their own perceived O/I ratio to their perceptions of the O/I ratio of *referent others*, or people whose situation is comparable to their own. As long as the ratios are similar, there's no problem, but someone who perceives the other person's ratio as greater than their own will feel an inequity. For example, if you discover that a coworker's salary is higher than yours, you may experience a sense of unfairness. People adopt several behaviors in the face of such **perceived inequity**.

Handling Perceived Inequity

Change Inputs

Suppose you find out a coworker who does exactly the same job as you and has the same level of experience gets paid $2.00 per hour more than you. You respond to this by slacking off and investing less effort, thereby lowering your inputs. Of the four components of the *O/I self* < *O/I other* equation, your own *I* is the one you have direct control over. When you're in a position of management and you come across an employee who appears unmotivated or seems to intentionally not do their job, it is very likely that their behavior is the result of a perceived unfairness or inequity. It is your job as a manager to try to find out what they think is unfair and restore a perception of fairness. While you might not think anything that has happened is actually unfair, people will act based on their perceptions of fairness, not on the actual equity of the situation. Sometimes all that's necessary is to help them see their misperception.

Attempt to Change Outcomes

Alternatively, if you find out you're underpaid, you could try to increase your *O* by approaching your manager and saying, "Hey, I found out that Jamal, who does the same job as me, makes $2.00 per hour more than me! I deserve a raise!" (This, incidentally, is one reason why discussing salaries is so taboo in many cultures. Companies and managers don't want to have this potential problem, so discussing salaries is viewed as inappropriate behavior. Do people still do it? Of course!)

Carry Out Cognitive Reevaluation

Suppose you find out that unbeknownst to you, your coworker went to night school and earned an MBA degree or perhaps they had 10 years' more experience than you while working at another company. Either of those could cause you to change how you perceive their inputs. You might realize, *Oh, they really do bring more compensable factors to the job than I do.* Because equity theory is based on one's perceptions, any of the four components of the equation can be adjusted cognitively. For example, one study showed that after a pay cut, employees increased their cognitive appraisal of nonmonetary job outcomes such as status, office furnishings, etc., in order to put the equation back in balance (*I may be getting paid less, but I sure do have a nice office!*).[44]

Attempt to Change Inputs or Outcomes

It's not easy to change the I or O of the referent other. You could ask your manager to cut their pay to match yours, but that would probably be met with icy indifference (at best). Even more ludicrously, you could ask your coworker to increase their inputs: "I found out recently that you make $2.00 per hour more than me, and I was wondering if you could just do a little extra work off the clock at night or on the weekends—that would make me feel much better about things!" But they probably wouldn't be impressed.

Pick Another "Other"

Employees might compare themselves to different coworkers to perceive a more equitable situation. Suppose you find out that your coworker does have an MBA degree, but instead of doing a cognitive reevaluation, you decide this person isn't an appropriate comparison for you anyway. This might lead you to choose another coworker who has a more similar educational or experience level with whom to compare yourself.

Leave the Field

Finally, if the inequity (in this case underpayment) is severe enough and the employee can find no other means to restore equity (such as getting the manager to give them a pay raise or doing some type of cognitive reevaluation), they may quit. Most people have quit a job or left an organization because they felt they were being treated unfairly. It's interesting to note that the term "leave the field" is based on some of the earliest equity theory studies, in which researchers had some boys gather in a field and play a game involving inequitable outcomes for certain boys.[45] They noted the boys responding in all the ways outlined above, but if the injustice was felt strongly enough, the boys would literally "leave the field."

One weakness of equity theory is that it doesn't specify which of these predictable outcomes a person will engage with. Will an employee simply slack off, or will they quit their job? This isn't predicted by the theory.

Organizational Justice

Equity theory includes the concept of **organizational justice**, which focuses on what people perceive as fairness in workplace practices.[46] In other words, the way an organization's behaviors, decisions, and actions are perceived by its employees influences their own attitudes and behaviors in the workplace. Organizational justice involves all matters of organizational behavior, including pay, access to training, and gender equality. Employees who perceive themselves as being treated unfairly may call in sick more often or become more unproductive and disengaged. It is essential that companies big and small promote a positive sense of organizational justice by building trust and encouraging communication among employees. Research shows that employees at high-trust companies report less stress, demonstrate higher productivity, and experience less burnout, leading to reduced turnover.[47]

There are four main kinds of organizational justice: distributive, procedural, interpersonal, and informational.

Distributive justice is the degree to which people perceive outcomes to be fairly allocated. For example, employees doing the same job as others expect to be compensated equally. The concept of distributive justice is based on equity theory. When equal work does not produce equal outcomes, or when one employee is paid more or less than another for doing the same job, then there is a lack of distributive justice. Although the gender pay gap is narrowing, it is still present. Women still earn less than men, and the pay gap widens further for women of color, women with children, and immigrant women (see Chapter 2). Organizations can promote distributive justice by taking the right steps to closing the gender pay gap, such as ending discriminatory hiring practices, readdressing promotional decisions, and removing obstacles to women so they can progress to leadership positions.[48]

Procedural justice is the degree to which people perceive the implementation of company policies and procedures to be fair. For example, if the organization has strict policies around dress code and tardiness, it can be frustrating to conscientious employees for a manager to turn a blind eye to an employee who has ignored the dress code or leaves work an hour earlier than the rest of the team.[49]

If a policy applies to all staff at every level, employees will be more likely to accept it as fair. If some workers are exempt, employees are unlikely to believe they're being treated equally. As CEO of U-Haul, Joe Shoen implements procedural justice by ensuring accessibility to both employees and customers. Their feedback allows Shoen to find out when policies aren't being implemented properly and put processes in place to resolve these issues.[50]

Interpersonal justice refers to the level of dignity, politeness, and respect employees receive by supervisors during change implementation. Mike Morini, the CEO of WorkForce Software, a small New York company that takes care of tasks such as payroll, worker schedules, and compliance on behalf of more than 4 million people in 80 countries, demonstrated interpersonal injustice during this post-pandemic era by offering employees flexible work schedules, listening to their concerns, and conducting surveys to better understand their needs.[51]

Informational justice refers to the degree to which employers provide truthful information and explanations to employees regarding why certain decisions are being made. Eugenie Fanning, vice president of people at real estate start-up SquareFoot in New York, believes in honesty and transparency when it comes to sharing information with employees. When the CEO of SquareFoot announced pay cuts during the COVID-19 crisis, Fanning engaged in one-on-one calls to explain what was happening and to reassure employees who had concerns about layoffs. Sharing information in this way helped Fanning to build solid relationships based on trust.[52]

A classic research study was conducted in a company that was implementing 15% across-the-board pay cuts in two plants.[53] In Plant A, the company president held a 90-minute meeting in which the president showed concern for the workers and provided detailed information about why the pay cuts were necessary, particularly so that the company wouldn't have to lay off any employees. In Plant B, a vice president spent only 15 minutes informing workers that the president had decided that 15% pay cuts were necessary. No additional information was provided except that the cuts were necessary because contracts had been lost. No apology or remorse was provided, and detailed information regarding the rationale for the cuts was not offered. Subsequently, employee theft (an interesting way that employees try to restore equity by increasing outcomes in their O/I ratio!) increased in both plants, but to a much greater magnitude in Plant B (a 1.5% increase in Plant A and a 5% increase in Plant B). Also, turnover increased substantially in Plant B, whereas in Plant A it remained unchanged. This was one of the first studies that helped us to begin to understand *interpersonal* and *informational* justice. The *distributive justice* was the same in both plants (15% pay cut), and the procedures to determine the pay cuts were the same in both plants (across the board for all employees). However, in Plant A the company president took time with the employees, showing concern and compassion (interpersonal justice) and providing detailed information regarding the reasons for the cuts (informational justice). In contrast, in Plant B the employees received an inadequate and impersonal explanation with much less of both types of justice, resulting in much different outcomes.

People who believe they're being treated poorly by an organization will become demotivated over time. However, organizations that meet or exceed employee expectations, reward good work, and treat people with respect have a greater chance of maintaining a more satisfied, productive workforce. This is where expectancy theory comes in.

EXPECTANCY THEORY

Expectancy theory holds that people will choose certain behaviors over others with the expectation of a certain outcome.[54] It was originally proposed by Yale School of Management professor Victor Vroom in 1964. Vroom's theory explores the motivation of individuals to maximize satisfaction and minimize dissatisfaction. In this context, motivation is a function of an individual's beliefs concerning effort-to-performance relationships (expectancy), work-outcome relationships (instrumentality), and the desirability of various work outcomes (valence).

Expectancy is the probability that the amount of work effort invested by an individual will result in a high level of performance. It could be phrased as "What's the probability that, if I work very hard, I'll be able to do a good job?" It is measured in a range from zero to +1. If someone believes strong effort won't result in a higher performance level, their expectancy is zero; however, if the person believes a good effort *will* lead to high performance, their expectancy is +1. For example, if you work hard on a project, you might expect to reach the required deadline. **Instrumentality** is the probability that good performance will lead to various work outcomes. Another way of saying this is "What's the probability that, if I do a good job, that there will be some kind of outcome in it for me?" It can range from −1 to +1. An instrumentality of +1 would apply to people who believe their performance will make an outcome likely, whereas people who think their performance will not result in outcomes would have an instrumentality of −1. For example, if you consistently reach your goals and perform well all year, then you might expect a bonus or a promotion (outcomes) as a reward for your efforts.

Valence is the value individuals place on work outcomes. Phrased a different way, it's "Is the outcome I get of any value to me?" Valences range from −1 to +1 and are positive or negative depending on the nature of the outcome. For example, if you expected a cash bonus as a reward but instead receive additional time off, you may see this as a negative outcome.

In addition, an article exploring the foundations of faking behavior reports that people may be motivated to engage in faking behavior as a means of successfully completing a test when (a) they believe that faking is essential for getting high scores on the test, thereby leading to positive work outcomes (instrumentality), or (b) they believe there is a high probability of faking behavior, resulting in increased test scores (expectancy).[55]

FIGURE 6.7 ■ Expectancy Theory

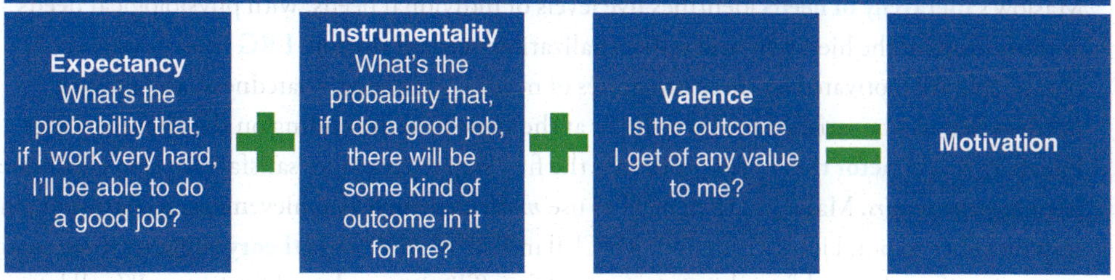

Source: Lunenburg, F. C. (2011). Expectancy theory of motivation: Motivating by altering expectations. *International Journal of Management, Business, and Administration, 15*(1), 1–6.

Expectancy theory can be summarized as follows: Say you work for a bank. The bank has a cross-sales incentive program. Cross-sales occur when someone comes in to buy one product and you sell them another. The classic example is, "Do you want fries and a drink with your burger?" So the bank has a cross-sales incentive program that works as follows: The top cross-sales person at each branch will be entered into a drawing (so as to give a chance to employees at small-volume branches) to win an all-expenses-paid trip for two to Hawaii. Is this motivational? Well, that depends on the person. You see, expectancy theory is based on the subjective assessments of each individual. For a married new-accounts representative who sees 30 customers per day, the program might be very motivational: They reason that because of their large number of customers and the ease of cross-selling related products (e.g., a savings account with a checking account), they have a good chance of being the top seller at their branch if they try (expectancy); they also often win prizes in drawings (instrumentality) and would love to take their spouse on a trip (valence). In contrast, a young, unmarried loan representative who sees three to four customers per day may *not* find the program motivational: Because of their low volume of customers and their difficulty in cross-selling other products at loan closings, they believe that even if they try, they will not be the top seller in their branch (expectancy); they never win anything in drawings (instrumentality); and they aren't especially interested in the trip for two because they don't currently have a significant other to take along on the trip (valence).

The theory is summarized in Figure 6.7.

As this chapter shows, motivation affects the way we behave in and outside the workplace. Motivation gives us energy, determination, and a sense of purpose. Without these motivational forces directed by clear goals, nothing would ever be achieved. Needs and contents theories help us to understand the complex nature of motivation by analyzing the underlying factors that drive us to successfully accomplish our goals. Equity theory and justice teach us about the importance of fair treatment in the workplace, and expectancy theory shows us the role our own expectations play when it comes to achieving our goals. As the next chapter shows, a large part of motivation comes from within us—a drive that incentivizes us to accomplish great things out of a sense of personal fulfillment. It is this feeling that empowers us to contribute to a larger purpose.

IN REVIEW

6.1 Explain the basic motivation process

Motivation is a process by which behavior is *energized*, meaning we have the strength to keep going even when things aren't going our way; *directed*, meaning the efforts we invest in our work also benefit our employer; and *maintained*, meaning we keep our intention to work over some period of time to achieve our objectives. **Content theories** of motivation explain why people have different needs at different times and how these needs motivate behavior. Maslow's hierarchy of needs, Alderfer's ERG theory, McClelland's need theory, and Herzberg's two-factor theory are all examples of content theories. **Process theories** describe the cognitive processes through which needs are translated into behavior. Examples of process theories include equity theory, expectancy theory, and goal-setting theory.

6.2 Compare the various needs theories of motivation

Maslow's **hierarchy of needs** identifies five levels of individual needs, with physiological needs at the bottom of the hierarchy and self-actualization needs at the top. **ERG theory** suggests that people are motivated by three categories of needs—existence, relatedness, and growth needs—that can be satisfied in any order or at the same time depending on the circumstances. Herzberg's **two-factor theory** proposes that the first step to employee satisfaction is to eliminate poor *hygiene factors*. Managers then need to use *motivators* such as achievement, recognition, and responsibility to build job satisfaction. McClelland's **acquired needs theory** suggests three main categories of needs: need for achievement, need for affiliation, and need for power. We all have a dominant motivator, and each of the motivators, in particular achievement, can be learned.

6.3 Apply goal-setting theory in organizational contexts

Goal-setting theory suggests that human performance is directed by conscious goals and intentions. Effective goals are specific, difficult, accepted by employees, and accompanied by regular feedback.

6.4 Examine equity theory in the context of organizational justice and distinguish among the predictable outcomes of perceived inequity

The concept of **equity theory**, introduced by psychologist J. Stacey Adams, holds that motivation is based on our perception of how fairly we're being treated in comparison with others. According to this theory, our perception of what's fair depends on the ratio O/I, where O = our outcomes, like the recognition, pay, and status we enjoy, and I = inputs, like our effort, experience, and ability.

Organizational justice describes how people perceive fairness in workplace practices. **Distributive justice** is the degree to which people perceive outcomes to be fairly allocated. **Procedural justice** is the degree to which people perceive the implementation of company policies and procedures to be fair. **Interpersonal justice** refers to the level of dignity, politeness, and respect employees receive by supervisors during change implementation. **Informational justice** refers to the degree of access people are given to information and the explanations they are provided to convey why certain decisions are being made.

6.5 Describe the expectancy theory of motivation and its practical implications

Vroom's **expectancy theory** holds that people will choose certain behaviors over others with the expectation of a certain outcome. The theory describes motivation as a function of an individual's beliefs concerning effort-to-performance relationships (expectancy), work-outcome relationships (instrumentality), and the desirability of various work outcomes (valence).

KEY TERMS

Acquired needs theory (p. 133)
Behavioral goals (p. 137)
Content theories (p. 131)
Distributive justice (p. 139)
Equity theory (p. 137)
ERG theory (p. 132)
Expectancy (p. 140)
Expectancy theory (p. 140)
Goal-setting theory (p. 135)
Hierarchy of needs theory (p. 131)
Hygiene factors (p. 132)
Informational justice (p. 139)
Interpersonal justice (p. 139)
Instrumentality (p. 140)
Motivation (p. 129)
Motivators (p. 132)
Need for achievement (p. 133)
Need for affiliation (p. 133)
Need for power (p. 134)
Organizational justice (p. 139)
Perceived inequity (p. 138)
Performance goals (p. 137)
Procedural justice (p. 139)
Process theories (p. 131)
Two-factor theory (p. 132)
Valence (p. 140)

UP FOR DEBATE: MONEY, MONEY, MONEY!

The best way to motivate employees to work harder and perform at a higher level is to offer them more money. Agree or disagree?

EXERCISE 6.1: UNDERSTANDING EQUITY THEORY

Objective

The purpose of this exercise is to gain a greater appreciation of the equity theory of motivation.

Instructions

In groups of two or three, discuss the following scenario:

> You discover that a student in the class currently has an A in the course. This student has the highest grades on every exam and has an A on every paper that has been assigned. In questioning the student, you find out that she attends every class, reads each chapter four times, creates flash cards of every definition and concept, and meets with the professor every two weeks to go over material from the book and from classes.

The equity theory of motivation would indicate that some students would see this particular student as receiving an "easy A" without knowing all the work and dedication she's putting into the course. However, after talking to her, you know she's putting a significant amount of time and effort into the course and it's not an easy A at all.

In your group, answer the following questions:

1. Would you put in as much effort and time as this student with the hopes of earning an A in the course? Why or why not?
2. Could an A still be earned in the course *without* taking all the steps this student is taking? Explain.
3. Would anyone in the group simply not take those actions, instead hoping for the best grade they can get by doing what they typically do? In other words, are you content with your current efforts even if the result is a B or C in the course?

Reflection Questions

1. How important is equity theory in organizations? What experience do you have with it in a job you have held?
2. If you see something as unfair at work—such as someone getting a better schedule than you or more money than you—would you change your behaviors so that you could also have a more accommodating schedule or additional money? Why or why not?
3. In what circumstances at an organization can equity theory backfire for managers? What scenarios might occur in which employees do *not* change their behaviors but instead "give up" or protest the unfairness?

Exercise contributed by Steven Stovall, Southeast Missouri State University.

EXERCISE 6.2: IS MONEY A MOTIVATOR?

Objective

The purpose of this exercise is to grasp the concept of money as a motivator.

Instructions

This exercise utilizes a debate format to discuss money as a potential motivator of employees. The instructor will ask the group to raise their hand if they believe money is a motivator, then ask them to raise their hand if they don't. Once everyone has raised their hand for one side of the issue or the other, move to the section of the room that believes the same as you.

Once you are with those who feel similarly to you, elect two spokespeople to represent your side. The group will offer suggestions, making the case that money is indeed a motivator or that it isn't. After ten minutes of preparation, the four representatives—two from each side—will come to the front of the classroom and begin the debate.

The format of the debate will be as follows:

> A coin is tossed to determine which side goes first.
>
> The first side has three minutes to make an opening statement. Then the other side has three minutes to make their opening statement.
>
> After the opening statements, the representatives who made the first opening statement have two minutes to respond. Then the other side has two minutes for rebuttal.
>
> This continues—two minutes per side—for thirty minutes (or an appropriate amount of time given any time constraints associated with the class).
>
> Finally, three-minute closing statements are made. The side that gave the first opening statement goes first, and then the side that gave the second opening statement has the final word.
>
> During opening and closing statements as well as responses and rebuttals, there can be no interruptions or distractions from the other side or the audience.
>
> Those who remain in the audience can still participate. If they readily see an opportunity for the perfect response, they should write their idea down and hand it to one of their representatives.

Reflection Questions

1. Based on what you saw and heard during the debate, where do you stand on this issue? Do you think money is a motivator? Why or why not?
2. What instances in an organization can you think of where money *might* be a motivator to some employees? In which instances would money absolutely *not* be a motivator?
3. Does the amount of money in consideration make a difference as to whether a person *might* be motivated ($5 versus $10,000)? Explain.

Exercise contributed by Steven Stovall, Southeast Missouri State University.

EXERCISE 6.3: YOUR MOTIVATION FOR SELECTING YOUR MAJOR

Objective

This exercise will help you develop your ability to *explain* the basic motivation process, *compare* the different needs motivation theories, and *select* a needs motivation theory that is most useful in understanding situations.

Instructions

This exercise will help you to apply chapter concepts in analyzing your decisions and give you a foundation for making choices that are more likely to fulfill your expectations. In this exercise, you will be applying decision-making models and concepts you've learned in this chapter to better analyze the process of choosing a major.

Step 1. Select a partner for the exercise. Ideally, this person should be someone you don't know well and don't work with on a regular basis. The person who has had a birthday most recently will take the role of the *teller*, and the other person will be the *analyzer*. Both partners will have a chance to play each role. Introduce yourselves to each other, and tell each other your majors. (5 minutes)

Step 2. The *teller* should describe the process they went through to choose a major, being as explicit as possible. It may be that the decision wasn't a direct decision about a major—the person may have been following the advice of a parent or older sibling. If this is the case, the decision to be analyzed is why the person chose to follow someone else's advice on major selection. (10 to 15 minutes)

The *analyzer* should restate the major selection in terms of chapter concepts. Specifically, select one of the chapter needs theories and describe the *teller's* needs in terms of the theory. Once you and the *teller* agree on the needs, describe the selection process based on *the motivation process* model.

Step 3. Switch roles and repeat step 2. (10 to 15 minutes)

Step 4. Be prepared to report your analyses to the class. (10 to 20 minutes)

Reflection Questions

1. How conscious and rational was your major selection?
2. Does your major selection meet the needs identified in this exercise?
3. After examining your major selection process using chapter concepts, do you see any way to improve future decision processes to better meet your needs?
4. How could you apply this process to selecting a career or new job?

Exercise contributed by Milton R. Mayfield, Professor of Business, Texas A&M International University, and Jacqueline R. Mayfield, Professor of Business, Texas A&M International University.

ONLINE EXERCISE 6.1: WHICH THEORY FOR YOUR FAVORITE CHARACTERS?

Objective

The purpose of this exercise is to gain an appreciation for various theories of motivation.

Instructions

For this exercise, you will be utilizing a discussion board. Think about one of your favorite TV shows. On the discussion board, choose three of the main characters from that show and talk about which theory presented in this chapter might be most applicable for motivating that particular character if they worked in your organization.

For example, if you chose *Family Guy*, you might say that Stewie, one of the characters on the series, might be motivated by power from McClelland's acquired needs theory because he seeks to take over the world. However, for Peter, equity theory could be more applicable because he sometimes sees that someone is getting something he's not, and he considers that unfair. If Chris were your employee, though, you might find Maslow's hierarchy of needs to be most relevant, as he attempts to satisfy his most fundamental needs first before moving on to the next need.

If you are familiar with the shows and characters that others post about, offer agreement or other theories you think would be more applicable.

Reflection Questions

1. Why is it important for managers to know various theories of motivation?
2. As you were learning about the theories of motivation, which of them did you readily grasp and see that you could apply in the workplace? Explain.
3. Which theory or theories of motivation do you feel would be difficult to understand and implement in the workplace? Explain.

Exercise contributed by Steven Stovall, Southeast Missouri State University.

ONLINE EXERCISE 6.2: IDENTIFYING MOTIVATION THEORIES

Objective

The purpose of this exercise is to recognize theories of motivation.

Instructions

Conduct an internet search of a video of someone giving a motivational speech or presentation. Try to find one with a dynamic speaker that inspires you. View that video and review the theories of motivation presented in this chapter. Which theory or theories does the motivational speakers seem to be utilizing in the video?

Reflection Questions

1. Is inspiration the same as motivation? Explain.
2. What was it in the video you selected that attracted you enough to choose it? Was it the speaker? The message? Something else?
3. If you were to give a motivational speech, which theory or theories of motivation would you utilize in your presentation? Explain.

Exercise contributed by Steven Stovall, Southeast Missouri State University.

CASE 6.1: CARIBU

Caribu is an educational entertainment platform for families. Like a cross between FaceTime and Kindle, the app's two-way video chat and library of thousands of books, games, and interactive activities enable long-distance families to read bedtime stories, color, and play with their kids from anywhere in the world in real time.

Maxeme Tuchman, the CEO and cofounder of Caribu, is a first-generation American and college graduate born into a family known as "Jewban," a term for Cubans of Jewish heritage. Tuchman's grandparents were Holocaust survivors who met in a refugee camp in Europe before escaping to Havana.[56] After the 1959 Communist revolution, nearly 95% of the Jewish Cuban population left the Castro regime for the United States and other countries.[57] The Tuchmans settled in Miami, Florida, where Tuchman was born.

Education, the Only Equalizer

"My family would always say, 'The only thing you can take with you when you flee in the middle of the night is what's in your head,'" Tuchman told *Entrepreneur* magazine.[58] "My family is the personification of the American Dream and I feel an incredible burden to pay it forward to them and to this country that has given us so much."[59]Tuchman is dedicated to educational equity and has seen it from all angles. Prior to founding Caribu, Tuchman was a public school teacher, an executive director of Teach for America, a consultant at the Bill and Melinda Gates Foundation, an educational project manager in New York City and Washington, DC, and a White House Fellow at the Department of the Treasury, appointed by President Barack Obama.[60] "I was looking for different ways I could make the most impact, and everywhere I went, whether it was non-profit, government, public school, or higher-ed, it was adults fighting adults about what's best for adults. I had it and that's how I ended up in EdTech."[61]

Tuchman realized technology could be a way to circumvent the bureaucracy and nepotism of educational institutions. A digital platform was the key to quickly reaching kids with personalized learning wherever they were, geographically and pedagogically. Inspiration for the app concept came from a viral image of a soldier reading a story to his daughter online, struggling to hold a picture book up to the webcam. "It looked awkward and the soldier had to choose between looking at the book or his daughter. There had to be a better way," Tuchman told Harvard Business School

Alumni.[62] "Adults are fine spending hours on video calls, talking and asking each other questions. Children learn and build relationships through activity and play, and until Caribu, there really was no great way to do that virtually."

Concordant with their mission to bring people together through video calls, the Caribu team is as dispersed around the globe as its users. Tuchman leads Caribu from Miami, to "be a big dolphin in a small pond," and without a company headquarters, keeps the team motivated with a Positive Feedback channel on Slack. "Whenever we get great feedback from our customers or a great app review, we put it in there, so that we always have a channel where we can share all of the great work that we're doing for our families."[63]

For Such a Time as This

Caribu's dedication to distance learning paid great dividends during the COVID-19 pandemic. In March 2020, Caribu suspended the app's paywall (unlimited subscriptions are typically $9.99 per month or $99.99 annually). As a result, the platform saw its user base grow over 10 times in one day. Apple named it an App Store Best of 2020 app, and as of this writing Caribu has over 1 million users across more than 200 countries and territories.

> Families told us they felt like we were an essential business. You needed Instacart to get your groceries, Zoom to do your work calls, and Caribu to keep your family together.[64]

In addition to the parents and grandparents who flocked to the platform in 2020, Caribu saw tremendous growth from kids using the app with other kids to stay connected during the lockdowns. Content creators took notice, and outbound licensing requests to publishers and authors gave way to big brands like Cartoon Network and DC Comics coming to Caribu asking to be featured on the platform.[65]

Reflecting on Caribu's success and its impact on families during the pandemic, Tuchman told *Authority Magazine*, "I am so proud that the product that I built is helping kids and their families stay connected across the globe during one of the most difficult years of their lives."[66]

Critical-Thinking Questions

1. Maxeme Tuchman's motivation to make education equitable and accessible stems from a family background. Can you think of a principle from your upbringing or ancestry that inspires you similarly and that you would use to motivate your team as a start-up founder or manager in an organization?
2. Do you have children or small younger siblings? If you were a director at Caribu, how would you motivate your team members who weren't first-generation college students or Jewish Cuban Americans like Maxeme Tuchman?
3. Can you think of a use case for an interactive educational video chat app like Caribu besides keeping families connected?

Lawrence Schiller/Contributor/Getty Images

7 MOTIVATION: PRACTICES AND APPLICATIONS

LEARNING OBJECTIVES

By the end of this chapter, you will be able to:

7.1 Explain the concept of intrinsic and extrinsic motivation and their primary determinants

7.2 Differentiate among the various types of extrinsic rewards

7.3 Discuss the various facets of job design

7.4 Discuss psychological empowerment and its components

7.5 Evaluate various approaches to nontraditional work schedules

Case Study: Spotify

Human resources departments at large organizations agonize over crafting the perfect incentive plans to attract and retain top talent. Silicon Valley tech firms are famous for extravagant on-premises amenities like nap pods, meditation spaces, yoga classes, free massages, and arcade lounges equipped with the latest and greatest gaming systems. Profit sharing and ESOPs (employee stock ownership plans) are a more familiar benefit to workers at closely held and publicly traded corporations alike and are a tried-and-true way to ensure employees are motivated by their firm's profitability. Both equity allocation and the snazzy campuses replete with trendy perks that are almost synonymous with venture-backed start-ups are extrinsic rewards, however—just one facet of the employee motivation equation.

Spotify's approach to empowering employees to take ownership of their professional development and customizable compensation packages with unmatched family benefits led to the company being named *Newsweek*'s #1 Most Loved Workplace in America in 2021.[1] As the most popular platform of its kind, the Swedish music streaming giant requires little introduction. if you survey your classmates about their streaming service of choice, you'll likely find more votes for Spotify than competitors like Apple, Amazon, or YouTube Music. You could well be listening to your favorite artists on Spotify as you read this text. As of Spring 2022, Spotify reports over 406 million active monthly users, 180 million of whom are premium subscribers.[2] To keep pace with its rapid user growth and expansion into new markets, Spotify hired over 1,000 new employees in 2020 alone. The company's workforce (which it calls "the band") is now nearly 7,000 strong in 79 offices around the globe. Even with thousands of new members playing, Spotify has stayed true to the original band. Ching-Wei Chen, director of machine learning engineering, says, "Spotify is the biggest company I've worked for and it feels like the smallest. In terms of red tape and hierarchy, it feels like a small company."[3]

People Growth = Company Growth

When our people grow, Spotify grows. This is one of our core beliefs and it shapes how we do things.

Johanna Bolin Tingvall is the global head of GreenHouse, Spotify's learning and development team. On the Spotify HR blog, Tingvall explains that developing the company's people internally is just as important as adding new band members. "We need every employee to work under the assumption that they will get better at anything if they practice," Tingvall says. Encouraging a growth mindset is a foundational aspect of Spotify's employee training package and how it fosters intrinsic motivation in its workforce. Directly referencing *Drive: The Surprising Truth About What Motivates Us*, Daniel Pink's popular book on self-determination theory research, Tingvall adds, "Giving people room to grow is a lot about creating an atmosphere where mastery, autonomy, and purpose are possible for everyone."[4]

One unusual area where Spotifiers enjoy autonomy is in their freedom to customize their long-term incentive plan. Eligible employees and candidates receive a grant amount in U.S. dollars, which they can allocate themselves. Program information, booklets, and calculators are provided to help employees choose among ESOs (both at-the-money and out-of-the-money options are available), RSUs (restricted stock units), and cash, all instruments with a similar life, vesting schedule, and terms and conditions. Seventeen different combinations are available in Spotify's equity system, including a default package with a mix of options and RSUs for those who don't want to choose.[5]

Spotify's customizable compensation program has been well received by employees and candidates, but perhaps its most long-term incentives are the company's benefits for growing families.

Growing the Band the Old-Fashioned Way

Appropriate for a company born in Sweden, the number-one-ranked nation for parental leave support, Spotify's family-forming benefits are among the most comprehensive in any industry. Michael Kim, Spotify's head of human resources for JAPAC & MENA (Japan, the Asia Pacific, the Middle East, and North Africa), says, "The way that country [Sweden] approaches things like family-friendly benefits weaves very much into our company culture."[6] All full-time employees worldwide are eligible for six months of paid parental leave, followed by a month of location and schedule flexibility to ease the transition back to work. Parental leave doesn't have to be taken all at once; employees can elect to redeem the time in separate periods until the child's third birthday.[7] The policy applies to birth, adoption, and surrogacy and is inclusive of same-sex couples and single fathers, who are often left out by corporate parental leave programs.

Spotify's family benefits also extend to workers affected by infertility. According to FertilityIQ's 2021 Family Builder Workplace Index, the sum of more than 50,000 user-submitted reports of employer fertility coverage policies, the vast majority of IVF (in vitro fertilization) patients did not have their costs covered by insurance and paid for most or all of their treatments out of pocket.[8] Spotify offers employees a generous allowance for fertility assessment, IVF treatments, elective egg freezing and fertility preservation, adoption and donor services, and fertility education.

Adam Winer, head of content strategy, insights, and analytics, also credits Spotify's Swedish heritage for its take on employee benefits: "With a lot of perks at other tech companies there's this sense that they're treating you nicely so you'll work hard, to keep you in the office. Here it's because they genuinely care about you as a human being: 'We're Swedish! We believe these things! Our culture is we all go to the beach for a month in the summer and shut everything down because Sweden is dark and terrible for nine months out of the year so we must all enjoy it. That's well-being and that's important to us.'"

Critical-Thinking Questions

1. How does GreenHouse, Spotify's learning and development team, promote employee psychological empowerment?
2. Spotify's growth mindset explicitly seeks to stimulate intrinsic motivation among the band. Can you think of ways the company utilizes job design to that effect as well?
3. Give an example of how Spotify's Swedish-inspired extrinsic rewards can validate feelings of competence and self-determination and thus boost intrinsic motivation among the band.

INTRINSIC MOTIVATION

Have you ever participated in a sport just for the excitement of playing, written a piece of music just for the pleasure of listening to it, or participated in a video game for the thrill of it? If so, you have been inspired by **intrinsic motivation**, which is the performance of tasks for one's own innate satisfaction.[9] As our case study shows, Spotify nurtures intrinsic motivation by encouraging a growth mindset, which teaches employees that they can always get better with practice. Studies show that intrinsic motivation is accelerated by doing things that are not for one's own benefit, such as contributing to a cause. For example, when university fundraisers were shown the impact of the money donated by the alumni on financially struggling students, they became even more motivated to raise money, which led to a 400% increase in productivity.[10]

Intrinsic motivation consists of two main mechanisms: need for competence and need for self-determination.[11] The **need for competence** is the motivation we derive from stretching and exercising our capabilities. For example, Spotify consistently challenges its employees by giving them the autonomy and the freedom to take ownership of their professional development.

The **need for self-determination** describes the feeling of motivation and control we get from efforts that don't rely on any external influences. For example, Spotify's efforts to encourage a growth mindset motivates employees to embrace challenges, learn from criticism, and take greater risks.

In contrast, **extrinsic motivation** is the performance of tasks or activities with the expectation of a reward or avoidance of punishment or negative outcomes.[12] Extrinsic motivators can be tangible, such as a financial reward, or intangible, such as fame or praise. A recent Hubspot survey showed that almost 70% of employees work harder when they're given constructive feedback and recognition.[13] Business communication platform Slack reported that daily greetings and regular check-ins for remote workers were also a powerful method of recognizing employees.[14] In the next section, we will further explore the different types of extrinsic awards in the workplace.

TYPES OF EXTRINSIC REWARDS

Extrinsic rewards are external awards offered to employees, such as salary, bonuses, and paid vacations.[15] Rather than simply playing a sport, writing music, or engaging in gaming for the "feel-good factor," you might carry out these activities for other incentives, such as money or recognition. Extrinsic rewards can either increase intrinsic motivation, if the rewards are high, or decrease it if they are low. On one hand, extrinsic rewards act as a source of competency information. That is, financial rewards directly and concretely show the employee they're valued and thus increase employee feelings of competence and self-determination and increase intrinsic motivation. For example, Spotify offers family-forming benefits as part of its compensation package, which includes generous parental leave in addition to policies for workers affected by infertility. These benefits show employees that the company cares about their personal and professional lives, which encourages them to work even harder for the company. On the other hand, when people feel they're being under-rewarded, their feelings of self-determination decrease, as does their intrinsic motivation.[16]

Let's explore the different types of extrinsic rewards.

Seniority-Based Pay

Guaranteed wages and salary increases based on the amount of time the employee has spent with the organization are called **seniority-based pay**.[17] These wages, which are paid at fixed intervals such as monthly or weekly, tend to encourage longevity and commitment, which reduces turnover. However, seniority-based

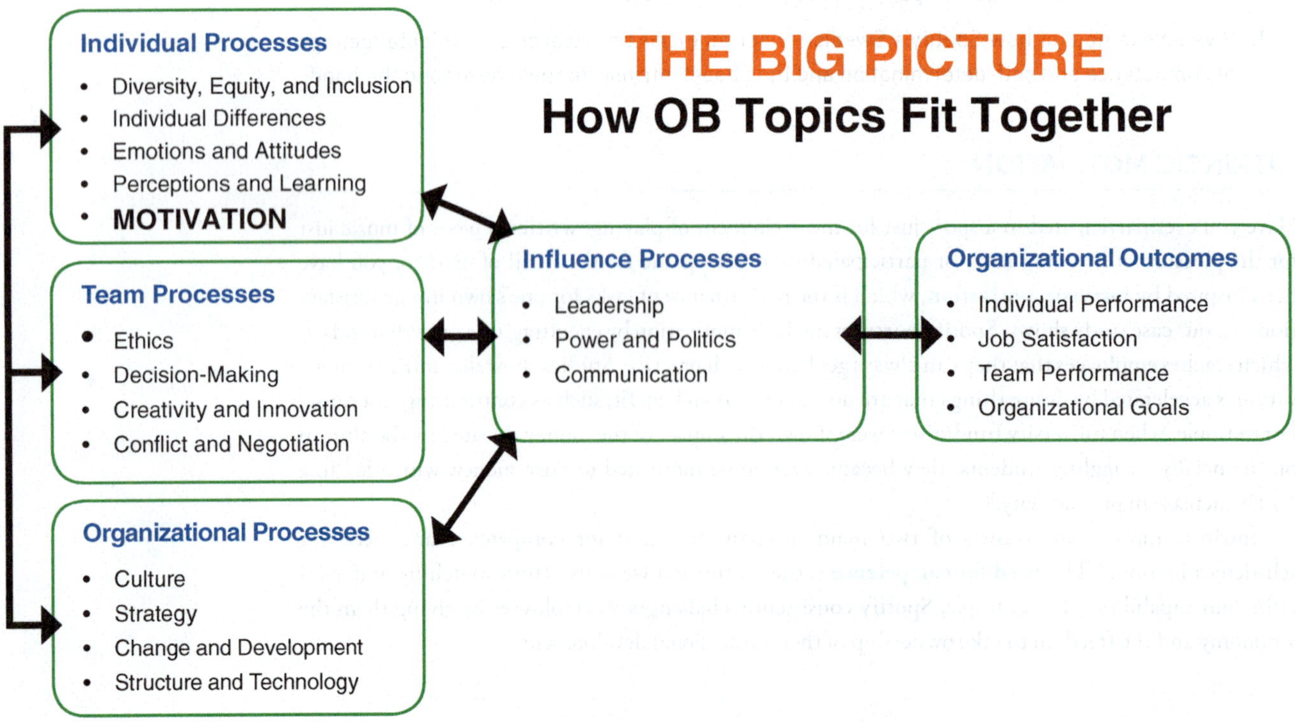

pay can also be demotivating when employees know they'll get paid regardless of how they perform, which also encourages poor performers to stay in an organization much longer. From the 1950s to the 1990s, Japanese companies rewarded the people who had been there the longest with the most money. In other words, the older you were, the more you were rewarded. As employees tended to stay in a job for life, the system worked by rewarding people for their loyalty. However, when the economic bubble burst in Japan, many employees were made redundant, and graduates were reluctant to join the first company that offered them roles. Today, despite the efforts of big companies like Sony, Hitachi, and Fujitsu to move away from this model, labor experts believe that seniority-based pay remains the norm.[18]

EXAMINING THE EVIDENCE

GAMIFICATION AS A MOTIVATOR IN THE WORKPLACE

Increasingly, companies are using "gamification" as a means of increasing employee motivation at work. Gamification involves the integration of game elements, such as points, badges, and leaderboards, into nongame work contexts. Proponents say it increases employee motivation by making basic work tasks more intrinsically motivating. In contrast, critics suggest that employees could view game elements such as points and leaderboards as an extrinsic form of behavioral control that might actually undermine their motivation. Recently, researchers Robert Mitchell, Lisa Schuster, and Hyun Seung Jin conducted a study aimed at determining when and how extrinsic feedback through gamification elements would be intrinsically motivating to employees.[19] Their findings suggest that extrinsic gamification elements can in fact decrease employee motivation, especially when they're perceived by employees as social pressures or as rewards and punishments. On the other hand, the researchers' results also show that gamification elements have the potential to satisfy employees' psychological needs, leading to intrinsic motivation when employees perceive personal benefits from the gamified elements. Consequently, organizations interested in using gamification should try to structure gamified work tasks in ways that bring value to both the organization and the individual. In this way, gamification can be both fun and motivational while providing meaningful and valuable benefits to both the organization and the employees.

Critical-Thinking Questions

1. What specific actions can managers take so that employees are less likely to view workplace gamification as controlling and more likely to view it as valuable and enjoyable?
2. Would you enjoy working in a gamified work environment? Why or why not?

Job Content–Based Pay

Job content–based pay is based on an evaluation of a job's worth to the organization and its relationship to other jobs within the organization.[20] It has been the most traditional compensation structure because it is thought to be one of the best ways to maintain pay equity. Employees under this structure also tend to be more motivated to compete for promotions and a higher rate of pay. At the same time, employees who are competing against each other may exaggerate their duties to their managers to try to impress, or they may hoard resources to get ahead. These activities can also create a psychological distance across teams and hierarchies.[21]

A restaurant manager and employees review changes to the menu.

hobo_018/Getty Images

Skill-Based Pay

Skill-based pay rewards employees for the acquisition of new skills that lead to enhanced work performance.[22] More and more companies are offering skill-based compensation programs to equip employees with the skills and knowledge they need to keep up with the demands of a constantly changing business landscape. This type of reward can be a useful way to motivate employees while providing them with an opportunity to showcase their new skills and competencies. As a result, workers are more flexible and productive. However, there can be some disadvantages. There is the high cost of additional bonuses and training to consider, not to mention that some people, regardless of how many skills they attain, may not have the desire or capability to manage a team.[23] This is why companies need to focus on personal development, not just skills-based development. Online employment service LinkedIn has created a skills-based hiring initiative to match employers and job seekers to roles that require particular skills. LinkedIn vice president of product Hari Srinivasan says, "We believe that by taking a skills-based approach to opportunity we can remove barriers for candidates that might not have the degree or network, while also increasing the size of employer talent pools, often letting them pinpoint quality applicants for hard-to-fill roles."[24]

Performance-Based Pay

Performance-based pay is a financial incentive awarded to employees for meeting specific goals or objectives.[25] Two levels of performance-based pay exist: individual level and team and organization level.

Individual-Level Performance-Based Pay

Individual-level pay options include piece rate plans, merit pay, and bonus pay.

- **Piece rate** is a pay plan in which workers are paid a fixed sum for each unit of production completed. In other words, people are rewarded for the quantity of goods they produce regardless of how long it has taken them. While this used to be the pay plan most common in the manufacturing and construction industries, it is less common now since the introduction of the minimum wage.
- **Merit pay** links pay increases directly to performance. In other words, it rewards high-performing employees with additional pay. Asset management firm Mercer reported that 90% of organizations measure performance as a basis for salary adjustments.[26] Studies have also found that companies that award merit pay to employees have higher levels of loyalty, morale, and staff retention.[27] Although merit pay is a useful method to show employees where they stand, companies must set out a clear and fair merit pay structure to prevent jealousy, favoritism, job insecurity, and unhealthy competition among employees.
- **Bonus pay** rewards employees for good performance in addition to their base salary. But bonuses aren't just given to people working within organizations. In the wake of COVID-19, there was an increase in sign-on bonuses across most sectors, with the healthcare sector offering lucrative sign-on bonuses to secure top talent for specialty jobs. For example, Ascension Health Alliance offered a sign-on bonus of up to $100,000 for a neurologist specializing in multiple sclerosis.[28]

Overall, research conducted by the University of East Anglia in the United Kingdom shows that performance-based pay can have negative effects on employee well-being. A study recently published in the *Human Resources Management Journal* based on a survey of almost 14,000 employees revealed that people who receive performance-based pay not only work harder but also end up with higher stress levels and lower levels of job satisfaction.[29] As head researcher Chidiebere Ogbonnaya says, "by tying employees' performance to financial incentives, employers send signals to employees about their intention to reward extra work effort with more pay. Employees in turn receive these signals and feel obliged to work harder in exchange for more pay."[30] The result? Overworked employees who end up feeling exploited by their employer.

Employers can try to decrease the negative effects of performance-based pay by providing a balance between the amount of work carried out by employees and the type of rewards on offer. Talking to employees about their compensation is a good way to gauge their thoughts and address any concerns they may have.

Team- and Organization-Level Performance-Based Pay

There are three types of team and organization performance-based plans:

- **Gain sharing** is a system whereby managers agree to share the benefits of cost savings with staff in return for their contribution to the company's performance.[31] French restaurant Bouillon Chartier based in Paris operates a voluntary gain-sharing plan whereby employees are rewarded a percentage of their annual wages when targets are met or surpassed.[32]
- **Profit sharing** is a pay system in which the organization shares its profits with employees.[33] Automaker Ford and airlines Delta and Southwest offer substantial profit-sharing programs.
- **Employee stock ownership plans** (ESOPs) allow employees to purchase company stock, often at below-market price, as one of their benefits.[34] Many small businesses use ESOPs because of their big tax benefits and because they allow the owner to keep control of the business until the time comes to hand over the reins to eligible employees. Supermarket chain Publix Super Markets is the largest employee-owned company in the U.S. Regardless of workers' position in the company, they all receive stock after 12 months of employment.[35]

Studies have shown that companies who give employees a stake in the business through profit-sharing programs and ESOPs tend to have a happier workforce, experience higher financial performance, and encounter less turnover than their peers.[36]

Motivation Over Time

Rewards can be either motivators or demotivators, depending on the situation and the individual. But when it comes to those employees who respond well to rewards, does it mean they stay motivated over time? Not necessarily. Research shows that as we get older, our ability to reason, focus, and remember (fluid intelligence) declines, yet our capacity to absorb educational and experiential knowledge (crystallized intelligence) increases (Figure 7.1).

In other words, as we reach middle age and above, we may struggle more with roles that demand high levels of fluid intelligence (e.g., engineering), which could affect our performance, motivation, and self-esteem. In contrast, we may perform better in roles that require crystallized intelligence, as it alleviates the pressure of the factors associated with fluid intelligence. So how does performance change

FIGURE 7.1 ■ Fluid Intelligence and Crystallized Intelligence Across the Life Span

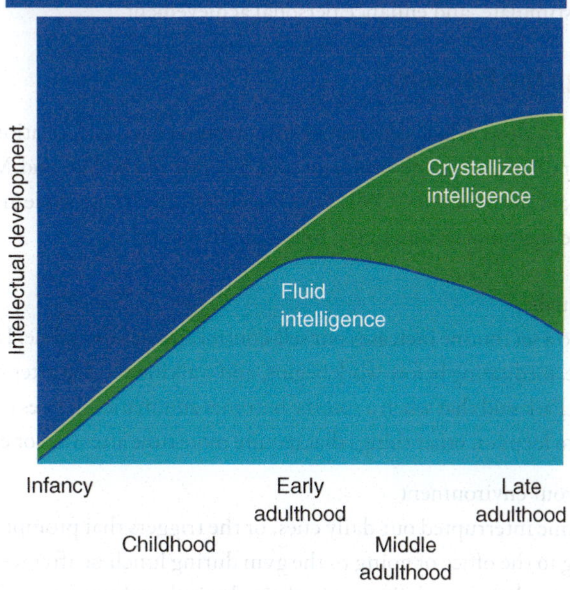

with age? Researchers propose that stronger rewards and incentives are necessary to motivate aging employees in jobs requiring crystallized intelligence.

However, despite the decline in fluid intelligence over time, further research shows that it is entirely possible to make up for this decline with crystallized intelligence. For example, say you're a student training to be a pharmacist. Learning about pharmacy requires high levels of fluid intelligence in order to absorb complex facts and procedures. However, after years of study, you will have gathered a huge body of information and knowledge (crystallized intelligence), which means you'll have less to learn over time. As you get older, you will be able to use this expert knowledge not only to function in your role as a pharmacist but also to advise others.

Yet there are some jobs that require consistent levels of fluid intelligence more suited to younger workers. In a 2009 study of U.S. air traffic controllers, researchers discovered that experienced controllers between ages 53 and 64 took around the same time to reroute two planes heading for a collision as the younger, more inexperienced controllers.[37] In contrast, the younger and experienced controllers took half the time. The study shows that in this particular role, where decisions have to be made quickly and problems need to be solved in uncertain situations, fluid intelligence is more valuable than crystallized intelligence. It also explains why the U.S. Federal Aviation Authority requires that air traffic controllers retire by the age of 56.[38]

However, that's not the only difference between generations when it comes to motivation. A study of U.S. high school seniors in 1976, 1991, and 2006 investigating the differences in work values between the baby boomer, Generation X, and millennial generations showed that leisure values increased while work values decreased steadily across the three generations.[39] Specifically, extrinsic values (status, money) were highest among Generation X, followed by millennials and then baby boomers. Millennials placed less importance on intrinsic values (having an interesting, results-oriented job) than baby boomers; in other words, millennials are more likely to value leisure activities over the workplace.

These researchers also discovered that millennials do not favor altruistic values (e.g., helping others, contributing to society), social values (e.g., making friends), or intrinsic values (e.g., intellectual stimulation, interesting job) more than previous generations.

It is important that employers take these findings into account when hiring people from different generations. For example, knowing that Generation X tends to value extrinsic rewards more than millennials should help managers recognize that millennials may need to be motivated by more than a paycheck and bonus.

Similarly, in order to recruit and retain millennials, companies need to focus on work/life balance and flexible schedules. Millennials who work under these conditions are more likely to stay with an organization and less likely to job hop.

While younger generations may need more than a bonus to become motivated, most people in the workforce, regardless of their generation, have one thing in common: their desire to work in a job designed to challenge, stimulate, and enhance personal achievement.

Motivation Through the Pandemic

Our motivation tends to drop when our autonomy, competence, and relationships are negatively impacted. In 2021, Lora Park, associate professor and director of the Self and Motivation Lab at the University of Buffalo, said she believed COVID has hugely affected these three areas.[40] Research shows that people can increase their motivation in the following five ways[41]:

- Create daily rituals

  Getting into a set routine increases our self-control and self-discipline. Laying your clothes out the night before, meditating before work begins, and walking the dog after work are all examples of small rituals. Park said that when a routine becomes automatic, "it frees up your mental energy to then be able to focus on other things that require more time attention or energy."

- Set up cues in your environment

  The pandemic interrupted our daily cues, or the triggers that prompt us to do something, such as walking to the office or going to the gym during lunch or after work. People working at home can set up their own daily cues in their physical environment—for example, by creating a designated work space that will mentally prepare them for work when they enter and disconnect them from work when they leave.

- Reward yourself

  Although rewards can motivate us, research shows that the timing of the reward also matters. Studies show that people are more intrinsically motivated by a task if they reward themselves during the task rather than waiting until they complete it. For example, treating yourself to some chocolate or a cup of coffee during a tedious work project might increase your motivation.

- Make time for positive moments

  During turbulent periods, it can be tough to stay positive, yet research has shown that positive emotions enhance our work performance, physical and mental health, social relationships, and income. Fostering positive moments during the day, such as texting a friend or watching a funny video, can increase our motivation.

- Recognize triggers that impact motivation

  It's important to recognize the triggers that lead to lack of motivation so you can make an attempt to boost your motivation levels. For example, being overworked or burnt out can lead to poor motivation, but you can address this by adjusting your schedule to working less hours or taking time off.

MOTIVATION THROUGH JOB DESIGN

Job design is a method of setting forth the duties and responsibilities of a job with the intention of improving productivity and performance.[42] The concept of job design can be traced back to the theory of **scientific management**, introduced in the early 20th century by Frederick Taylor and his colleagues, who analyzed workflow through systematic observation of the tasks to be performed. Taylor designed experiments to calculate the motions and time required to complete workplace tasks in order to improve efficiencies—for example, testing the various motions required for laying bricks to understand how workers could complete the task more quickly.

Through these "time and motion" studies, Taylor not only discovered better and faster ways to complete tasks but also found that certain people could work more efficiently than others, therefore concluding that selecting the right people for the job was another important part of workplace efficiency.

Also known as "Taylorism," scientific management focused on how to make people, assembly line workers in particular, more efficient at their jobs through training, monitoring, and detailed planning.

Job Design Approaches

There are three main approaches to job design: job enlargement, job rotation, and job enrichment.

Job enlargement is a method of job design that increases the range of interactive tasks and duties associated with a job.[43] For example, if you were a host at a restaurant, you might leave your station during quiet periods to collect glasses for the bar staff. In doing so, your job would have expanded to include other duties.

Job rotation is a process of periodically moving employees from one job to another.[44] Typically, rotational programs offer at least three different roles with a set amount of time assigned to each role. Dutch brewer Heineken provides a job rotation program where college graduates spend time in different departments such as packaging, brewing, and product development. After completing the program, the employees are given the option to choose which department they like best.[45]

Job enrichment means increasing the scope of a job to make it more complex, stimulating, and satisfying for employees.[46] Job enrichment differs from job enlargement based on the complexities of the tasks included in the role. In the example above, your tasks as a restaurant host may have been expanded to collecting glasses, but that duty in itself is unlikely to challenge you or allow for personal growth. However, if you were given more responsibility or empowered to work on your own ideas and make decisions that would normally have been made by senior management, you might experience the positive effects of job enrichment.

Job Characteristics Model

Job enrichment can be further explained through the Hackman and Oldham **job characteristics model** (see Figure 7.2), which identifies five core dimensions of jobs: skill variety, task identity, task significance, autonomy, and feedback.[47] Hackman and Oldham created a scoring system for employees based on these five characteristics; higher scores indicate more positive psychological states and outcomes.

Skill variety is the extent to which workers utilize a variety of skills. Employees are more likely to be motivated if they're using a range of skills in their roles rather than using one set repeatedly.

Task identity is the extent to which an employee completes an entire piece of work from start to finish. When employees identify with a task, they're more likely to be motivated enough to see the task through to completion. For example, furniture makers may have high task identity if they build a desk from start to finish, while factory workers on an assembly line may have low task identity if they have only one main task to perform.

Task significance is the extent to which employees see meaning in their roles on the organization. Employees are more motivated to do well when they feel their work is significant to the organization and they are shown recognition for their contributions. Employee referral platform Hireology, based in Chicago, holds weekly meetings to keep teams up-to-date on business performance and announce shout-outs to ensure employees feel appreciated.

Autonomy is the extent to which employees are given the freedom and independence to schedule and perform tasks. Studies show that employees are happier, more motivated, and feel more personally invested in a company when they're given the power to use their own initiative and make their own decisions.[48] California-based outdoor clothing company Patagonia allows its employees to create their own work schedules by choosing when they want to work. They are still expected to work full-time, but they have the freedom to take time off to go surfing or explore other outdoor pursuits. Patagonia's autonomous culture motivates employees by promoting a healthy lifestyle and giving them the freedom to tailor their working week in a way that suits them.[49]

Feedback is the extent to which employees are provided with timely information regarding their job performance. Yet it's just as important for employees to share feedback as it is for them to receive it, but only if they're given a safe space to raise any issues or concerns. Employee feedback management platform AllVoices reported that 74% of surveyed employees would feel more inclined to give honest feedback if it was truly anonymous.[50]

The Hackman and Oldham job characteristics model enables companies to design new jobs better and redesign existing ones in order to enhance employee motivation. According to the theory, an uninspiring, monotonous job tends to stifle motivation, whereas a more challenging, stimulating role increases it. Managers who ensure workers are exposed to a variety of skills, provide them with a sense of authority and ownership, impose on them an awareness of the significance of the task, and give regular feedback tend to have more motivated employees.

While it's important to design or redesign roles to motivate employees, this approach is unlikely to succeed without the benefit of psychological empowerment.

FIGURE 7.2 ■ Job Characteristics Model

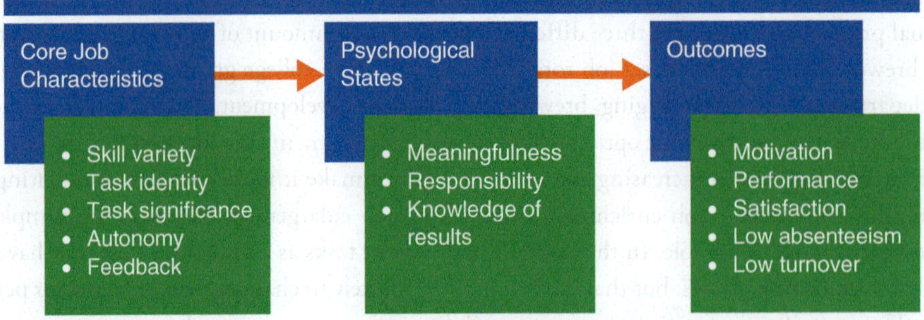

Source: Hackman, J. R., & Oldham, G. R. (1980). *Work redesign.* Addison-Wesley.

PSYCHOLOGICAL EMPOWERMENT

Another facet of the job characteristics model is the concept of **psychological empowerment**, the extent to which employees feel a sense of personal fulfillment and intent when carrying out tasks, along with the belief that their work contributes to some larger purpose.[51] There are four main factors associated with psychological empowerment: *competence, self-determination, impact*, and *meaningfulness*.

Competence is the ability to perform work tasks successfully.[52] It stands to reason that employees who are regarded as the most competent are assigned more tasks and responsibilities than the less competent. However, research from Duke University, the University of Georgia, and the University of Colorado shows that competent people may bear the burden of more work, especially in situations where other coworkers receive the same rewards for doing less.[53]

Self-determination is making use of one's skills, knowledge, and strengths to make choices and initiate work tasks.[54] Studies have found that employees who have a higher level of autonomy, the freedom to choose how to carry out their tasks and duties, and more control over decision-making tend to perform better than people who have less control.[55] This means that employees with self-determination tend to be more effective, motivated, and more satisfied with their jobs overall. Research has found the same principle to be at play in the sports world; self-determination in athletes leads to high performance, a drive to overcome obstacles and achieve goals, and an increased tendency to maintain a regular exercise regime.[56]

Impact is the degree to which an individual can influence work-related outcomes.[57] Rossanna Ceccato is the founder of disruptive clothing platform Redress, a Florida-based company that provides customers with an opportunity to swap barely used clothing for the styles available on the platform. Ceccato is a good example of someone making a valuable impact on the environment. Conscious fashion is the second-biggest polluting industry in the world, with over 5 billion pieces of clothing ending up in landfills, but through Ceccato's business model, customers have the ability to eliminate waste in order to create a more sustainable environment.[58]

Meaningfulness refers to the positive meaning and significance of an activity.[59] Research from the Brookings Institute found that people who believe their work to be meaningful make more of an effort in their roles, are less likely to call in sick, are more likely to postpone retirement, and are more inclined to engage in further training to improve their skills.[60] Meaningful jobs include those of teachers, surgeons, therapists, and members of the clergy.[61]

When a problematic issue in the workplace is resolved, employees are motivated to work harder.

NONTRADITIONAL WORK SCHEDULES

Flexible work schedules are becoming more popular with today's workers and their employers, particularly in the aftermath of the pandemic. According to a Microsoft Trend Report, the traditional nine-to-five working day is on the way out and remote working is becoming the more common choice.[62] Rather than putting in the traditional forty-hour week, many employees are permitted to work from home, choose their own working hours and how they want to work, and work remotely from different countries.

Free agents and part-time workers are two types of workers who adhere to nontraditional work schedules. **Free agents** are independent workers who supply organizations with short-term talent for projects that need to be completed within a certain amount of time.[63] Companies use free agents to fill gaps and add value in times of uncertainty. In sports, a free agent is an athlete who is not bound by any contract and is free to sign with another that offers the most money.

A **freelancer** is a type of free agent who can work for multiple employers, giving a limited amount of time to each. Freelancing gives people the opportunity to set their own schedules and create a better work/life balance. It has become a popular choice for younger generations in particular, with 50% of Gen Z and 44% of millennials working as freelancers. Growing industries such as accounting, customer service, digital marketing, and real estate offer opportunities to those looking for freelance roles.[64]

Similarly, **part-time workers** are workers who supply organizations with part-time talent for projects that need to be completed within a certain amount of time. Part-time workers work fewer hours than full-time workers but may supplement these hours by working for other employers. There are a number of reasons people may prefer to work part-time, such as to fulfill parenting responsibilities, to leave room for other hobbies and interests, or to pursue further training or study for a degree. Part-time jobs for students may include pet sitting, tutoring, cleaning, bar work, delivery driving, or babysitting.

Types of Nontraditional Work Schedules

There are four main nontraditional work schedules commonly adopted by employers in today's workplace (see Figure 7.3).

Flextime means flexible working hours. In a flextime arrangement, an employee can customize their own work hours within the limits established by management.[65] For example, an employee might work a 7 a.m. to 3 p.m. shift rather than the more traditional 9 a.m. to 5 p.m. workday.

Compressed workweeks give employees the benefit of an extra day off by allowing them to work their usual number of hours in fewer days per pay period.[66] For example, the employee might work four 10-hour days each week and then enjoy a three-day weekend, or work 80 hours in nine days and have an extra day off every other week.

Job sharing divides one full-time job among two or more people who work predetermined hours.[67] Job sharers can hand over their work to the next person when their part of the shift ends and the next begins. For example, you might work Monday to Wednesday and then hand over to your job share

FIGURE 7.3 ■ Examples of Nontraditional Work Schedules

WORK SCHEDULE	MONDAY	TUESDAY	WEDNESDAY	THURSDAY	FRIDAY
Flextime	7 a.m.–3 p.m.	8 a.m.–4 p.m.	10 a.m.–6 p.m.	8 a.m.–4 p.m.	9 a.m.–5 p.m.
Compressed Workweek	9 a.m.–7 p.m.	9 a.m.–7 p.m.	9 a.m.–7 p.m.	9 a.m.–7 p.m.	off
Job Sharing	Lucy 9 a.m.–2 p.m., Nathan 2 p.m.–6 p.m.	Lucy 9 a.m.–2 p.m., Nathan 2 p.m.–6 p.m.	Lucy 9 a.m.–2 p.m., Nathan 2 p.m.–6 p.m.	Lucy 9 a.m.–2 p.m., Nathan 2 p.m.–6 p.m.	Lucy 9 a.m.–2 p.m., Nathan 2 p.m.–6 p.m.
Telecommuting	9 a.m.–5 p.m.	9 a.m.–5 p.m.	9 a.m.–5 p.m.	Work from home	Work from home

partner, who then works from Wednesday to Friday, resulting in each of you working two and a half days per week. The U.S. federal government is a big advocate of job sharing because it benefits those who need a more flexible lifestyle.[68]

Remote work means working from home or from a remote location on a computer or other advanced telecommunications system linked to the main office.[69] This gives workers greater flexibility of working hours and location. Technological barriers could impede telecommuting for everyone. Although an estimated three-quarters of American adults have high-speed internet service at home, around 14% of households in urban areas and many in rural areas still remain disconnected.[70]

Though more companies are using at least one of these alternative work schedules, other businesses are coming up with even more creative ways to meet the needs of their employees.

Take the premise of unlimited vacation, for instance. Many companies, such as Mammoth, LinkedIn, and Netflix, are seeing the benefits of offering their employees as much vacation as they want or need as long as the job gets done. TV streaming app Roku doesn't track vacation days or have official holidays.[71] While this policy may sound easy to exploit, it does work in companies with a culture of respect and trust.

However, unlimited vacation may not be right for all companies. UK software firm CharlieHR revoked the unlimited vacation program in favor of an alternative as employees didn't make use of it, mainly because of their anxiety over not knowing the limit and stress about how to prepare for deadlines and handovers. As one CharlieHR employee explained, "unlimited means there's all this possibility . . . there's so much choice, that you never choose."[72]

As Table 7.1 shows, even the most flexible working arrangements have their drawbacks. Some people who work remotely or telecommute may feel isolated or cut off from coworkers, while others may not be suited to working from home and the potential distractions of family life. Job sharing can be frustrating if the sharers don't work well together, and holding down a multitude of part-time or free-agent jobs can lead to overwork and stress. This is why companies need to tailor their alternate work schedules to their employees with a view to retaining a productive, efficient, and committed workforce.

In this chapter, we have explored the application of motivation and its impact on employees, the difference between intrinsic and extrinsic motivation, the powerful effect of job design, and the motivational components of psychological empowerment and nontraditional work schedules. As we have seen, motivation is unsustainable without the support of teams and managers. In Chapter 8, we explore the nature of teams and the way people actively work together to achieve organizational goals.

TABLE 7.1 ■ Pros and Cons of Working Remotely

Pros of Working Remotely	Cons of Working Remotely
Flexible work schedule	Difficulty unplugging from work
No commute	Loneliness
More time with family	Technical issues
Ability to work from any location	Distractions from home
Better work/life balance	Difficulty staying motivated

IN REVIEW

7.1 Explain the concept of intrinsic and extrinsic motivation and their primary determinants

Intrinsic motivation moves us to perform tasks for our own innate satisfaction. The two main mechanisms of intrinsic motivation are *need for competence* and *need for self-determination*. The **need for competence** motivates us to gain satisfaction by stretching and exercising our capabilities. The **need for self-determination** motivates us to achieve feelings of satisfaction and control through efforts that don't rely on external influences. **Extrinsic motivation** is the performance of tasks or activities with the expectation of a reward or avoidance of punishment or negative outcomes. Extrinsic motivators can be tangible, such as a financial reward, or intangible, such as fame or praise.

7.2 Differentiate among the various types of extrinsic rewards

Extrinsic rewards are external contributions awarded to employees, such as salary, bonuses, and paid vacations. **Seniority-based pay** is guaranteed wages and salary increases based on the amount of time the employee has spent with the organization. **Job content–based pay** is a salary paid based on the evaluation of a job's worth. **Skill-based pay** rewards employees for the acquisition and development of new skills that lead to enhanced work performance. **Performance-based pay** is a financial incentive awarded to employees for meeting certain goals or objectives.

7.3 Discuss the various facets of job design

Job design is a method of setting the duties and responsibilities of a job with the intention of improving productivity and performance. **Job enlargement** increases the range of tasks and duties associated with a job. **Job rotation** is the process of periodically moving staff employees from one job to another. **Job enrichment** entails increasing the scope of a job to make it more complex, interesting, stimulating, and satisfying for employees.

7.4 Discuss psychological empowerment and its components

Psychological empowerment is the extent to which employees feel a sense of personal fulfillment and intent when carrying out tasks, together with a belief that their work contributes to some larger purpose. There are four main beliefs associated with psychological empowerment. **Competence** is a belief in a person's ability to perform work tasks successfully. **Self-determination** is making use of one's skills, knowledge, and strengths to make choices and initiate work tasks. **Impact** is the feeling of making a difference. **Meaningfulness** refers to the positive meaning and significance of an activity.

7.5 Evaluate various approaches to nontraditional work schedules

Free agents are independent workers who supply organizations with short-term talent for projects or time-bound objectives. **Part-time workers** (similar to free agents) are workers who supply organizations with part-time talent for projects or time-bound objectives.

There are four main nontraditional work schedules commonly adopted by employers. **Flextime** means flexible working hours that can be customized within the limits established by management. **Compressed workweeks** give you the benefit of an extra day off by allowing you to work your usual number of hours in fewer days per pay period. **Job sharing** is when one full-time job is divided among two or more people according to predetermined hours. **Remote work** means working from home or from a remote location on a computer or other advanced telecommunications system linked to the office.

KEY TERMS

Bonus pay (p. 154)
Competence (p. 159)
Compressed workweeks (p. 160)
Employee stock ownership plans (p. 155)
Extrinsic motivation (p. 152)
Extrinsic rewards (p. 152)
Flextime (p. 160)
Free agents (p. 162)
Freelancer (p. 160)
Gain sharing (p. 155)
Impact (p. 159)
Intrinsic motivation (p. 151)
Job characteristics model (p. 158)
Job content–based pay (p. 153)
Job design (p. 157)
Job enlargement (p. 157)
Job enrichment (p. 157)
Job rotation (p. 157)
Job sharing (p. 160)
Meaningfulness (p. 159)
Merit pay (p. 154)
Need for competence (p. 151)

Need for self-determination (p. 152)
Part-time workers (p. 160)
Performance-based pay (p. 154)
Piece rate (p. 154)
Profit sharing (p. 155)
Psychological empowerment (p. 159)
Remote work (p. 161)
Scientific management (p. 157)
Self-determination (p. 159)
Seniority-based pay (p. 152)
Skill-based pay (p. 153)

UP FOR DEBATE: WORK FROM HOME OR FROM THE OFFICE?

Given the recent pandemic, companies are grappling with the decision of whether to allow employees to continue to work from home. Employees who are *not* managers should be the ones making this decision. Agree or disagree?

Explain your answer.

EXERCISE 7.1: UNDERSTANDING JOB DESIGN

Objective

The purpose of this exercise is to gain a greater appreciation of job design.

Instructions

In groups of two to three, attempt to improve the overall job design of the following jobs. For each job title, decide whether you would use job rotation, job enlargement, job enrichment, or a combination of these. Explain how you would implement each form of job design.

- University president
- Cashier at a fast-food restaurant
- Janitor
- President of a major corporation
- College professor

Reflection Questions

1. What challenges did you have in enhancing the overall job design of each job? How did you overcome those challenges?
2. Which was the most difficult job to enhance the job design for? Explain.
3. Which was the easiest job to enhance the job design for? Explain.
4. Choose a job you have held either in the past or currently. If your supervisor gave you permission to enhance the job design of that job in any way you wanted, how would you change the job through effective job design?
5. Why do managers attempt to improve job design in the workplace? What benefit do managers receive from this?

Exercise contributed by Steven Stovall, Southeast Missouri State University.

EXERCISE 7.2: CHARITY BEGINS WITH MOTIVATION

Objectives

In completing this exercise, you will have practiced your ability to *explain* intrinsic motivation and its determinants, *differentiate* between various types of extrinsic rewards, and *discuss* work duties in terms of job design.

Background

You are part of a group that's in charge of recruiting and staffing a charity car wash to raise money for a university scholarship fund. The car wash is expected to last from 8 a.m. to 5 or 6 p.m., with lunch provided on a rotating basis for each volunteer. In addition to the free lunch, the university can provide a small fund for compensation (approximately $5 to $10 per volunteer) to be used in any reasonable way the committee decides is appropriate. The university is planning on posting the volunteers' names and pictures on the university website along with a brief story about the event.

From your OB class, you realize the importance of good job design in motivating people, both in terms of quality work outcomes and in terms of being able to better recruit people for tasks. Using this knowledge, you are able to convince everyone to hold a meeting just to develop a clear plan for maximizing the volunteers' motivation for this event. You are about to go into that meeting.

Instructions

Step 1. Form into groups (maximum seven members) and create a motivation plan for the volunteers. This plan should include intrinsic and extrinsic motivations as well as any job design aspects that are appropriate. Be creative in developing this plan, but also be sure to link your ideas back to chapter concepts, and use chapter terms in your descriptions. Then use this plan to make suggestions on how the job aspects can be used to promote the recruitment process. Also, provide information on how the job design and motivational aspects of the task are likely to affect volunteer outcomes. (20 minutes)

Step 2. Select a spokesperson to present your plan. (If possible, the spokesperson should be someone who has not had an opportunity to speak in front of the class before. If everyone has presented in front of the class, select the person who has presented the least.) Before the person presents, give your group a unique name. (20 to 30 minutes)

Step 3. Vote on the plan that should be the most motivational. (You can't vote for the team you were a member of.) In addition to writing the group's name on a sheet of paper, write down why you believe the plan will be the most motivational using chapter terms. (10 to 15 minutes)

Reflection Questions

1. What difficulties did you encounter in developing motivational methods with such constrained resources? How are these difficulties similar to what supervisors for entry-level personnel face?
2. Which type of motivations do you expect to be stronger in this situation—intrinsic or extrinsic?
3. How might that motivational balance differ for supervisors of entry-level personnel?
4. How did using chapter terms and concepts better help you frame and understand this situation?
5. What other teams came up with creative ways to motivate the volunteers? Were there motivators that you found difficult to classify as intrinsic or extrinsic?

Exercise contributed by Milton R. Mayfield, Professor of Business, Texas A&M International University, and Jacqueline R. Mayfield, Professor of Business, Texas A&M International University.

EXERCISE 7.3: ROLE-PLAYING JOB DESIGN

Objective

The purpose of this exercise is to grasp the concept of job design through a role play.

Instructions

There are three ways a manager could enhance the design of a job: job rotation, job enlargement, and job enrichment. Job rotation is periodically moving employees from one position to another; job enlargement is increasing the range of tasks and duties associated with a job; and job enrichment is increasing the scope of a job to make it more complex, interesting, stimulating, and satisfying for employees.

For this role play, a stack of blank paper will be needed, and the instructor will ask for four volunteers from the class. These four are the employees. In addition, two more volunteers will be the managers.

The task is simple. The four employees will use an assembly line to construct paper airplanes. The first employee will make a fold or two, the second employee will make another fold or two, and so on until the paper airplane is finished by the fourth employee (the managers will provide training on how to properly construct the airplane).

The role play consists of the following phases:

Phase 1: The managers determine one specific model of paper airplane and train the employees on how to make that particular model. The managers then divide the steps among the four employees.

Phase 2: The employees construct four paper airplanes identical to the one demonstrated during training.

Phase 3: The employees construct four more identical paper airplanes, but this time job rotation is used, whereby employees are assigned a different step along the production line than the one they originally had in Phase 1 (additional training from the managers may be necessary so that employees understand their new role).

Phase 4: Employees may remain in the same position or may move back to their original positions—this is entirely up to the managers. Four more planes will be constructed; however, for this phase, job enlargement will be introduced (additional tasks will be given to each employee). Managers can decide what these additional tasks will be—decorating the plane in a prescribed way, cleaning up around the area, etc.

Phase 5: For this phase, four more paper planes will be constructed and the managers will introduce job enrichment (they will give the employees more decision-making authority as to how their tasks are done). Again, it's up to the managers to decide how this should be implemented; for example, employees could be permitted to construct a different airplane of their choice, or managers might choose which tasks are to be completed by which employees to make the production process faster or more efficient.

Reflection Questions

1. How well did the managers introduce each method of job design? What did they do right, and what would you have done differently?
2. Take each method of job design—job rotation, job enlargement, and job enrichment—and think about a job for each that would benefit from that particular type of job design. For example, in which type of job would employees be most motivated if job rotation was available? Job enlargement? Job enrichment? Why did you choose those particular jobs?
3. What difficulty would managers have in implementing each method of job design? How could the manager overcome these difficulties?

Exercise contributed by Steven Stovall, Southeast Missouri State University.

ONLINE EXERCISE 7.1: FINDING EXAMPLES OF INDIVIDUAL PERFORMANCE-BASED PAY

Objective

The purpose of this exercise is to gain an appreciation for various forms of individual performance-based pay.

Instructions

Go to a job-listing website and look through the listings of available job postings. Read through the posts and find one example of each of the following forms of individual performance–based pay:

- Piece rate
- Bonus pay
- Merit pay

Keep in mind that many companies don't readily reveal their pay practices in these posts, so you may have to visit more than one career website to find an example of each. Once you've located one of each, copy the link or the post and submit that to your instructor, being sure to label it as an example of piece rate, bonus pay, or merit pay.

Reflection Questions

1. Which of these three forms of individual performance–based pay do you think is most common in the workplace? Explain.
2. Which form of individual performance–based pay would you like to receive/earn most? Why?
3. What are the advantages and disadvantages of each of these forms of pay?
4. Why are some companies secretive about their pay practices?

Exercise contributed by Steven Stovall, Southeast Missouri State University.

ONLINE EXERCISE 7.2: INTRINSIC MOTIVATION AND EXTRINSIC REWARDS

Objective

The purpose of this exercise is to understand intrinsic motivation and extrinsic rewards.

Instructions

This exercise is for an online discussion group. In your discussion group, think about the ideal organization for which you would like to work. Imagine that the culture, environment, and collegial atmosphere are what you would most enjoy. As you reflect on this, consider the intrinsic motivation and extrinsic rewards you'd prefer. Remember, intrinsic motivation is the performance of tasks for our own innate satisfaction, and extrinsic rewards are external awards such as salary, bonuses, and paid vacations. In the discussion group, post one "ideal" form of intrinsic motivation you would have in your optimal job/organization and two forms of extrinsic motivation you would like most to see.

Reflection Questions

1. Why did you choose what you did for intrinsic motivation? Why is this important to you?
2. Why did you choose the forms of extrinsic rewards you did? Why are these important to you?
3. How likely do you think it is that you'll find an organization that meets your ideals for intrinsic motivation and extrinsic rewards? Explain.
4. Think about the intrinsic motivation you discussed and the two extrinsic rewards you mentioned. Which of those are you willing to compromise to garner a job in an organization? Explain.

CASE 7.1: SEPHORA

French beauty product retailer Sephora operates more than 2,700 stores in 35 countries. Founded by Dominique Mandonnaud in 1970, the company was acquired by luxury conglomerate LVMH Moët Hennessy Louis Vuitton in 1997. Sephora offers cosmetics, fragrances, nail color, skin care, and other products from 340 brands as well as the company's own private label, Sephora Collection. The company is extremely committed to its employee experience, and Sephora consistently tops rankings of the best workplaces to work for, a testament to the loyalty its 39,000 employees feel toward the brand.[73]

"Data and insights are vital in understanding what drove customers and employees to engage with Sephora in the first place, and how to enhance those experiences to drive even deeper loyalty from both sets of people moving forward," Karalyn Smith, Sephora's global chief people officer told *Inside HR*.[74] Except for the items in the Sephora Collection, customers can buy nearly all the products the store sells at other retailers, so why do they shop at Sephora?

A look at Sephora's history gives insight into the brand's enduring popularity. Fifty years ago, the concept of letting consumers try cosmetics before they purchased them was unique. Founder Dominique Mandonnaud pioneered the idea of having production testers in each aisle at Sephora, a model that came to be known as "assisted self-service." The shopping experience that beauty consumers take for granted today was his first innovation at the company. Mandonnaud is a painter and sculptor, and the French entrepreneur's love of art is evinced by the theatrical nomenclature that permeates the company. At Sephora, the sales floor is the "stage" and the rest of the store is "backstage." Associates are called "cast members," and managers are referred to as "directors." Predictably, cast members' uniforms are "costumes." Beauty director Melinda Soares says, "We are the ultimate beauty destination, and our goal is to ensure that everyone feels like they belong."[75]

In a keynote presentation at the 2019 Qualtrics X4 Summit, Karalyn Smith shared how to nurture a sense of belonging among employees. "Our job is to find those moments that matter in the employee experience journey and make them special," Smith said at the gathering of experience management professionals. Smith offered five key needs that foster loyalty from the perspective of an employee:

- Train Me: I have the skills and knowledge I need to be successful
- Include Me: I feel a sense of belonging at Sephora
- Reward Me: I feel recognized and rewarded for my contributions and achievements
- Inspire Me: I am motivated to contribute at my very best
- Grow Me: I am growing and preparing for future opportunities[76]

At Sephora, training isn't a one-and-done stepping stone on the employee experience journey; employees are continually growing. "One of the things I love most about working for Sephora is the training," an employee told Business Insider. "You are trained when you are first hired, of course, then the rest of the training comes over time . . . I have learned so much over these last few months from working at a stand-alone store."[77] Sales associates or "cast members" aren't the only ones learning; "directors," even HR managers, grow in their employee experience journeys.

"We have this concept over here at Sephora—Teach, Inspire, Play," Stephen Bobko, vice president of human resources, told *HRD America*. "We need to be able to embody this fully—to inspire our colleagues with new ideas and collaborations every day." Many of the new ideas Bobko's team has implemented lately are direct responses to the pandemic. "In order to really engage our people digitally we have an education function under the HR umbrella. Along the way, we're continuing to look at ways to innovate our employee rewards offering. One of the big learnings over the course of COVID-19 was virtual medicine." Telemedicine is one of the best perks companies offered employees in 2020 and 2021. Companies that adapted to the digital-first, socially distant world made workers feel like their employers really cared about them. Bobko told the magazine that morale was high when the first pandemic restrictions were lifted and people were excited to return to work: "It was interesting to see employees return to the stores—especially to see how quickly the teams adapted to this new reality. All of our people are always eager to be involved in our brand and our ethos—which is what makes Sephora a great place to work."[78]

Critical-Thinking Questions

1. How does Sephora's employee experience journey cultivate employees' intrinsic motivation?
2. Give an example of how Sephora satisfies workers' need for competence.
3. Do you think the whimsical titles for staff and parts of the store at Sephora qualify as an example of job design? Why or why not?

PART III

TEAMS AND TEAMWORK

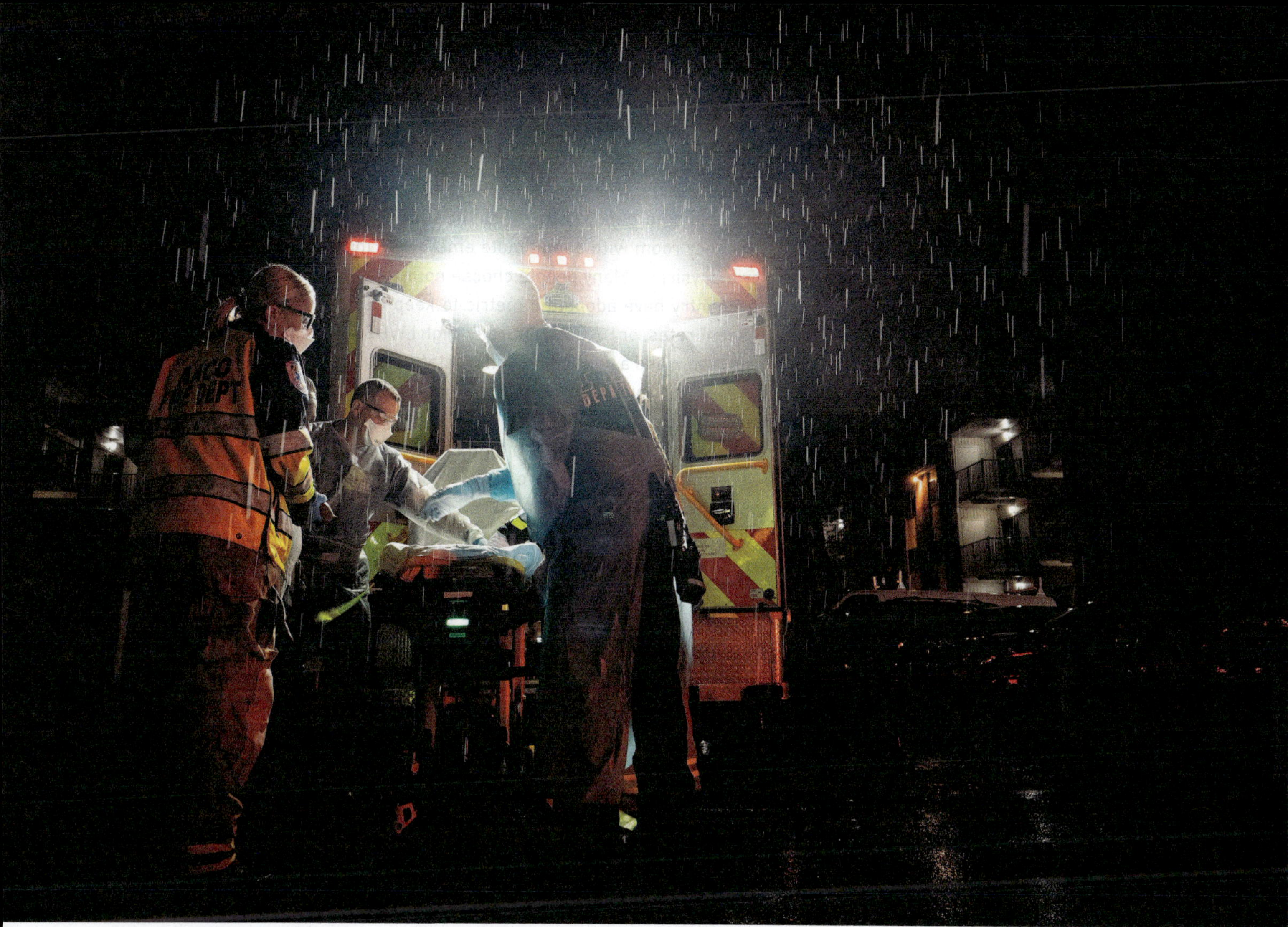

ALEX EDELMAN/Contributor/Getty Images

8 TEAMS

LEARNING OBJECTIVES

By the end of this chapter, you will be able to:

8.1 Distinguish between teams and groups

8.2 Explain how team processes affect team outcomes

8.3 Compare the various types of teams in organizations today

8.4 Apply the model of team effectiveness to evaluate team performance

8.5 Identify the advantages and disadvantages of different team decision-making approaches

Case Study: The Team at Thomas Jefferson University Hospital Emergency Department

Have you ever made a trip to the emergency room? If so, how long was your wait? Oftentimes, patients will go to the emergency room with a legitimate emergency medical condition but wait up to an hour to be seen by a physician. Many people choose not to wait and simply walk out the door. Hospitals around the country have adopted a metric to keep track of patients who leave, called "left-without-being-seen" rates, or LWBS.[1] Naturally, high LWBS rates correspond directly to an overcrowded emergency room and a poorly functioning staff of nurses and physicians. When patients leave without being seen, they put themselves in a situation where their health can decline further by not being treated.

Additionally, the nursing teams at hospitals with high LWBS rates typically perform below par due to the excessive sense of urgency they have when treating patients. Currently, it is not uncommon for the public to keep track of individual LWBS rates to avoid hospitals that have a history of long waits and poor service. In fact, the Centers for Medicare and Medicaid Services require hospitals to report the LWBS rates to the public on a quarterly basis.

This brings us to Thomas Jefferson University Hospital Emergency Department. This emergency department is located in Philadelphia, Pennsylvania, and saw around 124,536 emergency room visits during the fiscal year ending June 30, 2020.[2] The emergency department is made up of a team of physicians and nurses who run the day-to-day operations. The team at Thomas Jefferson Hospital decided to make it a goal of theirs to bring down LWBS rates below the national average of 2% along with decreasing door-to-provider times and improving overall service. This led to the creation of the Emergency Department 2.0 initiative at Thomas Jefferson.[3]

Indeed, this initiative seems to be paying off. According to recent reports, Thomas Jefferson University Hospital's door-to-provider time was less than 15 minutes.[4] This was a significant improvement over the 2015 indices, where door-to-provider time was 43 minutes. Additionally, recent reports show that the hospital's LWBS rate is at 1%. This again was a huge improvement from the 2015 numbers, where the hospital's LWBS rate was between 6% and 8%.[5]

Stephen McDonald, manager of the emergency department, said of the initiative, "We adopted it as our mantra and challenged ourselves to become a more patient—and family-centric—emergency department. Jefferson wants to be the best in all areas. It is a privilege to care for 65,000 people in the Philadelphia area, and we don't take that lightly."[6]

With a strong mission, the emergency department had the foundation it needed to make positive changes; however, without proper management, the team would likely have failed. The nature of this change called for increased interdependence between team members within the department, meaning teams would need to rely on each other, work closely together on a piece of work, consult with each other, provide each other with advice, and exchange information during the process of implementing the new process improvement strategies. The executive physicians stepped up to the plate and engaged deeply in the redesign of the operations in the department alongside the nurses and technicians. McDonald acknowledges, "The support [from leadership] was the only way we could institute such radical change."[7] While the leadership played a huge role in the ultimate success of the project, it was the integration of the nurses' perspectives that was the key factor in determining the best strategy moving forward. When it comes down to it, nurses in an emergency department know the operations better than anyone and have a much more useful perspective on how they can be improved than anyone else. The department leadership employed the Delphi technique, which is a method of decision-making in which information is gathered from a group of respondents within their area of expertise. Stephen McDonald recalls, "We wanted to leverage the amazing nursing staff and we really worked hard to engage them throughout the process. They were at the table and their voices were heard."[8]

This is by far one of the most important aspects of a successful team. Management that opens the floor to the perspectives of all team members and focuses on the perspectives of the people that make up the backbone of the team is much more likely to make better decisions.

Silencing and excluding team members from discussion will only cause harm to the team and the operation as a whole. Being inclusive to all team members gives everyone access to more knowledge and learning opportunities.[9] Also, empowering team members to contribute in their own special ways is sure to help any team succeed in accomplishing its goals. Teamwork has benefits that are both morale boosting and psychological: team members will be happier, more motivated, and more likely to contribute ideas that can improve productivity when they feel empowered.[10] A cohesive team with a strong mission, like the team at Thomas Jefferson, is a force to be reckoned with. Susan Cissone, administrative supervisor of the department, describes the instant benefits that including the nurses in decision-making had for the company as it pushed toward its goal. "Anyone looking to change their intake model needs to be bold; including our nursing staff in decisions led to our success."[11] In the first week of ED 2.0's implementation, Thomas Jefferson's emergency department saw a 0.42% LWBS rate, a number that far exceeded original expectations. The team at Thomas Jefferson has been able to sustain their early success with an LWBS rate under 1% and an average door-to-provider time hovering around 10 minutes which is among the best in the nation. Joseph Anton, VP of clinical support and services, explains, "We are extremely proud of what the team has accomplished. While ED 2.0 was a call to action to ensure we were putting the patients and their families at the center of all we do, it was also a tremendous example of the power of teamwork and staff engagement."[12]

Critical-Thinking Questions

1. What types of problems might the hospital have encountered had it not included the nursing staff in decision-making?
2. What was so valuable about seeing management engage in the new initiative alongside their subordinates?

THE DIFFERENCE BETWEEN TEAMS AND GROUPS

Teams and teamwork play a critical role in the success of 21st-century organizations. The Thomas Jefferson Hospital successfully reduced the LWBS rate by seeking different perspectives from all team members and including them in decision-making. By empowering and engaging different teams, the hospital created a cohesive team working together to achieve its goals. The most successful organizations value and understand the nature of teams and create a productive environment in which teams flourish. A **team** is a collection of people brought together to apply their individual skills to a common project or goal.[13]

Regardless of the type of organization, most employees work in some form of a team in today's workplace. Compared to a few decades ago, teamwork has become commonplace in contemporary organizations. But what has caused this dramatic shift to team structures? Global competition means that organizations need to respond quickly to competitive pressures. Efficient, collaborative teams are one way for organizations to meet the growing demands of their customers and stay ahead of the competition.

Organizational restructuring and downsizing have brought leaner, more efficient, and more productive structures to many companies. Rather than viewing layoffs as a negative, some companies perceive a trimmer organization as an optimal way for employees to collaborate more intensely, to become more engaged in the decision-making processes, and to contribute their own ideas and initiatives. In addition, employees have become more empowered through **decentralization**, the distribution of power across all levels of the organization.[14] Employees are encouraged to be creative and innovative and given more freedom to make decisions.

Many organizations, especially in the United States and Europe, are working in high technology or knowledge information industries where close collaboration is viewed as a positive forum for innovation and creativity. However, collaboration in today's working world doesn't necessarily mean physically sitting together in the same office. Thanks to increasing technology, people are more connected than ever before. For instance, for many organizations, the COVID-19 pandemic moved teamwork from in-person interactions to remote communication through videoconferencing technologies such as Zoom, Skype, and Microsoft Teams. As some organizations transition to a hybrid working structure, which gives people the option to work remotely or from the office, managers will need to figure out ways to keep teams engaged and connected.

Teams Versus Groups

The terms *teams* and *groups* are often used interchangeably, but there are subtle differences between them.[15]

A **group** usually consists of three or more people who work independently to attain organizational goals.[16] In other words, it focuses on achieving individual goals. For example, in a small business, there might be three people in the marketing department; one might be focused on sales, another on branding, and a third on the administration associated with those tasks. Each employee will work independently and produce individual projects, but all group members will still work toward the organization's common goals. Outside work, friends who come together to watch a football game on television would be classified as a group.

In contrast, teams consist of a number of people, usually between three and seven, who use their complementary skills to collaborate in a joint effort. Teams engage in interdependent, collaborative, and cooperative work to achieve goals. For example, players playing on a game of football would be classified as a team.

Teams with fewer than three people tend not to derive the benefits of a collaborative team, and teams with more than seven tend to have communication and control issues. In this chapter we focus on teams.

Are Teams Effective?

The effectiveness of work teams depends on how well they are managed and treated within the organization. A well-run team is usually productive, innovative, loyal, and adaptable. Organizations that consistently nurture teams tend to experience reduced turnover and absenteeism. Over a period of two years, researchers at technology giant Google carried out a study called Project Aristotle of over 180 teams at the company in an effort to discover the components of an effective team.[17] The results were

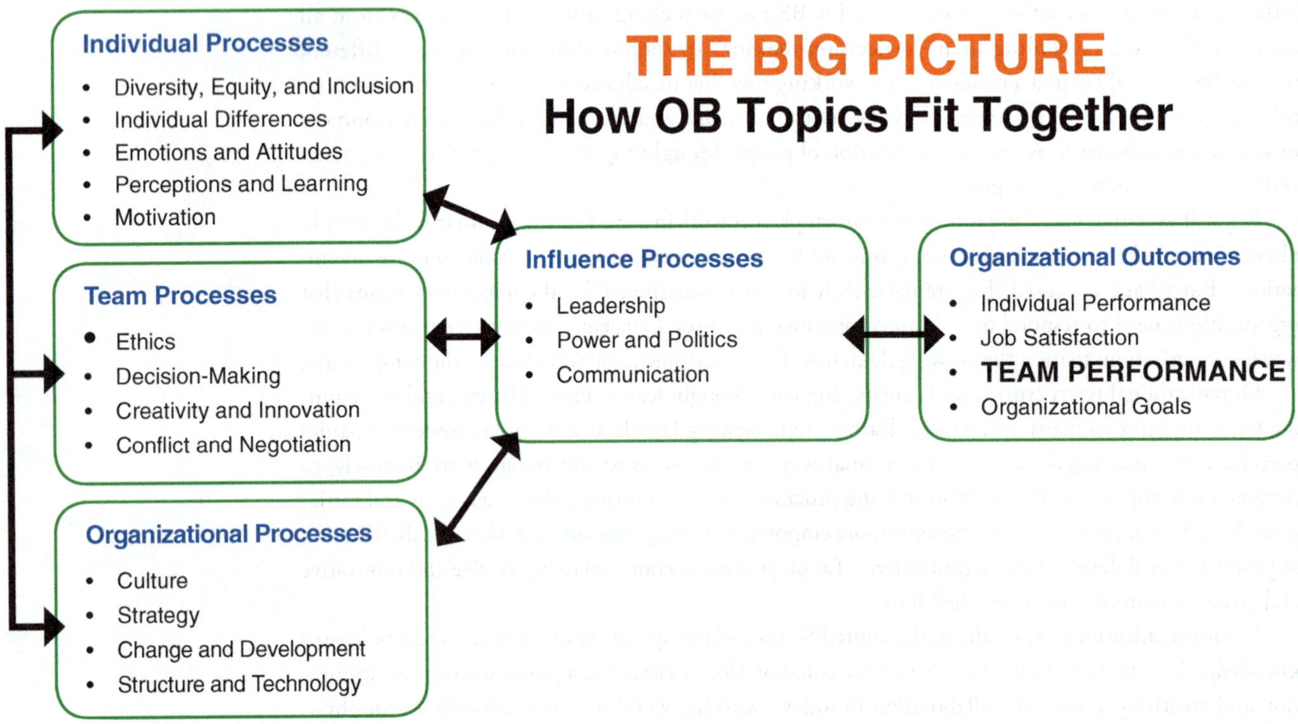

surprising. It turned out that it didn't matter so much who was on the team, but rather how team members interacted with each other, structured their work, and viewed their contributions.

Psychological Safety

The researchers found that most highly effective teams shared the same team dynamics. Teams were made up of dependable members who were clear about their roles and goals, attached personal meaning to their work, and understood the impact of their work. The findings showed that the most important component of an effective team was **psychological safety**, which is the shared belief among team members that it is safe for them to trust each other enough to take risks.[18] When people feel psychologically safe in a working environment, they will feel more inclined toward open communication, voicing their concerns, and actively seeking feedback.

A psychologically safe environment produces a number of positive outcomes on both the individual and team levels, such as better communication, knowledge sharing, greater reporting of errors, improved learning behaviors, and a higher ability to learn from failure. Vatsal Shah, founder of the all-in-one marketing platform Litmus based in California, said, "One of the keys to psychological safety in the workplace is creating a culture where mistakes are okay. Not only are they okay, they are essential and lead to growth."[19]

Research also shows a positive link between creativity and employees' perceptions of psychological safety, particularly in research and development teams where innovation performance is high.

While psychological safety may sound similar to trust, there is an important difference. Trust focuses on how one person might perceive another, but psychological safety is more focused on how team members perceive the behaviors of the team as a whole (see Figure 8.1).

FIGURE 8.1 ■ The Impact of Psychological Safety

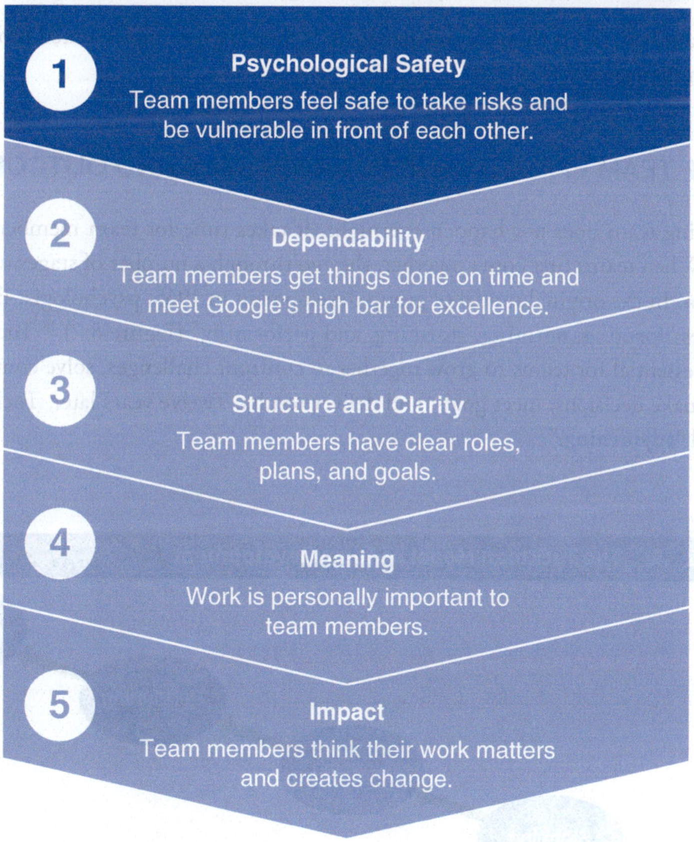

Source: Friedman, Z. (2019). *Google says the best teams have these 5 things.* Forbes. https://www.forbes.com/sites/zackfriedman/2019/01/28/google-says-the-best-teams-have-these-5-things/?sh=49825ae35a30

How to Build an Effective Team

All teams have the potential to be high-performing when they have the right manager. Here are a few tips that help managers get the most out of their teams[20]:

1. Nurture relationships
   It's not always easy to get along with everybody on the team, but investing in relationships builds trust and loyalty—both of which are key to a high-performing team.
2. Give honest feedback
   Some managers tend to shy away from giving "bad news" or negative feedback. Learning how to give honest feedback is a skill that must be adopted to cultivate a culture of openness.
3. Support remote workers
   Although over half of companies have remote teams in place, many companies do not have remote-working polices in place. Managers can support remote teams by aligning team members with the organization's mission and creating plans to ensure members feel motivated and engaged.[21]
4. Match people with purpose
   Teams are more effective when people are invested in a common purpose. For example, breakfast and brunch eatery Snooze, based in Denver, Colorado, introduced a Green Captains program where mentors educate staff on the company's sustainability initiatives around composting, recycling, and trash. Not only did this program encourage staff to be environmentally aware inside and outside work, but it also helped to improve employee retention in an industry commonly known for high turnover.[22]

However, teams can fail if they are mismanaged; if they are not implemented properly, they can cause more harm than good.

A MODEL OF TEAM EFFECTIVENESS: PROCESSES AND OUTCOMES

A high-performing team does not happen overnight. It takes time for team members to build rapport and trust. When teams first come together, they go through a number of stages in the process of becoming a team. In the original model of group development in 1965, psychologist Bruce Tuckman named the stages "**forming**, **norming**, **storming**, and **performing**" (Figure 8.2).[23] Tuckman believed these stages are essential for teams to grow together to confront challenges, solve complex problems, find solutions, make decisions, meet goals, and deliver results. Twelve years later, Tuckman created a fifth stage called "**adjourning**."

FIGURE 8.2 ■ The Tuckman Model of Team Development

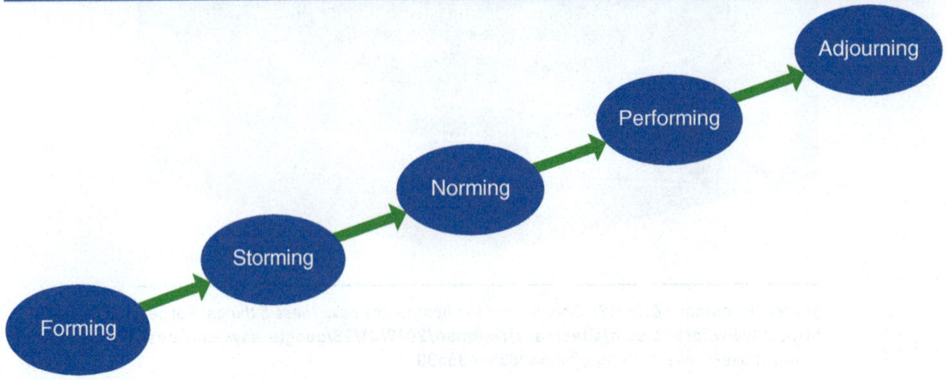

Source: Tuckman, B. (1965). Developmental sequence in small groups. *Psychological Bulletin, 63*, 384–399.

The Tuckman Model

Forming. In the first stage of group development, the members meet for the first time, get to know each other, and try to understand where they fit within the team structure. They may discuss opportunities and challenges ahead, decide on goals, and assign tasks. They may work independently from each other until they feel comfortable enough to raise difficult topics. During this period, team members focus on learning about each other, are polite to each other, and tend to avoid conflict.

Storming. After a period of time, tensions may arise between members and different personalities might clash, leading to conflict within the team. For instance, team members might question the actions of a team leader, perceive the leader as too weak or dominant, or feel annoyed with another team member for being frequently late or shirking responsibility. Tension and arguments may result when these opinions are voiced. However, if a team has any chance of being successful, the team members must find a way to manage these conflicts in order to resolve their differences and move past the issues. Some teams do not survive the storming stage, but the ones that do become all the stronger for it. By openly discussing and resolving issues, the team can put its differences aside and focus instead on the work at hand.

Norming. The team members resolve the conflict and begin to work well together and become more cohesive. Members become more tolerant and understanding of each other's differences and begin to appreciate different strengths. During this stage, team members may start to socialize together and make more of an effort to get to know each other. When rapport starts to build, team members feel more comfortable asking each other for help or providing constructive feedback. Because the team is becoming more cohesive, reaching goals, hitting milestones, and achieving deadlines become more realistic. However, it is not all smooth sailing during the norming stage. It is very common for the team to revert to the storming stage, especially when new tasks are assigned.

Performing. The team becomes invested in achieving its goals and operates as a unit. At this stage, there is high loyalty and trust between members. Team members are motivated to achieve common goals and can make decisions without supervision. Any dissent that occurs is handled easily, and members work in harmony in order to successfully complete common goals. Despite this congenial work environment, it is still possible for high-performing teams to lapse back into the storming stage, particularly if there is a change in leadership that challenges the team dynamics.

Adjourning. The final stage takes place when individuals either leave the team or have no reason to be in further contact with their teammates—successfully completing a group project, for example. Even long-standing teams may be forced to disband in the event of an organizational restructure. Although adjourning is usually inevitable, this can be a difficult stage for team members who have built relationships with fellow colleagues and grown used to the routine and norms of the team itself. When teams lose members who are then replaced by new members, the whole team development cycle is likely to start again.

FIGURE 8.3 ■ Gersick's Time and Transition Model

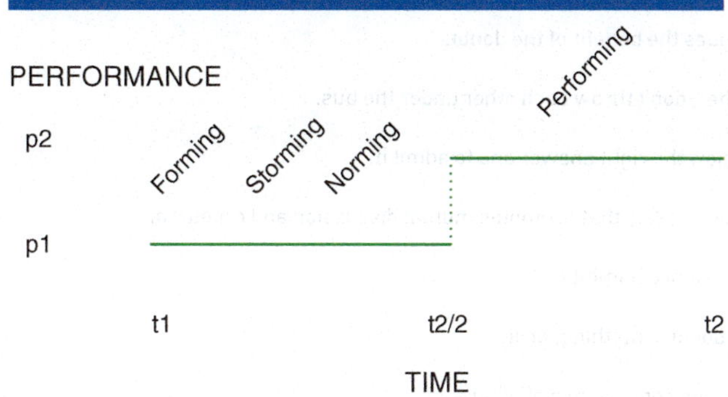

Source: Gersick, C. J. G. (1988). Time and transition in work teams: Toward a new model of group development. *Academy of Management Journal, 31*(1), 9–41.

Punctuated Equilibrium

While Tuckman's model is a popular theory for team formation, the punctuated equilibrium model developed by Connie Gersick suggests that teams do not develop in this sequence (see Figure 8.3). **Punctuated equilibrium** is a method of understanding organizational change by illustrating where change is relatively stable and where it becomes more volatile.[24]

For instance, when teams first come together, they tend to perform at a low level for a period of time that is more or less equal to half the time until the deadline or due date. At some point, the team transitions upward to a higher level of performance as the team task(s) are actually accomplished. Within the context of the Tuckman model, this means that teams tend to start off by combining the forming and norming stages before going through a period of low performance, followed by storming, a period of high performance, and then finally adjourning.

Tuckman's model is the most commonly used framework for team development today. It illustrates that team development is not always a linear process and provides a useful way for organizations to identify the reasons behind team behaviors in order to find ways to resolve issues and thereby optimize team performance and productivity.

Team Norms and Cohesion

The effectiveness of many teams depends on its **norms**, or the informal rules of behavior that govern the team.[25] Team norms are ground rules that impact the functioning of the team—for example, how team members communicate, email response times, how decisions are made, expected work hours, timekeeping, and so on. Teams that adhere to norms tend to perform better and are more cohesive. Table 8.1 outlines examples of positive team norms.[26]

Google's Project Aristotle study showed that team norms were more important than team smarts when it came to successfully completing an assignment.[27] Researchers found that dysfunctional teams failed more often because of wrong norms in spite of how many smart people were on it, whereas teams with healthy norms tended to succeed on every assignment. In sum, the right norms can increase a team's intelligence, whereas the wrong norms can hamper it.

TABLE 8.1 ■ Positive Team Norms
• Treat each other with dignity and respect.
• Avoid hidden agendas.
• Be genuine with each other about ideas, challenges, and feelings.
• Have confidence that issues discussed will be kept in confidence.
• Listen to understand.
• Practice being open-minded.
• Don't be defensive with your colleagues.
• Give your colleagues the benefit of the doubt.
• Support each other; don't throw each other under the bus.
• It's okay to not know the right answer and to admit it.
• Present problems in a way that promotes mutual discussion and resolution.
• Practice and experience humility.
• If you commit to doing something, do it.
• Respect the time and convenience of others.

Source: Karten, N. (2012, October 17). *How team norms can boost team effectiveness.* TechWell. https://www.techwell.com/techwell-insights/2012/10/how-team-norms-can-boost-team-effectiveness.

As Tuckman's team development model shows, teams need to be cohesive in order to perform well. **Cohesion** is the degree to which team members connect with each other.[28] In most cases, cohesiveness is essential for team effectiveness because it encourages members to work together to reach the same goal. Social and emotional bonds between members help to maintain consistent work efforts, steering everyone toward the same objective. A cohesive team is more motivated, communicates better, and reports higher levels of satisfaction than less cohesive teams.

However, there is such a thing as too much cohesion in a team, which can have negative consequences. For example, an overly cohesive team may be prone to inflexibility or resistance to change. It may also limit team members' ability to express their own personal thoughts and feelings for fear of upsetting the group dynamic. Too much cohesion can also lead to lack of accountability and decision-making.

Team Charters

Another good way to ensure good team communication and positive work cohesion is to provide team charters for every project.[29] A charter is a type of document that outlines the purpose of the team, the benefits of the project, the required objectives, and expected time frame. Ideally, team charters should be created in the early stages of team formation. Managers are responsible for ensuring that team members have been given clear direction and feel confident enough in their roles to achieve the goals of the project described in the charter efficiently and effectively.

Synergy: Process Gains and Losses

Team are more likely to perform well when they have good **synergy**, or the interaction that makes the total amount of work produced by a team greater than the amount of work produced by individual members working independently.[30] The Arizona Diamondbacks baseball team has good synergy, mostly because of its familial culture where every team member is given a voice.[31] Positive synergy is achieved by good leadership as well as by ensuring the right people are hired for the right roles. Teams with good synergy are more committed to goals, apply more diverse skills and abilities to tasks, and show greater willingness to share information and knowledge. Typically, teams that share common interests and values have a better chance of creating and maintaining positive synergy.

However, bad synergy within teams can lead to toxic negativity, especially when one or more team members exhibits negative behavior. Research has shown that it only takes one "bad apple" to impact a whole team.[32] These bad apples tend to work less than the other members, or attack and bully others. For example, in one study analyzing team dynamics in 50 manufacturing teams, researchers found that the teams with at least one irresponsible or negative team member were more likely to experience conflict, poor communication, and lack of cooperation.[33] Managers can address this issue by making an effort to try to change the negative behavior, but if this doesn't work, there may be little choice but to let the bad apple go.

Teams that achieve positive synergy will produce a number of **process gains**, which are the degree to which certain factors contribute to team effectiveness.[34] Process gains include a sense of shared purpose, plans, and goals; the confidence team members have in their own abilities to achieve objectives; a shared vision of the way the work should be carried out; and constructive task-focused conflict, which can help teams with their problem- solving and decision-making. In many cases, the level of process gains leads a team to exceed its performance.

In contrast, a team without good synergy can lead to **process losses**, the factors that detract from team effectiveness.[35] Team members who are afraid to disagree with other team members inhibit decision-making and problem-solving. Process losses include personality clashes or unproductive conflict and the inability to focus on certain tasks. They also include **social loafing**, also known as "free riding," which is the reduced effort people exert in a team compared to the amount they supply when working independently.[36] In fact, sometimes teams achieve less than people working alone. For example, in a brainstorming session, people may make less effort to contribute because they know that other people will put forward ideas instead.[37] People are more likely to engage in social loafing when they work in large teams where they can slip below the radar, when clear goals are not given, or when they believe they lack the skills and abilities necessary to complete the tasks.

Another form of social loafing facing today's organizations is **cyberloafing**, or accessing the internet for personal use during working hours.[38] Research shows that workers can spend up to a few hours a day checking social media, personal email, or watching YouTube.[39] According to a University of Nevada study, cyberloafing is estimated to cost U.S. businesses up to $85 billion per year.[40] Not only does it cost organizations money, but it also affects productivity, drains bandwidth, and makes systems vulnerable to computer viruses. In a different study conducted by online learning firm Udemy, six out of 10 people admitted they were unable to go through a whole working day without checking social media.[41] So how can organizations tackle this problem? Blocking employees from browsing sites unrelated to work may sound like the obvious solution, but there are some sites such as LinkedIn or Facebook used by organizations for legitimate work reasons. How can managers tell if employees are using a site for work purposes or cyberloafing?

In an effort to find a solution to cyberloafing, Jeremy Glassman and a team of fellow researchers at Arizona State University created software designed to prevent cyberloafing.[42] This system permitted employees to use certain sites and used on-screen warnings to remind employees not to access sites that were not work related. Sites that used up bandwidth (video sites) or could cause legal issues (pornography) were blocked. While employees were still allowed to access some leisure sites, they were limited to 10 minutes at a time, with a maximum limit of 90 minutes per day. When the 90 minutes expired, employees were blocked from those sites, and if they needed further access, they would have to explain to their managers why.

EXAMINING THE EVIDENCE

TEAM COHESION: IS TOO MUCH MORE THAN ENOUGH?

Team cohesion is a necessary prerequisite for effective team performance, as indicated by the model of team development. But is it possible to have too much team cohesion? The answer is yes!

In 1951, Solomon Asch of Swarthmore College published the results of the now-famous conformity study.[43] In the study, college students were asked to participate in a perceptual activity. Eight participants were shown a card with a single line, followed by another card with three lines (labeled A, B, and C, as shown).

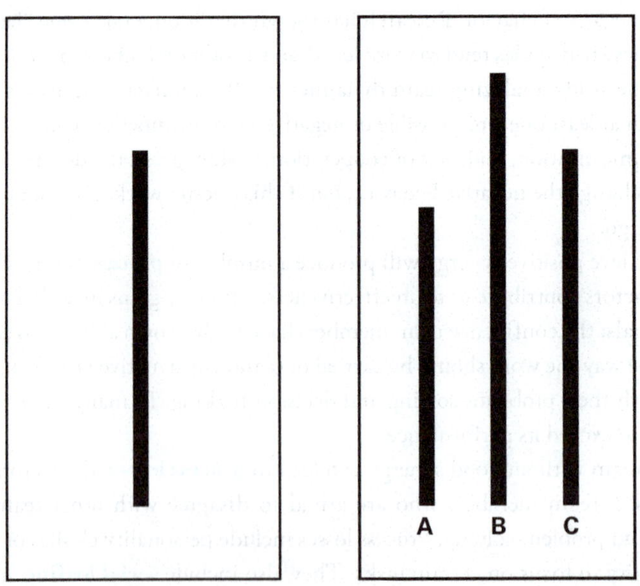

Participants were then asked to state which of the three lines matched the line on the first card in length. In the first couple of trials, all eight participants agreed it was C. However, in the third trial, the first seven participants all gave the same obviously incorrect answer, because they were actually confederates working in collusion with the researchers. The only true participant was the eighth student, and the real focus of the study was on how this student would react to the confederates' behavior. Remarkably, one of every three true participants responded with an obviously incorrect answer in order to conform to the answers given by the seven confederates! If there is that much pressure to conform in an ad hoc group brought together temporarily for a research study, imagine how much pressure there might be to conform in a permanent and highly cohesive work group. It's certainly possible that too much cohesion could be a bad thing. A more recent study provides additional support for this idea. The study of 180 teams in a national travel agency found that social ties within the teams had a curvilinear effect on team performance over time, first increasing and then decreasing performance as the negative effects of cohesion such as groupthink began to take a negative toll on team performance.[44]

Critical-Thinking Questions

1. How can managers recognize when there is too much cohesion on their teams?
2. What specific actions can managers take to reduce ineffective levels of team cohesiveness?

When Glassman tested this system at a real agricultural company, the results showed a significant decrease in cyberloafing.

"It provided them with a reminder of the acceptable uses for Internet resources while at work and what is expected of them," Glassman says. "With a greater amount of interaction with the system, the more likely they will be using the Internet resources for work-related purposes."[45]

While social and cyberloafing tend to negatively impact team dynamics, there are several factors that contribute to group effectiveness (see Figure 8.4). The first factor is **social facilitation**, which occurs when individuals perform tasks better in the presence of others.[46] However, social facilitation applies to simple rather than complex or novel tasks. For example, you may play soccer better when people are watching, but you might not be able to cook a meal as easily in front of an audience.

Another factor that contributes to group effectiveness is the number of favorable outcomes a team engineers. Effective teams usually produce high-quality goods and services, a satisfied customer base, a capacity to consistently work well together, and a high degree of team member satisfaction.

A team's effectiveness can be attributed to social facilitation when individuals perform better in the presence of others.

© iStockphoto.com/Izabela Habur

FIGURE 8.4 ■ A Model of Process Gains and Losses

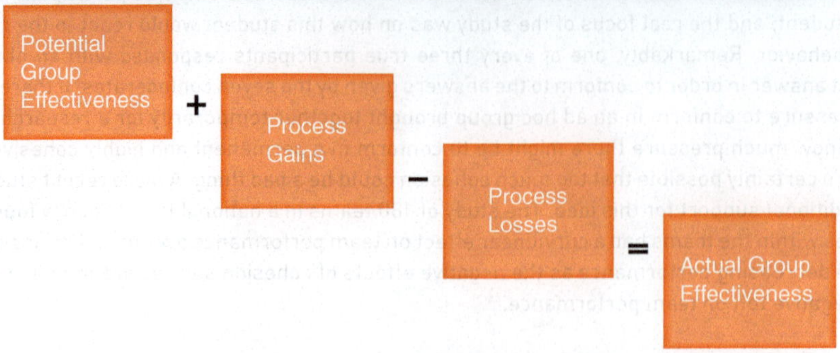

Sources: Miner, F. C. (1984, February). Group versus individual decision making: An investigation of performance measures, decision strategies, and process losses/gains. *Organizational Behavior and Human Performance, 33*(1), 112–124; Steiner, I. D. (1966). Models for inferring relationships between group size and potential group productivity. *Behavioral Science, 11*(4), 273–283.

TYPES OF TEAMS

Effective teams enhance organizational and individual performance, but not all teams are structured in the same way. Different types of teams include virtual teams, self-managing teams, problem-solving teams, and cross-functional teams.

Virtual Teams

The technological revolution has turned the original concept of what a team means on its head. Many global companies now operate in virtual teams, often in conjunction with remote work arrangements. A **virtual team** is a group of individuals who work together from different geographic locations and rely on communication technology, such as email, videoconferencing, instant messaging, and other electronic media, to collaborate.[47] See Figure 8.5 for the types of tools virtual teams use to communicate with each other. Virtual team members have great flexibility because they are able to work anywhere, including their own homes. Virtual working was already growing before the COVID-19 pandemic hit and is continuing to rise at an even faster pace. According to the Future Workforce Report, more than 36 million Americans will be working virtually by 2025.[48]

Organizations value the virtual team model because it saves on travel costs by eliminating in-person meetings, reduces the need for office space, and allows for greater sharing of information between employees from different countries.

However, there are several disadvantages to working in a virtual team. Lack of human contact can lead to social isolation, miscommunication due to technical issues or background noise, and higher stress levels and burnout due to lack of separation between work and home. For instance, Microsoft research found that during the pandemic, people were working longer hours, attending more meetings, and engaging in after-hours conversations between five p.m. and midnight.[49] Virtual teams located in different countries can also struggle with time differences and cultural differences. Managing a virtual team has become an essential management skill. Table 8.2 presents several tips on how to manage virtual teams.

Virtual team members don't have the opportunity to celebrate goal achievements together in person. Managers can reward high performers through praise or by highlighting their accomplishments in front of the whole team.

In many instances, virtual teams work successfully. Vivek Kumar is the cofounder of Qlicket, a startup that helps businesses to reduce employee turnover by collecting employee feedback in real time through a kiosk system, which filters through to managers for discussion. Kumar works virtually from Pittsburgh, Pennsylvania, with two other cofounders, one in San Francisco and the other in India. Kumar believes that the virtual team runs smoothly because of "a shared devotion to our mission of helping managers listen to employees."[50] Another example of a successful virtual team is the author team of this book. Chris Neck lives in Arizona; Jeff Houghton is in West Virginia; and Emma Murray

FIGURE 8.5 ■ Virtual Communication

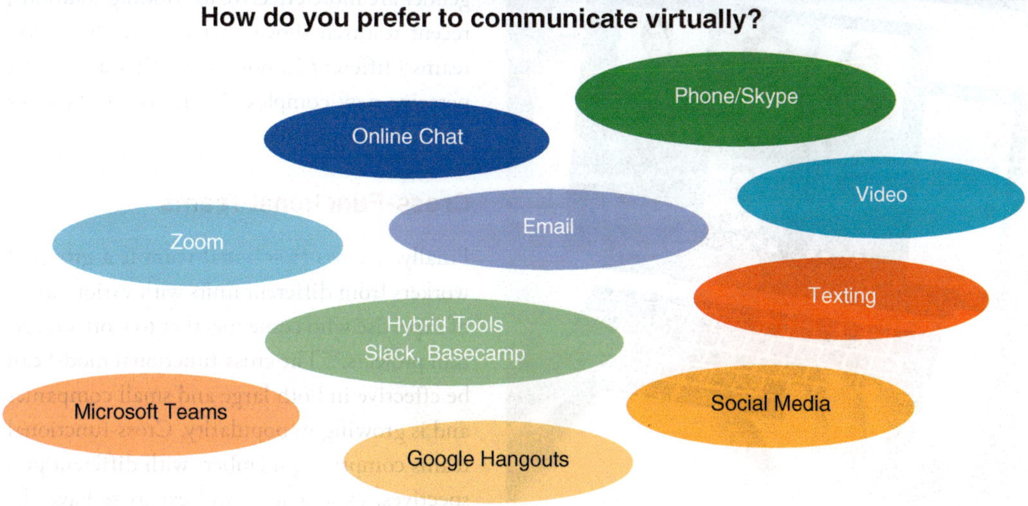

lives in London, United Kingdom. Despite their locations, the team has managed to successfully work together over a number of years, thanks to email, Zoom, and Microsoft Teams.

Self-Managing Teams

A **self-managing team** is a group of workers who manage their own daily duties under little to no supervision.[51] Manufacturing company W. L. Gore, online shoe delivery company Zappos, and tomato processing and packing company Morning Star are among many companies composed of highly effective self-managing teams, in which team members are expected to make decisions without consulting higher management.[52] The concept of self-managed teams is growing in popularity because of the benefits it brings to organizations. Numerous examples show that companies with self-managed teams grow faster, are more productive and profitable, have higher levels of engagement, and have a lower turnover of employees.[53] However, self-managing teams are not without their downsides. Research suggests that self-managing teams often struggle with internal conflict, trust, and accountability issues.[54]

Problem-Solving Teams

A **problem-solving team** consists of a small group of workers who come together for a set amount of time to discuss and resolve specific issues.[55] While it has been generally thought that teams comprising

TABLE 8.2 ■ 5 Tips for Managing Virtual Teams

1. Set expectations and stick to them
   Managers need to be clear on what they expect from the team and specify the goals that need to be achieved. Teams work more smoothly when everybody is confident about their individual tasks and roles.
2. Provide the right technological tools
   Virtual teams need to be equipped with the types of tools and technologies that enable them to work quickly and efficiently. IT support also needs to be in place to resolve any technical issues.
3. Organize regular online meetings
   As meeting in person is not an option for many virtual teams, it is essential to arrange frequent online meetings to discuss progress and listen to any issues raised by the team members.
4. Encourage a healthy work/life balance
   Managers can ensure that team members maintain a separation between work and personal life by encouraging them to work outdoors or engaging in hobbies or exercise outside working hours.
5. Reward achievement

Source: Atanacio, A. (2021, June 17). *Seven tips to lead a remote team successfully in 2021.* Forbes. https://www.forbes.com/sites/theyec/2021/06/17/seven-tips-to-lead-a-remote-team-successfully-in-2021/?sh=51d9c36a4743

Virtual teams can communicate with each other more easily with videoconferencing software like Skype.

members of different ages, ethnicities, and gender are more effective for finding solutions, recent research shows that cognitively diverse teams (different in how they think about and perceive new complex situations) are best for fast problem-solving.[56]

Cross-Functional Teams

Finally, a **cross-functional team** is a group of workers from different units with various areas of expertise who come together to work on certain projects.[57] The cross-functional model can be effective in both large and small companies and is growing in popularity. Cross-functional teams comprising members with different perspectives, experiences, and expertise have the ability to see the big picture and find innovative ways to achieve goals. Disadvantages of cross-functional teams include lack of trust (after the task is complete, teams often disband and re-form with new team members to work on a new goal), insufficient support from upper management, leading to low morale and failure, and growth limitations for team members working on a specific project for a certain period of time. Managers can address some of these issues by setting clear goals, minimizing conflict through team building and clear, honest communication, and rotating members from various departments into and out of the team to encourage further learning and growth.[58]

Cross-Cultural Diversity in Virtual Collaboration

Today's teams are likely to be composed of employees from different cultures with different languages. Diverse teams provide companies with a greater reach into global markets because of their ability to communicate with people from similar backgrounds. A wide range of diverse employees with different perspectives and knowledge also offer a variety of solutions that help boost creativity and productivity, and increasingly, organizations with diverse workforces have become desirable places to work because they are perceived as being fair and nondiscriminatory.

Due to globalization and the COVID-19 outbreak, it has become even more important for people working in a global economy to maintain cultural relationships, be open to other cultures, and develop a global mindset in order to fully understand cultural differences. In Chapter 1, we described the impact of COVID-19 on remote working and the importance of virtual collaboration. In a globalized world, virtual collaboration is more necessary than ever, but it can be complex for organizations to navigate different time zones, languages, cultures, and skill levels in addition to the economic and political climates in each country.

A recent study explored the behaviors and interactions between almost 6,000 people working in groups of six or eight in more than 800 remote teams in different countries all over the world during a period of several months.[59] Researchers focused on two main areas of diversity: **personal diversity**, diversity among individuals in relation to age, gender, values, and skills; and **contextual diversity**, diversity among individuals in relation to their circumstances and backgrounds and thus their economic and political viewpoints.[60]

The results showed that personal diversity has a negative impact on virtual collaboration. Teams comprising members from different cultures who speak different languages and are of different ages tend to experience more conflict and misunderstanding, communicate less, and have high levels of distrust. Teams low on personal diversity are more suitable for routine tasks where there is less of a need for innovation and complex problem-solving.[61]

In contrast, contextual diversity has a positive impact on virtual collaboration. Teams comprising members from countries with different economic and political systems are more likely to provide different perspectives, which supports decision-making, creativity, and problem-solving.[62]

Managers need to address any issues with teams with low personal diversity by providing training to increase cultural understanding and reduce prejudice and stereotypes with a view toward creating friendly interactions between team members. The degree of contextual diversity can also be enhanced by encouraging brainstorming, feedback, and constructive criticism, and offering a safe platform for knowledge exchange, discussion, and disagreement.

It is not always possible to separate contextual and personal diversity, but managing both areas effectively is likely to improve the way teams interact together.

Managing Cross-Cultural Diversity

Managing cross-cultural diversity isn't easy. It involves cultivating a deep appreciation and respect for other people's cultural differences and the willingness to change our behavior and perspectives in order to interact and communicate with other employees, teams, and even whole organizations. Research shows that people who are culturally competent tend to share certain characteristics (see Table 8.3).[63] Organizations that fail to implement successful cross-cultural diversity are often guilty of bias, lack of effort when it comes to recruiting and retaining diverse talent, and promoting a *we* versus *they* mentality. This is why it is so important that managers implement a healthy cross-culturally diverse workforce.

The first step to implementing a healthy diverse workforce is to understand how people experience cultural difference. Dr. Milton Bennett's Developmental Model of Intercultural Sensitivity (DMIS), comprising six world views, helps managers to assess the level of cultural awareness and sensitivity within different teams.[64] The six stages start from least developed to most developed.

- Denial: when people don't really believe there are differences between people and aren't particularly interested in cultural differences.
- Defense/reversal: when people recognize cultural differences exist but feel threatened by these differences (defense). In contrast, reversal takes place when people denigrate their own culture in favor of another culture; for example, people who have immersed themselves in a different culture may prefer the new culture to their own.

TABLE 8.3 ■ Characteristics of Culturally Competent People
Openness to cultural diversity
Flexibility and adaptability
Emotional resilience
Curiosity
Tolerance and respect for differences
Patience
A nonjudgmental attitude
Global identity
Cultural intelligence
Global leadership behaviors
Multicultural experiences, such as being multilingual and having lived in more than one country

Source: SHRM. (2015, November 30). *Understanding workplace cultures globally.* https://www.shrm.org/resourcesandtools/tools-and-samples/toolkits/pages/understandingworkplaceculturesglobally.aspx.

- Minimization: when people are aware of cultural differences but focus on the human element rather than differences between people. They have a sort of "live and let live" mentality.
- Acceptance: when people have a deep understanding of their own and others' cultural identities and appreciate the value of different cultural perspectives.
- Adaptation: when people have the ability to view a certain situation from a different cultural perspective and adapt their behavior in order to be more effective in managing that situation.
- Integration: when people have a deep understanding of one or more cultures and successfully integrate them into their own identity.

Once managers have a sense of the level of cultural awareness and sensitivity within their teams, they can begin to create training initiatives to increase the level of cultural intelligence. At the core of cultural intelligence is **cultural metacognition**, which refers to the level of conscious cultural awareness we possess during cross-cultural interactions.[65] Research has shown that people who interact with others across different cultures (intercultural) have higher levels of cultural metacognition than those who communicate with those in the same culture. This may be because people who are communicating with different cultures take into account cultural backgrounds and differences that influence their responses to certain situations. This is called *cultural perspective taking*—a process whereby we tend to imagine the world from someone else's perspective. The ability to put ourselves in the shoes of another means that we are more likely to see ourselves as similar to another person, which tends to reduce bias and stereotyping. Developing these metacognitive skills together with cross-cultural training could benefit managers who work from their native country as well as those who work internationally.

Cultural intelligence training goes further than honoring different customs but involves a full commitment to learning about different cultures. Spending time in a different culture, reading publications from other cultures, getting involved in global projects, learning a different language, socializing with an expatriate, and visiting an ethnic restaurant are all ways in which people can become more culturally intelligent.

Managers also need to be culturally aware in order to build relationships with foreign professionals. Managers need to be particularly conscious of pronouncing employees' names correctly and ensuring others do the same, learning cultural differences, assigning a new foreign professional a mentor to help navigate the organization and cultivate relationships, and engaging in role play in order to experience how the foreign professional might feel moving to a different country and working for a new organization.

The biggest challenge to successful cross-cultural diversity is communication. The following guidelines help to improve communications between multicultural teams:

- Be concise: words may be translated into several different languages, so keep your message short and to the point.
- Avoid jargon/slang: people outside the United States may have no idea what "hitting a home run" or "making a slam dunk" means. Use language that you are confident everybody understands well.
- Listen better: many people struggle with different accents, but listening well and having more patience will help you to further your understanding.
- Be respectful of cultural and religious differences: people from different cultures celebrate different holidays and different religions. Any signs of religious bias will not be well received.
- Understand different communication styles: people in the United States tend to favor a more informal style of direct communication, whereas people from the Middle East and Asia tend to prefer formal, indirect communication.

As the global cross-cultural training market continues to grow (by $1.46 billion between 2021 and 2025), more organizations are offering global cross-cultural training for their employees.[66]

Global training programs may include role play, training simulations (with feedback from managers, team members, etc.), global site visits where possible (which give employees opportunities to communicate with each other in person), and open discussion around cultural differences and how they influence behavior.

A MODEL OF TEAM EFFECTIVENESS: CONTEXT AND COMPOSITION

Not all teams are effective. Effective teams in an organization are characterized by their ability to improve quality, reach goals, and change processes. One classic way of understanding teams and their effectiveness is to consider teams in terms of the contextual influences that affect their functioning, their composition, the processes they use, and the outcomes they achieve.[67] Figure 8.6 shows how these factors influence team effectiveness.

Team Contextual Influences

There are three main contextual influences: team resources, task characteristics, and organizational systems and structures.

Team resources are important for effective teams because they equip the team members with the tools to successfully perform their roles. Resources consist of the equipment, materials, training, information, staffing, and budgets the organization supplies to support the team's goals.

Tasks are the specific steps the team must perform to achieve its goals. They can be structured or unstructured, complex or simple, and characterized by more or less interdependence among team members. **Interdependence** is the extent to which team members rely on each other to complete their work tasks.[68] For example, in the Thomas Jefferson University Hospital case study, the new initiative to improve patient service required team members to work closely together and depend on each other to complete work tasks. There are three levels of interdependence (see Figure 8.7):

FIGURE 8.6 ■ A Model of Team Effectiveness

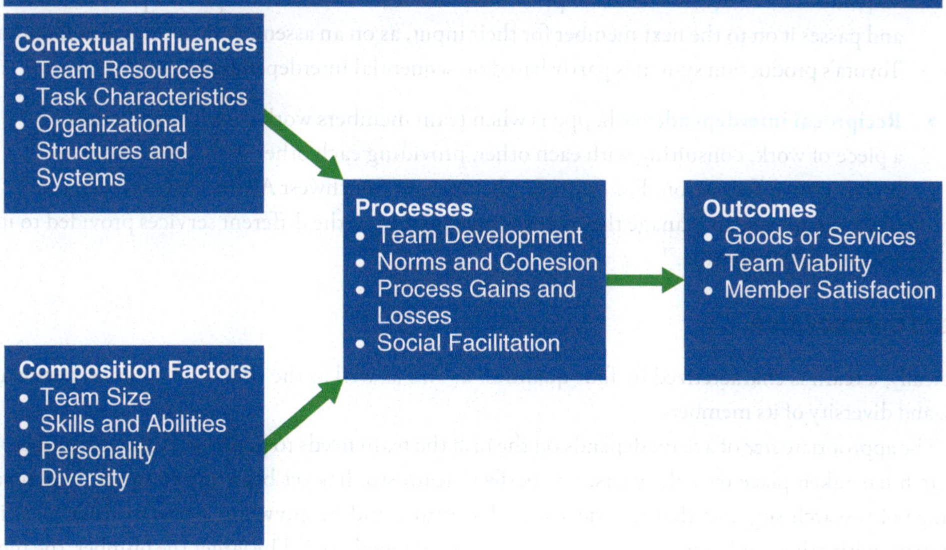

Sources: Hackman, J. R. (1987). The design of work teams. In J. W. Lorsch (Ed.), *Handbook of organizational behavior* (pp. 315–342). Prentice Hall; McGrath, J. E. (1964). *Social psychology: A brief introduction*. Holt, Rinehart & Winston; Resick, C. J., Dickson, M. W., Mitchelson, J. K., Allison, L. K., & Clark, M. A. (2010, June). Team composition, cognition, and effectiveness: Examining mental model similarity and accuracy. *Group Dynamics: Theory, Research, and Practice, 14*(2), 174–191; Doolen, T. L., Hacker, M. E., & Van Aken, E. M. (2003, August). The impact of organizational context on work team effectiveness: A study of production team. *IEEE Transactions on Engineering Management, 50*(3), 285–296.

FIGURE 8.7 ■ Levels of Task Interdependence

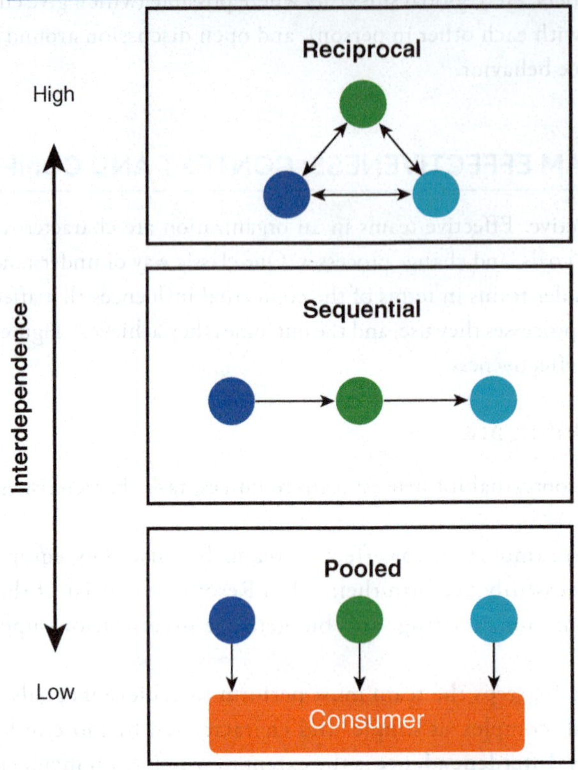

- **Pooled interdependence** occurs when each team member produces a piece of work independently of the others. Sandwich fast-food restaurant Subway and Bank of America branches are both examples of pooled interdependence. Though each restaurant unit is a part of the overall Subway organization, the units work independently of each other. Similarly, bank branches in different cities carry out the same duties but have no real need to interact with each other.[69]
- **Sequential interdependence** takes place when one team member completes a piece of work and passes it on to the next member for their input, as on an assembly line. Car manufacturer Toyota's production system is partly based on sequential interdependence.[70]
- **Reciprocal interdependence** happens when team members work closely together on a piece of work, consulting with each other, providing each other with advice, and exchanging information. For example, the teams at Southwest Airlines rely on reciprocal interdependence to manage the intense coordination of the different services provided to its customers in real time.[71]

Team Composition

Typically, a team is characterized by four qualities: its size as well as the skills and abilities, personalities, and diversity of its members.

The appropriate *size* of a team depends on the task the team needs to perform. Although numerous research has taken place over the years, no "perfect" team size has yet been agreed upon. In general, a range of research suggests that the ideal size of a team could be anywhere between three and five members, with other studies proposing anywhere up to 10 members.[72] The larger the number, the more problems arise. For instance, social loafing is more likely to occur in larger teams where members have the ability to "hide" behind the contributions and efforts of others.[73]

If all being a team player meant was having *skills* and *abilities*, professional baseball teams with the highest payrolls (like the New York Yankees) would win the World Series every year. Instead, it's the way talent interacts in the context of team processes that brings results.

Subway restaurants are an example of pooled interdependence. While all Subway restaurants are part of the larger organization, they operate independently of one another.

Brandon Bell/Staff/Getty Images

In terms of *personality*, teams typically need a balance between extraverts and introverts.[74] Having too many extraverts can mean too much talking and not enough listening, and having too many introverts can mean very little communication among the team members. Generally, people who are agreeable and conscientious are effective team members.[75]

Ensuring *diversity* on a team can be a challenge. Recall from Chapter 2 that diversity includes surface-level factors such as race and ethnicity, gender, sexuality, and age, as well as deep-level factors such as personality and beliefs. From a team composition perspective, managers are most concerned with the ways that deep-level diversity factors, like introversion and extraversion, affect team functioning. Typically, team members who share similarities in values, personalities, and interests tend to have positive social relationships with each other, which helps the team to be more effective.

Psychologist Benjamin Schneider's attraction-selection-attrition (ASA) model (see Figure 8.8) states that people are functions of three interrelated dynamic processes: attraction, selection, and attrition, all of which influence organizational culture.[76] For example, new employees are *attracted* to a team because of a perceived similarity in values, interests, and goals. New hires are *selected* based on how well they fit into an organization. Over time, *attrition* occurs when employees feel they do not fit in, causing them to leave the organization.

This theory explains why team members who are perceived as sharing similarities are selected as a good "fit," while those who do not fit in tend to leave the team.[77] However, there must be a balance between diversity and similarity, because too many people behaving in a similar way can stunt growth and have a negative effect on insight and creativity due to the lack of unique viewpoints.

While it may be tempting to congratulate or reward individual employees, this could create conflict or resentment among team members.

© iStockphoto.com/baramee2554

FIGURE 8.8 ■ Attraction-Selection-Attrition Model

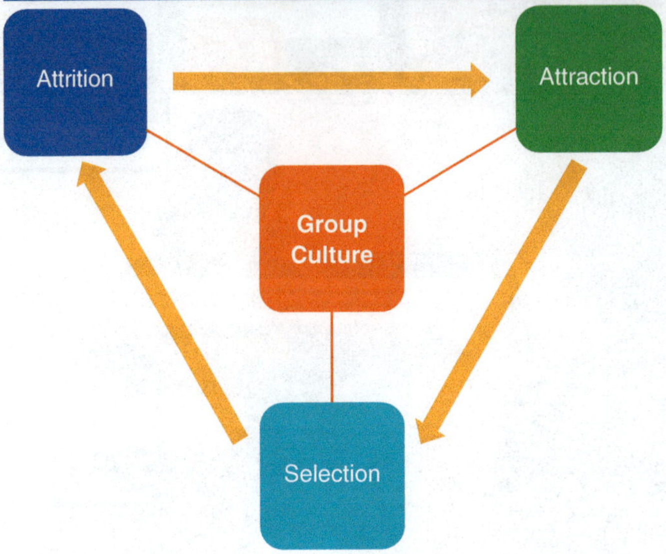

Sources: Schneider, B. (1987, September). The people make the place. *Personnel Psychology, 40*(3), 437–453; Schneider, B., Goldstein, H. W., & Smith, D. B. (1995, Winter). The ASA framework: An update. *Personnel Psychology, 48*(4), 747–773.

TEAM DECISION-MAKING

Decision-making is an essential part of a manager's daily responsibilities and has a direct impact on team and organizational success. Research shows that involving diverse teams composed of people with different backgrounds, experiences, and perspectives in the decision-making process gives rise to the types of decisions that prove critical to business success.[78] Although a recent study showed that 75% of employers perceived collaboration as very important, only 39% of employees believed their organization collaborated enough.[79] By involving team members, organizations foster collaboration; build employee engagement, which leads to less burnout and lower turnover; gain fresh perspectives; and enhance creativity. There are several types of team decision-making techniques: brainstorming, the nominal group technique (NGT), and the Delphi technique.

Brainstorming

One approach to team decision-making is the concept of **brainstorming**, which is generating creative, spontaneous ideas from all members of a group without making any initial criticism or judgment of them.[80] While brainstorming is a popular method of idea generation among many organizations, decades of studies have shown that simply gathering a group to toss out as many ideas as possible within a certain amount of time does not work.[81] In fact, studies show that people who follow this type of brainstorming produce fewer ideas (and fewer good ideas) than they would on their own. This is because people in a group setting are more likely to be influenced by the ideas of others, which causes them to think similarly, resulting in stagnation of creative and original thinking.

However, while the evidence points to flaws in the brainstorming process, this does not mean people should stop brainstorming altogether; it merely calls for a new approach.[82]

Brainstorm Alone—At First

Brainstorming alone is a useful way of coming up with new, creative ideas without being influenced by the group. Then, when everyone has had a chance to brainstorm alone, they can get together as a group and build on those ideas. One brainstorming technique includes the 6-3-5 method. Six people write down three ideas each. These ideas are passed to the person on their right, who builds on those ideas. The stack is passed around five times, ensuring that everyone in the group has a chance to develop each idea. When everyone is finished, the group gets together to discuss the ideas.

Slow Down the Creative Process

Some people don't like brainstorming. They would rather get the brainstorming process over with quickly in order to start implementing the solution. These people have a high level of the personality characteristic "need for closure." However, it is important that enough time is given to the brainstorming process so enough ideas are generated to find the right solution to the problem. The 6-3-5 method slows down the creative process by giving people individual turns to write down their ideas. This also helps people who have a need for closure, as it teaches them that everyone needs to wait until ideas are generated and built on.

Start Drawing

Studies show that a combination of drawing and writing is highly beneficial in generating ideas and coming up with creative solutions to problems. Drawing is useful because it helps describe ideas that are difficult to explain in words and also appeals to the part of the brain dedicated to visual processing. It is also helpful to include words in sketches or diagrams to aid interpretation. Google employees use pictures during their brainstorming sessions, believing that "pictures are usually louder than words and harder to misinterpret."[83]

Digital Brainstorming

Digital brainstorming is an effective way to gather ideas from virtual teams. Studies have shown that with the right approach, digital brainstorming can be more successful in generating high-quality ideas than traditional brainstorming.[84] By working independently rather than in person, brainstormers have more freedom to contribute in a way that removes feelings of self-consciousness and the social fear that sometimes occurs in a group setting.

The Nominal Group Technique

While using the right approach to brainstorming can be a useful way to make decisions, many organizations use other team decision-making techniques. The **nominal group technique** (NGT) is a structured way for team members to generate ideas and identify solutions.[85] Each member is asked the same question in relation to a work issue and requested to write down as many solutions as possible. Answers are read aloud and recorded for discussion. Then the ideas are put to a vote. No criticism or judgment of any ideas is allowed. The nominal group technique is particularly useful in bigger groups, where often only the loudest voices are heard. Using this technique allows each group member to put forward their ideas and solutions, thereby taking everyone's opinions into account.

The Delphi Technique

The **Delphi technique** is a method of decision-making in which information is gathered from a group of respondents within their area of expertise.[86] Questionnaires are sent to a select group of experts, whose responses are collated and reviewed, and then a summary is returned to the group with a follow-up questionnaire. Again, the experts provide their answers. The process continues until the group agrees on a common answer and a decision is reached. The Delphi technique was applied during the implementation of the new patient efficiency program at the Thomas Jefferson University Hospital profiled in our case study. This method allowed the group of executive physicians to gain new insights into the hospital's operations by gauging the thoughts and perspectives of the nurses in the emergency department.

Good-quality team decision-making has the power to drive business performance, which in turn positively impacts an organization's bottom line. However, there are both advantages and disadvantages of team decision-making.

Advantages and Disadvantages of Team Decision-Making

Team decision-making has its advantages. It often gives those involved a broader perspective, provides more alternatives, clarifies ambiguities, and brings about team satisfaction and support. By involving each team member in the decision, it also increases engagement, gains buy-in from the people who will have to do the work, and results in better decisions being made overall.

However, team decision-making also has its disadvantages. Meetings can be time-consuming; too much attention can be paid to simple matters; nobody may take responsibility for the decision; and team members might end up agreeing on a compromise that satisfies nobody.

One important factor that can negatively affect team decision-making is **groupthink**, a psychological phenomenon in which people in a cohesive group go along with the group consensus rather than offering their own opinions.[87] Groupthink is a major disadvantage to team decision-making, because the team members are more concerned with preserving harmony in the group than with risking opinions that may cause conflict or offense. In doing so, people lose the ability to "think outside the box" or think creatively in their decisions. This leads to an environment where ideas and perspectives simply remain unchallenged, which over time can prevent an organization from innovating, progressing, and competing. Being in this kind of group confers an illusion of immunity, an "us against the world" view in which the group members see themselves as knowing better than outsiders, even given evidence to the contrary. In the UK, Dominic Cummings, the former adviser to Prime Minister Boris Johnson, accused the UK government of groupthink for its slow response to the initial threat of COVID-19. Cummings believed that people working for Johnson felt too intimidated to challenge assumptions and share their doubts about the government's official plan.[88]

The rise of social media has also contributed to groupthink. For the first time in history, people are able to air their views to a large audience without the help of television networks, radio, or other media reserved for the select few.

Not only do we like to express our opinions on social media, but we are more willing to share our views with a like-minded audience, which has a tendency to cloud our judgment.[89] According to author Eli Pariser, this creates "filter bubbles" that contain people with the same views but, where those views go unchallenged, leads to polarization.[90] In fact, a study conducted by the University of Chicago discovered that "people held more-extreme positions after they spoke with like-minded others," which further cements groups together, limiting diversity of thought.[91] In a series of experiments, Berkeley researchers demonstrated how ideas—whether they are good, bad, or inaccurate—can spread on social media and lead to groupthink, even if those ideas are perpetuated by bots or fake users.[92] However, there is hope that social media will eventually become a tool that fosters wider discussion rather than restricting it to the shared views of like-minded groups.

In this chapter, we have focused on the different types of teams and how teams generate ideas and find solutions. In the next chapter, we will explore how managers make decisions and how organizations, teams, and individuals engage in creativity and innovation.

IN REVIEW

8.1 Distinguish between teams and groups

A **team** is a group of people brought together to use their individual skills on a common project or goal. Regardless of the type of organization, most employees work in some form of team in today's workplace. A **group** usually consists of three or more people who work independently to attain organizational goals.

8.2 Explain how team processes affect team outcomes

Process gains are factors that contribute to team effectiveness. They include a sense of shared purpose, plans, and goals; the confidence team members have in their own abilities to achieve objectives; a shared vision of how the work should be carried out; and constructive task-focused conflict that can help teams with their problem-solving and decision-making.

Process losses are factors that detract from team effectiveness. They include **social loafing**, wherein people in a group put in less effort than when working independently; personality clashes or conflict; and the inability to focus on certain tasks.

8.3 Compare the various types of teams in organizations today

Many global companies now operate in **virtual teams**, whose members are from different locations and work together through email, videoconferencing, instant messaging, and other electronic media. Diverse teams provide companies with a greater reach into global markets because of their ability to communicate with people from similar backgrounds. A **self-managing team** is a group of workers who manage their own daily duties under little to no supervision. A **problem-solving team** is a group of workers coming together for a set amount of time to discuss and resolve specific issues. A **cross-functional team** is a group of workers from different units with various areas of expertise.

8.4 Apply the model of team effectiveness to evaluate team performance

Team contextual influences include team resources, task characteristics, and organizational structures and systems. Team resources are the level of support provided by the organization, such as equipment, materials, training, information, staffing, budgets, and such. Task characteristics can be structured or unstructured; complex or simple; and measured by a degree of interdependence. Performance management systems, compensation and reward systems, and organizational and leadership structures must be aligned with team structures to maintain smooth running of operations.

Typically, a team has four main elements: team size, skills and abilities, personality of team members, and team diversity. Teams tend to consist of four to seven members. The skills and abilities of the team members are very important, but the way this talent interacts in the context of team processes is also important. Typically, teams need a balance between extraverts and introverts. Team members who share common interests or certain similarities tend to have positive social relationships with each other that help the team to be more effective.

8.5 Identify the advantages and disadvantages of different team decision-making approaches

Groupthink is a psychological phenomenon in which people in a cohesive group go along with the group consensus to preserve harmony rather than offering their own opinions.

Brainstorming generates creative, spontaneous ideas from all members of a group without any criticism or judgment.

The **nominal group technique** is a structured way for team members to generate ideas and identify solutions. Each member is asked the same question in relation to a work issue and requested to write as many answers as possible. Answers are read aloud and recorded for discussion. Then the ideas are put to the vote. No criticism or judgment of any ideas is allowed. The **Delphi technique** is a method of decision-making in which information is gathered from a group of respondents within their area of expertise.

KEY TERMS

Adjourning (p. 176)
Brainstorming (p. 190)
Cohesion (p. 179)
Contextual diversity (p. 184)
Cross-functional team (p. 184)
Cultural metacognition (p. 186)
Cyberloafing (p. 180)
Decentralization (p. 173)
Delphi technique (p. 191)
Forming (p. 176)
Group (p. 174)
Groupthink (p. 192)
Interdependence (p. 187)
Nominal group technique (p. 191)
Norming (p. 176)
Norms (p. 178)
Performing (p. 176)
Personal diversity (p. 184)
Pooled interdependence (p. 188)
Problem-solving team (p. 183)

Process gains (p. 179)
Process losses (p. 179)
Psychological safety (p. 175)
Punctuated equilibrium (p. 178)
Reciprocal interdependence (p. 188)
Self-managing team (p. 183)
Sequential interdependence (p. 188)
Social facilitation (p. 181)
Social loafing (p. 179)
Storming (p. 176)
Synergy (p. 179)
Team (p. 173)
Virtual teams (p. 193)

UP FOR DEBATE: "THERE IS NO 'I' IN TEAM"

A famous adage is "There is no 'I' in TEAM." This means that teams thrive when members focus on team functioning and outcomes as opposed to individual team members focusing on themselves. Do you agree or disagree with this quote?

EXERCISE 8.1: PRACTICING 6-3-5 BRAINSTORMING

Objective

The purpose of this exercise is to gain a greater appreciation of brainstorming.

Instructions

Brainstorming is ubiquitous in the business world. Companies use brainstorming for developing new products, adding features to existing products, crafting new marketing campaigns, improving services provided by human resources, and many more uses. One technique that has gained a foothold in businesses in recent years is the process of 6-3-5 brainstorming. With this method, team members spend some time alone developing ideas before bringing them to the group as a whole. It works like this: first, teams of six members are formed; second, each of the six team members writes down three ideas without input from anyone else; and third, the pieces of paper with the ideas are passed to the right, where new ideas are added (and this is done a total of five times).

This exercise utilizes the 6-3-5 method of brainstorming. Form teams of six people (if there aren't enough people to make this work exactly, it's okay if some groups have five or seven team members). The scenario is as follows: Your team works for a restaurant, and the dessert menu has been exactly the same for the last five years. The owner wants some new, fresh ideas for desserts. Using the 6-3-5 method, brainstorm as many new ideas as possible. Then, once the papers have been passed around five times, narrow the list down to the top three desserts you can all agree on to ultimately submit to the restaurant owner.

Reflection Questions

1. Traditional brainstorming simply has a group of people work together to develop as many ideas as possible. The 6-3-5 method is individual based first, and *then* the other team members get involved in adding ideas. What are the advantages and disadvantages of traditional brainstorming and the 6-3-5 method of brainstorming?
2. Which do you prefer as a brainstorming technique: traditional brainstorming or the 6-3-5 method? Explain.
3. What are ways you could utilize the 6-3-5 method of brainstorming at your current or most recent job?

Exercise contributed by Steven Stovall, Southeast Missouri State University.

EXERCISE 8.2: A NOMINAL BRAINSTORM ABOUT THE DELPHI TECHNIQUE

Objectives

This exercise will help you to *identify* the advantages and disadvantages of different team decision-making approaches.

Instructions

Form into a group of six to eight members. Your task is to develop a set of recommendations on using the Delphi technique and explain its appropriateness for generating management ideas. You will be developing these recommendations using the brainstorming and nominal group methods. To complete this task, complete the following steps:

Step1. Select a person to write down the ideas generated in this exercise and to tally votes in the later steps. (1 to 2 minutes)

Step 2. Use the brainstorming method to generate ideas about when using the Delphi technique would not be successful. These ideas can either be statements about the general characteristics of a situation or about a specific job situation. (5 minutes)

Step 3. Combine ideas where appropriate. Soliciting feedback from everyone in your group, determine whether an idea is relevant or not for your guidelines. To be considered relevant, an idea must be true (based on chapter concepts) and useful in a business setting. Write down the list of ideas that are voted as being relevant. (1 to 2 minutes)

Step 4. Use the nominal group technique to generate ideas about when the Delphi technique would be successful. These ideas can either be statements about the general characteristics of a situation or a specific job situation. (5 to 10 minutes).

Step 5. Repeat Step 3. (1 to 2 minutes)

Reflection Questions

1. Which idea generation method did you prefer? Why?
2. Which idea method generation method generated the most ideas?
3. Which idea generated the most relevant ideas?
4. What new ways of employing the Delphi technique did you discover?

Exercise contributed by Milton R. Mayfield, Professor of Business, Texas A&M International University, and Jacqueline R. Mayfield, Professor of Business, Texas A&M International University.

EXERCISE 8.3: CONSULTING AT BELLA NOTA

Objective

This exercise will help you to *distinguish* between teams and groups, *compare* different types of teams, and *apply* the team effectiveness model.

Background

You are in a consulting group who is working with Bella Nota—a company in Austin, Texas, that provides background and incidental music for commercials and industrial videos. The company has enough steady business to sustain 10 musicians, 2 composers, 2 sound engineers, and 1 conductor as full-time employees. The musicians and conductor usually work together on a regular basis, rotating between the composers and engineers. When business picks up or there is a call for a larger set of musicians, the local talent pool provides an easy source for short-term hires. While many of the same people are hired frequently, none of these people work for Bella Nota on an ongoing basis.

The company president, Natalie Bell, realizes how critically important high-quality team processes are to her business. She has brought in your consulting group to help design guidelines for developing effective teams. To form these guidelines, you will need to provide the following:

- Create a guideline that distinguishes between groups and teams. Include the differences between a team and a group, specifying when the use of teams would be more appropriate at Bella Nota.

- Develop a guideline for classifying different types of teams. While not all team types will be represented in the musical side of the company, there are other business activities and teams that will find these guidelines useful.
- Develop a guideline for evaluating the musical teams/groups on process. This guideline will be used for developing suggestions for future team/group improvements.

Instructions

Step 1. Form into teams to complete the three tasks outlined in the background section. (20 to 30 minutes)

Step 2. Present your guidelines to the class and be prepared to answer questions from the class and the instructor. (20 to 30 minutes)

Reflection Questions

1. How did using chapter terms and concepts help you to better structure your thinking about teams and team processes?
2. If you have been working in a team in this or another class, how can you use the guidelines in improving team outcomes?
3. How do processes differ in team work situations compared with individual work situations? How do team processes differ between different types of teams?

Exercise contributed by Milton R. Mayfield, Professor of Business, Texas A&M International University, and Jacqueline R. Mayfield, Professor of Business, Texas A&M International University.

ONLINE EXERCISE 8.1: VIRTUAL TEAM PROJECT

Objective

The purpose of this exercise is to gain an appreciation for virtual teams.

Instructions

Utilizing a discussion board, a virtual team will be created to complete a project. The scenario is as follows: You work for a very small company that had a very successful app for phones two years ago. The app was for runners who wanted to connect with other runners nearby for training or just to partner with someone to enjoy the company of a fellow runner. Though the app was free, income was garnered through ads on the app. However, the initial popularity of that app has faded, and sales of ads have diminished greatly. The president of the company desperately wants to introduce a new app to the public, and she doesn't care what that app is.

The president has asked all of you to develop a new app from start to finish. Using the discussion board, brainstorm a new cell phone app. Once you all agree on what the concept is, virtually partner with others on the discussion board and divide up the following roles among you:

- Sales (how the app will generate income)
- Images (what the graphics will look like)
- Text (what words and wording will be used)
- Functions (what the app will actually do)
- Marketing (how consumers will know the app exists)

After these roles have been divided among the discussion board participants, develop the app. Obviously, those working on functions will have to work closely with the images and text personnel to ensure the app's interface is attractive to users—which is important for marketing. And, if sales personnel want to place ads within the app, the salespeople will need to work closely with all the other groups to make the ads as seamless and unobtrusive as possible to the end users.

Reflection Questions

1. What difficulties did you have in building an effective team for this exercise? What successes did you have?
2. How did the team resolve conflict?
3. In what ways was this exercise similar to team-building projects you have had at your current or most recent job? How was it different?
4. What did you learn from this exercise that you can utilize in your current or most recent job? How will this help you as your career progresses?

Exercise contributed by Steven Stovall, Southeast Missouri State University.

ONLINE EXERCISE 8.2: OBSERVING EFFECTIVE TEAMS

Objective

The purpose of this exercise is to understand what makes a team effective.

Instructions

For this exercise, search online for a video that showcases what you consider to be effective teamwork. It might be a play in a football game, a military operation, a well-orchestrated basketball play, a band playing a piece of music, or a similar activity. Once you locate a short video, describe why you selected this as an example of effective teamwork.

Reflection Questions

1. Consider the video you selected. Why is this a demonstration of effective teamwork but a similar example isn't? How is your chosen video more demonstrative than others?
2. What do you think contributed to the success of the team in the video? Was it communication? Practice with teammates? Something else?
3. Imagine if one person were removed from the video. Do you think this would still be an example of effective teamwork? Why or why not?

Exercise contributed by Steven Stovall, Southeast Missouri State University.

CASE 8.1: PEPSICO

PepsiCo foods and beverages are consumed more than 1 billion times a day in over 200 countries and territories around the world. In 2021, 23 of the company's classic brands like Pepsi-Cola, Mountain Dew, Gatorade, and Doritos generated over $1 billion in sales each, contributing to PepsiCo's total net revenue of $79.5 billion across its portfolio for the year. With approximately 309,000 employees worldwide, effective teams are essential to PepsiCo's continued success.[93]

Matt Del Giudice, PsyD, MBA, was an organizational development consultant for the Department of Veterans Affairs (VA) before joining as the program lead for the company's Senior Leader Development Center (SLDC) in 2014. The VA role prepared Del Giudice well for the skepticism they would face when advising more than 150 senior vice presidents in five global cohorts at PepsiCo: "I spent a lot of time consulting with senior leaders, and often this included giving them difficult feedback." At PepsiCo, Del Giudice cautioned a senior leader about their intimidating communication style because it was impeding the team's effectiveness. The leader pushed back, telling Del Giudice they must be good at what mattered if they had been promoted so many times. The executive eventually acquiesced when they understood that nurturing relationships and building trust was key to performing at an even higher level.[94]

Del Giudice's tenure in executive assessment and development was marked by many such stories of leaders who were initially reticent to change their behaviors but enjoyed better team cohesion and elevated performance when they did. Del Giudice's program at the SLDC proved effective, with over 90% of participants showing improvement in key leadership metrics in a follow-up study. Today, Del Giudice is PepsiCo's senior director of global talent management and organization development and oversees succession planning, performance management, and HiPo (high-potential employee) assessment for thousands of employees across 20 departments worldwide.

Justin Wells, PepsiCo's director of global project management and innovation process, sought Del Giudice's expertise to address the innovation teams' lackluster performance. Upon examination, Del Giudice discovered overpopulated teams whose unnecessary members caused unproductive and inefficient meetings. Other teams were too streamlined and operated in silos, failing to effectively collaborate with specialized critical stakeholders like food scientists and lawyers. In addition, a dearth of communication between senior leadership and the innovation teams resulted in project delays and months of lost work. Del Giudice strove to get the teams quickly back on track by training one member of each group on team formation and project strategy, and those members in turn influenced the rest of their team members and communicated progress to senior leaders. "Matt helped me see that change is hard for people," Wells said. "Even if people knew something will make them more efficient, they may not like it. Matt helped with engaging the teams to make them open to change." This divide-and-conquer strategy proved successful. "When senior leaders reinforced that work products were 'works in progress' and did not need to be perfect, communication and feedback flowed more freely," Del Giudice said. "The dynamics become more iterative and focused on learning."

Tina Bigalke, PepsiCo's global chief diversity, equity, and inclusion officer, echoes Del Giudice's admonition to communicate freely instead of letting perfection stifle progress: "People stay silent or don't engage because they don't want to make a mistake, but you're going to make mistakes—that's part of the learning process." Bigalke's solution to fear of failure applies equally to apprehensive associates and intimidating senior vice presidents, explaining, "When you overcome that fear and engage with empathetic curiosity, you go beyond the surface and start making real connections, which in turn helps relationships grow and therefore inspires teams and people to deliver results." As the head of PepsiCo's DEI strategy, Bigalke believes that genuine curiosity and openness is the most powerful way to make one's voice heard and demands that staff advocate for others as well. "You have to have an authentic, personal commitment to inclusion and wanting to hear others' voices. Speak up for people, challenge the status quo, and engage in courageous decisions."[95]

Christine Daugherty, PepsiCo vice president of global sustainable agriculture and responsible sourcing, is no fan of the status quo either: "At PepsiCo we have the opportunity to really influence and change the global food system for the better . . . That gives me the opportunity to think, 'How can we use our voice, our influence, our technology, our diversity to drive positive change?'" Prior to joining PepsiCo, Daugherty was a NASA research scientist and a patent attorney and has abundant personal experience with the kind of courageous decisions DEI counterpart Tina Bigalke exhorts PepsiCo team members to engage in. Daugherty's current role involves traveling around the world, facing unfamiliar challenges, and meeting with supply partners to establish environmentally sustainable sourcing practices and ethically fair treatment for the farmers who grow the crops that become PepsiCo products. "If you don't get in a place where you are uncomfortable, you become stagnant. I have grown to be comfortable being uncomfortable," Daugherty says.[96]

PepsiCo's hiring and promotion of leaders with fearless temperaments and diverse experiences like Bigalke and Daugherty can be traced directly back to Matt Del Giudice. Del Giudice's evaluation of data from a survey designed to identify which senior leaders would be the best collaborators uncovered that breadth of experience in role responsibilities and locations was the best predictor of success. "This was a critical insight from Matt's work because it informed our talent management plans at the company," said Taylor Flake, former vice president of human resources. "It also highlights Matt's ability to toggle between psychological details and business knowledge to create programs that are very strategic for a large company."

Del Giudice credits these experiences at PepsiCo with sharpening their ability to view problems through different lenses. The minutiae of psychological assessments that fascinate Del Giudice are not always germane to the goals of business leaders, but they have learned to translate data into practical insights. "I consider it a privilege to work with leaders," Del Giudice says. "They wield a significant amount of influence over the lives of those who work with them. I believe that helping leaders create a positive work environment is not only good for business, it's also a moral imperative."

Critical-Thinking Questions

1. Describe some of the process losses Del Giudice diagnosed among the leaders and teams at PepsiCo and how the problems were remedied.
2. How many suboptimal contextual elements and team characteristics can you identify in the description of the innovation teams that Justin Wells and Matt Del Giudice partnered together to improve?
3. How can the behaviors Tina Bigalke and Christine Daugherty advocate lead to process gains and effective teams?

Doug Pensinger/Staff/Getty Images

9 DECISION-MAKING, CREATIVITY, AND INNOVATION

LEARNING OBJECTIVES

By the end of this chapter, you will be able to:

9.1 Identify the primary types of decisions managers make to solve problems

9.2 Identify factors that influence the way we make decisions in the real world

9.3 Discuss the critical nature of creativity and innovation in today's organizations

9.4 Describe the three-component model of creativity

9.5 Outline the steps in the innovation process

9.6 Identify the main types of innovations in organizations

Case Study: Creativity and Innovation, Arizona State University

"Let's go to the number-one party school in the U.S.!" Such an exclamation was typical of prospective Arizona State University students for many years through the 1990s and early 2000s. Including graduate and undergraduate enrollment, Arizona State University has more than 77,800 students, so it makes sense that ASU became primarily a symbol of social life.[1] There are almost 17,800 employees on staff, and that combined with the student body adds up to the size of a bustling city.[2] Arizona State University has become a behemoth of an organization, and it must answer to the taxpayers of an entire state; it is difficult for any person or group to run an organization with so many facets. Led by President Michael Crow and a carefully selected team, ASU is now regarded as the number-one university for innovation—a title they achieved by, not surprisingly, innovating.

Exploratory Innovation

In an attempt to pursue innovation and diversity, Arizona State University began adopting policies previously considered taboo in the world of higher education. Administrators decided to find ways to enroll as many capable students as possible; as seen through ASU's charter, "ASU is a comprehensive public research university, measured not by whom we exclude, but rather by whom we include and how they succeed."[3] Since setting aside the traditional industry metric of the acceptance rate, the university has seen record numbers of enrollment, and it is a place of cultural, social, economic, and ideological diversity. It is currently ranked near the very top in universities for veterans, and it is ranked at the very top of places to study for international students.[4]

The research funding at ASU has rapidly increased since 2002 to nearly $640 million in 2021.[5] In both 2021 and 2022, the widely trusted *U.S. News*report on higher education ranked ASU as the most innovative university in the country.[6] Arizona State University risked becoming a school known simply for its academic standards by bringing in so many students, but the leadership delivered on bringing in a huge supply of idea creation. This bold and innovative move to search for creativity through diversity plays a fundamental role in maintaining the university's accommodative approach to vast numbers of students.

Organizational Structure and Innovative Change

Arizona State University has many different vice presidents and directors, and they use this as a chance to bring about people innovation. There are 15 vice presidents of the university and 24 vice provosts and deans, so management at the university intentionally works in a large web to ensure diversity of ideas and creativity.[7] Many organizations struggle with silos and a lack of delegation, whereas the dozens of departments at ASU all run differently but with the same mission: to educate as many people as possible. In that way, ASU has taken tips from retailers and production corporations with similar structures, whose goal is to sell product to as many people as possible, and applied them to the pursuit of education.

Competitive Innovation

Another reason Arizona State University sticks out as an innovative institution compared to its peers is that it competes with other universities, and it does so through innovative means. Colleges and universities in the United States of America have always jousted for position in rankings and reputation, but ASU put a new twist on competition when they began accepting and educating so many thousands of undergraduate students. Instead of the traditional path of marketing their university in an attempt to increase application numbers and push acceptance rates down, the managers of Arizona State University market the university as a feasible path for any person genuinely seeking a higher education. This mindset is a form of innovation within the industry, as is the methodology propping it up.[8]

ASU tracks the statistics and benchmarks of dozens of nearby universities and community colleges, but not necessarily to find weaknesses. In fact, this process is an attempt to find strengths: Arizona State University partners with a number of universities across the United States; if a new, innovative program or research opportunity exists, the management at ASU hunts it down. This competitive edge extends into the business world. Arizona State University has one of the largest corporate sponsorships in the university world. Starbucks and ASU are partnered to bring education to thousands of baristas, and Starbucks CEO Howard Schultz spoke at the 2017 commencement.[9] In sum, Arizona State University exposes the cornucopia of opportunities for organizations led by innovative people and ideas, and its managers provide a useful exhibit of the constant search for improvement that goes hand in hand with innovation.

Innovation in Philanthropy

Universities such as ASU that strive to top the list of innovators often pride themselves on the work of their graduates. Recently, students out of Arizona State began a group called 33 Buckets, which traveled across South America installing affordable water filters and training local citizens on their maintenance. This was born out of a program called EPICS: Engineering in Community Service, where students and professors spend class time actively innovating and then launch as many real-world projects as possible. This program serves as an example for organizations who seek creative potential in their team members, and it shows that organizations can engage in practiced creativity by creating a space for it.[10]

Critical-Thinking Questions

1. What innovative decision boosted Arizona State University's enrollment?
2. How does ASU think about enrollment differently than competitors, and why do they do this?
3. How could the practices mentioned in this chapter and case report be integrated into your workplace?

DECISION-MAKING AND PROBLEM-SOLVING

The ability to make decisions and solve problems is a key aspect of organizational behavior. Every day, dozens of vice presidents, vice provosts, and deans working at ASU make pivotal decisions to align the university with its mission: to educate as many people as possible and to build diversity, innovation, and creativity.

We make decisions, big and small, every single day in our professional and personal lives. Living in the technology era means we are subject to a continuous flow of information that needs to be processed and absorbed. When we're deciding what to do with this abundance of information, our understanding of a rational decision-making process can guide us toward the right course of action. **Decision-making** is the action or process of identifying a strategy to resolve problems.[11] There is a tendency to use decision-making and problem-solving interchangeably, but they are not the same thing. Problem-solving is a method that requires analytical thinking and intuition to find a solution, whereas decision-making is a process that takes place during problem-solving and involves judgment to decide on the right course of action.

Amazon has a reputation for having high-quality customer service.

iStockPhoto/Julie Clopper

There are two main types of decisions: programmed decisions and nonprogrammed decisions.[12]

Programmed decisions are automatic responses to routine and recurring situations. Usually, these situations have occurred in the past and are familiar to the people dealing with them. Decisions are generally made by following company policies and guidelines that have been put in place to deal with specific issues. For example, Costco, Amazon, Apple, and Salesforce are just a few companies that are market leaders in customer service because of their excellent policy for responding efficiently to customer queries and resolving customer complaints. The COVID-19 pandemic encouraged many companies to change their company policies and guidelines to serve their customers. For example, Apple offered a Customer Assistance Program that allowed cardholders to skip monthly payments on Apple Cards without incurring interest.[13] Brick-and-mortar stores like Target introduced curbside pickup to make shopping safer and more convenient for customers during the pandemic—a policy that is predicted to stay.[14]

Nonprogrammed decisions respond to new or nonroutine problems for which there are no proven solutions. In these situations, employees won't find the answer they're looking for in the company handbook or policy guidelines. Very often, the problems are complex in nature, with few past occurrences for employees to draw on. For example, the rising number of cybersecurity threats and cybercrimes is an example of a complex problem that has not occurred so much in the past. Battling cybercrime will require serious decisions, given it is one of the biggest challenges facing organizations today, regardless of their size. For example, in 2021, meat processing company JBS Foods suffered a cyberattack that resulted in shutting down operations in its Canadian, Australian, and U.S. branches. JBS made the tough decision to pay the ransom demanded by the hackers—$11 million, one of the biggest payments ever paid out to hackers.[15]

We make dozens of decisions in our personal lives every day—from what we're going to wear to who we're going to meet to what we're going to eat for lunch. Some of these decisions are conscious, while others are instinctive. However, in business, decisions need to be made with more care and analysis. The skill of decision-making is one of the more important tools for managers and can make the difference between good and poor outcomes.

Managers often use the five-step decision-making process to help them make good decisions and resolve complex issues (Figure 9.1).

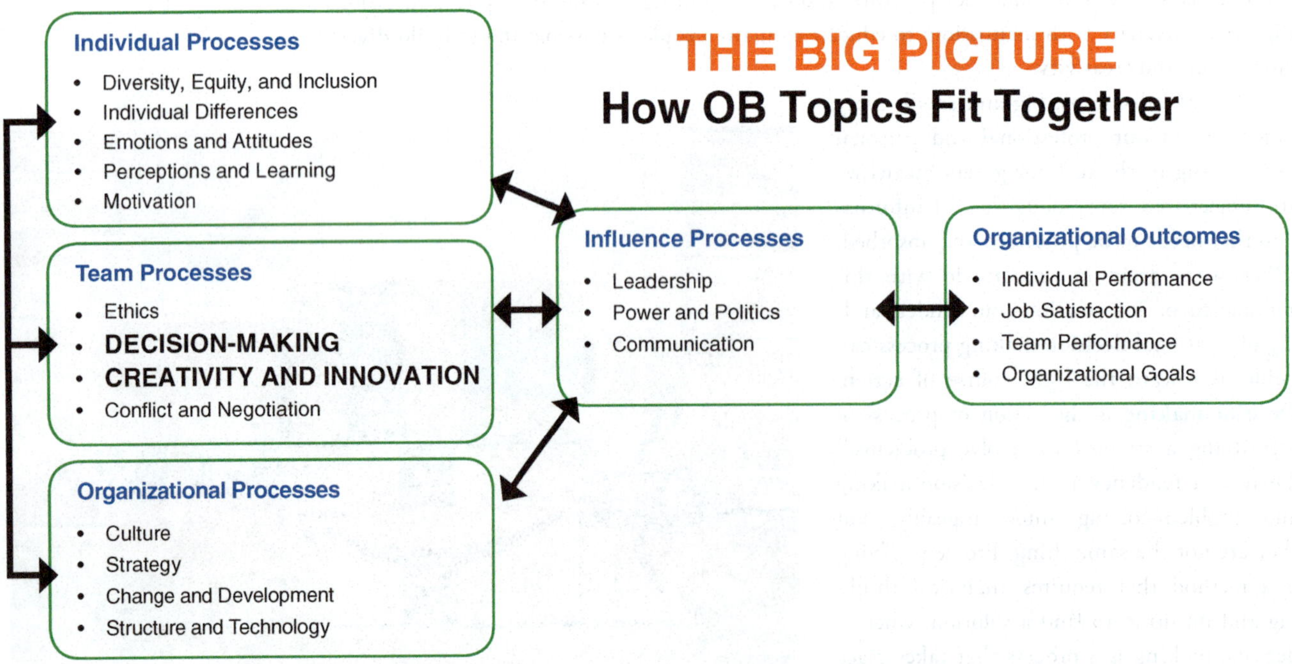

FIGURE 9.1 ■ A Five-Step Model of Decision-Making

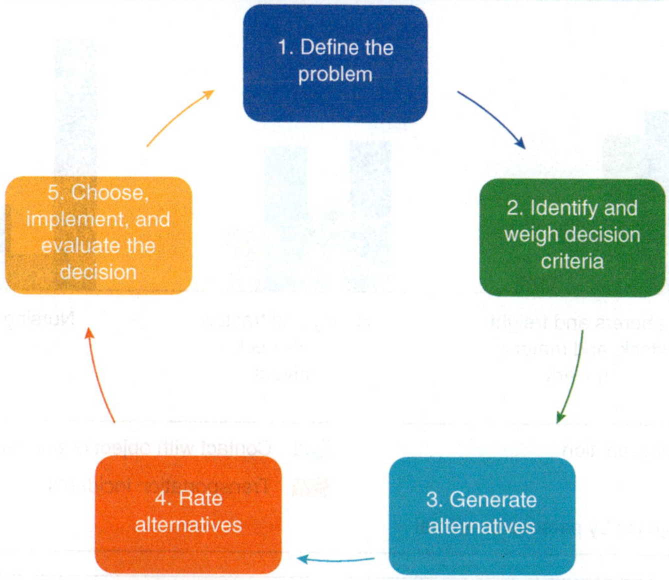

Define the Problem

The first step in the decision-making process is to define the problem. You need to fully understand the nature of the problem and be able to describe it in clear, concise terms in order to arrive at a solution. For example, say you are the manager of an assembly line in a manufacturing plant where work-related injuries have increased, leading to higher levels of absenteeism and falling profits due to reduced productivity. In this instance, the problem is the rise of work-related injuries and the goal would be to reduce the number of work-related injuries in the plant as soon as possible (Figure 9.2).

Identify and Weigh Decision Criteria

Now that the problem has been defined, you will need to identify and weigh the criteria in the decision—for example, the hazards and risks involved in the injuries, the degree to which employees follow safety procedures, and why injuries are becoming more common. One solution might be to increase employee focus on safety and encourage employees to care about safety procedures in a way that will not be viewed as a threat or a negative.

Generate Multiple Alternatives

Next, you may think of alternate solutions to the defined problem. Perhaps if you discover that employees are not adhering to safety guidelines, then stricter sanctions and punishments should be imposed for violations of safety standards. Alternatively, a reward system such as bonuses or vacation time for low injury rates would be a more beneficial way to highlight the safety initiative.

Rate Alternatives on the Basis of Decision Criteria

During this step, you might spend some time weighing the two possible solutions against each other and find they both rate poorly on the basis of the criteria. For example, sanctions and punishments could be viewed negatively and as a threat, and employees might fail to report injuries for fear of punishment. Similarly, though the reward system might be viewed more positively, there is also a concern that because rewards would be contingent on achieving a lower number of reported injuries, there is less incentive to report incidents that should be legally reported.

FIGURE 9.2 ■ Distribution of Selected Occupational Injuries for Selected Private Sector Occupations, 2013

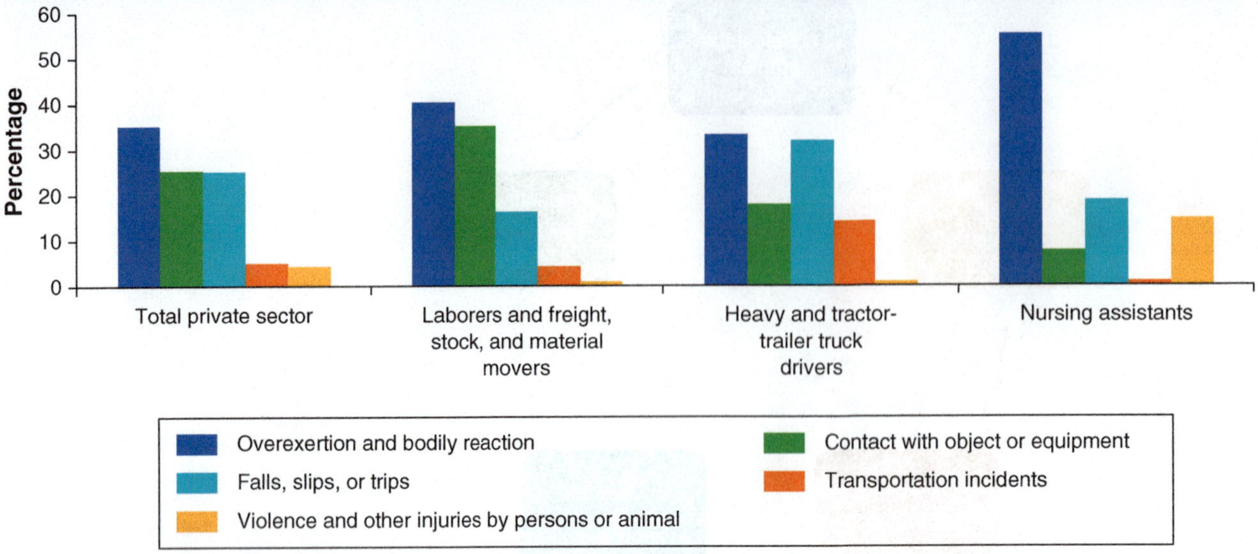

Source: Bureau of Labor Statistics. (2014). *Nonfatal occupational injuries and illnesses requiring days away from work, 2013* (p. 2). U.S. Department of Labor. www.bls.gov/news.release/pdf/osh2.pdf

Choose, Implement, and Evaluate the Best Alternative

Once the first four steps have been completed, it's time to make a decision on the basis of the information you've gathered. In this example, you might use a critical-thinking strategy to resolve the problem. This might involve designing a program around employee safety with specific attention to the plant's machinery. It could ask each employee to think critically about the work environment in terms of potential energy sources, including the plant's machines, which produce pressure, mechanical, chemical, electrical, gravity, and heat/cold energy. This initiative might encourage all employees to do three things relative to these energy sources: identify, act, and review. First, identify the energy source, and then take mitigating actions to eliminate it, control it, or if necessary, protect yourself from it. If that's not possible—for example, if the machine is malfunctioning—the employee should stop, call, and wait for a supervisor to review the situation. By making this decision, you have introduced a way to reduce work-related injuries in a nonthreatening way, as well as encouraging employees to think more seriously about their safety around machinery at work.

DECISION-MAKING IN THE REAL WORLD

We've seen that decision-making requires taking multiple steps to arrive at a clear solution. But what other factors affect an individual's ability to make rational decisions?

Bounded Rationality

Bounded rationality is the idea that we are restricted by a variety of constraints when making decisions.[16] This concept is in contrast with **complete rationality**, which assumes we take into account every single criterion or possible alternative when making a decision (see Figure 9.3).[17] In reality, most of us don't have the time or mental processing capacity to deal with so much information; instead, we tend to narrow the options to a few key criteria. For example, when buying a new car, we are more likely to use bounded rationality. First, we identify a few main benchmarks, like mileage, options, and price, and then we choose the models that meet our benchmarks to test drive. However, if we were to adopt a completely rational approach, we would need to consider every single car in production as a viable option, which is not realistic.

FIGURE 9.3 ■ Bounded Versus Complete Rationality

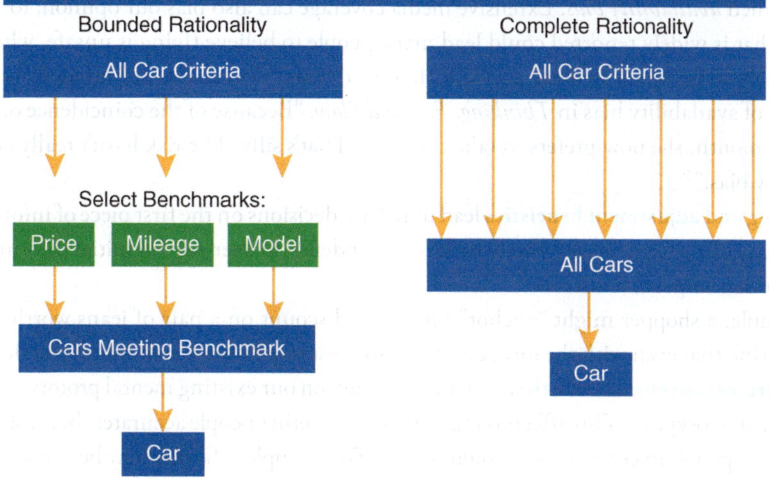

Satisficing Decisions

Satisficing decisions aim for acceptable results rather than the best or optimal solutions.[18] Satisficing is useful for less important decisions. For example, when purchasing a pack of chewing gum, we tend to choose something that looks good. We don't spend time researching the merits of all the different chewing gum brands and flavors on the market. If it turns out that we made a bad decision in choosing that particular brand, it's not a big deal, because gum isn't expensive. We simply make a different decision the next time. However, satisficing is not appropriate for important decisions. For example, when diagnosing illness, doctors can't afford to make an incorrect decision that causes harm; they need to consider a great deal of information to establish the right course of treatment for the patient.

Intuition

Intuition is the unconscious process of making decisions based on imagination and possibilities.[19] Relying on "a feeling" may not seem a totally reliable decision process. Some research suggests, however, that intuitive decisions often represent information we're already holding at an unconscious level, and thus it may lead to effective decisions.[20] In other words, the more stored knowledge we possess, the higher the quality of the decision-making. Take tennis players, for example. They have likely played tennis all their lives, so when they go onto the court, they tend to use their intuition to make split-second decisions rather than thinking through each stroke.[21]

Apple's classic slogan, "Think Different," alludes to founder Steve Jobs's tendency to rely on his intuition to make creative decisions and innovations.

Rob Janoff via Wikimedia Commons

Heuristics

Another aspect of decision making is **heuristics**, shortcuts or "rules of thumb" that allow us to make judgments and decisions quickly and efficiently.[22] There are three types of heuristics: availability heuristics, anchoring and adjustment heuristics, and representativeness heuristics.

Availability heuristics allow us to make judgments based on examples and events that are available and immediately spring to mind.[23] Sometimes we can make incorrect judgments about certain issues because of our reliance on information that is more readily available to us. This is called *availability bias*. Extensive media coverage can also bias our opinion; for example, a plane crash that is widely reported could lead many people to believe flying is unsafe, when it's actually more likely to be killed in a car accident than in the air.[24] Psychologist Daniel Kahneman uses this example of availability bias in *Thinking, Fast and Slow*: "Because of the coincidence of two planes crashing last month, she now prefers to take the train. That's silly. The risk hasn't really changed; it's an availability bias."[25]

Anchoring and adjustment heuristics lead us to base decisions on the first piece of information and then adjust it, leading to *anchoring bias*, which is the tendency to over-rely on initial information while overlooking other important criteria.[26]

For example, a shopper might "anchor" on a 25% discount on a pair of jeans worth $150 rather than considering that even with the discount, the jeans cost more than the shopper intended to spend.

With **representativeness heuristics**, we base a decision on our existing mental prototype and similar representative stereotypes.[27] This affects our ability to assess other people accurately because of our fixed ideas about how people in certain roles should behave. For example, a farmer may be perceived as tough, hardworking, and outdoorsy, whereas a librarian could be viewed as quiet, reserved, and efficient.[28]

We use representative heuristics to make decisions, using our existing expectations or experiences to predict an outcome. For example, you may expect someone dressed in a suit when interviewing for an office job to be a better fit for the company than someone who shows up in a sleeveless shirt and jeans.

Biases and Errors

Our decision-making is often influenced by different types of bias. Recognizing and minimizing these biases is crucial for making accurate decisions.

Common-information bias is the inclination to overemphasize information held by the majority of group members while failing to consider other perspectives held by the minority.[29] For example, in a voting situation, people often go along with the common or majority view rather than taking the time to learn about and discuss other views.

Confirmation bias is the tendency to seek out information that fuels or confirms our preexisting views and to discount information that conflicts with them.[30] For example, you might choose to follow people on social media only if they share your own viewpoints, or read only information that supports your views. Research shows that social media platforms such as Facebook and Twitter strengthen confirmation bias by exposing users to more of their preferred content rather than suggesting more diverse information with different viewpoints.[31]

Ease-of-recall bias is the propensity to over-rely on information recollected when making a decision.[32] For example, an investor might provide inaccurate information about a stock by plucking figures from memory instead of taking the time to locate the exact information.

Hindsight bias is the tendency to overestimate our ability to predict the outcome of an event.[33] For example, before a baseball game, you might "predict" that your favorite team is going to win. When your team does win, you might say, "I knew that was going to happen!" even though it's clearly impossible to predict these things.

Projection bias is the inclination to believe that other people think, feel, and act the same way we do (we project our thoughts and attitudes onto them).[34] For example, you might assume that all of your coworkers agree with your opinion of the company CEO, even though you've never asked them their opinion.

Escalation of commitment is the increased commitment we may make to a decision despite receiving negative information about the consequences.[35] For example, a manager may choose to invest in more and more training for an underperforming employee even though the evidence suggests that the employee's work is unlikely to improve. Figure 9.4 suggests a number of factors that can contribute to the escalation of commitment effect.

Sunk-cost bias is the decision to continue an unwise investment based on past investments of time, effort, and/or money.[36] For example, you might be reluctant to sell your car for a reasonable price because you spent so much to fix it (your sunk cost) and you think it's worth more than it is.

Framing bias is the tendency to highlight certain aspects of a situation to solve a problem while ignoring other aspects.[37] Framing bias can influence the decisions we make even when we're presented with the same information in different forms. For example, you may be more likely to choose a disinfectant that claims to kill 95% of bacteria over another product that states that only 5% of germs survive. The products say exactly the same thing, but the disinfectant with the higher percentage is framed more positively than the other option.[38]

Lack of participation error is the inclination to exclude certain people from the decision-making process. For example, in hierarchical companies, most of the lower-level employees aren't invited to partake in decision-making even though their feedback may prove very useful. Mike Kappel, founder

FIGURE 9.4 ■ Escalation of Commitment Effect

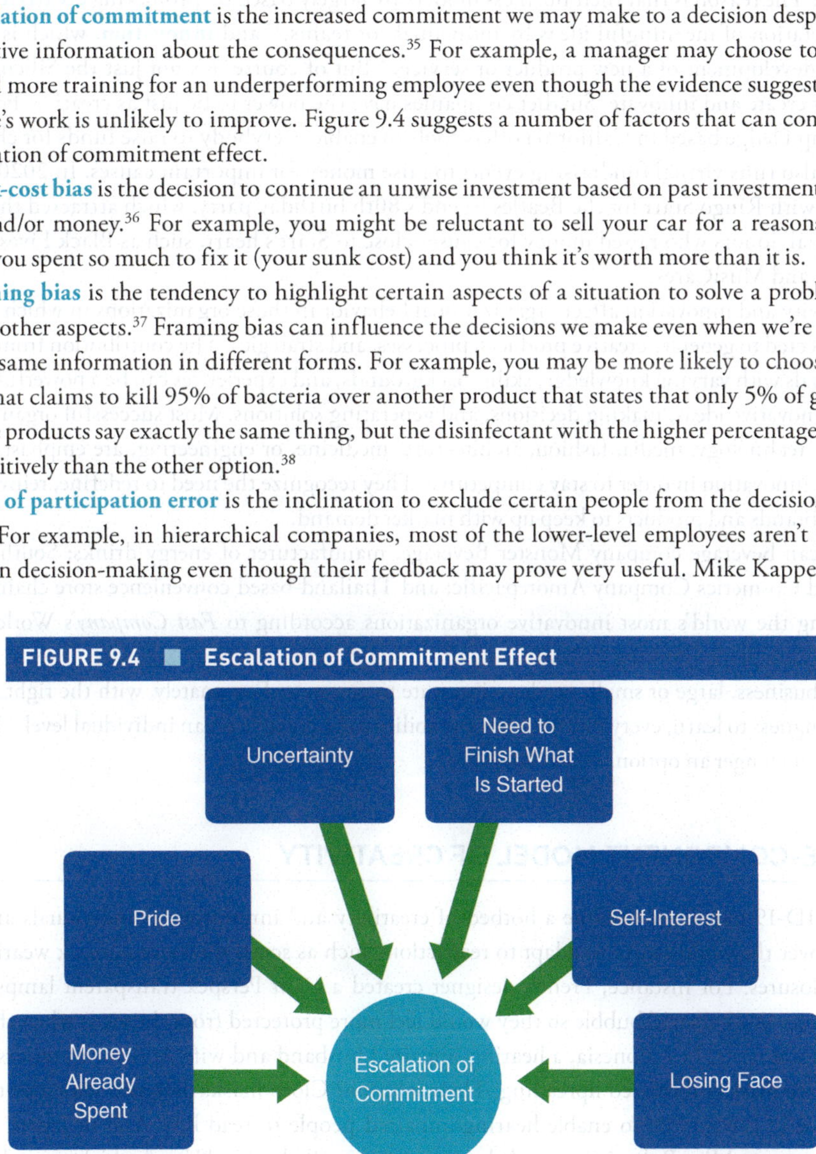

Source: Staw, B. M. (1981). The escalation of commitment to a course of action. *Academy of Management Review*, 6, 577–587.

and CEO of Patriot Software, believes that involving staff in decision-making leads to diverse opinions and fresh ideas, builds trust between senior management and employees, and boosts morale and engagement, as people feel more valued.[39]

Randomness error is the tendency for people to believe they can predict the outcome of chance events based on false information or superstition. For example, people believe it is possible to have a run of luck at the poker table, when in fact the probability of winning is the same every game.

CREATIVITY AND INNOVATION IN INDIVIDUALS, TEAMS, AND ORGANIZATIONS

In the previous sections, we have discussed the art of decision-making and its importance to today's organizations. Creativity and innovation can aid decision-making by giving people a greater understanding of the company's needs and its customers. Many of the world's leading organizations like Apple, Facebook, and Google have transformed the way we live and interact with others and encouraged us to want more. What do these organizations have in common, and why are they so wildly successful? The reason is that their business models are largely based on promoting **creativity**, which is the generation of meaningful ideas by individuals or teams,[40] and **innovation**, which is the creation and development of a new product or service.[41] But of course, it's not just the Silicon Valley giants that create and innovate. Smaller companies have the power to be just as creative. For example, start-up Pledge based in California offers tools to enable everybody to raise funds for charitable causes. It also runs virtual fundraising events to raise money for important causes. In 2020, Pledge partnered with Ringo Starr for the Beatles legend's 80th birthday party, which attracted thousands of individual donors who raised money for causes close to Starr's heart, such as Black Lives Matter, WaterAid, and MusiCares.[42]

Creativity and innovation affect organizational behavior in those organizations in which employees are expected to generate creative products, processes, and strategies. The contribution from a group of individuals with varying knowledge, skills, backgrounds, and experiences can be a powerful force in creating innovative ideas, making decisions, and generating solutions. Most successful organizations, whether in technology, media, fashion, architecture, medicine, or engineering, are emphasizing creativity and innovation in order to stay competitive. They recognize the need to redefine, reinvent, and repurpose brands and products to keep up with market demand.

American beverage company Monster Beverage, manufacturer of energy drinks; South Korean Beauty and Cosmetics Company Amorepacific; and Thailand-based convenience store chain CP All were among the world's most innovative organizations according to *Fast Company*'s World's Most Innovative Companies ranking in 2021.

Every business, large or small, needs to innovate to compete. Fortunately, with the right training and a willingness to learn, every one of us has the ability to be creative on an individual level. "Business as usual" is no longer an option.

A THREE-COMPONENT MODEL OF CREATIVITY

The COVID-19 pandemic became a hotbed of creativity and innovation as individuals and businesses all over the world strove to adapt to restrictions such as social distancing, mask wearing, and business closures. For instance, French designer created a giant Perspex transparent lampshade to enclose diners in a personal bubble so they would feel more protected from the virus when they were eating at restaurants. In Indonesia, a hearing-impaired husband and wife working as tailors discovered that face masks prohibited lipreading. Their solution? Cloth masks designed with a transparent plastic piece in the middle to enable hearing-impaired people to read lips. And in Japan, start-up robotics company Mira Robotics created the remote-controlled robot "Ugo," which uses ultraviolet rays to kill viruses on door handles.[43]

These individuals and businesses created innovations that filled a gap in the market and supported people through the pandemic. But what makes someone creative?

Cirque du Soleil constantly reinvents and innovates what we traditionally think about the circus, drawing on more high-end concepts like opera and theatre, to attract a higher-paying customer base.

Researchers have spent years trying to figure out what makes a person creative. Some theorists have focused on the personalities of history's most creative geniuses, such as Einstein, Plath, Edison, Plato, and Mozart, to try to find the common thread associated with creativity. Other theorists argue that the study of personality traits isn't sufficient to explain the foundations of creativity. Creativity researcher Teresa Amabile believes that creativity is a process rather than a list of traits and proposes a **three-component model of creativity** to describe the factors necessary for an individual to be creative. The three components of Amabile's model are domain-relevant skills and expertise, creativity-relevant processes, and task motivation (Figure 9.5).[44]

Domain-Relevant Skills and Expertise

Amabile argues that we must have *domain-relevant skills and expertise*—that is, knowledge about the subject and the skills and talent to provide the most creative and productive responses. An increase in

FIGURE 9.5 ■ Three Components of Creativity

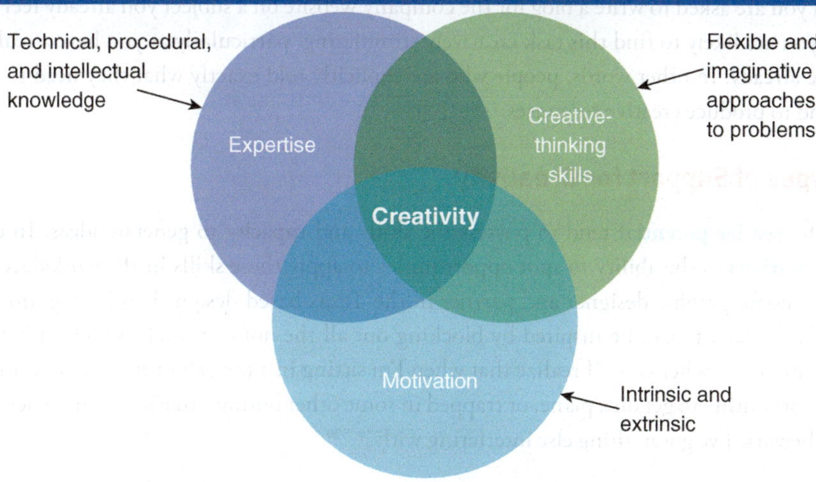

Source: Amabile, T. M. (1998, September). How to kill creativity. *Harvard Business Review, 76*(5), 76–87.

knowledge leads to higher levels of creativity. For example, say you work in the graphics section of your firm and your manager asks you to come up with a new product logo. If you are a brand expert, you will draw on your knowledge and experience of certain brands to come up with creative responses that accurately represent the product. Even without any brand knowledge, you can still produce creative responses, because such knowledge can be learned, but it usually takes longer to generate creative suggestions because it takes more time to acquire the relevant knowledge.[45]

Creativity-Relevant Processes

According to Amabile, *creativity-relevant processes*, work methods dependent on particular personality characteristics, methods of thinking, and knowledge of heuristics, are a second component needed for creativity. Personality traits such as self-discipline, perseverance, delayed gratification, and independence, for instance, appear to be associated with creative minds.[46] In addition, creative people tend to adopt a work style consisting of long periods of concentration and focus. They also have the ability to use **productive forgetting**, which allows them to abandon a solution that isn't working in favor of a new one.[47] People with creativity-relevant skills can also suspend judgment, adopt viewpoints different from their own, persist in overcoming obstacles, and ignore social approval. Finally, they use mental shortcuts or heuristics rather than strict rules to find creative ways to resolve a problem. For example, if you spend most of your day manually inputting data into a computer system, you might try to find practical ways to make the process more efficient. Like domain knowledge, creativity-relevant skills and processes can be learned through training and on-the- job experience.

Intrinsic and Extrinsic Motivation

People who have an innate interest in a chosen task tend to be more motivated to produce creative ideas. It stands to reason that if we find a task interesting and stimulating, we will be more inclined to engage with it. In contrast, a task that we perceive to be tedious and boring will not provoke the same degree of attention or inspiration.

In the past, it was believed that extrinsic or external factors that control the way a person deals with the task tend to inhibit creativity. For example, you might feel intimidated or overly cautious if your manager is looking over your shoulder while you answer emails. This level of control may indeed stifle your creativity and your willingness to take risks, while people who are given the freedom to explore creative options may feel less inhibited and more inclined to share their ideas. Similarly, extrinsic rewards such as bonuses or other monetary rewards may stunt employee creativity, because many people have a tendency to focus solely on the steps it takes to obtain the reward rather than thinking of creative ways to reach their work goal.

More recent research suggests that extrinsic motivation, when used in the right way, could support intrinsic or inner motivation, especially when the levels of intrinsic motivation are already high.[48] For example, if you are asked to write a blog for the company website on a subject you already feel passionate about, you are likely to find this task creatively stimulating, particularly as you have a real interest in the topic already. In other words, people who are explicitly told exactly what they need to do to be creative tend to produce creative responses.

Three Types of Support for Creativity

People with **creative potential** tend to possess the skills and capacity to generate ideas. In contrast, **practiced creativity** is the ability to spot opportunities to apply these skills in the workplace.[49] Paula Scher, a successful graphic designer and partner in the Texas-based design firm Pentagram, believes that practiced creativity can be inspired by blocking out all the noise around us and capitalizing on periods of boredom. Scher says, "I realize that when I'm sitting in a taxicab in traffic, or on my way to the airport, or waiting to get on a plane, or trapped in some other boring situation, that's when I get the best ideas, because I've got nothing else interfering with it."[50]

Research shows that creative people are more likely to flourish in a work environment that supports creativity.[51] If companies get it right, a creative mindset can lead to innovative thinking, better performance, increased job satisfaction, and a positive impact. For example, a recent Gallup analysis showed that companies that foster a culture of creativity engage workers who in turn become more creative. Employees need to be given the time, the freedom to create, and the opportunities to take risks for their ideas to come to fruition.[52]

Those who perceive their work environment to lack support for creative expression may feel reluctant to express their ideas. This may create a gap between the person's creative potential and the application of their creative skills.[53]

Organizations that do not cultivate an environment open to creativity are at a disadvantage because they are neglecting resources that could help the company operate and compete more effectively. Organizations can narrow the creativity gap by fostering an environment that employees perceive as supportive to creative expression.[54]

There are three main types of support for creativity in organizations: organizational support, supervisory support, and work group support, all of which have an influence on whether and how creativity flourishes in an organization.

EXAMINING THE EVIDENCE

ARE ADVANCED TECHNOLOGIES DESTROYING COLLABORATIVE CREATIVITY?

Creativity experts often argue that our ability to solve the most important challenges facing humanity depends on collaborative creativity—working with others to generate creative ideas and solutions. However, recent advances in technologies, including mobile technology, virtual technology, and artificial intelligence, may be negatively impacting our capacity for collaborative creativity. Researchers Sirkka L. Jarvenpaa and Liisa Välikangas recently explored this idea in a paper published in *Academy of Management Perspectives*.[55] They argue that successful collaborative creativity demands both *inner time*, or time to reflect on meaning, actions, and outcomes, and *social time*, or time spent discussing ideas with others. They suggest that advanced technologies could be suppressing both the inner time and social time of employees, resulting in less collaborative creativity. This problem could become even more severe in the increasingly commonplace context of remote work environments. Although more research is required to better understand the possible relationship between advanced technologies and collaborative creativity, managers should try to find ways to provide employees with opportunities for enhancing both inner and social time at work.

Critical-Thinking Questions

1. In what specific ways can advanced technologies interfere with the inner time and social time of employees?
2. What can managers do to help ensure that employees have ample inner time and social time, especially in virtual and remote work contexts?

Organizational Support for Creativity

Researchers have identified a range of environmental factors controlled by the organization that can either stimulate or stifle creativity.[56] Creativity flourishes when employees are provided with the autonomy and resources they need to implement their concepts and when they are given license to take risks. In addition, organizations that provide appropriate rewards and feedback and that encourage a collaborative environment tend to possess a more creative culture.[57]

In contrast, organizations that impose too many constraints or controls over their employees and do not provide feedback, resources, or sufficient rewards tend to create an environment that fails to encourage teamwork and collaboration. This type of organization stifles creativity.

Supervisory Support for Creativity

Employees who perceive their supervisor as supportive will feel more comfortable about speaking up and making suggestions. Supervisors who communicate, set clear goals, and are confident and protective of their teams tend to nurture a creative environment.[58] Michael Crow, president of Arizona State University, is an example of someone who is a good role model by supporting creativity through diversity in providing education to thousands of students.

Work Group Support for Creativity

Group members can support creativity by establishing certain norms, such as welcoming different perspectives, actively listening, fostering collaboration, being open-minded, and clearly communicating their views and approaches. Advertising company Quantcast supports creativity through collaboration. One Quantcast employee says, "Folks who are hungry for challenges, energized by a collaborative environment, and not afraid to get their hands dirty are going to be really successful here."[59]

THE INNOVATION PROCESS

Every innovation starts with an idea, and some of those ideas can have world-changing results. For example, to address the chronic problem of air pollution, Dutch inventor Daan Roosegaarde created a seven-meter-tall air purifier to tackle smog in cities all over the world. The giant air purifier has been installed in the Netherlands, Poland, China, and South Korea.[60]

Idea Generation

The first step in the innovation process, **idea generation**, is the creation of the idea itself (Figure 9.6). Usually an idea is born out of the recognition of a need for a solution and generated from existing information, experience, and knowledge. Bridget Levine, founder of pet accessory brand Frenchie Bulldog, based in London, UK, combined a keen love of dogs with her experience in fashion to create apparel for French bulldogs. Levine encourages idea generation in her team by regularly inviting them to contribute their thoughts and feedback.[61]

Sean Gallup/Getty Images

FIGURE 9.6 ■ A Model of the Innovation Process

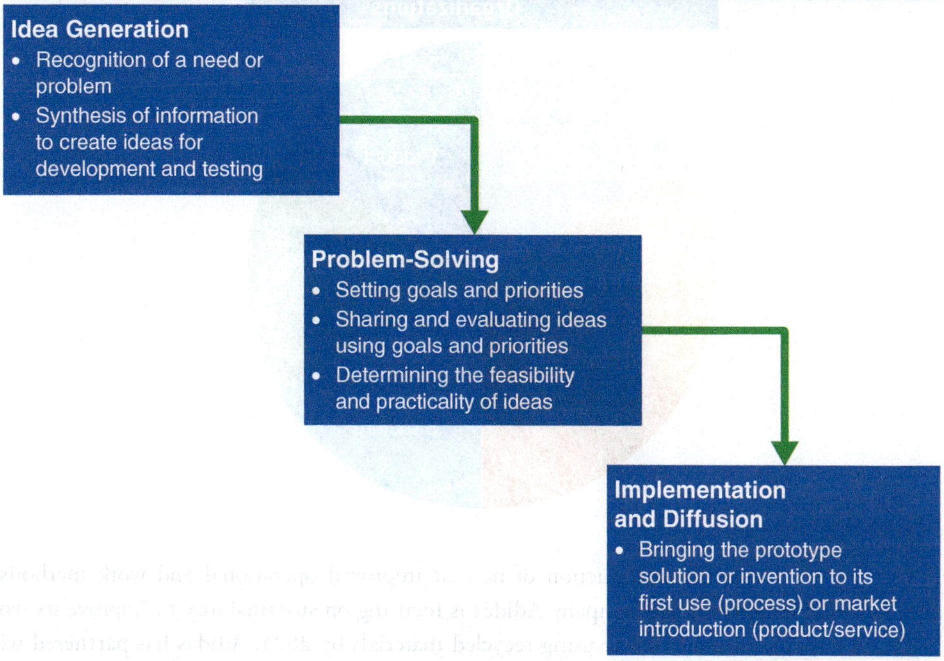

Source: Utterback, J. M. (1971, March). The process of technological innovation within the firm. *Academy of Management Journal, 14*(1), 75–88.

Problem-Solving

The second step of the innovation process is **problem-solving**: identifying any advantages and disadvantages associated with the innovation, exploring costs and value, and setting goals and priorities. One key lesson to keep in mind during this stage is that sometimes market demand doesn't correlate to customer usage. For example, during the pandemic, a contact tracing app was rolled out in France to notify users of whether they had come into contact with someone with COVID-19. Is spite of the anticipated demand, the app failed to attract users. Why? Because users didn't like the idea of being traced or volunteering their personal information as part of the signing-up process. Competitor NOVID solved these challenges by creating a similar app that doesn't require personal information and tracks users through GPS, thereby protecting their privacy.[62]

Implementation and Diffusion

The final stage of the innovation process, **implementation and diffusion**, entails producing and distributing the new product or idea. Without implementation, there is little chance of an idea becoming a reality. Apple implements its products through an efficient design process and distributes them through carefully staged events and conferences intended to create a buzz before the product is even officially launched.

TYPES OF INNOVATION IN ORGANIZATIONS

We often think of innovation as a process that produces a tangible product, but in fact there are six main types of innovations in organizations: product innovation, process innovation, organizational structure innovation, people innovation, exploitative innovation, and exploratory innovation (see Figure 9.7). Let's apply the six types of innovation to a manufacturing plant.

Product innovation is the development of new or improved goods or services that are sold to meet customer needs.[63] The Amazon Kindle would be an example of a new product innovation, while enhancing the new iPhone 13 models with brighter screens, more storage, and new cameras would be an example of an improved product innovation.[64]

FIGURE 9.7 ■ Types of Innovations in Organizations

Process innovation is the introduction of new or improved operational and work methods.[65] German footwear-manufacturing company Adidas is focusing on sustainability to improve its work methods and has committed to solely using recycled materials by 2024. Adidas has partnered with environmental organization Parley for the Oceans to design shoes from ocean plastic and has worked with biotech start-up Bolt Threads to create a vegan shoe made entirely from mushrooms.[66]

Organizational structure innovation is the introduction or modification of work assignments, authority relationships, and communication and reward systems.[67] Many organizations have evolved their traditional organizational office structure in response to the COVID-19 crisis. For example, outdoor recreation retailer REI sold its corporate headquarters in Bellevue, Washington, before staff had ever moved into the building and set up small branches in different locations instead. REI is also creating a working model that permits employees to work from home up to five days a week. Chris Putur, vice president of technology and operations, says, "We want to create an environment that's very flexible for our employees . . . We were amazed in 2020 at how incredibly agile and innovative and productive the team could be."[68]

People innovation includes the changes in beliefs and behaviors of individuals working in an organization.[69] Organizations use a variety of training methods to foster positive behavioral change in their employees. Studies have shown that there are effective methods managers can adopt to change

The Transit Elevated Bus in China is an example of how a problem can be solved through prototypes.
South China Morning Post/Contributor

behavior, such as inspiring employees rather than nagging them, recognizing and addressing problems to drive positive change, and providing clear collective goals to ensure everybody is on board.[70]

Exploratory innovation focuses on risk taking, radical thinking, and experimentation,[71] and **exploitative innovation** focuses on the enhancement and reuse (exploitation) of existing products and processes.[72] The first edition of the iPhone would be a good example of exploratory innovation, whereas subsequent editions based on the refinement of existing technology would be an example of exploitative innovation. To work, exploratory innovation has to be supported by a management team that advocates the freedom of radical thinking. For example, Arizona State University enrolls as many capable students as possible rather than adhering to the traditional acceptance rate, successfully creating a thriving, diverse culture. Researchers believe organizations need to strike a balance between the contradictory natures of exploitative and exploratory innovation. Many organizations play it safe by focusing on the refinement of existing products rather than taking risks to explore new avenues.

This approach can lead to **organizational cultural lag**, an effect that occurs when organizations fail to keep up with emerging innovations and so risk missing lucrative opportunities they could have capitalized on.[73] To avoid cultural lag, organizations need to continually focus on their existing products and processes at the same time they are investigating new innovations. For example, in 2021 Google acquired fitness tracking company Fitbit as a part of an initiative to enter the health care and wellness industry. Although Google will continue to focus on its existing offerings, it will be better positioned in the wearable technology market to compete against Apple's Apple Watch product.[74]

To achieve the desired combination of exploitation and exploration, senior managers need to achieve a balance, encourage their employees to think in terms of sustaining an existing product while developing innovation, provide a forum for creative discussion, assign roles and set goals to get the process in motion, and introduce a reward system to help motivate teams and reinforce the importance of the organization's strategy.

To be successful in today's workplace, organizations need to nurture an environment of creativity and innovation and give people a platform to share their thoughts and ideas as well as the confidence to make mistakes. Organizations also need good decision-makers to process and make sense of the continuous stream of information coming through every day.

IN REVIEW

9.1 Identify the primary types of decisions managers make to solve problems

The ability to make decisions and solve problems is a key aspect of organizational behavior. **Decision-making** is the action or process of identifying a strategy to resolve problems. There are two main types of decisions: programmed decisions and nonprogrammed decisions: **programmed decisions** are automatic responses to routine and recurring situations, and **nonprogrammed decisions** address new or nonroutine problems for which there are no proven answers. Managers often use the five-step decision-making process to help them make good decisions and resolve complex issues.

9.2 Identify factors that influence the way we make decisions in the real world

Bounded rationality is the idea that we are restricted by a variety of constraints when making decisions. This is in contrast with **complete rationality**, which assumes we take into account every single criterion or possible alternative when making a decision. **Satisficing decisions** aim for acceptable results rather than for the best or optimal solutions. **Intuition** is an unconscious process of making decisions based on imagination and possibilities.

Heuristics are shortcuts or "rules of thumb" that allow us to make judgments and decisions quickly and efficiently. **Availability heuristics** allow us to base judgments on examples and events that immediately spring to mind. The **anchoring and adjustment heuristic** is a process of basing decisions on the first piece of information we are given without taking other probabilities into account. Using **representativeness heuristics**, we base a decision on our existing mental prototype and similar stereotypes.

9.3 Discuss the critical nature of creativity and innovation in today's organizations

Creativity is the generation of meaningful ideas by individuals or teams. **Innovation** is the creation and development of a new product or service. Organizations need to redefine, reinvent, and repurpose brands and products to keep up with market demand. Creativity and innovation are the lifeblood of successful organizations.

9.4 Describe the three-component model of creativity

The **three-component model of creativity** proposes that creativity depends on the presence of domain-relevant skills and expertise, creativity-relevant processes, and intrinsic task motivation. *Domain-relevant skills and expertise* provide knowledge about the relevant subject and the skills and talent to provide the most creative and productive responses. *Creativity-relevant processes* are work methods dependent on certain personality characteristics, methods of thinking, and knowledge of heuristics. *Intrinsic task motivation* ensures that people who have an innate interest in a chosen task will be more motivated in producing creative ideas.

The three types of support for creativity includes *organizational*, which flourishes when employees are provided with autonomy to implement their concepts; *supervisory*, which is successful when employees perceive their supervisor as supportive; and *work group*, in which group members support creativity by establishing certain norms such as collaboration.

9.5 Outline the steps in the innovation process

Every innovation starts with an idea. **Idea generation** is the first step in innovation, followed by **problem-solving** and then **implementation and diffusion**. There are six main types of innovations in organizations: **product innovation**, **process innovation**, **organizational structure innovation**, **people innovation**, **exploitative innovation**, and **exploratory innovation**.

KEY TERMS

Anchoring and adjustment heuristic (p. 217)
Availability heuristic (p. 207)
Bounded rationality (p. 206)
Common-information bias (p. 208)
Complete rationality (p. 206)
Confirmation bias (p. 209)
Creative potential (p. 212)
Creativity (p. 210)
Decision-making (p. 203)
Ease-of-recall bias (p. 209)
Escalation of commitment (p. 209)
Exploitative innovation (p. 217)
Exploratory innovation (p. 217)
Framing bias (p. 209)
Heuristics (p. 207)
Hindsight bias (p. 209)
Idea generation (p. 214)
Implementation and diffusion (p. 215)
Innovation (p. 210)
Intuition (p. 207)
Lack of participation error (p. 209)
Nonprogrammed decisions (p. 204)
Organizational cultural lag (p. 217)
Organizational structure innovation (p. 216)
People innovation (p. 216)
Practiced creativity (p. 212)
Problem-solving (p. 215)
Process innovation (p. 216)
Product innovation (p. 215)
Productive forgetting (p. 212)
Programmed decisions (p. 204)
Projection bias (p. 209)
Randomness error (p. 210)
Representativeness heuristic (p. 208)
Satisficing decisions (p. 207)
Sunk-cost bias (p. 209)
Three-component model of creativity (p. 211)

UP FOR DEBATE: DECISION-MAKING AND BIAS

This chapter showed you that our decision-making is often influenced by different types of biases. It is possible for people to remove such biases from their decision-making and thus make better decisions. Agree or disagree?

EXERCISE 9.1: PRACTICING INNOVATION

Objective

The purpose of this exercise is to gain a greater appreciation of innovation.

Instructions

Innovation is the creation and development of a new product or service. In this exercise, you will be in groups of two to four students. The goal of each group is to practice innovation by developing a new course for college students. This new course will present "life lessons" for students, such as how to get a loan, what to look for when you need an attorney, how to pay taxes, how interest works, how to negotiate the price of a car, and so forth.

Your group should go through all three steps in the innovation process in developing this new course for your university:

1. Idea generation
2. Problem-solving
3. Implementation and diffusion

For the final step, obviously you won't be able to actually *implement* the new course, but describe *how* you would do so. The instructor will then ask each group to report on what they developed and how.

Reflection Questions

1. How did your group go through each of the three steps in the innovation process? Describe in detail how you approached each step.
2. What challenges did you have in developing this new course? How did you overcome those challenges?
3. Describe one way you could use the innovation process at your current or most recent job.
4. Discuss ways in which the innovation process might be difficult to perform in the workplace. In what circumstances would it be an easy process?

Exercise contributed by Steven Stovall, Southeast Missouri State University.

EXERCISE 9.2: DECISION-MAKING PROCESS ROLE PLAY

Objective

The purpose of this exercise is to grasp the concept of the five-step decision-making process.

Instructions

This exercise looks at the five-step decision-making process and has volunteers from the class role-play a simple decision-making scenario.

Three students will join the instructor at the front of the class. With the help of the rest of the class, the volunteers will proceed through all five steps of the decision-making process in an attempt to determine what they will have for lunch.

The five steps are:

1. Define the problem
2. Identify and weigh decision criteria
3. Generate multiple alternatives
4. Rate alternatives on the basis of decision criteria

5. Choose, implement, and evaluate the best alternative

As students tackle each step, the audience will provide suggestions, questions, and input. In the final step, a selection is made, but it is up to the volunteers to decide whether they want to report back an evaluation of the decision in the following class!

Reflection Questions

1. Though this was a very simple scenario, what challenges presented themselves during the decision-making process? How did the student volunteers overcome those challenges?
2. Think about a scenario at your current or most recent job. Mentally go through the five-step decision-making process for a decision you had to make. Evaluate that decision.
3. Provide three to five examples of when the decision-making process could be utilized in depth for an important work-related decision. Why is the decision-making for these kinds of situations more involved than it is for simple decisions (such as what to eat for lunch)?

Exercise contributed by Steven Stovall, Southeast Missouri State University.

EXERCISE 9.3: WATCH ME GET CREATIVE HERE

Objective(s)

This exercise will help you to better understand the various creativity and innovation concepts presented in this chapter.

Instructions

Step 1. Find a partner and select a concept you want to present to the class. (1 to 2 minutes)

Step 2. Develop a creative way to present this concept to the class. You will need to present the following elements of the concept:

- An overview of the concept
- The importance of the concept to organizations

The presentation needs to be brief (1 to 3 minutes), but it can take any creative form you want. Examples include writing a short story about the concept, singing a song about the concept, writing a poem about the concept, or performing a short skit demonstrating the concept.

When selecting a concept, you may want to use the major chapter headings as a guideline. (15 minutes)

Step 3. Present your concept in the selected creative way. (1 to 3 minutes)

Reflection Questions

1. How did the process of having to present a concept in a creative way aid your understanding of the creative process?
2. Which of your classmates' creative presentations were most memorable? Why?
3. What barriers did you face in developing a creative presentation?
4. How did completing a creative activity increase your confidence about future creative activities?
5. How could organizations use similar exercises to increase overall creativity in the organization?

Exercise contributed by Milton R. Mayfield, Professor of Business, Texas A&M International University, and Jacqueline R. Mayfield, Professor of Business, Texas A&M International University.

ONLINE EXERCISE 9.1: PROGRAMMED AND NONPROGRAMMED DECISIONS DISCUSSION

Objective

The purpose of this exercise is to gain an appreciation for programmed and nonprogrammed decisions.

Instructions

There are two types of decisions: programmed and nonprogrammed decisions. A programmed decision is one that is an automatic response to routine and recurring situations. Nonprogrammed decisions, on the other hand, are for new or nonroutine problems for which there are no proven answers. An example of a programmed decision would be what to wear to work, while a nonprogrammed decision might be whether or not you should look for another job.

On a discussion board, provide five programmed decisions you have made in the last week. Comment on others' posts about how similar or common their programmed decisions have been. Then post five nonprogrammed decisions you have made in your lifetime or will need to make in the coming years. Again, engage in a dialogue with other students about how their nonprogrammed decisions are like your own or how they are very different.

Reflection Questions

1. How easy was it to develop your list of programmed decisions versus nonprogrammed ones? Explain.
2. In your current or most recent job, what programmed decisions do you make? Nonprogrammed decisions?
3. What has been your most difficult nonprogrammed decision to make at this point in your life? Why was it so difficult? How did you ultimately make the decision?

ONLINE EXERCISE 9.2: CREATIVITY THROUGH A VISION BOARD

Objective

The purpose of this exercise is to understand creativity using a vision board.

Instructions

A vision board is a collage of images that weaves the pictures into a theme. For example, as you think about what your professional wardrobe might look like, you could search the internet and magazines for pictures of people and models wearing the clothes you would most like to wear in a professional setting. Grouping these together into a collage begins to show an overarching theme of how you would like to dress and the level of professionalism you would like to convey.

For this exercise, think of a business you would like to start (food truck, online boutique, dog walking service, and so on). Once you have a selected a new venture, search online for images of the type of business that appeals to you. Maybe it's a uniform employees are wearing, examples of logos, colors that inspire you, textures and fabrics you are drawn to, or ways of merchandising that are unique. Print these out and assemble a collage. Don't worry about how neat or symmetrical anything is—the objective is to simply create a theme. Pictures don't need to align with one another, and photos overlapping one another is common. Everyone's collage will look different.

Reflection Questions

1. What drew you to some images versus others? Why did you select the ones you did?
2. Describe your vision board. What do you think it conveys?

3. Have you ever created a vision board before? What was its purpose? If you haven't, is this something you would use again in the future? Explain.

Exercise contributed by Steven Stovall, Southeast Missouri State University.

CASE 9.1: MCDONALD'S DECISION-MAKING AND INNOVATION

McDonald's is home to far more than a good deal on a Big Mac, and the corporation engages in many effective practices, especially in the realm of decision-making and innovation. Created as one location in 1940 and turned into a corporate chain in 1955, McDonald's has been through some significant changes while at the same time holding on to its core offerings.[75] They are a unique company: there are about 38,000 locations worldwide, but only 7% of them are owned by the corporation—the rest are franchised to others, who pay a start-up cost and yearly franchise fees.[76] The chapter speaks about programmed decisions and nonprogrammed ones; these are both common at a company that must somehow manage the practices of around 35,000 locations that they don't physically own. To operate a consistent business, McDonald's must figure out how to program as many decisions as possible across the fleet, but at the same time each and every location presents its own financial, supply chain, hiring, and sales challenges, and each location must have leaders who use nonprogrammed decisions to solve them and provide a desirable offering to local customers.

Managing 38,000 Businesses

Managing a business is difficult. You always have to meet your minimum sales numbers to keep your doors open, but to get to that point, there are often dozens of problems that must be solved and decisions that must be made. For McDonald's, that applies to 38,000 storefronts. Corporate McDonald's has a solution for this, which they call their operations management unit. According to the Panmore Institute, "McDonald's Corporation's operations management (OM) supports the company's position as the largest fast food restaurant chain in the world. The ten decisions of operations management represent the various strategic areas of operations that must be coordinated for optimal productivity and performance."[77]

The text explains the fundamental process behind decision-making: define the problem, look at decision criteria to create alternatives, and then select the best option available. McDonald's goes through this process in each of their 10 primary operations management areas.[78] For example, McDonald's describes the vison shared by its founder, Ray Kroc: "Ray Kroc wanted to build a restaurant system that would be famous for providing food of consistently high quality and uniform methods of preparation. He wanted to serve burgers, fries and beverages that tasted just the same in Alaska as they did in Alabama. To achieve this, he chose a unique path: persuading both franchisees and suppliers to work not *for* McDonald's but *for*themselves, together *with*McDonald's, promoting the slogan, 'In business for yourself, but not by yourself.'"[79] This is a nearly insurmountable goal, but retailers today have made it look easy. To approach this goal, given the problems defined, McDonald's made a firm decision on quality management: they would provide the best food they could, as long as it was reasonably priced and could be duplicated everywhere using the same production line at every location.[80] After considering alternatives, like letting franchisors figure out production on their own or changing the nature of the business, the leadership at McDonald's picked their current strategy and committed to it. Implementing this decision has not been easy, and the team at corporate McDonald's and the leaders at all 38,000 locations have to continually work together to do so.

Quality

A common decision-making problem in the business world is that managers don't know precisely what they want. Either they become obsessed with too many goals and ideas at once and exhaust their resources, or they can't commit to anything consistently. McDonald's and its founder Ray made sure to avoid this tendency from the very beginning. Kroc famously said, "If I had a brick for every time I've repeated the phrase *Quality, Service, Cleanliness and Value*, I think I'd probably be able to bridge the Atlantic Ocean with them."[81] It seems simple: four goals, repeated so many times that they become an echo in the corporation. Saying them just once would never be enough—another franchise is always around the corner, or a long-standing location may hit a rough patch, and managers must find a way to implement the four goals time and time again.

By defining your mission, you can make the decisions necessary to support it. While it's not easy to keep track of quality in 38,000 restaurants, managers from the top down at McDonald's all agree on their primary focus. The decisions that go into maintaining the chain will never be simple, and they will never be uniform, but they can always be directed toward the goal: *Quality, Service, Cleanliness, and Value.*[82] With the end in mind, a manager can gather the right people, the right resources, and execute a plan. To the customer, McDonald's seems as basic as it gets—but it takes an immeasurable amount of hard work from the start and each coming day to make it seem that way. If the burger were different every day, the coffee cold one morning and hot the next, the booths messy one evening and clean the next, no customer would trust the brand. The person making the food and the person running the entire corporation must be on the same page, and they have to trust one another's decisions.

Next time you visit a McDonald's, ask yourself: How is the quality, service, cleanliness, and value for my dollar? If they are up to par, try to imagine the decade's worth of specialization and decision-making—some good, some bad—that went into creating the restaurant in which you sit. If they are lacking in one of those four departments, try to figure out why. It could have been a mistaken decision that an employee made five minutes ago, or it could have been an organizational mistake that a regional manager made months ago. Regardless of which scenario you find, your experience will be dependent on the ability of McDonald's employees to think critically about problems and solve them adequately.

Critical-Thinking Questions

1. Why is McDonald's uniquely challenged when it comes to decision-making?
2. What department at corporate McDonald's is in charge of making strategic decisions, and how many areas of focus does it have?
3. What were Ray Kroc's four original goals, and why are they still useful today?

Sean Gallup/Staff/Getty Images

10 ETHICS AND SOCIAL RESPONSIBILITY IN ORGANIZATIONS

LEARNING OBJECTIVES

By the end of this chapter, you will be able to:

10.1 Defend the importance of ethics in organizations and effectively evaluate and resolve ethical dilemmas

10.2 Compare and contrast various approaches to ethical decision-making

10.3 Differentiate between the challenges of ethical leadership and ethical followership

10.4 Describe the primary approaches to social responsibility in organizations

10.5 Identify the components of an ethical culture

Case Study: IBM's Ethical Supply Chains

For a long time now, high-flying tech start-ups have offered the best employment perks in business, encouraging employees to work more effectively and sustain a happier lifestyle while doing it. While it may seem like a concept that started at the dawn of the tech bubble in the nineties, this type of organizational culture was actually the brainchild of Thomas J. Watson Sr. of IBM from the early years of the 20th century.[1] Watson is pegged as the source of extravagant organizational culture as we know it today, having created IBM's own symphony, given employees country club memberships, and even created a songbook for IBM employees. At the same time, high-benefits corporations like IBM have a duty to ensure that employees are rewarded fairly and incentives are healthy.[2] The result of this strong organizational culture is a company devoted to continually showing itself to be the gold standard of ethical business practices.

To really understand how this can be, it is necessary to investigate the beginning of IBM and the beginning of Thomas Watson. In 1914, a man was confronted with a company that had recently been formed after the merging of three smaller firms that were geographically separated from one another. Watson's primary task was to integrate the three small firms operationally and organizationally toward a common initiative and is credited by many as the first business leader to consciously create a common organizational culture for a company. The company was the Computing-Tabulating-Recording Company (CTR), which became what we know today as IBM. The culture that Watson hoped to create for a company that was split between Washington, DC, New York, and Ohio was one that pressed innovation and outside-the-box thinking. Watson made the company motto "THINK" for a company that made devices that helped people work faster and more precisely. Watson knew the limitless potential of these types of machines and also knew the value of the people who could create and sell them. Encouraging each employee to be a thinker was what would knit this newly formed organization together. Over the years after this initiative, the newly renamed International Business Machines, or "IBM," developed a set of guidelines that would be the basis for their organizational culture. IBM called these "Basic Beliefs," and they were "Respect for the individual," "the best customer service in the world," and "excellence."[3]

Today, IBM is one of 30 companies included in the Dow Jones Industrial Average, and it employs nearly 380,000 people worldwide.[4] IBM employees have even been awarded five Nobel Prizes.[5] With yearly revenues of around $73 billion in 2020, it is hard to believe that even Watson could have predicted where the "THINK" motto would get them.[6] As all successful large companies do, IBM consistently finds ways to maintain an ethical work environment for employees and ethical relationships with suppliers, partners, investors, and all other market participants. According to their own corporate reports, one of the most useful tools in this pursuit has been communication. It is important that employees are trustworthy, that they trust each other, and that all those involved with the company give and receive respect. To monitor these character traits, IBM is in full communication at all times with all members of their business. Employees, partners, and suppliers always have a contact point within the company, so that everyone can report problems and expectations can be clear.[7]

IBM, for all its size and strength, however, has had its fair share of hills and valleys leading up to today. For much of the 20th century, IBM had a firm grasp on the business of corporate computing. This changed abruptly when the semiconductor ushered in a new era of personal computing and IBM lost market share to the likes of Microsoft and Apple. IBM didn't stay at the leading edge of technology and allowed itself to just follow along with the market. It lost its purpose and stopped developing new technologies of great significance, leading to its decline as the new millennium arrived.[8]

IBM stopped innovating, and the technology giant lost market share in an industry it had helped build. From the 1950s to the 1980s, under Thomas Watson, IBM had produced everything from the original computer languages to ATMs and even supermarket checkouts. IBM was a dominant force, and in 1990, the company was the second most profitable enterprise in the world. By 1991, earnings had dropped to –$2.8 billion, and they dropped 60% over the next two years.[9] By 1993, a newly appointed CEO decided that the company needed to reintegrate all of their systems and become "One IBM," saying, "[We had to change] the view that IBM was a group of fiefdoms. We needed to have a sense that we were going to operate as a team, as a global entity."[10] After over 80 years of doing business, the new CEO of IBM, Louis Gerstner, embarked on the same initiative that Thomas Watson had in 1914: to create an integrated company using corporate culture.

By the end of 1994, profits had risen to $5 billion, and by 2000, IBM Global Services had become the world's largest IT consulting and web services organization. IBM had clawed its way back to the top through the same practices that had put it there. IBM after 1994 was much leaner and much more devoted to its mission of making itself a leader in its industry.[11]

Since then IBM has become the gold standard of sustainable business practices, with one of the most ethically focused supply chains of any business and a culture motivated toward focusing on making a difference in places that need it. Now that it is so firmly rooted as a technology giant, it has an additional duty to promote ethical markets in ways that only become apparent upon critical thinking. Specifically, IBM purchases billions of dollars of supplies annually and has "more than 30,000 supplier locations spread out over more than 60 countries."[12] This means they have massive bargaining power in many companies and around the globe, including places where products can be sourced through unethical forms of labor. IBM puts out a report each year about its effort to ensure its suppliers are being socially responsible.

Current management says this about ethics: "Expectations and legislation are increasing, such as the growing concerns about conflict minerals, anti-slavery and human trafficking, and other important social responsibility issues."[13] So ethical concerns in today's business world affect all companies, and they have a social and legal responsibility to make money in the right way. IBM has taken the various sections of its business and united them behind a common initiative to be the guiding light of ethical practices to other large-cap technology giants. Due in part to this reintegration, IBM has climbed its way back to the top and prepared itself for another successful 100 years.

Critical-Thinking Questions

1. What was Thomas Watson's initial dilemma in uniting the Computing-Tabulating-Recording Company?
2. Why did IBM stagnate in the early nineties?
3. What is one tool that IBM uses to monitor the ethicality of decisions across their company and supplies?
4. What makes IBM very influential in the market regarding ethical supply chains?

ETHICS IN ORGANIZATIONS

IBM sets the gold standard for business practices through its firm commitment to ethics, which is applied to the culture of its organization as well as to its external partners, such as suppliers, to ensure social responsibility. **Ethics** are moral principles of duty and virtue that prescribe how we should behave.[14] We often hear that business people must be ruthless, willing to stab people in the back as they climb up the ladder of success. What place do ethics have in business decision-making? Should we even study ethics in a business class?

There are at least two good reasons to study ethics. First, there are reasons of virtue, meaning it's the right thing to do. Most people have learned values and developed character that steer them toward making the right ethical decisions over the wrong ones.

Second, there are reasons of prudence, meaning it's the smart thing to do. Even for people who don't care about doing the right thing, making ethical decisions tends to be in their own self-interest. People who cheat, lie, cut corners, and break trust rarely end up as successful in the long run when they're caught out by others. Overall, good things tend to happen to companies and individuals that consistently do the right thing, while bad things tend to happen to companies and individuals that even occasionally do the wrong thing.

Ethical behavior can also be influenced by world crises and turbulence. For example, accounting giant EY conducted a survey of 3,000 people from 33 countries to assess the impact of COVID-19 on company ethics, and 90% of respondents agreed that the disruption caused by the pandemic posed a risk to ethical company conduct. Examples of misconduct magnified by the pandemic included bribe taking, ignoring unethical behavior from third parties if it meant a boost to one's pay or career, and a willingness to mislead external parties. Respondents also suggested remote working as an area open to risk as a result of employees feeling detached from their colleagues, teams, and organizations and mistrustful of senior management.[15]

Despite the disruption caused by the COVID-19 crisis, the majority of respondents agreed that companies operating with integrity reaped huge benefits, such as bolstering their reputation, attracting new customers, and retaining talent. Andrew Gordon, EY's global forensic and integrity services leader, believes the pandemic offers a huge stimulus for ethical change: "Organizations that commit to doing the right thing, even when nobody is watching, will emerge from this pandemic stronger and more united."[16]

Ethical Corporate Scandals

Over the last couple of decades, the unethical behavior of some major U.S.-based organizations has hit the headlines worldwide. One of the most infamous unethical scandals involved the fall of energy giant Enron, which in 2001 was caught for using unethical accounting practices that ultimately led the team to commit one of the largest corporate frauds in U.S. history.[17] One of the biggest corporate casualties of the Enron scandal was the company's auditors, the accounting and consultancy firm Arthur Andersen, which until then had enjoyed a sterling reputation. Because of the unethical choices made by a few members of the Enron team, such as the decision to destroy evidence of wrongdoing, the company was eventually dissolved.

In 2016, Wells Fargo came under fire for creating fake bank accounts under the names of real customers, suffering more than $2 billion in losses after the scandal broke.[18] Ethical scandals can take place in all types of industries. Table 10.1 outlines some of the biggest ethical scandals over the last decade.

Yet it is not only enormous organizations that deal with ethical problems. Breaches of ethics happen all over the world; in many countries, corruption is prevalent and instances of bribery to win business are commonplace. Similarly, some organizations exploit labor by hiring children, paying very low wages, and forcing employees to work in poor conditions. An organization is unethical if it violates the basic rights of its employees and ignores health, safety, and environmental standards.

Ethics and Artificial Intelligence Technology

One of the more recent ethical debates springs from the rapid development of artificial intelligence (AI) technology. With enhanced speech recognition, robot dogs, "killer robots," solar-powered drones,

TABLE 10.1 ■ Biggest Ethical Scandals of the Last Decade

Industry	Organization	Ethical Scandal
Media	Fox News	Sexual misconduct
Pharmaceutical	Turing Pharmaceutical	Price inflation of a drug by more than 5,000%
Transportation	Volkswagen	Illegal devices to evade diesel emissions standards
Hospitality	Marriott	Data breaches leading to hackers stealing personal information from 500 million guests
Real Estate	WeWork	Toxic work culture where leaders were accused of discrimination and harassment

Source: Mohan, P. (2019, December 26). These are the worst scandals of the past decade. *Fast Company.* https://www.fastcompany.com/90444328/these-are-the-worst-scandals-of-the-last-decade

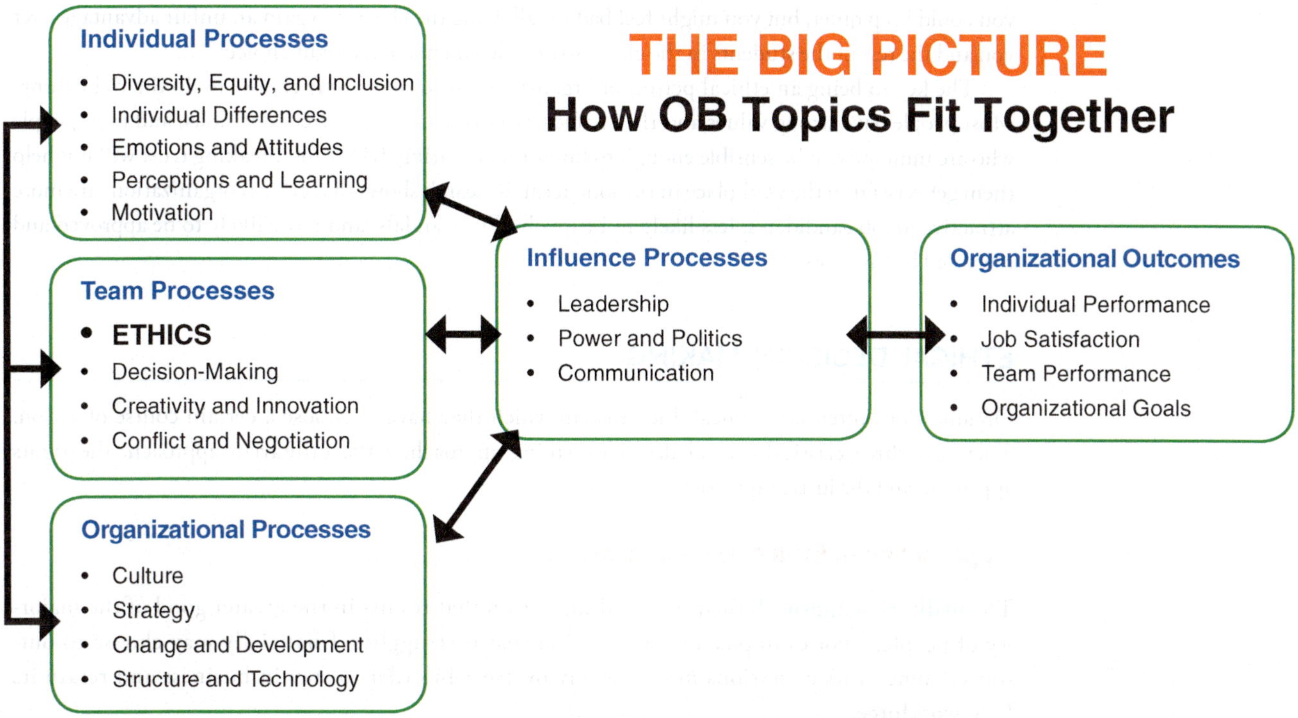

and self-driving cars on the horizon, the risks associated with AI have quickly come to the fore. Tesla Motors founder Elon Musk called AI the "biggest existential threat" to humanity, and the late physicist Stephen Hawking said, "The development of full artificial intelligence could spell the end of the human race."[19] Still to be answered are questions about the danger of building robots for military use, the safety of self-driving cars, the possibility that jobs will be lost to drones and robots, the general risk of creating software designed to help computers think like humans, and the damage to the environment caused by the huge amount of energy used to fuel the computers that train the algorithms. Companies also risk reputational and legal damage when using AI to create solutions. For example, an investigation was launched into health services company Optum, headquartered in Minnesota, for creating an algorithm that allegedly suggested that doctors and nurses should focus more of their attention on white patients rather than sicker Black patients.[20] Big tech companies such as Microsoft, Facebook, Twitter, Google, and more have begun to create teams to address the ethical issues associated with AI, such as the use of huge swaths of gathered data and the way it is used to train algorithms.[21]

Ethical Dilemmas

Individuals and companies frequently face large and small **ethical dilemmas**, or conflicts between two or more morally unpleasant alternatives.[22] Ethical dilemmas represent difficult ethical decisions. Many of today's organizations have committed to fostering an ethical culture and improving ethical behavior in the workplace by providing employee training programs, workshops, and seminars on dealing with ethical dilemmas. Managers have been faced with a number of ethical challenges due to the disruption to the workplace caused by COVID-19. For example, most white-collar workers previously based in offices had the ability to work from home, but may blue-collar workers in sectors such as agriculture, health, and hospitality were forced to do their jobs on the front lines, thereby exposing them to health risks. Organizations can demonstrate meaningful ethical actions to address the inequality and growing social divide highlighted by the pandemic by recognizing individual circumstances, using empathy, and being transparent with their employees.[23]

Many decisions include some sort of ethical choice. For instance, what would you do if you saw a good friend in your class cheating on an exam? It's tough to know the right decisions to make in certain circumstances. This is where ethical decision-making can be useful in guiding us to do the right thing.

The cheating example mentioned earlier represents an ethical dilemma. You could tell the professor you witnessed the student cheating, but then you might feel guilty for betraying a friend. However, you could keep quiet, but you might feel bad for allowing the cheater to gain an unfair advantage over you and the rest of the students in the class. So how do you make the right choice?

The key to being an ethical person or organization is to *consistently* choose to do the right thing. Most people have strong values and the character to make morally correct decisions, and even people who are immoral can be sensible enough to know that cheating, lying, and breaking trust will not help them get very far in the workplace in the long term. Research shows that ethical organizations are more attractive to job candidates, less likely to be involved in scandals, and more likely to be approved and rewarded by investors.[24]

ETHICAL DECISION-MAKING

Organizations often face ethical dilemmas in which they have to choose a certain course of action. There are three classical ethical decision-making approaches: the utilitarian approach, the rights approach, and the justice approach.

Approaches to Ethical Decision-Making

The **utilitarian approach** focuses on taking action that results in the greater good of the majority of people.[25] For example, an organization that is struggling financially may choose to outsource some of its operations more cheaply overseas in order to stay in business and retain its U.S. workforce.

The **rights approach** fosters decisions made on moral principles that infringe as little as possible on the entitlements of others.[26] For example, a business owner might believe it is morally wrong to pay overseas workers low wages and decide to close down a U.S.-based company rather than betray their principles.

The **justice approach** advocates basing decisions on fairness.[27] For example, a struggling organization might choose to turn down the best candidate for CEO if that person expects compensation that isn't in line with the company's fairness-based compensation structure.

There are no easy answers to most ethical decisions. The organization that saves its domestic workforce by outsourcing some functions to inexpensive labor overseas may discover that the overseas workers don't receive a fair wage or work in unsafe conditions. Similarly, the business owner who refuses to hire inexpensive labor because of ethical concerns will nevertheless lose the company, leaving current employees jobless. A struggling organization may choose a less-qualified candidate who is willing to accept their compensation structure, but to what extent is justice served if they fail to hire the candidate most likely to save the business?

Contemporary Views of Ethical Decision-Making

In the past, ethics researchers focused on what people *should* do when confronted with an ethical decision, but contemporary views explore what people *actually* do. Scientists have shown that our environment and our own psychological processes can influence our decision-making even when that decision goes against our own values.[28] And sometimes we're not even aware of our unethical behavior, especially when it is motivated by self-interest. Studies on ethical behavior in executive managers have shown that some senior managers unconsciously disregard corruption or wrongdoing in their company if it benefits them or the organization—a phenomenon known as *moral blindness*.[29] The following contemporary theories can help managers make ethical decisions.

Paine's "Moral Compass"

Lynn Paine, an ethics professor at Harvard, proposed a four-part "moral compass" to help managers make ethical decisions.[30] This involves factoring ethical considerations into every single part of organizational decisions. There are four types of lenses through which managers can explore the moral dimensions of their own decisions.

Lens 1: Is this action worthwhile?

This first lens explores the end results of the action. Does it serve a worthy purpose? Will it have an ethically successful outcome? To answer these questions, managers need to gather data and arm themselves with as much information as possible to reach the right conclusion.

Lens 2: Does this action comply with company principles?

Most companies have a set of ethical standards, a code of conduct, business norms, and values and ideals. Each action must be in line with the company's ethical standards.

Lens 3: What impact does this action have on others?

This involves analyzing how other people, such as stakeholders, may be affected by the decision. Learning about their different perspectives, how they might feel about the action, and preparing compensation if necessary are all important ways to research the decision before it is made.

Lens 4: Has this action been approved by the right authority?

There is little point in exploring the first three lenses unless the action has been signed off on by the relevant authority (such as a senior manager or CEO). It is also essential to check that the organization itself has the right to take this action, as well as the necessary resources.

The consequences of organizations making immoral decisions can be devastating. For example, in 2022, Elizabeth Holmes, founder of the blood-testing start-up Theranos, was found guilty of fraud over false claims made about the accuracy of the blood-testing model. During the trial, many former colleagues testified to telling Holmes about the flaws but said they had been dissuaded by Holmes from reporting their concerns for fear of putting off major investors. Theranos suffered irreparable damage because of the reported immoral decisions made by Holmes, ceasing all business operations in 2018 following news of the scandal.[31]

The Foursquare Protocol

The Foursquare Protocol is another contemporary ethical decision-making approach, proposed by Catholic University law professor Stephen Goldman.[32] Like the moral compass, this approach focuses on reaching the right ethical conclusions.

Protocol Element 1: Gathering all the facts

Information is key to making the right ethical decisions. Goldman equates this first step to a doctor diagnosing a patient. In the same way a doctor will gather information about a patient's symptoms, managers must follow the same process to identify relevant facts.

Protocol Element 2: Reflecting on past experiences

Just as doctors use past experience to treat patients, managers should follow the same process. How did the organization react to a similar case in the past? What was the outcome? How did other managers deal with the situation? How certain situations have previously been handled will influence the ethical culture going forward. For example, if sexual harassment has been tolerated in the past, it is likely there will be more cases in the future.

Protocol Element 3: Identifying the differences between the present and the past

It is important for managers to compare the similarities and differences between different cases in the past so they can come to a fair conclusion in the present. Just because one case was handled in a particular way before doesn't mean the same approach automatically follows for a similar case.

Protocol Element 4: Analyzing the situation

Once all the information has been gathered, three factors must be taken into consideration to reach the most ethical decision: First, do you have any self-interest that might compromise your judgment? For example, you may turn a blind eye to your top salesperson's tendency to accept corporate gifts (although this goes against company policies) because their sales contribute to your annual bonus. Second, consider how you would feel if you were on the receiving end of the decision being made. For example, if your decision involves layoffs, think about how you would feel if you were to be laid off. Third, listen to your own moral instincts and ask yourself some honest questions. Is the right thing to do overlooking a high performer's missteps? Or laying off people who have been with the company the longest?

Once all the steps of the Foursquare Protocol have been completed, you will have a much better chance of making the right ethical decision.

Kohlberg's Theory of Moral Development

Most of the decisions we make, we make as individuals. According to American psychologist Lawrence Kohlberg, we go through several stages of moral development that influence our decision-making—an adaptation of a theory originally introduced by Swiss psychologist Jean Piaget.[33] To illustrate these stages, Kohlberg carried out a famous experiment using a storytelling technique. One of the stories involved a man called Heinz whose wife was dying of cancer. Heinz found a local chemist who claimed there was a cure, but the chemist had priced the drug too far out of Heinz's reach. In desperation, Heinz borrowed enough money to pay half the price, promising the chemist the rest at a later date. The chemist refused. That night, Heinz broke into the chemist's and stole the drug.

Kohlberg used this story to monitor how moral reasoning changes from childhood to adulthood by interviewing a total of 72 boys from Chicago whose ages ranged between 10 and 16 years, 58 of whom were followed up for the next 20 years.[34] The results of these interviews formed the basis of Kohlberg's theory.

There are three main stages of moral development: preconventional morality, conventional morality, and postconventional morality (see Figure 10.1).[35]

1. Preconventional morality

   This stage applies to very young children whose morality tends to be based on obedience, self-protection, and self-interest. For instance, Heinz should never steal because stealing is wrong and against the rules.

2. Conventional morality

   During the second stage (adolescence and early adulthood), moral decisions are based on standards set by adult role models and societal norms. People who abide by these conventions are more likely to be accepted by society than those who do not. For instance, Heinz was right to steal the medicine to save a life, or wrong because he was breaking the law, which is against societal norms.

3. Postconventional morality

   In the final stage of moral development (mature adults), individual judgment is based on a chosen belief system that shapes moral views. In the Heinz example, people may consider the human rights side of the issue, such as the wife's right to the drug because human life has higher value than money. Equally, it could be argued it was not right to steal the drug, as Heinz's wife's life was no more precious than that of anyone else in the same position.

While Kohlberg's theory has given us a greater understanding of morality, the Heinz experiment in particular has been called into question. For instance, the story is clearly fictional, leading some experts to question if a group of boys between 10 and 16 years old, who have never experienced marriage or indeed ever been in a similar position, should have been involved in this sort of process.

Second, Kohlberg's theory has been criticized for gender bias, given that it is based on an all-male assessment, which neglects to take into account women's views of morality.

Finally, the Heinz dilemma is hypothetical and the boys' responses may not accurately reflect the decisions they would make if they were confronted with the same predicament in real life.

FIGURE 10.1 ■ Levels of Moral Reasoning

- Preconventional—moral reasoning is based on external rewards and punishments
- Conventional—laws and rules are upheld simply because they are laws and rules
- Postconventional—reasoning is based on personal moral standards

The Six Pillars of Character

Despite the challenges of ethical decision-making, having a clear ethical code that guides your actions will make it easier to choose the most appropriate path.

The Josephson Institute was founded in 1987 with a mission to change personal and organizational decision-making and improve ethics and character development in society.[36] CHARACTER COUNTS! is a program established by the institute to promote and teach the Six Pillars of Character that it believes define ethical behavior.[37] Today, this program is the most widely used approach to character education in the United States, reaching millions of young people through thousands of affiliated schools, agencies, and organizations.[38] Both Democratic and Republican presidential administrations have proclaimed the third week of October as CHARACTER COUNTS! Week, while a bipartisan group of U.S. senators forms the congressional CHARACTER COUNTS! Working Group.[39] In addition, dozens of mayors and governors have endorsed the CHARACTER COUNTS! framework and programming in their communities.[40]

The Six Pillars of Character are not based on political, religious, or cultural leanings in making ethical decisions. The Six Pillars are:[41]

Trustworthiness. Be trustworthy and willing to build trust with others. Honesty, sincerity, and loyalty are core qualities necessary for ethical behavior.

Respect. Treat others with courtesy, appreciation, and tolerance. Avoid judging others and using aggressive language.

Responsibility. Work hard, and be conscious of the way you behave and communicate toward others. Practice self-awareness and always strive toward self-improvement.

Fairness. Be impartial and make decisions based on sound knowledge. Follow the rules but question injustices when they arise.

Caring. Exercise forgiveness, compassion, gratitude, and kindness in relationships with others.

Citizenship. Be sure to vote and play your part in improving the lives of the people in your community. Be kind to the environment and make time to volunteer in social enterprises.

The Six Pillars of Character offer a framework of commonly held ethical values that may be useful in discussing ethical issues and making ethical decisions in the workplace. Josephson suggests the following process for making ethical decisions:[42] First, take into account the interest and well-being of all stakeholders. Next, put the core ethical values (the Six Pillars) above all other values. For example, a person may value money, success, or winning, but these values should not be put above core values such as integrity, courtesy, or kindness. Finally, this approach suggests that if you must violate one core value in order to honor another, do what you believe will provide the greatest amount of good in the long run (apply the utilitarian approach).

It is rare that the core values in the Six Pillars will conflict with one another, but it is possible, for example, that honesty might conflict with kindness and compassion; for example, if an employee asks for feedback and their manager does not want to stifle the employee's creativity in the long run, the manager may suggest to the employee that the idea is okay when in fact it is not.

Although ethics are useful in helping us make decisions and come to certain conclusions, they don't always give a clear answer to every moral question. For example, complex issues such as abortion and euthanasia have been the subject of strong debate over many years, yet people do not agree on a "right" or "wrong" moral answer to these issues. By following a code of ethics and a framework of ethical values, however, we can make many decisions at home and in the workplace based on sound guiding principles and good leadership.

ETHICAL LEADERSHIP AND FOLLOWERSHIP

Business leaders have greater responsibility for decision-making and organizational outcomes. Usually, leaders have a number of followers who have less responsibility but play a key role in implementing plans set out by the leader. Ideally, leaders and followers collaborate and work together to achieve common goals. However, sometimes ethical challenges can upset the dynamics of a relationship.

The Ethical Challenges of Followers

Leaders and Power

With leadership comes greater influence and power. Some leaders misuse that power to exert their influence over their followers. This sort of abuse can come in the form of bullying, verbal or physical abuse, and sexual harassment. Recent studies have reported that powerful people have little tolerance for mistakes and punish workers as a consequence, are more likely to blame others for perceived weaknesses or shortcomings, and are less concerned about reports of inequality.[43]

Further studies carried out by social scientists show the dangerous effects of power on the behavior of ordinary people.[44] They found that when certain people are put in a powerful position, they tend to lack empathy, are less able to detect emotion, and fail to understand other perspectives. In one experiment, the people in power were able to take candy from children without feeling any sense of guilt or remorse. In relation to inappropriate sexual behavior in men, studies show that the most powerful tend to believe that women are more attracted to them than they really are and are prone to looking for opportunities where they can engage in unacceptable sexual conduct. More than 40% of women say they have been sexually harassed in the workplace—a figure that has remained unchanged since the 1980s.[45]

Leaders and Privilege

The more power a leader possesses, the greater the privilege. Typically, top CEOs are paid enormous amounts, which some use to fund lavish lifestyles. For example, disgraced Theranos founder and CEO Elizabeth Holmes traveled on private jets, had multiple assistants, and stayed in luxury hotels.[46] Yet these high salaries are in stark contrast to those paid to the average worker. According to a 2021 report from the Economic Policy Institute, CEOs from the 350 companies studied made 351 times more than the average employee.[47]

This growing gap between the wealthiest and the poorest raises some interesting ethical questions. While CEOs bear the risk, pressure, scrutiny, and responsibility of their roles, do they deserve to get paid over 300 times more than the average employee? How can the pay gap be narrowed?

Some CEOs are already recognizing this massive disparity and making an effort to put it right. For example, Salesforce CEO Marc Benioff spent several years and more than $8 million equalizing pay to resolve the pay disparity at the software company. It may have been an expensive endeavor, but Benioff learned a great deal about ethics in pay and promoting equality. Benioff offered the following advice to leaders: "In the end, the most important thing leaders can do to promote equality is to open themselves up, take an honest inventory, listen to people, and never be too proud or defensive to make corrections."[48]

Leaders and Responsibility

While some CEOs enjoy considerable perks and wealthy lifestyles, they also have a huge amount of responsibility. In fact, due to the numerous instances of fraud and unethical conduct over the past few years, CEOs are being held to higher levels of accountability than ever before. Unethical behavior such as bribery, fraud, insider trading, environmental disasters, and sexual harassment no longer goes unnoticed or unpunished. The consequences for engaging in unethical behavior are serious, sometimes resulting in criminal indictments, dismissals, and huge financial penalties. Today's business leaders are

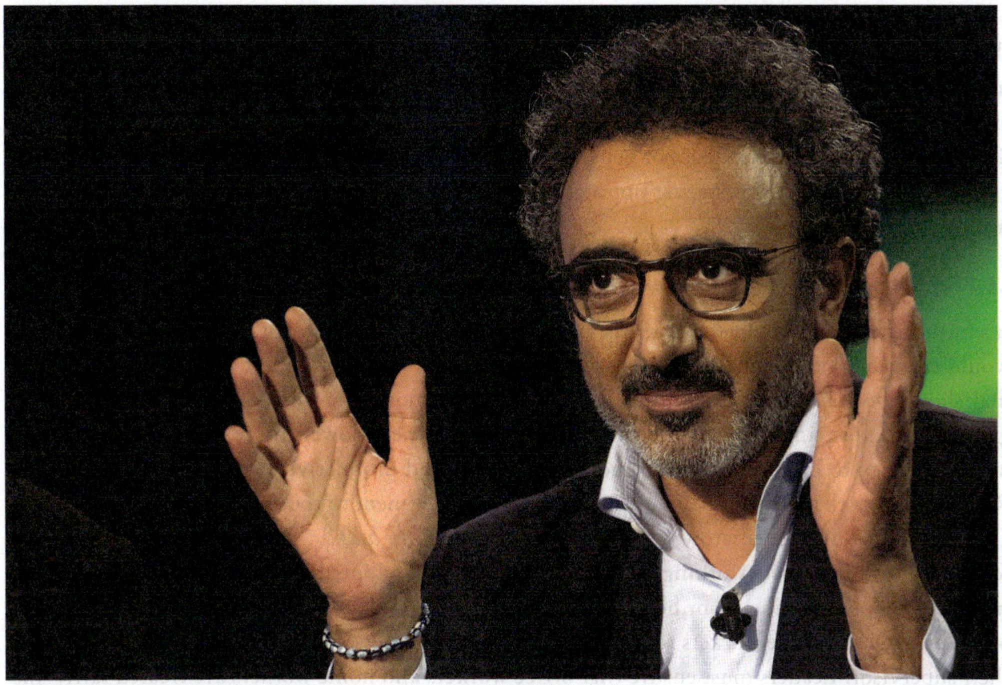

Chobani's CEO, Hamdi Ulukaya, is an example of a CEO who has taken action to reduce the pay gap between CEOs and their employees.

Reuters/Alamy Stock Photo

very much under the spotlight from the public and the media and cannot afford to engage in corporate misconduct if they want their organizations to survive.

During the pandemic, many organizations were considered a dependable news source, which helped to build trust between leaders and employees. According to the 2021 Edelman Trust Barometer, more than 60% of people surveyed considered CEOs and their organizations more credible than the American government and the media, with 72% stating that they trusted their employer to do the right thing.[49] Table 10.2 shows five ways leaders can build trust in organizations.

Leaders and Information Management

By the very nature of their senior positions, leaders tend to have more access to information than followers and are often the first to receive that information. The challenge for leaders is how to deal with that information. Do they share it immediately with followers or keep it to themselves? Consider the case of a senior manager who is told about upcoming layoffs but has been instructed to withhold this information until an official announcement is made. Yet rumors have started flying around about the layoffs and the team is agitated. Does the manager tell them the truth about the layoffs or stay silent until the announcement is made?

TABLE 10.2 ■ Five Ways Leaders Build Trust
Being a good role model by acting honestly, ethically, and legally
Being transparent with workers by always telling the truth, regardless of how uncomfortable it may be
Demonstrating loyalty to their teams by treating workers fairly and praising their achievements to upper management
Involving employees in decision-making by encouraging ideas, questions, and feedback
Showing confidence in teams by giving workers the autonomy to perform certain tasks by themselves

Source: Civitella, A. (2019, May 7). *How to build trust as a leader.* Forbes. https://www.forbes.com/sites/forbescoachescouncil/2019/05/07/how-to-build-trust-as-a-leader/?sh=174346853bfa

Leaders who fail to meet the ethical challenges of information management often behave in the following ways: lying about what they know, using the information for their own gain, denying having the knowledge at all, and telling certain followers to withhold information when others have a right to know. Researchers discovered that people who conceal knowledge are 17% less likely to flourish in the workplace or benefit from learning and growth. A poor knowledge-sharing culture can also have a devastating impact on the bottom line, costing large U.S. firms up to $47 million in lost productivity.[50]

Leaders and Consistency

It's human nature to prefer some people over others, and in an ideal world, leaders and followers would treat each other equally and respectfully. However, this is often not the case. Some leaders may show favoritism to certain followers by paying them more attention, overlooking tardiness, or giving them more time off when they need it. Treating some followers more favorably than others has a tendency to breed resentment and lower morale and productivity. It also stunts creativity. Research shows that we tend to give more preferential treatment to those we see the most and who are present in our immediate vicinity, known as *proximity bias*.[51] This raises ethical questions for leaders and managers working organizations that have adopted a hybrid working model. For instance, people working from home may feel more overlooked than their counterparts in the office because the office workers reap more benefits of close personal contact and "face time" with their supervisor. Leaders must ensure that office workers and home workers are treated fairly and equally to avoid instances of accidental favoritism.[52]

EXAMINING THE EVIDENCE

ETHICAL LEADERSHIP AND MORAL JUDGMENTS

The corporate scandals of recent years have highlighted the importance of both ethical leadership and ethical decision-making by all members of an organization. Recent research by University of Memphis researchers Robert Steinbauer, Robert W. Renn, Robert R. Taylor, and Phil K. Njoroge explores the possible relationship between these two processes.[53] Their research suggests that ethical leadership, which involves both demonstrating and promoting effective ethical conduct to organizational members, is likely to influence the moral judgments of organizational members. The effects of this type of leadership are likely enhanced by the extent to which organizational members perceive they will be held accountable for their ethical actions and the degree to which they engage in ethics-focused self-leadership, which entails leading and motivating one's own behavior to achieve goal-oriented outcomes. The research further suggests that the effects of ethics-focused self-leadership will be greater when coupled with conscious, active judgment processes rather than unconscious, reflexive, or intuitive approaches. This research suggests that organizations may be able to encourage better ethical decision-making by providing ethical leadership and self-leadership training for their leaders and other organizational members.

Critical-Thinking Questions

1. In what ways can ethical leaders encourage ethics-focused self-leadership in their organizations?
2. How might organizations best hold their members accountable for their ethical decisions and actions?

Leaders need to be consistent in their behavior toward their followers by learning how to cater to each individual's needs, how to choose appropriate times to bend the rules, and how to treat those followers that may not be as competent as others. They must also offer equal opportunities when it comes to promotions and bonuses and treat everybody around them with respect.

Leaders and Loyalty

From their followers and shareholders to investors, wider communities, and the environment, leaders have to juggle a range of loyalties. Ideally, all leaders would act in the best interests of their followers and prioritize the environment over financial gain, but as recent scandals have demonstrated, this is often not the case. For example, Steve Easterbrook, former CEO of McDonald's, is being sued $42 million by the fast-food chain—the amount originally given in the severance package—for not only engaging in intimate relationships with employees and destroying the evidence but also for potentially committing fraud. Easterbrook's unethical behavior abused the trust of followers and destroyed the company's reputation.[54]

The Ethical Challenges of Followers

Like leaders, followers face a number of ethical challenges in their working roles. As followers do not have the same power and status as their leaders, these challenges, if not met, can affect the dynamics of the leader-follower relationship. Here are some of the challenges that followers are confronted with.

Followers and Obligation

Good followers have a strong allegiance and commitment to their organizations, leaders, customers, and shareholders. For instance, workers at employee-owned supermarket chain Publix have an obligation to their organization to provide the best customer service possible, which is why the company is ranked as one of the best companies for customer service in the U.S. It is no coincidence that companies with happy, loyal, hardworking employees tend to offer the best customer service.[55]

However, followers also need to determine the extent of their obligation to a company. Should followers be expected to sacrifice their personal lives in favor of working long hours and weekends? Being overworked is a rising problem. According to a recent report, Hong Kong, Singapore, and Bangkok, Thailand, were among the cities with the biggest populations of overworked employees (working more than 48 hours a week) in the world.[56] Studies show that overwork can lead to physical and mental health problems.[57] Followers need to assess the degree of their own obligation to their companies and think about how much they want to give in order to strike the right work/life balance. In China, in response to the culture's societal pressures toward working long hours, young professionals began a social movement during the pandemic called *tang ping*, or "lying flat," a lifestyle choice that denounced the pressures of high-stress work by prioritizing health and well-being.[58]

Followers and Obedience

In the business world, followers are expected to carry out orders and demands in order to further the mission of the organization. However, there is a difference between carrying out orders and blind obedience. This is particularly important given society's belief that people can no longer resist responsibility for their actions by claiming they were merely following orders (known as the Nuremberg defense used by Nazi war criminals following World War II). However, a recent study shows that some people who have been coerced to do something they ordinarily wouldn't tend to experience a reduced sense of responsibility.[59] When faced with unethical situations, followers must ask themselves if obedience might lead to unethical behavior, dangerous consequences, or damage to the organization's mission.

Followers and Cynicism

In times of economic world turbulence, rising layoffs, corporate scandals, and continued austerity measures, it is easy for employees to become cynical. Research shows that cynical people tend to be irritable, more likely to engage in conflict, and less likely to support others.[60] Studies have also discovered a connection between cynicism and disrespect, reporting that cynical people are often more disrespectful toward others and have a greater tendency to believe they are victims of disrespectful treatment than less cynical people.[61] Too much cynicism can lead to lack of trust, lower commitment levels, reduced job satisfaction, and decreased performance and productivity. Further studies show that cynics suffer from poor physical and mental health and make less money.[62]

Yet cynicism does have its place when it comes to questioning the ethical decisions made by leaders. According to University of Toronto researcher Professor Kristin Scott, "People who are very cynical can ask the tough questions and examine decisions that their company is making with a critical lens. This kind of feedback may be beneficial for organizations if their own employees are holding them to account for their actions."[63]

In addition, Scott believes that too much cynicism can be alleviated when employees have the right support. A survey assessing workplace cynicism, carried out in partnership with Professor David Zweig, found that cynical employees tend to become more positive about their workplace when they have a supportive manager on board.[64] Zweig says, "Treating employees with respect, offering support and helping them understand the necessity of change within an organization are all the hallmarks of a good supervisor, but it also has the benefit of mitigating the negative effects of cynicism."[65]

Followers and Dissent

For most followers, there will be a time when they become dissatisfied with the organization in relation to areas such as organizational policies, pay, working conditions, promotions, bonuses, and so on. For organizations to be successful, employees need to be given the opportunity to express their dissent regarding organizational practices and to raise questions about unethical practices.[66] However, not all organizations encourage dissent, and not all followers feel comfortable expressing it. A recent survey of 1,000 full-time employees across the U.S. found that more than 60% were reluctant to share their concerns at work for fear of being seen as combative and uncooperative.[67] However, a failure to challenge the status quo can lead to poor financial performance, lack of growth in followers and managers, a decrease in productivity, and a decline in employee mental health.

Follower dissent is also likely to differ across cultures.[68] For example, in the Korean culture, challenging authority is very much discouraged. An investigation into the Korean airline Asiana Airlines crash in San Francisco in 2013, which killed three people and injured 181, showed that one of the copilots had been afraid to warn the captain about the low-speed landing.[69] This example proves that follower dissent can sometimes have fatal consequences.

When followers decide to express their dissent, they need to choose the right person to help solve the problem, suggest solutions to the issue, think about what they might say if their opinions are dismissed, and plan the steps they may have to take if they still want to be heard (such as escalating the problem to higher management). If the situation doesn't improve, followers may threaten to resign. However, resignation should be a last resort and only warranted if raised concerns have been repeatedly ignored by leaders over a lengthy period of time. Organizations can cultivate dissension by creating an environment of safety, curiosity, courage, and collaboration and providing forums that encourage feedback and empower followers to speak their minds.[70]

Followers and Bad News

Very few of us like to be the bearers of bad news, especially when we are directly at fault. Confessing a mistake may incur the wrath of our leaders, damage our reputations, and negatively influence our bonuses and promotional opportunities. However, organizations that don't provide a forum for sharing bad news can suffer catastrophic consequences. For example, the disastrous rollout of Canada's Phoenix payroll system for the Canadian federal government that caused huge payroll problems for tens of thousands of public servants was attributed to a working culture that doesn't encourage the sharing of bad news. Employees remained silent for fear of being accused of negativity or of not being team players.[71] As the Phoenix pay system disaster shows, followers must be given the freedom to report bad news to their leaders so those leaders can take corrective steps to address problems before they get out of hand.

Research shows that people prefer to receive bad news directly and honestly and value clarity and frankness over politeness and skirting the issue.[72] Delivering bad news takes courage and if possible is better communicated face-to-face to the most appropriate person rather than over email or the phone. During COVID-19, many companies were largely unable to give bad news in person to their employees and customers and were forced to use other forms of communication instead. For example, Florida-based fitness studio Orangetheory Fitness used thoughtful language to share bad news about the temporary closures of its 34 branches in an honest, compassionate, heartfelt email to all its customers. It also included elements of positivity in the messaging, offering customers free online workouts and explaining how patrons could help support the fitness studios and their employees.[73]

SOCIAL RESPONSIBILITY

While ethical values need to be upheld by both leaders and followers, it is even more important that organizations as a whole set a good example by behaving ethically and responsibly. One way organizations can do this is through practicing **corporate social responsibility** (CSR), defined as a business approach that delivers economic, social, and environmental benefits to stakeholders in order to contribute to sustainable development.[74]

Good CSR is especially important to today's consumers. According to the 2021 Global Sustainability Study, 60% of customers rated sustainability as one of their main criterion for buying from a company, and one-third of consumers, particularly those from the younger generations (Generation Z and millennials), are willing to pay more for sustainable products.[75] Table 10.3 lists examples of five companies considered to have excellent CSR reputations.

Traditionally, organizations have been measured against the profits they make, known as return on investment (ROI), or the amount of assets they have, called return on assets (ROA). In the last few years, organizations are now being monitored for their **return on ethics** (RoE), a mindset that promotes the highest standards of ethical behavior, which can lead to strong performance and competitive advantage.[76] Surveys show that companies with a positive ethical mindset experience a boost in sales, morale, and reputation.[77]

Carroll's Pyramid of Corporate Social Responsibility

Carroll's CSR pyramid is a simple framework that helps organizations define their social responsibilities. The CSR pyramid (Figure 10.2) was developed in 1991 by Archie Carroll, author and former associate dean of the University of Georgia, and consists of four levels: philanthropic responsibility, ethical responsibility, legal responsibility, and economic responsibility.[78]

FIGURE 10.2 ■ Carroll's Pyramid of Corporate Social Responsibility

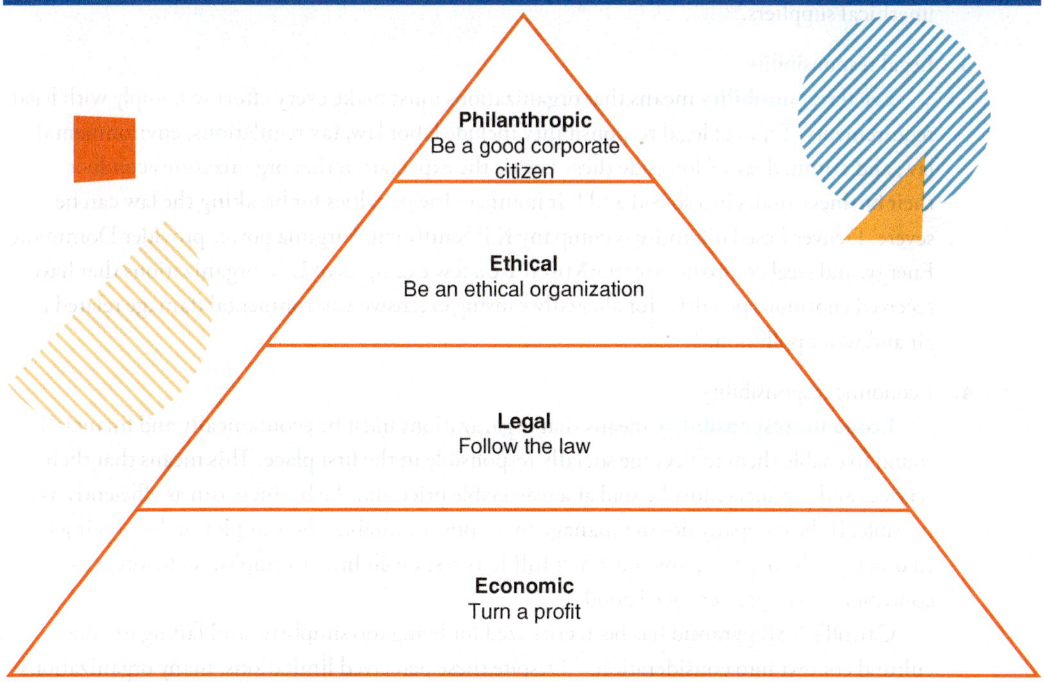

Source: Carroll, A. B. (1991). The pyramid of corporate social responsibility: Toward the moral management of organizational stakeholders. *Business Horizons, 34*(4), 39–48.

TABLE 10.3 ■ Top 5 CSR Companies in 2021

Company	CSR goals
Lego	Eliminating waste, diversity and inclusion initiatives
Disney	Protecting wildlife and the environment, eliminating waste, using solar energy
Rolex	Supporting conservation programs to gauge global warming and other impacts of climate change
Microsoft	Planning to become carbon neutral by 2030
Adidas	Recycling, respecting human rights, climate neutrality by 2050

Source: Gonçalves, A. (2020, March 4). *Top 10 companies with the best corporate (CSR) reputation in 2020.* You Matter. https://youmatter.world/en/top-10-companies-reputation-csr-2020/

1. Philanthropic responsibility

   Philanthropic responsibility involves going beyond the call of duty to benefit society. When an organization achieves its economic, legal, and ethical responsibilities, it can begin to focus on its discretionary responsibilities—that is, its philanthropic responsibilities. Examples are making charitable donations, running initiatives that benefit the community, engaging in projects that have a positive impact on the environment, and providing aid to people affected by natural disasters all over the world. For example, in 2021 Airbnb provided free housing to people who had been displaced by the devastating wildfires in Australia and also for those helping with relief efforts.[79]

2. Ethical responsibility

   Ethical responsibility means being morally aware enough to do the right thing in relation to the environment, fair wages, and who the company does business with. Buying from ethically responsible companies has increased in demand since the pandemic, and who these organizations work with really counts. A survey of nearly 30,000 people across the globe conducted by market research agency 3Gem revealed that almost two-thirds of respondents would never buy from a company again if it was discovered to be using unethical suppliers.[80]

3. Legal responsibility

   Legal responsibility means that organizations must make every effort to comply with legal requirements. Types of legal responsibility include labor law, tax regulations, environmental law, and criminal law. Alongside these laws is the expectation that organizations conduct their business affairs in a sound and fair manner. The penalties for breaking the law can be severe. Denver-based oil-and-gas company K P Kauffman, Virginia power provider Dominion Energy, and steel company ArcelorMittal are a few examples of U.S. organizations that have received enormous penalties for allegedly causing extensive environmental damage related to air and water pollution.[81]

4. Economic responsibility

   Economic responsibility means that organizations must be economically and financially sound to enable them to become socially responsible in the first place. This means that their services and products must be sold at a reasonable price and the business run as efficiently as possible. If the company doesn't manage to become profitable, then employees lose their jobs. In other words, the company must first fulfill its responsibilities to employees before it can contribute to the greater social good.

   Carroll's CSR pyramid has been criticized for being too simplistic and failing to take cultural context into consideration.[82] Despite these perceived limitations, many organizations have successfully integrated the model into their overall CSR strategy.

Social Entrepreneurs and CSR

While corporations tend to cycle through the various levels of responsibilities before being considered socially responsible, social entrepreneurs entrench CSR into their start-up business model. While there are similarities between traditional entrepreneurs and social entrepreneurs, there are differences too. For instance, although both traditional and social entrepreneurs found organizations, identify new opportunities, and create innovative products and services, they may differ in their original goals and objectives. Traditional entrepreneurs tend to start off with making profit as a goal, whereas a social entrepreneur may start off with the intention of tackling social and environmental problems to bring about social change. In 2021 the World Economic Forum reported that social entrepreneurs had improved the lives of 722 million people through health care initiatives and providing improved access to finance and education.

One of these social entrepreneurs is Eve Kekeh, founder of Bundlee, a baby clothing subscription company based in the UK. Babies outgrow their clothes up to seven times within the first two years of life, and a huge proportion end up in landfills or incinerators. Bundlee offers a more sustainable solution by allowing parents to rent rather than buy baby clothes. Each rental saves more than 40,000 gallons of water and 105kg of carbon dioxide.[83]

Some social entrepreneurs operate nonprofit companies, while others run for-profit businesses. For-profit organizations make a profit and benefit society at the same time. For example, The Right to Shower, headquartered in New Jersey, is a for-profit company that sells natural and ethically made soaps. The company donates 30% of its profits toward building mobile showers for people who are homeless all over the world.[84]

BUILDING ETHICAL AND SOCIALLY RESPONSIBLE ORGANIZATIONS

Regardless of the different types of organizations, building an ethical culture requires a shared sense of meaning to help positively influence ethical behavior. Some components of ethical behavior include core values, mission statements, codes of ethics, structure, boards of directors, reward and performance evaluation systems, reporting and communication systems, and ethics officers.

Core values are deeply held beliefs or guiding principles shared by everyone working at a particular company. They are the essence of a company's identity and help to support a company's vision. Common core values include integrity, honesty, perseverance, and accountability. Bayhealth, a not-for-profit health care company based in Delaware, uses core values to reflect its goal of providing the best health care for the communities it serves. Some of these core values include compassion, accountability, respect, integrity, and teamwork.[85]

Mission statements communicate the company's purpose as reflected by its members. It is essential that mission statements are continually reinforced to ensure every employee adheres to the message. For example, Cradles to Crayons, based in Chicago, provides children from age 0 to 12 living in low-income families with free essentials. Its mission statement represents its commitment to its determination to benefit communities by doing social good.[86]

Codes of ethics (sometimes called codes of conduct) are written sets of guidelines that define acceptable and unacceptable behavior. The main purpose of a code of ethics is to help employees make the right choices when confronted with difficult situations. Software recruitment company Workable enforces a strict code of ethics policy for every employee. The code emphasizes respect for others, integrity and honesty, accountability, teamwork, and the importance of treating everyone fairly.[87]

For a code of ethics to be successful, it must be supported by senior management, who should lead by example by behaving ethically at all times and acknowledging or rewarding those employees who follow the same code. Equally, leaders must also reprimand employees and suppliers who break the ethical code. For instance, in 2020 Apple penalized supplier Wistron Corp, a factory based in India that assembles the second-generation iPhone SE, for breaking the supplier code of ethics. The factory was shut down following acts of violence by contract workers due to anger over alleged unpaid wages. The workers destroyed property and equipment, causing millions of dollars' worth of damage.[88]

Some leaders believe that codes of conduct should be revisited, particularly in the aftermath of the pandemic. For example, Mark Coster, owner of STEM Toy Expert, believes that working from home during the pandemic has highlighted the positive impact of reducing one's carbon footprint and suggests that all companies should build a commitment to green values into their code of ethics.[89]

Organizational structure also influences ethical behavior. For example, a command-and-control structure, where leaders have a high amount of power and followers are expected to obey, sometimes inspires unethical behavior. Research shows that workers are more likely to behave ethically and challenge others about their unethical behavior if their managers are perceived as ethical leaders.[90]

Boards of directors sit at the head of the organizational structure and are responsible for overseeing top management and ensuring loyalty to shareholders. However, not all boards act in the best interests of the organization, and some have even approved unethical practices. Enron, HealthSouth, Tyco, Arthur Andersen, Siemens, Barclays, BP, General Motors, Takata, Volkswagen, Theranos, and Wells Fargo are just a few of the corporate scandals that have taken place over the last few years.[91] Because of these ethical failures, it has become even more important for board members to ensure that top management is practicing good ethical behavior.

Ethics hotlines allow employees to report unethical conduct anonymously without fear of retaliation. Many organizations use ethics hotlines to provide employees, who may not be comfortable reporting ethical incidents to management, with a safe place to share their concerns. Calls to ethics hotlines have increased significantly over the last decade. On the surface, it may appear that high numbers of complaints are a bad thing, but a recent study shows the opposite. When researchers conducted an extensive analysis of 2 million reports provided by Navex Global, a leader in employee hotline, risk, and compliance software, they found that companies that received more complaints through ethics hotlines were more profitable and more ethical than companies that did not. The results showed that employees felt engaged enough with the company to report unethical practices and trusted the company to investigate the complaints in a fair and thorough manner.[92]

Ethics officers are responsible for ensuring their organizations adhere to legal and ethical practices. Expanding organizations in particular can create challenges with respect to new employees and new regulations. Chief ethics officers need to continually convey the company's ethical code and values to ensure all employees work to the same ethical standards. Approximately 60% of the most ethical companies in the U.S., such as AT&T, LinkedIn, and U.S. Bancorp, have an independent chief ethics officers.[93]

Ethical Learning

One important way to prevent unethical behavior from occurring in organizations is to ensure that all employees have the opportunity to experience ethical learning. Ethical learning is a skill that can be developed over time through different forms of training and is considered a lifelong process.[94] Yet studies show that many organizations tend to provide ethics training infrequently, either on an annual basis or as part of the onboarding process.[95] According to management research, there are five ways to build an ethical company: (1) experiential ethics training, (2) reflection, (3) postmortem and premortem group discussions, (4) volunteer service, and (5) mentors.[96]

1. Experiential ethics training

   Experiential training is the process of learning through experience using real-world case studies as part of a classroom-based program rather than online or lecture-based ethics training. Aerospace organization Lockheed Martin is a good example of a company that uses experiential ethics training. Employees watch videos showcasing ethical challenges they might face at work before splitting into small groups where they have the opportunity to discuss the scenarios, ask questions, and develop a course of action about when and how to report unethical behavior. Despite the proven effectiveness of experiential learning, it is not commonly used in corporate training programs.

2. Reflection

   Research has shown that reflection is critical for developing ethical skills and expertise in the workplace. The process of reflection allows workers to think about their attitudes toward ethical situations, put themselves in the shoes of others, and evaluate their own traits and abilities in relation to others'. Organizations can promote reflection by creating an environment based on psychological safety (see Chapter 8: Teams), which allows people to speak up without fear, admit mistakes, and seek help when they witness unethical behavior. A psychologically safe environment for ethical learning gives people a safe space to reflect.

3. Postmortem and premortem group discussions

   To accelerate ethical learning, some organizations arrange postmortem meetings (also known as after-action reviews) to discuss the ethical outcomes of a project and whether the process aligned with the company values or code of conduct. Postmortem discussions are also useful for considering ethical dilemmas, such as whether to lay off a weak-performing employee caring for a sick child or whether to cancel a contract with a long-term supplier in favor of a more lucrative option. Discussing ethical issues in a group setting encourages different perspectives and broadens ethical worldviews.

   Groups can also hold a premortem discussion, where teams meet before the beginning of a project to discuss any ethical implications of the proposed business strategy or goals. This can be useful for identifying any biases, points of view, or other ethical considerations that may not have been previously accounted for.

4. Volunteer service

   Research has shown that serving others through volunteering reduces self-focus and increases awareness of moral and ethical concerns.[97] Volunteering has also proved to be beneficial to our well-being. In a recent study, undergraduates who took part in a summer volunteering program performed better in a moral-reasoning assessment compared to their peers who had not participated in the same program. The Savings Bank of Walpole, based in New Hampshire, provides teams with $700 to perform random acts of kindness and encourage employees to share these uplifting stories with others.[98]

5. Mentors

   Mentors are best known for offering career advice and supporting learning and growth, but they can also build ethical learning into their discussions. By sharing their own experiences, offering meaningful insights, and helping their mentees reflect on their own thoughts and actions, mentors can support ethical growth in an environment of psychological safety.

For organizations to remain ethical, leaders must ensure that ethical behavior is practiced throughout the organization by promoting ethical learning within an environment of psychological safety, staying in tune with how employees feel about the company, making sure that employees are being paid fairly and given opportunities for promotion, and building a diverse network to help circumnavigate cultural issues.

IN REVIEW

10.1 Defend the importance of ethics in organizations and effectively evaluate and resolve ethical dilemmas

Ethics are moral principles of duty and virtue that prescribe how we should behave. Individuals and companies frequently face large and small **ethical dilemmas**, or conflicts between two or more morally unpleasant alternatives. The key to being an ethical person or organization is to *consistently* choose to do the right thing.

10.2 Compare and contrast various approaches to ethical decision-making

There are three classical ethical decision-making approaches: the **utilitarian approach**, the **rights approach**, and the **justice approach**. Some contemporary approaches to help managers make ethical decisions include the four-part "moral compass" and the Foursquare Protocol.

10.3 Differentiate between the challenges of ethical leadership and ethical followership

Ideally, leaders and followers collaborate and work together to achieve common goals. However, sometimes ethical challenges in leadership, such as misuse of power, privilege, and abuse of responsibility, can upset the dynamics of a relationship. Like leaders, followers face a number of ethical challenges in their working roles, such as blind obedience, cynicism, and obligation. As followers do not have the same power and status as their leaders, these challenges, if not met, can affect the dynamics of the leader-follower relationship.

10.4 Describe the primary approaches to social responsibility in organizations
Organizations as a whole set a good example by behaving ethically and responsibly. One way organizations can do this is through practicing **corporate social responsibility** (CSR), a business approach that delivers economic, social, and environmental benefits to stakeholders in order to contribute to sustainable development. Carroll's CSR pyramid helps organizations define their social responsibilities, including their **philanthropic responsibility**, **ethical responsibility**, **legal responsibility**, and **economic responsibility**.

10.5 Identify the components of an ethical culture
Building an ethical culture requires a shared sense of meaning to help positively influence ethical behavior. Some components of ethical behavior include core values, mission statements, codes of ethics, structure, boards of directors, reward and performance evaluation systems, reporting and communication systems, and ethics officers.

KEY TERMS

Corporate social responsibility (p. 239)
Economic responsibility (p. 240)
Ethical dilemma (p. 229)
Ethical responsibility (p. 240)
Ethics (p. 227)
Justice approach (p. 230)
Legal responsibility (p. 240)
Philanthropic responsibility (p. 240)
Return on ethics (p. 239)
Rights approach (p. 230)
Utilitarian approach (p. 230)

UP FOR DEBATE: REPORTING ETHICAL VIOLATIONS

Chris has just finished grocery shopping and is loading the bags into the car. Then Chris realizes that the case of Gatorade in the bottom of the cart hasn't been paid for. Chris decides that it's okay to not go back into the store and pay for the Gatorade, reasoning that the store has probably overcharged for goods in the past. Agree or disagree?

EXERCISE 10.1: ETHICAL SITUATIONS

Objective

The purpose of this exercise is to gain a greater appreciation of ethics.

Instructions

We face ethical dilemmas everyday—some are broad in scope and some are relatively minor. These relatively minor ethical situations are just as important as the major ones. Below are several instances you may have found yourself in. In groups of three to five, discuss what you would do in each situation.

- You hand the cashier at a grocery store a $20 bill to pay for $16.50 worth of groceries. When the cashier hands you back the change, instead of giving you $3.50, they inadvertently give you $13.50 but don't realize their mistake.
- You borrow your grandmother's car for a few days. She has a "disabled driver" tag hanging from the rearview mirror. As you drive around town, you see several open parking spaces for cars with this disabled driver permit.

- At your favorite retail store, you put away the cart after placing your purchases in your car. As you do, you discover that someone left their purchases in a cart that was put away, including about $100 worth of merchandise.
- Your boss asks you to "pad" a report that you produce each week detailing the amount of overtime employees work. Your boss has been getting in trouble with the president of the company because of this particular report. If you would just pad the report for one week—showing there is actually less overtime—your boss feels he'll have more time to take actions that will ultimately reduce overtime for the company.
- You work in an office with 20 other employees. You have a fun, friendly work environment. However, you notice that the employee in the cubicle next to you is continually visiting pornographic websites. The manager isn't aware that your coworker is doing this on a regular basis.

Reflection Questions

1. How did you and your group members approach each of these ethical situations?
2. Was everyone in your group in agreement as to what should be done in each situation? Explain.
3. What similar examples of ethical dilemmas have you faced in your career? How did you handle those situations?

Exercise contributed by Steven Stovall, Southeast Missouri State University.

EXERCISE 10.2: CREATING A CODE OF ETHICS

Objective

The purpose of this exercise is to grasp the concept of a code of ethics.

Instructions

A code of ethics is a written set of guidelines that define acceptable and unacceptable behavior. It helps employees make the right choices when faced with difficult situations.

The instructor will invite two volunteers to come to the front of the class. One volunteer will write on the board, while the other will lead a brainstorming session with the students in the class. The purpose of the brainstorming is to develop a code of ethics for this course.

As participants in the brainstorming session, students will help craft a code of ethics that specifies what is acceptable conduct and behavior, how those who follow the code of ethics will be acknowledged or rewarded, and how those who break the ethical code will be reprimanded. As ideas are provided, the student volunteer at the board will capture each idea by writing it so that everyone can see it. Once there are enough ideas, the person leading the discussion will help the class craft a code of ethics specifically for this course.

Reflection Questions

1. Describe the process for developing this code of ethics.
2. Do you think codes of ethics are effective? Why or why not?
3. Does your current or most recent employer have a code of ethics? What is contained in the firm's code of ethics?

Exercise contributed by Steven Stovall, Southeast Missouri State University.

EXERCISE 10.3: WHAT IS FAIR?

Objectives

After successfully completing this exercise, you will be able to better *explain* different methods for resolving ethical dilemmas and *contrast* different approaches to ethical decision-making.

Background

You are the member of the board of directors for a medium-sized light-aircraft parts manufacturing plant. The company has been in operation for over 50 years and has been moderately successful throughout its history. However, due to changes in manufacturing processes, your current manufacturing methods are becoming obsolete and relatively costly compared to those of your competitors. You can upgrade your current manufacturing methods, but that will mean 20% of your workforce will no longer be needed.

Your company has always prided itself on supporting the community through providing well-paying jobs and strong employment guarantees to all of its workers. If you put the automation processes in place, you won't need to hire new workers for the foreseeable future. Additionally, all workers were promised (though not contractually guaranteed) lifetime employment as long as they did a good job.

If you don't implement the technological changes, your projections show a 20% chance of going bankrupt (and ceasing all operations) in the next five years due to increased competition.

Due to the nature of this decision, the company president has asked the company's board for advice on the ethical dimensions of this decision. You and the other board members have decided to meet to examine the situation using the utilitarian, rights, and justice approaches to the situation.

Instructions

Step 1. Form into groups of five to seven members. Examine the decision from all three ethical approaches and make a recommendation on what steps to take from one selected approach. You can bring up alternative solutions to those currently being considered, but those alternatives must fall within the presented business constraints and also be evaluated for ethical considerations. You will need to report your recommendation, and you will also need to report which approach you finally decided to use, why you chose it, the elements you used in making your decision, and if you would have made a different choice if you used another approach. (30 to 40 minutes)

Step 2. Choose a spokesperson to make your report to the entire class. However, all group members should be prepared to answer questions from the instructor and classmates. (5 minutes)

Reflection Questions

1. What difficulties did you have in making your recommendation?
2. Did using the different ethical approaches help you in making your decision?
3. What were the major ways in which your discussions differed using the different approaches?

Exercise contributed by Milton R. Mayfield, Professor of Business, Texas A&M International University, and Jacqueline R. Mayfield, Professor of Business, Texas A&M International University.

ONLINE EXERCISE 10.1: GOOD AND BAD EXAMPLES OF SOCIAL RESPONSIBILITY

Objective

The purpose of this exercise is to gain an appreciation for positive and negative examples of social responsibility.

Instructions

Corporate social responsibility is a business approach that delivers economic, social, and environmental benefits to stakeholders in order to contribute to sustainable development. There are four main levels—economic responsibility, legal responsibility, ethical responsibility, and discretionary responsibility. Your text explores these in detail.

Search online for one example of an organization that has exhibited social responsibility in a positive way and one example of another organization that has demonstrated social responsibility in a negative way. For each, write one double-spaced page detailing what the organization did and how the issue was resolved—if it was resolved. Submit these two pages to your instructor.

Reflection Questions

1. Which is more difficult to find: a good example of social responsibility or a bad one? Why?
2. For both the good and bad examples you found, which level of responsibility is represented—economic, legal, ethical, or discretionary?
3. For your positive example, what costs do you think the organization had to endure to take the action it did?
4. For the negative example, will the organization ever fully recover from this incident? Explain.

Exercise contributed by Steven Stovall, Southeast Missouri State University.

ONLINE EXERCISE 10.2: WRITING A SOCIAL RESPONSIBILITY STATEMENT

Objective

The purpose of this exercise is to understand what is included in a social responsibility statement.

Instructions

In an online discussion group of four to eight participants, develop a social responsibility statement for your university. Your institution may already have one; if you locate it, see if you can improve on it. As you craft your social responsibility statement, include economic responsibility, legal responsibility, ethical responsibility, and discretionary responsibility as outlined in the text.

Reflection Questions

1. Describe the process your team used to create a social responsibility statement. What was the most difficult part?
2. Were you able to find a social responsibility statement for your university? Evaluate that statement. If you couldn't find one, did you find a code of ethics or a similar statement? Explain.
3. Why is it important for an organization to have a statement about its social responsibility?

Exercise contributed by Steven Stovall, Southeast Missouri State University.

CASE 10.1: JETBLUE'S ETHICAL RESPONSE TO A CRISIS

Crisis happens to even the best companies, and the larger a company becomes, the more prone to crisis it will be due to more reach and more to lose. A crisis will quickly test the mettle of any company and will expose the relationship between corporate values and organizational processes in a very public way. The best CEOs are the ones who are students of the game of crisis management and public relations (PR) fiascoes, studying cases of mismanagement like many study basketball. Especially in the modern era of social media, where even the actions of a small-time employee could affect an entire brand and the way it's perceived, it's fundamental to have corporate processes in sync with corporate values. Small things matter more than ever now, and the companies that can consistently get ahead of PR mishaps are the ones that will continue to build brands that people trust.[99]

A good example of this lies within the airline industry. In an industry where power is consolidated and the main factor in deciding which brand to use is price, JetBlue has shone as a player that consistently goes above and beyond. JetBlue, founded in 1998 in one of the most competitive markets in the most competitive industry with the highest barriers to entry, has always sought to "bring the humanity back to air travel."[100] In the early days, this took better amenities, friendlier staff, and less emphasis on the bottom line. JetBlue modeled much of its philosophy off that of Southwest Airlines, a company with a very similar backstory. Commonly one of the highest-rated airlines in the United States for consumer satisfaction, JetBlue was faced with a serious dilemma one winter.[101]

In the middle of the winter of 2007, a major ice storm hit the East Coast, where JetBlue has the majority of its flights. This meant that in the span of just five days, JetBlue had to cancel over a thousand flights.[102] This left passengers caught all over the East Coast sleeping in airports with no way to get home. The entire industry was caught in what seemed like the worst-case scenario during holiday season. While JetBlue wasn't alone in this crisis situation, they knew they had to do something immediately or their brand would suffer. Founder and David Neeleman immediately expressed how "humiliated and mortified" they were that something like this could happen on such a scale[103] and immediately launched a full-fledged investigation into what had gone wrong internally and what could have been managed differently. On top of these actions, Neeleman was available on every media platform to answer questions and to walk customers through exactly how JetBlue would seek to make this right to them.[104]

Where most airlines would see a situation like this as an unavoidable part of doing business, JetBlue took it as a sign that they weren't doing nearly enough for their customers and for what JetBlue stood for. The findings of the internal investigation found that JetBlue had failed to equip itself with enough infrastructure to handle a situation like this. David Neeleman quickly announced amid the chaos that they had failed to provide themselves with reservation and employee communication systems large enough for a corporation their size. They had been using systems that were identical to the ones put together near the time of their founding. They stepped out in front of a crisis that could have been shaken off, instead using it as a way to strengthen their organizational communication systems and their brand in a single step.[105]

Going forward, JetBlue changed everything they could to better themselves. Neeleman announced once the investigation was completed, "This is going to be a different company because of this. It's going to be expensive. But what's more important is to win back people's confidence."[106] From then on, JetBlue focused on building a system that was scalable and that customers could depend on in difficult situations like storms.

In conclusion, JetBlue stepped out in front of an unfortunate situation and managed to make it a teaching moment for itself and for the industry. Its leadership could have blamed the weather or settled claims silently, but instead it re-formed itself as a company focused on overdelivering in easy times and hard. Other companies have a lot to learn from crises like this one, and the ones that can take lessons from situations like these are the ones that will continually succeed.

Discussion Questions

1. Describe the options JetBlue had when faced with the ice storm crisis.
2. What can any business learn from the mistakes JetBlue made?

Smith Collection/Gado / Contributor / Getty Images

11 EFFECTIVE COMMUNICATION

LEARNING OBJECTIVES

By the end of this chapter, you will be able to:

11.1 Describe the basic model of communication

11.2 Compare the types of communication channels

11.3 Identify key barriers to effective communication

11.4 Describe types of communication networks within organizations

11.5 Discuss the elements of effective cross-cultural communication

Case Study: Uber's Organizational Communication

With more than $11 billion in annual revenues in 2020, around 22,000 full-time employees, operations in more than 10,000 cities worldwide, and an innovative service that has changed the way we look at business, Uber has been an example of excellence in the tech start-up community since its inception in March of 2009.[1] In fact, the company's name has its roots in the German word *uber*, meaning super or topmost; a testament to the company's commitment to excellence.[2] However, Uber has run into some trouble that has tainted this image, stemming from recent trends in the organization's communication.

As Mike Isaac of the *New York Times* puts it, "The focus on pushing for the best result has also fueled what current and former Uber employees describe as a Hobbesian environment at the company, in which workers are sometimes pitted against one another and where a blind eye is turned to infractions from top performers."[3] Historically, the verbal communication practices that flow through the formal and the informal networks at Uber have been very detrimental to the company's image and productivity over time.

In any organization, there are two networks through which communication flows: formal networks and the informal networks. The formal networks represent the transmission of messages established and approved by the organizational hierarchy. This type of communication is typically imposed by the chain of command through policies and procedures and can be observed through a manager's downward communication.[4]

Downward communication is defined as messages sent from the upper levels of the organizational hierarchy to the lower levels.[5] Simply put, the way managers communicate with their subordinates is crucial to their effectiveness as managers. Managers who communicate expectations through clear, concise, and respectful messages are much more likely to receive the highest quality of work from their employees than managers who communicate very vague expectations and use verbal abuse toward employees whom they deem incompetent. An employee is much more responsive when receiving messages that make them feel empowered and cared for. Accusations of verbal abuse at Uber, like the claim that an Uber manager threatened to beat an underperforming employee's head in with a baseball bat, are an indication of a culture rooted in verbal abuse.[6] Managers have an ethical responsibility to provide verbal, nonthreatening constructive criticism to their employees. If nothing else, managers who communicate in this healthy way will, at the very least, see more improvement from their employees over time.

Additionally, there has been no room for employees to share their **differing perceptions** with one another. Differing perceptions are the way in which our interpretations of situations clash with the perceptions of others. What the management at Uber failed to realize is that the different perceptions of their employees is one of their most valuable assets. Some of the best ideas are brought to the tables by employees who see a situation a different way. By suppressing an employee's ability to do so, managers at Uber effectively put a halt to its internal creativity and hurt its own productivity. On one occasion, a director shouted a homophobic slur at a subordinate during a heated confrontation in a meeting.[7] This verbal abuse toward a subordinate not only is another example of the presence of faulty downward communication at Uber but it also likely sent a message to other subordinates that differing perceptions had no place in the company.

Informal communication is defined as a casual form of sharing information between employees across company divisions.[8] This is the everyday, free-ranging communication that employees partake in to build relationships and share opinions. Informal communication takes place through what is called the grapevine.[9] It is simply an unofficial line of communication between individuals or groups. Informal communication through the grapevine will happen naturally in any organization and it can be a healthy contributor to the well-being of employees. However, if informal communication is let loose in a belligerent workplace it can have some seriously adverse effects to the organization as a whole. The grapevine in an organization with a culture like Uber has the potential to give rise to gossip chains. Gossip chains are a type of communication that occurs when one individual creates and spreads untrue or inaccurate information through the organization.[10] At Uber, the excessively competitive culture has created an environment where stepping on the toes of fellow employees and damaging other's reputations is considered acceptable behavior. In Uber's case, "people wind up 'stepping on toes' in the wrong direction. Instead of challenging managers or superiors with bad ideas, they put down their peers."[11] The formal and informal communication networks of Uber have been tainted by these past trends. Currently, Uber is taking steps to remedy the situation and start fresh.

The corrupt culture of Uber started to be brought to light to the public in 2016 and since then the company has taken steps toward fixing the problems they have caused for themselves. There has been pushback from upper management and high employee turnover rates have made it difficult to get new culture initiatives to find a foothold within the company. In June of 2017, Uber hired HR consultant Frances Frei to serve as its senior vice president of leadership and strategy.[12] Prior to this engagement, Ms. Frei was a professor at Harvard University with a bio describing Frei as "a personal advisor to senior executives embarking on cultural change and organizational transformations."[13] This is exactly what Uber needs and the hiring of people like this is a true testament to Uber's commitment to changing its workplace culture by bringing in management who will actively challenge what used to be the status quo. Continued practices such as this are the key to any problems that originally stem from poor management. Many companies in the past, like Enron and WorldCom, have not been able to rebound from poor communication practices in management and this led to even larger problems like fraud and embezzlement. This is a huge step forward in the right direction for Uber, and the company should continue on this track as it strives to be a leader once again.

THE NEED FOR EFFECTIVE COMMUNICATION IN THE WORKPLACE

In an increasingly connected world, communication is more important than ever in the workplace. The Uber case demonstrates what can happen when communication breaks down in an organization. People hurling abuse at each other or making verbal threats brings down morale and can turn a culture toxic. We define **communication** as the act of transmitting thoughts, processes, and ideas through a variety of channels.[14] Efficient communication leads to better functioning of organizations, which benefits both employees and customers.

Today's organizations have no choice but to adapt quickly to the rise of new technologies and social networking tools to keep up with the competition and stay in touch with the needs of their customer bases and their employees. Inside the organization, effective communication must take place within and among peer groups and between different hierarchical levels. One of the most important roles of a manager is to encourage and nurture a collaborative working environment by effectively communicating with teams to ensure that tasks are accomplished and organizational goals achieved.

During the COVID-19 pandemic, the way we communicated with each other rapidly changed. For many of us, our in-person interactions shifted to online communication or wearing masks inside when social distancing was not a possibility. Although most people have adapted quickly to these changes, there are challenges and limitations to some of these methods of communication, which we will explore later in the chapter.

In 1947, mathematician Claude E. Shannon created a communication model that was later developed further by Warren Weaver. The Shannon–Weaver model (see Figure 11.1) is the cornerstone of communication models and is still in use today.[15]

FIGURE 11.1 ■ Shannon–Weaver Communications Model

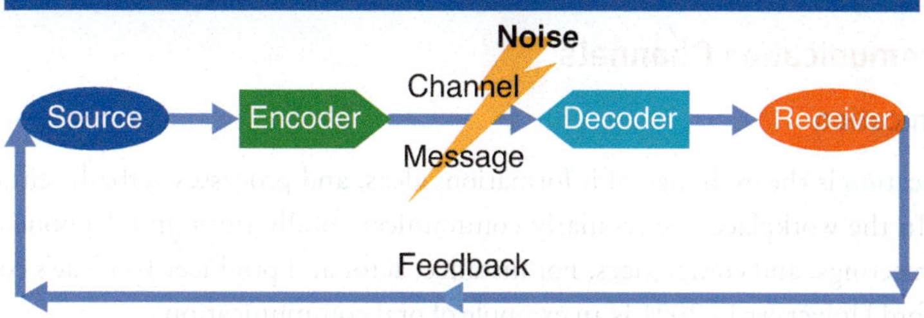

Source: Adapted from Shannon, C. E. & Weaver, W. (1949). *The Mathematical Theory of Communication.* University of Illinois Press.

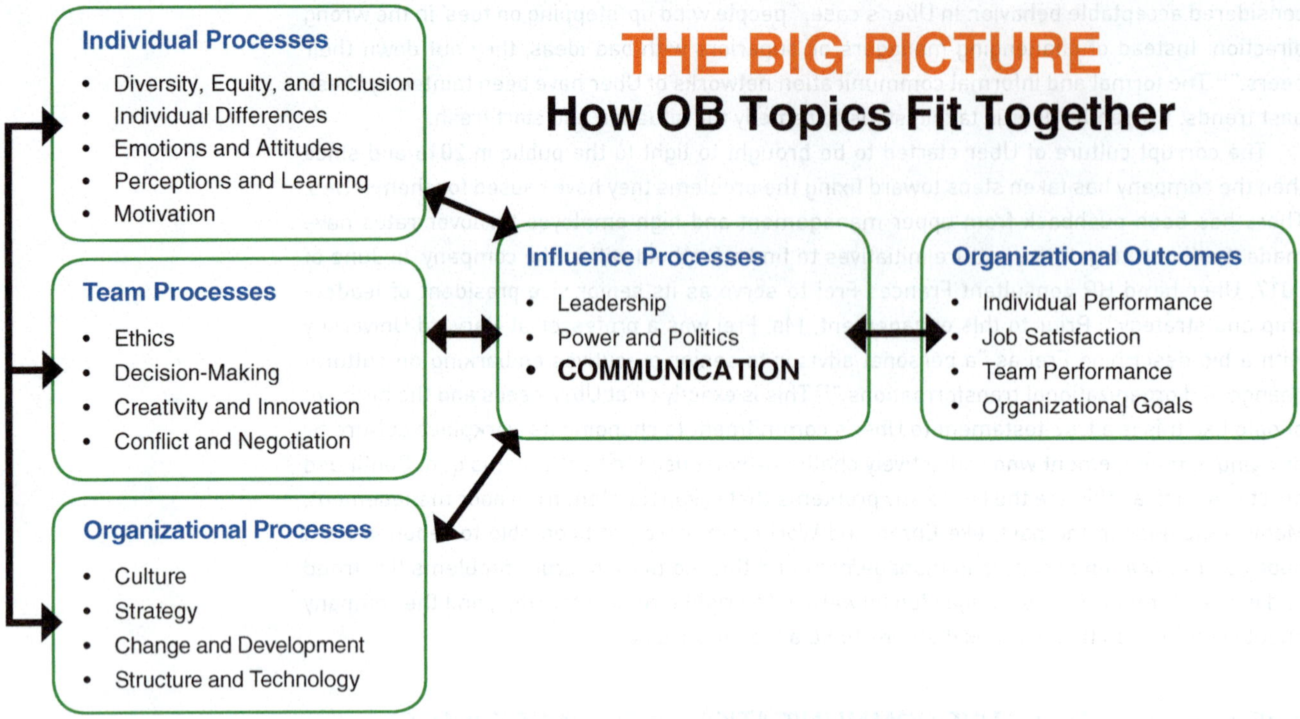

The Shannon–Weaver model assumes that communication relies on two main components: the *sender* of the message, also known as the source, and the *receiver* of the message. When the sender transmits a message through a communication channel—the route the message travels along—the content of the message is encoded into its intended meaning through different formats such as written, oral, or electronic; the receiver then decodes or interprets the message into a perceived meaning. The receiver provides feedback or a response to the sender to confirm the message has been received and its meaning understood.

Although this sounds like a fairly simple process, disturbances known as *noise* often occur. Background noise such as people talking loudly, construction work, or telephones ringing can all interfere with our ability to communicate effectively. Noise in the context of the Shannon–Weaver Model does not necessarily refer to sound, however; noise refers to interference that can muddy a message between the sender and receiver. In this context, noise might refer to complex or difficult language or cultural differences that distort meaning. It is essential for sender and receiver to clear their communication channels of any noise that may disrupt the meaning of the message.

COMMUNICATION CHANNELS

As recently as 30 years ago, only a handful of communication channels were available to us. But thanks to the rapid rise of technology, we now have myriad ways to send and receive messages (see Figure 11.2). Let's explore the different types of communication channels we use in daily life and the benefits and disadvantages of each.

Types of Communication Channels

Oral Communication

Oral communication is the exchange of information, ideas, and processes verbally, either one-on-one or as a group. In the workplace, we regularly communicate orally through telephone conversations, presentations, meetings, and conferences. For instance, actor and producer Issa Rae's commencement speech to Stanford University in 2021 is an example of oral communication.

FIGURE 11.2 ■ Communication Channels

Source: Neck, C. P. (2013). *Management*, p. 379. Wiley.

Advantages and Disadvantages. Talking to people in person or on the phone or in a video chat is an excellent way to network and build relationships. Another major advantage of oral communication is that messages are sent and received almost instantaneously, and feedback is given just as fast, so misunderstandings can be quickly cleared up. However, sometimes the informal nature of oral communication means that messages or parts of messages are forgotten or misunderstood later. Mask-wearing also impacted oral communication during the pandemic by muffling our speech and concealing our facial cues. This was especially difficult for the Deaf and hard-of-hearing community who rely on lip-reading and facial expressions to communicate effectively.

Written Communication

Written communication makes use of the written word in the form of reports, memos, employee manuals and letters to communicate messages. Notice of acceptance to college or a formal job offer is usually delivered in a written letter.

The State of the Union is one example of oral communication, when the president of the United States gives a speech to the country about the status of the country and its government.

Spencer Platt / Staff / Getty Images

Advantages and Disadvantages. Effective written communication minimizes misunderstandings when messages to recipients are delivered clearly and concisely. Senders also have the opportunity to review written messages before sending and record and archive them if necessary. However, written communication is less personal than oral communication and should not be used to convey emotional messages. When delivering negative feedback, it is always best to do it over the phone or in person. In addition, unless the receiver provides instant feedback, the sender will not always know whether the message has reached its destination or has been interpreted correctly.

Electronic Communication

Electronic/digital communication is the transmission of messages through email, videoconferencing, blogs, fax, instant messaging, live chat, texting, and social media (Twitter, Snapchat, TikTok, LinkedIn, Facebook, YouTube, Pinterest, Instagram, and more). Many companies and social activist groups use "hashtag campaigns" to quickly and broadly disperse information and start conversations around certain topics, events, and products. During COVID-19, more than half of global organizations increased their use of digital communication channels, with live chat, email, and video the most popular choices in staying connected with their employees.[16]

Advantages and Disadvantages. There is no better way of instantly reaching a large audience across a global network than through forms of electronic communication. Videoconferencing has become a staple in our everyday lives and looks as though it is here to stay. Table 11.1 lists some tips for videoconferencing etiquette.

However, there are also inherent disadvantages to electronic communication. The vast amount of data being delivered from multiple platforms can lead to content overload which can be overwhelming. Electronic communication can be hindered by technical problems, misinterpretation, and privacy breaches. In 2021, data breaches in health-care data compromised over 40 million patient records.[17] Many health-care

TABLE 11.1 ■ Video Conferencing Etiquette

1. Make sure everything is working
To avoid technical hitches, give yourself a few minutes before for the meeting to check that everything is working, including your camera, microphone and the videoconferencing tool itself. Make sure you're also on time for the meeting—traffic jams and car trouble are not acceptable excuses when you're working remotely.
2. Dress appropriately
When working from home, there may be a temptation to dress overly casually. Although not as many companies require formal wear such as a suit, it is important to look professional by wearing clean, smart clothes.
3. Check your background
Before you join the meeting, make sure you clear your background of any distractions such as piles of dirty dishes or other clutter in the kitchen, or an unmade bed and dirty laundry if you're working from the bedroom. Ideally, your background should be well lit and as blank as possible to avoid distractions.
4. Avoid multitasking
Treat a virtual meeting as you would an in-person meeting. In other words, resist the temptation to check social media, emails, or texts while other members are talking. And only snack or eat lunch if it has already been agreed with your team mates. You may be behind a screen but it is very easy for others to spot when someone isn't paying attention.
5. Use the mute button appropriately
Microphones can pick up on anything from coughing, typing, a dog barking, or other background noise, so it is best to mute yourself when you're not speaking, to avoid distracting other participants. When it is your time to speak, take a moment to check that you have pressed the unmute button. This will save you effort of repeating yourself.
6. Make eye contact
The screen can be quite busy during a virtual meeting particularly meetings with many attendees. Images of colleagues, your own image, text-based chat and other movement in the background can make it difficult to focus. However, it is important to try and maintain eye contact with the person you are addressing as best you can to ensure your message is being communicated.
7. Speak Clearly
Account for connection quality and minor delays by speaking clearly and slowly. Wait until others have finished speaking and avoid interrupting where you can.

providers were so consumed by responding to the COVID-19 crisis and addressing patient needs that they failed to report breaches or were unaware of them, leaving their systems vulnerable to malicious attacks.[18]

Nonverbal Communication

Nonverbal communication is the transmission of wordless cues between people. Examples of nonverbal cues include facial expression, eye gaze, gestures, tone of voice, head-nodding, smiling, and body language such as the way we walk, stand, dress, and position ourselves.[19] From the way we shake hands to the color of the clothing we wear, nonverbal details show others who we are and influence the way we are perceived. The type of body language we use in the workplace is especially important when communicating with our colleagues.[20] For example, fidgeting, hair-twirling, or face-touching may be perceived by others as boredom, nervousness, or some other insecurity. Similarly, failure to make eye contact might make the other person think that you're not interested in what they have to say. Being aware of our body language and what it means goes a long way toward building good working relationships. Figure 11.3 illustrates how different types of body language may be interpreted by others.

Nonverbal communication occurs in popular sitcoms like *The Office* and *Emily in Paris* as in many sitcoms, where the characters often engage in different facial expressions and gestures to convey thoughts and emotions.

Advantages and Disadvantages. Nonverbal communication can be an important way of interacting with others because it allows for transmission of subtle messages through eye contact, vocal tone, and posture. However, because we are usually unaware of the nonverbal messages we are sending, we are at risk of unintentionally conveying the wrong message, which, in turn, may give the wrong impression. There can also be confusion and discrepancies between the nonverbal cues we convey and the words we are saying. For example, you might tell your professor you are happy to stay after class and take on an extra assignment, but defensive body language such as folded arms, downcast eyes, and legs crossed away from your professor will suggest otherwise.

Health workers rely on positive nonverbal communication, such as smiling, and direct eye contact to show empathy to their patients. Research shows that patients who receive high nonverbal support demonstrate a greater tolerance for pain and recover more quickly.[21] Showing nonverbal communication was particularly challenging for health workers during COVID-19; face masks and personal

FIGURE 11.3 ■ Different Types of Body Language

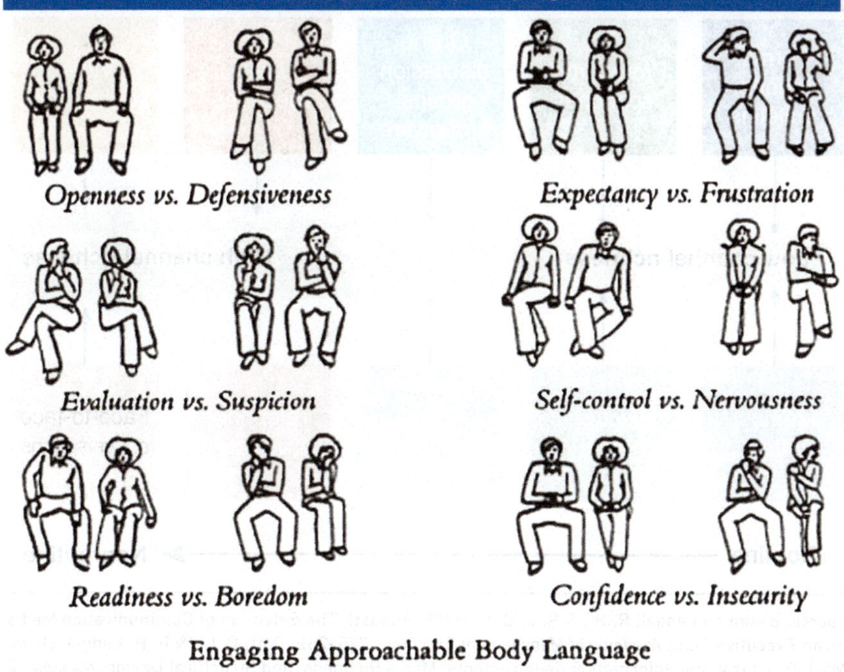

Source: Tutorials Point. "Cracking Interviews—Quick Guide." https://www.tutorialspoint.com/cracking_interviews/cracking_interviews_quick_guide.htm

protective equipment interfered with nonverbal communication by suppressing facial expressions and body movements.[22] Dr. Sharan Chugani made an effort to overcome these limitations by creating a novel way to comfort patients, build trust, and better interpret their emotions and feelings.

"I write my name on my gown and draw a smiling face . . . It makes a difference in that people like putting a face to a name and them being able to see you smile makes a big difference with trust and reassurance."[23]

Characters on ABC's *Modern Family* often convey their thoughts and emotions through nonverbal communication such as facial expressions and body language.
Album/Alamy Stock Photo

Channel Richness

With so many communication channels to choose from, how do we choose the most appropriate one for certain situations? One way is to weigh **channel richness**, the degree to which a channel allows us to easily communicate and understand information sent between people and organizations (Figure 11.4).[24] Face-to-face communication is considered to be very high in channel richness as it allows for immediate feedback, the understanding of verbal and nonverbal cues, and

FIGURE 11.4 ■ Channel Richness

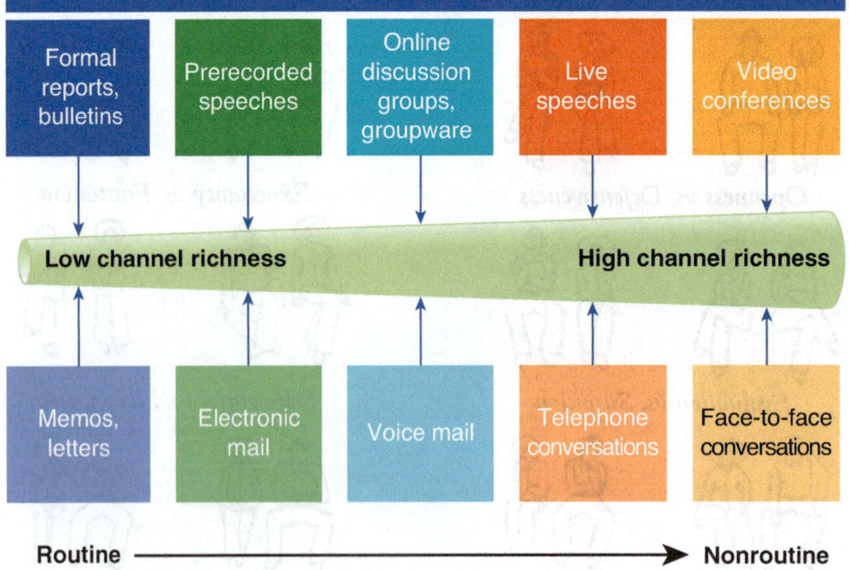

Source: Based on Lengel, R. H., & R. L. Daft. (1988, August). The Selection of Communication Media as an Executive Skill. *Academy of Management Executive*, 225–232; Daft, D. L., & R. H. Lengel. (1996, May). Organizational Information Requirements, Media Richness, and Structural Design. *Managerial Science* 554-572. Reproduced from R. L. Daft & R. A. Noe, *Organizational Behavior*, p. 311. Harcourt. Copyright © 2007 Prentice Hall Inc. All rights reserved.

opportunities for building relationships. Videoconferencing is also thought to be one of the richest forms of communication, but as we have explored it does have its disadvantages such as technical hitches, hacking, and time lags which sometimes make smooth communication difficult.

The second-richest channel is the phone. During phone conversations we are able to listen to verbal cues, detect levels of emotion, and pick up on nonverbal cues such as tone of voice. Despite their popularity, emails, text messages, blogs, memos, e-bulletins, and so on are considered to be at the lower end of channel richness, especially when the information becomes sensitive or complex. By far the most effective way of resolving a situation or dealing with a difficult issue is to call a face-to-face meeting or pick up the phone.

BARRIERS TO COMMUNICATION

Because communication is central to our relationships with others, it is essential that we understand the barriers that can hamper our ability to communicate successfully and learn how to overcome them.[25] Here are some of the barriers most often encountered at work.

Filtering occurs when the sender deliberately manipulates a message before passing it on to the intended receiver to manage the receiver's reactions. People tend to filter information for two main reasons: a fear of passing on bad news and a desire to please the receiver—for example, a sales manager who withholds low sales figures from senior management for fear of a negative reaction.[26]

Emotions. Our emotions have an effect on the way we communicate. When we are happy and relaxed, we are more likely to accept constructive criticism in a positive way and convey our messages succinctly and accurately. However, when we are stressed or angry, we might snap at others or feel attacked or defensive when someone tries to offer advice. It is essential that we are aware of our emotions and keep them in check before they spiral out of control. For example, in 2021, KPMG chairman Bill Michael was forced to apologize for an outburst during a virtual meeting to discuss the impact of the COVID-19 pandemic. In a video which was shared publicly, Michael told staff to "stop moaning" and to stop "playing the victim card" in relation to lockdown and other pandemic-related issues. Michael ultimately resigned after the outburst.[27]

Information overload is a phenomenon that occurs when we become overwhelmed by the wealth of information surrounding us, from social media, television, radio and our mobile devices. Studies have found that information overload reduces creativity and innovation, decreases productivity, interrupts natural thought processes, impacts workflow, inhibits logic, and also causes headaches, nausea, and irritability.[28] Studies show that 98% of people do not have the ability to focus on more than one thing at a time, so it is essential to put the right measures in place to avoid being overpowered by information.[29] Limiting our news resources, filtering social media and switching off notifications, shutting down your devices and silencing your phone, and physically removing yourself from information generators (such as going for a walk or grabbing a coffee) are all useful ways to prevent information overload.[30]

Differing perceptions. Sometimes the way we interpret situations clashes with the perceptions of others, leading to confusion and misconception. For example, over the past five years, there has been a perception that younger and older generations have been clashing over climate change with younger people perceived as ecowarriors fighting against the uncaring older generations.[31] A recent study disproved this perception by showing that older people care about the planet just as much as younger people, finding that older generations are more likely to act in environmentally conscious ways.[32]

We can overcome this communication barrier by challenging our own assumptions about other people and situations, making an effort to understand different perspectives and by seeking advice from others to clarify our perceptions.

Poor Listening

The Greek philosopher Epictetus once said, "We have two ears and one mouth so we should listen twice as much as we speak." This quote references one of the biggest obstacles to successful communication:

poor listening. Within organizations, failure to listen properly can lead to misunderstandings that can damage personal and work relationships. Ineffective listening also comes at a high price—it is estimated that millions of dollars are wasted every year due to the time it takes to repeat information, correct misunderstandings, and make up for loss of productivity.[33]

A way to overcome poor listening is through **active listening**, which consists of concentrating on the true meaning of what others are saying.[34] It is an essential skill for employees in the workplace because it allows the receiver to hear and understand the message and reassures the speaker that the message has been heard in the same terms in which it is delivered. Good active listeners remove all distractions so they can concentrate on what is being said, show a real interest in the message the speaker is trying to deliver, and provide appropriate responses to the speaker at suitable times. Fred Halstead, author of *Leadership Skills that Inspire Incredible Results* believes that being a good active listener is particularly important for leaders as ". . . it establishes your role as effective and empathetic—someone who keeps an open mind and is willing to learn from others."[35]

There are three main components to active listening: processing, sensing, and responding (see Figure 11.5).[36] **Processing** involves actively understanding and remembering what is being said as well as making an effort to empathize with the speaker's feelings and thoughts and the situation at hand. Active listening also requires looking for nonverbal cues such eye contact or lack thereof, poor posture (slouching, sitting upright, and tense), and tone of voice (sarcastic, angry, confident) to really understand the entire message.

Sensing involves paying attention to the signals sent from the speaker. The listener avoids forming an opinion or interrupting the speaker until they have finished and consciously remains attentive to what the speaker is saying.

Finally, **responding** is the way active listeners provide feedback to the speaker ("I see what you mean") and clarify the message by repeating some of the key points at appropriate breaks ("So, you're saying that . . .").

As we have illustrated, communication between individuals can be complex and is often the cause of conflicts and misunderstandings. In the next section, we explore how the different directions of communication affect the functioning of organizations.

FIGURE 11.5 ■ The Active Listening Process

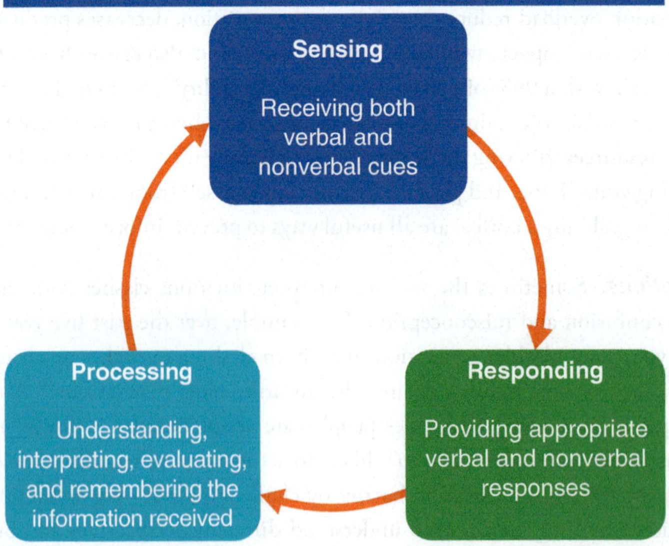

Source: Based on Comer, L. B. & Drollinger, T. (1999). Active empathetic listening and selling success: A conceptual framework. *Journal of Personal Selling and Sales Management, 19*(1), 15–29.

EXAMINING THE EVIDENCE

ELECTRONIC COMMUNICATION DURING NONWORKING HOURS

Increases in electronic communication technologies such as smartphones, tablets, laptops, and wireless internet have made it easier than ever for organizations to communicate with their employees outside of working hours. But what are the effects of these after-hour communications on employee well-being? In a recent study, researchers Marcus M. Butts of the University of Texas at Arlington, William J. Becker of Texas Christian University, and Wendy R. Boswell of Texas A & M University explored this question.[37] They found that the emotional reaction and amount of work–nonwork role conflict experienced by employees receiving after-hours communications depended on the affective content and time demands of the messages. Messages with a positive affective tone involving encouragement, support, and recognition and that demanded less communication time resulted in more employee happiness and ultimately less work–nonwork conflict. In contrast, messages with a negative affective tone involving uncivil, degrading, or hostile content and those that demanded more communication time resulted in greater employee anger and more work–nonwork conflict. These findings suggest that communications sent outside of regular working hours should focus on positive feedback and accomplishments and not focus on problems, criticisms, and deficiencies. Organizations may be well advised to provide employees with training and guidelines on the appropriate use of electronic communications outside normal working hours.

Critical-Thinking Questions

1. Would it be advisable for organizations to implement policies prohibiting electronic communication after normal working hours? Why or why not?
2. Specifically, what types of messages would be best delivered electronically outside of working hours? Provide some examples of effective after-hour communications.

COMMUNICATING IN ORGANIZATIONS

The flow of communication in an organization can move in three main directions depending on how an organization is structured.[38] (See Figure 11.6.)

Downward communication sends messages from the upper levels of the organizational hierarchy to the lower levels. For example, in hierarchical organizations like the military, there is a tendency to use downward communication. One of the major functions of downward communication is to maintain discipline and employee compliance through positive influence. When downward communication is successful, it is totally transparent. This means that lower-level employees consistently receive clear messages and feedback from their superiors regarding organizational performance, strategies, developments, and goals. Sharing information down the levels provides employees with a sense of involvement and minimizes doubt and insecurity about how the company is performing. However, when downward communication goes wrong and messages fail to be transmitted effectively down the chain of command, it can cause confusion, distrust, and anxiety among the rest of the workforce.

Upward communication is the process in which employees from the lower levels of the organizational hierarchy communicate with the higher levels by sharing their feedback, ideas and concerns.

If lower-level employees do not effectively communicate with their superiors and instead withhold or filter information, this can leave those at the higher levels ignorant of what is really going on in the organization. Studies show that effective upward communication improves employee retention, increases engagement, morale, and job satisfaction, creates a sense of purpose, and promotes an inclusive environment. More than 75% of employees agreed that they would prefer to work in a company where their voices are being heard.[39]

Lateral communication is the process in which employees send messages between and among similar hierarchical levels across organizations. Lateral communication can be an effective way for people from

FIGURE 11.6 ■ Three Directions of Communication in Organizations

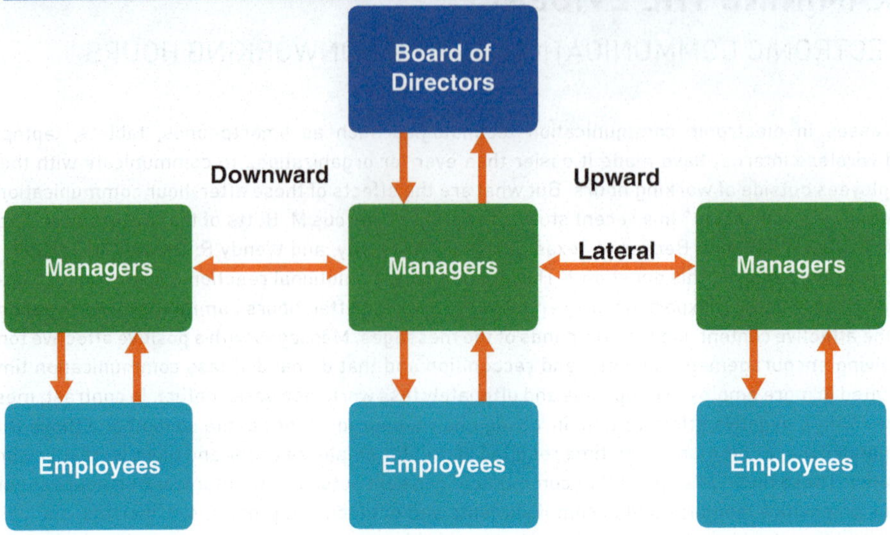

Source: Based on Lunenburg, F. C. (2010). Formal communication channels: Upward, downward, horizontal, and external. *Focus on Colleges, Universities, and Schools, 4*(1). www.nationalforum.com/Electronic%20Journal%20Volumes/Lunenburg,%20Fred%20C,%20Formal%20Comm%20Channels%20FOCUS%20V4%20N1%202010.pdf.

different departments to communicate the information they need to their peers quickly and accurately. Although lateral communication supports teamwork, encourages innovation, fosters empowerment, and helps build morale, it requires managerial control to minimize potential interpersonal conflict that may arise as a result of many participants collaborating at once.

Regardless of the direction of the flow of communication within organizations, most messages are sent through two main communication networks: formal and informal.[40] **Formal networks** transmit the messages established and approved by the organizational hierarchy. Usually, formal networks are imposed by the chain of command, which sends official messages such as policies and procedures to the rest of the staff. For example, when a CEO needs to tell employees about a new company policy, management might send the information in the form of an email.

Informal networks handle the unofficial sharing of information between employees and across company divisions. Informal networks can help employees communicate freely with one another, build relationships, exchange opinions, and share grievances. For instance, informal networks allow minimum wage workers to share their grievances about low pay, teachers to share classroom management strategies, and students to rate their professors and study for a major exam.

One of the main forms of informal networks is the **grapevine**, the unofficial line of communication between individuals or groups.[41] Grapevines are a useful method of communicating messages quickly and efficiently in person, or through technological tools such as email, blog or social media, or via digital channels like WhatsApp groups. They can bring about a sense of unity among the employees who share information. However, they are more common where management keeps employees in the dark about what is going on in the organization or when the culture is aggressively competitive. Uber took

Companies like IDEO utilize lateral communication to increase collaboration across departments and to promote creativity.

iStockPhoto / fizkes

steps to address the level of informal communication in the organization after the company grapevine became rife with rumors and inaccurate information.

Grapevines also give rise to **gossip chains**, communication networks in which one individual creates and spreads untrue or inaccurate information to others through the organization.[42] Each person who hears the gossip has the choice to keep it confidential or to pass it on. For example, one employee might spread gossip to others to discredit an unpopular supervisor. In contrast, a **cluster chain** consists of a group of people who broadcast information only within their group.[43] In both gossip chains and cluster chains, the information moves very quickly and can be damaging to an organization regardless of management's confirming or denying the rumors. Successful organizations actively control rumors and gossip through effective, honest, and consistent communication.[44]

Trader Joe's employees at all levels are encouraged to contribute thoughts and ideas about how the store is run.

Pat Greenhouse/The Boston Globe via Getty Images

Teachers share stories and tips with each other as part of an informal network of communication.

© iStockphoto.com/kali9

CROSS-CULTURAL COMMUNICATION

The success of global organizations depends on the quality of cross-cultural communication, and without the necessary preparation, it can be a minefield. Cultural misunderstandings are all too common. When is kissing a business associate appropriate? Or bowing to a colleague? When is it of the utmost importance to arrive on time for a business meeting? And what sort of behavior is expected during a meal? When it comes to advertising, it is imperative that the message not get lost in translation through cultural error. For example, KFC's "Finger-Lickin' Good" was interpreted as "Eat your fingers off" in China; Swedish vacuum maker's ad campaign for Electrolux centered on the slogan "Nothing sucks like an Electrolux," which understandably failed to appeal to many U.S. consumers; and Braniff Airlines advertised its leather seats with the slogan "Fly in leather," which was translated in Mexico as "Fly naked"—not what the airline intended to convey.

To avoid these costly blunders, many organizations encourage their employees to learn a second language and carry out extensive research to increase their understanding of other cultures. In answer to the questions mentioned, by the way, it is appropriate in France to greet business associates with a kiss on the cheek; bowing is a traditional form of greeting in East Asia; and punctuality is essential when attending meetings in the United Kingdom, Germany, and Switzerland, among others.

One of the major barriers to cross-cultural communication is **ethnocentrism**, the tendency to believe your culture or ethnicity is superior to everyone else's.[45] For example, members of Western cultures might judge negatively people from other cultures in which it is customary to use the hands to eat rather than use utensils, or they might belittle other cultures for their passive or formal nature. Figure 11.7 shows a map of the world.

Why does this map appear "wrong" to many people? Because it is shown from a different perspective than what one normally sees on a map. The famed Uruguayan artist Joaquin Torres-Garcia painted South America in this way in the art piece *América invertida* to contrast the South with the North, where an ethnocentric perspective lead many in the so-called dominant northern hemisphere to look down on their southern neighbors. For those in the South, however, including Torres-Garcia, that view is simply upside-down.[46]

Low-Context versus High-Context Cultures

The role of language has a major influence on culture and vice versa. In the United States, it is common to use sports references in a business environment. "They are team players," "You're way off base," and "That manager threw me a curve" are all popular phrases that are familiar in the United States but might be confusing to people from other cultures. Anthropologist Edward T. Hall studied the variety of ways different cultures use language and divided cultures into two main groups on that basis: low-context and high-context.[47]

FIGURE 11.7 ■ "Southside Up" Global Map

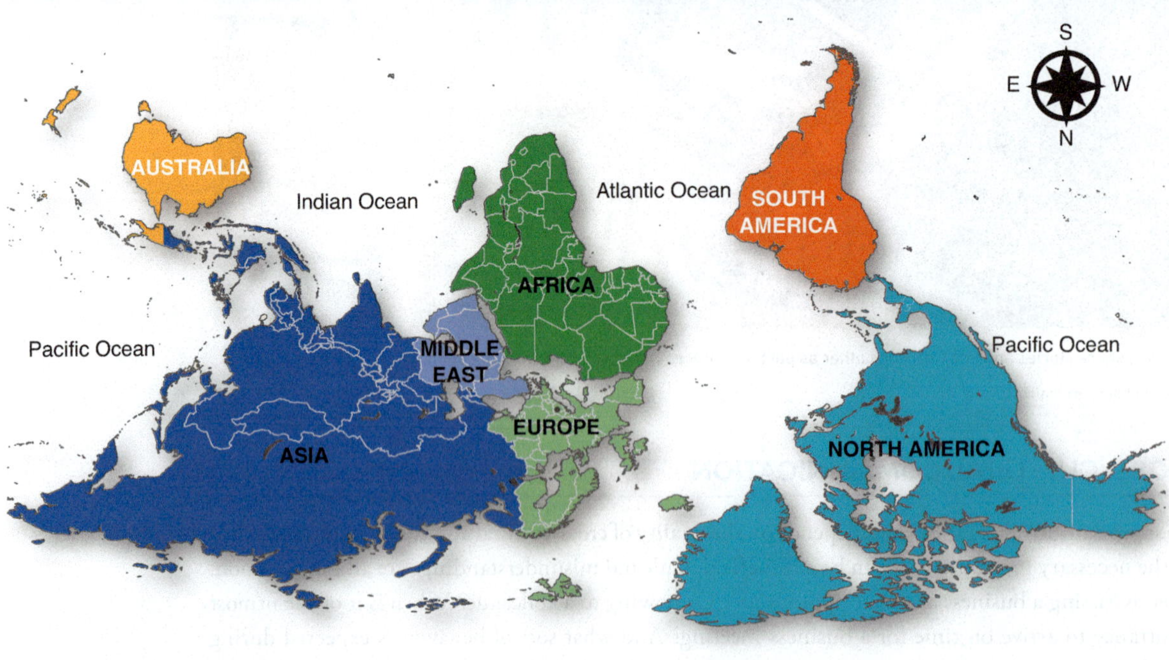

Source: Anna Versluis/SAGE

Low-context cultures depend more on explicit messages conveyed through the spoken or written word. Most English-speaking and Germanic countries have a fast, direct, logical, efficient, "What you say is what you mean" communication style. In business environments in these countries, there is less emphasis on interpersonal relationships and more on the individual.

In contrast, in **high-context cultures**, most messages are conveyed through body language, nonverbal cues, and the circumstances in which the communication is taking place. According to Hall, many Middle Eastern and Asian cultures fall into this category. The Japanese, for example, have an indirect, intuitive, unemotional, contemplative, and passive style of negotiation. In short, what you say is not necessarily what you mean. High-context cultures value silence as a way of absorbing information and getting a sense of the people they are communicating with.

Over the years, there have been many well-documented clashes between low-context and high-context cultures. For example, when Kentucky whiskey distillery Jim Beam merged with Japanese brewing and distillery group Suntory, the management teams experienced a culture clash in relation to how decisions were made. Although U.S. culture largely favors quick, flexible decision-making with the manager having the final say, Japanese culture relies on a system where decisions are made by group consensus. As soon as the Jim Beam managers understood this process, they were able to work more collaboratively with the Suntory team.[48]

Social Context

Communication also depends on the social setting. We tend to use different vocabulary depending on the situation or the person we are talking to, and our response to these social contexts differs by culture. For example, you are unlikely to greet your professor the same way you would your baseball teammate or fellow student.

The way people from different cultures use language can provide a richer understanding of their society. For example, the Japanese base their linguistic styles on status and choose from three different styles to express the appropriate level of social respect: basic speech, average speech, or elegant speech. Novice speakers of Japanese might inadvertently offend someone to whom they are speaking if they mistakenly choose the incorrect linguistic style.[49]

Gender categories can be reflected in language and can, in turn, affect communication. In some areas of the West Indies, for example, women and men use different words to refer to the same thing.

Other Complicating Factors

Several other factors can further complicate our communication with members of other cultures.[50]

Slang and Idioms

Slang is informal language applied in a particular context or group. Although it is not usually appropriate in business communication, slang is often used in daily life. For example, in the United Kingdom and Ireland, "knackered" means "exhausted," while in the United States the slang phrase "in a New York minute" means to do something very fast.

An *idiom* is a word or group of words used to convey a meaning other than its literal one. For example, U.S. businesspeople sometimes use expressions such as "dead in the water" for a project or action that has stalled. Even native English-speakers communicating with people from other English-speaking countries may encounter difficulties with idioms. For example, in a business setting, the U.S. expression, "Table it" means not to discuss a matter further, whereas in the United Kingdom, it means to bring the matter to the table for discussion.

Euphemisms

Most languages include *euphemisms*, vague or general words used in place of those considered to be too blunt or harsh. Popular business euphemisms include "giving (someone) their marching orders" instead of firing the person; "under the table" to describe an illegal or concealed transaction; and "pushing the envelope," which means going beyond the limits of performance. Without understanding euphemisms and the social context in which to use them, businesspeople have difficulty appreciating and successfully integrating into different cultures.

Proverbs

Proverbs or wise sayings are common to many different cultures. Common proverbs used in a U.S. business environment include, "A fool and their money are soon parted," "Too many cooks spoil the broth," and "Better late than never." Once again, it is essential to understand the way different societies use proverbs and how they are applied to behavior.

Verbal Dueling

Certain cultural subgroups engage in *verbal dueling*, a form of competitive communication in which the participants exchange insults until one "wins." Although verbal dueling is generally associated with male adolescents (African American adolescents in the United States verbally duel in a game called "The Dozens," and Turkish adolescents play a similar game), verbal battles also take place among political leaders and in a number of societies where exchanging insults is regarded as a better way of diffusing conflict than using weapons.[51] When you are interacting with other cultures, it is useful to become aware of different forms of verbal dueling to truly understand the nature of cross-cultural communication.

Humor

Most cultures value humor, but what is perceived to be funny in one culture can easily fall flat in another because some jokes are inappropriate for the audience or get lost in translation. While it is common for a British or US businessperson to begin a speech or a presentation with some light humor or an anecdote, that is not the case in Asia where humor is less pervasive in formal business settings. When presenting to people from different cultures, it is essential to know the audience and avoid jokes that could be perceived as inappropriate—or not to joke at all if that is the better course. Comedian, author and activist Chelsea Handler was praised for giving a humorous commencement speech broadcast on the iHeartMedia podcast that addressed all the graduating classes of 2020 who missed the commencement ceremonies because of the pandemic.[52]

Conversational Taboos

Regardless of the participants' cultural background, a degree of small talk usually takes place before the beginning of a meeting, especially when people are meeting for the first time. U.S. businesspeople tend to talk about the weather or sports and avoid taboo or contentious subjects such as religion, politics, and personal matters. Members of other cultures are accustomed to openly discussing religion and politics or asking personal questions in a business setting. What qualifies as taboo varies from culture to culture, so it is vital to know what to expect before the initial meeting.

Overcoming Difficulties in Cross-Cultural Communication

With so many potential obstacles to avoid, communicating with different cultures can seem a daunting prospect. The more knowledge and understanding we have, the smoother and more successful the communication will be. With this in mind, what can we do to reduce misunderstandings and misinterpretations?

- Do your homework and make sure you are familiar with the language and customs of different cultures.
- Never make assumptions; it is better to believe there are differences until similarities have been established.
- Be an active listener and summarize points to confirm you understand what the other party has said.
- Make an effort to be supportive, encouraging, and empathic, particularly toward those interacting in an English-speaking nation for whom English is a second language.
- Avoid slang, jargon, and euphemisms; they often cause confusion.

The most successful cross-cultural teams work in an environment which cultivates openness, trust, and respect. However, in many organizations, communication does not go so smoothly. Researchers have identified three work situations where communication most commonly breaks down. They are eliciting ideas, surfacing disagreement, and giving feedback.[53]

Eliciting Ideas

The level of participation in discussions which involve the sharing of ideas varies across different cultures. For example, people from low-context cultures like the United States and Australia are used to openly expressing their thoughts and opinions, while those from high-context cultures like Japan tend to wait until the more senior colleagues voice their thoughts before speaking up. Similarly, Finnish people are more hesitant in contributing, for fear of looking foolish, and prefer to think before they speak. In contrast, Americans are more confident in "shooting from the hip."

One way to ensure that all participants are contributing is to go around the table at least once, so everyone is given a chance to speak. Another solution is to rein in our own thoughts at first in favor of hearing what the others have to say, and asking plenty of open-ended questions to further explore their ideas. Research based on teams of Americans and East Asians showed these tactics significantly increased the contributions from both sides.

"Instead of taking five times as many opportunities to speak and using nearly ten times as many words as their Chinese, Japanese, Korean, or Taiwanese colleagues, Americans took just 50 percent more turns and spoke just 4 percent more words when an inclusive team leadership approached was used."

Surfacing Disagreement

When conflict arises during business discussions, some cultures are more comfortable with it than others. For example, people from Latin and Middle Eastern countries may be used to engaging in fiery exchanges and making loud arguments, whereas people from Asia or Scandinavia may employ the power of silence and rigid body language to convey their opposition.

To motivate participants to engage in healthy debate, it is a good idea to designate a devil's advocate—someone who is responsible for encouraging each party to discuss the different challenges associated with each of the proposals. Another tactic would be to ask each participant to share their pros and cons to enable both parties to freely argue both sides.

Giving Feedback

Providing feedback is essential for personal development, collaboration, and productivity, but it can also be a cultural minefield. In the United States, feedback is generally received as an opportunity to develop, and well received in front of a group. In contrast, people from other cultures may prefer meeting one-on-one to save face in front of their colleagues. Cultures also differ in the language they use to deliver feedback. In low-context cultures like the Netherlands or the United States, managers tend to use direct language, while in high-context cultures, such as India, managers use more subtle language.

When delivering feedback across different cultures, it is important to find a middle ground. This might involve using positive language to soften the critical aspects or, where appropriate, delivering feedback to the whole team rather than one particular individual.

In this chapter, we have explored communication in organizations and its importance across different cultures. In the next chapter, we explore how communication plays a significant role in building trust, dealing with conflict, and preparing for negotiation.

IN REVIEW

11.1 Describe the basic model of communication

Communication is the act of transmitting thoughts, processes, and ideas through a variety of channels. The Shannon–Weaver Model of communication is based on two components: the sender of the message, known as the *source*, and the receiver of the message. The sender encodes and then transmits a message through a communication channel where it is decoded by the receiver. The receiver must then provide feedback or a response to the sender to confirm that the message has been received and its meaning understood. Disturbances in the communications process are called *noise*.

11.2 Compare the types of communication channels

Oral communication is the verbal exchange of information, ideas, and processes one on one or as a group. **Written communication** makes use of the written word through reports, memos, letters, and other channels. **Electronic communication** transmits messages through email, Skype, videoconferencing, blogs, fax, instant messaging, texting, and social networking. **Nonverbal communication** is the transmission of wordless cues through posture, facial expression, gestures, tone of voice, and so on.

11.3 Identify key barriers to effective communication

Filtering is screening and manipulating a message from a sender before passing it on to the receiver. Our *emotions* have an effect on the way we communicate. The wealth of information surrounding us can lead us to make hasty decisions or prioritize poorly because of *information overload*. Because of *differing perceptions*, the ways we interpret situations can clash with the perceptions of others, leading to confusion and misconception. We can overcome this communication barrier by challenging our own assumptions about other people and situations for accuracy and by seeking advice from others to clarify our perceptions.

11.4 Describe types of communication networks within organizations

Downward communication sends messages from the upper levels of the organizational hierarchy to the lower levels, and **upward communication** sends messages from the lower levels of the organizational hierarchy to the higher levels. **Lateral communication** flows between and among similar hierarchical levels across organizations. **Formal networks** transmit messages established and approved by the organizational hierarchy. In contrast, **informal networks** are a means of unofficially sharing of information between employees across company divisions.

11.5 Discuss the elements of effective cross-cultural communication

Strategies for effective cross-cultural communication include doing your homework and making sure you know the language and customs of different cultures; never making assumptions; believing there are cultural differences until otherwise established; being an active listener; and summarizing points to confirm you understand what the other party has said; being supportive and empathic toward those for whom English is a second language; and avoiding slang, jargon, and euphemisms.

KEY TERMS

UP FOR DEBATE: THE IMPORTANCE OF COMMUNICATION

Former US President Gerald Ford wrote: "If I went back to college again, I'd concentrate on two areas: learning to write and to speak before an audience. Nothing in life is more important than the ability to communicate effectively." Do you agree or disagree with President Ford regarding the importance of the ability to communicate?

EXERCISE 11.1: OVERCOMING BARRIERS TO EFFECTIVE COMMUNICATION

Objective

The purpose of this exercise is to gain a greater appreciation of the barriers to communication.

Instructions

The text discusses four different barriers to effective communication. They are:

- **Filtering**—the process of screening and then manipulating a message from a sender before passing it on to the intended receiver
- **Emotions**—a state of feeling that affects the way we communicate
- **Information overload**—exposure to an overwhelming amount of information
- **Differing perceptions**—the way in which our interpretations of situations clashes with the perceptions of others

In groups of three to five students, discuss each of these barriers in the context of the workplace. For each barrier, provide an example where this barrier has occurred and ways it could have been avoided or ameliorated altogether. Approach each example from the standpoint of the sender of the message as well as the receiver.

Reflection Questions

1. How similar were your experiences to those of the others in the group? Discuss.
2. If you were the manager and you discovered that employees were not receiving a message from you accurately due to information overload, what steps would you personally take to correct the situation?
3. Describe a situation at work or in the classroom where you engaged in filtering.

Exercise contributed by Steven Stovall, Southeast Missouri State University.

EXERCISE 11.2: THERE'S AN APP FOR THAT

Objectives

Identify key barriers to effective communication.

Discuss the elements of effective cross-cultural communication.

Instructions

Step 1. Write down as many barriers to intercultural communication as you can think of. (1 to 3 minutes)

Step 2. Find a partner and combine lists. Then, for as many barriers as possible, write down one communication or information technology that can help overcome each barrier. (5 to 10 minutes)

Step 3. Each pair should find another pair and form a quad. These quads should combine lists and reconcile any differences. Then they should examine the combined list and look for areas where information or communication technology *cannot* help to overcome intercultural communication barriers. (5 to 10 minutes)

Step 4. Choose a spokesperson for your quad and be prepared to discuss your list when called upon by your instructor. (3 to 5 minutes)

Reflection Questions

1. In what ways do you think using information or communication technologies could actually hurt intercultural communications?
2. What was the most interesting technology use you heard?
3. Were there any overall trends in technology use that you heard from the exercise?
4. Are there any ways that you have personally used information or communication technologies to overcome intercultural communication barriers? If so, which were most effective?

Exercise contributed by Milton R. Mayfield, Professor of Business, Texas A&M International University, and Jacqueline R. Mayfield, Professor of Business, Texas A&M International University.

EXERCISE 11.3: THE TELEPHONE GAME

Objective

The purpose of this exercise is to grasp the concept of how a message can be easily altered as it travels through a communication channel.

Instructions

This is a very old exercise known as the "telephone game," as it refers to a message that is told to one person over the phone, who then calls someone else to relay the message, who in turn, calls someone else, and so on.

Starting at one corner of the back of the room, have that person secretly think of a sentence to whisper to the student sitting next to them. Sentences should be somewhat complex, such as, "Carl collected coins, coincidentally, Sarah sought stamps," or "Three foxes brought five loaves of bread to eight little pigs," and similar statements.

The rules are simple. As the message is whispered to the next person, it is spoken only once. The goal is to try and be as accurate as possible—intentionally garbling the message is not as fun. The message continues to work its way to the front of the room. When the last student hears the message, that student stands up and announces the sentence as it was heard. The student who originated the message then stands up and repeats the message as it was intended initially.

Reflection Questions

1. How different was the final sentence from the original sentence? Why does this happen?
2. What examples have you experienced at work where an intended message gets mixed up or completely altered during the communication process?
3. Discuss ways a situation like the one that played out during the telephone game could be avoided in the workplace.

Exercise contributed by Steven Stovall, Southeast Missouri State University.

ONLINE EXERCISE 11.1: EXAMPLES OF POOR COMMUNICATION

Objective

The purpose of this exercise is to gain an appreciation for examples of poor communication in the workplace.

Instruction

Conduct an online search, seeking an example of when a company communicated poorly with customers or employees. It might be a sale that was incorrect, or a new policy that went into effect, or even where employees were terminated from their positions via a text message or email.

Once you discover an example of poor communication in an organization, draft a report to your instructor. Assume that you work for the organization in question and your instructor is the CEO of the company. In the report, describe the situation that occurred and what steps you will be taking to ensure that this does not happen again. The report should be approximately two to three double-spaced pages.

Reflection Questions

1. Why does poor communication happen in the workplace? With some companies employing tens of thousands of employees, how could poor communication still occur with customers? With employees?
2. What examples of poor communication have you experienced so far in your career? Describe at least two.
3. Discuss a time when you did not utilize effective communication at work. What lessons did you learn from the experience?

Exercise contributed by Steven Stovall, Southeast Missouri State University.

ONLINE EXERCISE 11.2: ASSESSING NONVERBAL COMMUNICATION

Objective

The purpose of this exercise is to understand nonverbal communication.

Instruction

Search the internet for a 4- to 10-minute video of someone talking. It might be an individual speaking directly to the screen or a dialogue between two or more people. Try to find one that has someone being very demonstrative with their nonverbal movements. Then, assess the nonverbal communication of the primary person speaking in the video.

Make observations about what gestures they use, their posture, eye contact, and so on. How do you interpret these nonverbal communications? Do these make the person seem nervous, confident, afraid, happy, or some other emotion? Write one double-spaced page about your observations and assessment and answer the questions below on a separate page.

Reflection Questions

1. Obviously, you'll never know exactly what emotion the speaker had at the moment captured in the video, but how accurate do you think your assessment is? Explain.
2. What cues did you observe in the speaker that gave the most indication about emotion? Was it hand gestures? Eye contact? Or something else?
3. What nonverbal behaviors do you often catch yourself doing when speaking to others? What do you think those convey about you?

Exercise contributed by Steven Stovall, Southeast Missouri State University.

CASE 11.1: STAGECOACH GROUP

Stagecoach Group is the largest bus and coach operator in the UK. Around 2.5 million passengers ride Stagecoach's 8,400-bus fleet daily on routes that connect more than 100 towns and cities in England, Scotland, and Wales.[54] In the transportation industry, prompt, high-fidelity communication is critical. Through the introduction of a robust employee experience app and a reliable new radio network, Stagecoach can instantly communicate with all of its 20,000 drivers and deliver a safe, dependable experience for passengers.

Prior to adopting Blink, a mobile and desktop app that allows employees to access critical information, communicate with colleagues, and view company news, Stagecoach operated an intranet across its 19 sites. "[It] was very old and dilapidated," business analyst Ricky Sickelmore said. "No one even remembered their usernames or passwords. It was almost impossible to get any messages out to everyone at once."[55] Before Stagecoach committed to moving internal communications for its nearly 25,000 employees to a new platform, the company ran a four-week proof of concept of Blink with 500 drivers, including one depot that did not even use the existing intranet.[56]

"When we first introduced the platform, we were unsure how people would take it. But adoption was huge from day one. That's testament to how easy it is to use," Sickelmore said. By the last week of the pilot program, 89% of drivers opened the app at least six times per day, and 100% of drivers surveyed said they would recommend Blink to a colleague.

Sickelmore shared a story of how Blink enables Stagecoach to listen to employees and respond immediately. "One of our MDs (managing directors) read that there were issues with city center routes. Without Blink, it would have taken him three weeks of sitting in the canteen listening to drivers chat to get that information," he said. "Instead, he went and changed the routes that very same day. And in doing so, made a better service for passengers and drivers."

Martin Griffiths, the CEO of Stagecoach Group is personally active on Blink. "Supporting employees so they can manage work pressures is key . . . and keeping lines of communication open is vital for any CEO," Griffiths said. "Making sure you understand what your staff are going through and recognizing those pressures over the long term will always give you positive results."[57]

The results of Stagecoach Group's collaboration with Blink did not go unnoticed by the business community. Stagecoach was named Digital Workplace of the Year at the 2019 Digital Workplace Awards and received the Gold Prize in the Social, Collaboration and Communication category at the 2019 Intranet and Digital Workplace Awards, where intranet consultancy Step Two applauded the company for "successfully driving efficiency and engagement."[58]

Lesley Ashman, Director of Technology and Change at Stagecoach commented on the awards, "We've worked hard with the Blink team to deliver the platform to thousands of our employees in a relatively short space of time, so we're really pleased to receive these awards. Blink has helped increase the level of employee engagement across the business and is a valuable internal communications tool that we look forward to using even more comprehensively in the future."

Stagecoach Group's adoption of Blink transformed employee communication and engagement, but drivers cannot pull out their phones to look at the app while behind the wheel. Stagecoach Manchester experienced high failure rates with its more than 20-year-old radio network that required expensive and time-consuming repairs, hindering the operator's ability to run its routes on schedule. Even when the legacy network did work, spotty wireless coverage in the area surrounding Manchester resulted in poor communication quality and delayed updates until a driver returned to an area with a stronger signal.

Stagecoach Manchester, the Group's largest subsidiary outside of Greater London, partnered with UK-based ICT (information and communications technology) provider Affini to modernize the aging radios in its coaches. Affini delivered a future-proofed Digital Mobile Radio (DMR) solution that provided many new features to enhance the growing Stagecoach Manchester fleet. First, the new system operates over microwave, which enables voice and data to be carried over the same network and facilitates future infrastructure expansion to extend coverage when necessary. The DMR delivers better voice quality than the old system, hands-free control (drivers activate the DMR by pressing an overhead button and subsequently operate it with a foot pedal), and improved safety features like the ability to interrupt transmissions in emergency situations.[59]

Between Stagecoach Manchester's modern, feature-rich DMR system and the Group-wide Blink app, Stagecoach leverages effective, real-time communication with its drivers to deliver a high-quality experience to passengers. "Blink is a compendium of information. It's probably going to be the most important tool that we have," says Peter Daly, a driver for Stagecoach. "Blink has made my job easier. It's been a godsend."

Critical-Thinking Questions

1. Give an example of how Blink facilitates upward, downward, or lateral communication at Stagecoach Group, and how that results in better employee outcomes.
2. Describe how Stagecoach's implementation of Blink increased the channel richness of the company's internal communication.
3. Ricky Sickelmore's story of the managing director who changed the routes after reading drivers' feedback is an example of how Blink absorbed communication that would previously have occurred on the grapevine. Do you think the app is better described as a formal or informal communication network in that instance? Why?

Jonathan Bachman / Stringer / Getty Images

12 TRUST, CONFLICT, AND NEGOTIATION

LEARNING OBJECTIVES

By the end of this chapter, you will be able to:

12.1 Outline the bases of trust and predictable outcomes of trust in organizations

12.2 Describe the conflict process and the various types of conflict

12.3 Identify the five basic conflict management strategies

12.4 Describe the negotiation process

12.5 Compare distributive and integrative bargaining approaches

Case Study: Distrust in the National Football League (NFL)

The National Football League (NFL) is the most profitable professional sports association in the United States and arguably the most profitable in the world. The sport of American football was invented over the course of about 20 years between 1869 into the 1880s.[1] As the sport grew in popularity throughout America's universities, graduates started to form their own clubs. These individual clubs were the beginnings of what would later become the first professional teams.

To look at the history of the National Football league, one must go to Canton, Ohio, where, in August of 1920, representatives from the largest professional football clubs met to form the American Professional Football Conference. According to the *Canton Evening Repository*, the purpose of the meeting was to "raise the standard of professional football in every possible way, to eliminate bidding for players between rival clubs and to secure cooperation in the formation of schedules."[2] The organization allowed for the franchising of each team, which meant that each team operates under its own corporate model and is responsible for its own operations; however, a portion of its profits are paid back to the league which handles regulations, officiating, scheduling, and countless other logistical measures that lift a burden of the individual team owners. In 1922, the American Professional Football Conference changed its name to the National Football League.[3]

The competition for the best talent and the best schedules often resulted in conflicts between two different clubs. There are times where conflict can be healthy and improve the functionality of an organization or group; however, in the case of the unorganized world of professional football, the conflict was very dysfunctional meaning it had negative effects on individuals and teams. The creation of an organized league improved the working relationships between the teams, which by late 1920 grew in number to 14. Only two of the original 14 teams remain today: the Decatur Staleys (now the Chicago Bears) and the Chicago Cardinals (now the Arizona Cardinals).[4]

As the professional sport started to increase in popularity, the league began to grow with more clubs vying for a spot in the mix. Yet, the NFL faced an unusual dilemma. Between the 1930s and the 1950s, many rival leagues began to sprout up. There was the American Football League (AFL), the All-America Football Conference, and various regional leagues. In 1966, the NFL and the AFL merged (keeping the NFL name) to create what is now a 32-team league that hosts the largest sporting event in the nation, the Super Bowl.[5]

Today, with NFL's revenue at $16 billion, it ranks #1 in the world of professional sports.[6] The sport seemingly has the United States wrapped around its finger. So much so that back in 2012, 200 million unique viewers tuned in every Sunday to watch the NFL's games on television.[7] With such high popularity and revenues, the NFL has enabled its individual teams to pay some of the world's largest salaries to their players. Becoming an NFL player is no small feat. These men (and potentially women in the near future) have mastered the art of physical and mental toughness in addition to pinpoint accuracy in various athletic skillsets. Because of the sport's popularity, NFL players have become cultural icons, hometown heroes, spokespersons for social justice, famous actors, and expensive but effective marketing tools. In 2021, the highest paid NFL player received $45 million.[8] However, the average earnings of an NFL player ranks last in comparison to the other major American professional sports leagues behind the NBA, MLB, and the NHL. This statistic and others that essentially put a greater burden on the NFL players and increase the profits for the various team owners became antecedents to conflict. Essentially, these are factors that set the scene for potential conflict and in the end, they resulted in the 2011 NFL Player Lockout.[9]

In 2011, a meeting between the NFL Players Association and the owners resulted in a disagreement on a new collective bargaining agreement which is the process of negotiation between employers and employees on salary regulation, benefits, working conditions, for example. Because a consensus was not reached, the NFL owners "locked out" all the NFL players from all practices, facilities, and coaching. In the case of the NFL lockout, negotiations took 18 weeks and four days before a consensus was reached. It required time in court, player testimonies, and millions of dollars to pay for the services of arbitrators, conciliators, and mediators.[10]

On July 30, 2011, the lockout officially ended and the NFL along with its players resumed operations. The end result of the lockout was that both parties, the players and the owners, achieved maximum value from the negotiations. The players received better benefits from increased minimum salaries, access to health care for life, newly allocated retirement benefits, improved player safety procedures, and increased roster size. The owners received more equitable revenue sharing between teams, avoidance of fines if they pay over the salary cap, franchise tags, increased share of revenue from regular season games, and increased credit for stadium upgrades. Essentially, rather than both parties trying to claim a "fixed pie" of resources, the negotiations were administered so that the pie was enlarged to ensure everyone got a piece.[11]

Many people claim that this lockout stemmed from the general lack of trust that the NFL players had toward the league. The distrust seems to have been well placed given the unfair conditions that the players found themselves in. The NFL has learned its lesson and today works toward better relationships with its players. However, the lack of trust still lingers throughout the league and the NFL is constantly trying to repair it. They should continue to try to gain back the players' trust because trust has great benefits to an organization. Rather than focusing on commotion surrounding the league and spiraling negativity, when trust is high people tend to work better together and are better focused on the task at hand. Trust plays a huge role in preventing conflicts like the 2011 lockout from ever arising in the first place.

TRUST IN ORGANIZATIONS

Trust is a critical factor for organizational performance. Lack of trust between the NFL players and the league was considered to be at the heart of the disagreement that led to the 2011 lockout. Although that event occurred several years ago, lack of trust still exists between the two parties and the damage has been difficult to repair.

For people to successfully work together and build relationships, they need to have a high degree of trust in one another. We define **trust** as dependence on the integrity, ability, honesty, and reliability of someone or something else.[12] In U.S. celebrity culture, Tom Hanks ranks as the most trustworthy celebrity, according to a 2021 poll conducted by culture and entertainment site *Ranker*.[13] Actor Morgan Freeman and actor and author Betty White also ranked high on the list. In contrast, other public figures have lost our trust, such as Silicon Valley blood-testing startup, Theranos founder Elizabeth Holmes, who was convicted for criminal fraud in 2022, and Greg Glassman, founder and CEO of fitness franchise CrossFit was forced to step down after making incendiary comments about the murder of George Floyd.[14]

Public trust was also a key factor during the COVID-19 pandemic. According to a poll conducted by the Wellcome Global Monitor, more than three-quarters of people globally said they trusted science and scientists to provide information and guidance.[15] In contrast, a global survey conducted by the Edelman Trust Barometer found than nearly 60% of people had lost faith in government leaders, business leaders, and journalists, believing them to be responsible for spreading falsehoods during the pandemic.[16] Despite this criticism of corporate and governmental institutions, more than two-thirds of respondents wanted CEOs to step in when the government fails to address problems or issues. Experts believe that trust in leaders will rise in the coming years once the pandemic is under control and the economy begins to improve.[17]

Types of Trust

Trust is one of the key factors in successful personal or professional relationships. How do we know when to trust someone? Say a new team leader has been appointed to your work team. How do you make up your mind that your team leader is someone you can trust?

Generally, we can form three types of trust: disposition-based trust, cognition-based trust, and affect-based trust (see Figure 12.1).[18]

FIGURE 12.1 ■ Three Types of Trust

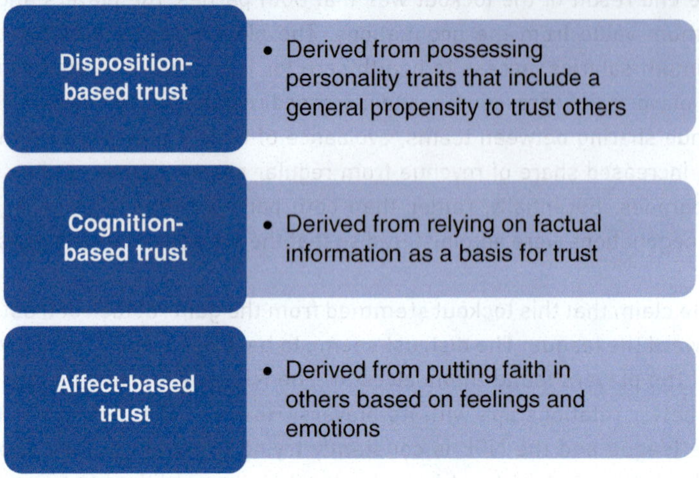

Sources: Based on Mayer, Roger C., James H. Davis, and F. David Schoorman. "An Integrative Model of Organizational Trust." *Academy of Management Review* 20, no. 3 (July 1995): 709–34; McAllister, Daniel J. "Affect- and Cognition-Based Trust as Foundations for Interpersonal Cooperation in Organizations." *Academy of Management Journal* 38, no. 1 (February 1995): 24–59.

Disposition-based trust exists when people possess personality traits that encourage them to put their faith in others. For instance, you might be the kind of person who will trust the new team leader unless you are given a reason not to.

In contrast, in *cognition-based trust*, people rely on factual information such as someone's past experience and track record as a basis for trust. You might be wary of a new team leader until you recognize that they demonstrate the character, integrity, abilities, and benevolence to lead the team.

Finally, *affect-based trust* occurs when people put their faith in others based on feelings and emotions. For example, you are more likely to trust a new team leader if you feel you have made an emotional connection with them, such as by finding out you grew up in the same town.

Outcomes of Trust

When trust is high in the workplace, people tend to work better together and are more focused on their duties. Recent research found that people working in high-trust environments experience less stress, have more energy, demonstrate higher levels of productivity, satisfaction and engagement, take less sick days, and are less likely to burnout.[19] In contrast, employees working in a low-trust organizational environment are less collaborative, have less loyalty to the company, lack engagement in their tasks, exhibit defensive behaviors, display apathy toward organizational goals, and have higher levels of absenteeism.[20] Trust is key when it comes to building and maintaining relationships, increasing morale and productivity, and effectively preventing unhealthy conflict.

The Trust Triangle

Leaders need to build up stores of trust to foster healthy relationships with their teams. Recent research has identified three core drivers of trust: authenticity, logic, and empathy called the trust triangle (see Figure 12.2).[21] Breakdowns in trust can usually be traced to one of these drivers in managers or leaders. Uber is a good example of a company that struggled with all three drivers of trust as demonstrated in the following sections.

Authenticity: We tend to trust others when we believe we are in engaging with their "real" selves. A lack of authenticity is usually detected when people are not being their true selves. For instance, your work persona may be very different to how you behave around friends and family. However, it is not so easy to be truly authentic or your "real self" in the workplace by sharing everything you're thinking and feeling. For example, women are more likely to be penalized for demonstrating negative emotions than

FIGURE 12.2 ■ The Trust Triangle

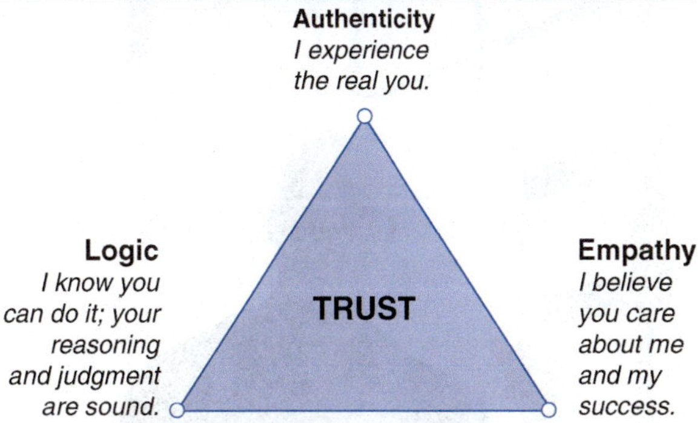

Source: Frei, F. X. & Morriss, A. (2020, May/June). Begin with trust. *Harvard Business Review.* https://hbr.org/2020/05/begin-with-trust

men, and Black men tend to be unfairly stereotyped for being predisposed to anger.[22] The key to being authentic is to share the parts of you that are different to other people, show your true personality, and reassure your team that it is okay to make mistakes. Authentic managers and leaders have the power to build trust and create an environment where team members feel seen and valued, and feel more comfortable displaying their authentic selves. Uber's "us versus them" culture undermined authenticity as people from opposing sides suspected they were not being told the whole truth about what was going on at the company.[23]

Logic: People tend follow leaders when they have confidence in their ideas, judgment, and knowledge. If they lose faith in the ability of a leader to deliver either of those three areas, then poor logic is likely to be the problem. Leaders who continuously make the effort to learn from other people, admit that they don't have all the answers, absorb other people's experiences, and communicate their ideas clearly and effectively are more likely to engage people into following their logic. Uber failed to address questions regarding the long-term viability of its business model and whether its managers had the skills to lead a rapidly expanding organization which led to logic problems and confusion among investors and regulators.[24]

Empathy: Empathetic leaders build trust when they show a genuine interest in the feelings and thoughts of others. A lack of empathy is a major barrier to fostering long-lasting relationships. If you give the impression that you care more about yourself than your team, then you won't be trusted to lead them. Lack of empathy and a growth-at-all-costs culture drove destructive leadership behavior at Uber resulting in strained relationships with investors, drivers and employees.[25]

Uber has since worked towards building a culture of trust by installing a new CEO, rewriting the company's cultural values, strengthening the relationship with regulators, upskilling thousands of employees, and actively listening to workers.[26]

Psychological Contract

Just as the drivers of trust are important in how we interact with others in our personal lives, we also have expectations about how we are treated within an organization. This type of unwritten expectation between employees and organizations is called a **psychological contract**.[27] Essentially, this contract determines the degree to which employees trust their organizations to value their efforts, and how well employees meet the expectations of the organization in terms of their work contributions. For instance, if employees do not feel they are being treated fairly, then this might affect their work performance, commitment, and overall job satisfaction. Similarly, if the organization does not feel that employees are fulfilling their side of the contract, then they are likely to be reprimanded or let go.

Social Networks

Trust also plays an important part in how we relate to others in work through our social networks. In this context, **social networks** describes the recurrent patterns of interaction with others that take place when

Some employees use cognition-based trust, or evidence of someone's qualifications, when deciding to entrust new leaders.

carrying out work activities (for example, exchanging information or working on projects).[28] People who demonstrate their *ability* (the skills and abilities to successfully support the completion of a task), *integrity* (the ability to keep confidence, respect others, and stand up for what's right), and *benevolence* (the ability to listen, offer positive remarks, and provide gentle encouragement) in their interactions with others tend to be perceived as being trustworthy.[29] However, those who fail to portray these characteristics can come across as untrustworthy, regardless how skilled they are at their roles. For example, in 2022 Bobby Kotick, CEO of California video gaming company Activision Blizzard, was pressured to resign after employees alleged that Kotick was aware of the culture of sexual harassment at the company but failed to take action. These accusations have resulted in a lack of trust among Kotick's employees, peers, and investors.[30]

Trust is essential for building relationships as well as our own reputations. Lack of trust can lead to serious conflicts between teams and organizations. The next section describes the conflict process and different types of conflict.

CONFLICT IN TEAMS AND ORGANIZATIONS

Teams and organizations of all types face many challenges and it is inevitable that conflicts will naturally arise, especially when there is a significant lack of trust. We define **conflict** as a clash between individuals or groups because of different opinions, thought processes, and perceptions.[31] Many types of clashes can occur within organizations and between them and their constituents. For instance, the NFL (featured in our case study) has experienced its fair share of conflict over the years, particularly in relation to salary and benefits which eventually culminated in a lockout until an agreement between the owners and players was reached. As another example, in 2021, hundreds Netflix employees walked out in protest of the company's handling of a Dave Chappelle special where the comedian made comments about the transgender community which caused offence to some employees and Netflix subscribers. Although Netflix did not remove the special, CEO Ted Sarandos admitted "screwing up" in his communication with his employees in defending the special and should have "led with a lot more humanity."[32]

As a member of an organization you will have opinions that differ at times from those of other teams or individuals. Disagreements and clashes generally cause stress and discomfort, but does this mean all conflict is bad? Not necessarily. Studies show that teams that work too much in harmony are more likely to drift towards inaction and complacency.[33] Indeed, there are times when conflict helps teams and organizations be more creative and innovative. Research shows that teams that engage in productive conflict such as expressing opposing views, and working under a certain level of tension tend to be more creative and innovative.[34] As chewing gum tycoon William Wrigley Jr. once said, "When two men always agree, one of them is unnecessary."[35]

A business park owner sits outside the former New York offices of Kodak after the company paid millions in fines for violating state environmental laws.

Carolyn Thompson via Associated Press

Functional and Dysfunctional Conflict

When conflict is constructive it can help improve work performance, redefine company goals, and encourage people to communicate better. Such **functional conflict** consists of productive and healthy disputes between individuals or groups.[36] For functional conflict to be successful, individuals from opposing sides need to be genuinely interested in finding a resolution to the problem and willing to listen to each other. Providing individuals with a forum to express their opinions often gives rise to critical thinking and helps to generate new ideas and solutions.

In contrast, **dysfunctional conflict** consists of disputes and disagreements that negatively affect individuals or teams.[37] This type of conflict often arises from an unwillingness to listen to each other or a reluctance to agree on a resolution or goal. High levels of dysfunctional conflict can lead to absenteeism, turnover, and a substantial drop in work performance, all of which can have a devastating effect on organizational goals and objectives.

Types of Conflict

The three main types of conflict in organizations are task conflict, relationship conflict, and process conflict.[38]

Task conflict refers to a clash between individuals about the direction, content, or goals of a work assignment. High task conflict can lead to disagreements that may raise negative emotions such as resentment, anger, and aggression. In contrast, low levels of task conflict are believed to have the most positive effect on organizations by stimulating creativity, healthy competition, and critical thinking among the individuals discussing the various ways to approach a task. Another benefit of low-level task conflict is that, if handled appropriately, it allows every viewpoint to be heard and discussed, giving the individuals a sense of recognition and job satisfaction.

Relationship conflict refers to personality conflicts between two or more individuals in the workplace. This type of conflict can be useful in resolving disputes if the parties are willing to communicate in a constructive and effective way. However, overall, it is considered the most destructive and harmful to organizations because it can give rise to hostility, mistrust, fear, and negativity. Managing relationship conflicts can also be time consuming and take resources away from other goals and priorities. A challenge for organizations today is that workforce diversity brings together a greater number of people from different backgrounds with different personalities, attitudes, and viewpoints, and managers must be vigilant to ensure that workplace relationships remain as harmonious as possible both in the office and in a remote working environment.

Process conflict refers to the clash in viewpoints about how to carry out work. Like task conflict, process conflict can be beneficial to organizations as long as it operates at a low level. When individuals and groups are given the chance to express their thoughts and opinions, they are more likely to generate new ideas regarding the best way to approach and define the process. However, high levels of debate about process can lead to resentment, apathy, and job dissatisfaction.

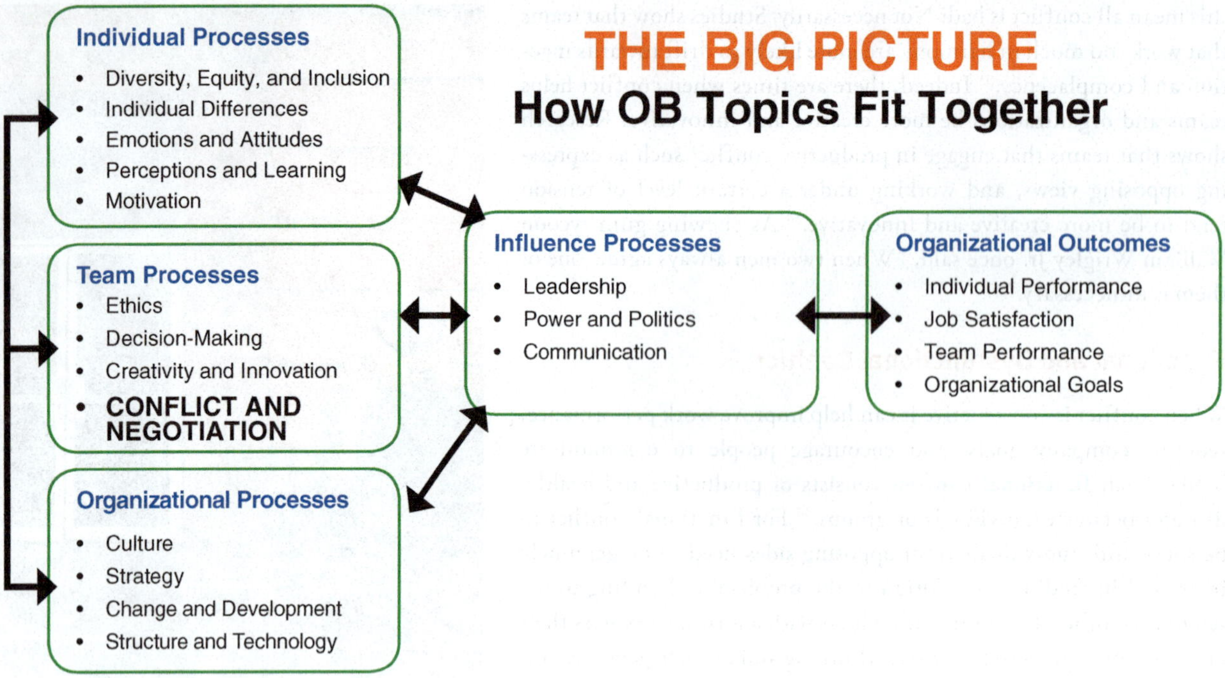

The Conflict Process

As we have learned, conflicts can have positive or negative outcomes depending on how the situation is managed. The following example illustrates the four different stages of the conflict process: *antecedents of conflict, perceived/felt conflict, manifest conflict*, and *outcomes of conflict*.[39]

You join a virtual team meeting at 9:00 a.m. even though your manager and your team has strict rules on punctuality. You don't communicate the reason for your tardiness to the rest of your team and this isn't the first time this has happened. Without your realizing it, your tendency to arrive later to the meeting than everyone else is an **antecedent of conflict**. You have set the scene for potential disputes. Antecedents of conflict include lack of communication, incompatible personalities, and collisions in value systems. In this case, your tendency to arrive late is clashing with the rest of the team's value of timeliness.

Shortly after you have joined the meeting, one of your coworkers says, "Glad you could join us," which prompts a chuckle from the rest of the team. You perceive that the team has a problem with your tardiness and you feel their disapproval directed toward you. This is the **perceived/felt conflict stage**, during which emotional differences are sensed and felt.

Now you have a choice. Do you address the conflict head on or do you ignore it? In the **manifest conflict stage** people engage in behaviors that provoke a response. You can either try to resolve the conflict by bringing the matter out into the open, or you can suppress it, which may temporarily solve the problem but may also leave the situation open to future conflict and escalation.

The final stage is the **outcomes of conflict stage**, which encompasses the consequences of the dispute. Depending on how you and the rest of the team handle the manifest conflict stage, there will be either functional or dysfunctional outcomes. For example, if you choose to address the team in a professional manner and open up the lines of communication by explaining your lateness then you are more likely to bring about a positive outcome. In contrast, if you decide to angrily retort to the sarcastic comment that your tardiness isn't such a big deal, you may make the situation even worse, which will lead to a dysfunctional outcome.

While conflict can be difficult to deal with, there are ways in which it can be resolved. The next section focuses on some useful strategies managers can adopt when challenged with conflict in the workplace.

CONFLICT MANAGEMENT STRATEGIES

Conflict is inevitable in the workplace. But we often focus more on how the other person responds rather than how we respond. Given that statistics show that workplace violence is on the rise (almost 2 million U.S. workers report some level of violence in the workplace every year) it is more important than ever for organizations to set strategies in place to help manage conflict.[40] By analyzing and understanding the following five basic conflict-management strategies, employees will be able to choose how to respond to others and manage conflicts so they are productive and don't escalate out of control.

There are five conflict management strategies (see Figure 12.3): *avoidance, accommodation, competition, compromise,* and *collaboration*.[41]

Avoidance

Avoidance is an attempt to suppress a conflict and pretend it doesn't exist. People who avoid conflict often hope that the problem will go away by itself or that someone else will take responsibility and confront the issue instead. Avoidance is a lose/lose situation. If you don't address the conflict then the people around you will have no idea how you're really feeling, or think that you don't care enough to get involved, and most likely, the problem will continue to go unresolved. The longer the issue is left unaddressed, the unhappier and frustrated you may feel, which may ultimately lead to an angry or negative outburst. However, there are certain situations in which avoidance makes sense. For example, rather than rushing into making a decision, you may benefit from taking some time to think more about it; or if you've had a difficult conversation with a coworker, giving that person space to calm down may be more sensible than trying to resolve the issue there and then.

Accommodation

Accommodation is an attempt to adjust our views to play down differences between parties. People who accommodate others tend to neglect or hide their own true feelings or opinions about a certain issue to keep the peace or avoid rocking the boat. In sum, accommodating means giving people what they want. For example, say your manager gives you a 5% raise rather than the 10% you were expecting. Instead of voicing your disappointment and communicating that your needs aren't being met, you accept the raise without argument, thereby giving in to your manager, rather than fighting for what

FIGURE 12.3 ■ Conflict Management Strategies

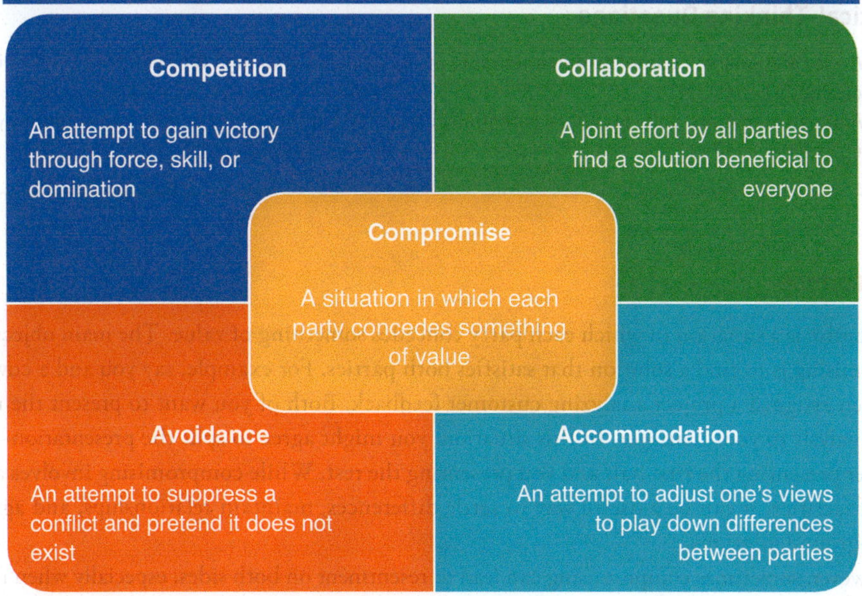

you want. In doing so, you are sacrificing your own personal needs to please your manager. This will give rise to resentment and anger over time. However, accommodation can be useful in certain situations, particularly when it comes to areas you're fairly relaxed about. For instance, if some people on the team feel strongly about choosing a virtual murder mystery day as a team bonding activity and you don't, then it's appropriate to accommodate those people by agreeing to their choice.

Competition

Competition is an attempt to gain victory through force, skill, or domination. When people compete against each other, it is at the other person's expense: one side wins and the other loses. In the workplace, a competing style of managing conflict is a way to gain power and pressure others into falling into line with certain methods and beliefs. People who use a competitive style tend to communicate aggressively, try to control discussions, and have little regard for preserving future relationships.

However, competing has its place in certain situations, for example, when it comes to important issues such as standing up for rights in the workplace or implementing a controversial decision regarding layoffs. However, both these scenarios regardless of their importance are likely to lead to divisions and resentment.

EXAMINING THE EVIDENCE

TASK AND RELATIONSHIP CONFLICT

Researchers and practitioners have long asserted that task-related conflict can be beneficial by stimulating creativity and critical thinking in group decision-making. However, two recent meta-analyses examining the effects of task-related conflict across multiple studies failed to find support for an overall positive relationship between task conflict and group performance.[42] These findings led researchers Frank R. C. de Wit and Daan Scheepers of Leiden University and Karen A. Jehn of the Melbourne Business School to delve a little deeper into the relationships between task conflict, relationship conflict, and decision-making.[43] They found that when relationship conflict was present during task conflict, group members were more likely to rigidly hold onto less than optimal starting positions during group interactions, leading to poor decision outcomes. The findings suggest that task conflict is neither universally good nor universally bad. Instead, its potential benefits in group decision-making may depend on whether relationship conflict is also present.

Critical-Thinking Questions

1. Why is relationship conflict so detrimental to group decision-making? Why can task conflict be potentially beneficial?
2. What can managers do to facilitate potentially beneficial conflict while minimizing potentially detrimental conflict?

Compromise

Compromise is a situation in which each party concedes something of value. The main objective of compromising is to find a solution that satisfies both parties. For example, say you and a coworker have been assigned a project analyzing customer feedback. Both of you want to present the results of the analysis to your manager. In this situation, you might agree to split the presentation—your coworker presenting the first half and you presenting the rest. While compromising involves an element of sacrifice, it can be a useful way to settle differences, maintain relationships, and agree on middle-ground solutions.

However, sometimes compromising can lead to resentment on both sides, especially when neither party gets exactly what it wants. Using the example above, while you may have reached an agreement with your coworker, you may not feel totally happy to split the presenting responsibilities especially if you think you are the better presenter. Furthermore, compromising often and too easily can also stunt creativity when it comes to finding deeper solutions to the issue.

Collaboration

Collaboration is a joint effort by all parties to find a solution beneficial to everyone. Parties that engage in collaboration take the time to truly understand each other's underlying needs, wants, and goals. Collaborations between two people might involve analyzing the source of a disagreement to generate new insights or working together on creative solutions to a shared problem. Successful collaboration involves good communication and cooperation resulting in a better solution than either party could have achieved alone. It also helps to maintain and build long-term relationships.

However, collaboration takes a lot of time and commitment and may not be appropriate in all situations, for example, when it comes to minor issues or relationships that you don't regard to be beneficial or important.

While each of the five strategies can be applied to different situations, some people are more comfortable using certain approaches over others. However, when it comes to handling conflict, take a moment to ask yourself whether you are using the best conflict strategy to resolve the problem. If not, you may need to go in a different direction.

Overall, relationships that are based on trust and respect tend to have less conflict. When conflict arises, it is often resolved quickly and effectively thanks to negotiation skills.

NEGOTIATION AND DISPUTE RESOLUTION

We may not realize it, but most of us negotiate on a daily basis in every aspect of our lives, with family members, friends, classmates, roommates, and partners, as well as with our coworkers, team leaders, and bosses. We define **negotiation** as the process of reaching an agreement that both parties find acceptable.[44] Since disagreements are common in a range of OB issues, including task allocation, work schedules, and salaries, the art of negotiation is a necessity in life as well as in the workplace. With the shift to remote working, virtual negotiations are also likely to take place. To ensure successful remote negotiations, managers must have a good knowledge of digital tools and follow the ten useful tips for negotiation (which can be applied to face-to-face and virtual negotiations), outlined in Table 12.1.

Let's explore the negotiation process.[45]

Getting Ready to Negotiate

Before any negotiation, it is critical for each party to outline the goals and objectives they would like to achieve. It is also essential for each party to do its homework on its opponent—to consider the other party's position and decision-making power, the length of time it has been in business, and whether it has any other negotiating history. Professor Jared Curhan of MIT Management Sloan School also advises preparing for an alternative outcome or **BATNA** (Best Alternative to Negotiated Agreement) should the deal not work out as planned. Curhan suggests the following question should be asked during the preparation stage: "Before any negotiation, ask yourself, 'What am I going to do if I don't reach a deal?'"[46]

Shaping Expectations

Defining the ground rules of negotiation before talks begin is key to shaping expectations. It is essential that each party understands the rules and agrees to adhere to them during the negotiation process. Opening with something like "Let's agree on some ground rules for our negotiation before we get started" is a good way to set expectations. These rules might include an agreement that the parties involved must only talk one at a time, listen to each other, treat one another with respect, and share a mutual intolerance of derogatory language or any other kind of verbal attacks.

TABLE 12.1 ■ 10 Tips for Negotiation

Do your homework. Make sure you carry out some research on what is to be discussed and spend some time thinking through various outcomes before the meeting.
Consider different points of view. Think about the situation from the other person's perspective, not just your own. Try and understand their needs and concerns.
Clarify your goals. Make sure you define your main objectives before the discussion and have a clear BATNA in mind.
Choose the time for discussion carefully. Make sure there is enough time for the discussion to take place and during a period where both parties are relaxed.
Try to control your emotions. Remain calm and avoid getting emotional. Remember—high emotions can confuse our thinking which hampers the negotiation process.
Listen! Make sure you actively listen to the other parties, and do not interrupt until it is your turn to talk.
Explain your needs. Tell the other side what you would prefer the outcome to be, and why. Explain your needs calmly and concisely.
Avoid laying blame. Even if you have some misgivings toward the other party, do not air them during the negotiation process. Focus on the facts, and never make your comments personal.
Collaborate to find a creative solution. Try to not think of negotiation as one party winning and the other losing. The best negotiations end with each party walking away satisfied. Working together to find creative ways to meet everyone's needs is also a good way to build and sustain long-term relationships.
Remember that tomorrow is another day. If emotions start to run high and tempers flare, then it's reasonable to table the discussion for another day. The space gives the parties involved some time to calm down and think through the issues more rationally.

Source: "Seven Keys to Effective Negotiation." www.mitsloan.mit.edu, February 17, 2016. http://mitsloan.mit.edu/newsroom/articles/seven-keys-to-effective-negotiation/

The rules may also include conditions for termination and an agreement that either party can halt the discussion at any time. With the ground rules set, the parties can begin their negotiation. Often, the ground rules can take longer than the negotiation itself, but establishing the rules before the conversation starts encourages cooperation, prevents misunderstandings, and overall makes for a smoother negotiation.

Providing Supporting Evidence

Providing supporting evidence is key to a successful negotiation. Parties entering a negotiation must show supporting evidence as proof to back up their arguments. Each party should describe the evidence and explain the facts clearly and concisely using jargon-free language. This is a good opportunity for each party to educate each other about their position.

Negotiating the Deal

Once each party has a chance to explain their positions, it is time to negotiate the deal. The goal during this stage is for the parties to convince each other of the validity of their demands and to persuade the other side to concede to those demands. Each argument must be presented logically and clearly. It is possible for the discussion to become heated as each party strives to win the best deal, but too much emotion may negatively impact the negotiation. In fact, recognizing our own emotional triggers is a good way to defuse negative emotions in the heat of the moment. A study led by author and Nobel Laureate Daniel Kahneman showed that Americans experience the most distress when they are speaking to their bosses or commuting.[47] Being aware of these negative emotions and their potential to impact your ability to negotiate goes a long way to minimizing emotional behavior during the crucial stages.

When engaging in negotiations, both parties should outline their goals for the discussion and understand the other party's position.

Reaching an Agreement and Implementing the Deal

With the bargaining process complete, the parties move on to the final stage of negotiation—formalizing an agreement and implementing the deal. They spend time clarifying the deal and ensuring that everyone understands the outcome of the negotiations and the specifications of the final agreement. Pending due diligence, the agreement will be formalized in writing and signed by each party by an agreed-upon date. Following the process, it is important that each party keeps its promises and adheres to the terms of the agreement.

Resolving Disputes Using a Third Party

What if the parties had reached a stalemate in their negotiations or failed to find a mutually beneficial solution to the price war that was harming both their companies? In these instances, it is useful to introduce a neutral third party to help settle disputes. There are three types of third party roles: mediator, arbitrator, and conciliator (see Table 12.2).[48]

A **mediator** is a neutral third party who attempts to assist parties in a negotiation to find a resolution or come to an agreement using rational arguments and persuasion. The chief role of mediators is to get the opposing parties to communicate rather than provide a solution or a decision. A mediator has no right to impose their views on the parties.

An **arbitrator** is a neutral third party officially assigned to settle a dispute who listens to both sides of the argument as stated by the parties. Unlike a mediator, an arbitrator has the power to issue a judgment, which is final and binding for all parties.

TABLE 12.2 ■ Third-Party Dispute Resolution Approaches

Mediator	Arbitrator	Conciliator
Reinstates communication between two parties	Issues judgment based on statements from both parties	Persuades opponents to communicate
Offers no opinions or judgment	Judgment is binding for all parties	Offers nonbinding opinion

Major League Baseball players' salary arbitrations are complicated processes where a player's market salary is compared against offers from the player and the team.

George Nikitin via Associated Press

Finally, a **conciliator** is a neutral third party who is informally assigned to persuade opponents to communicate. The conciliator is allowed to offer an opinion, but unlike that of an arbitrator, this judgment does not carry any legal weight.

Many businesses in conflict choose one or more of these third-party dispute resolution approaches because they can be a useful way to resolve differences and can prevent an issue from escalating.

For example, Major League Baseball teams and players often engage in arbitration to determine a player's salary. The process begins with both the team and the player's agent submitting their "last best" salary offer. Each side then presents their case and a rebuttal to the opposing side's case in a salary hearing to a panel of three arbitrators chosen from a slate of sixteen arbitrators determined jointly by Major League Baseball and the players association. The panel considers the evidence presented to reach a decision on what they consider to be the correct "market salary" for that player. This figure is compared to the two "best final offers," and whichever figure is closest is likely to be selected. For example, suppose that a player's agent submits a best final offer of $20 million, and the team submits a best final offer of $15 million. Theoretically, the panel of arbitrators would need to determine whether the player's market value is more or less than $17.5 million, the midpoint figure. If the arbitrators find the correct price to be higher than the midpoint, they will choose the $20 million figure requested by the player; if they determine that the player's market value is lower than the midpoint, then they will select the team's offer.[49]

The ultimate goal of a negotiation should be to provide an agreement that satisfies everyone and leaves all the parties on good terms. But in reality, the process is not always straightforward. Negotiators may use different types of bargaining strategies to influence certain outcomes.

BARGAINING APPROACHES

Bargaining and negotiating are often thought to be one and the same, but there are important differences. Although a subset of negotiation, bargaining focuses more on price, where one party may agree to give the other a lower price than initially suggested. In contrast, negotiation goes further than just the price; it is a process of give and take, where each side engages in thoughtful discussion to reach an agreement to satisfy both parties.

In general, people use two main bargaining strategies: distributive bargaining and integrative bargaining (see Figure 12.4).

Distributive bargaining occurs when two parties both try to claim a "fixed pie" of resources.[50] For example, say you are trying to buy a used car. You know you will need a certain amount of

FIGURE 12.4 ■ Bargaining Approaches

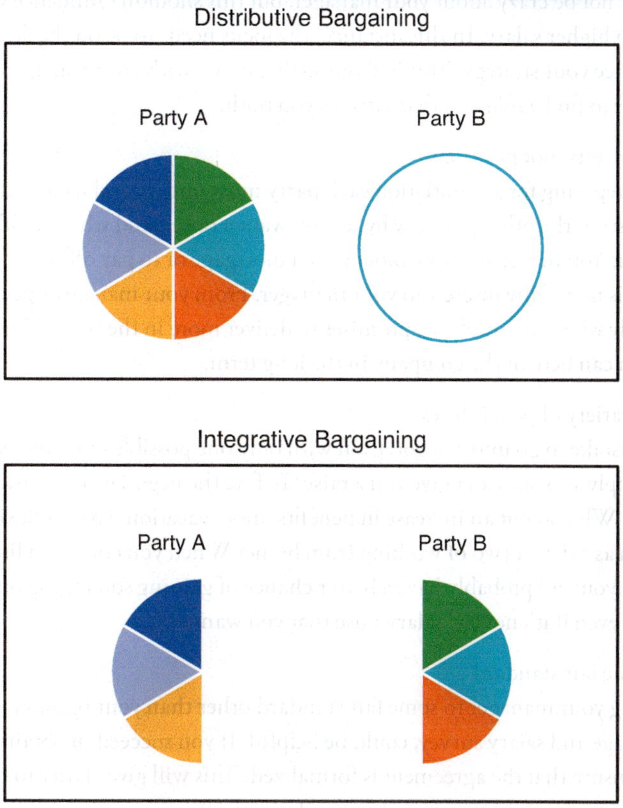

money to fix the car up the way you want it, and for that reason you want a reduction in the price. However, the car salesperson wants the maximum price he can get for the car and tells you to take it or leave it. This is known as a win/lose situation, in which one party only gains and the other one only loses.

Another approach to distributive bargaining is to compromise just for the sake of ending the negotiation. For example, say you and the car salesperson have been haggling for a long time and each of you is getting frustrated. The rep agrees to let you have a small percentage off the price, but you do not feel it is enough. Eventually you both give up something to agree on a price, but neither of you is satisfied with the outcome.

In many instances, distributive bargaining can be time consuming and inefficient. It can lead to a contest of wills, especially when egos get in the way. It is better suited to short-term bargaining with people you are unlikely to deal with again than to the building of long-term relationships, which require a degree of give and take.

Integrative bargaining occurs when both parties negotiate a win/win solution.[51] It is about enlarging the pie so everyone gets a piece. This type of bargaining applies to businesses that want to build long-term relationships with each other. For example, a clothing manufacturer is looking to negotiate with its fabric supplier to reach a mutually beneficial agreement. The manufacturer wants the supplier to consistently provide it with high-quality fabrics at a fair price within the allotted time frames. The fabric supplier agrees and a formal contract is arranged. In the end, both parties win: the clothing manufacturer has negotiated a long-term contract with the fabric supplier at a fair price, and the fabric supplier is guaranteed a stream of business from the clothing manufacturer. Both parties have achieved the maximum value from the negotiation.

Integrative Bargaining Strategies

There are four basic strategies for integrative bargaining.[52] The best choice will vary depending on the situation. For example, let's say you are preparing to negotiate a salary raise at work and are looking for the best ways to approach the situation.

- Separate the people from the problem

  You may not be crazy about your manager, but this shouldn't influence your approach to negotiating a higher salary. In this instance, the focus needs to be on the facts; emotion should never influence your strategy. This is about sitting down with your manager and putting your feelings aside to find a solution that satisfies you both.

- Focus on interests, not positions

  When preparing for a negotiation each party must understand its own interests as well as the interests of the other party. Why do you want a raise? And why should your manager give it to you? You may need more money for a mortgage or to pay off your college loans, but frankly this is not of any interest to your manager. From your manager's perspective, a raise is deserved only when the employee promises to deliver more in the future. You need to list all the ways you can benefit the company in the long term.

- Generate a variety of possibilities

  It is a mistake to go into a negotiation with only one possible outcome. What if your manager simply says she can't give you a raise? Before the negotiation, consider some other possibilities. What about an increase in benefits, more vacation days, or flexible work options such as a day or two of working from home? When you compile a list of acceptable possibilities, you will probably have a better chance of gaining something out of the negotiation, even if it's not the salary raise that you wanted.[53]

- Insist on some fair standard

  Referring your manager to some fair standard other than your opinion, such as a published wage and salary survey, could be helpful. If you succeed in obtaining the salary raise, then ensure that the agreement is formalized. This will give clarity to the negotiations and prevent any misunderstandings further down the line.

Other Negotiating Strategies

It is always wise to have a best possible alternative to a negotiable agreement (BATNA), which is the best outcome you could achieve if the negotiation fails and you must follow another course of action.[54] For example, say you want a salary raise of $5,000 per year, but you will accept $3,000 if it is offered. What will you do if you are unable to get the $3,000 raise? Will you settle for your current salary? Will you quit your job and try to find a higher-paying job in another organization? Once you have identified your BATNA, you will be in a better position to figure out your zone of possible agreement (**ZOPA**) (see Figure 12.5), which is the area where two sides in a negotiation may find common ground.[55] For example, say you request your $5,000 salary raise and your manager tells you that the best offer will be $3,500. Since this figure lies within the zone that both parties find acceptable, then it is likely an agreement will be reached.

FIGURE 12.5 ■ Zone of Possible Agreement

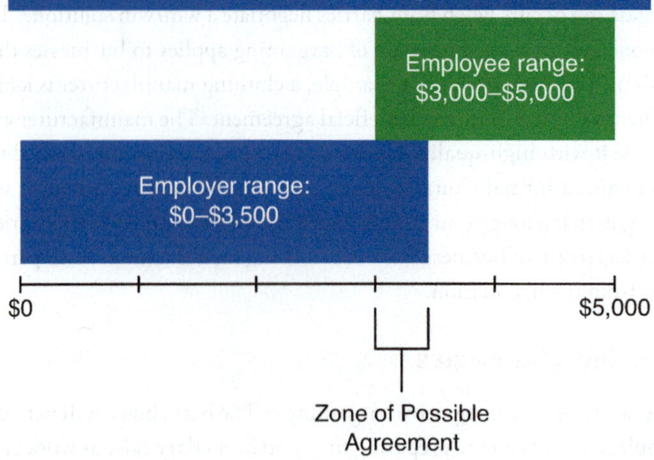

In this chapter, we have explored the complexities of conflict and negotiation and examined the different types of negotiation strategies that can help resolve conflict. In the next chapter, we explore the concept of leadership.

IN REVIEW

12.1 Outline the bases of trust and predictable outcomes of trust in organizations

We define **trust** as the dependence on the integrity, ability, honesty, and reliability of someone or something else. Generally, there are three types. People with *disposition-based trust* tend to possess personality traits that encourage them to put their faith in others. In contrast, people with *cognition-based trust* base their faith in others on factual information such as the person's past experience and proven track record. Finally, *affect-based trust* occurs when people put their faith in others based on feelings and emotions.

When trust is high in the workplace, people tend to work better together and are more focused on their duties. They tend to take more risks, display citizenship behaviors, and exhibit fewer ineffectual or counterproductive behaviors.

12.2 Describe the conflict process and the various types of conflict

We define **conflict** as a clash between individuals or groups in relation to different opinions, thought processes, and perceptions. **Functional conflict** consists of constructive and healthy disputes between individuals or groups. In contrast, **dysfunctional conflict** consists of disputes and disagreements that have negative effects on individuals or teams. It often arises from an unwillingness to listen to each other or a reluctance to agree on a resolution or goal.

Task conflict refers to the clash between individuals in relation to the direction, content, or goal of a certain assignment. **Relationship conflict** refers to the clash in personality between two or more individuals. This type of conflict is considered to be the most destructive and harmful to organizations because it can give rise to hostility, mistrust, fear, and negativity. **Process conflict** refers to the clash in viewpoints about how to carry out work. It can be beneficial to organizations as long as it operates at a low level.

The four different stages of the conflict process are antecedents of conflict, perceived/felt conflict, manifest conflict, and outcomes of conflict. **Antecedents of conflict** are the factors that set the scene for potential disputes: lack of communication, incompatible personalities, and collisions in value systems. In the **perceived/felt conflict stage**, emotional differences are sensed and felt. The **manifest conflict** stage consists of behaviors that provoke a response. The final stage is the **outcomes of conflict stage**, which describes the consequences of the dispute.

12.3 Identify the five basic conflict management strategies

Avoidance is the attempt to suppress a conflict and pretend it does not really exist. **Accommodation** is one party's attempt to adjust their views to play down the differences between the parties. **Competition** is the attempt to gain victory through force, skill, or domination. **Compromise** is a situation in which each party concedes something of value. **Collaborating** occurs when all parties work together to find a solution beneficial to everyone.

12.4 Describe the negotiation process

We define **negotiation** as the process of reaching an agreement that both parties find acceptable. Before any negotiation, it is critical that each party get ready to negotiate by outlining the goals and objectives they would like to achieve. The second step is to shape the expectations for the negotiation. Next, both parties take turns in bolstering their demands with supportive evidence. Then the parties bargain back and forth until they both agree upon a deal. This leads to the final stage of the process, known as the agreement and implementation stage. During this stage, the agreement will be formalized in writing.

There are three types of neutral third-party roles in the event of a stalemate. A **mediator** attempts to assist parties to find a resolution using rational arguments and persuasion. A mediator has no right to impose their views on the parties. An **arbitrator** listens to both sides before issuing a judgment considered final and binding for all parties. Finally, a **conciliator** is informally assigned to persuade opponents to communicate. The conciliator is allowed to offer an opinion but it does not carry any legal weight.

12.5 Compare distributive and integrative bargaining approaches

Distributive bargaining occurs when two parties try to claim a "fixed pie" of resources. It is more suitable for short-term bargaining with people you are unlikely to deal with again than for long-term relationships, which require give and take. **Integrative bargaining** occurs when both parties negotiate a win-win solution by enlarging the pie so everyone gets a piece.

KEY TERMS

Antecedents of conflict (p. 289)
Arbitrator (p. 285)
Avoidance (p. 281)
BATNA (p. 283)
Conciliator (p. 286)
Conflict (p. 278)
Distributive bargaining (p. 286)
Dysfunctional conflict (p. 279)
Functional conflict (p. 279)
Integrative bargaining (p. 287)
Manifest conflict stage (p. 280)
Mediator (p. 285)
Negotiation (p. 283)
Outcomes of conflict stage (p. 280)
Perceived/felt conflict stage (p. 280)
Process conflict (p. 279)
Psychological contract (p. 277)
Relationship conflict (p. 279)
Social networks (p. 277)
Task conflict (p. 279)
Trust (p. 275)
ZOPA (p. 288)

UP FOR DEBATE NEGOTIATION TACTICS

Some business people believe that a "those who speak first lose" philosophy is the best negotiation tactic. They hope silence will make the other party feel uncomfortable and continue talking, possibly revealing unfavorable information. Do you agree that this is the best negotiation tactic?

EXERCISE 12.1: WHICH IS MORE IMPORTANT? HANDLING CONFLICT

Objective

The purpose of this exercise is to gain a greater appreciation of conflict and how to work through it.

Instructions

In groups of three to five, rank the following items in order of their importance to society. Clearly, there will be conflict among group members. Your group should probably first determine what the word *importance* means—affecting the most people, impacting in a negative way, impacting in a positive way, for instance. Also, you should define *society*—the local or regional society, American society, the world, and so forth. Remember to utilize concepts regarding conflict from this chapter as your group ranks the following from the most important to the least important:

- Abortion rights
- Diversity in the workplace
- Terrorism preparedness
- Equal pay for equal work
- Sexual harassment
- Welfare
- Labor unions

- Cure for cancer
- Unemployment
- Compensation of CEOs

Reflection Questions

1. How did your group determine a strategy for ranking these? Describe.
2. What challenges did you have in accomplishing the task? How did you overcome those challenges?
3. Did you use negotiation at any point during the process? Explain.
4. Describe an example of conflict at your current or most recent job. How has that conflict been resolved?
5. Discuss instances in which conflict resolution might be difficult to accomplish in the workplace.

Exercise contributed by Steven Stovall, Southeast Missouri State University.

EXERCISE 12.2: TENSION, CONFLICT, RESOLUTION

Objectives

This exercise will help you to be able to better *describe* the conflict process, *describe* the various types of conflict, and *identify* the five basic conflict management strategies.

Instructions

Step 1. Think of a conflict you are currently in (one that you are willing to share with the class), or, if you are not currently in any conflict, one that you have recently been in but were not able to resolve satisfactorily. Write this conflict down in as much detail as possible. (Note, you can give other parties in this description pseudonyms if you want to.) (5 minutes)

Step 2. Find a partner and give each other a brief overview of your conflicts. Choose the conflict that you both agree is the most interesting, and closely related to chapter topics on conflict management. (If one person has chosen an ongoing conflict, and the other person has chosen a past conflict, choose the ongoing conflict.) Both partners should then analyze the conflict for the following elements:

- Determine if the conflict is functional or dysfunctional.
- Determine the type of conflict (task, relationship, or process).
- Describe the conflict development using the four stages of conflict (antecedents of conflict, perceived/felt conflict, manifest conflict, and outcomes of conflict).
- Identify which of the five conflict management strategies were used in the conflict. (10 to 15 minutes)

Step 3. Be prepared to present your analysis to the class or provide details on specific aspects of the analysis when asked by your instructor. (5 minutes)

Reflection Questions

1. How did analyzing your conflict help you to better understand the reasons for your conflict?
2. How did working through the conflict with someone else help you to understand the conflict more clearly?
3. What new insights did you gain about avoiding dysfunctional conflicts, or better resolving functional conflicts?
4. How could you use this process in future conflicts?

5. As a manager, how could you use this or similar methods to help workers in dealing with a conflict?
6. In what ways would it be beneficial to have all parties in a conflict work through a similar process?

Exercise contributed by Milton R. Mayfield, Professor of Business, Texas A&M International University, and Jacqueline R. Mayfield, Professor of Business, Texas A&M International University.

EXERCISE 12.3: WIN AS MUCH AS YOU CAN

Objective

The purpose of this exercise is to grasp the concept of trust in group settings.

Instructions

This exercise is based on the "prisoner's dilemma" activity and involves trust of others as well as negotiation. The class will be divided into four groups. Each group should elect two representatives. Those four pairs of representatives will come to the front of the room. If the size of the class is small enough, the students should sit near their elected representatives (if this is not possible, the representatives will be seated by themselves). The four pairs of representatives should be seated far enough away from one another to ensure that conversations cannot be heard.

Each pair of representatives will receive from the instructor a single card that has a large "A" on one side and a large "B" on the other. The instructions are as follows:

- Both pairs of representatives will be reminded that the name of this exercise is "win as much as you can."
- There will be 10 rounds and each pair of representatives will determine for each round whether they will hold up the "A" side or the "B" side of their card (if it is a smaller class, the other students will help confer with the representatives; in larger classes, the representatives will simply confer with each other).
- Each pair of representatives must agree on whether they will hold up an "A" or a "B."
- Scoring is as follows:
  - 4 Bs = each team loses 1 point
  - 3 Bs = each team wins 1 point
  - 1 A = that team loses 3 points
  - 2 As = each team wins 2 points
  - 2 Bs = each team loses 2 points
  - 1 B = that team wins 3 points
  - 3 As = each team loses 1 point
  - 4 As = each team wins 1 point

Here is the format for the 10 rounds:

Round 1:

1. Pairs of representatives discuss only with one another which card they will show (for each round, if the class is small, the other students associated with the representatives may also provide input). There can be no communication—verbal or nonverbal between the pairs of representatives. After conferring, each pair of representatives holds up the card showing either an "A" or a "B" to the other pairs. This must be done at the exact same time to avoid cheating (the instructor will say something along the lines of "Ok, on the count of three, hold up your card . . . one, two, three!").
2. Again, representatives confer with one another and after about a minute of conferring, hold up the cards at the same time.

3. Same as Round 2.
4. Here, the pairs of representatives may discuss with other pairs. They can negotiate, agree to hold up a certain card, meet with one pair separately from the other pairs, and so forth. After a few minutes of discussion and negotiations, the pairs of representatives return to their seats. They then confer with one another and determine whether they will do what was agreed or hold up a different letter. However, keep in mind, that in this round, the points are *doubled.*
5. Same as Round 2.
6. Same as Round 2.
7. Same as Round 4. However, the points are 4 times the amount.
8. Same as Round 2.
9. Same as Round 2.
10. Same as Round 4. However, the points are 8 times the amount.

At the conclusion of Round 10, the instructor will total the points to see who won the most points. Discussion will then ensue as to the process, negotiations, and how trust played a role.

Reflection Questions

1. What did you learn from this game about trust and negotiations?
2. How important is trust in the workplace? When it comes to negotiations, what role does trust play?
3. The name of this exercise is "win as much as you can." You probably noticed that at least one team could not be trusted despite agreeing to hold up a particular card—they had the approach that they wanted to *win as much as they could.* Does this happen in the workplace? Explain.
4. What can we do as employees to earn trust and maintain trust among those with whom we work?

Exercise contributed by Steven Stovall, Southeast Missouri State University.

ONLINE EXERCISE 12.1: WHAT CONFLICT MANAGEMENT STRATEGY DO YOU USE?

Objective

The purpose of this exercise is to gain an appreciation for different conflict management strategies.

Instructions

Take a look at the following five conflict management strategies:

- **Avoidance**—an attempt to suppress a conflict and pretend it doesn't exist
- **Accommodation**—an attempt to adjust our views to play down differences between parties
- **Competition**—an attempt to gain victory through force, skill, or domination
- **Compromise**—a situation in which each party concedes something of value
- **Collaboration**—a joint effort by all parties to find a solution beneficial to everyone

Be sure to read the chapter, as the text delves into each of these in more detail. After studying these five types of conflict management strategies, which one or ones do you tend to use when faced with conflict? On a discussion board, post which strategy or strategies you utilize most often and give an example. After each participant has had a chance to post something, comment on others' posts. For those who use the same strategy as you, discuss why you tend to find that strategy helpful. For those who use a different strategy than you, ask how and why their strategy is useful.

Reflection Questions

1. Do you utilize a different conflict management strategy in your personal life versus at work? Explain.
2. Which conflict management strategy would you never use in the workplace? Why?
3. Think of a current or recent manager you have had. Which conflict management strategy did they use? How effective was that manager in resolving conflicts?

Exercise contributed by Steven Stovall, Southeast Missouri State University.

ONLINE EXERCISE 12.2: WHO DO YOU DISTRUST? AND WHY?

Objective

The purpose of this exercise is to gain an understanding of trust.

Instructions

Search online for a short video (under 10 minutes) of someone doing or saying something where you have a sense of distrust of that individual. Perhaps it is their tone of voice, their posture, or even the specific words they are saying. Review the video and make notes about their verbal and nonverbal behavior, then answer the questions below.

Reflection Questions

- In your observation of the subject in the video, what did you see or hear that caused you to distrust this individual? Be as specific as possible.
- Even after viewing the video and having a level of distrust for this person, what *could* they say or do that would cause you to consider trusting that person? Explain.
- The person in the video is likely a stranger to you. Why are we so quick to distrust someone based only on a few moments with that person? Discuss.

Exercise contributed by Steven Stovall, Southeast Missouri State University.

CASE 12.1: ALLIED GRAPE GROWERS

California produces 85% of the United States' wine and is the fourth largest wine producer in the world after Italy, France, and Spain. Wine grapes are one of California's top five crops and more than 110 varieties are grown on approximately 600,000 acres in 49 of the state's 58 counties. 325,000 Californians are employed by the wine and wine grape sector, which generates $60 billion in annual economic activity.[56] The state's wineries typically attract more than 23 million visitors each year, but a perfect storm of challenges brought the California wine industry to a standstill in 2020.

In addition to the lost tourism revenue and reduced restaurant sales that were direct effects of the COVID-19 pandemic, a record-breaking wildfire season threatened to wipe out the entire 2020 vintage. "It is one of the saddest years ever," winemaker Philippe Melka, founder of Atelier Melka in Napa Valley told *Wine Spectator*. "Usually harvest is a happy time. We have very, very little hope."[57]

Melka's pessimism about the 2020 harvest stemmed from the effects of smoke exposure on grapes in vineyards near the fires. "Smoke taint is pretty obvious," says Rick Davis, owner of Calstar Cellars in Santa Rosa. "The best descriptor I've heard for the flavor profile of a smoke-tainted wine was that if you're particularly fond of licking wet ash trays, you'll like this wine."[58] There's no evidence that smoke-tainted wine can make you sick, but the risk of ruined flavor is so unpalatable that many wineries refuse to buy smoke tainted grapes, putting growers in a very difficult position.

Allied Grape Growers (AGG) is a 500-member grower-owned marketing association that has been negotiating grape purchase agreements between growers and buyers since 1951.[59] While wine grape purchase contracts have long addressed quality loss due to smoke exposure, the timing of the fires right at the beginning of harvest season and pandemic-related schedule delays made the 2020 crop exceptionally unfruitful. Furthermore, growers alleged that wineries exploited vague quality standards provisions to reject grapes in breach of contract, causing them substantial economic injury. AGG and the California Association of Winegrape Growers (CAWG) commissioned Sacramento law firm Downey Brand, LLP to prepare a legal analysis of the 2020 wine grape rejections and provide guidance to growers so they would never find themselves in such a disastrous position again.

In the analysis, Downey Brand quotes industry sources who estimated 165,000 to 325,000 tons of wine grapes went unharvested "due to actual or perceived concerns of quality loss due to wildfire smoke exposure." The U.S. Department of Agriculture's Risk Management Agency paid $187,920,862 in crop insurance claims to growers, consistent with growers' claim that they had sustained $601 million in total losses due to the wildfires and smoke exposure.[60]

Wineries applied inconsistent rejection standards and testing methods, and in some instances the rejection letters they sent cited previously unwritten quality criteria, leaving growers scrambling with little time to find replacement buyers. "A lot of people forget that anytime you're dealing with agriculture, dealing with nature, you can't control it. We still have to deal with a vagary of Mother Nature, and it's a very humbling thing," world-renowned vintner Bill Harlan said.[61]

The firm prepared the following recommendations for growers to clearly define smoke exposure provisions when negotiating future purchase contracts with wineries, provided in Table 12.3 below:

TABLE 12.3

- Sampling of grapes: How will it be conducted? By whom? When? What are the chain of custody requirements for samples pulled from a vineyard or truck?
- Testing of samples: How will it be conducted? By a certified, third-party lab? When? What methodology will be applied? How will results be shared?
- Smoke exposure standards or criteria: What thresholds for chemical compounds will be applied? What standards or criteria will apply if sensory analysis is part of the winery's decision to accept or reject grapes, and will sensory analysis be coupled with lab results and not a standalone factor in the decision?
- Test results: How will the results of the tests affect the winery's right to reject grapes or impose a price adjustment, if at all?

Growers' bargaining position is not as strong as that of the wineries to whom they sell their grapes, making fair negotiation of quality standards and testing provisions difficult, but growers are not completely without leverage. A winery may save money in the short term by rejecting grapes, canceling a vintage, and avoiding the risk of unsalable, smoke-tainted wine, but if they ruin relationships with their growers, who will supply grapes next year?

Some buyers focused on the long term and sought ways to share the fire and smoke risk with their suppliers. Pete Richmond's Silverado Farming Company farms grapes for Atelier Melka and many other Cabernet-focused wineries in Napa. Some of his grapes were picked prior to receiving test results, he says: "Our wineries are working on sliding scale, meaning they'll pay the full amount if the grapes are OK, and if not, they'll pay less." Some of Richmond's wineries were so committed to their shared values, they paid $1,500 per ton to leave grapes on the vine, unharvested. "Paying growers not to pick is pretty innovative and helps maintain relationships. We're in this together." The Harvard Law School Program on Negotiation included this example of integrative bargaining between the wineries and Richmond in their "10 Notable Negotiations of 2020."[62]

Despite suffering the greatest losses of his over 40-year career in winemaking, Bill Harlan remains optimistic about the future: "Napa County is resilient, each time we come out even better. Even though it's pretty devastating right now, I look at it as one more learning lesson, and we'll come out even better."

Critical-Thinking Questions

1. Describe a novel antecedent of conflict that arose between the growers and wineries in their grape purchase contract disputes as a result of the COVID-19 pandemic in 2020.

2. Some wineries that chose a conflict management strategy of competition succeeded in 2020. Now that AGG and CAWG growers have regrouped and developed a collaborative plan to resolve quality standards disputes, do you think that strategy will work for them again in the future?

3. Do you think the integrative bargaining that Pete Richmond and the wineries that Silverado Farming Company contracts with will reap benefits beyond their continued supplier agreement? Why?

PART

IV

LEADERSHIP AND INFLUENCE PROCESSES

iStockPhoto / Geber86

13 LEADERSHIP PERSPECTIVES

LEARNING OBJECTIVES

By the end of this chapter, you will be able to:

13.1 Explain the basic concept of leadership

13.2 Distinguish between formal and informal leadership and between leadership and management

13.3 Contrast the four basic types of leadership

13.4 Describe the trait, behavioral, and contingency leadership perspectives

13.5 Compare the inspirational, relational, and follower-centered leadership perspectives

13.6 Discuss the power-distributing leadership perspectives of empowering, shared, and self-leadership

13.7 Describe the values-based leadership perspectives of authentic, spiritual, servant, and ethical leadership

13.8 Discuss leadership across cultures

13.9 Identify gender issues in the context of leadership

Case Study: Procter and Gamble's Leadership Training Program

Whether you realize it or not, there is a company that has quietly inserted itself into most aspects of your day-to-day routine. To some it may seem like a soap and shampoo company but those that know its past know that it has created the market that it now leads. It has ridden the wave of modern hygiene to what it is today and is responsible for many of the consumable products you use every day in your home. This company is Procter and Gamble. Originally founded by William Proctor and James Gamble in 1837 as a soap company, P&G's products really took off during the Civil War when it won contracts with the Union army to provide supplies to its soldiers.[1] Back then, most consumer products were made using home remedies with recipes passed down for generations. P&G were the first to streamline the process and to make brands with consistent ingredients. It was through this effort, that they effectively invented branding as we know it.[2]

With over $76 billion in sales and 65 brands in its portfolio, Procter and Gamble is the world's largest advertiser.[3] They sell all types of consumer goods—from cleaning agents to razors. You may not know it, but Gillette, Febreze, Vicks, and Olay are all P&G brands.

Today, Procter and Gamble products sell around the world (apart from North Korea and Cuba) and P&G employs over 101,000 people.[4] While it all started with soap, over the last 150 years, P&G have created new products by using out-of-the-box thinking. Before 2014, its portfolio included foods, snacks, and beverages. However, since then, they decided to cut 100 of their brands and kept the 65 brands that made 95% of their profits.[5] With this streamlining, we have the modern-day Procter and Gamble.

As a leader in new and innovative products, P&G knew it would constantly need to reinvent itself to keep up with the competition and meet the needs of consumers. If it only sold soap, it would quickly have its business stolen away by another company making a newer kind of soap. According to former chairman Richard Deupree, "The Procter & Gamble Company never has gone in circles, never followed footsteps, but rather has continually broken new trails, entered new fields, set new records, even raised its own high standards."[6]

P&G also adopted this mindset in its approach to advertising. It knew that reinventing its product line along with how it was presented would be crucial. For that reason, P&G is regarded by many as the inventor of advertising as we now know it and seen as the first household name brand. Its desire to advertise neatly coincided with the age of the newspaper and the rise of print advertising.[7]

Along with being at the forefront of product innovation and advertising, P&G has also been a leader in its field for product testing and the proper vetting of all its products. It set a standard for the importance of safety, and even in the early days of mainstream advertising it made the safety of its product a huge priority. Thanks to the early groundwork laid by P&G, consumers rarely have to worry about the safety of cleaning products.[8]

P&G has been the proud recipient of many awards, including being #1 on Fortune's Global Top Companies for Leaders or #15 for World's Most Admired Brands.[9] It is consistently ranked a top company for its organizational culture, brand recognition, and leadership development programs. It has one of the most efficient employee training programs of any major companies and prides itself on mentorship and leadership skills even at entry level. As a result, P&G has become a very sought-after place to work. Its leadership in the industry applies to everything it does, from how it treats its workforce to how it manages its brand and its success shows no sign of slowing down.

Critical-Thinking Questions

1. Why does Procter and Gamble draw so many job applicants?
2. How did Procter and Gamble influence the creation of their industry as it pertains to safety?

WHAT IS LEADERSHIP?

Our Proctor & Gamble (P&G) case shows the different ways in which organizations can lead. P&G is a leading brand because of its commitment to innovation, branding, safety, and excellent leadership training programs. Organizations this successful need good leaders. But what does it mean to be a good leader? The search for what makes a good leader has been going on for centuries and, despite myriad studies, there are no conclusive answers. Although many definitions exist, for our purposes, **leadership** is a process of providing general direction from a position of influence to individuals or groups toward the successful attainment of goals.[10]

The internet has revolutionized society by giving millions of people a voice and the ability to communicate across cultural and geographical barriers. With enough online resources to access most corners of the world, almost anybody can be a leader, with or without formal authority, given the right skills and a strong initiative. In our global world, effective leaders need to connect and collaborate with people from different types of social groups through global networks to be heard.

The COVID-19 pandemic has also impacted leadership. The blurring of boundaries between work and family lives forced business leaders to reframe their attitudes towards their employees. This involved taking a more holistic approach by recognizing that employees wear many different hats and have many competing priorities, such as a parent juggling work with homeschool, a recent graduate living in shared accommodation, or a caregiver looking after sick relatives.[11] For example, image-sharing social media company Pinterest showed compassionate leadership by introducing a four-week paid leave program for working parents to take time out of work to homeschool their children.[12]

Leader Emergence

What makes a great leader? Would you single out presidents and prime ministers, sports coaches, or CEOs as examples of iconic leaders? On what basis do you identify them as leaders? Popularity? Achievement? The way they communicate? The way they engage with you through social media? For example, do you like leaders who tweet? Perhaps it's something intangible, like a leader's charisma. Coca Cola former CEO Indra Nooyi has been described as a charismatic leader who has inspired women all over the world by overcoming cultural, social, and gender challenges to rise to the top.[13]

Societal norms and media influence have much to do with our perceptions about what makes an effective leader, and sometimes they create a false impression of **leader emergence**, which occurs when someone naturally becomes the leader of a leaderless group.[14] As a result, we can fall prey to stereotypes. Dianne Bevelander, professor of management education at Erasmus University's Rotterdam School of Management, has challenged business schools to drop the tendency to stereotype leaders when teaching business courses. Bevelander said, "New leadership no longer looks like a white man

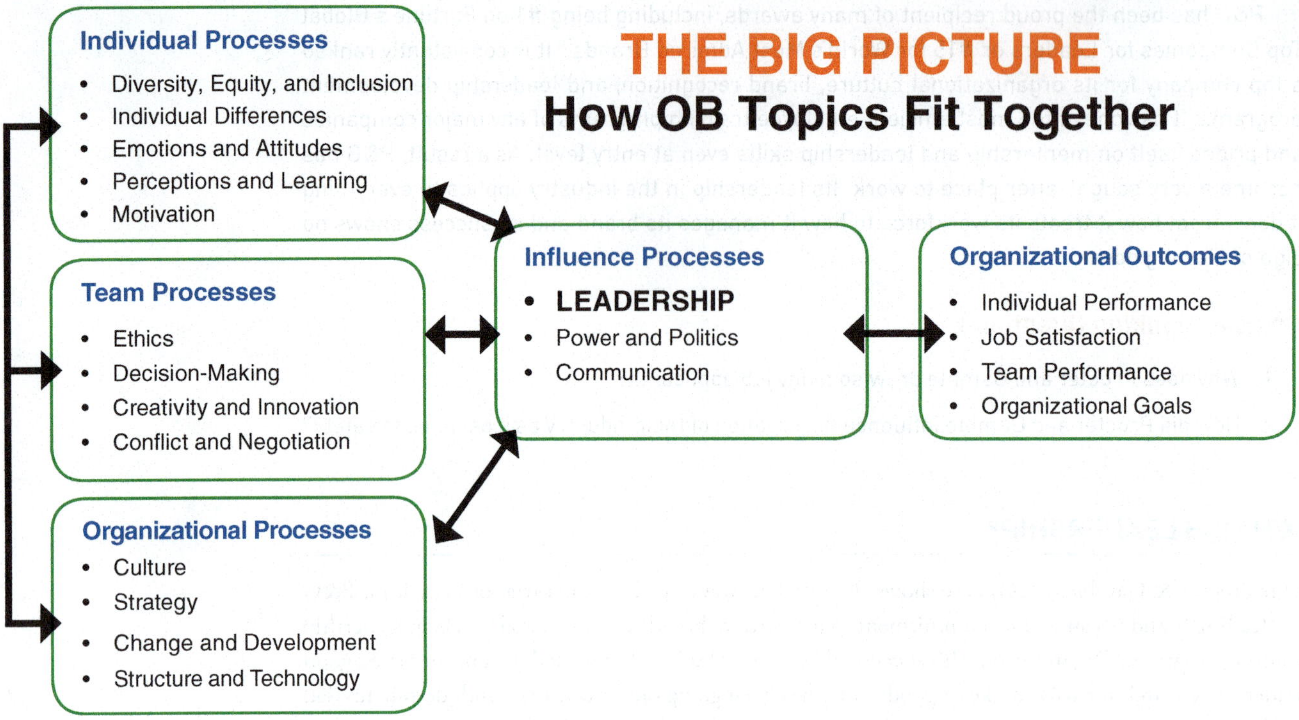

rescuing companies . . . It is far more diverse and includes women, people of color, and people with different sexual orientations."[15]

Despite numerous debates regarding the nature of leadership, there is a general view that today's leaders are most likely to be critical thinkers who lead from a position of influence rather than power, and who use their decision-making, motivational, and communication skills to inspire others with their vision to generate results. Researchers have discovered that can produce astonishing results in terms of increasing a company's profits, maintaining a successful corporate culture, motivating employees through good times and bad, increasing production levels, connecting with the community, and leading the charge on sustainability. Recent research has also shown that companies led by leaders who demonstrate empathy toward their employees present higher levels of morale, productivity, and work performance.[16] President and CEO of employee benefits administration company Businessolver, Jon Shanahan said: "After years of decline, workplace empathy has improved—alongside overall attentiveness to issues long considered to be among the most difficult to discuss in the workplace, including our lives outside of work, mental health, and race."[17]

FORMAL AND INFORMAL LEADERSHIP

Within most organizations there are two types of leaders: formal and informal.[18] A **formal leader** is a person officially designated by the organization, like a CEO who is appointed by the board of directors. For example, Lynsi Snyder CEO of In-N-Out Burger company is an example of a formal leader and was named as one of the best performing CEOs in the world by the 2021 Glassdoor Employees' Choice Awards.[19] An **informal leader** is a person who does not receive a title but is perceived by others as a leader. In the teaching profession, teachers hold both formal and informal roles to provide leadership by example for their peers.[20]

Formal leaders must act in the best interests of the organization and have certain rights and privileges that allow them to reward or discipline employees. Informal leaders do not have official appointments and therefore do not have the same rights as formal leaders, but team members may rely on them to motivate and help them realize their goals. Research shows that although informal leadership duties can help some employees feel more valued and supported, taking on extra tasks can also cause a decrease in job satisfaction and energy levels when informal leaders are not adequately supported by formal leaders despite long-term benefits.[21] Formal leaders can support informal leaders by communicating expectations, inviting feedback, and ensuring other people are in place to share the workload.

Management versus Leadership

Although management and leadership share some similarities, they do not mean the same thing. Both leaders and managers work with people, set goals, and influence others to achieve those goals, but several distinctions separate the two functions (see Figure 13.1).

First, leadership has been around far longer than management. History records the strategies employed by military leaders such as Alexander the Great (336–323 bcE) and Attila the Hun (406–453 bcE). Managers, in contrast, are mainly a product of industrialization in the 20th century, an era when large-scale production and manufacturing demanded the organizational skills necessary to plan, organize, staff, and control the operation. These skills are still highly relevant in the 21st-century workplace.

Second, leadership consists of creating a vision, introducing change and movement, and influencing others to achieve goals, while managers maintain the status quo, promote stability, and ensure the smooth running of operations.[22] There is an overlap between managers and leaders, however. For example, if you are a manager running a project and setting goals for your team, then you are leading your team. Similarly, if you are a leader and you are engaged in the daily organization of operations, then you are fulfilling management functions. In each case, both managers and leaders are leading from a position of influence. Harvard Business School Dean Nitin Nohria described the distinction between leadership and management: *"I think of management as working with other people to make sure the goals an organization has articulated are executed . . . Leadership is about developing what the goals should be. It's more about driving change."*[23]

However, realistically, not all managers are leaders, nor for that matter all leaders managers. For example, managers who put their own interests above those of their employees or who fail to motivate, guide, or positively influence their teams would not be classified as good leaders.

However, although it is useful for leaders to have managerial skills, it is not essential; certainly, it is advantageous for leaders to understand the discipline of management and have a background in the management functions, but it doesn't mean they need to be managers as well as leaders. Their primary

FIGURE 13.1 ■ Comparison of a Leader and a Manager

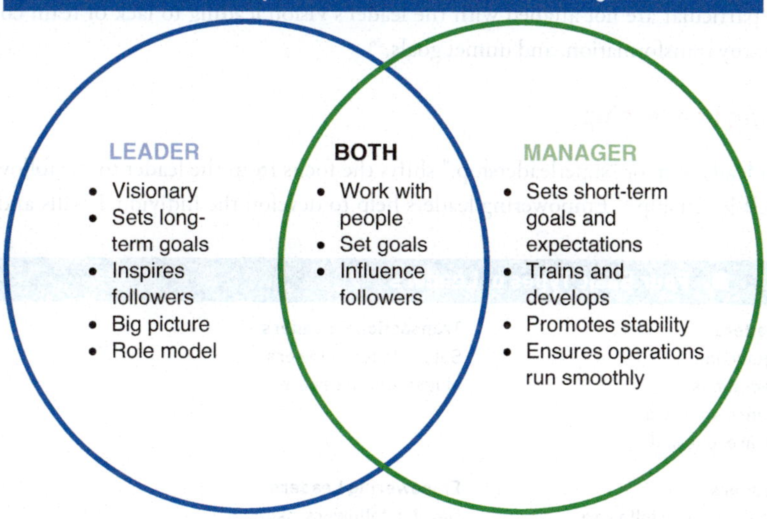

strength lies in the ability to influence the behaviors and work of others to realize their vision and achieve set goals by choosing between certain leadership types.

BASIC LEADERSHIP TYPES

Today's leaders tend to choose between four distinct types of leadership behavior based on the work environment and overall goals of the organization. Originally proposed by Charles C. Manz and Henry P. Sims Jr., and since refined by other leadership theorists, the four types include directive leadership, transactional leadership, visionary leadership, and empowering leadership (also known as "superleadership").[24] (See Table 13.1.)

Directive Leadership

Directive leadership behavior consists of implementing guidelines, providing information about what is expected, setting performance standards, and ensuring that individuals follow rules. Directive leaders are sometimes known as **production-oriented leaders** because they tend to focus more on the technical or task aspects of the job. Directive leaders also tend to rule with an **autocratic style**, making decisions without asking for suggestions from others. They also rely on the power to use their authority to command, reprimand, or intimidate to get the desired results from their subordinates. Directive leadership is most common in military settings to ensure compliance to strict guidelines. It is not recommended in corporate settings as it discourages idea-sharing and feedback.

Transactional Leadership

Transactional leadership is a rewards-and-punishment system based on the assumption that employees are motivated by goals and equitable rewards. The transactional leader offers clear and objective goals for followers to gain **compliance**, which occurs when the targets of influence readily agree to carry out the leader's requests. Although this type of leadership can create a sense of fairness as all employee performance is measured the same way, transactional feedback can stifle creativity and risk-taking by punishing employees for not meeting their goals and not making allowances for mistakes.[25]

Visionary Leadership

Visionary leadership often contrasted with transactional leadership, creates visions to motivate, inspire, and stimulate employees. A visionary leader uses charisma to encourage followers to share in the mission and expects them to commit and work toward their desired goal. Employees must be on board for the vision to succeed. Research shows that visionary leadership breaks down when middle managers in particular are not aligned with the leader's vision leading to lack of team commitment, delayed company transformation, and unmet goals.[26]

Empowering Leadership

Empowering leadership or "superleadership," shifts the focus from the leader to the follower through the idea of self-leadership.[27] Empowering leaders help to develop the individual skills and abilities of

TABLE 13.1 ■ Four Basic Types of Leaders

Directive Leaders Implement guidelines Provide expectations Set performance standards Ensure rules are followed	**Transactional Leaders** Set goals for followers Motivate with rewards
Visionary Leaders Create vision to motivate followers Utilize charisma to gain support Expect commitment from followers	**Empowering Leaders** Develop followers' skills Encourage followers to take ownership of their work Lead others to lead themselves

their followers, allowing them to utilize these skills, take ownership of their work, and contribute to organizational performance. The idea of "superleadership" has been defined as the "process of leading others to lead themselves."[28] Companies that empower their employees tend to experience increased growth, trust, job satisfaction, and creativity. Norma Watenpaugh, CEO of Phoenix Consulting Group (Phoenix CG) provided this advice for empowering employees: "Give them autonomy, respect, and resources, then stand back. I've been amazed at how energized and creative people can be when you give them ownership."[29]

EARLY LEADERSHIP PERSPECTIVES

As we have learned, there is no set definition or combination of characteristics that describes a good leader. However, to support our current understanding of leadership, it is useful to explore the early theories of leadership, each of which focuses on different ways in which a great leader is created. These include trait, behavioral, and contingency theories.

Trait Leadership Perspective

The **trait leadership perspective** is a theory that explores the relationship between leaders' personal qualities and characteristics and the way their traits differentiate them from nonleaders. In other words, the theory assumes effective leaders are born, not made. Famous leaders such as Gandhi, Churchill, Lincoln, Joan of Arc, and Alexander the Great were studied by early trait theorists, who explored characteristics such as physical appearance, personality, and ability and sought to link them to individuals' leadership qualities. However, trait theory has since been widely criticized for its limiting methodology and inaccurate conclusions.[30] Researchers believed that traits in isolation could not predict leadership success.

Despite skepticism about early trait theory, the study of leadership traits has made a bit of a comeback in recent years since researchers have discovered patterns of traits.[31] Modern theorists now believe that leadership characteristics can be nurtured and developed over time, and that leaders must use a combination of these traits effectively to become successful leaders. The following is a list of leadership core traits identified in more recent research studies:[32]

Early trait theorists studied famous leaders like Winston Churchill and Joan of Arc to determine whether certain characteristics were indicative of strong leadership qualities.

Keystone / Stringer / Getty Images

- **Drive.** Leaders are ambitious and motivated and have a natural desire to succeed.
- **Desire to lead.** Leaders are motivated by a keen desire to lead and influence others, and to gain power.
- **Integrity.** Successful leaders are honest, trustworthy, and ethical and maintain behavior consistent with these values.
- **Self-confidence.** Leaders have a high degree of self-confidence in their leadership abilities.
- **Cognitive ability.** Leaders who have a wide range of cognitive skills have the ability to gather, integrate, and process complex information.
- **Knowledge of domain.** Leaders who possess a keen knowledge of their field are better at making decisions, predicting potential problems, and understanding the impact of their actions.
- **Openness to new experiences.** Leaders must be flexible, open to new experiences, and willing to adopt the ideas of others.
- **Extraversion.** Leaders who enjoy engaging with others tend to form relationships that support them in problem-solving and in seeking new opportunities.

Although modern trait theory proposes that leadership traits can be nurtured over time, the behavioral leadership perspective focuses on a set of specific behaviors displayed by leaders in any given situation.

Behavioral Leadership Perspective

The **behavioral leadership perspective** proposes that specific behaviors distinguish leaders from nonleaders. During the 1950s, independent researchers at both Ohio State University and University of Michigan conducted studies of leadership behavior (see Table 13.2).

Kean Collection / Staff / Getty Images

Ohio State University Studies

In the 1940s, researchers at Ohio State University administered a questionnaire to hundreds of people working in the military, business, and educational fields to assess leadership styles. The aim was to ascertain how employees perceived the types of leadership behavior exhibited by their superiors. From the results, researchers proposed a two-dimensional view of leadership behavior based on leadership styles they called initiating structure, and consideration.[33] **Initiating structure** is a behavior demonstrated by leaders who define the roles of the employees, set clear guidelines and procedures, and establish distinct patterns of organization and communication. **Consideration** is a behavior demonstrated by leaders who develop mutual trust and respect and actively build interpersonal relationships with their followers.

These two dimensions are similar to the theories proposed by the Michigan studies a few years later.

University of Michigan Studies

In an effort to identify the patterns of leadership behavior, University of Michigan researchers under the general direction of Rensis Likert in the 1950s interviewed leaders from both private and public companies and asked them to complete a questionnaire. The results helped the researchers establish two

TABLE 13.2 ■ Behavioral Leadership Perspective Studies

The Ohio State Studies	The University of Michigan Studies
1. Initiating structure	**1.** Job-Centered Leadership Style
2. Consideration	**2.** Employee-Centered Leadership Style

Sources: Based on Hemphill, J. K., and A. E. Coons, *Leader Behavior: Its Description and Measurement*. Research Monograph No. 88 (Columbus: Ohio State University, Bureau of Business Research, 1957); Likert, Rensis. *New Patterns of Management* (New York: McGraw-Hill, 1961).

styles of leadership behavior: *job-centered leadership style*, a behavioral leadership style that emphasizes employee tasks and the methods used to accomplish them, and *employee-centered leadership style*, a behavioral leadership style that emphasizes the personal needs of employees and the development of interpersonal relationships.[34]

Researchers investigated the impact each leadership style had on rates of productivity, staff turnover, job satisfaction, and absenteeism and concluded that because employee-centered leaders had better results in these areas, they were more effective than job-centered leaders. However, there were some inconsistencies within the studies, mainly due to the fact that researchers were skeptical that leaders could possess characteristics from both styles rather than just one, which other theorists thought cast doubt on the results.

The two dimensions of initiating structure and consideration suggested in the Ohio studies are similar to the theories proposed by the Michigan studies. For example, initiating structure is similar to job-centered leadership because both behaviors place an emphasis on assigning tasks and getting the job done, and consideration is comparable to employee-centered leadership, with its focus on employee welfare and development. Although there are similarities between the Michigan and Ohio State studies, the Ohio State studies offer a more rounded view of leadership behavior by demonstrating that leaders could exhibit characteristics from both dimensions rather than just one.

The Leadership Grid

As an extension of the results published from the Ohio State studies, management researchers Robert R. Blake and Jane S. Mouton designed the **leadership grid**, an approach that plots concern for production on the horizontal axis and concern for people on the vertical axis (see Figure 13.2). Each axis is a scale, with 1 representing the least concern and 9 the most. The five leadership styles are country club, produce or perish, impoverished, middle-of-the-road, and team leader.[35]

Leaders who get a low score for production and a high score for people are known as "country club" leaders. This style of leader is more concerned about the well-being of employees than about production and feels confident that a happy, relaxed workforce is the most productive. However, because of the lack of control and direction, this type of leadership can inhibit productivity.

"Produce or perish" leaders emphasize production over people and lead with an authoritarian rule, using punishment as a motivator. "Impoverished" leaders have very little concern for production *or* for people, which means they are ineffective for the most part. Leaders who are "middle-of-the-road" appear to have achieved the right balance between concern for people and concern for production, but this requires compromise; the problem with compromise is that the needs of both factions are not fully met, resulting in an average performance. Finally, the "team leader" rates production needs and people needs equally highly. According to the Blake–Mouton model, the team leader is the ideal leader, because they create an environment in which teams are motivated and committed to furthering the success of the organization, leading to high production and satisfied employees.

The leadership grid reaffirmed the findings of the Ohio State studies that consideration of employees leads to a higher-performing workforce; however, it also introduced the idea that both people and production should be treated with the highest concern for the organization to achieve optimal results.

FIGURE 13.2 ■ The Blake Mouton Leadership Grid

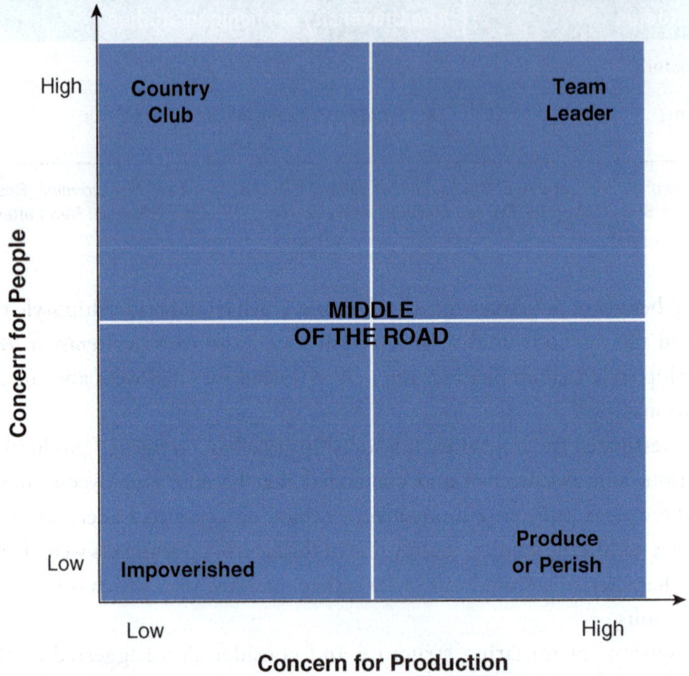

Source: Adapted from Blake, R. R. & Mouton, J. S. (1964). *The managerial grid.* Gulf Publishing.

Contingency Leadership Perspective

The **contingency leadership perspective**, pioneered by Fred E. Fiedler, claimed that the effectiveness of the leader depended on there being an appropriate match between the leader's traits or behaviors and the demands and characteristics of the contingency or situation.[36] Fiedler sought to identify the different types of leadership styles in certain situations and devised a scale called **least-preferred coworker (LPC)**, an instrument that evaluates whether a person is task oriented or relationship oriented.

To use the LPC scale, leaders were asked to think of a work situation in which they encountered a person they least enjoyed working with and rate that person's standing based on adjectives such as *friendly* or *unfriendly*, *considerate* or *inconsiderate*, and so on (see Figure 13.3).

Leaders who gave high scores on the LPC scale were thought to be relationship motivated, because they tended to describe their least preferred coworker in a positive light. Those who had a more negative view of their coworkers received a low LPC score and were believed to be more task motivated.

In the next stage of this theory, Fiedler set out to prove that leadership style was dependent on the following situational variables:

- **Leader–member relations** describe the degree of confidence, trust, and respect that exist between subordinates and their leaders. Leaders who are well regarded can better influence events and outcomes.
- **Task structure** is the degree to which job assignments are defined. Leaders who provide clear, structured tasks are viewed more favorably.
- **Leader's position power** is the level of power a leader possesses to reward or punish, or promote and demote.

Fiedler's contingency model (see Figure 13.4) is designed to predict the effectiveness of leadership styles in certain situations, on a scale from 1 to 8. For example, in instances of high situational control where leader–member relations are good, task structure is low, and the leader has strong position power, the model gives a score of 3, suggesting a low LPC leadership or task-driven style is most effective. Conversely, in instances of low situational control when leader–member relations are poor, task structure is high, and the leader has weak position power, the model assigns a rating of 6, suggesting a high LPC leadership or relationship-driven style is best. Fiedler found that the most favorable situations occurred when leader–member relations, task structure, and position power are all high because then leaders have the most control over the situation.

Although Fiedler's model is useful for matching optimal leadership styles to certain situations, it has been criticized for its lack of flexibility, primarily its assumption that leadership styles cannot be changed. For example, according to the theory, leaders with low LPC ratings (more task driven) in situations where a high LPC approach (relationship driven) would be more suitable should be replaced by leaders with a natural flair for building relationships, even though it might be equally effective to encourage the low LPC leaders to adopt a different style or to develop their skills through training or other measures.

FIGURE 13.3 ■ Least-Preferred Coworker Scale

Unfriendly	1 2 3 4 5 6 7 8	Friendly
Unpleasant	1 2 3 4 5 6 7 8	Pleasant
Rejecting	1 2 3 4 5 6 7 8	Accepting
Tense	1 2 3 4 5 6 7 8	Relaxed
Cold	1 2 3 4 5 6 7 8	Warm
Boring	1 2 3 4 5 6 7 8	Interesting
Backbiting	1 2 3 4 5 6 7 8	Loyal
Uncooperative	1 2 3 4 5 6 7 8	Cooperative
Hostile	1 2 3 4 5 6 7 8	Supportive
Guarded	1 2 3 4 5 6 7 8	Open
Insincere	1 2 3 4 5 6 7 8	Sincere
Unkind	1 2 3 4 5 6 7 8	Kind
Inconsiderate	1 2 3 4 5 6 7 8	Considerate
Untrustworthy	1 2 3 4 5 6 7 8	Trustworthy
Gloomy	1 2 3 4 5 6 7 8	Cheerful
Quarrelsome	1 2 3 4 5 6 7 8	Harmonious

FIGURE 13.4 ■ Fiedler's Contingency Model

Leader-Member Relations	GOOD				POOR			
Task Structure	High		Low		High		Low	
Position Power	Strong	Weak	Strong	Weak	Strong	Weak	Strong	Weak
	1	2	3	4	5	6	7	8
Preferred Leadership Style	Low LPCs Middle LPCs			High LPCs				Low LPCs

Source: Adapted from Fiedler, F. E. (1967). *A theory of leadership effectiveness*. McGraw-Hill.

Hersey and Blanchard's Situational Leadership Model

Developed in 1969 by Paul Hersey and Ken Blanchard, the **situational leadership model** proposes that leaders should adapt their leadership style based on the types of people they are leading and the requirements of the task.[37] Drawing from the findings of the Ohio State studies, Hersey and Blanchard applied concepts similar to "initiating structure" and "consideration" to the following four main leadership styles:

- **Telling** (S1). Telling is a directive approach in which leaders give clear instructions and guidance to followers, informing them exactly how and when to complete the task. This leadership style works best within environments that have high initiating structure and low consideration, where the completion of the task takes precedence over the relationship with employees. For example, in an emergency people would rather be told what to do to deal with the situation as quickly and safely as possible.
- **Selling** (S2). Leaders who adopt the selling style provide support to followers through communicating and "selling" the goals of the task to gain commitment. This style is appropriate for issues with high initiating structure and high consideration. For example, a leader of a sales team has to meet regular sales targets but also needs to foster a good relationship with the sales reps to motivate them to meet their goals.
- **Participating** (S3). Leaders and followers work together and share in the decision-making responsibilities of the task in the participating style. It works best in situations where there is low initiating structure and high consideration. For example, an employee may have picked up some skills on the job but needs more guidance to complete a task. In this case, the leader will include the follower in decisions and help develop their knowledge base.
- **Delegating** (S4). Leaders give most of the responsibility to followers in the delegating style yet still monitor progress. Delegating occurs in instances of low initiating structure and low consideration. For example, when employees are fully functional and skilled to complete a task, there is little need for leadership involvement.

Telling and selling are more task-oriented leadership styles, whereas participating and delegating are more focused on the development of team members' ability to work independently to complete the task.

But which leadership style is most appropriate? And how do leaders know which one to use? According to Hersey and Blanchard, the choice of leadership style depends on the willingness and ability of followers, in other words, their level of readiness to get the job done.

The Hersey–Blanchard model expands on previous theories by emphasizing the importance of the readiness or maturity of followers when completing a task. It also allows for greater flexibility in leadership behaviors when it comes to dealing with different types of people in the workforce.

House's Path–Goal Theory

Originally developed by Robert House in 1971, **path–goal leadership theory** suggests that leadership effectiveness is the degree to which the leader enhances the performance of followers by guiding them on a defined track toward achieving their goals.[38] Leaders can help followers by clarifying the routes they need to take to achieve their goals, removing obstacles, and providing incentives at certain milestones. The level of support and assistance provided to followers depends on the situation, the complexity of the task, and the motivational capabilities of the followers.

House describes how leadership effectiveness is influenced by the interaction among the four main leadership styles:

- **Directive leadership**. Leadership behavior characterized by implementing guidelines, managing expectations, setting definite performance standards, and ensuring that individuals follow rules. This type of leadership is appropriate in the military, where commands are expected to be followed immediately and without question.

- **Supportive leadership**. A type of leadership behavior characterized by friendliness and concern for the welfare of others. For example, a leader might work with followers struggling with a task until they feel empowered enough to carry out the task themselves.
- **Participative leadership**. Leadership behavior that consists of consulting with followers and considering their input in decision-making. For example, a marketing leader might gather their followers to collect input about the possibility of launching a new product or taking a product off the market.
- **Achievement-oriented leadership**. Leadership behavior characterized by setting challenging goals, improving performance, and assisting in employee training. This style of leadership is often used by football quarterbacks, who are expected to direct the team to perform certain plays at the right time to win the game.

According to House, certain styles of leadership may be more suitable in some situations than others to influence follower satisfaction, motivation for the task, and acceptance of the leader. There are two main situational contingencies:

- **Subordinate characteristics** such as anxiety, inflexibility, perceived ability, locus of control, and close-mindedness.
- **Task characteristics** outside the follower's control such as team dynamics, authority systems, and task structure.

The theory suggests that leaders can adjust their leadership styles to compensate for employee limitations. For example, a leader may take a supportive approach with a disgruntled employee in an effort to get to the root of the problem and find a resolution.

In contrast to the Fiedler contingency model, the path–goal model states that the four leadership styles are flexible, and that effective leaders can possess and adopt more than one style to help, motivate, and support their employees by removing obstacles on the path to achieving goals (see Figure 13.5). Unlike earlier theories, the path–goal model also offers specific suggestions for how leaders can help employees by taking into account relevant contingency factors such as employee characteristics and environmental factors.

Substitutes for Leadership Model

Although path–goal theory focuses on the centrality of the leadership role to employee satisfaction and work performance, the **substitutes for leadership model**[39] proposes that certain characteristics of individuals, the job, or the organization can act as substitutes for leadership or neutralize leadership impact altogether. In this context, **neutralizing** means replacing leadership attributes that do not affect followers' outcomes.

FIGURE 13.5 ■ Path-Goal Theory Model

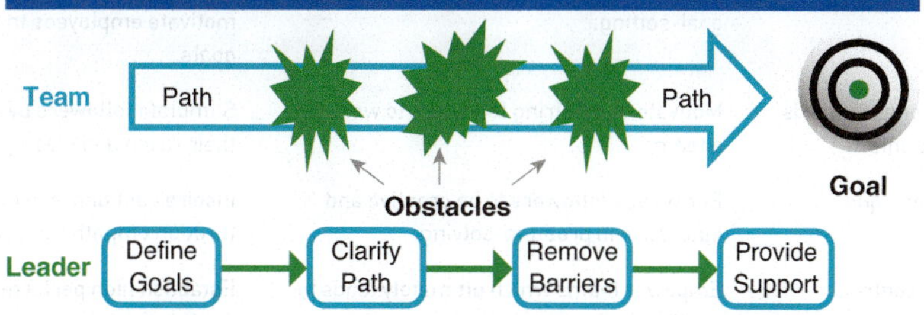

Sources: House, R. "Path-Goal Theory of Leadership: Lessons, Legacy, and a Reformulated Theory." *Leadership Quarterly* 7, no. 3 (1996): 323–352; model adapted from Northouse, P. G. *Leadership: Theory and Practice* (4th ed.) (SAGE, 2007): 128.

A team that is well run, experienced, and organized might substitute for or neutralize the need for a task-oriented leader because the team already knows how to carry out the requirements of their roles. For example, Dutch nursing organization Buurtzorg cultivates environments in which teams are largely left to manage themselves. Research has shown that Buurtzorg has the highest rates of employee satisfaction than any other Dutch company with over 1,000 employees.[40]

CONTEMPORARY LEADERSHIP PERSPECTIVES

Although early leadership perspectives enhanced our understanding of leadership and follower behavior, more recent inspirational and relational leadership perspectives have built on these theories to explain how leaders motivate and build relationships with followers to achieve performance beyond expectations. Popular contemporary perspectives include leader–member exchange (LMX), transformational leadership, and charismatic leadership (see Table 13.3).

Leader–Member Exchange (LMX) Theory

The **leader–member exchange (LMX) theory**[41] builds on the idea that leaders develop different relationships with different followers. The quality of the relationship determines whether the leader (often subconsciously) places the follower in the "in-group exchange" or the "out-group exchange" (see Figure 13.6).

- **In-group exchange**. Typically, team members who are loyal, trustworthy, and skilled have high-quality relationships with leaders. The leader devotes more attention to this in-group, assigns challenging tasks, and often spends more one-to-one time with members. People in this group are given more opportunities for growth and advancement and often mirror the leader's work ethic and characteristics.
- **Out-group exchange**. People who are perceived to be incompetent, unmotivated, untrustworthy team members have low-quality relationships with their leaders. Leaders tend to assign simple, limited tasks to this group, communicate with them only when necessary, and often withhold opportunities for growth or advancement.

LMX theory demonstrates the dangers of overclassifying individuals. Once an individual is in the out-group and the leader's perception of that person has been sealed, it is almost impossible to change that perception, and often the individual has no recourse but to leave the team or organization. Leaders need to nurture all relationships with their followers to draw out everyone's best efforts and achieve organizational success.

TABLE 13.3 ■ Differences Between Transactional, Transformational, and Charismatic Leaders

Transactional Leaders	Transformational Leaders	Charismatic Leaders
Set goals for followers.	Involve followers in collaborative goal-setting.	Use charm and personality to motivate employees to achieve goals.
Motivate through rewards and punishments.	Motivate by inspiring followers to work as a team.	Stimulate followers by sharing their vision and ideology.
Maintain status quo.	Encourage followers to be creative and innovative in problem-solving.	Inspire confidence in followers through empathy and support.
Monitor and control.	Empower teams which ultimately leads to employee engagement.	Establish high performance expectations.
Work within an existing organizational culture.	Work toward changing an organizational culture by implementing new initiatives.	

FIGURE 13.6 ■ LMX Theory

Source: Gupta, A. (2009, June 6). Leader member exchange. *Practical Management.* http://practical-management.com/pdf/Leadership-Development/Leader-Member-Exchange.pdf?format=phocapdf. Copyright © practical-management.com.

Transformational Leadership

Transformational leadership is a leadership style that inspires followers to transcend their self-interests for the good of the organization and commit to a shared vision. Transformational leadership is becoming an increasingly popular model for today's leaders. Amazon CEO Jeff Bezos, media mogul Oprah Winfrey, and Satya Nadella CEO of Microsoft, are good examples of transformational leaders who have transformed their companies by inspiring their teams to achieve goals.[42] The four dimensions of transformational leadership are[43]

- **Idealized influence** (also referred to as *charisma*) is behavior that gains the admiration, trust, and respect of followers.
- **Inspirational motivation** promotes commitment to a shared vision of the future.
- **Intellectual stimulation** encourages people to view problems from a different perspective and to think about innovative and alternative ways to address them.
- **Individualized consideration** creates mutual respect or trust and a genuine concern for the needs and desires of others.

In direct opposition to transformational leadership is **laissez-faire leadership**, in which a leader fully delegates responsibility to others.[44] This type of leader has little involvement with followers, almost no control over the task, and little interest in making decisions unless forced into it. Investor Warren Buffett is an example of a laissez-faire leader, who gives management teams the freedom to make decisions and take risks rather than closely monitoring them like many other CEOs.[45]

Charismatic Leadership

Transformational leadership theory was inspired by Max Weber's concept of **charismatic leadership**, which is the ability of a leader to use their personality or charm to inspire, motivate, and acquire loyalty and commitment from employees.[46]

Charismatic leaders are similar to transformational leaders in that they both use inspirational techniques to energize and motivate their followers. They can certainly use their exceptional leadership skills for good. However, though transformational leaders are focused on the best interests of the individuals and the organization, charismatic leaders may place more emphasis on their own needs and interests[47] and become caught up in their own hype. Leaders who follow their own agendas become inflexible, believe they can do no wrong, and tend to dismiss advice from others if it diverges from their own convictions. Osama Bin Laden, Saudi terrorist and founder of militant organization al-Qaeda is an example of a charismatic leader who inspired devotion in others to carry out an extreme political agenda—to horrifying and tragic results.

In addition, serious repercussions can occur when charismatic leaders become convinced of their own infallibility—their followers may also buy into this belief and perceive such leaders as invincible. The danger is that followers will relate their own personal job satisfaction and the success of the organization directly to the presence of the leader. In this situation, the departure of a charismatic leader can have a devastating effect on followers. Therefore, the charismatic leader needs to be an appropriate role model for followers.

Follower-Centered Leadership Perspective

Recently, researchers have begun to explore a more follower-centered approach that focuses less on different types of leaders and their behaviors. **Followership** is the capacity of individuals to cooperate with leaders.[48] The theory that studies it stems from cognitive categorization theory, which explores the idea that people tend to label others on the basis of a first impression.[49]

The follower-centered leadership perspective focuses on how followers view leaders and how they view themselves. There are two types of theories in this approach: implicit leadership theories, and implicit followership theories.

According to **implicit leadership theories**, we have a natural tendency to apply traits and attributes to others to determine whether they are leaders.[50] Relevant traits and attributes include charismatic, attractive, intelligent, dedicated, tyrannical, and strong. These traits are called **leadership prototypes** and are behaviors we associate with leadership.[51]

Implicit followership theories are preconceived notions about the types of behaviors that leaders believe characterize followers and nonfollowers.[52] Common prototypes ascribed to good followers included enthusiasm, industriousness, and being a good citizen. Ineffective or nonfollowers are characterized as easily influenced, lacking humility, lacking experience, working slowly, and behaving unprofessionally. Like LMX theory, followership theories show that opinions based on first impressions or very quick judgments can prejudice our views of others and create negativity within groups.

Although transformational and empowering leadership approaches may dominate today's views on leadership, a number of cutting-edge perspectives are quickly gaining ground. Recent theorists have criticized directive leaders for using fear as a motivator, questioned the "carrot-and-stick" methodology of transactional leadership, and argued that transformational leaders may impede independent thinking in followers.

It may be impossible to wrap the constituents of leadership into a neat package. Perhaps, however, we can conclude from the evolution of leadership theories that different situations require different kinds of leaders. Next we focus on emerging leadership perspectives, and how they enhance the skills and improve the effectiveness of 21st-century leaders.

POWER-DISTRIBUTING LEADERSHIP PERSPECTIVES

The concept of "distributed leadership" has grown in popularity over the past few years and serves as an alternative to those theories that have focused on leadership traits, characteristics, and behaviors. Instead, distributed leadership calls for sharing the power and influence within organizations. Let's return to our narrative to further explore the three main facets of power-distributing leadership: empowering, shared, and self-leadership.

Bill Gates demonstrated empowering leadership by encouraging employees to share their ideas, innovate, and build on their strengths.

Luke Sharrett/Bloomberg via Getty Images

Empowering Leadership

Empowering leadership is the practice of delegating power that motivates employees and inspires them to achieve goals.[53] Monty Moran, former co-CEO of Chipotle Mexican Grill believes that leaders who empower employees through connection, inspire through a vision, instill confidence in workers, and are full transparent with knowledge and information have the ability to create a happier workforce. Moran said, "When people feel confident, encouraged, and motivated, they are happier, more motivated, and more effective at their jobs. They become the best version of themselves while performing at their full potential."[54]

Empowering leadership is similar to participative leadership, in which leaders allow their employees to partake in decision-making processes and provide them with the resources and support to carry out their roles. Empowering leaders encourage their employees to act independently and make decisions without the presence of a formal leader. Here are some of the behaviors they use:

- **Leading by example.** Empowering leaders inspire their employees by influencing others by exhibiting positive behaviors in and outside the workplace. For example, Sara Blakely, CEO of women's underwear maker Spanx, donated $5 million in personal funds to support female entrepreneurs operating small businesses that had been impacted by the COVID-19 pandemic. Blakey's mentee Brian Towey said, "Leading by example includes recognizing that others may not be in the same fortunate position as you and doing everything possible to help . . . [Blakely] has shown that empathy and kindness are the two most important qualities during these times."[55]
- **Coaching.** Empowering leaders take active steps to educate and train their employees so they can become more independent. Studies show that good coaching can increase team effectiveness, productivity, and self-awareness.[56]
- **Participative decision-making.** Empowering leaders encourage employees to make decisions and express their opinions. For example, worldwide clothing and accessories retailer Gap Inc.

empowers their employees by giving them the autonomy to make decisions and to speak up and take action on any issues they may have.[57]

- **Informing.** Empowering leaders keep their employees up to date with company information and goals. For example, social media management tool Buffer has fostered a culture of transparency and makes sure its employees are kept well informed about big organizational changes. Transparency is one of Buffer's core values and is key to building trust within its remote workforce.[58]
- **Showing concern**. Empowering leaders take an interest in the well-being of their employees and treat them with respect. Studies show that employees who experienced empathy from their leaders were more engaged, innovative, and felt more capable of meeting the demands of personal, family, and work duties, compared with those workplaces with less empathetic leadership.[59]

Shared Leadership

Shared leadership distributes influence among groups and individuals to achieve organizational or team goals.[60] Rather than being solely responsible for decision-making, the leader shares responsibility with the group as members strive to achieve common goals (see Figure 13.7).

Shared leadership is becoming more frequent in-patient care and top management teams. For shared leadership to be effective, employees must share the same vision and goals, be provided with the right resources to carry out their tasks, maintain similar levels of knowledge and skills, work in a collaborative environment that fosters trust and cooperation, and be flexible enough to adapt to changing conditions. Recent research shows that teams with shared leadership experience less conflict, more cohesion, and higher levels of trust than teams that not have shared leadership.[61]

FIGURE 13.7 ■ Traditional Leadership versus Shared Leadership

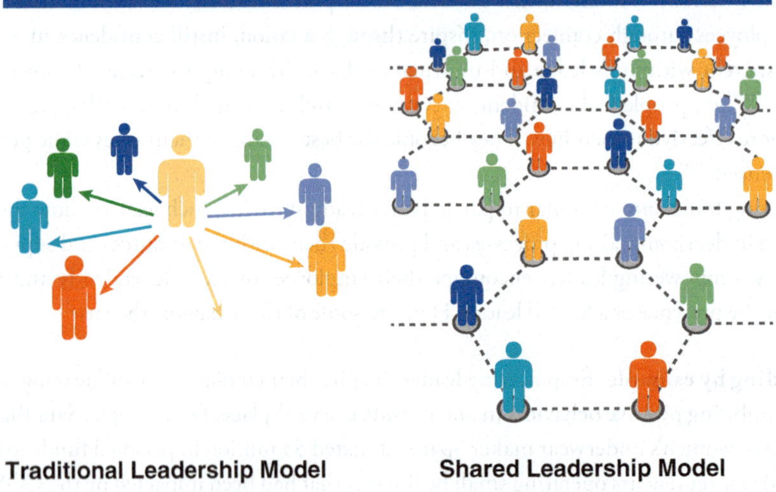

EXAMINING THE EVIDENCE

EMPOWERING LEADERSHIP: THE PARADOX OF SIMULTANEOUSLY MAINTAINING AND LETTING GO OF CONTROL

Empowering leadership involves sharing power and decision-making authority in ways that motivate employees to achieve goals and work autonomously. However, leadership scholars have noted that empowering leadership involves a paradox of giving up power to followers while still training to maintain influence over them. A recent study published in the journal *Organizational Behavior and Human Decision Processes* by Eric Kearneya, Meir Shemlab, Daan van Knippenberg, and Florian A. Scholz addresses this paradox.[62] Their findings suggest that visionary leadership and empowering leadership are synergistic and that leaders will be more effective when they engage in visionary leadership and empowering leadership simultaneously, adopting a "both-and" approach rather than using one approach or the other separately. More specifically, the study showed that using visionary leadership and empowering leadership together enhances follower goal clarity and ultimately follower performance. In short, this research suggests that leaders may be most effective when they present their followers with a clear, inspirational vision (visionary leadership) while also working to motivate followers to carefully consider and take ownership of the vision as it relates to their own work (empowering leadership).

Critical-Thinking Questions

1. How difficult is it to simultaneously engage in visionary and empowering leadership? What challenges might leaders face in trying to use both approaches at the same time?
2. Give some specific examples of how a leader could be visionary and empowering simultaneously.

Self-Leadership

Both empowering and shared leadership facilitate and encourage self-leadership. **Self-leadership** is a process through which people intentionally influence their thinking and behavior to achieve their objectives.[63] In other words, people can deliberately guide themselves toward attaining favorable outcomes. Examples of self-leadership behaviors include self-awareness, inclusion, mindfulness, empathy, and social intelligence. Author and management expert Ken Blanchard uses self-leadership techniques to remove constraints, identify points of power, and collaborate with others.[64] There are three main categories of self-leadership strategies.[65]

Behavior-focused strategies are targeted toward increasing our self-awareness and managing our own conduct. They include self-observation, self-goal setting, self-reward, self-correcting feedback, and self-cueing.[66] Self-observation entails analyzing our own behaviors for the purposes of identifying those that need to be adjusted, enhanced, or eliminated altogether. For example, setting goals that challenge us motivates us to achieve them. Self-reward helps us motivate ourselves and improve performance by mentally praising our own achievements and giving ourselves positive feedback and corrections. Self-cueing strategies, such as writing to-do lists or keeping an efficient record of information, helps to focus our attention on assigned tasks.

Natural reward strategies help us to find pleasure in certain aspects of our roles, leading to an enhanced sense of competence, self-discipline, and application.[67] For example, if you are given a particularly tedious assignment, you could decide to complete the most onerous part of the task first before turning your attention to the more rewarding part. Even external reward strategies can make a difference in the way we work. For example, adding personal touches to your desk can have a calming effect when work becomes frustrating.

Constructive thought pattern strategies focus on the modification of certain key mental processes.[68] That is, the more positive and optimistic our thinking patterns, the better our work performance. Mental imagery is one strategy we can use to shape our thought processes by visualizing the successful attainment of the goal before we begin. This is a common technique among top athletes; for example, 18-gold-medal Olympic swimmer Michael Phelps used mental imagery to succeed. Coach Bob Bowman described how Phelps used visualization to gain advantage: "For months before a race Michael gets into a relaxed state. He mentally rehearses for two hours a day in the pool. He sees himself winning. He smells the air, tastes the water, hears the sounds, sees the clock."[69]

VALUES-BASED LEADERSHIP PERSPECTIVES

Following the economic, political, and societal turbulence over the last few years, there has been a shift from power-based leadership to values-based leadership. Values-based leaders act in concert with a set of principles to equip others with the right tools to unleash their potential so that they can act for the greater good.[70] There are four types of values-based leadership: authentic, spiritual, servant, and ethical.

Authentic Leadership

Authentic leadership is a pattern of leadership behavior based on honesty, practicality, and ethicality.[71] Support for this type of leadership has been gaining ground as a reaction to the number of corporate scandals and blunders made by high-profile leaders.

Authentic leaders find their "true north" or moral compass, they are more focused on empowering their employees, forming meaningful relationships, and fostering an ethical environment.[72] Authentic leadership has been associated with improved job performance, increased job satisfaction, greater trust in the leader–follower relationship, and organizational commitment.[73] Marriott International CEO Arne Sorenson is a good example of an authentic leader. During COVID-19 when face-to-face communication was not possible, Sorenson released a video, speaking honestly and openly about the crisis, empathizing with employees, and reassuring them that they will always come first. Sorenson won huge acclaim for the speech by being genuine, humble, candid, emotional, and hopeful for the future.[74]

Spiritual Leadership

Spiritual leadership is a values-based style of leadership that motivates employees through faith, hope, and vision and encourages positive social emotions such as forgiveness and gratitude.[75] The concept of spirituality is not necessarily connected with religion; rather it is communicated in the workplace through shared values, attitudes, and behaviors. Spiritual leaders use their charisma to unite followers and to encourage them to view their roles as an opportunity for growth and meaningful contribution. Research shows that spiritual leadership has a positive impact on organizational commitment and productivity and helps align employees to the company's vision and values.[76]

Servant Leadership

Servant leadership is a pattern of leadership that places an emphasis on employees and the community rather than on the leader.[77] Servant leaders share their power and tend to "lead from behind," ensuring

Richard Murphy's legacy of servant leadership lives on in successful programs like the Harlem Children's Zone in New York, providing services for children and families in need.

Frances Roberts / Alamy Stock Photo

the team (not the leader) receives recognition for hard work. They are usually empathic, good listeners, perceptive, and committed to growth in the organization and the community. New research shows that servant leadership improves morale and increases company profit.[78] Melissa Reiff, former CEO of specialty retail chain The Container Store is a good example of a servant leader. Reiff demonstrated servant leadership by sharing information with every single employee to ensure they feel fully included in the company. Reiff said, "Nothing makes someone feel more a part of a team than knowing everything has been communicated to them. We know that some information we share could fall into competitors' hands, but the advantages far outweigh the risks."[79]

Ethical Leadership

Ethical leadership is a means of influencing others through personal values, morals, and beliefs.[80] By following their own values as well as the organization's values, ethical leaders are role models for ethical conduct. They communicate honestly and openly about the importance of ethical behavior and hold their followers accountable for failing to uphold organizational values, often rewarding those who consistently demonstrate ethical behavior. Typically, they are fair, honest, principled people who excel at making fair, balanced decisions and who practice what they preach. Dan Amos, chairman and CEO of American Insurance Company, Aflac—a 15-time recipient of Ethisphere's World's Most Ethical Companies award—is an ethical leader who believes that "ethics is a mindset, not an option."[81]

CROSS-CULTURAL LEADERSHIP

All leaders, regardless of the leadership style, must be able to lead multicultural teams. **Cross-cultural leadership** is the process of leading across different cultures.[82] Many companies and organizations of all sizes employ people from different cultural backgrounds, have branches in other countries, outsource parts of their business abroad, or use foreign suppliers. The rise of remote working has further removed geographical boundaries thereby enabling leaders to work more collaboratively with a globalized workforce. For 21st-century leaders to lead effectively, they need to be proficient at managing people from different cultural backgrounds, in the office and remotely. Leaders who are mindful of cultural norms, encourage greater collaboration between cross-border teams, and maintain regular contact with overseas leaders have a higher chance of cultivating a successful multinational company culture.[83] Joshua Zerkel Head of Global Engagement Marketing at Asana, a San Francisco company that designs tools to improve work collaboration, leads Asana's global marketing team comprising of 14 members across five countries. According to Zerkel, building a personal understanding of different cultures and communication styles is the key to cross-cultural team success: "I can say with 100% certainty that most places and most people do not function in the way folks in San Francisco do. Even though I'm used to the way we communicate in San Francisco, it's important to remember that not all of my teammates are."[84]

Project Globe

Project GLOBE (Global Leadership and Organizational Behavior Effectiveness) is the largest research study to date on cross-cultural leadership.[85] Conducted over the course of eleven years, the project surveyed 17,300 managers from 951 organizations, in 62 societal cultures, and relied on about 140 country coinvestigators. It concluded that individuals from different cultures or "societal clusters" associate certain sets of beliefs or preconceived notions with leaders. This is in line with *implicit leadership theory* or ILT, which explains our tendency as individuals to assign personality characteristics, skills, and behaviors to certain leaders. Our personal belief systems (also referred to as prototypes, mental models, and stereotypes) are thus thought to influence the extent to which we accept leaders. The GLOBE project researchers wanted to discover whether societal and organizational culture has a bearing on how people perceive leadership. In short, they tested the same concept as ILT but on a universal level.

The key findings of the GLOBE project centered around six global leadership attributes perceived by businesspeople worldwide to either contribute to or inhibit leadership; these are known as *culturally endorsed leadership theory* or CLT.[86]

The six dimensions of the CLT leadership profiles are[87]

- **Charismatic/value based**. This dimension captures the leader's capacity to inspire, motivate, and expect high performance outcomes from others. All cultures believed this CLT profile to be a key contributor to outstanding leadership.
- **Team oriented**. Team orientation highlights effective team building and the implementation of a common purpose or goal among team members. Again, all cultures surveyed found this dimension to be a major contributor to outstanding leadership.
- **Participative**. This CLT describes the extent to which managers engage others in making and implementing decisions.
- **Humane oriented**. The leadership dimension that signifies supportive, considerate, compassionate, and generous leadership was thought to be only a moderate contributor to outstanding leadership across all the cultures.
- **Autonomous**. This CLT describes independent and individualistic leadership. Unlike the other dimensions, autonomous leadership is thought to impede or only slightly facilitate outstanding leadership.
- **Self-protective.** This leadership dimension describes the self-interests of the leader in terms of face-saving, safety, and security and is generally reported to inhibit outstanding leadership.

The findings of GLOBE's empirical study have improved our knowledge of what professionals across 62 societies perceive to be the key contributors to outstanding leadership. This evidence is essential to today's leaders who will be expected to exhibit cross-cultural skills in most aspects of their roles.

LEADERSHIP AND GENDER

Gender inequality remains a source of much discussion and debate. In Chapter 2 Diversity, Equity and Inclusion (DEI) we discussed the gender pay gap, inequality in hiring practices, and the difficulty women experience in breaking through the glass ceiling to progress to more senior positions. Although more women are achieving leadership positions, there is no doubt that in the United States and other countries they are still underrepresented in the higher levels of organizations. As of September 2021, there were 26 women leaders serving as heads of state or in leadership positions in government in 24 countries.[88] History shows that there has never been a female leader as president. In the business world, there are 74 women CEOs in the Fortune 500 which translates to just 15% of the female representation at the biggest companies in the United States.[89]

Studies show that women are more likely to lead democratically, be a role model, listen to others, show transformational leadership, and display more humility, emotional intelligence, and moral sensitivity than men.[90] If women have more potential as leaders, then why are they still so unrepresented in organizations and other institutions? Research suggests that gender inequality in organizations is due to several likely causes.[91]

Leadership style and expectations. Some studies suggest that men and women differ in their overall leadership styles. Men tend to be autocratic while women employ a more transformational style.[92] Given widespread expectations of leaders employing more traditionally masculine styles of leadership, women may be perceived as less suited for leadership positions. In cases where women do embrace more autocratic styles, however, they may be perceived more negatively than a man displaying similar characteristics. More of today's leaders, regardless of gender, are adopting a participative approach to leadership because it is considered to be more effective. This trend may help to accelerate the promotion of more women to leadership positions.

Family and career demands. The burden of balancing domestic and child and elder care responsibilities with work falls heavily on women.[93] In fact, the United States is the only developed country in

FIGURE 13.8 ■ Maternity Leave Policies Around the World

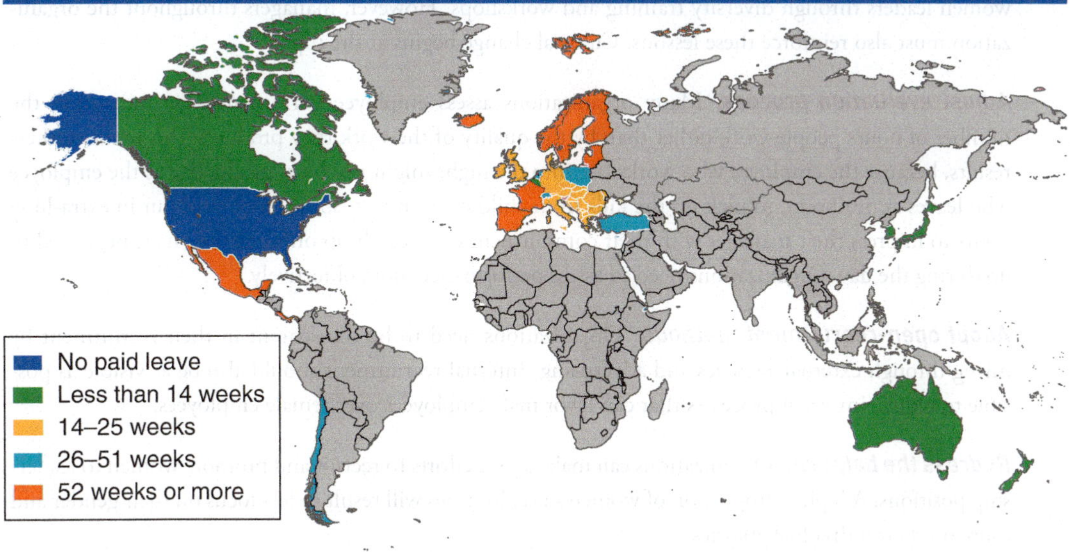

the world that doesn't guarantee paid maternal leave. As Figure 13.8 shows, it shares this policy only with Papua New Guinea, Suriname, and five small Pacific Island nations.[94] However, in 2022, the Biden administration pushed for its proposal to provide 12 weeks of paid parental leave nationwide. If the proposal becomes policy, it will be a major development in the issue of paid leave.[95]

Studies also find that employers may elect not to assign more challenging tasks to women because of assumed domestic responsibilities.[96] Less challenging work assignments generally result in fewer promotions and contribute to the glass ceiling effect discussed in Chapter 2. A recent survey found that women were significantly more likely to feel that taking maternity leave had a negative impact on their career, yet only a small number of men reported the same experience following paternity leave.[97] This research highlights the need to address gender equality in parental leave.

Professional networks. Another line of research suggests that women who juggle familial and work duties have less time for socializing with colleagues and building professional networks.[98] When career advancement depends largely on who you know, inability to network can be a drag on advancement. However, even when women devote time to building relationships outside work, they may still face an uphill struggle—many of the most powerful and instrumental organizational networks are composed of men who typically engage in male-bonding activities. For example, in 2021 a gender discrimination lawsuit was filed against Sony Playstation by nine women employees claiming that the company allegedly promoted male-oriented activities such as visiting strip clubs during lunchtime, ranking female colleagues on their appearance, and sharing inappropriate jokes and images of women.[99]

Discrimination and stereotypes. Discrimination and stereotypical views of women may provide barriers to advancement.[100] Over the decades, numerous sexual harassment cases have been brought in which women have been passed over for promotion in favor of their male counterparts, and many more instances have gone unreported. Tesla has been sued for failing to address sexual harassment claims made by women employees. Tesla CEO Elon Musk has also been criticized for inappropriate behavior such as dubbing a line of cars "S3XY" after the Models S, 3, X and Y. Former Tesla worker Eden Mederos believed that Musk's lewd comments seemed to directly influence the behavior of male colleagues: "He would make 69 or 420 jokes . . . which caused the technicians to be even worse."[101]

How Organizations Can Support Women Leaders

Organizations can play a big part in addressing gender inequality by altering the attitudes and perceptual distortions of women in the workplace.

For example, they can

Eliminate prejudice. Organizations can raise awareness of the stereotypes and prejudices toward women leaders through diversity training and workshops. However, managers throughout the organization must also reinforce these lessons. Cultural change begins at the top.

Adjust evaluation process. Many organizations assess employee performance by measuring the number of hours people work rather than by the quality of the work they produce. This tends to skew results, because the employee who works late into the night might not be as productive as the employee who leaves at 5:00 p.m. to pick up the kids from child care. In fact, some employees put in extra-long hours to impress their manager with their commitment or to catch up on work they have neglected to do during the day. Organizations need to assess performance more objectively.

Adopt open-recruitment methods. Organizations need to be transparent in their recruitment by hiring through external agencies and advertising. Internal recruitment should also be as visible as possible to reduce informal processes that can favor male employees over female employees.

Redress the balance. Organizations can make active efforts to recruit and promote women to leadership positions. A higher proportion of women in senior roles will result in less focus on their gender and more on their individual abilities.

Encourage networking. Socializing and network building are key to career advancement. Organizations can provide more opportunities for informal socializing and encourage all employees to participate. They can also establish mentoring programs to help women take advantage of networking opportunities and create new ones.

Provide management opportunities. If organizations do not provide an opportunity for employees to develop the skills and knowledge required for promotion, employees will find it difficult to advance to the next level. They may instead be forced to change companies to find more challenging roles with broader responsibility and better compensation.

Establish family-friendly practices. The high cost of full-time child care can work out to more than an average working salary, leading many working parents to question the point of having one parent work at all. More women are leaving traditional organizations to pursue entrepreneurial ventures or to work for more flexible companies that allow employees to create their own hours. However, organizations can encourage both parents to stay in the traditional workforce by providing flextime, job sharing, telecommuting, child care benefits, and on-site child care. Allowing both parents to work more flexible hours helps them balance the vigorous demands of children with a working life. Insurance company Zurich experienced a 16% increase in job applications from men and women after it advertised part-time, job-share, or flexible roles.[102]

Encourage men to use family-friendly benefits. Although parental leave and part-time work provide valuable support to mothers, taking advantage of them can also delay career progression. To even the playing field, organizations should encourage men to choose these options if desired, giving more women the opportunity to access managerial roles.

Allow time to achieve. Some organizations expect employees to ascend the career ladder at a rapid pace and ask those who do not keep up—often those with parental responsibilities—to leave. This is not to say employees with children are not capable of performing as well as those without children; they are simply unable to put in the same hours. Firms should capitalize on their initial investment in employees by giving the parents of young children—especially young mothers, who typically bear greater childcare responsibilities—more time to prove themselves and achieve promotion.

Have women mentor men. Mentoring is a valuable way for people to help others progress in their careers. Research shows that women mentoring men could benefit both parties as each party would have the opportunity to learn about different working and leadership styles.[103] Cindi Schipani, professor of business law at the University of Michigan said, "We're hoping that if we encourage more women mentoring men, maybe we can generate more empathy, more co-operation and just more willingness to see each other as people and to work for everybody's success."[104]

Keep the door open. Organizations should stay in touch with high-performing women who leave their roles because of changing personal circumstances. Keeping the lines of communication with former employees open conveys a message that it is still possible to return to work if and when the situation allows.

Although more progress is needed, organizations clearly have a variety of options for fostering a more gender diverse workforce. Achieving more representative numbers of women in leadership positions will encourage nuanced assessments of individual leadership styles.

While there may be a large and varied set of theories surrounding leadership, we still do not have a set definition. However, these theories help us to separate good leaders from bad, and further our understanding of what effective leadership really means. While leadership styles tend to vary according to the context or the situation, we would argue that someone who uses critical thinking, leads from a position of influence, cultivates a culture of diversity, equity and inclusion, and uses decision-making and motivational skills to inspire others, is likely to be an effective leader.

IN REVIEW

13.1 Explain the basic concept of leadership

Leadership is a process of providing general direction, from a position of influence, to individuals or groups toward the successful attainment of goals. Effective leaders lead from a position of influence rather than power, and use their decision-making, motivational, communication, and critical-thinking skills to inspire others with their vision to generate results. **Leader emergence** occurs when someone naturally becomes the leader of a leaderless group.

13.2 Distinguish between formal and informal leadership and between leadership and management

Within most organizations there are two types of leaders: formal and informal. A **formal leader** is a person officially designated by the organization. An **informal leader** is a person who does not receive a title but is perceived by others as a leader. Both leaders and managers work with people, set goals, and influence others to achieve those goals, but several distinctions separate the two functions.

13.3 Contrast the four basic types of leadership

Today's leaders tend to choose between four distinct types of leadership behavior based on the work environment and overall goals of the organization. **Directive leadership** is characterized by implementing guidelines, providing information on what is expected, setting definite performance standards, and ensuring that individuals follow rules. **Transactional leadership** is a behavioral type of leadership that proposes that employees are motivated by goals and equitable rewards. **Visionary leadership** uses charisma to encourage followers to share in the mission and commit to and work toward the desired goal. **Empowering leadership** shifts the focus from the leader to the follower through the idea of self-leadership.

13.4 Describe the trait, behavioral, and contingency leadership perspectives

The **trait leadership perspective** explores the relationship between leaders and personal qualities and characteristics, and how we differentiate leaders from nonleaders. It assumes effective leaders are born, not made. The **behavioral leadership perspective** proposes that specific behaviors distinguish leaders from nonleaders. Subsequently, the **contingency leadership perspective** suggests the effectiveness of the leader relates to the interaction of the leader's traits or behaviors and situational factors.

13.5 Compare the inspirational, relational, and follower-centered leadership perspectives

Popular contemporary perspectives include **leader–member exchange (LMX)** a theory that builds on the idea that leaders develop different relationships with different followers, **Transformational leadership** a leadership style that inspires followers to transcend their self-interests for the good of the organization and commit to a shared vision, and charismatic leadership, and **charismatic leadership** the ability of a leader to use their personality or charm to inspire, motivate, and acquire loyalty and commitment from employees.

13.6 Discuss the power-distributing leadership perspectives of empowering, shared, and self-leadership

Empowering leadership gives or delegates power to employees that motivates and inspires them to achieve goals. **Shared leadership** distributes influence among groups and individuals to achieve organizational or team goals, or both. **Self-leadership** is a process through which people intentionally influence their thinking and behavior to achieve their objectives, using behavior-focused strategies, natural reward strategies, and constructive thought pattern strategies.

13.7 Describe the values-based leadership perspectives of authentic, spiritual, servant, and ethical leadership

Authentic leadership is a pattern of leadership behavior based on honesty, practicality, and ethicality. **Spiritual leadership** is a values-based style of leadership that motivates employees through faith, hope, and vision and encourages positive social emotions such as forgiveness and gratitude. **Servant leadership** emphasizes employees and the community rather than the leader. **Ethical leadership** is the influence of others through personal values, morals, and beliefs.

13.8 Discuss leadership across cultures

Cross-cultural leadership is the process of leading across different cultures. The key findings of the GLOBE project centered around six global leadership attributes: (1) charismatic/value based, (2) team oriented, (3) participative, (4) humane oriented, (5) autonomous, and (6) self-protective.

13.9 Identify gender issues in the context of leadership

Although more women are achieving leadership positions, they are still underrepresented in higher levels of organizations around the world. Factors that contribute to gender inequality include: leadership style and expectations, family and career demands, lack of access to professional networks, and discrimination and stereotypes.

KEY TERMS

Participating (p. 310)
Participative leadership (p. 311)
Path–goal leadership theory (p. 310)
Production-oriented leader (p. 304)
Self-leadership (p. 317)
Selling (p. 310)
Servant leadership (p. 318)
Shared leadership (p. 316)
Situational leadership model (p. 310)
Spiritual leadership (p. 318)
Subordinate characteristics (p. 311)
Substitutes for leadership model (p. 311)
Supportive leadership (p. 311)
Task characteristics (p. 311)
Task structure (p. 308)
Telling (p. 310)
Trait leadership perspective (p. 305)
Transactional leadership (p. 304)
Transformational leadership (p. 313)
Visionary leadership (p. 304)

UP FOR DEBATE: LEADERSHIP CULTURE

Most employees would prefer to work in an organization that demonstrates an empowering leadership culture as opposed to a more directive one. Agree or Disagree?

EXERCISE 13.1: IDENTIFYING TYPES OF LEADERSHIP

Objective

The purpose of this exercise is to be able to identify the four basic types of leaders.

Instructions

Your text identifies four types of leaders:

- **Directive leadership**—leadership style characterized by implementing guidelines, managing expectations, setting definite performance standards, and ensuring that individuals follow rules
- **Transactional leadership**—a behavioral type of leadership that proposes that employees are motivated by goals and equitable rewards
- **Visionary leadership**—a behavioral type of leadership that creates visions to motivate, inspire, and stimulate employees
- **Empowering leadership**—a behavioral type of leadership that empowers leaders to help develop the individual skills and abilities of their followers

The instructor will ask for eight to 12 volunteers from the class for a series of role-plays (two to three participants for each type of leader). Each group of participants will be given one of the four leadership types above. Then, each group will take 5 to 10 minutes to devise a scenario or skit that demonstrates that particular type of leader. For example, one group will create a role-play demonstrating directive leadership, another, transactional leadership, and so on.

The student volunteers will then take turns performing their role-play in front of the class.

The remaining students will attempt to guess which type of leadership is being shown based upon the words and interactions of the students at the front of the room. Students should write down their opinion as to which type of leadership is shown and the correct identification is not given until all four groups of students have completed their skit.

Reflection Questions

1. For each group of students, how could you tell which type of leader was being demonstrated? What cues or clues were given that showcased that particular type of leader?
2. Which of the four types of leaders is your current or most recent supervisor? Explain.
3. What type of leader do you think of yourself as? Why?
4. What type of leader would you like to be in the future? Why?
5. Exercise contributed by Steven Stovall, Southeast Missouri State University.

EXERCISE 13.2: LEADERSHIP JOLT

Objectives

This exercise will help you to better explain basic leadership concepts.

Instructions

While standing in line and talking about your organizational behavior class with some friends at a local coffee house, the person in front of you overhears and asks you a question about leadership. She is the head of a moderate-size, but extremely well-connected office supply company and wants to improve the leadership of her managers. She asks you what the most important leadership concept is for making improvements in workplace outcomes, and also says that many other CEOs she knows would be interested in having a presentation on the same subject. She turns around to pay for and pick up her order, so you have a few minutes to collect your thoughts. But you also know that she will not have too long to listen to your idea, and this is your chance to make some very good contacts for your future career.

Step 1. Choose the leadership concept you feel is the most useful for improving workplace outcomes. Write an overview of this concept, what outcomes can be improved by adopting the leadership behavior, and why it is practical to try and model the leadership behavior. (5 minutes)

Step 2. Be prepared to present your description to the class. (1 to 3 minutes)

Reflection Questions

1. How did framing a description of a leadership concept in terms of a persuasive presentation change your view of the concept?
2. What new insights did you gain from having to make such a succinct overview of the concept?
3. What new ways of applying the concept did you discover through this process?
4. What surprised you most about your classmates' presentations?

Exercise contributed by Milton R. Mayfield, Professor of Business, Texas A&M International University, and Jacqueline R. Mayfield, Professor of Business, Texas A&M International University.

EXERCISE 13.3: THE CHALLENGE OF LEADERSHIP

Objectives

Successful completion of this exercise will help you to better explain basic leadership concepts and distinguish between formal and informal leadership.

Instructions

Step 1. Select a person that you feel is (or was) a leader in an organization, but did not have a formal leadership position. (This person should be someone that you have had personal interactions with.) Develop an argument about why that person was a leader using chapter concepts and terms. In your description, make sure that you describe the circumstances and environment relevant to this person's informal leadership role. (5 minutes)

Step 2. Find two other people and select one person to act as a judge. (If no one wants to volunteer, select the person who has had the most recent birthday.) Have each of the contestants present their argument for the selected person being an informal leader. If someone selects a person who actually holds a formal leadership role, that person is automatically disqualified. Otherwise, judge the arguments based on how well the argument is supported with chapter concepts.

The judge should award each person 1 point for every argument that is supported by a relevant chapter concept. If no concept is used for support, or if a concept is used incorrectly, then the person has one point deducted from their score. After each person has had a chance to present their argument, then the judge should tally the scores. Whoever has the highest score wins. In case of a tie, the winner is the person who has the highest proportion of supported arguments to total arguments. (10 to 15 minutes)

Step 3. The judge should be prepared to present the winning person's argument to the class. (5 minutes)

Reflection Questions

1. What new insights did you learn about informal leadership?
2. Did you notice any recurring circumstances that lead to someone becoming an informal leader?
3. What were the aspects of informal leadership that surprised you?

Exercise contributed by Milton R. Mayfield, Professor of Business, Texas A&M International University, and Jacqueline R. Mayfield, Professor of Business, Texas A&M International University.

ONLINE EXERCISE 13.1: ASSESSING LEADERSHIP OF A CEO

Objective

The purpose of this exercise is to gain an appreciation for current business leaders.

Instructions

Conduct an online search of a current CEO or president of a large for-profit company. Once you have identified this individual, learn as much as you can about them through further online research. Based upon what you discover, write a two- to three-page paper for your instructor where you assess the following:

- How long has this person been with this company? Did they become president by working up to that position from lower ranks within the company or arrive at the position from outside the firm?
- Discuss the person's ability to manage versus ability to lead.
- Which of the four basic types of leadership is this president (directive, transactional, visionary, or empowering)?
- Would this person be considered a charismatic leader? Why or why not?

Reflection Questions

1. How did you choose a CEO for this assignment? What criteria did you use in your selection?
2. Without personally knowing this individual, describe the difficulty of this assignment.
3. If you were to conduct this same analysis of your current or previous manager, what would your analysis state about this person?
4. What if you were to conduct this same analysis of yourself? What would be your response for each question?

Exercise contributed by Steven Stovall, Southeast Missouri State University.

ONLINE EXERCISE 13.2: HOW DO YOU DEFINE LEADERSHIP?

Objective

The purpose of this exercise is to gain an understanding of the definition of leadership.

Instructions

In an online discussion group, post your definition of leadership. In the text, several theories about leadership are presented, but what is *your* personal definition of leadership? What does that word mean to you? Post your definition and provide commentary or questions to two other posts by members of your discussion group.

Reflection Questions

1. How did you determine your definition of leadership? Was it based on something in your upbringing or experiences you've had with leaders?
2. What theory of leadership in this text most closely aligns with your definition of leadership? Explain.
3. You were asked to post a comment or question on two other posts within your discussion group. How would you assess the other two definitions of leadership? How similar or dissimilar to yours are they?
4. Do you think your definition of leadership has changed during the course of your life? Do you think it will continue to change? Explain.

Exercise contributed by Steven Stovall, Southeast Missouri State University.

CASE 13.1: LEADERSHIP PERSPECTIVE AT CHOBANI

Chobani's story is that of a fairy tale. What started as an immigrant's risky venture has become a market-consuming conglomerate worth billions of dollars. Hamdi Ulukaya, a Turkish immigrant of Kurdish ethnicity, opened a wholesale feta cheese plant in 2002 after tasting the inferior local American cheese. Over the years, this small local plant expanded its operations and its vision as it took risks to deliver a product that was simply better. The company has also made headlines for its investment in its people.[105] Its management philosophy has proven successful, as the company now owns over 20% of the market share in the yogurt space. This would not be possible without the man leading the operation.[106] The chapter seeks to define what makes a great leader. It defines leadership as the process of providing general direction from a position of influence to individuals or groups toward the successful attainment of goals. It asks the question, however, what part of the process separates an average leader from a great leader. Communication? Popularity? Achievement? Looking closely at Chobani's leadership, it's clear that a great leader cannot be defined by a set of specific attributes; rather, great leaders are defined by what makes them different from everyone else.

Taking Risks and Defining Moments of Leadership

Starting a business of your own is a daunting task. To say that it takes hard work and commitment is an understatement. It takes blood, sweat, tears, and sometimes a little bit of luck to be a successful entrepreneur. In fact, 70% of businesses started in the United States fail after the first 10 years of operation.[107] These are massive odds to go against for anyone. Now imagine that you're an immigrant in a foreign country. Hamdi Ulukaya permanently immigrated to the United States in 1994 with the intention of studying English and taking business courses at a small college in upstate New York, finding work as a hand on a farm nearby. In 2002, Ulukaya's father visited the States and was disgusted with the quality of cheese being served, suggesting that Ulukaya import cheese from Turkey to sell around town. Upon doing so, the cheese became popular and Ulukaya decided to produce it. After two years of barely breaking even, an interesting opportunity presented itself to Ulukaya on a piece of junk mail advertising the sale of an old Kroger cheese manufacturing plant that had just been shut down. Ulukaya toured the plant the following day, took out a loan from the U.S. government, and bought it within five months.[108] This was arguably a risky move, but it was necessary to expand the operations and improve efficiencies of the cheese business.

Ulukaya needed employees to run a new cheese manufacturing plant and hired up all the recently fired Kroger employees, but had concerns that they would have their doubts about working for an immigrant entrepreneur with no experience in the cheese business. While this position of authority involved behaving like a formal leader, a leader who is officially designated by the organization, Ulukaya needed to be a different type of leader for the new workforce to buy into the operation.[109]

Formal leaders must act in the best interests of the organization and have certain rights and privileges that allow them to reward or discipline employees. Informal leaders, on the other hand, are relied on by team members for motivation and to help them realize their goals. Knowing that position of authority was not enough at this stage of the operation, Ulukaya paid new employees significantly more than they were receiving while they worked at Kroger. According to Ulukaya, "Finding and training new members of our team is ultimately a tax on our productivity. And replacing an employee can cost up to double their salary in lost knowledge, not to mention hiring and training time. With many of our original employees still working with us at our plants, we're proof that the long-term benefit to our company and our community far outweighs the short-term cost. . . . Because Chobani is a private and independent company, we have the freedom of following our own conscience when it comes to our business practices."[110] Ulukaya complemented formal leadership with qualities to become an excellent informal leader.

Manager versus Leader

Hamdi Ulukaya's business philosophy is evident when you look at all aspects of the Chobani brand. The product itself is made out of all natural, healthy ingredients. There are no preservatives, gelatine, or dairy used from cows injected with growth hormones.[111] Ulukaya is an extremely generous employer, giving every employee an ownership stake in the company. The company also sponsors numerous worldwide initiatives.[112] As an immigrant, Ulukaya has made Chobani a leader in hiring refugees who come to look for asylum and a fresh start and has consistently maintained that companies should focus on their impact on humanity as a whole and not just their profit margins, believing that "business is still the strongest, most effective way to change the world."[113]

The common theme surrounding all of these ventures is that Ulukaya is always doing things differently and is much more than a manager. This chapter examines the similarities and differences between managers and leaders. Managers set short-term goals, train and develop employees, promote stability, and ensure operations run smoothly. Leaders are visionaries, they set long-term goals, they inspire followers, they maintain a big-picture mindset, and they are role models. Ulukaya is both a leader and a manager and has been a huge influence in the industry and in the communities in which the business operates.

Sean Gallup / Staff / Getty Images

14 INFLUENCE, POWER, AND POLITICS

LEARNING OBJECTIVES

By the end of this chapter, you will be able to:

14.1 Discuss the concept of power and its relationship to leadership

14.2 Identify the various sources of power

14.3 Describe tactics for influencing others and outline the results of the various influence tactics

14.4 Identify the causes and possible consequences of organizational politics

14.5 Discuss the four different types of organizational politics

Case Study: Managerial Power at NextEra Energy, Inc.

All large companies which are traded publicly on stock exchanges must constantly engage in the process of organizing effective organizational influence, power, and politics. A single mistake or lie among management can devastate an entire company's standing in the public market. One company pairs that duty with its own huge renewable energy production arm which must heavily engage with both federal and state governments: NextEra Energy, Inc. (NYSE: NEE). A $153 billion market cap company, NextEra Energy, based in South Florida, is a member of the Forbes 200 business list.[1] It has a subsidiary which provides publicly regulated electricity to nearly half of Florida, it produces more megawatts of renewable electricity than any company in the world and NextEra Energy, Inc., and its subsidiary companies have around 14,900 employees.[2]

Power Structures in a Large Cap Incorporation

The first challenge for managers at NextEra is simply adequately leading a company with so many employees and interests. They confront this by employing many layers of legitimate power, and, in fact, operating separate subsidiary businesses. First, NextEra Energy, Inc. operates Florida Power and Light, the largest electricity utility in Florida. NextEra also created NextEra Energy Resources, which is the group in charge of national and international energy production, which engages in many renewable energy ventures. In addition to those, NextEra Energy Capital Holdings provides capital management support. In spite of the vast array of engineers, project managers, financial experts, accountants, and more, NextEra Energy, Inc. has a chain of command. The CEO is James "Jim" Robo whose vison for Next Era is to "Be North America's Leader in the Generation and Delivery of Clean Energy."[3] In operating, their stated corporate values are as follows: "We Are Committed to Excellence. We Do the Right Thing. We Treat People with Respect."[4]

A corporate structure with legitimate power, paired with these vision and values statements, is a key component in managing the organizational behavior at NextEra Energy. Managers in businesses of all sizes must enforce legitimate power, but they often should do so through stated goals and values. In this way, NextEra cares for its employees, and their hard work is a willful return for the respect of their leaders. To adequately manage all of its arms, there are separate CEOs from NextEra Energy, Inc. for both NextEra Energy Resources and Florida Power and Light. Beyond that, there are multiple executive vice presidents, each with an entire section of the company to look after.[5] Businesses of all sizes can engage in this type of structure: Whether or not a business is large enough to justify splitting into separate entities, a single leader always has to delegate to other managers or to their employees.

Corporate Referent Power

NextEra Energy says to future employees, "We will reward your time, talent, and commitment with pay, benefits, career development opportunities, a supportive work environment, and many more advantages."[6] And they mean it. Employees at many of their locations enjoy free or highly discounted access to wellness centers, doctor's checkups, gymnasiums, and relaxing corporate environments. This is a form of referent power—in a sense, NextEra is a corporation to which the employees are referent. NextEra dedicates millions of corporate dollars to human resources departments and comprehensive employee benefits, and in return employees show loyalty to the company and its executives. This attitude trickles down among managers, leading to a widespread coherence among managers and employees.

In large-scale business operations, it is paramount that employees enjoy their work. It is easier to fall into anonymity in large corporations, so any managing directors in such places must constantly remember to show their team the care and hard work that reap referent power. In all industries and scales of operations there are employee–manager relationships that must go beyond simple legitimate power structures. Whether a manager employs benefits to create reward power or to simply engage with their employees, a manager is in charge of finding ways to add value to work beyond a paycheck.[7]

A clear description of the importance of influencing the behavior of employees can be seen in the consequences listed in this chapter. There are entire organizational effects that differ when employees behave out of either resistance, compliance, or commitment. Resistance to proper management is purely a negative progress; successful companies and employees spend time organizing projects and making deals, not arguing among themselves to a harmful extent about how to do it. Even compliance alone fails to fuel a successful team. Without committed employees and managers, a company will always struggle to succeed, so NextEra Energy and other companies devote countless resources to cultivating a committed group of employees—all 14,900 of them. And the final piece to achieving the same results NextEra achieves, which cannot be forgotten, is that an employer provides benefits and rewards out of sincerity as opposed to contrived manipulation. From the CEO to the lowest level of employee on the organizational chart, members of all businesses recognize respect and good treatment just as easily as they recognize when they're being used.[8]

Risk Factors

Organizational politics become more important as the intensity of the larger external global political climate escalates, and this is true at NextEra as much as in any organization. Oftentimes members of organizations like NextEra Energy, which produces huge amounts of renewable energy, or any organization in a heavily regulated industry, make the news for giving in to corrupt organizational politics.[9] There are important lines between acceptable benefits for employees, whether they are gifted by governments or private parties such as investment banks. NextEra Energy has consolidated revenues over $17 billion a year—this means they constantly spend money and borrow money to operate a massive conglomerate of ever-growing projects.[10] This presents one of the biggest organizational political risks: With this much money moving around, outside sources are always trying to gain access to the corporation. This industry often involves forms of bribery, and NextEra wholeheartedly attempts to remain a neutral, fair business partner. On a smaller scale, employees and managers can monitor their own risk of inappropriate organizational politics by treating all members of their organizations and other organizations with equal respect and care, but not with inappropriate gifts. Lastly, employees and managers can mitigate the risk of bribery by setting clear, articulated guidelines on the types of rewards that may be given and accepted, a practice in which NextEra Energy engages.

NextEra Energy and its subsidiaries provide a useful template for all managers in maintaining a professional corporate environment that rewards employees. Accordingly, the management is effective, and NextEra continues to post better results while producing happy, hardworking employees. This template is only useful to an extent: All forms of management require a unique mixture of power forms, and one of the best ways to discover them is by finding ways to make employees feel appreciated.

Critical-Thinking Questions

1. Why should managers employ more than legitimate power to influence workers?
2. What is the purpose of monitoring organizational politics?
3. Describe how NextEra Energy maintains professional organizational politics.

POWER: DEFINITION AND OVERVIEW

The concept of **power**, the capacity to influence the actions of others, is inextricably linked with leadership.[11] Leaders have power for different reasons. In organizations, some leaders may be perceived as powerful by their followers because of their ability to give raises or bonuses, assign important tasks, or hire and fire. The power of other types of leaders may lie in their professional or technical expertise, or they may have personal qualities that inspire admiration in their followers. Being aware of why you are influenced by someone else helps you recognize your own power, decide whether you want to accept the way the power is being used, and build on your own leadership skills to learn how to be a positive influence in your organization. NextEra Energy is a good example of an organization that uses its power for good. Not only is the organization determined to be the leader of clean energy, but its CEO Jim Robo is also committed to treating employees with fairness and respect. In return, workers at NextEra Energy work hard together toward the fulfillment of the company's vision and goals.

However, there are different ways in which leaders can use their influence. For example, in Chapter 13, we learned about the power that authoritarian leaders wield over their followers to force compliance. But we also learned about transactional, transformational, and charismatic leaders, who are just as influential but instead obtain results by initiating shared goals, building meaningful relationships, and gaining the respect and esteem of others.

Indeed, psychological research has suggested that coercive power is a less effective method for gaining power, and that *social intelligence*, or our ability to negotiate, resolve conflicts, and understand the goals of others as well as group norms is the key to moving up in hierarchies.[12] Drawing from this theory, "leaders that treat their subordinates with respect, share power, and generate a sense of camaraderie and trust are considered more just and fair."[13] We might conclude that depending on their psychological make-up, different types of leaders may exert their power to influence in different ways, which can lead to positive or negative outcomes.

BASIC SOURCES OF POWER

To truly understand the concept of power, we need to explore the underlying sources of power (see Figure 14.1). There are two: organizational power and personal power.[14]

Organizational Power

Organizations are political structures that operate in a system for distributing power and authority among individuals and teams. Depending on how it is used, power can lead to either positive or negative outcomes in an organization.

There are three main aspects of power within organizations:

- **Legitimate power** is the leader's officially sanctioned authority to ask others to do things. For example, an organization such as the military that operates within a hierarchical structure places managers in a position of legitimate power. This means that by virtue of their organizational position managers have the formal authority or power to give orders and approve or deny employee requests. James "Jim" Robo, CEO of NextEra Energy, is an example of a leader with legitimate power because of the senior position.

- **Reward power** is the use of incentives to influence the actions of others. For example, some managers may inspire employees by promising salary raises, bonuses, promotions, while others prefer to take a novel approach. Interactive entertainment and mobile gaming company Scopely based in California rewards employees with self-portrait oil paintings that are then hung around the office. This unique reward system has not only provided humor to the workplace but has also helped to retain talent.[15] When used appropriately, reward power can motivate, but if rewards are used unethically or distributed based on favoritism, they can lead to demoralization and apathy.

FIGURE 14.1 ■ Sources of Power

Organizational Power	Personal Power
Legitimate Power	Expert Power
Reward Power	Referent Power
Coercive Power	

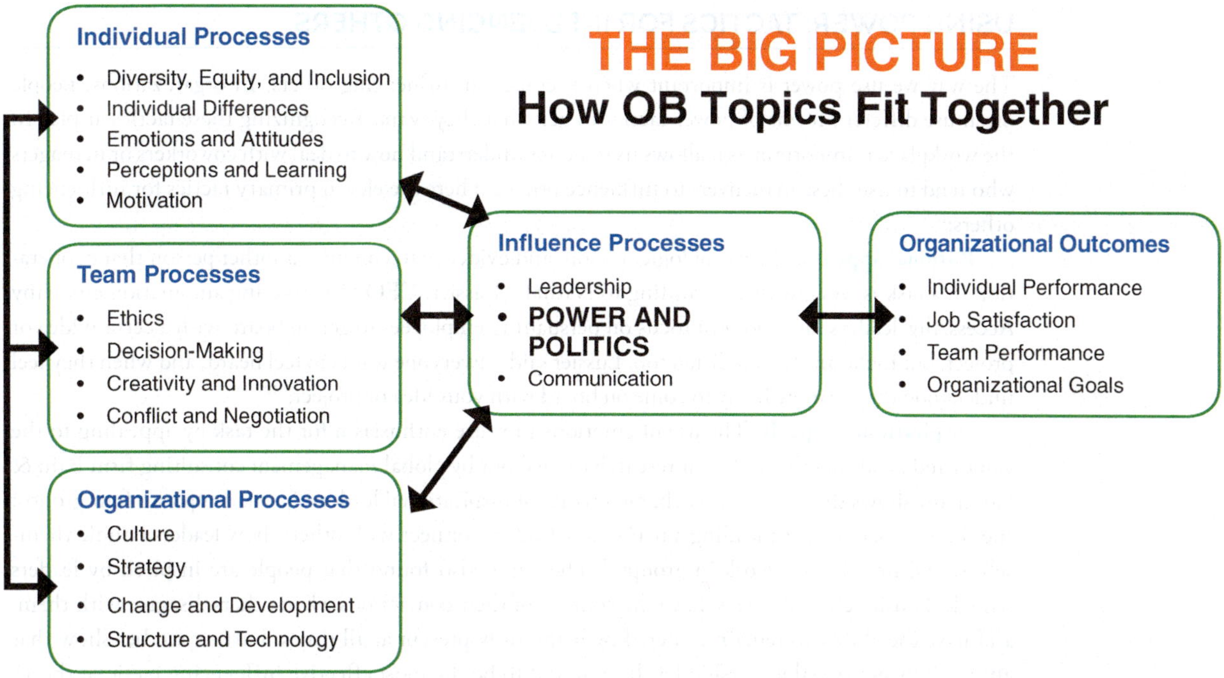

- **Coercive power** is the means by which a person controls the behavior of others through punishments, threats, or sanctions. For example, a manager might have the power to fire or punish employees if they are perceived as violating the organization's policies and norms. In today's organizations, coercive power is perceived by many leaders as a negative power and is usually used as a last resort. Although coercive power is often used in crisis situations—during COVID-19 coercive power was used enforce restrictions such as school and business closures, lockdowns, the wearing of face masks, and other strict regulations—it can also backfire, particularly when leaders fail to lead by example. For example, leader of the House of Representatives, Nancy Pelosi caused public outrage when spotted without a face mask in a hair salon that was supposed to be closed. Research shows that leaders who break the rules can have a negative effect on societal behavior.[16]

Personal Power

Personal power comes from within the individual and is independent of the position they hold in an organization. Personality and specialist knowledge in a certain area can be useful tools of personal power and influence. There are two main types of personal power:

- **Expert power** is the ability to influence the behavior of others through the possession of knowledge or expertise on which others depend. For example, team members working on an unfamiliar task may turn to their leader for guidance and expertise. Expert power is easily gained by using the wealth of information resources around us. For a start, you can develop expert power in an organization by reading the company's annual report, company blogs, social media posts, and tuning into leadership speeches. Once you have developed your own expert base, you get the opportunity to share your own knowledge and contribute to important topics.

- **Referent power** is the influence a leader gains over others when they desire to identify and be associated with them. For example, people will naturally gravitate toward a leader who comes across as fair, approachable, and adept at handling certain situations. The leadership team at NextEra Energy uses referent power by rewarding employees for their hard work by providing comprehensive perks and benefits. In return, employees show loyalty, work hard, and actively find ways to add value to the organization.

USING POWER: TACTICS FOR INFLUENCING OTHERS

The way we use power is important when it comes to influencing others. In organizations, people often use different forms of power tactics to get what they want. Recognizing these tactics at play in the workplace is important as it allows us to better understand how to deal with coworkers or managers who tend to use these maneuvers to influence others. There are eleven primary tactics for influencing others:[17]

Rational appeals: The use of logic, reason, and evidence to convince another person that cooperation in a task is worthwhile. According to Nathalie Lussier, CEO of marketing automation company AccessAlly, leaders must not just focus on persuading employees to get on board with a certain idea or project, but make an effort to listen too. Lussier said, "Everyone wants to feel heard, and when they feel understood they're more likely to come on board with your idea or project."[18]

Inspirational appeals: The use of emotions to rouse enthusiasm for the task by appealing to the values and ideals of others. Recent research carried out by global management consulting firm Bain & Company shows that there are 33 characteristics of inspirational leadership, made up into four groups: the skills associated with leading a team; how leaders connect with others; how leaders handle themselves; and how leaders work in groups.[19] The study also found that people are inspired by leaders who deal positively with stress, have the courage of their convictions when others disagree with them, and have the ability to remain centered by being fully present at all times. Further studies show that although inspirational leadership has been found to be the most effective influencing tactic of the 11 tactics, it is the least used influencing method.[20]

Upward appeals: The argument that the task has been requested by higher management, or a request to higher management to assist in gaining cooperation. For example, when trying to persuade a colleague to complete a task, you might use the argument that the request has come from the top, and that's why it needs to be done.

Personal appeals: A request to cooperate on the basis of friendship or as a personal favor. However, asking for or accepting favors requires a degree of caution. For example, employees accepting gifts from clients may expose the company to bribery or compromise personal and professional integrity by giving the impression that employees will be open to carrying out special favors for their clients in the future.

Consultation: The offer of participation or consultation in the decision-making process. Research shows that companies that involve employees in decision-making experience higher levels of engagement, increased productivity, and greater revenue.[21]

Exchange: The promise of rewards to persuade another person to cooperate. NextEra Energy, featured in our case study, rewards its employees for their hard work with generous salaries, benefits, career development opportunities, and additional perks such as free or highly discounted access to wellness centers, doctor's checkups, gymnasiums, and relaxing corporate environments.

Coalition building: Reference to the support of others as a reason for someone to agree to a request. For example, unions often build coalitions to make collective demands on an organization, and may threaten to strike if demands are not met.

Ingratiation: An effort to win favor and the good graces of others before making a request. Although this tactic may help give employees a career boost, ingratiation should only be taken so far. For instance, recent research shows that managers who use ingratiation as a tactic with their CEOs may start to feel resentment against their bosses, especially when they believe the CEO is benefiting at their expense.[22] Another study found that employees that ingratiate themselves with their managers may experience a depletion in energy resources resulting in the temptation to slack off or behave badly in the workplace.[23]

Silent authority: A passive tactic that relies on unspoken but acknowledged power. For example, when leaders use silence as a tactic, they are better able to hear what is being said and what remains unsaid, which allows them to reach the truth much more easily.

Information control: Withholding key information to influence outcomes. Research suggests that people withhold information from fear of losing power or status.[24] Other studies show that employees who withhold information may do so through a fear of speaking their minds.[25] Overall, research has

Influencing employees by explaining how their efforts contribute to a greater good is an example of an inspirational appeal.

©iStockphoto.com/Geber86

shown that there are no benefits to withholding information. On the contrary, organizations where employees are allowed to speak freely and share information, tend to experience a higher rate of retention and performance.[26]

Assertiveness: The use of demands or threats to persuade someone to carry out a task. Assertiveness could also involve setting unreasonable deadlines, becoming angry or impatient with employees, and making the same demands over and over again. Min-Liang Tan, CEO of Razer, a gaming company based in California, has been accused of creating a hostile work environment by humiliating, threatening, and being verbally abusive toward employees.[27]

Choosing a particular tactic depends on the situation. Effective leaders know when to choose "hard" tactics such as assertiveness and information control, and when they should tread more carefully and adopt "soft" tactics such as personal appeals, inspirational appeals, or exchange. The key to influencing others is to identify which situation calls for a particular type of tactic.

Consequences of Influence Tactics

When employed successfully, influence tactics can motivate employees, help managers obtain support and resources, and instigate effort, commitment, and cooperation. One of the best ways of choosing the right influence tactic is to understand how people react to different forms of influence. We can explore the effectiveness of an influence tactic by looking at three different possible outcomes: commitment, compliance, and resistance (see Figure 14.2).[28]

Commitment occurs when people are enthusiastic and fully in agreement with an action or decision and are motivated to put in the extra effort to successfully reach a goal. This is the best reaction to an influence tactic.

Compliance occurs when people are indifferent to a task and make only the minimal effort necessary to complete a goal. Although this reaction is not ideal for tasks that require more commitment, compliance has its place, especially when it comes to simple requests. For example, a manager telling an employee to do a routine, monotonous task like scanning a stack of documents may not receive an enthusiastic response, but the task will ultimately get done. In this scenario, compliance may be considered a successful outcome.

FIGURE 14.2 ■ Consequences of Influence Tactics

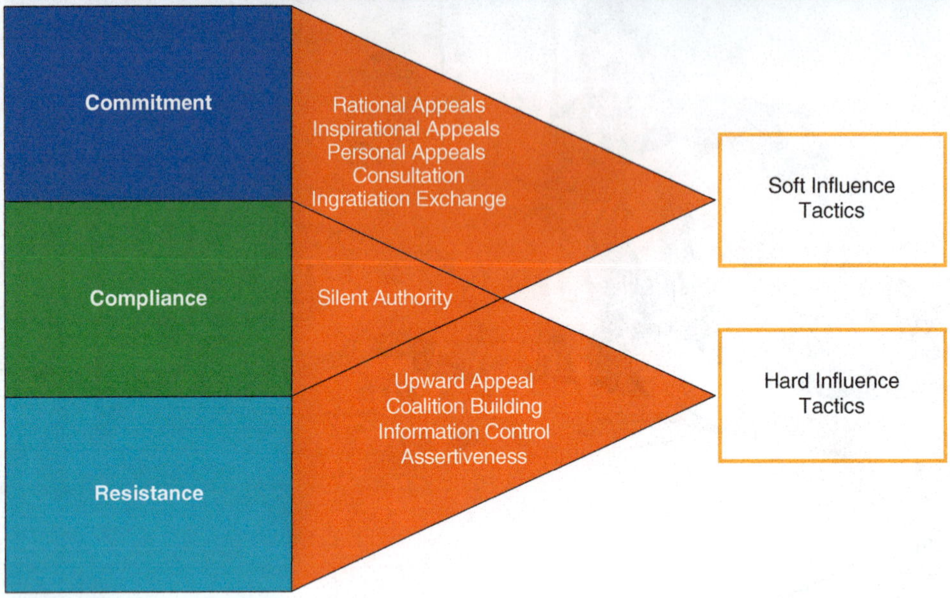

Source: Based on Falbe, C. M., & Yukl, G. (1992, August). Consequences for managers of using single influence tactics and combinations of tactics. *Academy of Management Journal, 35*(3), 638–652.

Resistance takes place when people oppose the influencer's request by refusing to do it or arguing against carrying out the task. This is the worst reaction to an influence tactic, and it also causes bad feeling and distrust.

In general, people tend to react better to "soft" rather than "hard" tactics. Soft tactics are more likely to result in commitment and are a frequent choice of leaders with personal sources of power such as expert and referent power. In contrast, hard tactics are more likely to generate compliance or resistance, and they are used by leaders with position power such as legitimate, reward, and coercive power.

It's helpful to know which soft influence tactics are the most effective in a given situation and why. For example, people with more knowledge and expertise tend to achieve better results through rational appeals because they have the necessary factual and logical evidence to support their requests. The success of ingratiation, inspirational appeals, or personal appeals largely depends on the sincerity of the person making the request. False behavior displayed by leaders tends to cause their staff to lose respect. Similarly, exchange and consultation as soft influence tactics must be meant sincerely to achieve the desired reaction.

What about hard tactics? People with strong legitimate power usually have more success using silent authority to have their requests fulfilled. For example, a CEO of an organization might expect subordinates to immediately carry out requests even if they might not necessarily agree.

The choice of the most suitable influence tactic depends on personal, organizational, and cultural values. For example, people with an inclination toward power may prefer to use assertiveness to get their demands met, whereas those who prefer to toe the line may seek support from others higher up in the organization through upward appeals. At an organizational level, people in companies with a competitive culture are more likely to build coalitions to protest or debate an issue, or they may deliberately control information to manipulate; both these tactics can generate resistance, and ultimately damage future relationships.

Influence tactics also vary across different cultures. Though extensive studies have been carried out to identify which cultures use certain influence tactics more commonly than others, the results are mixed at best. Some studies suggest information control is more common in Hong Kong than in the United States,[29] while others propose that coalition building is more effective in the United States and Switzerland than in China.[30] Despite these studies, knowledge gaps still exist, and further research is necessary to explain the cultural variations and effectiveness of influence tactics.

Compliance is the lowest level of commitment an employee can make as a result of influence tactics. However, compliance is just the right level of commitment an employee needs to make for simple tasks, like making photocopies.

EXAMINING THE EVIDENCE

POLITICAL BEHAVIOR: A VIABLE COPING STRATEGY FOR ORGANIZATIONAL POLITICS?

Research suggests that political behavior often results in negative outcomes for individuals and organizations. But in certain situations, it may have positive outcomes. Researchers Shuhua Sun of Tulane University and Huaizhong Chen of West Virginia University found that when employees choose to "play the political game" and engage in political behavior, it can serve as a coping mechanism that reduces the negative effects of perceived organizational politics on employee psychological empowerment and ultimately on employee task performance.[31] However, it appears that these positive benefits may come with an associated cost. Their findings also suggest that political behavior also *increases* the negative effects of perceived organizational politics on employee emotional exhaustion, thereby reducing task performance. These researchers suggest that employees should be aware of both the positive and negative effects of political behavior as a coping strategy, while managers should attempt to minimize employee perceptions of organizational politics. As long as employees perceive organizational politics, they are likely to suffer one way or the other. If they actively "play the political game," they may gain a sense of greater control, but at the cost of more emotional exhaustion. On the other hand, if they choose not to politick, they will likely experience lower levels of psychological empowerment.

Critical-Thinking Questions

1. How can managers most effectively leverage the positive effects of organizational politics?
2. In what ways can managers minimize employee perceptions of organizational politics?

ORGANIZATIONAL POLITICS

The word *politics* often elicits more negative than positive connotations. Popular culture generally portrays politicians as underhanded, power hungry, and ruthless in their ambition to make it to the top. Yet all people are capable of engaging in self-serving behavior. Politics exist wherever there is conflict and competition between employees in the scramble up the career ladder. We define **organizational politics** as behavior that is not formally sanctioned by the organization and that is focused on maximizing our self-interest, often at the expense of the organization or other employees.[32] Whether you choose to engage in it or avoid it, organizational politics is inescapable in the workplace and can occur in the office or online. Although many people don't realize it, "taking something offline," or "just having a chat" with decision-makers outside a formal setting is a sign of political engagement. As authors and researchers Lee G. Bolman and Terrence E. Deal said, "the question is not whether organizations will have politics but rather what kind of politics they will have."[33]

The vast majority of research evidence suggests that organizational politics has negative effects, including increased strain and stress, higher organizational turnover, decreased job satisfaction and performance, lower morale, and reduced organizational commitment.[34] However, politics can be used for positive means when people possess **political skill**, the ability to understand and influence others for the good of the organization.[35] In other words, when people hold the interests of the organization above their own interests, provide high levels of feedback to colleagues and direct reports, and maintain good working relationships to achieve results, then organizational politics can have positive results. Studies show that individuals with political skills tend to do better in gaining more personal power as well as managing stress and job demands, than their politically naive counterparts.[36] They also have a greater impact on organizational outcomes. Yet as the Examining the Evidence feature shows, playing the political game can also come at a price.

How do people behave when they are engaging in political behaviors? Political behaviors include ingratiation, self-promotion, strong influence tactics, coalition building, the forging of connections with powerful allies, taking credit for positive events and the success of others, and the circumvention of legitimate channels to secure resources that would otherwise be unattainable.[37] You may notice that some of these terms appeared in Section 14.3; political behaviors are indeed closely aligned with tactical influence. People who "play the game" seek to influence others to get ahead, whether it's for their own interests or for the best interests of the organization. Some people think they don't need to engage with work politics because they think their work should speak for itself, yet as Carla Harris, vice chairman at Morgan Stanley said, "You can't let work speak for you; work doesn't speak."[38] Promoting yourself and your work and the impact it is having on the organization is a necessary and healthy way to build relationships, increase your influence, and grow and progress in the workplace.

Why is organizational politics an inevitable part of working life? There are two main factors at play: organizational factors and individual factors.[39]

Organizational Factors

People are more likely to engage in political behavior in organizations where resources such as monetary rewards or promotions are limited. In today's uncertain economy, many companies have implemented austerity measures and cut back on overhead, often by conducting layoffs. Many companies have suffered a decline since the COVID-19 pandemic and have been forced to announce massive layoffs as a result. Airbnb, American Airlines, and Hilton Hotels are among the biggest companies who have laid off thousands of employees due to the economic fallout of the pandemic for businesses operating in the travel and leisure industry.[40]

These cost-cutting steps can fuel political behavior as employees compete for dwindling resources and rewards. "Zero-sum rewards," programs that compensate only one or a few team members at the expense of the others, can have negative consequences for those who do not receive anything, creating bad feeling and driving unhealthy competition. Similarly, organizations going through periods of organizational change tend to have more politically centered workforces. For example, rumors of layoffs may encourage some employees to use political tactics to ensure that their jobs are secure.

An organization's environment or culture is a good indicator of the extent of politics that exists in it. For example, in organizations that fail to implement formal rules, that tolerate a lack of trust between employees and management, or that put employees under serious pressure to perform, competition and politics prevail.

Individual Factors

Even if your organization is highly political, the extent to which you engage in political behavior depends on your personality. For example, you may be someone who has a strong desire for power and operates with a high internal locus of control (the belief that you can control outcomes). Or you could be a high self-monitor, someone who is more sensitive to social cues, can relate well to others, and inspires trust and confidence. Finally, you might have a Machiavellian personality and be willing to manipulate others and use power to advance your own self-interests. Kathleen Kelley Reardon, an expert on organizational politics believes that political players can be classified into four types:[41]

The Purist: People who avoid politics and just want to get on with the job

The Street Fighter: People who use underhand or Machiavellian tactics to get ahead

The Team Player: People who believe that the key to getting ahead is to work well with others and progress as a group

The Maneuverer: People who play politics in a way that isn't obvious to others who tend to take things at face value

Different types of political players may not thrive in certain political environments. For instance, a purist is unlikely to be content working in a highly political organization, and a street fighter will not be easily accepted in an organization with minimal politics. Overall, political intelligence is a skill that can be practiced and mastered. People who invest their time building connections inside and outside the workplace are more likely to gain recognition from peers and people of influence and have a greater of being rewarded with bonuses and promotions as a result.

Politics and Visibility

If you are aiming for a promotion, you will need to network with the right people and take on high-profile projects to increase your **visibility**, which is others' awareness of your presence in an organization.[42] Ultimately, your rewards, bonuses, and promotional prospects depend on the relationships you have with others. You don't need to behave in an underhanded way to stand out, but with so much competition in the workplace there is nothing wrong with ensuring that your hard work is acknowledged and fairly rewarded. Of course, you can choose to stay out of politics altogether, but this may mean getting passed over for promotions simply because the people responsible for promotional decisions and rewards are unaware of your skills, talents, and contributions.

As the preference for remote working rises, there are concerns that contributions will go unrecognized and people are at risk of fading into the background. Questions have been raised when working remotely. Table 14.1 outlines some tips on maintaining visibility when you're working from home, or remotely, or as a part of a hybrid structure.

The next section provides a greater understanding of the political landscape that exists in most organizations.

FOUR DIFFERENT TYPES OF ORGANIZATIONAL POLITICS

In organizations, political behavior can either be destructive or a force for good. Regardless of the situation, it is important to understand the four main types of organizational politics to navigate the political landscape. These are the weeds, the rocks, the high ground, and the woods.[43] Two dimensions operate across these four types. The first dimension involves just one person who engages in political activity, which expands to group-level politics as others get involved, before evolving into organizational politics. The second dimension is the degree to which the power is used; it can either be "soft" power, where people make informal use of their own influence or relationships or "hard" power where people use their own authority and expertise to engage in political activity. Being aware of these two dimensions can help us to understand the types of politics around us.

TABLE 14.1 ■ How to stay visible when not in the office

• Reinforce your reliability and commitment to deadlines: There can sometimes be an assumption that people working remotely have a tendency to "goof off." You can dispel this notion by emailing your manager with the complete assignment and stating that you have delivered on your assignment by the agreed deadline, as promised.
• Maintain social connections: Remote workers don't have the opportunity to have informal conversations to connect with colleagues but it is important to build relationships nonetheless. Research shows that colleagues are more willing to support each other when they feel a personal connection with others. Remote workers can build these connections by initiating one-to-one video chats or hosting virtual networking events.
• Be physically visible when you can: When geographically possible, try and come into the office now and then to meet your colleagues and introduce yourself to new hires. If geography doesn't permit it, then make sure you present yourself will in video meetings; for example, always keep your video on so people can get a sense of your appearance and body language.
• Make yourself easy to work with: Remote workers aren't as accessible people working in an office, sitting a few feet away from teams and managers. Setting out rules early on preferred communication styles (Slack, phone, email etc.), laying out assumptions around response times, and holding weekly check-in meetings with your boss will give the impression you are a valuable asset to the team.

Source: Clark, D. (2021, July 30). Staying visible when your team is in the office . . . but you're WFH. *Harvard Business Review.* https://hbr.org/2021/07/staying-visible-when-your-team-is-in-the-office-but-youre-wfh

The Weeds

The weeds describes a place where people engage in politics using personal influence and informal networks. For example, a not-for-profit organization relies on donors to keep the business afloat. The secretary general starts behaving unethically and underperforming. There is a concern among the staff that this behavior will put off current and future donors. A group of employees gets together to discuss the problem informally. Over time, the problem gets worse, but the group's influence grows stronger, and within a year the secretary general is removed from the role to protect the company's reputation. This shows that informal groups have the political power to be a force for good.

However, informal groups can be destructive if they are set up to hamper legitimate change or disrupt the long-term interests of the organization. To counteract the negative aspect of groups operating in "the weeds," managers need to understand the nature of the politics, identify the key players, and communicate with them to find the source of their discontent.

The Rocks

When in "the rocks," people in authority use hard power to enforce decisions. Often these people operate in high-status groups such as finance committees or senior management teams. While using hard power can be a stabilizing force particularly during turbulent times when tough decisions need to be made, there are also downsides to using this type of political behavior. For example, a mid-size advertising agency is implementing a growth strategy, but the CEO is using formal power to block the changes, questioning decisions, changing opinions, and taking people off projects without telling them. This type of political behavior is destructive and self-serving.

In this situation, it is better to try and find a way to persuade the CEO that these changes are positive in the long-term. For instance, growth is in the interests of the company and the CEO will be leaving behind an impressive legacy if they steer the company in the right way.

The High Ground

The high ground describes a type of organizational politics where the rules, structures, and policy guidelines are set formally in place. While rules and regulations are necessary for a well-functioning organization, too much formal authority can lead to overly bureaucratic structures which impede innovation and change. One way of tackling this level of rigidity is to set up task forces, or separate groups outside the formal structure of the organization to analyze the problem and make a case for change. For example, one public agency was failing to collect millions of tax revenues because of its cumbersome internal structures and policies. A dedicated task force was created outside of the formal organizational structure to discuss a solution. The group's suggestions were implemented over time, leading to a change in processes and a much higher recovery rate.

The Woods

Besides their rules and regulations, organizations have certain norms (see Chapter 8 for further information on norms), which can sometimes prove to be a political minefield. Organizations can get lost in "the woods" by focusing on the issues rather than the hidden, unseen, underlying norms that could well be the key source of the problem. One way of identifying these unspoken habits is to ask people outside the organization such as clients, temporary contractors, or recent hires to share their thoughts on how the company operates. Their feedback will determine whether the cultural norms are hindering or helping the organization.

For example, a newly merged telecoms company engaged in a simple exercise where people from both companies were asked to describe their respective cultural norms and those of the other parties. Discussing these norms openly bridged the gap between the two parties, who began to work as a team to roll out a key project.

Each type of organizational politics has a positive and negative aspect. It is essential that managers understand the drivers of these behaviors to avoid getting drawn into the dark side of politics.

So far, we have explored the role of power and politics and how it influences relationships in organizations. In the next chapter, we will illustrate the importance of positive culture and its impact on organizational behavior.

IN REVIEW

14.1 Discuss the concept of power and its relationship to leadership

The concept of **power**, which is the capacity to influence the actions of others, is inextricably linked with leadership. Recent psychological research has suggested that coercive power is a myth, and that true power lies in social intelligence or our ability to negotiate, resolve conflicts, and understand the goals of others. Depending on their psychological make-up, different types of leaders may exert their power to influence in different ways, which can lead to positive or negative outcomes.

14.2 Identify the various sources of power

Organizational power can be broken into three main aspects: **legitimate power**, **reward power**, and **coercive power**. Legitimate power is the right to ask others to do things within the scope of the leader's authority. Reward power is the use of incentives to influence the actions of others. Coercive power controls the behavior of others through punishments, threats, or sanctions.

Personal power can be broken into two main types: expert power and referent power. Expert power is the ability to influence the behavior of others through the possession of knowledge or expertise on which they depend. Referent power is influence over others based on their desire to identify and be associated with the leader.

14.3 Describe tactics for influencing others and outline the results of the various influence tactics

There are several different types of tactics we can use to influence others:

- **Rational appeals**: The use of logic, reason, and evidence to convince another person that cooperation in a task is worthwhile
- **Inspirational appeals**: The use of emotions to rouse enthusiasm for the task by appealing to the values and ideals of others
- **Upward appeals**: The argument that the task has been requested by higher management, or a request to higher management to assist in gaining cooperation
- **Personal appeals**: Requests to cooperate on the basis of friendship or as a personal favor
- **Consultation:** The offer of participation or consultation in the decision-making process

- **Exchange:** The promise of rewards to persuade another person to cooperate
- **Coalition building:** Reference to the support of others as a reason for someone to agree to a request
- **Ingratiation:** An effort to win favor and the good graces of others before making a request
- **Silent authority:** A passive tactic that relies on unspoken but acknowledged power
- **Information control**: Withholding key information to influence outcomes
- **Assertiveness:** The use of demands or threats to persuade someone to carry out a task

The three basic outcomes of influence tactics are commitment, compliance, and resistance. *Commitment* occurs when people are enthusiastic and fully in agreement with an action or decision and are motivated to put in the extra effort to successfully reach a goal. *Compliance* occurs when people are indifferent to a task and make only the minimal effort necessary to complete a goal. *Resistance* takes place when people oppose the influencer's request by refusing to carry out a task or arguing against carrying out a task.

14.4 Identify the causes and possible consequences of organizational politics

Organizational politics is behavior that is not formally sanctioned by the organization and that is focused on maximizing our self-interest, often at the expense of the organization or other employees.

Some negative effects of organizational politics include increased strain and stress, higher organizational turnover, decreased job satisfaction and performance, lower morale, and reduced organizational commitment. Organizational politics can also be used for positive means when people possess **political skill**, the ability to understand and influence others for the good of the organization, and hold the interests of the organization above their own interests, provide high levels of feedback to employees, and maintain good working relationships to achieve results.

14.5 Discuss the four different types of organizational politics

It is important to understand the four main types of organizational politics to navigate the political landscape. These are the weeds, the rocks, the high ground, and the woods. The weeds describes a place where people engage in politics using personal influence and informal networks. When in the rocks, people in authority use hard power to enforce decisions. The high ground describes a type of organizational politics where the rules, structures, and policy guidelines are set formally in place. Finally, organizations can get lost in the woods by focusing on the issues rather than the hidden, unseen, underlying norms that could well be the key source of the problem.

KEY TERMS

Assertiveness (p. 337)
Coalition building (p. 336)
Coercive power (p. 335)
Consultation (p. 336)
Exchange (p. 336)
Expert power (p. 335)
Information control (p. 336)
Ingratiation (p. 336)
Inspirational appeals (p. 336)
Legitimate power (p. 334)
Organizational politics (p. 340)
Personal appeals (p. 336)
Personal power (p. 343)
Political skill (p. 340)
Power (p. 333)
Rational appeals (p. 336)
Referent power (p. 335)
Reward power (p. 334)
Silent authority (p. 336)
Upward appeals (p. 336)
Visibility (p. 341)

UP FOR DEBATE: IS POLITICS GOOD OR BAD?

The word *politics* tends to have a negative connotation in that any politics in an organization is a bad thing. Agree or Disagree?

EXERCISE 14.1: TACTICS FOR INFLUENCING OTHERS

Objective

The purpose of this exercise is to gain a greater appreciation of the 11 primary tactics for influencing others.

Instructions

The text discusses 11 primary tactics for influencing others (rational appeals, inspirational appeals, etc.). In groups of three to five students, select any two of the tactics. Then, brainstorm a TV show or online series that has a character who utilizes your selected tactics. You may have two different shows or characters for the two tactics.

Once you have identified the two tactics and characters, what examples can you cite or behaviors these characters exhibit that demonstrate their use of these influencing tactics? How do other characters react to these tactics? In other words, are the tactics effective?

Reflection Questions

1. What tactics does your current or previous supervisor use to influence employees? How effective are these tactics?
2. Which tactics do you rely on to influence others? Why?
3. Which of the 11 tactics do you not respond to well? Which is a tactic that works on you most of the time? Explain.

Exercise contributed by Steven Stovall, Southeast Missouri State University.

EXERCISE 14.2: I HAVE THE POWER

Objectives

This exercise will help you to be able to better *discuss* the concept of power and *identify* various sources of power.

Instructions

Step 1. Think of an organization of which you are a member. For each power type (legitimate, reward, coercive, expert, and referent), describe why you do or do not have that particular power. Since power is an exchange process and differs in various relationships, you may also need to specify with who (or what group of people) you have that power. (5 minutes)

Step 2. Find a partner (ideally someone who you do not work with on a regular basis), and prepare a list of similarities and differences in your influence relationships. (10 minutes)

Step 3. Choose a spokesperson for your pair and be prepared to discuss your comparison with the class. (1 to 3 minutes)

Reflection Questions

1. How would you expect your power bases to change in a different organization?
2. How do you expect your power bases to change after you graduate from your program?
3. What power bases do you prefer to use? How could you improve those power bases?
4. What power bases would you expect to transfer between organizations and positions?

Exercise contributed by Milton R. Mayfield, Professor of Business, Texas A&M International University, and Jacqueline R. Mayfield, Professor of Business, Texas A&M International University.

EXERCISE 14.3: GRAPPLING WITH ORGANIZATIONAL POLITICS

Objective

The purpose of this exercise is to grasp the concept of the four different types of organizational politics.

Instructions

Your text identifies four types of organizational politics:

- **The weeds**—a place where people engage in politics using personal influence and informal networks
- **The rocks**—a place where people in authority use hard power to enforce decisions
- **The high ground**—situation where the rules, structures, and policy guidelines are set formally in place
- **The woods**—a situation where members of the organization focus on issues rather than the hidden, unseen, underlying norms that could well be the source of the problem

The instructor will ask for eight to 12 volunteers from the class for a series of role-plays (two to three participants for each type of organizational politics). Each group of participants will be given one of the four types above. Then, each group will take 5 to 10 minutes to devise a scenario or skit that demonstrates that particular type of organizational politics. For example, one group will create a role-play demonstrating the weeds, another, the rocks, and so on.

The student volunteers will then take turns performing their role-play in front of the class.

The remaining students will attempt to guess which type of organizational politics is being shown based upon the words and interactions of the students at the front of the room. Students should write down their opinion as to which type of politics is shown and the correct identification is not given until all four groups of students have completed their skits.

Reflection Questions

1. For each group of students, how could you tell which type of organizational politics was being demonstrated? What cues or clues were given that showcased that particular type?
2. Which of the four types of organizational politics are you currently experiencing in your job or at a previous job? Explain.
3. What type of organizational politics would you most thrive in? Why?
4. What type of organizational politics would you least like? Why?

Exercise contributed by Steven Stovall, Southeast Missouri State University.

ONLINE EXERCISE 14.1: UNDERSTANDING THE CONSEQUENCES OF INFLUENCE TACTICS

Objective

The purpose of this exercise is to gain an appreciation for the possible outcomes of influence tactics.

Description of Exercise

This exercise utilizes a discussion board to explore the three possible outcomes a person may have to influence tactics. Those three outcomes are as follows:

- **Commitment**—occurs when people are enthusiastic and fully in agreement with an action or decision and are motivated to put in the extra effort to successfully reach a goal
- **Compliance**—occurs when people are indifferent to a task and make only the minimal effort necessary to complete a goal

- **Resistance**—occurs when people oppose the influencer's request by refusing to do it or arguing against carrying out the task

On the discussion board, post an example from your experience where commitment was the outcome to an influence tactic of a supervisor. Allow others to also post their experiences as well. Once everyone has posted, discuss the similarities of tactics and responses people had. Explore how there may also be differences. Then, repeat this discussion with compliance and resistance.

Discussion Questions

1. What did you learn about others' responses to various influence tactics that will help you in the future as you encounter these?
2. Do you think the type of outcome to influence tactics is a result of the manager's behavior and words or the entire culture of the organization? Explain.
3. How can organizations move away from a resistance outcome to one that is more commitment focused?
4. If you were hired as a new manager and you discover that the previous supervisor used harsh tactics in attempting to influence the employees which have resulted in a climate of compliance and resistance, what steps would you take to change the situation?

ONLINE EXERCISE 14.2: UNDERSTANDING ORGANIZATIONAL POLITICS

Objective

The purpose of this exercise is to gain an understanding of organizational politics.

Description of Exercise

Think about organizational politics you have experienced at your current or previous jobs. We've all encountered various forms of organizational politics—whether it was when we were first hired and we were trying to be accepted by others or we noticed who was getting promoted or preferential schedules and thought it might be due to savvy organizational politicking. In a discussion group, post the worst example of organizational politics from your experience. Describe not only what happened, but the thoughts and feelings you had about the situation.

Discussion Questions

- With the example you provided, at the time did you think the situation was fair to you or to others? What about now? Explain.
- Do you consider yourself strong in organizational politics? Why or why not?
- Can you imagine an organization without any organizational politics? If yes, describe it, and if no, explain why.

Exercise contributed by Steven Stovall, Southeast Missouri State University.

CASE 14.1: STARBUCKS

Celebrity endorsements have been an advertising mainstay for generations. Companies pay stars large sums to be seen with their products in the hopes that consumers will associate their positive feelings toward the endorser with their brand. This strategy of using referent personal power in marketing has adapted to social media and persists today, but new trends are calling the efficacy of formal influencer programs into question.

The digital native Generation Z values transparency, authenticity, and online influence, according to a recent McKinsey & Company report.[44] Millions of young people express an interest in becoming social media influencers themselves and their platform of choice is clear: TikTok. Less saturated than

Instagram and more accessible than YouTube, corporate savvy and sophisticated production are not prerequisites for a TikTok to go viral—in fact, they're often counterproductive. The platform where everyday teens' spontaneous recordings can instantly be seen by millions levels the influencer playing field between individuals and global brands. In true, authentic Gen Z spirit, many young people are posting right from where their careers are beginning: in green aprons behind the counter of the #1 coffee chain.

Starbucks is a lifestyle on TikTok, and the company harnesses the influential power its nearly 350,000 partners wield online. In addition to the company's official "Starbucks Partners" accounts on TikTok and other social media channels, Starbucks encourages partners to post from their personal, non-blue-checked accounts using the hashtag #starbuckspartners. Videos of new "secret menu" drinks frequently accumulate millions of views in days. Mae Karwowski, CEO of influencer marketing agency Obviously, says, "Employees can be your best advocates because they know and love the brand, they know all the 'hacks' and insider info."[45]

The benefits of employee influencer marketing are twofold and work together synergistically: Content created by individual employees is more personal (and thus more trustworthy) than stilted corporate communication, and their real insider experience at the company affords them a degree of expert power to persuade consumers.

"The first step is to give guidelines to employees," Karwowski says. "Show that corporate actually knows that this is an app that exists, then monitor and reward positive behavior." Of course, corporate social media guidelines are nothing new, but most standard practices either explicitly prohibit or indirectly discourage employees from posting about their job online. In contrast, the first line of Starbucks' Social Media Guidelines for Canada and U.S. Partners reads, "**Share your passion.** We're called partners, because this isn't just a job, it's our passion. So, go ahead and share it!"[46] Starbucks' more relaxed social media policy than most companies of its size is the right approach, Karwowski says. "Why don't you capture the good and create parameters for the rest?"

Many baristas jump at the chance to gain social media notoriety with the company's blessing, an example of commitment to the organization's employee influencer goals, while others worry Starbucks' explosive online popularity is making their jobs harder.

Starbucks marketing proudly states that beyond its standard menu items, there are over 170,000 possible beverages by combining all the stores options and add-ons. On TikTok, custom drink recipes go viral, often to the chagrin of the baristas who have to prepare them. In April 2022, #starbuckssecretmenu had over 318 million views. In an article titled "The Rise of the Appucino: How TikTok Is Changing Starbucks," company spokesperson Erin Shane Riley told BuzzFeed News that "secret menu" items have gone viral before, like the "Pink Drink" that was popular on Instagram and Pinterest that Starbucks officially added it to the menu in 2016. "TikTok is a great way to listen to our customers," Riley said.

Mary Davies, president of Beanstalk Internet Marketing, says that "People are looking for connections on a personal level with businesses and brands that feel like part of their community." Indeed, the line between authentic content and advertising blurs when customers know the baristas who post "#starbuckspartner" TikToks, but some employees feel Starbucks is taking its quest for personal influence too far.

Each Starbucks location is required to receive high "customer connection scores" to stay in good standing with the company, but what the customer connection score measures is meeting resistance from partners who feel it is an illogical appeal (at least in its current implementation). A partner or store's customer connection score boils down to just one question asked of Starbucks Rewards members after a purchase: "Did your barista try to get to know you?" A customer answering "no" reflects poorly on an employee, even if the encounter was one where "getting to know you" was not appropriate or even possible, like picking up a completed online order to go. Besides, baristas are asked to keep point-of-sale interaction times under 30 seconds, a goal that seems at odds with establishing much of a connection, making the customer connection score push feel like a use of coercive power and a source of resentment for partners.[47]

In *Onward: How Starbucks Fought for Its Life Without Losing Its Soul*, three-time Starbucks CEO Howard Schultz writes, "Employees are the true ambassadors of our brand, the real merchants of romance and theater, and as such the primary catalysts for delighting customers."[48] Founded in Seattle, Washington, in 1971, Starbucks' stalwart roast made the city's Pike Place Market a household name. More than 50 years later, the company boasts over $29 billion in annual revenue and Starbucks' iconic green twin-tailed siren adorns nearly 35,000 locations in 83 countries and territories worldwide.[49]

Critical-Thinking Questions

1. Organizational and personal power are typically inward focused between employees and managers. Describe a way in which Starbucks turned its power outside, facing consumers.
2. How are the beliefs of Generation Z consumers changing companies' behavior in influence and marketing?
3. The case contrasts examples of commitment (to the employee influencer program) and resistance (to the customer connection score requirements). Think about a time you saw different influence tactic outcomes among your coworkers. How did your manager respond? How would you try to bring employees to compliance or commitment?

PART V

ORGANIZATIONAL CONTEXT

Robert Alexander / Contributor / Getty Images

15 ORGANIZATIONS AND CULTURE

LEARNING OBJECTIVES

By the end of this chapter, you will be able to:

15.1 Describe the basic characteristics of organizational culture

15.2 Discuss the various artifacts and functions of organizational culture

15.3 Compare various types of organizational cultures

15.4 Identify key ways in which organizations adapt their practices across cultures

15.5 Contrast differing approaches for shaping organizational culture

Case Study: Recreational Equipment Incorporated's (REI) Organizational Culture

REI started as a Seattle-based equipment shop for experienced climbers back in 1938. Founded by Lloyd and Mary Anderson, REI was a cooperative to help outdoor enthusiasts acquire good quality climbing gear at reasonable prices.[1] From the beginning, they both knew that for customers to buy their products they would need all employees to be experienced with whatever they were selling. In any business, especially one like REI, disengaged employees drag down others and impact customer service, sales, and quality. REI created a culture of engaged employees and continues to lead the way in doing so even today.

To take on the most experienced staff, they have always prioritized the well-being of their employees, hoping that the employees would then care for the well-being of each and every customer. With this in mind, it is no surprise then that their first full-time employee was also the first American to summit Mount Everest, and would also become their CEO during the 1960s.[2] What was a small gear rental co-op had diversified into the family camping market focused more on consumer goods by the '80s. With a new less experienced market of customers required a shift in employee type that made each store member an even more vital piece of the operation. Now that their clientele was made up of fewer mountaineers and more family campers, they needed a staff whose advice families could depend on, making REI a prime example of employee-focused organizational culture.[3]

Today, REI is one of the largest stores of their kind with billions of revenues and nearly 15,000 employees.[4] While no longer a small company, REI maintains its small-store feel where employees are required to have an intimate knowledge of each product they are selling for the sake of the customer. REI has experienced restructuring over their long history such as their above change in the 1980s from a "co-op" style retailer to a more standard format that offered a wide range of sporting products. Then again, in 2014, REI made another shift back toward that of a cooperative-style store, even rebranding to reflect the new change of business model.[5] All of these changes reflect what the consumer wants at the time and show REI's intimate connection with the needs and wants of their customers. It is important to note that REI's focus on its employees and customers is also illustrated by the fact that just one of its stores out of 170 in the United States is unionized.[6]

Innovation is required to manage organizational culture long term, and while many companies try to create new fun ideas to handle this, many fail in doing so. REI has something called "company campfire" where associates and executives have the ability to share their thoughts and participate in debates on social media. More than 4,500 of its 15,000 employees have logged on and contributed since its creation.[7] Ideas like this are at the essence of organizational culture. For employees, it offers a voice on things that matter in the most direct way, and for managers, it gives a direct line to the conversations, worries, and complaints of all employees. This is corporate innovation at its finest but without an organizational culture that fits with this method, employees could feel afraid of speaking their minds on important topics, but not at REI.

REI is continually changing and improving, yet the aspect about the retailer that has never changed is how REI treats its customers and employees. While they have an excellent culture and method for managing employees, they understand the need for incentives. Employees in any business are greatly affected by incentives; however, the types of incentives and the way they influence employees varies from industry to industry. REI is consistently a top-ranked company to work for and has been ranked in the top 100 Companies to Work for in the United States since the list's creation in 1998.[8] Of course, there is a reason that REI is in the Fortune Magazine Employer Hall of Fame: in fact, there are many. Of its 15,000 employees, all of them have access to health-care benefits. While many employers give employees discounts on products, REI gives discounts on merchandise, outdoor classes, and also "Yay Day" passes which entitle employees to spend six hours outdoors for pay.[9] When more and more retailers were opening their doors on Thanksgiving to accommodate for Black Friday shopping, REI chose to close their stores for Black Friday altogether. They halted all business both online and in-store and gave employees a paid day off.[10] These are just some of the things that REI does to make sure that its employees are taken care of and happy with their jobs.

These initiatives by REI are what make them a leader in retail, thanks to their satisfied and motivated staff of outdoor enthusiasts. REI understands that the best way to sell outdoors gear is to build itself a staff that is experienced in the outdoors so that they know what they would buy. They create the best employees by hiring the most loyal customers. They aren't just hiring a workforce, they are hiring a walking opinion on all things outdoors. By doing everything they can to incentivize employees to frequent the outdoors, REI shows that it is committed to providing a helpful staff with enough experience to comfortably recommend products on a customer-by-customer basis. These perks along with benefits for all employees and a handful of other incentives leaves REI a large enough pool of potential employees to always have a quality staff on hand.[11]

With programs like "company campfire" in the place of water-cooler conversations and "#optoutside" in the place of Black Friday frenzies, REI shows that they have always been committed to putting their organizational culture above all else.[12] It shows that REI is committed to their future by protecting their two most vital resources: a place to use their products and employees to sell them. With these two resources intact, REI's business should be a lasting one and should continually grow and change. They continually innovate new ideas to do this more efficiently and to effectively manage their image and it has paid off immensely.

Critical-Thinking Questions

1. Why does REI need employees who are experienced with their equipment just to sell products?
2. Why doesn't REI take part in Black Friday even though it is many stores' most successful day?

WHAT IS ORGANIZATIONAL CULTURE?

The culture of an organization often influences its degree of success or failure. REI profiled in our case study measures its success by the level of knowledge exhibited by its employees when selling equipment to outdoor enthusiasts. We define **organizational culture** as a pattern of shared norms, rules, values, and beliefs that guides the attitudes and behaviors of its employees.[13]

The COVID-19 Pandemic forced a renewed focus on organizational culture and how culture can keep and attract employees by triggering employees to question their value to the organization and their purpose in life. As a result, many workers have left the workforce in pursuit of a better work/life balance. Recent studies show that companies that prioritize a flexible working culture, value employee health and well-being, celebrate recognition, embrace advanced technology, and foster people-focused initiatives such as diversity, equity, and inclusion strategies, experience higher levels of retention, engagement, and job satisfaction.[14]

People are the most important asset to an organization, and the behavioral side of a culture is as important as, if not more important than, the financial side. REI shows appreciation for its employees by giving them discounts on merchandise, paid days off, and "Yay Day" passes. As we will see, a company that neglects its internal culture is likely to suffer economically.

On a more personal level, the type of organizational culture also affects an employee's chance of fitting in and doing well. So how do you know which kind of culture is best for you? Some corporate cultures encourage long hours with few breaks, while others are more relaxed and informal. This is why doing your research on different organizations before you join one is essential. Finding out how employees rate their companies can be a good way of determining whether an organization is the right one for you. Take the 2022 Employees' Choice Awards conducted by online jobs and career community Glassdoor, for instance. Multinational technology company NVIDIA topped the list, followed by

Facebook employees enjoy a strengths-based organizational culture where they believe in what they are doing and value their relationship with others.

©iStockphoto.com/PeopleImages

software products provider Hubspot, and consulting firm Bain ranking second and third, respectively, on the list of top 50 best companies to work for in the United States. While NVIDIA and Bain employees credited supportive culture as one of the main reasons they enjoyed work, Bain employees also commented that it could be a high-pressured work environment. Perhaps one of the most surprising results involved Zoom which fell from number 22 in 2021 to number 100 in 2022. This big slip in the rankings highlights the pressure on employees during high periods of business demand and the stress of working in a fast-paced work environment.[15]

Components of Culture

Organizational culture can be subtle, with some of its components hidden beneath the surface. As illustrated in Figure 15.1, there are two main components of culture: observable and unobservable.

Observable culture refers to the components of culture that we can see in an organization. For example, personal appearances and dress codes, processes and structures, behaviors and attitudes, and *artifacts* of the culture like awards, myths, and stories[16] (described in more detail following) are all observable parts of organizational culture.

Unobservable culture consists of the components that lie beneath the surface of an organization, such as company values and assumptions.[17] For instance, Dottie Herman, CEO of America's third largest real estate company Douglas Elliman, believes in a values-based company culture that integrates transparency, empowerment, commitment, and inclusiveness.[18]

The components of unobservable culture are often demonstrated in employee behaviors and attitudes. In some cases, the assumptions and values that make up unobservable culture can become so ingrained in employees' mindsets that their perspectives and behaviors become difficult to change.

The Competing Values Framework

One popular way of approaching the study of organization culture is the **competing values framework (CVF)**, which provides a means to identify, measure, and change culture.[19] It is a useful tool to help managers develop the behavioral skills required to deal with the issues arising from an increasingly complex workplace.

FIGURE 15.1 ■ The Cultural Iceberg: Components of Organizational Culture

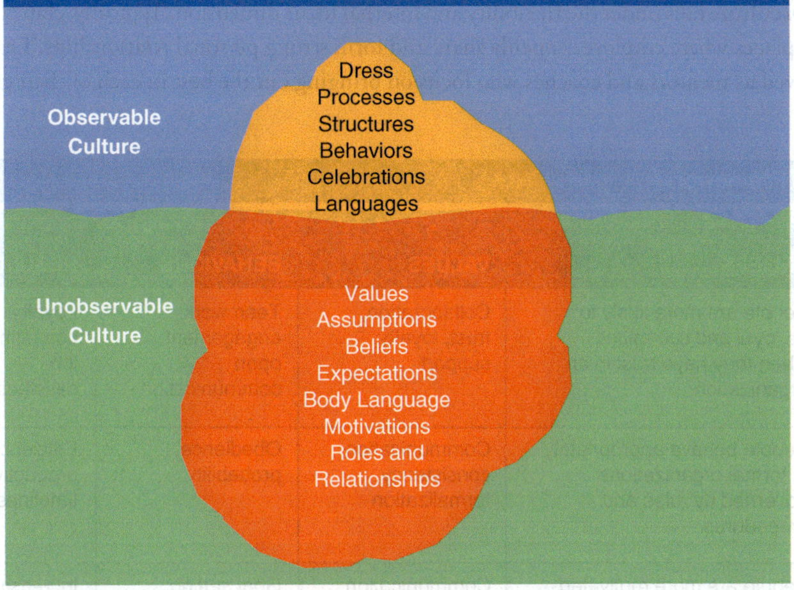

Source: Based on Hall, E. T. (1976). *Beyond Culture*. Anchor.

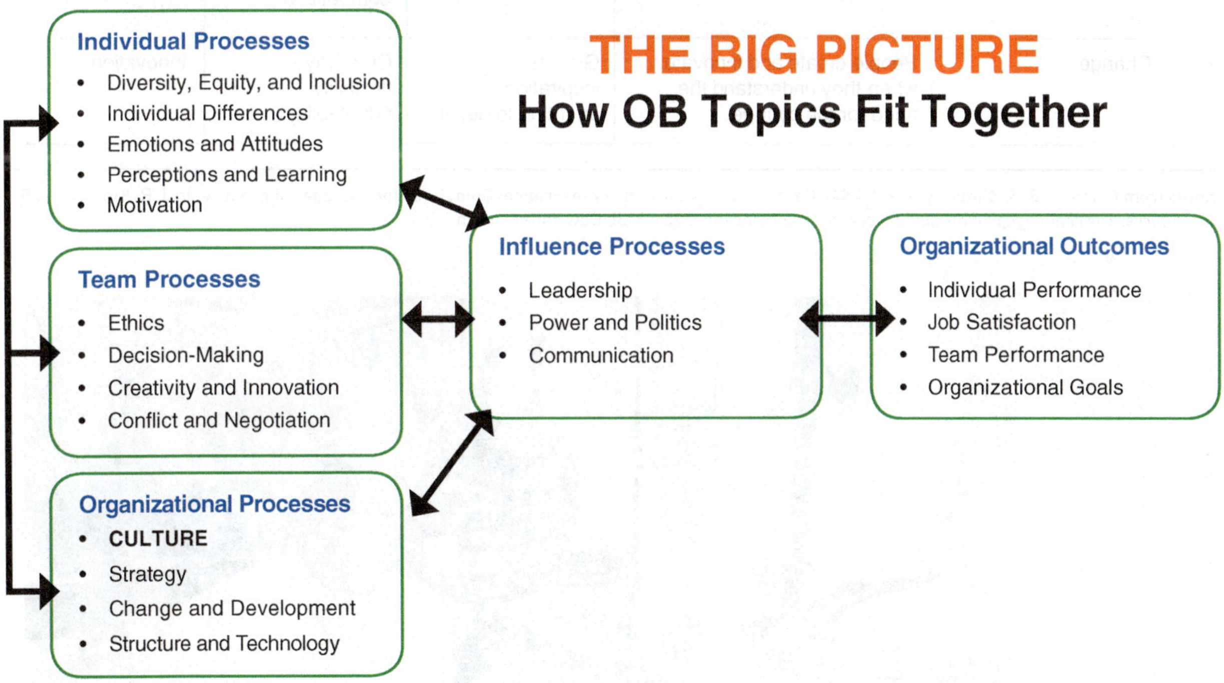

This model highlights two main value dimensions: the first dimension differentiates *flexibility* and *discretion* from *stability* and *control*. This means that some organizations benefit from a more adaptable, flexible culture whereas others might thrive on a more stable and mechanical culture. The second dimension differentiates *internal focus* and *integration* from an *external focus* in the workplace. In other words, some organizations are effective if they focus on the internal culture, for example, ensuring that employees share the same values, integrate well, and work harmoniously, while other organizations focus on building successful relationships outside the organization such as with suppliers, clients, and customers to make themselves more competitive. Publix, Zappos, Nordstrom, and Lexus are examples of organizations that have focused on enhancing the customer experience to build excellent customer relationships.[20] These two dimensions combined result in four different types of culture: clan, hierarchy, adhocracy, and market (see Figure 15.2).

The *clan* culture falls under the flexibility and internal focus dimension. Typically, clan cultures are welcoming places where employees openly share and form strong personal relationships. Leaders tend to be perceived as mentors and coaches who focus on bringing out the best in each of their employees.

FIGURE 15.2 ■ Competing Values Framework

CULTURE TYPE	ASSUMPTIONS	BELIEFS	VALUES	BEHAVIORS	RESULTS
Clan	Human relationships	People are more likely to be loyal and committed when they have trust in an organization.	Collaboration, trust, loyalty, support	Teamwork, engagement, open communication	Loyalty, commitment, job satisfaction
Hierarchy	Stability	People behave appropriately in formal organizations governed by rules and procedures.	Communication, consistency, formalization	Obedience, probability	Efficiency, productivity, timeliness
Market	Accomplishment	People are more motivated to reach goals when they are rewarded for their achievements.	Communication, capability, achievement	Goal setting, competitiveness, planning, researching the competition	Increasing market share and profit, productivity
Adhocracy	Change	People create and innovate when they understand the need for the change.	Growth, inspiration, attention to detail	Creativity, flexibility, adaptability	Innovation

Source: Adapted from Quinn, R. E. & Kimberly, J. R. (1984). Paradox, planning, and perseverance: Guidelines for managerial practice. In J. R. Kimberly & R. E. Quinn, *New futures: The challenge of managing corporate transitions* (pp. 295—313). Dow Jones-Irwin.

Tom Chappell, founder of Tom's of Maine, fosters a company culture that feels more like a family. This is an example of clan culture.

Gregory Rec/Portland Press Herald via Getty Images

The clan culture also furnishes a collaborative environment in which loyalty and commitment are high. Organizations with a clan culture primarily gauge their success against the performance and satisfaction of their employees. Specialist software company Breathe based in the United Kingdom is a good example of clan culture. Breathe puts employees first by encouraging them to speak openly, share honest feedback and ideas, and involve workers in every role to make suggestions relating to every part of working life. For example, when Breathe decided to redesign the office, employees were invited to contribute inspirational quotes and mottoes to help boost morale.[21] Speaking of clan culture, Breathe CEO Jonathan Richards' said, "It's not the values written on the walls, nor the office fruit bowls, bean bags, or pool table. It's also not the leadership style alone. It is all of the above and more."[22]

The *hierarchy* culture exhibits a combination of stability and an internal focus. Unlike organizations adopting the clan culture, hierarchical organizations like the military can be formal and structured places where employees are primarily guided by processes, rules, and procedures. Hierarchical cultures are run via a formal chain of command populated by leaders who use their positions to manage their employees and to emphasize the importance of efficiency, productivity, and organization in the day-to-day running of operations. Amazon is a good example of a company with a hierarchical culture where the chain of command runs from the top to the bottom levels of the organization. Organizations that are too rigid and bureaucratic, however, tend not to react well to change.

Like the hierarchy culture, the *market* culture is also positioned under the control and stability dimension but places more emphasis on interactions conducted outside the organization with a view to increasing company competitiveness. Leaders tend to be driven and goal oriented and to gauge success on the basis of market performance. Hubspot is an example of an organization that drives employees hard to beat the competition by hiring people who have a shared passion for metrics. Results-driven cultures also lead to unhealthy competition between employees when leadership is weak at the top.

The *adhocracy* culture focuses on flexibility and discretion with an external emphasis. These organizations are fast moving and the quickest to adapt to changing markets. Leaders tend to be entrepreneurs and risk-takers who encourage their employees to experiment and generate innovative ideas. Success is measured by company growth and the production of unique, cutting-edge, and innovative products and services. Online ordering and food delivery platform DoorDash demonstrates its adhocracy culture by being agile and encouraging rapid innovation.[23]

Oracle uses a market culture to justify demanding work schedules, keeping their eye on the competition.

©iStockphoto.com/drserg

Although most organizations have elements of all four of these cultural types, some emphasize one type over another. For example, a small family-run business might exhibit characteristics of a clan culture; an investment bank with a strong emphasis on the bottom line may operate as a hierarchy; a results-driven company such as a call center that makes hundreds of sales every day is characterized by elements of a market culture; and start-ups and high-tech firms often have an adhocracy culture.

Though most organizations require different elements from each of the four cultures to operate effectively, none of the elements should be taken to extremes. For example, an organization that is too bureaucratic tends to stifle creativity and can be slow to react to change. Similarly, organizations that are rigidly results driven can damage relationships between competing employees. In the current business environment, we find a focus on clan and adhocracy cultures, with an emphasis on strong relationships based on mutual respect built inside and outside the workplace, and in the most successful organizations an environment that nurtures creativity and innovation.[24]

Dominant Culture, Subculture, Counterculture

Every cultural group has its distinctions. The **dominant culture** is the set of core values shared by the bulk of organizational employees.[25] So, for instance, recreational equipment and maker of children's wagons Radio Flyer based in Chicago has a "Smile Squad" that spreads the word about volunteering opportunities in the community. In 2021, Radio Flyer was featured in Fortune's "50 Best Workplaces for Giving Back."[26]

In addition to this dominant culture, **subcultures** may spring up, which are groups in an organization that share different values from those held by the majority (see Figure 15.3).[27] For example, the Department of Defense consists of different branches such as the Army, Marines, and the Navy. Overall, the dominant culture pervades, but each individual branch has its own subculture made up of unique characteristics. However, it is more common for subcultures to arise in companies where there is no dominant culture, or in the merger of two companies, each of which has a different culture. For example, in 2018 United Airlines unintentionally violated the values of its employee subculture by scrapping a quarterly bonus plan in favor of a prize draw which only benefited a small group of employees. The airline company pulled the program within a day in response to negative feedback from workers.[28]

An extreme type of subculture whose values strongly differ from those of the larger organization is a **counterculture**.[29] Such groups openly reject the company's values, embrace change, and challenge the status quo. It might seem that these "rebel" groups would be bad for an organization, but a counterculture can also produce positive results. It can instigate a revolution that brings about much-needed change, and contribute valuable perspectives and creative ideas. For example, John DeLorean, division head at General Motors in the 1970s, took steps to create a counterculture that was in direct opposition to GM's corporate culture. The GM culture at that time was based on hierarchy, bureaucracy, and conformity; employees were expected to defer to seniority and be conservative in their choice of work

FIGURE 15.3 ■ The Relationship Among Dominant Culture, Subculture, and Counterculture

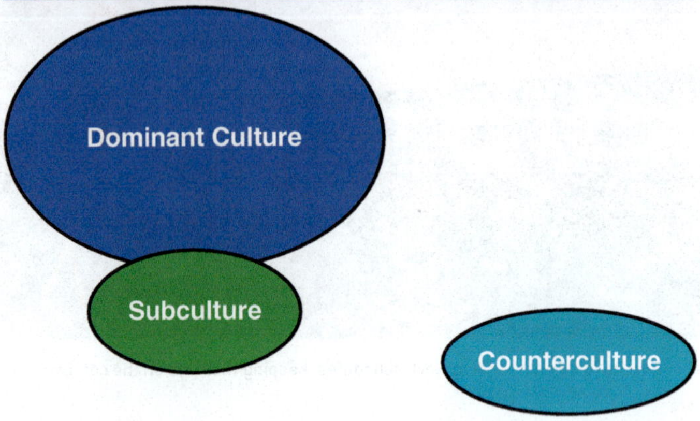

clothes and office decoration. DeLorean sought to change all this by rallying a group of followers to reject the bureaucratic decision-making and conformity, dressing in modern styles and redecorating their offices in bright colors. Although GM tolerated this counterculture for a while, it fell apart when DeLorean left to start the DeLorean Motor Company (producer of the famous DeLorean DMC-12, featured in Hollywood's blockbuster *Back to the Future* series).

Strong and Weak Cultures

When the majority of employees are aligned with the values of an organization, the organization has a strong culture; there is less need for detailed policies and procedures because the rules are accepted and understood.[30] Core values are fundamental for company success and many businesses' values were put to the test during the COVID-19 pandemic. Dr Yemisi Bolade-Ogunfodun, a lecturer and program director at Henley Business School said, "The moment of truth for many organizations has been revealed in how employers express the culture in supportive attitudes to employees, in initiatives developed to cushion the adverse effects of the pandemic and in living out their core values; in other words, 'walking the talk.'"[31] Social media solutions company Sprout Social based in Chicago used its core values of communication, accountability, and care to energize teams to drive each other and the business forward, achieving growth and success as a result.[32]

In contrast, an organization with a weak culture is one whose core values are not embraced or shared by its employees. This occurs mainly because the core values are not defined or communicated well, which can lead to inconsistent behavior among employees, which in turn can lead to bad service. Toxic work cultures have been identified as the leading cause of the huge number of resignations that took place during COVID-19. Other reasons for weak cultures include burnout and failure to recognize or appreciate performance.[33]

Although strong organizational cultures are valuable for nurturing a sense of unity and providing direction, they usually take a long time to develop and can be difficult to adapt in a rapidly changing environment. In addition, employees can become conditioned to think the same way as their peers and become reluctant to share different views—a phenomenon known as **groupthink**.[34] Too much groupthink in an organization can lead to stifled creativity, lack of innovation, and cultural clashes.

After a number of White House lawn security breaches in 2015, an independent investigation into the culture of the Secret Service showed that the organization needed new cultural leadership.

©iStockphoto.com/Thomas Faull

ARTIFACTS AND FUNCTIONS OF ORGANIZATIONAL CULTURE

The artifacts or identifiable elements of an organization provide members and outsiders with a better understanding of its culture.[35]

Newcomers to the company are often told **stories**, narratives based on real organizational experiences that have become embellished over time and illustrate core cultural values. Research shows that information is up to 20 times more memorable when it is delivered through the medium of storytelling. Stories can also increase our feelings of care, connection, and empathy.[36]

Organizations may also have a number of **symbols**, which are objects that express meaning about a culture. For example, an office dress code is an example of a symbol that can also impact how a company culture is perceived. Recent studies show that more than half of respondents have positive associations with companies that have a casual dress code, while 60% of workers reported a negative perception of companies that impose a formal dress code.[37]

The culture is also supported by **rituals**, formalized actions, and planned routines. Moringa food company Kuli Kuli, based in Oakland, California, has a ritual which celebrates employee achievements by banging a gong.[38] Research shows that workplace rituals can increase employee engagement, create bonds between different generations, and give people a sense of purpose.[39]

Another cultural artifact includes **ceremonies**, events that reinforce the relationship between employees and the organization. For example, Massachusetts consulting firm ALKU launched the "Corporate Cup Program" during the COVID-19 pandemic to honor employees for their achievements while working from home. The company also started a weekly "Top Ten Plays" showcasing 10 employee Zoom highlights and awarded outstanding employees with T-shirts that represented ALKU's business goals such as #BeAPro, #PitchYourNiche, and #FollowMyLead.[40]

Some companies have a particular **organizational language** which involves the staff using certain words or metaphors and expressions regularly in conversation with each other. For example, in the Google culture, Google employees are called "Googlers," new employees are called "Newglers," and employees who bike together are called "Bikeglers."[41] Candidates must also possess an element of "Googley-ness" which involves a combination of conscientious and intellectual humility.[42]

Organizations with the most positive cultural artifacts are ones which cultivate independent and innovative thinking, provide meaningful feedback, and emphasize personal responsibility.

Functions of Organizational Culture

Two major functions of organizational culture imperative to an organization's survival are external adaptation and internal integration.[43] **External adaptation** is the way an organization reacts to outside influences. To achieve external adaptation to its environment, the organization must arrive at some basic shared assumptions about its mission and strategy, about the goals, tasks, and methods the organization needs to achieve, and about ways of managing both success and failure.[44] For example, British–Swedish multinational pharmaceutical company AstraZeneca responded to the COVID-19 pandemic by adapting a range of business models to meet urgent needs, such as developing vaccines, refining testing and screen processes, and using AI to gather new insights into new diseases.[45]

Internal integration, in contrast, is the process of creating a shared identity among employees by adopting a common language, group boundaries, an accepted distribution of power and status, and norms of trust, rewards, and punishment.[46] Every company, regardless of size, needs a degree of internal integration to succeed. Internal integration allows teams to communicate effectively, develop friendships and norms, and define acceptable and unacceptable behaviors. Research shows that team members with a shared sense of identity are more likely to feel part of a team, have greater emotional well-being, and are less likely to suffer burnout.[47]

Potential Dysfunctions of Culture

What happens when cultures become a liability rather than an asset? There are at least three situations in which organizational culture can become dysfunctional and create hindrances: during organizational change, under organizational diversity, and during mergers and acquisitions.

Change hindrances are cultural obstacles that impede progress and make it difficult for the organization to adapt to different situations.[48] Examples of change hindrances are ineffective communication with employees, unclear processes and procedures, disorganized leadership, failure to involve employees, and inadequate resources. For managers to effectively implement change, such as introducing a new system or restructuring a team, they need to minimize resistance by communicating clear objectives, engaging their employees in decision making, equipping them with the necessary resources to support the change, and keeping them fully informed about how and why the change is taking place.

Diversity hindrances are cultural obstacles that limit the range of employee demographics in organizations.[49] As we explored in Chapter 2, diversity can span a wide range of areas, including age/generation, race/ethnicity, gender, and ability. Many of today's organizations cultivate a diverse workforce because of the benefits diversity can bring.

However, despite the trend toward creating more diverse workplaces, managers at many organizations must still overcome cultural and other obstacles to achieve this ideal. Organizations with strong cultures tend to select the same types of employees because they are perceived to best fit the culture. Technology companies in particular score low on workplace diversity, including Zoom and Tesla who have been identified as two of the worst companies for gender diversity at the senior leadership level with only two women sitting on the board of directors for each company.[50]

Organizations that continue to hire the same types of people limit the level of diversity in their organization, which often leads to inequality. For example, the pay inequity between men and women in the workplace has been well documented, as has the lack of minorities in senior positions. Organizations that work hard to overcome diversity hindrances and recognize the value of differences are more likely to have a rich, varied, and productive workforce.

Mergers and acquisitions hindrances are cultural obstacles that make it difficult for two organizations to join together.[51] Mismatched cultures can lead to a "culture clash" that can have a devastating impact on the success of the merger.[52] For example, French luxury goods company LVMH's acquisition of American jeweler Tiffany in 2021, resulted in a major culture clash following an unofficial memo circulated by Tiffany staff outlining some tips on "Franco-American cultural nuances and etiquette." One of these tips stated that French people were more likely to provide negative feedback, were "less warm and fuzzy" and not inclined to use excessively positive comments such as "amazing" and "fabulous."[53] Although the memo was denounced by Tiffany, it highlighted the cultural divide between the two companies.

An organization that encourages innovation through informal interaction may not blend well with one that follows more formal processes and procedures. To break down these cultural barriers, managers in both organizations need to adopt cultural initiatives, which include promoting open communication with and among employees, providing a forum for questions and concerns, and engaging employees in major decisions.

TYPES OF ORGANIZATIONAL CULTURES

Earlier in this chapter, we explored the different types of organizational cultures, namely the adhocracy, clan, hierarchy, and market cultures, through the competing values framework. As we see next, however, many more types of culture exist in the workplace (see Figure 15.4).

Positive Organizational Culture

Organizations with positive organizational cultures focus on supporting employees' strengths, increasing morale, and providing rewards for good work.[54] In this type of culture, employees are active in decision-making and kept informed of the organization's vision and direction. They tend to be productive, engaged, and committed to the company. File hosting services company Dropbox is a good example of an organization with a positive culture. Dropbox fosters an environment which focuses heavily on diversity, and celebrates different backgrounds and perspectives by encouraging people to share their stories. The company also has an internal post service called Gratitude Post which allows employees to send handwritten messages of gratitude to each other, which helps to build and strengthen relationships between team members.[55]

FIGURE 15.4 ■ Organizational Cultures

CULTURE	ATTRIBUTES
Positive Organizational Culture	• Employees' strengths are supported • Morale is high • Good work is rewarded
Communal Culture	• Employees think alike • Employees share knowledge • Employees have a clear focus on goals • Goals are achieved as a team
Fragmented Culture	• Socializing is minimal • Individuals work independently
Mercenary Culture	• Employees are measured based on their performance and productivity • High commitment is expected • Financial goals are top priority • Socializing is minimal
Networked Culture	• Trust is high • Employees communicate openly and share information • Employees work mostly independently, but come together to share ideas • Work is highly creative
Ethical Culture	• Managers act as ethical role models • Ethical standards are clear • Employees are trained to behave ethically
Spiritual Culture	• Tasks contribute to the good of society • Caring, compassion, and support are prioritized over profit

Communal Culture

Organizations that nurture a communal culture environment are home to employees who tend to think alike, are happy to share knowledge, and have a clear focus on the direction of the task.[56] They are sociable and responsive and work well together to achieve goals.

Medical devices company Eargo, based in San Jose, California, has been praised for its positive, nurturing, fun culture. One Eargo employee said, "Fantastic. One of the best companies ever. Great fun people to work with. To infinity and beyond."[57]

Fragmented Culture

Fragmented culture is found in companies where employees tend to keep to themselves, avoid socializing, and work as individuals rather than as part of a team.[58] For example, during the COVID-19 pandemic, there was a large-scale shift to remote/hybrid working leading to fears that the company culture might become weaker and more fragmented. Despite these concerns, research shows that nearly 70% of employees reported that their organization's culture had a positive effect on their role, compared to just over 50% of employees working on-site.[59]

Mercenary Culture

As the name suggests, mercenary cultures exist in organizations where making money is the top priority.[60] Employees are measured by their levels of performance and productivity and are expected to have a high commitment to achieving organizational goals. In 2018, Netflix came under the spotlight for its hugely competitive and mercenary culture, where employees were expected to work long hours, under intense pressure within a cutthroat environment.[61]

Networked Cultures

Networked cultures are characterized by a high degree of trust between employees and a willingness to communicate and share information.[62] Employees may work independently of each other, but they come together on an informal basis to swap and exchange ideas. Highly creative organizations such as Apple, Pixar, and website building and hosting company Squarespace in which people are encouraged to think differently, tend to have networked cultures.

Ethical Culture

Because of well-documented ethical scandals during the past few years, many organizations are focused on creating more ethical cultures.[63] This means managers need to be role models themselves, communicate ethical standards, and train employees to behave in an ethical manner. To reinforce this type of culture, employees should be rewarded for ethical behavior and punished for unethical behavior. An example of an organization with a strong ethical culture is Kao, a Japanese company that manufactures personal care, household, and cosmetics products, which has been recognized by the Ethisphere Institute as the most ethical company in the world 14 years in a row because of its strong commitment to integrity, sustainability, and social responsibility.[64]

Spiritual Culture

Spiritual culture focuses on opportunities for employees to grow in the workplace by carrying out meaningful tasks that contribute to the good of society as a whole.[65] Organizations with a spiritual culture prioritize caring, compassion, and support for others over profit. There has been some debate over the effectiveness of spiritual organizations, with supporters believing that workplace spirituality enhances the value of the organization, and critics questioning the legitimacy of this type of culture as well as its effectiveness in terms of profit and financial success.[66] Research and design consultancy Sacred Design Lab fosters a spiritual culture by embedding values into every part of the organization with the goal of creating a sense of "belonging and becoming."[67]

EXAMINING THE EVIDENCE

LINKING ORGANIZATIONAL CULTURE AND PERFORMANCE

Organizational culture emerged in the 1970s and 1980s as a concept popularized by practitioner-focused books such as Tom Peters and Robert Waterman's *In Search of Excellence* and Edgar Schein's *Organizational Culture and Leadership*. Two basic premises developed from these and other similar writings. The first is that organizational culture is derived primarily from the personalities, values, and behaviors of the founders and top executives of organizations. The second premise is that organizational culture is a key determinant of an organization's performance.

Nearly 50 years later, these fundamental assumptions about organizational culture remain largely in place, although they have been subject to some degree of skepticism. Recently, however, researcher Boon-Seng Tan of the Nanyang Business School in Singapore synthesized research studies across multiple disciplines to assess these basic assumptions.68 Results of the analyses show that more homogeneous organizational cultures that encourage teamwork and have a clear mission, tend to enhance organizational performance across multiple economic models. These findings provide support for the presumed linkage between organizational culture and performance along with a theoretical explanation for why and how culture matters.

Critical-Thinking Questions

1. If organizational culture is a key resource for shaping firm performance, what other parameters could affect firm performance?
2. What are the implications for senior leadership's responsibility for building high performance organizational cultures?

Many organizations strive to build an organizational culture that promotes respect and trust for others, loyalty and commitment to the company, and positivity and creativity. Yet achieving a desired organizational culture does not happen overnight; indeed, building culture is a slowly evolving process shaped over time.

ADAPTING ORGANIZATIONAL PRACTICES ACROSS CULTURES

One of the main criteria for a successful global expansion is an understanding of different organizational cultures.

One of the most valuable studies in measuring culture was conducted by Dutch sociologist Geert Hofstede. Hofstede identified five ways of measuring culture based on research analyzing the interactions between people from different cultures all over the world.[69] Known as Hofstede's dimensions, these five measures, each of which is shown as a continuum in Figure 15.5, have been used by organizations to improve understanding and cooperation between cultures.

Hofstede's Dimensions

The **individualist–collectivist** dimension focuses on the degree to which citizens in a given culture believe they have the right to live their lives as they see fit, choose their own values, and act on their own judgment. This dimension is usually high in individualist cultures like the United States. In collectivist cultures such as Thailand, people are more likely to value the welfare of the group over that of any particular individual and suspend personal values and judgment for the sake of the "greater good." **Power distance** expresses the extent to which people in different societies accept the way power is distributed. People in countries with *high power distance* such as Mexico and Singapore are more likely to accept the idea of hierarchy and depend on those with power to make the decisions. At the organizational level, high power distance is most common in hierarchical structures where there is very little interaction between lower- and higher-level employees. In *low power distance* countries such as the United States and Sweden, in contrast, people tend to prefer consultation with others and strive to ensure the distribution of power is equalized as fairly as possible.

Uncertainty avoidance measures the degree to which people are able to deal with the unexpected and how they cope with uncertainty in unstructured environments. As Figure 15.5 shows, Italy and Mexico have cultures that emphasize more predictable structures, while the United States and Singapore emphasize variable environments. In countries with a competitive culture, such as Austria and China, employees generally tend to display more assertive, striving, merit-oriented personality

FIGURE 15.5 ■ Hofstede's Dimensions

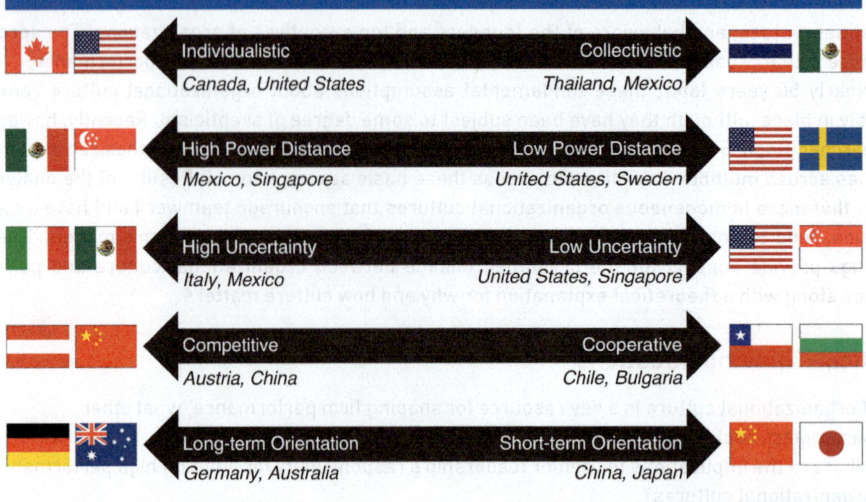

Source: Neck, C. P. (2013). *Management.* Wiley.

traits. In contrast, countries with cooperative cultures such as Chile and Bulgaria tend to take a more compassionate, tolerant, and caring approach. Hofstede used the terms *masculine* and *feminine* to denote the competitive versus cooperative continuum in work, but the authors consider this nomenclature outdated. Cultures that lean toward **long-term orientation** measure values such as perseverance, respect for tradition, and thrift against **short-term orientation** values such as meeting social obligations and avoiding embarrassment or shame.

Hofstede has been criticized for using surveys to measure cultural differences, and overgeneralizing national populations on the basis of the limited size of the model, in that there weren't enough respondents to the questionnaires to draw the conclusions that Hofstede had made. Hofstede has responded to these criticisms by defending the use of surveys, noting that the results closely correlated with other data that represented whole national populations.[70]

Although Hofstede's cultural dimensions provide a useful guideline for organizations considering branching out into new territories, every organization is different and will need to take its own particular traits into consideration. At the same time, an understanding of Hofstede's cultural dimensions may help management in one culture determine how best to launch a business in another culture and support new employees.

Global Integration versus Local Responsiveness

International companies face challenges in two major areas when they operate in foreign countries: global integration and local responsiveness.[71] This means they often have to strike a balance between following their own global strategies—determining how their products are made and marketed and how employees are treated—and meeting the legal, financial, employment, and other requirements of their host government. Firms may have to change or tailor their operations to remain in compliance with those requirements. As a result, they have to consider how much they should either standardize or localize their practices.

Standardization is the degree to which employees are expected to follow the same rules and policies everywhere.[72] For example, in a manufacturing plant, teams might follow best practices that are applied globally, such as adhering to certain protocols for safety reasons and ensuring operations go smoothly. When introducing a new product under a global standardized process, teams may perform *upstream functions* such as identifying the market need, devising strategies, and brainstorming ways to bring the product to market. These functions take place behind the scenes and are invisible to the customer.

Singaporeans are more suited to dealing with a variable environment. This cultural characteristic is reflected in their unique and modern skyline.

©iStockphoto.com/FabVietnam_Photography

Localization, in contrast, is the process of adapting certain functions to accommodate the language, culture, or governing laws of a different country.[73] In the case of a new product, teams working in a foreign country might step in to manage the *downstream functions* that focus on sales and marketing of the product after the launch. These functions are centered on improving the flow of the product to the customer.

International Assignments and Career Development

Sometimes employees are sent abroad on international assignments to further their personal and career development. An **expatriate** is an employee who lives and works in a foreign country on a temporary basis.[74] As of 2021, there are an estimated 9 million American expatriates living abroad according to the U.S. Department of State.[75] High-potential employees or **HIPOs** are employees who are flexible, committed, and motivated.[76] Such employees are often chosen to work on international assignments as part of their career development.

Although international assignments sound like exciting prospects, they can have downsides. Many people underestimate the difficulty of moving to a different country as an expatriate and experiencing **culture shock**, a feeling of nervousness, doubt, and confusion arising from being in a foreign and unfamiliar environment.[77]

If you ever have the opportunity to work on a long-term foreign assignment, avoid culture shock by doing your homework. Research the culture and the language, talk to people who have been in that country to get their advice and feedback, and make sure the job you will be doing is clear from the very beginning. Many employees have accepted assignments overseas only to find the role or the culture (or both) to be nothing like they envisioned. Ideally, organizations should offer support and provide cultural knowledge and language training if necessary to prepare their employees for an overseas experience.[78]

Stages of Cultural Adaptation

Typically, there are five stages of cultural adaptation.[79] (See Figure 15.6.) The first is the *honeymoon* stage that takes place soon after arrival in the new country. Everything is exciting and novel and there is an immediate impulse to explore and soak up the new culture. However, after a few weeks, the *disintegration* stage sets in, the gloss starts to wear off, and feelings of nervousness and insecurity may appear. It might be difficult to communicate with the residents, the food might seem strange, business and social etiquette might be a struggle, and the local laws may seem confusing. For example, business attire in China is typically conservative with men in suits and women in high necklines; in the Middle East, West Africa and Latin America, giving a "thumbs up" gesture to signal your approval is

FIGURE 15.6 ■ Stages of Cultural Adaptation

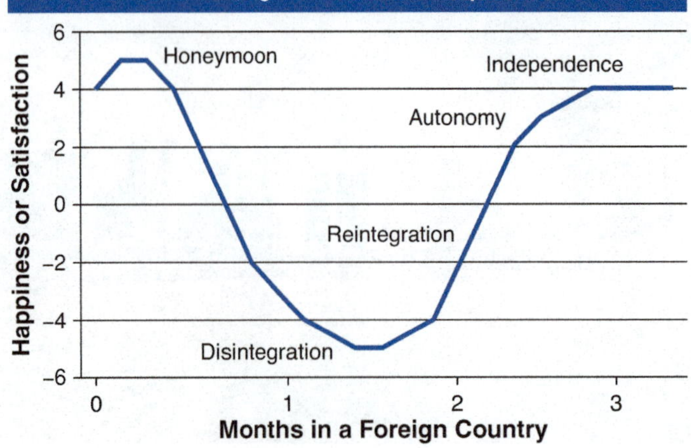

Source: Adapted from Winkleman, M. (1994). Cultural shock and adaptation. *Journal of Counseling and Development, 73*(2), 121–126.

considered rude; and backing away from physical contact in Brazil where it is customary to stand close to the person you are talking to, is regarded as disrespectful.[80]

The third stage is *reintegration*, which typically occurs after a few months in the foreign location. At this stage, you probably have reached an understanding about how the business and social cultures operate and have accepted the factors that seemed strange in the beginning. You may still have mixed feelings about living and working in the society, but you are starting to adjust. During the *autonomy* stage you are more confident about knowing how to function in your new environment, you know how to interact with people and where to socialize, and you have a clearer understanding of business practices. In short, you are beginning to settle in.

This leads to the *independence* stage, in which you understand how the culture operates, feel confident that you can handle most situations, and value the culture for its differences from as well as its similarities to your own.

Expatriate Failure

Global firms hope that most employees who are sent on foreign assignments, particularly expatriates who might be expected to last for a couple of years or more, will reach the independence stage. However, expatriates sometimes return home early for a variety of reasons. There are several reasons why expatriates fail to complete the duration of their stay in a different country.[81] The most common is family stress.[82] Although the employee is experiencing a novel and exciting environment and making new friends at work, the spouse, who may have left a job or career behind at home, may be lonely and struggling to adjust to the new culture, which can put an enormous amount of pressure on a relationship.

Another factor is that foreign assignments often come with a higher degree of responsibility, which some people find overwhelming. Managing people from different cultures can be frustrating and perplexing, especially if the expatriate is not familiar with local customs. If an expatriate is unable to fulfill the requirements of their role or does not possess the emotional maturity to handle additional responsibility, then the organization itself may choose to terminate the assignment.

Finally, another reason for expatriate failure is inability to adjust to cultural or language differences, which often occurs because of poor advance preparation. This can lead to severe homesickness and an early return home.

Benefits and Costs of International Assignments

Are expatriate assignments worth the cost and extra effort to the employee, the family, and the firm? In some companies, a person's career development depends on them taking international assignments. For example, an employee working in a U.S. investment bank in New York with branches located globally can gain great experience and make valuable new contacts in one of the firm's international offices. However, "out of sight, out of mind" can also operate. In other words, sometimes expatriates can return home to find they have been overlooked for career opportunities or promotions while away. To combat this issue, employees working abroad must manage their careers by staying in touch with their mentors and remaining in close contact with their biggest work champions back at headquarters, either through video conferencing tools like Zoom or Skype or making face-to-face appointments when returning to the main office on scheduled trips, or both.[83]

SHAPING ORGANIZATIONAL CULTURE

Organizational culture can be difficult to change. Unlike many other management functions, shaping organizational culture requires changing mindsets. In short, it is an emotional process rather than a rational or analytical one, and as we have learned, dealing with emotions in the workplace can be tricky.

Consultancy firm Booz & Co. has outlined a concept called "the critical few" that presents managers with ways to implement effective change within the organizational culture.[84] First, organizations need to define a few *critical behaviors* that managers would like their employees to embody—for example, hire only people who energize others, or make sure employees provide excellent customer service.

Ryan Roslansky's values and behaviors are embraced by LinkedIn employees, who are encouraged to follow their passions and take action.

David Paul Morris/Bloomberg via Getty Images

Once these critical behaviors have been identified, they can be strengthened and nurtured through training until they become a natural part of the company ethos.

Second, focus on a few *cultural traits* that have an emotional effect on employees. What makes employees take pride in their work? What kinds of traits motivate them—loyalty, commitment, trust? Once these traits have been identified, managers can promote them with the goal of encouraging every employee to embrace them.

Finally, managers need to identify the *informal leaders* in the organization. These leaders can exist at every level. They are well liked, trusted, and respected and have a natural way of influencing the behavior of others. Managers need to get these informal leaders motivated to help champion changes and get buy-in from others.

However, change starts at the top, and one of the most important catalysts for change is the behavior of top management.

Influence of Founders and Top Management

Successful organizations tend to be led by top managers and leaders who embody certain beliefs, values, and assumptions, thereby influencing employees to do the same.[85] Shoei Yamana, the CEO of Konica Minolta, the Japanese manufacturer of planetariums is a good example of a leader whose behaviors and values have been embraced by the Konica Minolta staff and have become the core of the company's mission. Shoei Yamana said, "My belief is that people don't work for numbers . . . they need to share the same belief that they are creating value in some way."[86]

Selection Practices

Managers working in organizations with a certain culture tend to select candidates whose personalities, behaviors, values, and attitudes best match that culture and values.[87] This match is called **person-organization fit**. Netflix is an example of a company that hire on the basis of person–organization fit and uses the saying "Always be recruiting." Candidates can come from all sorts of different places, anywhere from conversations on the sideline of a soccer game, to chance meetings on an airplane. Even when the candidate doesn't quite fit the role, Netflix makes sure that the interview experience is efficient, effective, and enjoyable.[88]

Socialization Methods

New hires are integrated into the company's corporate culture through **socialization**, the process through which an organization communicates its values to new employees.[89] For example, when you were hired for your current or most recent job, training probably happened as part of your socialization process. There are three main forms of socialization: context, content, and social dynamics.[90]

Context

Socialization depends on the *context* in which the information is imparted. For example, organizations can choose to socialize new hires through an informal or formal process, and on an individual or collective basis. During an informal process, new hires are put to work immediately so they can learn the company's values through on-the-job training.

Most organizations advocate a more formal approach, including a ceremonial induction or orientation program that introduces new hires to the specifics of the culture and helps build a sense of cohesiveness and identity. Cloverleaf, a human resources consulting company based in Kentucky, socializes new hires remotely by providing them with personality profiles of team members and conducting Zoom weekly meetings that allow employees to give shoutouts to their colleagues and share their personal and professional concerns. These meetings help new hires to get to know their colleagues better and figure out what motivates them. When this happens, they are more willing to support their team members and perform at a higher level as a result.[91]

Content

Organizations often provide new hires with *content*, information regarding the activities and tasks they may be expected to carry out, and the time each activity should take to complete. Examples of content might include an employee handbook; a document that describes the company's goals, policies and expectations; or documentation outlining details about the new hire's department and the role and responsibilities. This information gives new hires a sense of career direction and provides them with an understanding about what they are expected to do and why they are doing it.

New Red Hat employees receive special group training and are each given a red fedora to show that they are now part of the team.

Timon Schneider / Alamy Stock Photo

Social Dynamics

Socialization also depends on the nature of *social dynamics*.[92] Teams with good dynamics consist of team members who positively interact with each other, and work towards a common goal. Teams with poor dynamics tend to be low performing and are more likely to being about negative outcomes.[93] Some organizations assign new hires to specific employees who act as role models or mentors and help to advise on both the formal and informal aspects of the organizational culture. For example, Microsoft runs an "onboarding buddies" program that educates new hires on the type of information that won't be found in the employee handbook, such as cultural norms, unspoken rules, and how team members are expected to engage with each other. Microsoft's buddy system has provided organizational context, greater employee satisfaction and a boost in productivity.[94]

However, in many cases, new hires do not receive formal social support from team members. Left to their own devices, they are forced to figure out the dynamics by themselves, which can result in uncertainty and confusion.

Organizations with successful socialization strategies are more likely to have a positive organizational culture and perform better as a result.

Feldman's Model of Organizational Socialization

Researcher Daniel Feldman identified three phases of organizational socialization experienced by an employee before and after entering an organization.[95] These three phases are anticipatory socialization, encounter phase, and change and acquisition phase. (See Figure 15.7.)

Anticipatory Socialization

Anticipatory socialization takes place before the individual joins the organization. This can happen in several ways. For example, the individual may have talked to current employees to get their opinions about what they like and dislike about the organization, or they may have researched the company online to get a better sense of the working environment.

Encounter Phase

The encounter phase begins when the individual signs an employment contract and learns more about what the organization is really like. During this phase, the organization may use a number of socializing techniques to help the new employee become better acquainted with the working environment, such as introductions to key members of the organization, classroom or online training, or written guidelines about the company.

Change and Acquisition Phase

When socialization is successful, the employee will have a clear understanding of their role and will have learned how to confidently carry out new tasks and skills. This is also the period when new employees adjust to group values and norms and come to understand where they fit into the team dynamic.

FIGURE 15.7 ■ Feldman's Three Stages of Organizational Socialization

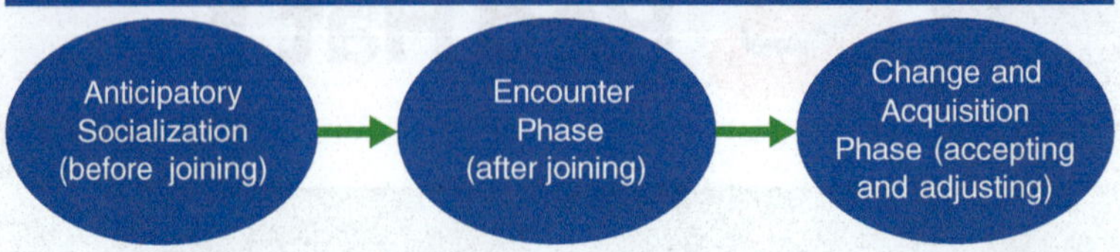

Source: Based on Feldman, D. C. (1976). A contingency theory of socialization. *Administrative Science Quarterly, 21*(3), 433–452.

Successful organizations work hard to shape the culture by building trust and leading by example. They foster an environment where employees are treated like accountable adults who want to take responsibility for their work processes and do good work. Organizations that take the right steps to nurture a positive culture will go a long way toward maintaining employee engagement, morale, and overall happiness.

IN REVIEW

15.1 Describe the basic characteristics of organizational culture

Organizational culture is a pattern of shared norms, rules, values, and beliefs that guide the attitudes and behaviors of its employees. Observable culture refers to the components that can be seen in an organization such as dress, structures, behaviors, and artifacts. **Unobservable culture** consists of the components that lie beneath the surface, such as company values and assumptions.

15.2 Discuss the various artifacts and functions of organizational culture

The artifacts or identifiable elements of any organization can include: **symbols** objects that provide meaning about a culture; **rituals** formalized actions and planned routines; **ceremonies** events that reinforce the relationship between employees and the organization; and **organizational language** a type of verbal communication that consists of certain words or metaphors, and expressions used regularly by staff. There are two main functions of organizational culture: **external adaptation** is a shared understanding of the goals, tasks, and methods that need to be achieved, together with ways of managing success and failure; and **internal integration** a shared identity with agreed-upon methods of working together.

15.3 Compare various types of organizational cultures

Organizations with a *positive organizational culture* focus on building on employee strengths, increasing morale, and providing rewards for good work. Employees in a *communal culture* tend to think alike, are happy to share knowledge, and have a clear focus on the direction of the task. Organizations with a *fragmented culture* have employees who tend to keep to themselves, avoid socializing, and work as individuals rather than part of a team. As the name suggests, *mercenary cultures* exist in organizations where making money is the top priority. In *networked cultures*, there is a high degree of trust between employees and a willingness to communicate and share information. In an *ethical culture*, managers need to be role models themselves, communicate ethical standards, and train employees to behave in an ethical manner. Organizations with a *spiritual culture* focus on the opportunities for employees to grow in the workplace by carrying out meaningful tasks that contribute to the good of society as a whole.

15.4 Identify key ways in which organizations adapt their practices across cultures

One of the main criteria for a successful global expansion is an understanding of different organizational cultures. Hofstede's five dimensions have been used by organizations to improve understanding and cooperation between cultures.

International companies face challenges in two major areas when they operate in foreign countries: global integration and local responsiveness. **Standardization** is the degree to which all employees are expected to follow the same rules and policies. **Localization** is the process of adapting certain functions to accommodate the language, culture, or governing laws of a country.

15.5 Contrast differing approaches for shaping organizational culture

Managers working in organizations with a certain culture tend to select candidates whose personalities and attitudes best match that culture and values. This match is called **person–organization fit**. New hires are integrated into the company's corporate culture through a process of **socialization**, which is a way an organization communicates its values to employees.

KEY TERMS

Ceremonies (p. 362)
Change hindrances (p. 363)
Competing values framework (p. 356)
Counterculture (p. 360)
Culture shock (p. 368)
Diversity hindrances (p. 363)
Dominant culture (p. 360)
Expatriate (p. 368)
External adaptation (p. 362)
HIPOs (p. 368)
Individualist–collectivist (p. 366)
Internal integration (p. 362)
Localization (p. 368)
Long-term orientation (p. 367)
Mergers and acquisition hindrances (p. 363)
Observable culture (p. 356)
Organizational culture (p. 355)
Organizational language (p. 362)
Person-organization fit (p. 370)
Power distance (p. 366)
Rituals (p. 362)
Short-term orientation (p. 367)
Socialization (p. 371)
Standardization (p. 373)
Stories (p. 362)
Subcultures (p. 360)
Symbols (p. 362)
Uncertainty avoidance (p. 366)
Unobservable culture (p. 373)

UP FOR DEBATE: ORGANIZATIONAL CULTURAL FIT

Many organizations feel that the culture of an organization is so important that they even fire top performers who don't "fit" the culture. This is a good thing. Agree or Disagree?

EXERCISE 15.1: THAT'S THE WAY WE DO THINGS AROUND HERE!

Consider an organization with which you are very familiar. Ideally, it is one for which you have worked, volunteered, or otherwise served as a member.

Observable Aspects of Culture

If an outsider were to come into your organization, what would they see? What would appear striking and characteristic of your organization?

1. List some specific structures and processes, behaviors, and dress and personal appearance factors an outsider might find striking.

____

____

____

____

2. What cultural artifacts (stories, rituals, symbols, language) are especially representative of your organization's underlying culture?

____

____

____

____

Unobservable Aspects of Culture

What aspects of the culture would be less visible to an outside observer? What values, norms, and assumptions are hidden beneath the surface?

1. List the core values, the primary or dominant values that are accepted throughout your organization.

____

____

2. What are the basic underlying assumptions of your organization, the taken-for-granted beliefs and philosophies that are so ingrained that members act on them in a given situation without questioning the validity of their own actions?

CATEGORIZING YOUR CULTURE

1. Which type of culture does your organization most resemble according to the competing values framework (clan, adhocracy, hierarchy, market)?

2. Perhaps your organization's culture more closely resembles one of the other types of cultures discussed in the chapter (positive, communal, fragmented, mercenary, networked, ethical, spiritual).

3. Or possibly you would categorize your organization's culture in terms different from any of the following categories described:

Thinking Critically About Your Culture

1. What aspects of your organization's culture have enabled it to be successful?

2. What aspects of your organization's culture have constrained or inhibited it from succeeding?

EXERCISE 15.2: WHAT ARE THE ARTIFACTS OF YOUR UNIVERSITY?

Objective

The purpose of this exercise is to grasp the concept of cultural artifacts of organizations.

Instructions

For members of an organizational culture to fully understand their culture, artifacts help articulate the culture in ways that the members can readily appreciate and, in some cases, explain to outsiders.

The text discusses five typical artifacts of organizational culture. They are explained in more detail in the text, but here are short definitions of each:

- **Stories**—narratives based on real organizational experiences that have become embellished over time and illustrate core cultural values
- **Symbols**—objects that provide meaning about a culture
- **Rituals**—formalized actions and planned routines
- **Ceremonies**—events that reinforce the relationship between employees and the organization
- **Organizational language**—words or metaphors and expressions specific to an organization

In this exercise, a student will lead a discussion with the class to determine how each of the artifacts is demonstrated at your university. Once a volunteer student is selected, that student will come to the front of the room and proceed through each of the five artifacts mentioned above as they relate to your university. In other words, what stories are told about the university that truly represent the culture? What symbols exist on campus that express the university's culture? And so on.

Reflection Questions

1. How does your, and even the class's, view about the university's culture differ from that of an employee of the university? Would a student and a university employee completely agree on the culture of the university? Why or why not?
2. Choose an organization you have either worked with in the past or which you are currently employed. What stories, symbols, rituals, ceremonies, and organizational language can you identify in that organization?
3. Who is more likely to *accurately* identify the cultural artifacts of an organization: employees within that organization or outsiders? Explain.

Exercise contributed by Steven Stovall, Southeast Missouri State University.

EXERCISE 15.3: YOU GOT LUCKY

Objectives

1. Describe the basic characteristics of organizational culture.
2. Contrast differing approaches for shaping organizational culture.

Background

Upon completing your university degree, you have been hired as a store manager for Clover Supermarkets, and can expect to be promoted to a district manager for McQueen Foods (the corporate owner of Clover Supermarkets) in six to 18 months if you can show success at Clover. McQueen Foods is a large grocery store chain that has been buying out smaller grocery store chains such as Clover Supermarkets over the past few years. During college, you had worked at a McQueen store and worked your way up to shift manager. You know that McQueen prides itself on caring for its employees and providing excellent customer service while still selling groceries at competitive prices.

You have been managing one of the last free-standing Clover Supermarkets for about a month, and you have noticed a big difference between the cultures of McQueen and Clover stores. While all of the Clover employees are polite, none of them seem to have any special drive to provide the extra customer service that McQueen is known for. When customers call, they can be left on hold for long periods of time, and it is very difficult for customers to find help with locating items when they are in the store. Many customers have to bag their own groceries, and it is rare that there is someone who can help customers carry their groceries out to the car. In addition, when workers are asked questions about products, they will rarely be able to answer such questions. And while the store does have a system in place to add new items based on customer requests, such items rarely appear on store shelves.

You are convinced that this lack of customer service has hurt Clover's performance, and that it needs to be changed. Such a change will also help bring the Clover culture in line with the McQueen culture. You are aware of the difficulty in changing any culture, and that if you want to align the Clover culture with the McQueen culture, then you cannot change the service aspect by hurting the respect for company employees or by making prices noncompetitive.

However, you also see this change as a career opportunity for you. If you can successfully change the Clover culture, and provide a blueprint for similar changes at the other stores that McQueen has recently acquired, this accomplishment will greatly help your career progression at McQueen Foods.

To help generate ideas for this change, you have invited other new McQueen store managers that you met in your training program to discuss possibilities.

Instructions

Step 1. Form into groups of five to seven members and develop an outline for the cultural change. The plan must include a clear description of the current culture, a vision for the desired future culture, and methods for changing the current culture to match the future culture. Because of the difficulty in changing cultures, you will want to list multiple methods for changing the key cultural aspects. Also, sequence the cultural change steps as necessary, and list where expected resistance to change can come from. Describe what approaches you might take to overcome these roadblocks. (15 to 30 minutes)

Step 2. Be prepared to present your change plan to the class. (5 to 10 minutes)

Reflection Questions

1. What insights did you gain from thinking of organizational cultures from a change perspective?
2. What disagreements arose about cultural diagnosis in your team?
3. What cultural change ideas were the most difficult for your team to develop?
4. How did the constraints of maintaining worker support and competitive prices make the cultural change more challenging?

Exercise contributed by Milton R. Mayfield, Professor of Business, Texas A&M International University, and Jacqueline R. Mayfield, Professor of Business, Texas A&M International University.

ONLINE EXERCISE 15.1: EXAMPLES OF POOR COMMUNICATION

Objective

The purpose of this exercise is to gain an appreciation for organizational culture.

Instructions

In addition to social media, there are many websites available that give a window into the culture of a particular organization. Sites such as glassdoor.com, indeed.com, and careerbliss.com have reviews written about thousands of companies and what it is like to work in those firms.

Choose a large company you are familiar with. Next, go to that company's website—especially the part of the website that describes career opportunities and what the culture is like at that organization. Also, read posts the company has placed on various social media platforms describing what it is like to work at that firm.

Then, read about the company on the career websites just mentioned. Write a two- to three-page report to your instructor that demonstrates what the organization says the organizational culture is like and then compare/contrast what is on the company's website with the anonymous reviews posted on websites such as glassdoor.com.

Reflection Questions

1. Did the company you chose describe an organizational culture that is congruent with what you found on the career websites? How were they similar? Different?
2. How does the firm you currently work for (or your most recent employer) describe its organizational culture? How does that differ from what you have experienced at the organization?
3. Why is there sometimes a difference between what a company promotes on its website and in social media to potential employees about its positive culture and what current and former employees state about the culture?
4. What is the best way to know what an organization's culture is like? Explain.

Exercise contributed by Steven Stovall, Southeast Missouri State University.

ONLINE EXERCISE 15.2: UNDERSTANDING CULTURES IN FOREIGN COUNTRIES

Objective

The purpose of this exercise is to gain an understanding of the culture of a foreign country.

Description of Exercise

Search online for a full-time, on-site job in a foreign country. There are numerous websites you might use such as goabroad, easyexpat, gooverseas, idealist, indeedworldwide, expatnetwork, and others. Again, you're looking for a full-time position that requires that you move to that country. However, don't worry about your level of experience, education, or other qualifications. Simply locate a job in a country that you find appealing. Once you have selected the job, answer the questions below.

Discussion Questions

- How did you select the job? What attracted you to it? Was it the job itself or the country it was located in?
- Reading the job description, does it appear that the company is open to an expatriate filling role? Did the description provide any information about training or orientation for someone relocating to this country? Explain.
- Research the country that the job you selected is located in. Describe the culture.
- Using Hofstede's five dimensions of culture, evaluate the country you selected.

Exercise contributed by Steven Stovall, Southeast Missouri State University.

CASE 15.1: HUBSPOT'S ORGANIZATIONAL CULTURE

Entrepreneurs often say "we hire for culture fit" without even defining the company culture their recruits are fitting into. In a 2016 Entrepreneurial Thought Leaders seminar at Stanford University, HubSpot co-founder and CTO Dharmesh Shah said, "That's awesome that you hire for culture fit. What's your culture? Just describe it," adding, "If you can't tell me what your culture is, that means when you say 'we hire for culture fit' that means you hire people just like yourself. You have all sorts of biases that kick in and that's a very, very dangerous thing."[96]

> *"If you can't tell me what your culture is, when you say, 'we hire for culture fit' that means you hire people just like yourself."*

But the self-described introvert was not always so invested in organizational beliefs, values, and behaviors. "The first two years of HubSpot, the word *culture* was a dirty word for Dharmesh and I," former HubSpot CEO Brian Halligan told Jungle Ventures. Halligan and Dharmesh Shah met as classmates in MIT's MBA program and founded HubSpot, a suite of inbound marketing and sales software tools in 2006. "When anyone would talk about culture, we would roll our eyes like, 'Ah, it's a bunch of crap. Who cares about that stuff? It's about the numbers and what's going on. We're shipping product; let's go!'" A conversation with iRobot CEO and founder Colin Angle provided a new perspective: "Brian, culture is how you build a big company. Culture is how people make decisions when you're not in the room," Halligan recalls. After the meeting, Halligan convinced Shah of the merits of prioritizing culture and began drafting the HubSpot Culture Code.[97]

Culture Is a Product

According to Shah, "We obsess over our culture just like our product. Because culture *is* a product."[98] With a transparent, open-source mindset, Shah published HubSpot's Culture Code in 2013. The 128-page slide deck has attracted over six million views and inspired countless similar statements in the decade since. The deck describes a virtuous circle of building culture as a company builds its product: A great product attracts customers; a great culture attracts talented employees who build great products and strengthen the culture, perpetuating the loop.

Shah elucidated the *culture as product* analogy further in an article on OnStartups.com, the 700,000-member community and startup blog.[99] An organization's employees are the customers of its culture "product" and thus many elements of product development methodology can be easily translated to building culture. A company must seek feedback on culture from its people, understand their needs, and measure and analyze its performance. As a software company, HubSpot categorizes its responses to eNPS (employee Net Promoter Score) surveys as "bug reports and feature requests." Just as markets are dynamic and competitive products are never "done," culture must evolve to meet the changing demands of a growing, maturing organization. A company should strive to preserve its core values and spirit as it scales, but what works in a startup context is not always appropriate for a larger organization. For example, many startups, HubSpot included, eschew job titles in their early days but recognize the need to delegate decision-making authority as teams grow and projects increase in complexity. The HubSpot Culture Code specifically addresses this point in its slides on transparency, noting that openness to and acceptance of all input does not equal democracy and that not all decisions may be made by consensus. Ultimately, a culture must be "shipped" like a product to be used by its constituents. A 128-page slide deck like the HubSpot Culture Code may not be necessary for every organization, but a statement of company culture must exist in a manifestation that is usable and accessible by its employees.[100]

"Compromising on Culture Is Mortgaging the Future"

The HubSpot Culture Code includes five tenets, listed in Table 15.1 and described below:

TABLE 15.1 ■ The HubSpot Culture Code Tenets

1. We solve for the customer.
2. We work to be remarkably transparent.
3. We favor autonomy and accountability.
4. We believe our best perk is amazing peers.
5. We lean towards long-term impact.

HubSpot's mission is to "help millions of organizations grow better." HubSpot provides a CRM platform for scaling businesses and makes decisions by asking, "What's in it for the customer?" To solve for the customer effectively, every employee of HubSpot has insider access to information like company financials, diversity goals (and shortcomings), and management meeting decks. According to the

Culture Code, "Remarkable transparency helps us make decisions and take ownership." HubSpot's emphasis on employee autonomy is evinced by its three-word policy on everything from social media use to sick days or even buying team lunches: "Use good judgment." Good judgment is clarified as "customer > company > individual", that is, employees are expected to prioritize the customer's needs, those of the company, and then their own. When these goals are not aligned in order, Dharmesh writes, "The interest rate on culture debt is crushingly high." HubSpot defines its "amazing peers" as people with HEART: those who are humble, empathetic, adaptable, remarkable, and transparent. Finally, the company aspires to have long-term impact by questioning the status quo, continually simplifying and refactoring processes to remain agile, able to deliver exceptional products without regressing to the mean of large, established tech companies.

HubSpot's commitment to defining and publishing its Culture Code leaves no room for doubt about its internal values and behaviors, nor the possibility of "culture fit" being used as a shield to hire a homogeneous workforce. The company has been featured on numerous "Best Places to Work" rankings by *Forbes, Fortune, Inc.*, and Glassdoor, as well as being named as having the #1 Best Company Culture by Comparably in 2021.[101]

Critical Thinking Questions

1. Do you agree with Dharmesh's supposition that culture is a product? Why or why not?
2. Have you been a member of an organization with a great culture statement? How do you think it was put into practice?
3. Have you ever been on the wrong end of a "culture fit" hiring or firing decision? Would a clearer explanation of that organization's values have helped in that situation?

iStockPhoto / SpVVK

16 ORGANIZATIONAL CHANGE AND STRUCTURE

LEARNING OBJECTIVES

By the end of this chapter, you will be able to:

16.1 Compare and contrast various conceptualizations of the change process

16.2 Identify the forces for change in organizations

16.3 Describe where resistance to change comes from and how to reduce it

16.4 Discuss how organizational structure helps shape behavior in organizations

16.5 Describe the concept of organizational development in organizations and identify different types of OD change interventions

Case Study: Google's Organizational Development and Change

There have been very few companies in the world's history that have had as profound an impact on human life in such a short period of time as Google. In the past 24 years, Google has grown from a two-man start-up based in a garage to having Alphabet as its parent company and over 156,000 employees in 2021.[1] In addition, this worldwide tech conglomerate is located in 50 different countries and has made around $257.6 billion in revenues.[2] This kind of growth seems unsustainable. However, Google has shown the world that all it really takes is tireless dedication to corporate adaptability and complete commitment to smooth organizational change and development. Over the course of its life, Google has displayed these attributes excellently through its structural interventions, in terms of altering its rewards systems, changing its culture, and reorganizing the structure itself through job design and division of labor. The tech industry is, by far, the most competitive industry on the planet right now. Tens of thousands of highly qualified candidates from around the world are constantly vying for an opportunity to work at Google. Google not only has greater prestige and growth opportunities than other tech companies but it also has some of the best, if not the best, compensation packages in the world with entry-level employees earning six-figure salaries right off the bat.[3]

In one instance, a Google software engineer was offered a $500,000 salary to leave Google and work for a tech start-up in Silicon Valley, but turned it down because at Google they were being paid a salary worth $3 million![4] Additionally, around the world Google is known for providing some of the best accommodation allowances in the industry. Thousands of employees have moved from country to country working for the Google brand across the globe and the company has vowed to make this a stress-free activity by essentially paying for all of it. This is one of Google's best offerings to prospective employees in almost every corner of the planet. However, this remuneration philosophy has proven to be, surprisingly, ineffective in the southernmost regions of the Middle East, particularly the United Arab Emirates. According to Marc Schoenen, who has moved from the headquarters in California to the United Kingdom and travels frequently, "We try to have a globally consistent model, but it wasn't working in Dubai, so we changed it. Situations like this highlight ongoing discussions about global uniformity and local customization."[5] To gain a competitive advantage in the recruiting space in Dubai, Google needed to change how they compensated their employees completely.

After much deliberation, Google decided that the right strategy moving forward was to pay their employees "unfairly," as some have called it, when in reality employees' compensation is entirely based on the impact they have in the organization. This means that, potentially, lower level employees could earn more than senior employees. "There have been situations where one person received a stock award of $10,000 and another working in the same area received $1,000,000. This isn't the norm, but the range of rewards at almost any level can easily vary by 300% to 500%, and even then, there is plenty of room for outliers," says Lazlo Bock, Google's Senior Vice President of People Operations.[6]

In the highly competitive tech industry, paying star employees above the average is the only way to ward off competitors such as Uber, Facebook, LinkedIn, and Twitter. Similarly, in the film and sports industries, it simply makes sense to pay top performers top dollar. Schoenen argues, "We believe you can apply the same sports structure to engineering, coding and legal expertise. If you have the right metrics, you can identify star performers in every function. It might only be three people out of one thousand, but these are the people driving your organization and you need to appreciate them."[7] The strategy Google implemented in Dubai is a fantastic example of how important it is to adapt the ways that employees are rewarded to the times. Google identified that, in its competitive industry, allowing competition to continue to thrive within the workplace is what drives maximum output in Dubai. The structure of the employee rewards was altered and now Google is reaping the benefits of its own adaptability.

One of Google's more well-known initiatives is that of its workplace culture. Walking into Google's headquarters to see the swings dangling from the ceilings and beanbags on the floors might make one question if they are actually looking at a Fortune 100 company, but they would be mistaken if they came to any other conclusion.[8] Google identified a very interesting opportunity to be different from every single one of their competitors simply by changing their culture. Years ago, Google set out on a mission to have its various offices and campuses around the globe "reflect the company's overarching philosophy, which is nothing less than 'to create the happiest, most productive workplace in the world,'" according to a Google spokesperson, Jordan Newman.[9] Google's mission was and still is inherently in the favor of every single one of its employees so when this change was implemented there was almost no resistance to it. Often times, widespread organizational change comes with a significant amount of resistance from employees who are accustomed to the status quo. This status quo can lead to what is called structural inertia which makes the process of changing a huge pain for companies. Google was able to steer clear of this barricade by implementing new changes every day, effectively forcing the employees to adapt. That may seem like a very aggressive strategy, however, when you are pushing to make your culture more playful and relaxing by bringing puppies into work and buying thousands of bean bags for your employees, there isn't much pushback from the start. More recently, Google has undergone even more change following a decision to restructure its many components into a series of companies under a new umbrella corporation called Alphabet.[10]

Organizational development, change, and structure is often a very grueling process for even the most successful companies. Yet, Google has mastered the art of OD by integrating a philosophy of adaptability that has become second nature to its workforce as it has swept through all of the silos in the company. Especially in the competitive tech industry, companies like Google must continue to be both agile and adaptive to deal with the pressure of continual change and development.

Critical-Thinking Questions

1. Why might Google's tactics for employee compensation need to vary in different places in the world?
2. Why do companies often run into resistance when trying to implement new organizational development and changes?

THE CHANGE PROCESS

Organizations have undergone enormous changes over the past couple of years. The COVID-19 pandemic has forced many companies to rethink their public safety policies, adapt to new technological changes, increase cultural understandings, and find ways to meet the demands of customer and stakeholders. The ability to manage change is one of the key skills leaders need today when operating in an environment of continuous uncertainty.[11]

Google is a great example of an organization which implements changes to stay current. Its advocacy for change has been at the forefront of its success in becoming a global technology giant. Like Google, organizations must be both agile and adaptive to deal with the pressure of continual change. During the COVID-19 pandemic, Google became one of the first companies to impose a work from home policy and plans to create a hybrid work option after surveys showed that most workers showed a preference to be in the office some days, just not every day.[12] Table 16.1 lists some more big corporate changes that took place during the pandemic.

Change Management

It's not easy to implement change inside an organization, however, and successful change requires careful planning, hard work, cooperation, and excellent communication through the process of **change management** a method of overseeing and implementing change to support the transformation of organizational goals, processes or technologies.[13]

Change management has been around for more than 50 years, yet studies show that 60% to 70% of organizational change projects fail, despite huge investments in training and education to support

TABLE 16.1 ■ Five Corporate Transformations During Covid.

1. Commercial Airlines Switching to Cargo Flights
Due to the dramatic fall in airline passengers, large airlines such as Virgin Atlantic, Lufthansa, United, and American Airlines swapped commercial flights for cargo flights, using the planes to transport grocery items and health-care provisions.
2. Restaurants Selling Fresh Groceries
Many restaurants forced to close during the pandemic began to sell fresh groceries to create another source of income. Panera, California Pizza Kitchen, and Subway are among the restaurant chains that provided groceries like fresh vegetables, meat, and eggs to their customers.
3. Retailers Moving to Curbside Pick-Up and Digital Ordering
To ensure customers were able to buy the items they needed, retailers such as Dick's Sporting Goods and Best Buy offered curbside pick-up for online and phone orders. A number of stores have partnered with tech companies to enhance their digital ordering capabilities. For example, Walgreens partnered with Facebook to offer an instant ordering service which allows customers to place their orders quickly and easily.
4. Hotels Offering Day Rates for Remote Workers
With transport at a standstill and the majority of people working from home, many hotels chose to fill up the empty space by offering day rates for remote workers seeking to work in a more peaceful and private environment. For example, Red Roof Hotels provided remote workers with access to hotel rooms converted into office suites, for $29 per day.
5. Fitness Companies Moving To Online Workouts
When fitness centers and gyms closed, many fitness companies moved online to provide access to their services to people working from home. For example, Planet Fitness live-streamed exercise classes for their members, and fitness apparel company Under Armour hosted a 30-day Healthy at Home fitness challenge to motivate their customers to stay active.

Source: Adapted from Morgan, B. (2020, May). 10 examples of how COVID-19 forced business transformation. *Forbes*. https://www.forbes.com/sites/blakemorgan/2020/05/01/10-examples-of-how-covid-19-forced-business-transformation/?sh=3607c05b1be3

them.[14] What are the reasons for these failures? One theory proposes that too many organizations hire outside consultants or experts to design the change projects rather than assigning the responsibility to the managers inside the organization. This means that managers do not get the opportunity to fully embrace the changes, and it weakens their ability to implement the changes effectively.[15]

What happens when a whole industry needs to change? In 2017, sexual harassment claims were made against movie director mogul Harvey Weinstein igniting the #MeToo movement on social media. Over 30 women came forward to tell their stories about the abuse they had suffered from the now-disgraced Hollywood legend, including major movie stars Angelina Jolie, Gwyneth Paltrow, and Ashley Judd. Since the news broke, dozens of other women have come forward with claims of sexual harassment made by other studio executives. Lack of diversity and the low number of women in powerful positions have been considered as some of the reasons for the abuse that managed to span so many decades without being addressed. In 2021, researchers studying the impact of the #MeToo movement found some meaningful change had occurred. For instance, more women had been hired as film writers than before the scandal, with 35% of producers who had former connections to Weinstein more likely to work with women writers. Although these changes are positive, the study reported that female producers, rather than male producers, were the main drivers of this shift to hire more women.[16]

The DADA Process

Managers must tread carefully when addressing concerns; otherwise, they run the risk of inciting the **DADA syndrome**, experienced by individuals faced with unwanted change. The syndrome consists of four stages: denial, anger, depression, and finally acceptance.[17] During the denial stage, people deliberately ignore the change; in the anger stage, they begin to express rage about the change; in the depression stage, they often experience low emotional states and lack of motivation; and finally, in the acceptance stage, they begin to come around to the idea of the change and try and make the best of it. In worst-case scenarios, people will leave an organization if they are unable to accept the changes being implemented.

Lewin's Basic Change Model

Lewin's basic change model is a comprehensive change model that helps organizations facilitate the change process. Kurt Lewin was a German American psychologist who developed a three-stage model of planned change that explained how to initiate, manage, and stabilize the change process. The three stages are known as *unfreezing, transforming*, and *refreezing*.[18]

Unfreezing

Unfreezing requires explaining the rationale for change, breaking down the status quo, challenging existing beliefs, and understanding how starting on a new path is essential for the company's survival. This is the most difficult and stressful part of the change process, because challenging deeply held beliefs about the way things are done can provoke strong reactions from people. The Walt Disney company is undergoing the process of unfreezing through its commitment to inclusivity. In 2022, Disney announced its intention to eliminate gender references by no longer using words such as "ladies," "gentlemen," "girls," and "boys," in its theme parks.[19] Disney also launched a "Reimagine Tomorrow" campaign to make its content more inclusive by ensuring more Disney characters represent the LGBTQIA community.[20] Disney's diversity and inclusion program supports the unfreezing process by ensuring employees are educated and trained to deal with this change.

Transforming

After the unfreezing stage comes the **transforming** stage, in which people begin to make peace with their doubts and uncertainties and embrace the new direction of the company. However, transformation does not happen overnight. Managers need to give employees time to adjust to change and ensure they are communicating with them consistently and effectively. They need to reinforce their vision for change by providing evidence such as research, documentation, and success stories of other companies that have implemented similar changes. Employees who are still struggling with the changes must be offered more support through training and additional resources when necessary.

Chicago Bears quarterback Jay Cutler, along with head coach Marc Trestman, spoke out against hazing new team members and instead promoted a culture of respect in the locker room.

Icon Sports Wire / Contributor / Getty Images

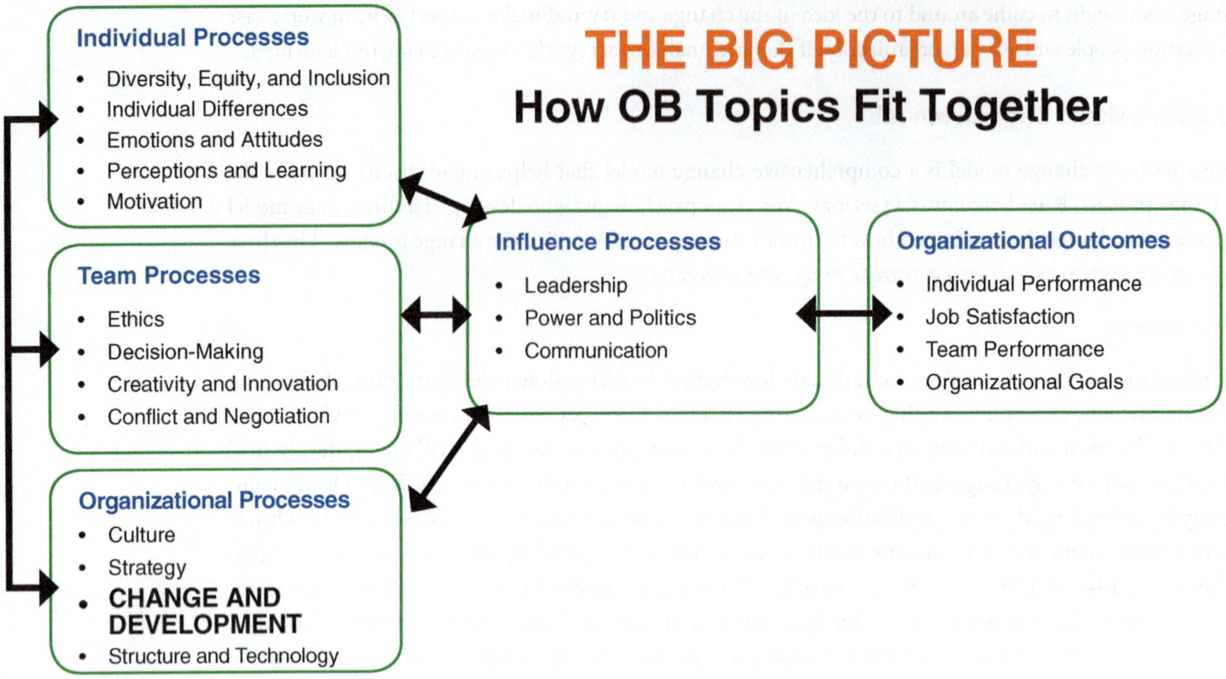

Refreezing

When employees appear to have embraced the change, managers use refreezing to reinforce the new approach and help people internalize the changes. This is done by creating reward systems, tracking behaviors, and setting up continuous training to further enhance skills. During this stage, it is very important for managers to promote a sense of stability and consistency for the changes to be fully incorporated into daily working life.

Lewin's Force Field Analysis

Before implementing any changes, organizations need to assess the validity of the change. Force field analysis (see Figure 16.1) is a useful decision-making technique that helps to assess the reasons for and against making certain changes.[21] The drivers for change must be stronger than the restraining forces for the change to work.

FIGURE 16.1 ■ Lewin's Force Field Analysis Model

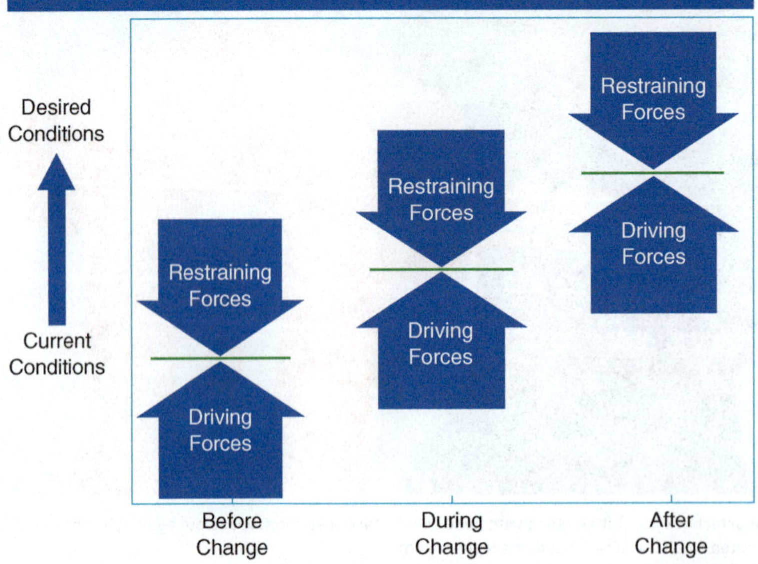

FORCES FOR CHANGE

Every day, employees are affected by a range of internal and external forces as they try to perform their roles in organizations. Managers who promote an awareness of these forces and make an effort to counteract them have a better chance of creating a more productive and loyal workforce. This means organizations need to adapt to **external forces**, which are outside influences such as competitors' actions and customers' changing preferences, and to **internal forces**, which are inside influences such as company culture and employee diversity.[22]

External Forces for Change

Organizations cannot function in a vacuum—they need to be aware of and respond to events and trends in the outside world. Some examples of these external forces are customers' demographic characteristics, technological advancements, customer and market changes, social and political pressures, and generational changes. Let's consider each.

Demographic Characteristics

Organizations need to adapt to demographic changes such as aging and increasingly diversified customer populations. To deal with these changes, many organizations have tailored their marketing strategies to appeal to a variety of different consumers and to ensure fair treatment for people regardless of age, religion, sexual orientation, gender, or race and ethnicity. For example, New York-based unisex clothing company, MUXE, promotes gender-fluid clothing such as T-shirts and tank tops designed to challenge gender norms and stereotypes. MUXE donates a percentage of its profits to Live Out Loud, an LGBTQ+ youth organization also based in New York City.[23]

Technological Advancements

The rapid rise of and continuous innovation in computer and wireless technology means that organizations must move equally fast to compete. Many organizations now use digital marketing such as Instagram, livestreaming, and podcasts to promote their products, build awareness of their brands, and connect more fully with their consumers. For instance, cosmetics giant Sephora launched a podcast

Companies like Banana Republic have begun featuring same-sex couples in their advertisements, including TV personality Nate Berkus and husband Jeremiah Brent.

Steve Mack / Alamy Stock Photo

called #LIPSTORIES featuring real stories from influential women aimed to resonate with customers on a personal level, and to help spread product awareness.[24] Another example of a recent technological advancement is the workplace metaverse, virtual reality spaces that offer an alternative office space where people can work, attend training, or chat with their colleagues. Walmart, Nike, and Gucci are among some of the major organizations exploring the opportunities raised by the metaverse.[25]

Customer and Market Changes

Customer expectations have increased since the COVID-19 pandemic. Research shows that customers want more human interaction when dealing with a company, prefer simpler and faster service, have a lower tolerance threshold for delayed resolution, and tend to share more feedback on social media—positive and negative.[26] Negative feedback from customers that has the potential to reach countless others online can immediately influence sales, and it can also enhance or damage the organization's reputation in the long term. For example, customer comments on review sites like Tripadvisor, Trustpilot, and Yelp can help or hurt hotels, local businesses, tourist attractions, and restaurants. Organizations that listen to their customers, request feedback, and make the effort to fix problems immediately have a higher chance of keeping up with the evolving market landscape than those who don't.

Social Trends and Political Pressures

Changing social trends and values can often pressure organizations into adjusting how they operate. For instance, driven by concerns around climate change and other environmental issues, more and more customers are aligning themselves with companies that match their own values by producing sustainable goods and services. In 2022, a study on consumer trends relating to sustainable products and packaging reported that more than 70% of respondents said they were buying more environmentally friendly products than five years ago, while more than 80% stated they intended to buy even more over the course of the next five years.[27] Activewear company Girlfriend Collective caters to these values by producing eco-friendly, durable and stylish clothes made from recycled materials such as plastic water bottles thereby addressing the issues of wastefulness and pollution caused by the "fast-fashion" industry.[28]

Organizations can also be subject to political pressures that force them into taking action. For example in 2022, Putin's invasion of Ukraine and the subsequent outrage from Ukraine supporters all over the world prompted many organizations to cut ties with Russia. A poll reported that the majority of Americans perceived companies that took a stand against Russia as authentic leaders and tended to be more critical of those that stayed on the sidelines of the international crisis.[29] Since the Ukraine invasion, organizations from different industries all over the world have distanced themselves from Russia by suspending or removing their operations, including Spotify, Shell, Nestlé, Renault, TikTok, Boeing, Roku, and more.

Generational Changes

Today's workforce is made up of five different generations (see Chapter 2, Diversity, Equity, Inclusion DEI, for more on generations) which presents both opportunities and challenges for managers. Baby boomers are already retiring and millions more will start exiting their companies over the next few years. When they go, they take with them years of talent, skills, and experience, leaving companies to find ways to bridge the enormous talent gap. During the early days of the COVID-19 pandemic, nearly 30 million baby boomers left the job market and retired, leaving many organizations struggling to fill vacancies.[30] Some organizations have put strategies in place to fill the roles such as promoting millennials to higher management, and creating partnerships where boomers take on roles as mentors and transfer their extensive knowledge to the younger generation.[31]

Internal Forces for Change

Although it is essential that organizations respond to external forces, it is just as important to look inside the organization at the internal forces at play. Issues such as low job satisfaction can influence productivity and cause conflict or strikes. Organizations must address internal problems as soon as they arise and strive to build a positive working environment based on mutual respect, teamwork, and collaboration.[32] Management changes, organizational restructuring, and intrapreneurship are some examples of the internal forces that affect organizations.

Management Change

New CEOs or executive management can have a significant impact on an organization's culture and strategy. People at the higher levels tend to introduce big changes across the whole organization in line with their own vision. For example, Sonia Syngal made big plans for change following her move to Gap Inc. in 2020, such as strengthening the performance of the company by becoming more efficient and less bureaucratic. Syngal credits success to getting stuck in, and offered the following advice to Stanford students: "And, it's cliche, but get in the muck and follow your passion and know that you can change the world. Watching others or helping others do it is not nearly as fun."[33]

Organizational Restructuring

There may be instances when organizations need to change their organizational structure to adapt to new strategies, new product lines, or global expansion. The shift to remote working during the COVID-19 pandemic forced many companies to redesign their organizational structures by devising ways to adapt to different working conditions. For example, citing the economic impact of the pandemics, Mozilla Corp., the developer of the Firefox web browser, restructured its organization by laying off over more than 250 employees, closing its operations in Taiwan, and moving 60 employees to different teams, to strengthen its "ability to build and invest in products and services that will give people alternatives to conventional Big Tech."[34]

Changing structures means disruption for employees. Communication and training are essential during a reorganization to ensure that employees understand the reasons for the change and the implications it will have for their daily duties.

Intrapreneurship

Many organizations foster a spirit of **intrapreneurship** in their employees by encouraging them to come up with new ideas and new ways of doing things.[35] When an employee suggests something innovative, the organization must consider the best way of implementing the idea, which may mean allocating more resources, putting more people to work on the initiative, or coming up with different branding in the case of a new product. Research shows that companies that champion intrapreneurship experience higher levels of employee engagement and productivity.[36] Another study reported that some of the most successful innovations introduced over the last few decades were invented by existing employees.[37]

Apple, 3M, Toyota, and Google are organizations known for encouraging intrapreneurship. Gmail, Google News, Google Maps, AdWords, AdSense, Driverless Cars, Google Glasses are just a few examples of innovations devised by Google employees from inside the organization.[38]

Although organizations must be aware of both external and internal forces for change, they must also be able to manage resistance to change and understand how to reduce it. We look at this challenge next.

RESISTANCE TO CHANGE

One of the main obstacles to implementing organizational changes is **resistance to change**, people's unwillingness to accept or support modifications in the workplace.[39] According to management consulting company McKinsey, 70% of change programs fail because of resistance to change and poor management support.[40] When people resist change it can affect their productivity, performance, and relationships (see Figure 16.2).

FIGURE 16.2 ■ Sources of Resistance to Change

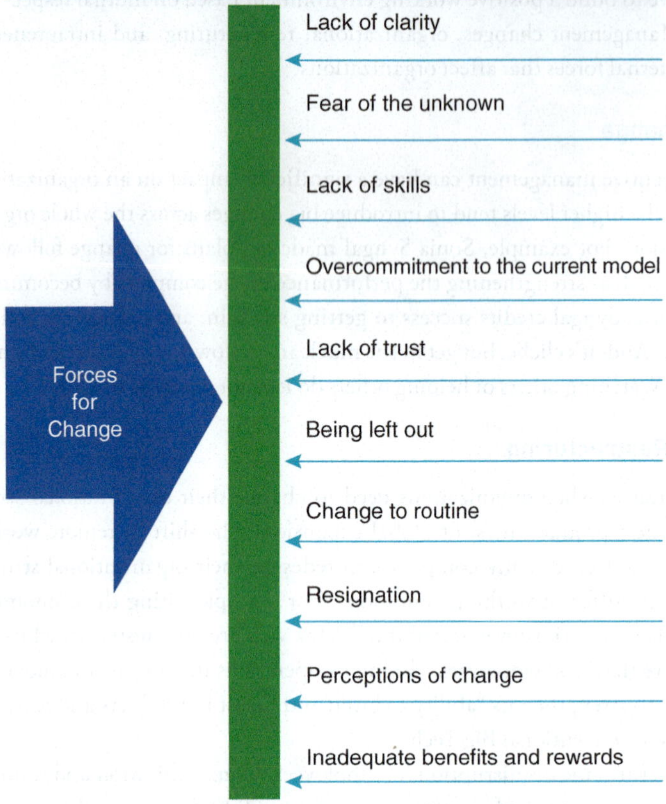

Individual Sources of Resistance to Change

There are ten main reasons for employees resisting change:[41]

1. **Lack of clarity:** When the argument for change is not communicated clearly, there can be cause for misunderstandings and resistance—especially from long-standing employees, used to the current model who do not see why things have to change at all.
2. **Fear of the unknown:** Concerns about what may lie ahead are a common reason why people resist change. This barrier will only be removed when people are reassured that moving forward is better than standing still.
3. **Lack of skills:** Some people worry that they won't have the right skills to cope with the change. The right communication and appropriate training help to assuage these concerns.
4. **Overcommitment to the current model:** Some people are so invested in the "old way" of doing things, that they perceive any suggested changes as a threat.
5. **Lack of trust:** If employees don't have any trust in their organization, then it is less likely for them to get on board with the changes.
6. **Being left out:** People are more likely to support change if they are well informed and made aware of the reasons that have led to the changes. This is especially important if their jobs are going to be affected.
7. **Change to routine:** It can be difficult to coax people out of their comfort zones to embrace new changes, especially if they have been with the company over a long period of time.
8. **Resignation:** Some people go along with change because they are too jaded to resist it. However, compliance does not lead to job satisfaction. For the changes to really work, people have to be motivated enough to support them properly.

9. **Perceptions of change:** People may resist change if they believe the change is more beneficial to another department or area or if they feel that they will be worse off once the change has been implemented.

10. **Inadequate benefits and rewards:** Many employees will oppose change if they feel unfairly compensated for making the change.

As Figure 16.3 illustrates, poorly communicated policies for change can raise a number of strong emotions such as denial, anger, confusion, and depression. A successful change management model will help to lead employees toward acceptance and provide them with the confidence to cope with the changes.

Kotter's 8-Step Change Model

Research conducted by Harvard business school professor and change expert John Kotter shows that only 30% of organizations successfully implement organizational change. As a result of these findings, Kotter created an 8-Step Change Model for leading change in organizations (see Figure 16.4).[42]

1. **Create a Sense of Urgency**
   During the first step, employees must be made aware of how important the change is to them and the organization. This requires honest and open dialogue, outlining the threats and risks of not making the change, and the importance of taking action at this time.

2. **Create a Guiding Coalition**
   It is important to create a project team, preferably composed of employees from different roles and positions, that focuses on the changes required by the organization. This team would encourage the rest of the employees to get on board with the changes and act as a sounding board for those who have any questions or concerns.

3. **Create a Vision for Change**
   For change to work, people need a clear vision of what the organization is trying to achieve. Employees will need to be a part of that vision for them to accept the changes ahead.

4. **Communicate the Vision**
   Once the vision has been formulated, it is essential that it is communicated effectively to all employees across the entire organization. Talking to employees and keeping them informed increases the chances of acceptance, especially when their opinions and concerns are taken into account.

FIGURE 16.3 ■ Psychological Reactions to Change

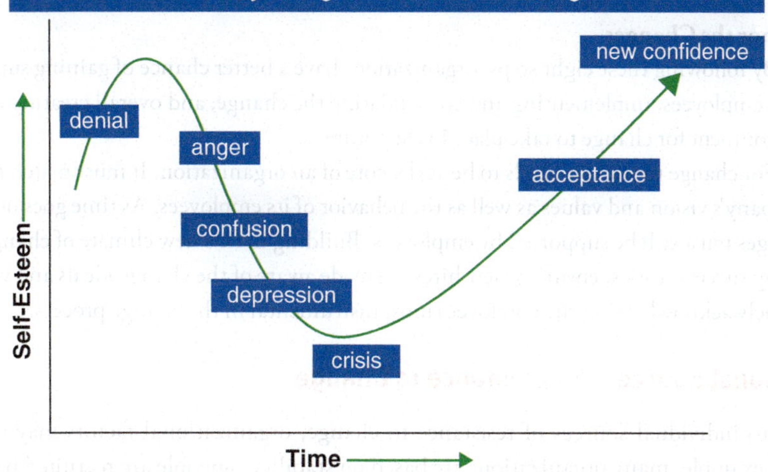

Source: Rick, T. (2011). Top 12 reasons why people resist change. *Meliorate.* https://www.torbenrick.eu/blog/change-management/12-reasons-why-people-resist-change/

FIGURE 16.4 ■ Kotter's 8-Step Change Model

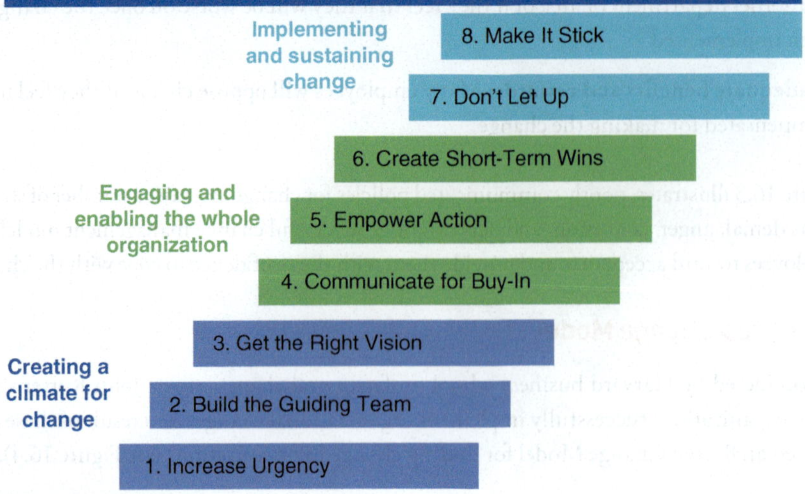

Source: Kotter, J. P. & Cohen, D. S. (2012). *The heart of change*. Harvard Business School Press.

5. **Remove Obstacles**

   Change will not be successful unless all obstacles are removed beforehand. In this context, the obstacles are usually employees who are resisting the change. Talking to these employees is the best way of understanding the reasons why they don't want the changes to go ahead. Incorporating their ideas into the change process is also a powerful way to get them onboard.

6. **Create Short-Term Wins**

   Change can be a long process, and employees need to be motivated to go the distance. This is why it is important to create short-term goals, where employees are given rewards and acknowledgment when they have successfully achieved their targets. Not only will this encourage employees to continue to pursue long-term goals, but it sends a message to the rest of the organization that the change is definitely going ahead.

7. **Consolidate Improvements**

   Kotter believed that many change processes tend to fail because victory is declared too soon. Change is an ongoing process which needs to be incorporated into the overall organizational culture. Therefore, organizations must promote the idea of continuous change and constantly look for ways to improve processes.

8. **Anchor the Changes**

   By following these eight steps, organizations have a better chance of gaining support from employees, implementing and consolidating the change, and overall creating the right environment for change to take place in the future.

   For change to stick, it needs to be at the core of an organization. It must match the company's vision and values as well as the behavior of its employees. As time goes on, the changes must still be supported by employees. Building in this new climate of change involves telling success stories, ensuring new hires are made aware of the change ideals and values, and publicly acknowledging the employees most instrumental in the change process.

Organizational Sources of Resistance to Change

In addition to individual sources of resistance to change, organizational factors may prove to be barriers. For example, many organizations are based on stability—people are recruited because they fit in with the organizational culture and are then socialized to behave in certain ways through training, rules, processes, and procedures. However, this uniformity can lead to *structural inertia*, which makes an organization slow to change after having followed the same rules and procedures for many years.

Organizations can also fall prey to *limited focus of change*, which arises when only a small number of departments apply the change rather than the whole organization. Confusion often results because the change is not being fully enforced. Another organizational source of resistance to change is *group inertia*. This means that even if individuals agree with the change, they may be constrained by group norms—a situation that often occurs in unions.[43] Groups may also feel that organizational changes are a *threat to expertise*. For example, a data analysis department may feel threatened when a computer program is brought in to perform many of the data functions. The group may resist learning the program for fear it will render their roles obsolete. Furthermore, the group may not want to entertain *decisions that disrupt cultural traditions or group relationships*, which means they will cling to the familiar way of doing things.

Finally, an organization can experience *threat to established power relationships*, particularly when it is undergoing a reorganization. Companies moving from an autocratic structure to a participative or self-managed one are likely to experience opposition from middle managers who may feel their source of power is being threatened.

Reducing Resistance to Change

Typically, organizations use different types of methods to deal with resistance to change.[44]

Education and Communication

One of the most common approaches to addressing resistance to change is education and communication. It is best to teach people about the change before it takes place and ensure the message is communicated clearly and effectively. For instance, Google CEO Larry Page made the significant decision to restructure Google into a series of companies under a new umbrella corporation called Alphabet, and made sure everyone at Google understood the reasons for such a radical change. Page clearly explained why the changes made sense: Under the new model, employees would be free to focus on their own goals without being concerned with Google's overall mission, as well as benefiting from more purposeful innovation. While Page acknowledged that change wasn't easy, it was fundamentally necessary to restructure such a diverse organization, "in the technology industry, where revolutionary ideas drive the next big growth areas, you need to be a bit uncomfortable to stay relevant."[45]

Participation

When employees are involved in the change, they are more likely to support it rather than resist it. Research shows that companies that give their employees a voice are more likely to succeed.[46] Managers can engage employees in proposed organizational changes by listening to their feedback and providing responses to their questions. Table 16.2 lists some common questions from employees about change.

Negotiation

The negotiation method is generally useful when the employees resisting the change feel they have something to lose. Through negotiation, managers can offer them an improved compensation package or other incentives in exchange for agreeing to implement the changes. However, this approach can be expensive and might encourage others to seek the same treatment.

Manipulation

In certain circumstances, corporate management may use manipulation to encourage their employees to accept changes. For example, an influential figure of seniority might be drafted into the change process, not necessarily to play an active role, but to give endorsement to the change and convince the rest of the staff that the change is a good idea. However, if employees suspect they are being manipulated, it can lead to even more disruption.

TABLE 16.2 ■ Frequent questions from employees during change

- Why is the change happening right now?
- What happens if the change doesn't take place?
- How will the change affect me and my role?
- What choices do I have if I disagree with the change?
- What are the benefits the change to the organization?
- What if the change fails?
- What happens if I have to take on more work for the same pay?

Source: Adapted from Creasy, T. (2022, May 18). 10 questions employees will have about any change. *Prosci.* https://blog.prosci.com/10-questions-employees-have-about-change

Involving employees in organizational changes will make them more invested and more likely to support them.

iStockPhoto / fizkes

Coercion

Coercion is most commonly used in a crisis when leaders need everyone on board with the changes and right away. However, although threatening job losses or providing poor performance evaluations might work in the short term, it usually leaves employees bitter and ultimately less committed to the changes. Research has shown that companies that threaten to fire their employees as a means of motivation can result in insecurity, poor health, burnout, and reduced levels of job satisfaction and performance.[47]

ORGANIZATIONAL STRUCTURE

So far, we have focused on organizational change. Although change is fundamental to many of today's organizations, it would not be possible without the support of an underlying structure. For instance, implementing change requires installing and empowering people at the right levels of authority, and reacting to change is possible only when the organization's structure reflects its business goals and objectives. We define **organizational structure** as the framework of work roles and functions that helps shape and support employee behavior.[48] There are many different ways to organize work. For instance, Burger King's global corporate structure is organized around four geographical regions: North America; Europe, Middle East and Africa; Latin America and the Caribbean; and Asia-Pacific.[49]

In contrast, organizations in the retail industry such as superstores like Walmart or Target are structured into departments like pharmacy, grocery, housewares, outdoor, and clothing.

Lines of reporting that define who reports to whom are also examples of organizational structure. Workers can report to a direct superior who reports to a manager, as at Walmart;[50] they can function as a team that manages itself, as at Zappos, Google, and Facebook;[51] or they can simultaneously report to multiple managers in different areas of the firm, as at Starbucks.[52] We take a closer look at all these structures later in the chapter.

For now, note that the structure of an organization has a significant influence on the behavior of its employees. It groups and separates people geographically, hierarchically, or both; it builds and limits relationships by setting up lines of reporting and teams; and it defines employees' responsibilities by outlining their areas of influence and accountability. Many types of organizational structures are possible, and the most successful choices of structure are made with knowledge of the way each structure shapes behavior, including work performance and, to a degree, working relationships. Organizations can undertake rapid reorganizations to make themselves more competitive and adaptable to change. For example, in 2020, following the delays in releases of several blockbuster movies caused by the COVID-19 pandemic and the subsequent closures of movie theaters, Disney announced a major reorganization of its studio and entertainment businesses by focusing on its streaming services such as Disney+. Disney's reorganization aims to grow its direct-to-consumer business and better position the company for a future based on streaming.[53]

An organization's structure affects how successfully it can coordinate and accomplish its work activities. (Think about why elementary and high schools organize their students by age rather than by height, for instance.) Several different organizing concepts, such as how specialized a given job is and how many people report to an individual manager, describe the kinds of choices an organization's top managers must make in choosing the most appropriate structure. Let's look at these.

Specialization and Division of Labor

Work specialization, also known as **division of labor**, is the degree to which jobs are divided into specific tasks.[54] When work is specialized, employees who work in a certain department carry out only the

A hostess at a restaurant performs different skills from a server or a chef. These specializations allow each employee to be more skilled and efficient at their designated jobs.

tasks that relate to their roles. For example, at a restaurant there might be someone greeting the customers, another person showing them to their table, someone taking their orders, and another person bussing the tables, but all the employees would not perform all these tasks to accomplish the job of feeding customers. The advantages of specialization may include increased efficiency and more accurate production as workers become more skilled in a particular task.

However, many organizations are moving away from specialization because too much of it—as when employees repeatedly perform the same few tasks—can lead to bored employees with narrow skill sets. Instead, many companies are widening the scope of their employees' roles and creating environments in which employees can rotate among tasks to broaden their skill base.

Departmentalization

Departmentalization is a process of grouping people with related job duties, skills, and experiences into the same area within the overall organizational structure.[55] Many mid-size and larger companies structure their organizations in this way. Starbucks is one example of a large company that groups its business functions into different departments including an HR department, a finance department, and a marketing department.

For example, a manufacturing plant may be divided into production, sales and marketing, accounting, and human resources with very little crossover between the departments (see Figure 16.5).

Chain of Command

Some organizations devise a **chain of command**, a flow of authority and power from the highest to the lowest levels of the organization (see Figure 16.6).[56]

The conventional top-down chain of command structure begins with executive level officers (CEO, CFO, president), followed by department managers and employees. The main advantage of a chain of command is that it gives senior management control over the company and ensures that orders are carried out by people in the lower levels of the chain. The U.S Army operates a strict chain of command to ensure a smooth flow of communication between the higher and lower ranks. In contrast, **unity of command** is a management technique where employees report to one, and only one designated manager. The premise behind unity of command is to ensure clear communication, less work duplication, and quicker decision-making.

Span of Control

When organizations expand by hiring more people, the number of direct reports to a given manager usually increases, giving that manager a wider span of control.[57] Some of the advantages for both

FIGURE 16.5 ■ Example of Departmentalization Structure

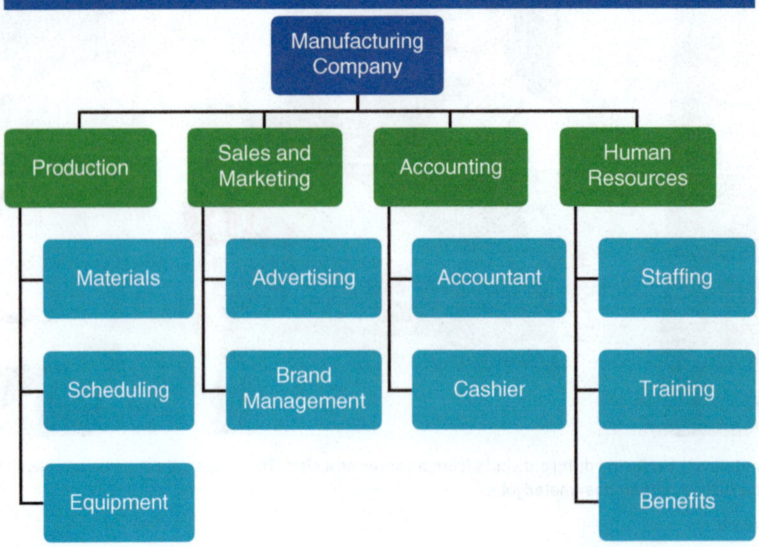

FIGURE 16.6 ■ Example of Chain of Command

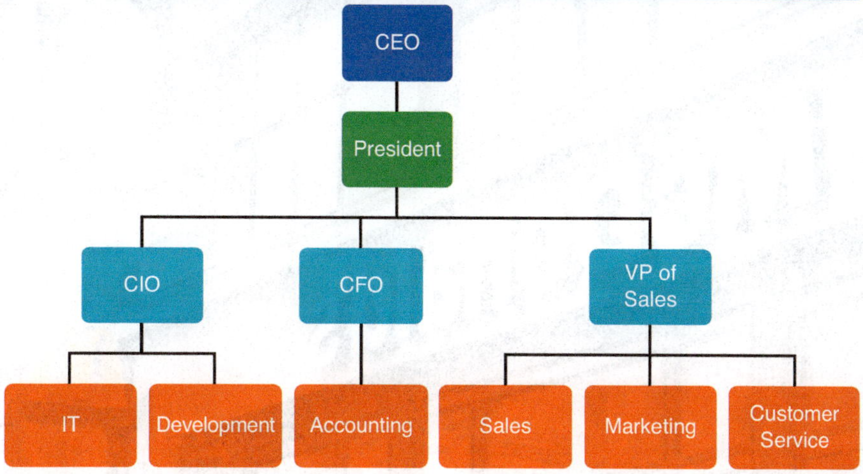

employees and managers of a wide span of control are better communication and collaboration as more employees are included in the decision-making process, and higher morale as employees are given more responsibility and less supervision. Google has a wide span of control where only one supervisor is needed to monitor a number of employees because skilled Google workers are given the autonomy to work under minimal supervision. In contrast, fast-food chains like KFC have a narrow span of control where employees are closely monitored by supervisors to ensure hygiene standards are being maintained and customer needs are being met.[58] Some of the disadvantages of a wide span of control is that are that managers may lose control over what employees are doing, and employees may lack discipline if they are given too much autonomy. Similarly, a narrow span of control may limit teams from taking the initiative and making independent decisions.

Centralization and Decentralization

Decision-making can be either centralized or decentralized.[59] In a centralized organizational structure, such as Pizza Hut, McDonald's and Burger King, senior management makes all the major decisions, whereas in a decentralized organization, like Chicago–based food manufacturing company Kraft Foods, employees are empowered to make decisions without seeking approval from senior management. Again, many organizations are seeking to move toward a decentralized approach because the evidence suggests that empowered employees are a key factor of organizational success.[60]

Mechanistic and Organic Models

The **mechanistic model** is a formalized structure based on centralization and departmentalization.[61] There is a definite chain of command, employees tend to work separately rather than collaborating, and there is very little communication between lower-level employees and upper-level management. This sort of model is predominant in manufacturing, where everyone is assigned specific tasks and expected to follow certain rules and procedures. Although the mechanistic structure is relatively easy to implement, it can be difficult to adapt it to rapid change given the number of layers and depth of the reporting structure.

The **organic model** is a less formalized structure based on decentralization and cross-functional teams.[62] Decision-making is participative and distributed throughout the organization. Typically, communication is open and frequent, and employees are more likely to accept and adapt to the inevitable changes that arise from operating fast-moving industries such as fashion or technology.

Formalization and Bureaucracy

Formalization is the degree to which rules and procedures are standardized in an organization.[63] Tesla is an example of an organization whose employees are expected to follow strict rules. An email from

McDonald's operates with a centralized organizational structure, with decisions and standards being handed down to individual stores from the corporate office.

©iStockphoto.com/albertobrian

CEO Elon Musk, outlined six rules for employees to follow. Some of these guidelines included "getting rid of frequent meetings," avoiding the use of acronyms or "nonsense words" to communicate, and leaving company meetings or drop off a call if employees aren't adding value.[64] Although there are some benefits to having strict rules, such as less confusion about how and why things are done, employees may become frustrated at the lack of opportunity to exercise their own judgment. Today's organizations tend to follow a less formalized structure to manage employee behavior.

EXAMINING THE EVIDENCE

FORMALIZATION AND CENTRALIZATION: CAN ORGANIZATIONAL STRUCTURE SUBSTITUTE FOR LEADERSHIP?

In the late 1970s, leadership researchers Steven Kerr and John M. Jermier suggested that certain organizational characteristics could substitute for leadership.[65] Recently, researchers Nathan Eva, Sen Sendjay, Daniel Prajogo, and Karryna Madison built on the idea of substitutes for leadership by exploring whether organizational structure components of formalization and centralization moderate the effects of servant leadership on follower job satisfaction.[66] Their findings suggest that servant leadership behaviors will have a greater effect on followers in organizations with lower levels of organizational structure. More specifically, they found that formalization tends to serve as a substitute for servant leadership while centralization tends to neutralize the influence of servant leadership. These findings suggest that the popular servant-leadership approach will be most effective in organic organizations with less formalization and decentralized organizational structures.

Critical-Thinking Questions

1. What are the implications for organizational leaders regarding the best way to structure their organizations relative to the predominant leadership styles in their organizations?
2. Would these findings apply to other types of leadership (e.g., visionary leadership or empowering leadership)? Why or why not?

Bureaucracy is characterized by formalized rules and regulation, specialized routine tasks, division of labor, and centralized authority.[67] Bureaucratic structures, such as the IRS or the Motor Vehicle Bureau, tend to follow a chain of command with decision making and power firmly at the top.

There are four main types of organizational structures: simple structures, functional structures, divisional structures, and matrix structures.[68]

Simple structures (see Figure 16.7) are more common in small organizations where there is one central authority figure, usually a business owner, who tends to make the decisions. For example, the owner of a small clothing store might have to manage a cashier and salespeople. Because there are no layers of management, decisions can be made and implemented quickly. However, this structure has its drawbacks. The business owner may become overloaded with work or may be reluctant to delegate when necessary, which could slow down the progress of the organization.

Functional structures group employees according to the tasks they perform for the organization, such as marketing, finance, and human resources. Here employees are managed by means of clear levels of authority. In general, this structure works well for smaller organizations, but there is a risk of lack of communication between the departments because of their tendency to work separately from each other (see Figure 16.8).

The **divisional structure**—sometimes called *multidivisional structure*—groups employees by products and services, by geographic regions, or by customers (see Figure 16.9). Although divisional structures are ideally placed to meet external demands, divisions that are performing similar tasks—in different locations, for example—may be at risk of duplicating their work. They may also compete for shared resources. PepsiCo is an example of a company with a divisional structure. It is made up six divisions each positioned in different locations with its own way of doing business: PepsiCo Beverages North America; Frito-Lay North America; Quaker Foods North America; Latin America; Europe Sub-Saharan Africa; and Asia, Middle East and North Africa.[69]

The **matrix structure** is an organizational structure that combines both functional and divisional departmentalization, with dual lines of authority (see Figure 16.10).[70]

Employees tend to have dual reporting relationships to both *functional managers* who are people who have authority over specific departments and *product managers* who are the people responsible for the development of products in an organization. Some benefits to the matrix structure include the freedom to collaborate and innovate with coworkers across different departments, and the opportunities to learn new skills through this process. For example, high-technology firms like aerospace company Boeing use a matrix structure, which is more suited to its flexible working environment.[71]

FIGURE 16.7 ■ Simple Structure

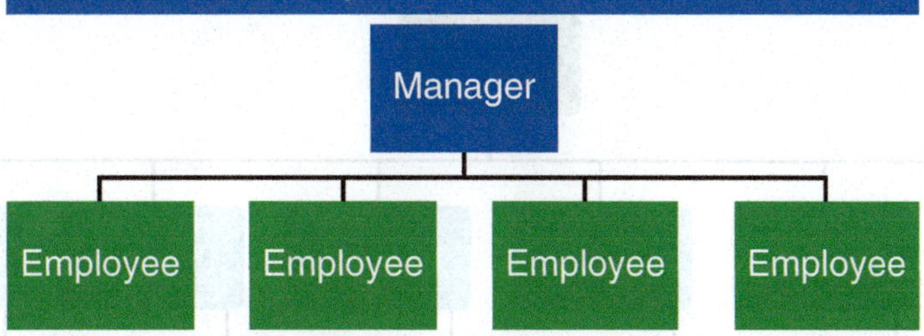

FIGURE 16.8 ■ Current Pioneering Health Frankfurt Organizational Structure

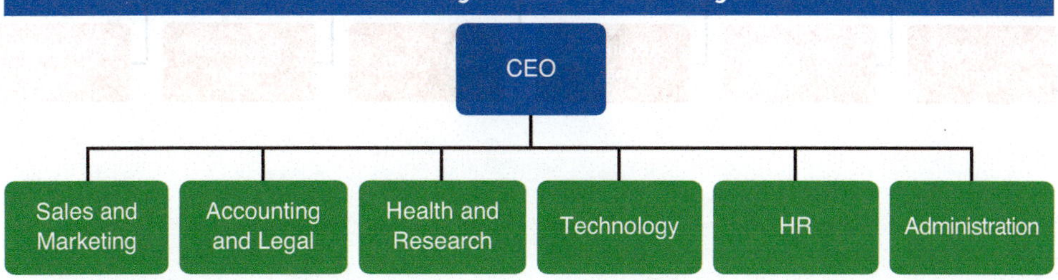

FIGURE 16.9 ■ Domestic and Global Organizational Structure

FIGURE 16.10 ■ Matrix Structure

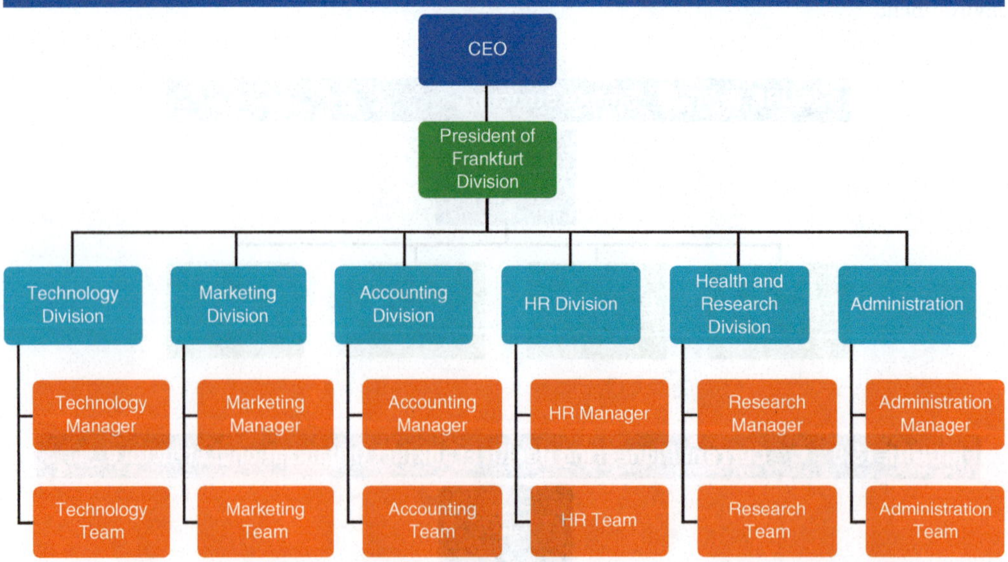

ORGANIZATIONAL DEVELOPMENT

To further reinforce organizational learning, many organizations use **organizational development (OD)**, a planned system that uses behavioral science knowledge to increase an organization's efficiency and effectiveness[72] to cope with internal and external changes. OD researchers and practitioners observe the culture, strategy, and climate of an organization and try to answer questions such as how do employees communicate? What are their cultural norms, attitudes, and beliefs? How are problems resolved? What is the mood or personality of an organization? Once they have identified these factors, they can begin to work out how to influence the employees' behavior.

Researchers tend to follow three basic steps in an OD model: diagnosis, interventions, and progress monitoring (see Figure 16.11).[73] First they seek to *diagnose* the problem and bring any issues to the surface so they can be resolved. The most common diagnostic techniques are employee surveys (such as job satisfaction surveys), questionnaires, and interviews.

Once this feedback has been collated, *interventions* can be used that are designed to address the underlying problems. For example, OD specialists may recommend team-building exercises, additional training, or role restructuring for employees who appear to be experiencing job dissatisfaction.

Finally, OD specialists *monitor* the effects of the intervention after it has been implemented to gauge its effectiveness. Often, they ask the employees to complete the same survey post-implementation. This helps identify the change objectives that have and have not been met. When goals have not been reached, the OD specialists analyze the situation, try to determine why they failed, and introduce modifications to the process. In the following section, we take a more in-depth view of the types of OD interventions adopted in organizations.

Types of OD Change Interventions

OD interventions are plans consisting of specific steps to address problems and create solutions to implement change in some facet of an organization, with the overall goal of improving the entire organization. Five different types of change interventions are commonly used in organizations: **structural interventions**, **task-technology interventions**, sociotechnical systems design, quality of work life interventions, and **people-focused interventions**.[74] Let's explore how these interventions work.

Structural Interventions

Structural interventions focus on job design, tasks, and division of labor. Typically, structural intervention is carried out in three different ways: changing rewards systems, changing the culture, and reorganizing the structure itself.[75]

FIGURE 16.11 ■ Organizational Development Techniques

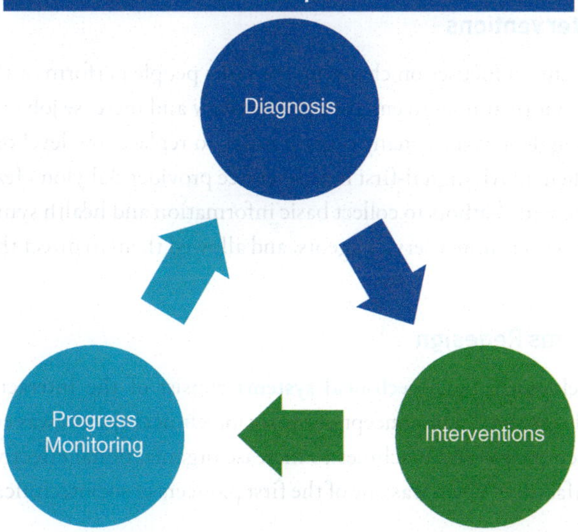

A new generation in the workforce responds more positively to praise as motivation, encouraging many companies to integrate praise into their day-to-day operations.

Jacob Lund / Alamy Stock Photo

German utility company E.ON introduced a reward system where employees received recognition for their efforts through digital and physical thank-you notes. This simple and inexpensive method resulted in increased motivation, a rise in employees "feeling valued" and an enhanced understanding of E.ON's business vision.[76]

Another type of intervention employed in organizations is *changing the culture*. For example, global medical technology maker Becton Dickinson addressed the lack of constructive conflict and engagement in its company culture by encouraging open communication, collaboration, and giving high-potential employees the opportunity to identify and solve challenges.[77]

Finally, organizations may choose to *change the structure* of the organization to improve communication, problem-solving, and goal-setting techniques. For example, companies Zappos advocates a flat, more open organizational structure people do not have job titles and are able to create their own guidelines. Zappos engages employees by giving them more freedom and autonomy which encourages growth and productivity and the motivation to achieve goals.[78]

Task-Technology Interventions

Task-technology intervention focuses on changing the tasks people perform or the technological processes they use to carry out their roles to enhance productivity and increase job satisfaction.[79] Artificial intelligence (AI) is being deployed by many organizations to replace low-level or unproductive tasks. For example, with the help of AI, digital-first health service provider Babylon Health headquartered in London, U.K., implemented chatbots to collect basic information and health symptoms from patients, which took the pressure off customer service agents, and allowed them to direct their attention towards more important tasks.[80]

Sociotechnical Systems Redesign

In organizational development, **sociotechnical systems** consist of the interaction between human behavior and technical systems.[81] The concept of the sociotechnical system was established to improve the relationship between people and machines to increase organizational effectiveness and efficiency. For example, car manufacturer Volvo was one of the first pioneers of sociotechnical systems redesign. It ended its mechanistic approach—in which people worked separately on a production line, specializing in one task—by creating a sociotechnical system in which a group of highly skilled employees worked together to assemble the cars using a collection of parts. As a result, people no longer felt like they were "machines" and became more motivated, productive, and effective.

Thus, if a company is introducing a new technical system, its managers need to consider the people who will be learning and using it. Unlike technology, people are not mechanistic and cannot be "programmed" in the same way. However, many organizations treat the technical system and the users as two separate entities. This is why the organizational change team and the technical team need to communicate regularly throughout the process of redesigning their sociotechnical system to ensure that the new system meets both organizational and human needs. Studies have shown that organizations like Volvo that focus on improving both technical and human systems have a better chance of adapting and responding to change.

Quality of Worklife Interventions

Another type of OD intervention is **quality of worklife (QWL)**, which alters the relationship between the employees and the workplace.[82] QWL efforts focus on improving employee satisfaction with pay, compensation, job security, responsibilities, performance, work/life balance, health, and career opportunities. For example, U.K.–based housebuilder Taylor Wimpey nurtures a QWL intervention by providing flexible work hours, family-friendly policies, opportunities to purchase additional vacation days, and time off for charity days.[83]

People-Focused Interventions

Finally, organizations can use different types of people-focused interventions during times of change. **Sensitivity training** is a type of program designed to raise awareness of group dynamics and any existing prejudices toward others.[84] Typically, the members of an organization are encouraged to participate in group discussions, exercises, and role-plays. They are also invited to share their perspectives and to raise any issues that concern them about dealing with different groups. Then they are shown productive ways to alleviate tensions without causing conflict. In 2021, The National Association for Stock Car Auto Racing (NASCAR) showed its intolerance for thoughtless, ill-considered language by ordering NASCAR Cup Series driver Kyle Busch to undergo sensitivity training after using an insensitive term that denigrates people with intellectual disabilities.[85]

We've seen that organizations sometimes use *survey feedback* to assess the level of job satisfaction in the workplace and take steps to reduce any problems that may hinder success. **Process consultation** is another form of intervention, which attempts to increase groups' awareness or understanding of their behaviors in the workplace.[86] Usually, an outside observer such as a trainer will study the way groups interact with each other and then provide feedback to members in the hope of making them more aware of their attitudes and behaviors and to develop practical solutions to identified problems.

Most organizations use *team-building* exercises to help improve the relationship between groups of employees.[87] These exercises might include physical challenges such as obstacle courses or rowing, or weekend retreats designed to bond employees and teams by giving them a place away from the office to spend time together in informal activities. Team building is also a fundamental part of **intergroup development**, which is finding ways to change the attitudes, perceptions, and stereotypes that employees may have of each other.[88] Part of this approach is to gather different groups together, listen to their perspectives on others, and seek to resolve these views through exercises and discussion.

Over the course of this textbook, we have explored many different facets of organizational behavior supported by the latest theory and research, media, and firsthand accounts. As you have learned, organizational behavior isn't just about "common sense"—it is a way of understanding the people you may work with: people who you will likely spend more time with than anybody else—and navigating all their different learning styles, personality traits, and other complexities. Learning the language of OB is an essential skill to master in managing your own behavior as well as the behavior of others.

IN REVIEW

16.1 Compare and contrast various conceptualizations of the change process

The **DADA syndrome** experienced by individuals faced with unwanted change consists of four stages: denial, anger, depression, and acceptance. Lewin's basic change model is a three-stage model of planned change that explains how to initiate, manage, and stabilize the change process by *unfreezing, transforming*, and *refreezing*. Lewin's force field analysis model is a decision-making technique that helps assess the reasons for and against making certain changes.

16.2 Identify the forces for change in organizations

For organizations to succeed, they need to adapt to **external forces**, or outside influences such as customers' demographic characteristics, technological advancements, customer and market changes, and social and political pressures, and **internal forces**, or inside influences such as management changes, organizational restructuring, and intrapreneurship.

16.3 Describe where resistance to change comes from and how to reduce it

Some individual sources of **resistance to change** are fear of the unknown, insecurity, and habit. Organizational sources include structural inertia, limited focus of change, group inertia, threat to expertise, and threat to established power relationships.

One of the most common ways to address resistance to change is education and communication before the change takes place. Other methods include participation, negotiation, manipulation, and coercion.

16.4 Describe how organizational structure helps shape behavior in organizations

Organizational structure is a framework of work roles that helps shape and support employee behavior. The structure of an organization has significant influence over the behavior of its employees. It groups and separates people geographically, hierarchically, or both; it builds and limits relationships by setting up lines of reporting and teams; and it defines employees' responsibilities by outlining their area of influence and accountability.

16.5 Describe the concept of organizational development in organizations and identify types of OD change interventions

Organizational development (OD) is a planned system that uses behavioral science knowledge to increase the efficiency and effectiveness of an organization. OD researchers tend to follow three basic steps in an OD model: diagnosis, interventions, and progress monitoring.

Structural intervention is carried out in three different ways: changing rewards systems, changing the culture, and reorganizing the structure itself. **Task-technology interventions** restructure tasks, redesign roles, or reconfigure sociotechnical systems. **Sociotechnical systems** redesign improves the interaction between human behavior and technical systems. **Quality of worklife (QWL)** interventions focus on employee satisfaction with pay, compensation, job security, responsibilities, performance, work/life balance, health, and career opportunities. Finally, organizations use different types of **people-focused interventions** during times of change.

KEY TERMS

Bureaucracy (p. 399)
Chain of command (p. 396)
Change management (p. 383)
DADA syndrome (p. 384)
Departmentalization (p. 396)
Division of labor (p. 395)
Divisional structure (p. 399)
External forces (p. 387)
Formalization (p. 397)
Functional structures (p. 399)
Intergroup development (p. 403)
Internal forces (p. 387)
Matrix structure (p. 399)
Mechanistic model (p. 397)
Organizational development (OD) (p. 401)
Organizational structure (p. 394)

People-focused intervention (p. 401)
Process consultation (p. 403)
Quality of worklife (QWL) (p. 403)
Resistance to change (p. 389)
Sensitivity training (p. 403)
Simple structures (p. 399)
Sociotechnical systems (p. 402)
Structural intervention (p. 401)
Task-technology intervention (p. 401)
Transforming (p. 385)

UP FOR DEBATE: MANAGEMENT'S ROLE IN ORGANIZATIONAL CHANGE

In the United States, when companies want to execute a major change in the company (e.g., changing a major product or implementing a new system for employee bonuses), upper-level management is under zero obligation to consult employees at all organizational levels to have a voice in the change. What do you think? Agree or disagree? Explain your answer.

EXERCISE 16.1: OVERCOMING RESISTANCE TO CHANGE

Objective

The purpose of this exercise is to understand resistance to change.

Instructions

This exercise is a class discussion based upon employees' resistance to change. The text discusses 10 individual sources of resistance to change. The 10 reasons are provided below and are explained in detail within the text:

- Lack of clarity
- Fear of the unknown
- Lack of skills
- Overcommitment to the current model
- Lack of trust
- Being left out
- Change to routine
- Resignation
- Perceptions of change
- Inadequate benefits and rewards

Your instructor will write each on the board or provide a slide with the 10 reasons delineated. As a class, discuss each one from a manager's perspective. As you proceed through the reasons, offer suggestions for steps a manager could take to lessen or remove that particular resistance to change. Be as specific as possible with detailed actions or words the manager could employ in combating each resistance to change.

Reflection Questions

1. Which of the 10 reasons for resistance to change is the most challenging for a manager to address? Why?
2. Which of the 10 reasons for resistance to change do you engage in most often at work? Explain.
3. What successful strategies have you personally experienced that a manager utilized to combat two or more of the reasons listed above? Why were they so effective?

Exercise contributed by Steven Stovall, Southeast Missouri State University.

EXERCISE 16.2: THE STRUCTURE VERSUS STRATEGY DEBATE

Objective

The purpose of this exercise is to grasp the synergies of structure and strategy.

Instructions

Among organizational behavior researchers, there is often a debate as to which comes first: organizational structure or organizational strategy. On one hand, those who believe that structure is set first suggest that to effectively determine the strategy of an organization, organizational structure must be established. In other words, the only way strategy could be crafted is if a structure is in place first. But, on the other hand, those who posit that strategy is implemented first believe that the structure of the organization is created based upon the strategy that the top managers of the organization want to execute. This position of the debate requires that first strategy must be determined before any structure could be created.

This exercise utilizes a debate format to consider the importance of structure and strategy. The instructor will ask the group who believes structure is first priority and who feels that strategy is the first priority. Once everyone has raised their hand for either side of this issue, move to the section of the room that believes the same as you about structure and strategy.

Once you are with those who feel similarly as you, elect two spokespeople to represent your side. The group will offer suggestions, making the case that either structure comes first, or that strategy does. After 10 minutes of preparation, the four representatives—two from each side—come to the front of the classroom and begin the debate.

The format of the debate is as follows:

A coin is tossed to determine which side goes first.

The first side has 3 minutes to make an opening statement. Then, the other side has 3 minutes to make their opening statement.

After the opening statements, the representatives who made the first opening statement have 3 minutes to respond. Then, the other side has 3 minutes for rebuttal.

This continues—2 minutes per side—for 30 minutes (or an appropriate amount of time, given any time constraints associated with the class).

Finally, 3-minute closing statements are made. The side that gave the first opening statement goes first and then the side that gave the second opening statement has the final word.

During opening and closing statements as well as responses and rebuttals, there can be no interruptions or distractions from the other side or the audience.

Those who remain in the audience can still participate. If they readily see an opportunity for the perfect response, they should write their idea down and hand it to one of their representatives.

Reflection Questions

1. Based upon what you saw and heard during the debate, where do you stand on this issue? Do you think structure determines strategy or that strategy determines structure? Explain.
2. Is your stance on this debate the same if the organization is new (such as an entrepreneurial start-up) or if it is a well-established company (over 100 years old) that suddenly hires a president from outside the company who wants to establish new strategies and restructure the organization? Explain.
3. In your current or most recent place of employment, has structure taken precedence or has strategy? Explain.

Exercise contributed by Steven Stovall, Southeast Missouri State University.

EXERCISE 16.3: ROAD TO CHANGE AND DEVELOPMENT

Objectives

This exercise gives you practice in *identifying* organizational change forces, and *describing* change resistance and methods for reducing this change resistance.

Instructions

Background—It is five years in the future and you are working for your state's department of transportation. You have been placed on a task force to provide a smooth transition to automating highway and road maintenance tasks. This change is expected to take two years to implement, and is expected to enable the department to increase efficiency and reduce costs for many maintenance tasks. It is projected that through a combination of retraining and normal workforce attrition, the department can keep 80% of the existing workforce and see a 20% reduction in its operational budget. As an alternative, 100% of the workforce can be retained, but operational savings will be only 10%. All cost reductions will be beneficial, but there are political forces that are pushing for the maximum savings possible. In addition, there is a high level of cohesion and solidarity among the road maintenance workers, and they see these potential changes as threats to their and their colleagues' jobs.

For the initial meeting of your task force, you will need to identify the forces that are promoting change, and the forces that will resist the change. In identifying these elements, be sure to discuss both the technical and nontechnical issues related to change, and discuss methods for reducing change resistance. You should concentrate your discussion on concepts from this chapter, but you will also need to bring in relevant concepts from other chapters when developing your plan. You should include both change methods (80% and 100% worker retention) in your discussion.

You will also find it useful to start with identifying and specifying the desirable future state of your organization.

To develop this plan, you should form into teams of five to seven people. Once you have formed a team, take 20 to 30 minutes to develop the plan and be prepared to have a team spokesperson present your plan in a 5- to 10-minute presentation.

Reflection Questions

1. How did the change plans differ under the two scenarios?
2. What elements remained consistent between the two scenarios?
3. What disputes about the change plans arose in your team?
4. What were the easiest change elements to identify and decide upon?
5. How would you expect the change resistance elements to differ if the change time period was substantially longer or shorter?

Exercise contributed by Milton R. Mayfield, Professor of Business, Texas A&M International University, and Jacqueline R. Mayfield, Professor of Business, Texas A&M International University.

ONLINE EXERCISE 16.1: ANALYZING ORGANIZATIONAL STRUCTURE

Objective

The purpose of this exercise is to gain an appreciation for aspects of organizational structure.

Instructions

Conduct an online search of a large company you are familiar with. Try and locate an organizational chart that illustrates the structure of the firm. Once you have found a recent organizational chart, write an analysis for your instructor that describes the organizational structure.

Specifically, your analysis should address the following:

- Discuss the division of labor—Does the company seem to employ primarily specialists or generalists?
- Describe the departmentalization—How is the firm departmentalized?
- Assess the chain of command—Is chain of command from the front-line associates to the president clearly defined?
- Discuss the span of control—Are managers supervising an appropriate number of employees?
- Determine the degree of centralization—Based upon the organizational chart, is this company centralized or decentralized?
- Describe the structural model—Does the company exhibit a mechanistic or organic model?

Reflection Questions

1. What was the most challenging aspect of organizational structure for you to assess in this assignment? Why?
2. For the organization you currently work for, or a recent employer, assess the organizational structure you have experienced.
3. What kind of organizational structure would you most like to work in? Least? Explain.
4. Why do companies have varying organizational structures? Why are they not all the same?

Exercise contributed by Steven Stovall, Southeast Missouri State University.

ONLINE EXERCISE 16.2: UNDERSTANDING FORCES FOR CHANGE

The purpose of this exercise is to gain an understanding of external and internal forces for change.

Instructions

Think about your current job or a previous job where a major change occurred. It may have been a policy change related to human resources (for example, when you could take a break and when you couldn't or a change in health-care providers). It may have also been something on a broader scale such as the company adding a new service or product line or changing its name or logo. Try to recall a change that occurred that impacted you.

In a discussion group, describe the change you experienced. Share not only what the change was, but how you felt at the time about that change.

Reflection Questions

1. For the change you described in the discussion post, what was your initial reaction? Did you think "this will never work" or did you embrace the change? Discuss.
2. Did you or someone you work with steadfastly resist the change? If so, why? Also, what could or did managers do to assuage the resistance to change?
3. How would you have rolled out the change described in the discussion group? What would you have done differently?

Exercise contributed by Steven Stovall, Southeast Missouri State University.

CASE 16.1: ORGANIZATIONAL CHANGE AND STRUCTURE AT GENERAL ELECTRIC (GE)

General Electric (NYSE: GE), headquartered in Boston, is one of the most storied and successful corporations in American history. They have roots all the way back to Thomas Edison's invention of the incandescent light bulb, when they purchased Edison's company Edison General, in 1892.[89] General

Electric can be found all across homes, consumer products markets, and business-to-business transactions around the world; they are involved in providing everything from refrigerators to wind turbines to financial services and banking. As impressive as their history is, GE must constantly adapt and change their business to stay alive.

The Change Process

Jeff Immelt, the Chief Executive Officer of GE from 2000 until 2017, saw huge success and huge failure, and found ways to help General Electric adapt to the world around it.[90] The text speaks about internal and external forces, which are forces from inside and outside a company, respectively, that demand action. GE, with Immelt in the corner office, saw much of both. For example, the 2008 financial crisis did not leave GE unscathed: their stock price in 2007 was $40, and by 2009 it was below $10.[91] It makes it difficult for a large conglomeration of companies like General Electric to function effectively when their share price is so low and equity markets are ineffective for raising capital to continue growth and operations, but this external force led to positive organizational change. According to Jeff Immelt, "The changes that took place in the world from 2001, when I assumed the company's leadership, to 2017 are too numerous to mention. The task of the CEO has never been as difficult as it is today."[92] When the internet came around, and with it a technology boom, General Electric could have easily been left in the dust as an old industrial corporation. To adapt, GE has become an innovator in technology, began investing in many new businesses, and redesigned old ones.

Immelt remarked, "It's the leader's job to connect the dots for everyone in the organization."[93] This is a tough task, but an important one. The text mentions resistance to change: a very common phenomenon where employees or managers refuse to embrace change; sometimes they do not want to learn a new method, or they simply do not believe there is a need for a change. Part of connecting the dots, as Immelt puts it, is "to get people in your organization to see the need for change as existential."[94] All future managers should be aware of that fact—that without their full dedication and leadership, they will never get their team to get on board with serious organizational change.

GE Transformations

There is no way for a company to survive 100 years, or even 10, without undergoing some changes in their identity or services. There are three elements of Lewin's Basic Change model, and General Electric has become familiar with the one in the middle: transformation. This occurs when managers accept the need for change, and begin the difficult process of implementation; this involves important things, like making sure employees are aligned with the transformation.[95] For example, GE started a branch named GE Capital as far back as 1932, and it has grown into a very large financial services operator and financier. The management found, though, that their company had gone astray with too many subsidiaries involved in their essential business offerings, so they defined their core business as industrial businesses and technology. After defining the change, they spent years reframing GE Capital and many other business units to put an emphasis on supporting the core industrial activities.[96]

GE has done a few more things to promote a transformation in the 2000s.[97] They doubled investment in research and development (R&D) to ensure they are at the front of the pack in the technology they manufacture; a longstanding company can be disrupted by a start-up on any day unless they transform and innovate constantly. Changes like that require convincing: Management has to agree to spend the money, the funds have to be found somewhere, and new teams of employees must be created and work well together. GE also transformed into a global company, and they have operations in over 130 countries.[98] This, too, is part of their core mission to add value in the digital age and stay ahead of disruptors and external forces.

General Electric: Still an Open Case

Charles Dow created the still-famous Dow Jones Industrial index out of 12 companies in 1896, and GE was the only original member still standing up until 2018.[99] Their removal after such a long stay on the list of companies used to measure the health of the American market is only one of General Electric's new problems and largely occurred in response to their recent poor performance in some areas. They have the biggest pension deficit of any company on Standard and Poor's 500 index, meaning that they have outstanding debt to their employees of over $28 billion.[100] They have had to make cuts to their dividends, the money they pay shareholders quarterly, and they will have to raise capital and sell off business units until they can manage both problems, and return to their historic profitability.

GE has seen times worse than these, and they have learned to adapt all throughout the 21st century. The open case now is whether they will change, transform, and fix their problems like they have in the past.

Case Questions

1. Name two transformations that GE has undergone since the turn of the century.
2. What is an external force? Describe one which GE had to react to.
3. Why is GE an open case?

GLOSSARY

Ability diversity: The representation of people with different levels of mental and physical abilities within an organization

Achievement-oriented leadership: Leadership behavior characterized by setting challenging goals, improving performance, and assisting training

Acquired needs theory: A theory that suggests three main categories of needs: need for achievement, need for affiliation, and need for power

Active listening: The act of concentrating on the true meaning of what others are saying

Adjourning: The stage when individuals either leave the team or have no reason to be in further contact with their teammates

Affective commitment: an employee's perceived positive emotional attachment to the organization

Affects: The range of feelings, in the form of emotions and moods, that people experience

Affirmative action: Proactive steps taken by organizations to counteract discrimination against underrepresented groups and women

Anchoring and adjustment heuristic: A process whereby people base their decisions on the first piece of information they are given without taking other probabilities into account

Antecedents of conflict: Factors that set the scene for potential dispute

Anthropology: The study of people and their activities in relation to societal, environmental, and cultural influences

Arbitrator: A neutral third party officially assigned to settle a dispute

Assertiveness: The use of demands or threats to persuade someone to carry out a task

Attitude: A learned tendency to consistently respond positively or negatively to people or events

Attribution theory: A theory that holds that people look to explain the behavior of others in two ways: by making *internal attributions*, attributing behavior to personal characteristics, or by making *external attributions*, attributing behavior to situational factors

Authentic leadership: A pattern of leadership behavior based on honesty, practicality, and ethicality

Autocratic style: A leadership style based on making decisions without asking for suggestions from others

Availability heuristic: A rule of thumb for making judgments that uses examples and events that immediately spring to mind

Avoidance: An attempt to suppress a conflict and pretend it does not exist

Awareness of others: A consciousness of other people's feelings, behaviors, personalities, likes, and dislikes

BATNA: The best possible alternative to a negotiable agreement

Behavioral goals: Short-term goals

Behavioral leadership perspective: The belief that specific behaviors distinguish leaders from nonleaders

Bias: The tendency to show prejudice against another person or group

Big Five model: Five basic dimensions of personality—Extraversion, Agreeableness, Conscientiousness, Neuroticism (or Emotional Stability), and Openness to Experience—frequently used to evaluate people in the workplace

Bonus pay: A pay plan that rewards employees for recent performance rather than historical performance

Bounded rationality: The idea that we are restricted by a variety of constraints when making decisions

Brainstorming: The process of generating creative, spontaneous ideas from all members of a group without any criticism or judgment

Bureaucracy: An organizational style characterized by formalized rules and regulation, specialized routine tasks, division of labor, and centralized authority

Ceremonies: Events that reinforce the relationship between employees and the organization

Chain of command: The flow of authority and power from the highest to the lowest levels of the organization

Change hindrances: Obstacles that impede progress and make it difficult for the organization to adapt to different situations

Change management: A method of overseeing and implementing change to support the transformation of organizational goals, processes or technologies

Channel richness: The capacity to communicate and understand information between people and organizations

Character strengths: Positive qualities that benefit oneself and others

Charismatic leadership: The ability of a leader to use their personality or charm to inspire, motivate, and acquire loyalty and commitment from employees

Classical conditioning: A conditioning concept developed by Russian physiologist Ivan Pavlov that suggests that learning can be accomplished through the use of stimuli

Cluster chain: A type of communication that occurs when a group of people broadcast information within a larger group

Coalition building: Gathering the support of others as a reason for another person to agree to a request

Coercive power: A strategy by which a person controls the behavior of others through punishments, threats, or sanctions

Cognitive dissonance: Inconsistency between a person's beliefs, attitudes, or behaviors

Cohesion: The degree to which team members connect with each other

Common-information bias: The inclination to overemphasize information held by the majority of group members while failing to consider other perspectives held by the minority

Communication: The act of transmitting thoughts, processes, and ideas through a variety of channels

Competence: The ability to perform work tasks successfully

Competing values framework: A procedure that provides a way to identify, measure, and change organizational culture

Competitive advantage: The edge that gives organizations a more beneficial position than their competitors and allows them to generate more profits and retain more customers

Complete rationality: The assumption that we take into account every single criterion or possible alternative in making a decision

Compliance: The behavior of targets of influence who agree to readily carry out the requests of the leader

Compressed workweeks: A work arrangement that gives employees the benefit of an extra day off by allowing them to work their usual number of hours in fewer days per pay period

Concealable stigmatized identities: Identities that are kept hidden because they carry negative stereotypes

Conceptual skill: The capacity to see the organization as a whole and understand how each part relates to the others and how it fits into its overall environment

Conciliator: A neutral third party who is informally assigned to persuade opponents to communicate

Confirmation bias: The tendency to seek out information that fuels our preexisting views and to discount information that conflicts with our worldview

Conflict: A clash between individuals or groups in relation to different opinions, thought processes, and perceptions

Consideration: A behavioral leadership style demonstrated by leaders who develop mutual trust and respect and actively build interpersonal relationships with their followers

Consultation: The offer of participation or consultation in the decision-making process

Content theories: Theories that explain why people have different needs at different times and how these needs motivate behavior; examples are Maslow's hierarchy of needs, Alderfer's ERG theory, McClelland's need theory, and Herzberg's two-factor theory

Contextual diversity: Diversity among individuals in relation to their circumstances and backgrounds and thus their economic and political viewpoints

Contingency leadership perspective: The view that the effectiveness of the leader relates to the interaction of the leader's traits or behaviors with situational factors

Contingency thinking: The approach that describes actions as dependent on the nature of the situation; one size does not fit all

Continuance commitment: The need to remain in an organization because the perceived losses of leaving are greater than the benefits that would be gained in a new organization

Continuous reinforcement: A reinforcement schedule in which a reward occurs after each instance of a behavior or set of behaviors

Contrast effect: An effect that takes place when people rank something higher or lower than they should as a result of exposure to recent events or situations

Coping: The effort to manage, reduce, or minimize stressors

Corporate social responsibility: A business approach that delivers economic, social, and environmental benefits to stakeholders in order to contribute to sustainable development

Correlation: A reciprocal relationship between two or more factors

Counterculture: Values that differ strongly from those of the larger organization

Counterproductive work behaviors: Voluntary behaviors that purposefully disrupt or harm the organization

Creative potential: The skill and capacity to generate ideas

Creativity: The generation of meaningful ideas by individuals or teams

Critical thinking: The ability to use intelligence, knowledge, and skills to question and carefully explore situations and arrive at thoughtful conclusions based on evidence and reason

Cross-cultural leadership: The process of leading across cultures

Cross-functional team: A group of workers from different units with various areas of expertise

Cultural metacognition: The level of conscious cultural awareness we possess during cross-cultural interactions

Culture shock: Feelings of nervousness, doubt, and confusion arising from being in a foreign environment

Cyberloafing: A phenomenon whereby people access the internet for personal use while pretending to work

DADA syndrome: Four stages—denial, anger, depression, and acceptance—experienced by individuals when they are faced with unwanted change

Decentralization: The distribution of power across all levels of the organization

Decision-making: The action or process of identifying a strategy to resolve problems

Deep acting: Efforts to change your actual emotions to better match the required emotions of the situation

Deep-level diversity: Differences in verbal and nonverbal behaviors that are not as easily perceived because they lie below the surface, such as differences in attitudes, values, beliefs, and personality

Delegating: The act of giving most of the responsibility to followers while still monitoring progress

Delphi technique: A method of decision-making in which information is gathered from a group of respondents within their area of expertise

Departmentalization: A process of grouping people with related job duties, skills, and experiences into different areas within the overall organizational structure

Dependent variables: Factors affected by independent variables

Differing perceptions: The way in which our interpretations of situations clashes with the perceptions of others.

Directive leadership: A leadership style characterized by implementing guidelines, managing expectations, setting definite performance standards, and ensuring that individuals follow rules

Disability: A physical or mental impairment that substantially limits one or more of their major life activities

Discrimination: The unfair treatment of people and groups based on certain characteristics, such as race, age, gender, religion, disability, or sexual orientation

Display rules: Basic norms that govern which emotions should be displayed and which should be suppressed

Distress: High levels of stressors that have destructive and negative effects on effort and performance

Distributive bargaining: A strategy that involves two parties trying to claim a "fixed pie" of resources

Distributive justice: The degree to which people think outcomes are fair

Diversity, equity, and inclusion: A term used to describe programs and policies that encourage the representation and participation of diverse groups of people, including people of different genders, races and ethnicities, abilities and disabilities, religions, cultures, ages, and sexual orientations and people with diverse backgrounds, experiences, and skills and expertise.

Diversity: The presence of differences within a given setting

Diversity hindrances: Obstacles that limit the range of employees in organizations

Divisional structure: (sometimes called *multidivisional structure*) An organizational structure that groups employees by products and services, geographic regions, or customers

Division of labor: The degree to which certain jobs are divided into specific tasks

Dominant culture: Set of core values shared by the majority of organizational employees

Downward communication: Messages sent from the upper levels of the organizational hierarchy to the lower levels

Dysfunctional conflict: A dispute or disagreement that has negative effects on individuals or teams

Ease-of-recall bias: The propensity to over-rely on information recollected from memory when making a decision

Economic responsibility: Means that organizations must be economically and financially sound to enable them to become socially responsible in the first place

Electronic communication: The ability to transmit messages through email, videoconferencing, blogs, fax, instant messaging, texting, and social media

Emotional contagion: A phenomenon in which emotions that are experienced by a few people in a work group are spread to the others

Emotional dissonance: A discrepancy between the emotions a person displays and the emotions they actually feel

Emotional intelligence: The ability to understand emotions in oneself and others in order to effectively manage one's own behaviors and relationships with others

Emotional labor: The process of managing one's feelings to present positive emotions even when they are contrary to one's actual feelings

Emotional regulation: A set of processes through which people influence their own emotions and the ways in which they experience and express them

Emotional stability: The extent to which someone can remain calm and composed

Emotion-focused coping: An effort to change your emotional reaction to a stressor by using positive language and distracting techniques

Emotions: Intense feelings directed at a specific object or person

Employee engagement: A connection with the organization and passion for one's job

Employee stock ownership plans: Plans that allow employees to purchase company stock, often at below-market price, as one of their benefits

Empowering leadership: A behavioral type of leadership that empowers leaders to help develop the individual skills and abilities of their followers. Also known as "superleadership"

Equality: The process of ensuring that everyone is given the same opportunities and resources regardless of individual need

Equity: The process of ensuring that processes and programs are impartial and fair and provide equal access to new opportunities so as to enhance the success of all employees

Equity theory: Theory that holds that motivation is based on our perception of fairness in comparison with others

ERG theory: Theory that suggests that people are motivated by three categories of needs arranged in the form of a hierarchy

Escalation of commitment: Increased commitment to a decision despite negative information

Ethical dilemma: A conflict between two or more morally unpleasant alternatives

Ethical leadership: A means of influencing others through personal values, morals, and beliefs

Ethical responsibility: Means being morally aware enough to do the right thing in relation to the environment, fair wages, and who the company does business with

Ethics: Moral principles that guide our behavior

Ethnicity: Sociological factors such as nationality, culture, language, and ancestry

Ethnocentrism: The tendency to believe that your culture or ethnicity is superior to everyone else's

Eustress: Moderate levels of stressors that have constructive and positive effects on effort and performance

Evidence-based management: The practice of using a variety of sources of evidence to make decisions

Exchange: The promise of rewards to persuade another person to cooperate

Expatriate: An employee who lives and works in a foreign country on a temporary basis

Expectancy: The probability that the amount of work effort invested by an individual will result in a high level of performance

Expectancy theory: Theory that holds that people will choose certain behaviors over others with the expectation of a certain outcome

Expert power: The ability to influence the behavior of others through the amount of knowledge or expertise possessed by an individual on which others depend

Exploitative innovation: The enhancement and reuse of existing products and processes

Exploratory innovation: Risk taking, radical thinking, and experimentation

External adaptation: A pattern of basic assumptions shared between employees of the goals, tasks, and methods that need to be achieved, together with ways of managing success and failure

External forces: Outside influences for change

External locus of control: The believe that outside influences are responsible for one's fate

Extinction: The absence of any consequences for a behavior, which reduces the likelihood that the behavior will be repeated in the same or similar situations

Extraversion: The personality trait of obtaining gratification from outside stimulation

Extrinsic motivation: The performance of tasks or activities with the expectation of a reward or avoidance of punishment or negative outcomes

Extrinsic rewards: External contributions awarded to employees, such as salary, bonuses, and paid vacations

Filtering: The process of screening and then manipulating a message from a sender before passing it on to the intended receiver

Flextime: Flexible working hours that can be customized within the limits established by management

Followership: Individuals' capacity to cooperate with leaders

Formalization: The degree to which rules and procedures are standardized in an organization

Formal leader a person officially designated as a head of a group or an organization

Formal networks: The transmission of messages established and approved by the organizational hierarchy

Forming: A process whereby team members meet for the first time, get to know each other, and try to understand where they fit into the team structure

Framing bias: The tendency to highlight certain aspects of a situation to solve a problem while ignoring other aspects

Free agents: Independent workers who supply organizations with short-term talent for projects that need to be completed within a certain amount of time

Freelancer: A type of free agent who can work for multiple employers, giving a limited amount of time to each

Functional conflict: A constructive and healthy dispute between individuals or groups

Functional structures: Organizational structures that group employees according to the tasks they perform for the organization

Fundamental attribution error: The tendency to underestimate the influence of external factors and overestimate the impact of internal factors when making judgments about the behavior of others

Gain sharing: A system whereby managers agree to share the benefits of cost savings with staff in return for their contribution to the company's performance

Gender diversity: The equal representation of men, women, and nonbinary people in the workplace

Glass ceiling: An invisible barrier that limits one's ability to progress to more senior positions

Glass cliff: A phenomenon whereby women or ethnic minorities are given leadership positions during periods of crisis without any support

Goal-setting theory: Theory that suggests that human performance is directed by conscious goals and intentions

Gossip chains: A type of communication that occurs when one individual creates and spreads untrue or inaccurate information through the organization

Grapevine: An unofficial line of communication between individuals or groups

Group: Three or more people who work independently to attain organizational goals

Groupthink: A psychological phenomenon in which people in a cohesive group go along with the group consensus rather than offering their own opinions

Halo effect: A perception problem through which we form a positive or negative bias of an individual based on our overall impressions of that person

Heuristics: Shortcuts or "rules of thumb" that allow us to make judgments and decisions quickly and efficiently

Hierarchy of needs theory: Maslow's theory that suggests people are motivated by their desire to satisfy specific needs and that needs are arranged in a hierarchy, with physiological needs at the bottom and self-actualization needs at the top

High-context cultures: Cultures in which meaning is conveyed through body language, nonverbal cues, and the circumstances in which the communication is taking place

High-involvement management: The way managers empower employees to make decisions, provide them with extensive training and the opportunities to increase their knowledge base, share important information, and provide incentive compensation

Hindsight bias: The tendency to overestimate the ability to predict an outcome of an event

HIPOs: High-potential employees who are flexible, committed, and motivated

Human capital: People's skills, knowledge, experience, and general attributes

Human capital inimitability: The degree to which the skills and talents of employees can be emulated by other organizations

Human capital rareness: The skills and talents of an organization's people that are unique in the industry

Human capital value: The way employees work toward the strategic goals of an organization to achieve competitive advantage

Human skills: The ability to relate to other people

Hygiene factors: Sources of job satisfaction such as salary, status, and security

Hypothesis: A statement that specifies the relationships between variables

Idea generation: The first step in the innovation process—creation of the idea itself

Idealized influence: Behavior that gains the admiration, trust, and respect of followers, who in turn follow the leader's example with their own actions

Impact: The feeling of making a difference

Implementation and diffusion: The final stage of the innovation process, which entails producing and distributing the new product or idea

Implicit bias: A set of positive or negative stereotypes someone may unconsciously hold toward a person or group

Implicit followership theories: Preconceived notions about the types of behaviors that characterize followers and nonfollowers

Implicit leadership theories: Hypotheses that explore the extent to which we distinguish leaders and nonleaders based on underlying assumptions, stereotypes, and beliefs

Impression management: The process by which we attempt to influence the perceptions others may have of us

Inclusion: The practice of ensuring that people are welcomed and feel a sense of belonging in the workplace

Independent variables: Factors that remain unchanged

Individual differences: The behavioral and cognitive similarities and differences among people

Individualist–collectivist: The degree to which employees believe they have the right to live their lives as they see fit, choose their own values, and act on their own judgment

Individualized consideration: Leader behavior associated with creating mutual respect or trust and a genuine concern for the needs and desires of others

Informal leader a person who does not receive a title but is perceived by others as a leader

Informal networks: A casual form of sharing information between employees across company divisions

Informational justice: The degree to which employers provide truthful information and explanations to employees regarding why certain decisions are being made

Information control: A hard influencing tactic in which key information is withheld to manipulate outcomes

Information overload: Exposure to an overwhelming amount of information

Ingratiation: A strategy of winning favor and putting oneself in the good graces of others before making a request

Ingratiation: An effort to win favor and the good graces of others before making a request

In-group exchange: Interaction that occurs when leaders and followers develop good working relationships based on mutual trust, respect, and a sense of sharing common fates

Initiating structure: A behavioral leadership style demonstrated by leaders who define the roles of the employees, set clear guidelines and procedures, and establish distinct patterns of organization and communication

Innovation: The creation and development of a new product or service

Inspirational appeals: The use of emotions to raise enthusiasm for the task by appealing to the values and ideals of others

Inspirational motivation: Leadership behaviors that promote commitment to a shared vision of the future

Instrumentality: The probability that good performance will lead to various work outcomes

Integrative bargaining: A strategy that involves both parties negotiating a win/win solution

Intellectual stimulation: Stimuli that encourage people to think and promote intelligence, logic, and problem-solving

Interdependence: The extent to which team members rely on each other to complete their work tasks

Intergroup development: The process of finding ways to change the attitudes, perceptions, and stereotypes that employees may have of each other

Intermittent reinforcement: A reinforcement schedule in which a reward does not occur after each instance of a behavior or set of behaviors

Internal forces: Inside influences for change

Internal integration: A shared identity with agreed-upon methods of working together

Internal locus of control: The belief that one is responsible for influencing events in one's life

Interpersonal justice: The level of dignity, politeness, and respect employees receive by supervisors during change implementation

Intersectionality: A term describing how different types of discrimination—against race, class, gender, religion, sexual orientation, disability, or other individual characteristics—may overlap with one another, manifesting in negative outcomes

Intrinsic motivation: The performance of tasks for our own innate satisfaction

Introversion: The personality trait of focusing on internal feelings rather than outside stimulation

Intuition: An unconscious process of making decisions based on imagination and possibilities

Job characteristics model: Five core dimensions of jobs: skill variety, task identity, task significance, autonomy, and feedback

Job content–based pay: A salary paid based on the evaluation of a job's worth

Job design: A method of setting the duties and responsibilities of a job with the intention of improving productivity and performance

Job enlargement: An increase in the range of tasks and duties associated with a job

Job enrichment: An increase in the scope of a job to make it more complex, interesting, stimulating, and satisfying for employees

Job rotation: A process of periodically moving staff employees from one job to another

Job satisfaction: The degree to which an individual feels positive or negative about a job

Job sharing: An employment option in which one full-time job is divided among two or more people according to predetermined hours

Justice approach: Making decisions on the basis of fairness

Lack of participation error: The inclination to exclude certain people from the decision-making process

Laissez-faire leadership: Leadership behavior that fully delegates responsibility to others

Lateral communication: Messages sent between and among the same hierarchical levels across organizations

Leader emergence: The natural occurrence of someone becoming the leader of a leaderless group

Leader-exchange theory: A theory of leadership that focuses on the relationships between leaders and their group members.

Leader–member relations: Relationships that reflect the degree of confidence, trust, and respect that exists between subordinates and their leaders

Leadership: The process of providing general direction, from a position of influence, to individuals or groups toward the successful attainment of goals

Leadership grid: An approach that plots concern for production on the horizontal axis and concern for people on the vertical axis where 1 is the least concern and 9 is the greatest concern

Leadership prototypes: Behaviors that people associate with leadership

Leader's position power: The level of power a leader possesses to reward or punish, or promote and demote

Learning: An ongoing process through which individuals adjust their behavior based on experience

Least-preferred coworker (LPC) questionnaire: An instrument that purports to measure whether a person is task oriented or relationship oriented

Legal responsibility: Means that organizations must make every effort to comply with legal requirements

Legitimate power: The degree to which a person has the right to ask others to do things that are considered within the scope of their authority

Localization: The process of adapting certain functions to accommodate the language, culture, or governing laws of a country

Locus of control: The extent to which people feel they have influence over events

Long-term orientation: The measurement of values such as perseverance, respect for tradition, and thrift

Low-context cultures: Cultures that depend on explicit messages conveyed through the spoken or written word

Machiavellianism: A philosophy that describes the behavior of people who manipulate others and use unethical practices for personal gain

Manifest conflict stage: The stage at which people engage in behaviors that provoke a response

Matrix structure: An organizational structure that combines both functional and divisional departmentalization together with dual lines of authority

Meaningfulness: Refers to the positive meaning and significance of an activity.

Mechanistic model: A formalized structure based on centralization and departmentalization

Mediator: A neutral third party who attempts to assist parties in a negotiation to find a resolution or come to an agreement using rational arguments and persuasion

Mergers and acquisition hindrances: Obstacles that make it difficult for two organizations to join together

Merit pay: A pay plan in which pay raises are linked directly to performance

Microaggressions: Verbal, behavioral, or environmental slights or insults made against a target person or group

Model: A simplified snapshot of reality

Moods: Generalized positive or negative feelings of mind

Motivation: Forces from within individuals that stimulate and drive them to achieve goals

Motivators: Sources of job satisfaction such as achievement, recognition, and responsibility

Need for achievement: Need to perform well against a standard of excellence

Need for affiliation: Need to be liked and to stay on good terms with most other people

Need for competence: The motivation derived from stretching and exercising our capabilities

Need for power: Desire to influence people and events

Need for self-determination: The feeling of motivation and control we get from making efforts that don't rely on any external influences

Negative affect: A mood dimension that consists of emotions such as boredom, lethargy, and depression

Negative reinforcement: The removal of a particular item or stimulus following the demonstration of a certain behavior in order to increase that behavior

Negotiation: The process of reaching an agreement that both parties find acceptable

Neuroticism: A personality trait that involves being tense, moody, irritable, and temperamental

Neutralizing: The substitution of leadership attributes that do not affect follower outcomes

Nominal group technique: A structured way for team members to generate ideas and identify solutions in which each member is asked the same question in relation to a work issue and requested to write as many answers as possible; answers are read aloud and voted on

Nonprogrammed decisions: New or nonroutine problems for which there are no proven answers

Nonverbal communication: The transmission of wordless cues between people

Normative commitment: The degree to which employees feel they should stay in the organization because of a feeling of loyalty or obligation

Norming: The process by which team members resolve conflict and begin to work well together and become more cohesive

Norms: The informal rules of a team's behavior that govern the team

Observable culture: The components of culture that can be seen in an organization

Open systems theory: The assumption that organizations are systems that interact with their environments to obtain resources or inputs and transform them into outputs returned to the environment for consumption

Operant conditioning: The process of forming associations between learning and behavior by controlling its consequences

Oral communication: The ability to give and exchange information, ideas, and processes verbally, either one on one or as a group

Organization: A structured arrangement of people working together to accomplish specific goals

Organizational behavior: A field of study focused on understanding, explaining, and improving attitudes of individuals and groups in organizations

Organizational behavior modification: The use of behavioral techniques to reinforce positive work behavior and discourage unhelpful work behavior

Organizational citizenship behavior: Discretionary and voluntary behavior that is not a part of the employee's specific role requirements and is not formally rewarded

Organizational commitment: an employee's psychological connection to an organization

Organizational cultural lag: The deficit in organizations that fail to keep up with new emerging innovations

Organizational culture: A pattern of shared norms, rules, values, and beliefs that guides the attitudes and behaviors of its employees

Organizational development (OD): A deliberately planned system that uses behavioral science knowledge to increase the efficiency and effectiveness of an organization

Organizational justice: The perception of fairness in workplace practices

Organizational language: Words or metaphors and expressions specific to an organization

Organizational politics: Behavior that is not formally sanctioned by the organization and that is focused on maximizing our self-interest, often at the expense of the organization or other employees

Organizational structure: A framework of work roles that helps shape and support employee behavior

Organizational structure innovation: The introduction or modification of work assignments, authority relationships, and communication and reward systems within an organization

Outcomes of conflict stage: The stage that describes the consequences of the dispute

Out-group exchange: Interaction that occurs when leaders and followers fail to create a sense of mutual trust, respect, or common fate

Participating: Leadership behavior in which both leaders and followers work together and share in the decision-making responsibilities of the task

Participative leadership: A leadership style that favors consulting with followers and considering their input in decision-making

Part-time workers: Workers who supply organizations with part-time talent for projects that need to be completed within a certain amount of time

Path–goal leadership theory: A theory that proposes that leadership effectiveness depends on the degree to which the leader enhances the performance of followers by guiding them on a defined track toward achieving their goals

People-focused intervention: An attempt to support employees through organizational change by engaging in team-building activities, skill-training and group discussions

People innovation: Changes in the beliefs and behaviors of individuals working in an organization

Perceived/felt conflict stage: The stage at which emotional differences are sensed and felt

Perceived inequity: The sense of feeling under-rewarded or over-rewarded in comparison with others

Perception: The process by which we receive and interpret information from our environment

Performance-based pay: A financial incentive awarded to employees for meeting certain goals or objectives

Performance goals: Long-term goals set into the future

Performing: The way in which a team is invested toward achieving its goals and operates as a unit

Personal appeals: Requests to cooperate on the basis of friendship or as a personal favor

Personal conception: The degree to which individuals relate to and think about their social and physical environments and their personal beliefs regarding a range of issues

Personal diversity: Diversity among individuals in relation to age, gender, values, and skills

Personality: A stable and unique pattern of traits, characteristics, and resulting behaviors that gives an individual their identity

Personality traits: The characteristics that describe people's thoughts, feelings, and behaviors

Personal power: The ability to influence the behavior of others

Person-job fit: The process of identifying the skills, experiences, and competencies needed to fulfill job description requirements

Person-organization fit: The degree of compatibility between job candidates and organizations

Philanthropic responsibility: Going beyond the call of duty to benefit society

Piece rate: A pay plan in which workers are paid a fixed sum for each unit of production completed

Political science: The study of the behavior of individuals and groups within a political environment

Political skill: The ability to understand and influence others for the good of the organization

Pooled interdependence: An organizational model in which each team member produces a piece of work independently of the other members

Positive affect: A mood dimension that consists of emotions such as excitement, self-assurance, and cheerfulness

Positive organizational behavior: The strengths, virtues, vitality, and resilience of individuals and organizations

Positive reinforcement: The use of positive consequences to reinforce positive behaviors and make someone more likely to behave in similar ways in the same or similar situations

Power: The capacity to influence the actions of others

Power distance: The extent to which people in different societies accept the way power is distributed.

Practiced creativity: The ability to spot opportunities to apply creative skills in the workplace

Primacy effect: A perception problem in which an individual assesses a person quickly on the basis of the first information encountered

Proactive personality: The tendency for individuals to take the initiative to change their circumstances

Problem-focused coping: A type of coping that aims to reduce or eliminate stressors through understanding the problem and seeking practical ways to resolve it

Problem-solving: The second step of the innovation process—identifying any advantages or disadvantages associated with the innovation, exploring costs and value, and setting goals and priorities

Problem-solving team: A group of workers coming together for a set amount of time to discuss specific issues

Procedural justice: The degree to which people perceive the implementation of company policies and procedures to be fair

Process conflict: The clash in viewpoints in relation to how to carry out work

Process consultation: An intervention that involves increasing group awareness or understanding

Process gains: Factors that contribute to team effectiveness

Processing: The act of understanding and remembering what is being said as well as making an effort to empathize with the speaker's feelings and thoughts and the situation at hand.

Process innovation: The introduction of new or improved operational and work methods

Process losses: Factors that detract from team effectiveness

Process theories: Theories that describe the cognitive processes through which needs are translated into behavior, such as equity theory, expectancy theory, and goal-setting theory

Product innovation: The development of new or improved goods or services that are sold to meet customer needs

Production-oriented leader: A leader who tends to focus more on the technical or task aspects of the job

Productive forgetting: The ability to abandon a solution that isn't working in favor of a new one

Profit sharing: A pay system in which the organization shares its profits with employees

Programmed decisions: Automatic responses to routine and recurring situations

Projecting: A process in which people transfer their own personal attributes to others

Projection bias: The inclination to believe other people think, feel, and act the same way we do

Psychological contract: An agreement that determines the degree to which employees trust their organizations to value their efforts, and how well employees meet the expectations of the organization in terms of their work contributions

Psychological empowerment: The extent to which employees feel a sense of personal fulfillment and intent when carrying out tasks, together with a belief that their work contributes to some larger purpose

Psychological safety: The shared belief among team members that it is safe for them to trust each other enough to take risks

Psychology: The scientific study of the human mind that seeks to measure and explain behavioral characteristics

Punctuated equilibrium: A method of understanding organizational change by illustrating where change is relatively stable and where it becomes more volatile

Punishment: The administration of unpleasant consequences or the removal of positive ones for the purpose of discouraging undesirable behavior

Quality of worklife (QWL): The relationship between the employees and the workplace

Race: Identifying biological factors such as skin, hair, or eye color

Randomness error: The tendency for people to believe they can predict the outcome of chance events based on false information or superstition

Rational appeals: The use of logic, reason, and evidence to convince another person that cooperation in a task is worthwhile

Recency effect: A perception problem in which we use the most recent information available to assess a person

Reciprocal interdependence: An organizational model in which team members work closely together on a piece of work, consulting with each other, providing each other with advice, and exchanging information

Referent power: The degree to which a leader can influence others through their desire to identify and be associated with them

Reinforcement: The application of consequences to establish patterns of behavior

Reinforcement theory: A theory that states that behavior is a function of its consequences and is determined exclusively by environmental factors such as external stimuli and other reinforcers

Relationship conflict: The clash in personalities between two or more individuals

Remote work: Working from home or from a remote location on a computer or other advanced telecommunications system linked to the main office

Representativeness heuristic: A shortcut for forming a decision that uses existing mental prototypes and similar stereotypes

Resistance to change: The unwillingness to accept or support modifications in the workplace

Responding: The way active listeners provide feedback to the speaker

Return on ethics: A mindset that promotes the highest standards of ethical behavior, which can lead to strong performance and competitive advantage

Reward power: The extent to which someone uses incentives to influence the actions of others

Rights approach: A decision-making method based on using moral principles that least infringe on the entitlements of others

Risk-taking propensity: The tendency to engage in behaviors that might have positive or negative outcomes

Rituals: Formalized actions and planned routines

Satisficing decisions: Solutions that aim for acceptable results rather than for the best or optimal ones

Scientific management: Early-20th-century theory introduced by Frederick Taylor and his colleagues that analyzes workflow through systematic observation or reasoning

Selective attention: The tendency to selectively focus on aspects of situations that are most aligned with our own interests, values, and attitudes

Self-awareness: Being aware of one's own feelings, behaviors, personalities, likes, and dislikes

Self-concept: The beliefs a person has about who they are and how they feel about themselves

Self-determination: Making use of one's skills, knowledge, and strengths to make choices and initiate work tasks.

Self-efficacy: A person's belief in their ability to succeed in a specific task or situation

Self-efficacy: The belief we have in our ability to succeed in a specific task or situation

Self-esteem: The beliefs people have about their own worth following the self-evaluation process

Self-fulfilling prophecy: The way a person behaves based on preexisting expectations about another person or situation so as to create an outcome that is aligned with those expectations

Self-leadership: A process whereby people intentionally influence their thinking and behavior to achieve their objectives

Self-managing team: A group of workers who manage their daily duties under little to no supervision

Self-monitoring: The degree to which people adjust their behavior to accommodate different situations

Self-regulation: A process whereby people set goals, creating a discrepancy between the desired state and the current state

Self-serving bias: The tendency for individuals to attribute their own successes to internal factors and blame their failures on external factors

Selling: Leadership behavior characterized by support provided to followers through communication and "selling" them the aims of the task to gain commitment

Seniority-based pay: Guaranteed wages and salary increases based on the amount of time the employee has spent with the organization

Sensing: The way listeners pay attention to the signals sent from the speaker

Sensitivity training: A type of program designed to raise awareness of group dynamics and any existing prejudices toward others

Sequential interdependence: An organizational model in which one team member completes a piece of work and passes it on to the next member for their input, similar to an assembly line

Servant leadership: A pattern of leadership that places an emphasis on employees and the community rather than on the leader

Sexual orientation: A person's sexual identity and the gender(s) to which they are attracted

Shared leadership: A style of leadership that distributes influence among groups and individuals to achieve organizational or team goals

Short-term orientation: The measurement of values such as meeting social obligations and avoiding embarrassment or shame

Silent authority: An influencing tactic that relies on unspoken but acknowledged power

Simple structures: Organizational structures, common in small organizations, where is there is one central authority figure, usually a business owner, who tends to make decisions

Situational leadership model: A leadership model that proposes leaders should adapt their leadership style based on the types of people they are leading and the requirements of the task

Skill-based pay: A system of pay that rewards employees for the acquisition and development of new skills that lead to enhanced work performance

Social cognitive theory: A theory that proposes that learning takes place through the observation, imitation, and the modeling of others within a social context

Social facilitation: The tendency for individuals to perform tasks better when they are in the presence of others

Socialization: The process through which an organization communicates its values to new employees

Social loafing: A phenomenon wherein people put forth less effort when they work in teams than when they work alone

Social networks: The recurrent patterns of interaction with others that take place when carrying out work activities

Social norms: The informal rules that govern behavior in groups and societies

Social psychology: The social science that blends concepts from sociology and psychology and focuses on how people influence each other in a social setting

Sociology: The study of the behavior of groups and how they relate to each other in a social setting

Sociotechnical systems: The interaction between human behavior and technical systems

Spiritual leadership: A values-based style of leadership that motivates employees through faith, hope, and vision and encourages positive social emotions such as forgiveness and gratitude

Standardization: The degree to which employees are expected to follow the same rules and policies everywhere

Stereotypes: An individual's fixed beliefs about the characteristics of a particular group

Stereotype threat: Fear of confirming a negative stereotype about one's own group

Stereotyping: The tendency to believe that certain people or things share the same characteristics

Stories: Narratives based on real organizational experiences that have become embellished over time and illustrate core cultural values

Storming: A phase during which, after a period of time, tension may arise between members and different personalities might clash, leading to tension and conflict in the team

Strain: The physiological and psychological reactions to stress

Strategic OB approach: The idea that people are the key to productivity, competitive edge, and financial success

Stress: A response that occurs when a person perceives a situation as threatening to their well-being when their resources have been taxed or exceeded

Stressors: Environmental stimuli that place demands on individuals

Structural intervention: An attempt to alter the organizational structure through job design and division of labor

Subcultures: Groups in an organization who share different values to those held by the majority

Subordinate characteristics: Situational contingencies such as anxiety, inflexibility, perceived ability, locus of control, and close-mindedness

Substitutes for leadership model: A model that suggests certain characteristics of the situation can constrain the influence of the leader

Sunk-cost bias: The decision to continue an investment based on past investments of time, effort, and/or money

Supportive leadership: A leadership behavior characterized by friendliness and concern for the welfare of others

Surface acting: Suppressing one's true feelings while displaying the organizationally desirable ones

Surface-level diversity: The easily perceived differences between us, such as age and generation, race and ethnicity, gender and sexual orientation, and physical and/or mental ability

Symbols: Objects that provide meaning about a culture

Synergy: The concept that the total amount of work produced by a team is greater than the amount of work produced by individual members working independently

Task characteristics: Situational contingencies outside the follower's control, such as team dynamics, authority systems, and task structure

Task conflict: The clash between individuals in relation to the direction, content, or goal of a certain assignment

Task structure: The degree to which job assignments are defined

Task-technology intervention: An attempt to change the tasks people perform or the technological processes they use to enhance productivity and increase job satisfaction

Team: A group of people brought together to use their individual skills on a common project or goal

Technical skill: The aptitude to perform and apply specialized tasks

Telling: A leadership behavior characterized by giving clear instructions and guidance to followers, informing them exactly how and when to complete the task

Theory: A set of principles intended to explain behavioral phenomena in organizations

Three-component model of creativity: A model proposing that individual creativity relies on domain-relevant skills and expertise, creativity-relevant processes, and intrinsic task motivation

Trait leadership perspective: A theory that explores the relationship between leaders and personal qualities and characteristics and how they differentiate leaders from nonleaders

Transactional leadership: A behavioral type of leadership that proposes that employees are motivated by goals and equitable rewards

Transformational leadership a leadership style that inspires followers to transcend their self-interests for the good of the organization and commit to a shared vision

Transforming: The process that occurs when people begin to make peace with their doubts and uncertainties and begin to embrace the new direction of the company

Triadic reciprocal model of behavior: A model that shows human functioning shaped by three factors that are reciprocally related: reinforcement, cognitive processes, and behavior

Trust: The dependence on the integrity, ability, honesty, and reliability of someone or something else

Two-factor theory: The impact of motivational influences on job satisfaction

Type A orientation: A personality that is competitive, impatient, aggressive, and achievement oriented

Type B orientation: A personality that is relaxed, easygoing, patient, and noncompetitive

Uncertainty avoidance: The degree to which people are able to deal with the unexpected and how they cope with uncertainty in unstructured environments

Unobservable culture: The components that lie beneath the surface of an organization, such as company values and assumptions

Upward appeals: The argument that the task has been requested by higher management, or a request to higher management to assist in gaining cooperation

Upward communication: Messages sent from the lower levels of the organizational hierarchy to the higher levels

Utilitarian approach: Action that results in the greater good for the majority of people

Valence: The value individuals place on work outcomes

Value chain: The sequence of activities carried out by organizations to create valued goods and services to consumers

Vicarious learning: A process of learning by watching the actions or behaviors of another person

Virtual teams: Groups of individuals from different locations who work together through email, videoconferencing, instant messaging, and other electronic media

Visibility: The awareness of others regarding your presence in an organization

Visionary leadership: A behavioral type of leadership that creates visions to motivate, inspire, and stimulate employees

Well-being program: A holistic approach taken by organizations to provide support in the areas of physical and mental health

Workplace diversity: The degree to which an organization represents different cultures

Written communication: Messages communicated through the written word, such as email, reports, memos, letters, and other channels

ZOPA: The zone of possible agreement, the area where two sides in a negotiation may find common ground

ENDNOTES

FM

1. Kuncel, N. R., & S. A. Hezlett. (2010, December). Fact and fiction in cognitive ability testing for admissions and hiring decisions. *Current Directions in Psychological Science, 19(6)*, 339–345.

CHAPTER 1

1. Hilton. (2022). *Hilton brands*. https://www.hilton.com/en/corporate/
2. Great Place to Work. (2019). *Fortune 100 best companies to work for® 2019*. https://www.greatplacetowork.com/best-workplaces/100-best/2019
3. Heath, C., & Starr, K. (2018). *The Hilton effect*. https://www.hospitalitynet.org/news/4090352.html
4. Brownlee, D. (2019, September 4). *How the "best companies to work for" engage employees and retain top talent*. Forbes. https://www.forbes.com/sites/danabrownlee/2019/09/04/how-the-best-companies-to-work-for-engage-employees-and-retain-top-talent/?sh=57578fd1ecae
5. Lambrano, L. (2020, May 21). *A brief history of the corporate culture transformation at Hilton | Part 3: listening*. LinkedIn. https://www.linkedin.com/pulse/brief-history-corporate-culture-transformation-hilton-lambrano-1e/
6. Tyko, K. (2020, March 26). Hilton CEO forgoing salary as part of company's coronavirus response. *USA Today*. https://www.usatoday.com/story/money/2020/03/26/coronavirus-furloughs-job-cuts-hilton-ceo-forgoing-salary/2922894001/
7. Frauenheim, E. (2020, October 27). *How world's best workplace Hilton showed creativity in caring during COVID-19*. Great Place to Work. https://www.greatplacetowork.com/resources/blog/how-world-s-best-workplace-hilton-showed-creativity-in-caring-during-covid-19
8. Rivera, J. (2020, March 23). Furloughed Hilton workers offered access to other jobs during coronavirus pandemic. *USA Today*. https://www.usatoday.com/story/money/2020/03/23/hilton-employees-furloughs-coronavirus-covid-19-jobs/2893323001/
9. For an overview of the field of organizational behavior, see Latham, G. P. (2019). Perspectives of a practitioner-scientist on organizational psychology/organizational behavior. *Annual Review of Organizational Psychology and Organizational Behavior, 6*, 1–16; Mitchell, T. R. (2018). A dynamic, inclusive, and affective evolutionary view of organizational behavior. *Annual Review of Organizational Psychology and Organizational Behavior, 5*, 1–19.
10. Minahan, T. (2021, May 31). What your future employees want most. *Harvard Business Review*. https://hbr.org/2021/05/what-your-future-employees-want-most
11. Fayol, H. (1916). Industrial and general administration. Dunod.
12. Diokpa, L., Swift, A., Afe, O., & Lentini, A. (2021, June 8). *The impact of COVID-19 on the five functions of management*. Institute for Public Relations. https://instituteforpr.org/the-impact-of-covid-19-on-the-five-functions-of-management/
13. Katz, R. L. (1956, March). Skills of an effective administrator. *Harvard Business Review, 34*(2), 127. Sutanto, R. (2021). Strategic management technical skills, interpersonal skills and conceptual skills of officers in manning KRI. *Open Access Indonesia Journal of Social Sciences, 4*(6), 483–491.
14. Ibid.
15. Ibid.
16. Salovey, P., & Mayer, J. D. (1989). Emotional intelligence. *Imagination, Cognition and Personality, 9*(3), 185–211. Miao, C., Humphrey, R. H., & Qian, S. (2017, June). A meta-analysis of emotional intelligence and work attitudes. *Journal of Occupational and Organizational Psychology, 90*(2), 177–202.
17. Katz, R. L. (1956, March). Skills of an effective administrator. *Harvard Business Review, 34*(2), 127. Cai, H. (2014, September). Management development: A principles framework and critical skills approach. *Human Systems Management*, 33(4), 207–212.
18. Crook, T. R., Todd, S. Y., Combs, J. G., Woehr, D. J., & Ketchen, D. J., Jr. (2011, May). Does human capital matter? A meta-analysis of the relationship between human capital and firm performance. *Journal of Applied Psychology, 96*(3), 443–456. Hamilton, R. H., & Sodeman, W. A. (2020). The questions we ask: Opportunities and challenges for using big data analytics to strategically manage human capital resources. *Business Horizons, 63*(1), 85–95. Wright, P. M., Coff, R., & Moliterno, T. P. (2014, February). Strategic human capital: Crossing the great divide. *Journal of Management, 40*(2), 353–370.
19. Hatch, N. W., & Dyer, J. H. (2004, December). Human capital and learning as a source of sustainable competitive advantage. *Strategic Management, 25*(12), 1155–1178. Kryscynski, D., Coff, R., & Campbell, B. (2021). Charting a path between firm-specific incentives and human capital–based competitive advantage. *Strategic Management Journal, 42*(2), 386–412. Campbell, B., Coff, R., & Kryscynski, D. (2012, July). Rethinking sustained competitive advantage from human capital. *Academy of Management Review, 37*(3), 376–395.
20. Ibid.
21. Calma, A., & Davies, M. (2021). Critical thinking in business education: Current outlook and future prospects. *Studies in Higher Education, 46*(11), 2279–2295. Dwyer, C. P. (2017). *Critical thinking: Conceptual perspectives and practical guidelines*. Cambridge University Press. Lack, C. W., & Rousseau, J. (2016). *Critical thinking, science, and pseudoscience: Why we can't trust our brains*. Springer.
22. Forbes Human Resource Council. (2020, November 9). *The top 10 skills recruiters are looking for in 2021*. Forbes. https://www.forbes.com/sites/forbeshumanresourcescouncil/2020/11/09/the-top-10-skills-recruiters-are-looking-for-in-2021/?sh=32be3f907e38

23. Plummer, M. (2019, October 11). A short guide to building your team's critical thinking skills. *Harvard Business Review, 10*, 11–19. https://hbr.org/2019/10/a-short-guide-to-building-your-teams-critical-thinking-skills

24. Nguyen, C. (2021, May 31). *The importance of building critical thinking skills.* Market Games. https://www.marketgames.io/blog-posts/importance-of-building-critical-thinking

25. Orrell, B. (2021, May 27). *"Soft skills" are essential: Why college may not have prepared you for success at work.* American Enterprise Institute. https://www.aei.org/op-eds/soft-skills-are-essential-why-college-may-not-have-prepared-you-for-success-at-work/

26. Stubbings, C., & Sethi, B. (2020). Upskilling: Building confidence in an uncertain world. *PwC,* 1–25. https://www.pwc.com/gx/en/ceo-survey/2020/trends/pwc-talent-trends-2020.pdf

27. Whiting, K. (2020, October 21). *These are the top 10 job skills of tomorrow—and how long it takes to learn them.* World Economic Forum. https://www.weforum.org/agenda/2020/10/top-10-work-skills-of-tomorrow-how-long-it-takes-to-learn-them/

28. Forbes Human Resource Council. (2020, November 9). *The top 10 skills recruiters are looking for in 2021.* Forbes. https://www.forbes.com/sites/forbeshumanresourcescouncil/2020/11/09/the-top-10-skills-recruiters-are-looking-for-in-2021/?sh=32be3f907e38

29. Ibid.

30. For an overview of the scientific method and theory testing in the behavioral sciences, see Marczyk, G., DeMatteo, D., & Festinger, D. (2005). *Essentials of research design and methodology.* Wiley.

31. Rousseau, D. M. (2012). Envisioning evidence-based management. In D. M. Rousseau (Ed.), *The Oxford handbook of evidence-based management* (pp. 3–24). Oxford University Press.

32. Pfeffer, J., & Sutton, R. I. (2006, January). Evidence-based management. *Harvard Business Review, 84*(1), 62–74.

33. Rousseau, D. M. (2012). Envisioning evidence-based management. In D. M. Rousseau (Ed.), *The Oxford handbook of evidence-based management* (pp. 3–24). Oxford University Press.

34. Rousseau, D. M. (Ed.). (2012). *The Oxford handbook of evidence-based management.* Oxford University Press.

35. Emery, M. (2010, November). Refutation of Kira and van Eijnatten's critique of the Emery's open systems theory. *Systems Research and Behavioral Science, 27*(6), 697–712. Zagier Roberts, V. (2019). The organization of work: Contributions from open systems theory. In A. Obholzer & V. Zagier Roberts (Eds.), *The unconscious at work* (pp. 37–48). Routledge. Rosen, N. A. (1970). Open systems theory in an organizational sub-system: A field experiment. *Organizational Behavior and Human Performance, 5*(3), 245–265.

36. Acquier, A., Valiorgue, B., & Daudigeos, T. (2017, August). Sharing the shared value: A transaction cost perspective on strategic CSR policies in global value chains. *Journal of Business Ethics, 144*(1), 139–152. Gertner, M. I. (2013, October). The value chain and value creation. *Advances in Management, 6*(10), 1–4. Kano, L., Tsang, E. W. K., & Yeung, H. W. C. (2020). Global value chains: A review of the multi-disciplinary literature. *Journal of International Business Studies, 51*(4), 577–622.

37. Mutikani, L. (2021, January 27). *COVID-19 savages U.S. Economy, 2020 performance worst in 74 years.* Reuters. https://www.reuters.com/article/us-usa-economy-idUSKBN29X0I8

38. Choi, J. N., Sung, S. Y., & Zhang, Z. (2017, October). Workforce diversity in manufacturing companies and organizational performance: The role of status-relatedness and internal processes. *International Journal of Human Resource Management, 28*(19), 2738–2761. Lee, H. W., & Kim, E. (2020). Workforce diversity and firm performance: Relational coordination as a mediator and structural empowerment and multisource feedback as moderators. *Human Resource Management, 59*(1), 5–23.

39. Kalwani, S., & Mahesh, J. (2020). Trends in organizational behavior: A systematic review and research directions. *Journal of Business & Management, 26*(1), 40–78.

40. Zhao, M. S. (2020, January 7). *10 Successful women leaders share what they do to create a fantastic work culture.* Medium. https://medium.com/authority-magazine/10-successful-women-leaders-share-what-they-do-to-create-a-fantastic-work-culture-c05580d6ea30

41. Pegley, R. (2019, August 19). What business leaders can learn from sports coaches. *CEO Magazine.* https://www.theceomagazine.com/business/management-leadership/business-leaders-learn-sports-coaches/

42. Whiting, K. (2020. August 26). *The future of flexible working, according to 6 companies.* World Economic Forum. https://www.weforum.org/agenda/2020/08/flexible-remote-working-post-covid19-company-predictions/

43. Quick, J. C., Cooper, C. L., Gibbs, P. C., Little, L. M., & Nelson, D. L. (2010). Positive organizational behavior at work. In G. P. Hodgkinson & J. K. Ford (Eds.), *International review of industrial and organizational psychology* (Vol. 25, pp. 253–291). Wiley-Blackwell. Kim, M., Kim, A. C. H., Newman, J. I., Ferris, G. R., & Perrewé, P. L. (2019). The antecedents and consequences of positive organizational behavior: The role of psychological capital for promoting employee well-being in sport organizations. *Sport Management Review, 221*, 108–125. Luthans, F., & Avolio, B. J. (2009, February). The "point" of positive organizational behavior. *Journal of Organizational Behavior, 30*(2), 291–307.

44. Celestine, N. (2022, May 9). *Positive organizational behavior: Applying positive psychology at work.* PositivePsychology.com. https://positivepsychology.com/positive-organizational-behavior/

45. Ying, Z., & Min, Z. (2016, January). The effect of high involvement management on employee well-being in Britain. *Academy of Management Annual Meeting Proceedings, 2016*(1), 1. Wood, S., & Ogbonnaya, C. (2018). High-involvement management, economic recession, well-being, and organizational performance. *Journal of Management, 44*(8), 3070–3095. Wood, S. A., van Veldhoven, M., Croon, M., & de Menezes, L. M. (2012, April). Enriched job design, high involvement management and organizational performance: The mediating roles of job satisfaction and well-being. *Human Relations, 65*(4), 419–445.

46. Forbes Business Council. (2021, October 12). *15 ways to empower your employees.* Forbes. https://www.forbes.com/sites/forbesbusinesscouncil

/2021/10/12/15-ways-to-empower-your-employees/?sh=757bd50230c8

47. Japsen, B. (2017, February 21). *After CVS stopped cigarette sales, smokers stopped buying elsewhere, too.* Forbes. https://www.forbes.com/sites/brucejapsen/2017/02/20/after-cvs-stopped-cigarette-sales-smokers-stopped-buying-elsewhere-too/?sh=15a349fec8f5
48. Japsen, B. (2015, September 3). *Year after cigarette ban, CVS says 95 million fewer packs sold at "all retailers."* Forbes. https://www.forbes.com/sites/brucejapsen/2015/09/03/year-after-cvs-cigarette-ban-95-million-fewer-packs-sold-by-all-retailers/?sh=7dd4c79a6835
49. CVS Health. (2015, February 10). *CVS Health reports strong profit growth for full year 2014; fourth quarter adjusted EPS at high end of company's expectations.* https://cvshealth.com/news-and-insights/press-releases/cvs-health-reports-strong-profit-growth-for-full-year-2014-fourth. CVS Health. (2021, February 16). *CVS Health reports fourth quarter and full-year 2020 results and provides 2021 full year guidance.* https://cvshealth.com/news-and-insights/press-releases/cvs-health-reports-results-2020-q4
50. Velasco, S. (2016, June 23). She's been instrumental in CVS taking a stand against tobacco. *The Christian Science Monitor.* https://www.csmonitor.com/World/Making-a-difference/2016/0623/She-s-been-instrumental-in-CVS-taking-a-stand-against-tobacco
51. CVS Health. (2014). *Code of conduct.* https://cvssuppliers.com/sites/default/files/CVS%20Code%20of%20Conduct_External.pdf
52. Fortune 500. (2021, June 8). *Fortune.* https://fortune.com/fortune500/

CHAPTER 2

1. Goldin, R., & Rouse, C. (1997). *Orchestrating impartiality: The impact of "blind" auditions on female musicians* (NBER Working Paper No. 5903). National Bureau of Economic Research. https://www.nber.org/papers/w5903
2. Grothaus, M. (2016, March 14). How "blind recruitment" works and why you should consider it. *Fast Company.* https://www.fastcompany.com/3057631/how-blind-recruitment-works-and-why-you-should-consider
3. Smith, J. (2015, May 31). *Why companies are using "blind auditions" to hire top talent.* Business Insider. https://www.businessinsider.com/companies-are-using-blind-auditions-to-hire-top-talent-2015-5
4. Bortz, D. (2019, August 16). *Can blind hiring improve workplace diversity?* Society for Human Resource Management. https://www.shrm.org/hr-today/news/hr-magazine/0418/pages/can-blind-hiring-improve-workplace-diversity.aspx. Salinas, B. (2015, May 28). *Blind auditions could give employers a better hiring sense.* NPR. https://www.npr.org/sections/alltechconsidered/2015/05/28/410264592/blind-auditions-could-give-employers-a-better-hiring-sense
5. Dolby. (n.d.). *Diversity, inclusion, and belonging.* https://www.dolby.com/about/corporate/diversity-inclusion-and-belonging/
6. Dolby (n.d.). *Advancing diversity, inclusion, and belonging.* https://www.dolby.com/about/corporate/sustainability-at-dolby/diversity-inclusion-and-belonging/
7. Definition adapted from Rosencrance, L. (2021, March). *Diversity, equity and inclusion.* TechTarget. https://www.techtarget.com/searchhrsoftware/definition/diversity-equity-and-inclusion-DEI. For an overview of the importance of DEI in the workplace, see Westover, J. H. (2021, February). The importance of diversity, equity, inclusion, and belonging in the workplace: Maximizing the human capital potential of our people. *Leadership Excellence, 38*(2), 24–27.
8. Dixon-Fyle, S., Dolan, K., Hunt, V., & Prince, S. (2020, May 19). *Diversity wins: How inclusion matters.* McKinsey. https://www.mckinsey.com/featured-insights/diversity-and-inclusion/diversity-wins-how-inclusion-matters
9. Bernstein, R. S., Bulger, M., Salipante, P., & Weisinger, J. Y. (2020). From diversity to inclusion to equity: A theory of generative interactions. *Journal of Business Ethics, 167*(3), 395–410.
10. Van Laar, C., Meeussen, L., Veldman, J., Van Grootel, S., Sterk, N., & Jacobs, C. (2019). Coping with stigma in the workplace: Understanding the role of threat regulation, supportive factors, and potential hidden costs. *Frontiers in Psychology, 10*, 1879.
11. American Psychological Association. (2019, October 31). *Discrimination: What it is, and how to cope.* https://www.apa.org/topics/racism-bias-discrimination/types-stress
12. University of Michigan. (n.d.). *Defining DEI.* https://diversity.umich.edu/about/defining-dei/
13. For a recent review of diversity research, see del Carmen Triana, M., Gu, P., Chapa, O., Richard, O., & Colella, A. (2021, January). Sixty years of discrimination and diversity research in human resource management: A review with suggestions for future research directions. *Human Resource Management, 60*(1), 145–204.
14. Good, B. (2021, May 10). *DiversityInc announces the 2021 top 50 companies for diversity list.* DiversityInc. https://www.diversityinc.com/diversityinc-announces-the-2021-top-50-companies-for-diversity-list/
15. Ellingrud, K., Krishnan, M., Krivkovich, A., Kukla, K., Mendy, A., Robinson, N., Sancier-Sultan, S., & Yee, L. (2020, November 17). *Diverse employees are struggling the most during COVID-19—Here's how companies can respond.* McKinsey. https://www.mckinsey.com/featured-insights/diversity-and-inclusion/diverse-employees-are-struggling-the-most-during-covid-19-heres-how-companies-can-respond
16. Jansen, A. E., & Searle, B. J. (2021, December 15). Diverse effects of team diversity: A review and framework of surface and deep-level diversity. *Personnel Review, 50*(9), 1838–1853. Harrison, D. A., Price, K. H., Gavin, J. H., & Florey, A. T. (2002, October). Time, teams, and task performance: Changing effects of surface- and deep-level diversity on group functioning. *Academy of Management Journal, 45*(5), 1029–1045.
17. Szatmari, B. (2021, October 21). Supplementary material for "Young Stars and Red Giants: The Moderating Effect of Age Diversity on the Relationship Between the Proportion of High Performers and Team Performance." *Journal of Applied Psychology.* https://doi.org/10.1037/apl0000971.supp. Seong, J. Y., & Hong, D.-S.

(2018, May 25). Age diversity, group organisational citizenship behaviour, and group performance: Exploring the moderating role of charismatic leadership and participation in decision-making. *Human Resource Management Journal, 28*(4), 621–640. Stone, D. L., & Tetrick, L. E. (2013). Understanding and facilitating age diversity in organizations. *Journal of Managerial Psychology, 28*(7–8), 725–728.

18. Waldmeir, P. (2021, March 22). Employers use COVID as cover for age discrimination. *Financial Times*. https://www.ft.com/content/2b22593a-26ea-4377-ad7d-3e93ad0061f9
19. Waldman, E. (2021, August 31). How to manage a multi-generational team. *Harvard Business Review*. https://hbr.org/2021/08/how-to-manage-a-multi-generational-team
20. Ibid.
21. Byars-Winston, A., Fouad, N., & Wen, Y. (2015, April). Race/ethnicity and sex in U.S. occupations, 1970–2010: Implications for research, practice, and policy. *Journal of Vocational Behavior, 87*, 54–70. Humes, K., & Hogan, H. (2015). Do current race and ethnicity concepts reflect a changing America? In *Race and social problems: Restructuring inequality* (pp. 15–38). Springer Science + Business Media. Zhang, L., Goldberg, C. B., & McKay, P. F. (2020, September). From new hires to their supervisors: The influence of newcomer race/ethnicity on the leader–member exchange conveyance. *Journal of Occupational and Organizational Psychology, 93*(3), 767–789.
22. Ellingrud, K., Krishnan, M., Krivkovich, A., Kukla, K., Mendy, A., Robinson, N., Sancier-Sultan, S., & Yee, L. (2020, November 17). *Diverse employees are struggling the most during COVID-19—Here's how companies can respond.* McKinsey. https://www.mckinsey.com/featured-insights/diversity-and-inclusion/diverse-employees-are-struggling-the-most-during-covid-19-heres-how-companies-can-respond
23. Burns, T., Huang, J., Krivkovich, A., Rambachan, I., Trkulja, T., & Yee, L. (2021, September 27). *Women in the workplace 2021.* McKinsey. https://www.mckinsey.com/featured-insights/diversity-and-inclusion/women-in-the-workplace
24. See, for example, Furtado, J. V., Moreira, A. C., Mota, J., & Dundes, L. (2021, February). Gender affirmative action and management: A systematic literature review on how diversity and inclusion management affect gender equity in organizations. *Behavioral Sciences (2076-328X), 11*(2), 21; Roh, H., & Kim, E. (2016, May). The business case for gender diversity: Examining the role of human resource management investments. *Human Resource Management, 55*(3), 519–534.
25. See, for example, Manzi, F., & Heilman, M. E. (2021, February). Breaking the glass ceiling: For one and all? *Journal of Personality and Social Psychology, 120*(2), 257–277; Ng, E. S., & Sears, G. J. (2017, January). The glass ceiling in context: The influence of CEO gender, recruitment practices and firm internationalisation on the representation of women in management. *Human Resource Management Journal, 27*(1), 133–151.
26. Zillman, C. (2020, October 19). How Jane Fraser broke banking's highest glass ceiling. *Fortune*. https://fortune.com/longform/citi-ceo-jane-fraser-first-woman-wall-street-bank-citigroup-glass-ceiling/
27. Milenkovic, M. (2021, September 24). *The leadership gap: 20 revealing male vs. female CEO statistics.* SmallBizGenius. https://www.smallbizgenius.net/by-the-numbers/male-vs-female-ceo-statistics/#gref
28. Bruckmüller, S., & Branscombe, N. R. (2010). The glass cliff: When and why women are selected as leaders in crisis contexts. *British Journal of Social Psychology, 49*(3), 433–451. Ryan, M. K., & Haslam, S. A. (2005). The glass cliff: Evidence that women are over-represented in precarious leadership positions. *British Journal of Management, 16*(2), 81–90. Ryan, M. K., Haslam, S. A., Morgenroth, T., Rink, F., Stoker, J., & Peters, K. (2016). Getting on top of the glass cliff: Reviewing a decade of evidence, explanations, and impact. *Leadership Quarterly, 27*(3), 446–455.
29. Ibid.
30. Cook, A., & Glass, C. (2013). Glass cliffs and organizational saviors: Barriers to minority leadership in work organizations? *Social Problems, 60*(2), 168–187.
31. Oakes, K. (2022, February 6). *The invisible danger of the "glass cliff."* BBC Future. https://www.bbc.com/future/article/20220204-the-danger-of-the-glass-cliff-for-women-and-people-of-colour
32. Barroso, A., & Brown, A. (2021, May 25). *Gender pay gap in U.S. held steady in 2020.* Pew Research Center. https://www.pewresearch.org/fact-tank/2021/05/25/gender-pay-gap-facts/
33. Ellingrud, K., Krishnan, M., Krivkovich, A., Kukla, K., Mendy, A., Robinson, N., Sancier-Sultan, S., & Yee, L. (2020, November 17). *Diverse employees are struggling the most during COVID-19—Here's how companies can respond.* McKinsey. https://www.mckinsey.com/featured-insights/diversity-and-inclusion/diverse-employees-are-struggling-the-most-during-covid-19-heres-how-companies-can-respond
34. Cerullo, M. (2021, February 5). *Nearly 3 million U.S. women have dropped out of the labor force in the past year.* CBS News. https://www.cbsnews.com/news/covid-crisis-3-million-women-labor-force/
35. Jones, J. M. (2021, February 24). *LGBT identification rises to 5.6% in latest U.S. estimate.* Gallup. https://news.gallup.com/poll/329708/lgbt-identification-rises-latest-estimate.aspx
36. Zurcher, A. (2020, June 15). *US Supreme Court backs protection for LGBT workers.* BBC News. https://www.bbc.com/news/world-us-canada-53055632
37. Ellingrud, K., Krishnan, M., Krivkovich, A., Kukla, K., Mendy, A., Robinson, N., Sancier-Sultan, S., & Yee, L. (2020, November 17). *Diverse employees are struggling the most during COVID-19—Here's how companies can respond.* McKinsey. https://www.mckinsey.com/featured-insights/diversity-and-inclusion/diverse-employees-are-struggling-the-most-during-covid-19-heres-how-companies-can-respond
38. Golden, R. (2021, March 2). *2020 marked 7-year high unemployment rate for people with disabilities.* HRDive. https://www.hrdive.com/news/2020-marked-7-year-high-unemployment-rate-for-people-with-disabilities/595959/
39. Smith, A. (2020, August 28). *A million people with disabilities have lost jobs during the pandemic.* SHRM. https://www.shrm.org/resourcesandtools/legal-and-compliance/employment-la

w/pages/coronavirus-unemployment-people-with-disabilities.aspx

40. Casey, C. (2020, March 19). Do your D&I efforts include people with disabilities? *Harvard Business Review.* https://hbr.org/2020/03/do-your-di-efforts-include-people-with-disabilities

41. Miller, C. (2019, May). Affirmative action and its persistent effects: A new perspective. *California Management Review, 61*(3), 19–33. Selmi, M. (2003, April). The price of discrimination: The nature of class action employment discrimination litigation and its effects. *Texas Law Review, 1,* 1249. Neathey, F., Dench, S., & Thomas, L. (2003). Monitoring progress toward pay equality. In *Institute for Employment Studies report on behalf of the Equal Opportunities Commission.* http://www.equalityhumanrights.com/.../code_of_practice_equal-pay.pdf

42. Telwatte, A., Anglim, J., Wynton, S. K. A., & Moulding, R. (2017, February). Workplace accommodations for employees with disabilities: A multilevel model of employer decision-making. *Rehabilitation Psychology, 62*(1), 7–19. Clevel, J. N., Barnes-Farrell, J., & Ratz, J. M. (1997). Accommodation in the workplace. *Human Resource Management Review, 7,* 77–108. Colella, A., Paetzold, R. L., & Belliveau, M. A. (2004). Factors affecting coworkers' procedural justice inferences of the workplace accommodations of employees with disabilities. *Personnel Psychology, 57,* 1–23.

43. U.S. Equal Employment Opportunity Commission. (n.d.). *Overview.* https://www.eeoc.gov/overview

44. Diamond, B. M. (2022, May 11). *2021 EEOC charge statistics: Retaliation & impact of remote work.* Lexology. https://www.lexology.com/library/detail.aspx?g=97e76ae0-ac54-4754-98d4-ccc31bfd3efa

45. Crenshaw, K. W. (2017). *On intersectionality: Essential writings.* New Press. Cho, S., Crenshaw, K. W., & McCall, L. (2013). Toward a field of intersectionality studies: Theory, applications, and praxis. *Signs: Journal of Women in Culture and Society, 38*(4), 785–810.

46. Tulshyan, R. (2019, July 1). Do your diversity efforts reflect the experiences of women of color? *Harvard Business Review.* https://hbr.org/2019/07/do-your-diversity-efforts-reflect-the-experiences-of-women-of-color

47. Baglini, A. (2020, July 22). *5 ways intersectionality affects diversity and inclusion at work.* World Economic Forum. https://www.weforum.org/agenda/2020/07/diversity-inclusion-equality-intersectionality/

48. Washington, E. F., Birch, A. H., & Roberts, L. M. (2020, July 3). When and how to respond to microaggressions. *Harvard Business Review.* https://hbr.org/2020/07/when-and-how-to-respond-to-microaggressions

49. Ward, M., & Premack, R. (2021, March 1). *What is a microaggression? 14 things people think are fine to say at work—but are actually racist, sexist, or offensive.* Business Insider. https://www.businessinsider.com/microaggression-unconscious-bias-at-work-2018-6?r = US&IR = T

50. Spanierman, L. B., Clark, D. A., & Kim, Y. (2021). Reviewing racial microaggressions research: Documenting targets' experiences, harmful sequelae, and resistance strategies. *Perspectives on Psychological Science, 16*(5), 1037–1059.

51. Follmer, K. B., Sabat, I. E., & Siuta, R. L. (2020). Disclosure of stigmatized identities at work: An interdisciplinary review and agenda for future research. *Journal of Organizational Behavior, 41*(2), 169–184.

52. Jones, K. P. (2017). To tell or not to tell? Examining the role of discrimination in the pregnancy disclosure process at work. *Journal of Occupational Health Psychology, 22*(2), 239.

53. Follmer, K. B., Sabat, I. E., & Siuta, R. L. (2020). Disclosure of stigmatized identities at work: An interdisciplinary review and agenda for future research. *Journal of Organizational Behavior, 41*(2), 169–184.

54. Ibid.

55. Bril-Barniv, S., Moran, G. S., Naaman, A., Roe, D., & Karnieli-Miller, O. (2017). A qualitative study examining experiences and dilemmas in concealment and disclosure of people living with serious mental illness. *Qualitative Health Research, 27*(4), 573–583. Ragins, B. R., Singh, R., & Cornwell, J. M. (2007). Making the invisible visible: Fear and disclosure of sexual orientation at work. *Journal of Applied Psychology, 92*(4), 1103.

56. Jans, L. H., Kaye, H. S., & Jones, E. C. (2012). Getting hired: Successfully employed people with disabilities offer advice on disclosure, interviewing, and job search. *Journal of Occupational Rehabilitation, 22*(2), 155–165. Peterson, D., Currey, N., & Collings, S. (2011). "You don't look like one of them": Disclosure of mental illness in the workplace as an ongoing dilemma. *Psychiatric Rehabilitation Journal, 35*(2), 145.

57. Spencer, S. J., Logel, C., & Davies, P. G. (2016). Stereotype threat. *Annual Review of Psychology, 67,* 415–437.

58. Cohen, G. L., & Garcia, J. (2008). Identity, belonging, and achievement: A model, interventions, implications. *Current Directions in Psychological Science, 17*(6), 365–369.

59. Ibid.

60. Carr, P. B., & Steele, C. M. (2009). Stereotype threat and inflexible perseverance in problem solving. *Journal of Experimental Social Psychology, 45*(4), 853–859. Steele, C. M., & Aronson, J. (1995). Stereotype threat and the intellectual test performance of African Americans. *Journal of Personality and Social Psychology, 69*(5), 797.

61. Cadaret, M. C., Hartung, P. J., Subich, L. M., & Weigold, I. K. (2017). Stereotype threat as a barrier to women entering engineering careers. *Journal of Vocational Behavior, 99,* 40–51. Shapiro, J. R., & Williams, A. M. (2012). The role of stereotype threats in undermining girls' and women's performance and interest in STEM fields. *Sex Roles, 66*(3), 175–183.

62. Croizet, J.-C., & Claire, T. (1998). Extending the concept of stereotype threat to social class: The intellectual underperformance of students from low socioeconomic backgrounds. *Personality and Social Psychology Bulletin, 24*(6), 588–594.

63. Kaye, S. (2021, June 28). *Stereotype threat: Are you making it harder for your underrepresented staff to succeed?* HRZone. https://www.hrzone.com/lead/culture/stereotype-threat-are-you-making-it-harder-for-your-underrepresented-staff-to-succeed

64. Konrad, A. M., Richard, O. C., & Yang, Y. (2021). Both diversity and meritocracy: Managing the diversity-meritocracy paradox with organizational ambidexterity. *Journal of Management Studies, 58*(8), 2180–2206.

65. Kabanoff, B. (1991, April). Equity, equality, power, and conflict. *Academy of Management Review, 16*(2), 416–441. Mannix, E. A., Neale, M. A., & Northcraft, G. B. (1995, September). Equity, equality, or need? The effects of organizational culture on the allocation of benefits and burdens. *Organizational Behavior and Human Decision Processes, 63*(3), 276–286.

66. GW Online Public Health. (2020, November 5). *Equity vs. equality: What's the difference?* https://onlinepublichealth.gwu.edu/resources/equity-vs-equality/

67. L'Oréal USA. (2021, August 26). *L'Oréal USA becomes first company worldwide to receive new EDGEplus certification addressing intersectional gender equity* [Press release]. PR Newswire. https://www.prnewswire.com/news-releases/loreal-usa-becomes-first-company-worldwide-to-receive-new-edgeplus-certification-addressing-intersectional-gender-equity-301363448.html

68. Jordan, S. L., Ferris, G. R., & Lamont, B. T. (2019, September). A framework for understanding the effects of past experiences on justice expectations and perceptions of human resource inclusion practices. *Human Resource Management Review, 29*(3), 386–399. Roberts, R. (2021, July). From snacking on diversity and inclusion to systemic organizational consumption. *Strategic HR Review, 20*(4), 141–144.

69. Romansky, L., Garrod, M., Brown, K., & Deo, K. (2021, May 27). How to measure inclusion in the workplace. *Harvard Business Review*. https://hbr.org/2021/05/how-to-measure-inclusion-in-the-workplace

70. Ibid.

71. Ibid.

72. Ibid.

73. Schooley, S. (2022, February 1). *7 ways to improve workplace diversity and inclusion*. Business.com. https://www.business.com/articles/diversity-and-inclusion-examples/

74. Barton, L. (2021, September 6). What is DEI doing for the formerly incarcerated? *Harvard Business Review*. https://hbr.org/2021/09/what-is-dei-doing-for-the-formerly-incarcerated

75. Ibid.

76. Ibid.

77. Perkins, E. (n.d.). *Second Chance employment for ex-cons at Dave's Killer Bread*. Cafferty & Scheidegger. https://racinelaw.com/second-chance-employment-for-ex-cons-at-daves-killer-bread/

78. Ellingrud, K., Krishnan, M., Krivkovich, A., Kukla, K., Mendy, A., Robinson, N., Sancier-Sultan, S., & Yee, L. (2020, November 17). *Diverse employees are struggling the most during COVID-19—Here's how companies can respond*. McKinsey. https://www.mckinsey.com/featured-insights/diversity-and-inclusion/diverse-employees-are-struggling-the-most-during-covid-19-heres-how-companies-can-respond

79. Nathoo, Z. (2021, June 16). *Why ineffective diversity training won't go away*. BBC. https://www.bbc.com/worklife/article/20210614-why-ineffective-diversity-training-wont-go-away

80. Ibid.

81. Friedman, E. (2020, November 13). *How to leverage skills tests to reduce unconscious bias in hiring*. Forbes. https://www.forbes.com/sites/forbeshumanresourcescouncil/2020/11/13/how-to-leverage-skills-tests-to-reduce-unconscious-bias-in-hiring/?sh=1b7323145d6f

82. Ibid.

83. Ibid.

84. Asare, J. G. (2019, September 26). *The key to diversity and inclusion is mentorship*. Forbes. https://www.forbes.com/sites/janicegassam/2019/09/26/the-key-to-diversity-and-inclusion-is-mentorship/?sh=3975f63c7fbd

85. Rezvani, S., & Gordon, S. A. (November 1, 2021). How sharing our stories builds inclusion. *Harvard Business Review*. https://hbr.org/2021/11/how-sharing-our-stories-builds-inclusion

86. Pedulla, D. (2020, May 12). Diversity and inclusion efforts that really work. *Harvard Business Review*. https://hbr.org/2020/05/diversity-and-inclusion-efforts-that-really-work

87. Ibid.

88. CBRE. (2021, January 26). *CBRE recognized as an outstanding diversity & inclusion organization* [Press release]. https://www.cbre.ca/press-releases/cbre-recognized-as-an-outstanding-diversity-and-inclusion-organization. News Direct. (2021, July 20). *CBRE named as "Best Place to Work for Disability Inclusion" by the Disability Equality Index*. News Direct. https://newsdirect.com/news/cbre-named-a-best-place-to-work-for-disability-inclusion-by-the-disability-equality-index-338533616

89. CBRE. (2020, June 24). *CBRE Group, Inc. promotes Tim Dismond to chief diversity officer*. Business Wire. https://www.businesswire.com/news/home/20200624005786/en/CBRE-Group-Inc.-Promotes-Tim-Dismond-to-Chief-Diversity-Officer

90. Bodamer, D. (2020, September 10). *Catching up with CBRE's new chief diversity officer*. WealthManagement.com. https://www.wealthmanagement.com/brokerage/catching-cbre-s-new-chief-diversity-officer

91. Rosario, I. (2021, October 28). *CBRE's Tim Dismond on doing the work in ESG*. Commercial Property Executive. https://www.commercialsearch.com/news/cbres-tim-dismond-on-doing-the-work-in-esg

92. CBRE. (2020, October 7). *CBRE Group, Inc. announces $3 billion commitment to supplier diversity* [Press release]. https://www.cbre.com/about/media-center/cbre-announces-3-billion-commitment-to-supplier-diversity

93. Billion Dollar Roundtable. (n.d.). *Supplier diversity | United States | Billion Dollar Roundtable*. https://www.billiondollarroundtable.org/

94. CBRE. (2020, October 7). *CBRE Group, Inc. announces $3 billion commitment to supplier diversity* [Press release]. https://www.cbre.com/about/media-center/cbre-announces-3-billion-commitment-to-supplier-diversity

95. Rosario, I. (2021, October 28). *CBRE's Tim Dismond on doing the work in ESG*. Commercial Property Executive. https://www.commercialsearch.com/news/cbres-tim-dismond-on-doing-the-work-in-esg

CHAPTER 3

1. PEAK Fleet. (n.d.). *The PEAK Fleet*. Retrieved September 4, 2020, from https://www.thepeakfleet.com/

2. McCraren, S., & Neis, J. (Hosts). (2020, November 24). All about values: Markitors and PEAK Fleet (No. 4) [Audio podcast episode]. In *People+Profit Show: Elevating humanity through business*. Conscious Capitalism Arizona. https://ccarizona.or

g/podcast-brett-farmiloe-markitors-brian-stinson-peak-fleet-episode-4/

3. Ibid.

4. Ibid.

5. Burwell, J., & McIntosh, K. (Hosts). (2021, January 14). The future of team health with Jen Coyne and Brian Stinson (No. 19) [Audio podcast episode]. In *The future of work: Water cooler conversations*. MAC6. https://mac6.com/blog/episode-19-the-future-of-team-health-with-jen-coyne-and-brian-stinson/

6. Hering, T. (2020, February 10). *How a purpose-driven consulting firm took it up another notch*. Benefit Corporations for Good. https://benefitcorporationsforgood.com/blog/2019/5/28/how-a-purpose-driven-consulting-firm-took-it-up-another-notch

7. Burwell, J., & McIntosh, K. (Hosts). (2021, January 14). The future of team health with Jen Coyne and Brian Stinson (No. 19) [Audio podcast episode]. In *The future of work: Water cooler conversations*. MAC6. https://mac6.com/blog/episode-19-the-future-of-team-health-with-jen-coyne-and-brian-stinson/

8. PEAK Fleet. (n.d.). *PEAK Values®*. https://www.thepeakfleet.com/peak-values/

9. Burwell, J., & McIntosh, K. (Hosts). (2021, January 14). The future of team health with Jen Coyne and Brian Stinson (No. 19) [Audio podcast episode]. In *The future of work: Water cooler conversations*. MAC6. https://mac6.com/blog/episode-19-the-future-of-team-health-with-jen-coyne-and-brian-stinson/

10. For an overview of individual differences research, see Zeigler-Hill, V., & Shackelford, T. K. (Eds.). (2018). *The SAGE handbook of personality and individual differences: The science of personality and individual differences*. SAGE; Mikulincer, M., Shaver, P. R., Cooper, M. L., & Larsen, R. J. (2015). *APA handbook of personality and social psychology: Vol. 4. Personality processes and individual differences*. American Psychological Association.

11. Carver, C. S. (2012). Self-awareness. In M. R. Leary & J. P. Tangney (Eds.), *Handbook of self and identity* (2nd ed., pp. 50–68). Guilford Press. Proust, J. (2015). *The philosophy of metacognition: Mental agency and self-awareness*. Oxford University Press.

12. Figurski, T. J. (1987). Self-awareness and other-awareness: The use of perspective in everyday life. In K. M. Yardley & T. Honess (Eds.), *Self and identity: Psychosocial perspectives* (pp. 197–210). Wiley. Reddy, V. (2008). Experiencing others: A second-person approach to other-awareness. In B. Sokol, J. I. M. Carpendale, N. Budwig, & U. Mueller (Eds.), *Social life and social knowledge: Toward a process account of development* (pp. 123–144). Erlbaum.

13. Johnson, R. E., Chang, C.-H. (Daisy), Kim, Y. J., & Lin, S.-H. (Joanna). (2018). Employee self-concept and identity. In D. S. Ones, N. Anderson, C. Viswesvaran, & H. Kepir Sinangil (Eds.), *The SAGE handbook of industrial, work & organizational psychology: Organizational psychology* (Vol. 2, 2nd ed., pp. 25–45). SAGE. Har, S. S., & Kyrios, M. (2016). The self-concept: Theory and research. In G. Doron, M. Nedeljkovic, M. Kyrios, & R. Moulding (Eds.), *The self in understanding and treating psychological disorders* (pp. 8–18). Cambridge University Press.

14. Wyland, C. L., & Shaffer, E. S. (2019). Assessing self-esteem. In M. W. Gallagher & S. J. Lopez (Eds.), *Positive psychological assessment: A handbook of models and measures* (2nd ed., pp. 203–218). American Psychological Association. MacKinnon, N. J. (2015). *Self-esteem and beyond*. Palgrave Macmillan. Ferris, D. L., Lian, H., Brown, D. J., & Morrison, R. (2015, February). Ostracism, self-esteem, and job performance: When do we self-verify and when do we self-enhance? *Academy of Management Journal, 58*(1), 279–297.

15. Bandura, A. (1997). *Self-efficacy: The exercise of control*. W. H. Freeman/Times Books/Henry Holt. Schunk, D. H., & DiBenedetto, M. K. (2021). Self-efficacy and human motivation. In A. J. Elliot (Ed.), *Advances in motivation science* (Vol. 8, pp. 153–179). Elsevier Academic Press. Beck, J. W., & Schmidt, A. M. (2018, February). Negative relationships between self-efficacy and performance can be adaptive: The mediating role of resource allocation. *Journal of Management, 44*(2), 555–558.

16. For an overview of personality theory and research, see Cervone, D., & Pervin, L. A. (2018). *Personality: Theory and research* (14th ed.). Wiley.

17. McKie, R. (2018, November 11). What makes us? Nature or nurture? The DNA debate comes back to life. *The Guardian*. https://www.theguardian.com/science/2018/nov/11/nature-or-nurture-debate-three-identical-strangers-film

18. Ibid.

19. Bornstein, R. F. (2016). Personality traits and dynamics. In J. C. Norcross, G. R. VandenBos, & D. K. Freedheim (Eds.), *APA handbook of clinical psychology: Applications and methods* (pp. 81–101). American Psychological Association. Paunonen, S. V., & Hong, R. Y. (2015). On the properties of personality traits. In M. Mikulincer & P. R. Shaver (Eds.), *APA handbook of personality and social psychology: Vol. 4. Personality processes and individual differences* (pp. 233–259). American Psychological Association.

20. Jung, C. G. (1971). Collected works of C. G. Jung: Vol. 6. Psychological types. Princeton University Press. (Original work published 1921). Crellin, C. (2014). Jung's theory of personality: A modern reappraisal. Routledge.

21. Ibid.

22. McCaulley, M. H. (1990, January). The Myers-Briggs Type Indicator: A measure for individuals and groups. *Measurement and Evaluation in Counseling and Development, 22*(4), 181–195.

23. See for example, Quenk, N. L. (2009). *Essentials of Myers-Briggs Type Indicator® assessment* (2nd ed.). Wiley.

24. Bower, K. M. (2015, Winter). Coaching with the Myers Briggs type indicator: A valuable tool for client self-awareness. *Journal of Practical Consulting, 5*(2), 10–18. Mi-Ran, K., & Su-Jeong, H. (2014, December). Relationships between the Myers-Briggs type indicator personality profiling, academic performance and student satisfaction in nursing students. *International Journal of Bio-science and Bio-technology, 6*(6), 1–11. McCaulley, M. H. (1990, January). The Myers-Briggs type indicator: A measure for individuals and groups. *Measurement and Evaluation in Counseling and Development, 22*(4), 181–195.

25. Hackston, J. (2020, June 25). How different personality types cope with an always-on culture. *Harvard Business Review*. https://hbr.org/2020/06/how-different-personality-types-cope-with-an-always-on-culture

26. Barbuto, J. E., Jr. (1997, April). A critique of the Myers-Briggs Type Indicator and its operationalization of Carl Jung's psychological types. *Psychological Reports, 80*(2), 611. Pittenger, D. J. (Spring 2005). Cautionary comments regarding the Myers-Briggs type indicator. *Consulting Psychology Journal: Practice and Research, 57*(2), 210–221.

27. Ibid.

28. Moyle, P., & Hackston, J. (2018). Personality assessment for employee development: Ivory tower or real world? *Journal of Personality Assessment, 100*(5), 507–517.

29. Gholipour, B. (2019, May 19). *How accurate is the Myers-Briggs personality test?* Livescience.com. https://www.livescience.com/65513-does-myers-briggs-personality-test-work.html

30. Ibid.

31. Ibid.

32. Eysenck, H. (1998). *Dimensions of personality*. Transaction. (Original work published 1947)

33. Eysenck, H. J., & Eysenck, S. B. (1977). *Psychoticism as a dimension of personality*. Carne & Russak.

34. Cattell, R. B. (1943). The description of personality: Basic traits resolved into clusters. *Journal of Abnormal and Social Psychology, 38*(4), 476.

35. See, for example, Block, J. (1977, December). The Eysencks and psychoticism. *Journal of Abnormal Psychology, 86*(6), 653–654; Howarth, E. (1976, May). Were Cattell's personality sphere factors correctly identified in the first instance? *British Journal of Psychology, 67*(2): 213–230; Saville, P., & Blinkhorn, S. (1981). Reliability, homogeneity and the construct validity of Cattell's 16PF. *Personality and Individual Differences, 2*(4), 325–333; Jackson, C. J., Furnham, A., Forde, L., & Cotter, T. (2000, May). The structure of the Eysenck personality profiler. *British Journal of Psychology, 91*(2), 223.

36. Barrick, M. R., & Mount, M. K. (Spring 1991). The Big Five personality dimensions and job performance: A meta-analysis. *Personnel Psychology, 44*(1), 1–26. John, O. P., & Srivastava, S. (1999). The Big Five trait taxonomy: History, measurement, and theoretical perspectives. In D. Cervone & L. A. Pervin (Eds.), *Handbook of personality: Theory and research* (2nd ed., pp. 102–138). Guilford Press.

37. See, for example, Gurven, M., von Rueden, C., Massenkoff, M., Kaplan, H., & Vie, M. L. (2013, February). How universal is the Big Five? Testing the five-factor model of personality variation among forager-farmers in the Bolivian Amazon. *Journal of Personality and Social Psychology, 104*(2), 354–370.

38. See, for example, Saucier, G., & Srivastava, S. (2015). What makes a good structural model of personality? Evaluating the Big Five and alternatives. In M. Mikulincer & P. R. Shaver (Eds.), *APA handbook of personality and social psychology: Vol. 4. Personality processes and individual differences* (pp. 283–305). American Psychological Association.

39. Chang, C.-H. (Daisy), Ferris, D. L., Johnson, R. E., Rosen, C. C., & Tan, J. A. (2012, January). Core self-evaluations: A review and evaluation of the literature. *Journal of Management, 38*(1), 81–128. Mäkikangas, A., Kinnunen, U., Mauno, S., & Selenko, E. (2016, October 7). Factor structure and longitudinal factorial validity of the core self-evaluation scale: Exploratory structural equation modeling. *European Journal of Psychological Assessment, 34*(6), 444–449.

40. McDonald, R., Tempone, V. J., & Simmons, W. L. (1968). Locus of control as a personality and situational variable. *Perceptual and Motor Skills, 27*(1), 135–141. Rotter, J. B., & Mulry, R. C. (1965, October). Internal versus external control of reinforcement and decision time. *Journal of Personality and Social Psychology, 2*(4), 598–604.

41. Ashton, M. C., Lee, K., & de Vries, R. E. (2014, May). The HEXACO honesty-humility, agreeableness, and emotionality factors: A review of research and theory. *Personality and Social Psychology Review, 18*(2), 139–152. de Vries, R. E., Ashton, M. C., & Lee, K. (2019). New developments in HEXACO personality research. *Zeitschrift für Psychologie, 227*(3), 163–165.

42. Ibid.

43. Wiltshire, J., Bourdage, J. S., & Lee, K. (2014, June). Honesty-humility and perceptions of organizational politics in predicting workplace outcomes. *Journal of Business and Psychology, 29*(2), 235–251.

44. Lee, K., & Ashton, M. C. (2012, April). Getting mad and getting even: Agreeableness and honesty-humility as predictors of revenge intentions. *Personality and Individual Differences, 52*(5), 596–600.

45. Scipioni, J. (2021, April 22). *Ray Dalio gives employees a personality test—here's one Dalio created that you can take for free*. CNBC. https://www.cnbc.com/2021/04/22/ray-dalio-created-principleyou-personality-test-anyone-can-take-free.html

46. Ibid.

47. Edwards, J. R. (1991). *Person-job fit: A conceptual integration, literature review, and methodological critique*. Wiley. Sylva, H., Mol, S. T., Den Hartog, D. N., & Dorenbosch, L. (2019). Person-job fit and proactive career behaviour: A dynamic approach. *European Journal of Work and Organizational Psychology, 28*(5), 631–645.

48. Kristof, A. L. (1996). Person-organization fit: An integrative review of its conceptualizations, measurement, and implications. *Personnel Psychology, 49*(1), 1–49. Semrau, T., & Biemann, T. (2022). When sergeants can outrank generals: Person-organization fit and the performance of franchisees as agents of their franchisor. *Journal of Business Venturing, 37*(2), 106177.

49. Iyer, P. V., Oostrom, J. K., Serlie, A. W., van Dam, A., & Ph Born, M. (2020). The criterion-related validity of a short commensurate measure of personality-based person-organization fit. *International Journal of Selection and Assessment, 28*(2), 143–162.

50. Johnson, A. (2020, February 13). *8 ways to ensure person-organization fit when hiring new employees*. Harver.com. https://harver.com/blog/person-organization-fit/

51. Ibid.

52. Ibid.

53. Duckworth, A. L., Peterson, C., Matthews, M. D., & Kelly, D. R. (2007). Grit: Perseverance and passion for long-term goals. *Journal of Personality and Social Psychology, 92*(6), 1087.

54. Luthans, F., Youssef, C. M., & Avolio, B. J. (2007). *Psychological capital: Developing the human competitive edge* (Vol. 198). Oxford University Press.

55. Luthans, K. W., Luthans, B. C., & Chaffin, T. D. (2019). Refining grit in academic performance: The mediational role of psychological capital. *Journal of Management Education, 43*(1), 35–61.

56. Peterson, C., & Seligman, M. E. P. (2004). *Character strengths and virtues: A handbook and classification.* American Psychological Association.

57. Peterson, C., & Park, N. (2006, December). Character strengths in organizations. *Journal of Organizational Behavior, 27*(8), 1149–1154. Peterson, C., Stephens, J. P., Park, N., Lee, F., & Seligman, M. E. P. (2010). Strengths of character and work. In P. A. Linley, S. Harrington, & N. Garcea (Eds.), *Oxford handbook of positive psychology and work* (pp. 221–231). Oxford University Press.

58. Linley, P. A., Maltby, J., Wood, A. M., Joseph, S., Harrington, S., Peterson, C., Park, N., & Seligman, M. E. P. (2007, July). Character strengths in the United Kingdom: The VIA inventory of strengths. *Personality and Individual Differences, 43*(2), 341–351.

59. Peterson, C., & Seligman, M. E. P. (2004). *Character strengths and virtues: A handbook and classification.* American Psychological Association.

60. Macdonald, C., Bore, M., & Munro, D. (2008, August). Values in action scale and the Big 5: An empirical indication of structure. *Journal of Research in Personality, 42*(4), 787–799.

61. See, for example, Höfer, S., Hausler, M., Huber, A., Strecker, C., Renn, D., & Höge, T. (2020, April). Psychometric characteristics of the German Values in Action Inventory of Strengths 120-item short form. *Applied Research in Quality of Life, 15*(2), 597–611; Azañedo, C. M., Fernández-Abascal, E. G., & Barraca, J. (2014, July). Character strengths in Spain: Validation of the values in action inventory of strengths (VIA-IS) in a Spanish sample. *Clínica y Salud, 25*(2), 123–130.

62. Marston, W. M. (1999). *Emotions of normal people.* Routledge. (Original work published 1928)

63. Everything DiSC. (2013). Research report for adaptive testing assessment. Wiley.

64. Buckingham, M., & Clifton, D. O. (2001). *Now, discover your strengths.* Simon & Schuster. Rath, T. (2007). *StrengthsFinder 2.0.* Gallup.

65. Asplund, J., Lopez, S. J., Hodges, T., & Harter, J. (2007). The Clifton StrengthsFinder 2.0 technical report: Development and validation. Gallup.

66. Fuglestad, P. T., & Snyder, M. (2009). Self-monitoring. In M. R. Leary & R. H. Hoyle (Eds.), *Handbook of individual differences in social behavior* (pp. 574–591). Guilford Press. Oh, I.-S., Charlier, S. D., Mount, M. K., & Berry, C. M. (2014, January). The two faces of high self-monitors: Chameleonic moderating effects of self-monitoring on the relationships between personality traits and counterproductive work behaviors. *Journal of Organizational Behavior, 35*(1), 92–111. Pillow, D. R., Hale, W. J., Jr., Crabtree, M. A., & Hinojosa, T. L. (2017, October 1). Exploring the relations between self-monitoring, authenticity, and well-being. *Personality and Individual Differences, 116*, 393–398.

67. Cherry, K. (2021, May 20). *What is self-monitoring?* Verywell Mind. https://www.verywellmind.com/what-is-self-monitoring-5179838

68. Li, W.-D., Fay, D., Frese, M., Harms, P. D., & Gao, X. Y. (2014, March 17). Reciprocal relationship between proactive personality and work characteristics: A latent change score approach. *Journal of Applied Psychology, 99*(5), 948–965. Park, J. H., & DeFrank, R. S. (2018, February). The role of proactive personality in the stressor–strain model. *International Journal of Stress Management, 25*(1), 44–59.

69. Parker, S. K., & Wang, Y. (Lena). (2019, August 21). When to take initiative at work, and when not to. *Harvard Business Review.* https://hbr.org/2019/08/when-to-take-initiative-at-work-and-when-not-to

70. Ganster, D. C., Schaubroeck, J., Sime, W. E., & Mayes, B. T. (1991, February). The nomological validity of the Type A personality among employed adults. *Journal of Applied Psychology, 76*(1), 143–168. Billing, T. K., & Steverson, P. (2013, November). Moderating role of Type-A personality on stress-outcome relationships. *Management Decision, 51*(9), 1893–1904. Naseer, S., Raja, U., & Donia, M. B. L. (2016, July). Effect of perceived politics and perceived support on bullying and emotional exhaustion: The moderating role of type a personality. *The Journal of Psychology: Interdisciplinary and Applied, 150*(5), 606–624.

71. Josef, A. K., Richter, D., Samanez-Larkin, G. R., Wagner, G. G., Hertwig, R., & Mata, R. (2016, September). Stability and change in risk-taking propensity across the adult life span. *Journal of Personality and Social Psychology, 111*(3), 430–450. Gardiner, E., & Jackson, C. J. (2012, November). Workplace mavericks: How personality and risk-taking propensity predicts Maverickism. *British Journal of Psychology, 103*(4), 497–519.

72. Casselman, B. (2013, June 2). Risk-averse culture infects U.S. workers, entrepreneurs. *Wall Street Journal.* http://online.wsj.com/article/SB10001424127887324031404578481162903760052.html

73. InsideEVs. (2019, December 11). *Tesla, Elon Musk, and how risk-taking has led to success.* https://insideevs.com/features/387249/tesla-elon-musk-art-of-risk/

74. Schwartz, B. (2004). *The paradox of choice: Why more is less.* HarperCollins.

75. Paulhus, D. L., & Williams, K. M. (2002, December). The dark triad of personality: Narcissism, Machiavellianism and psychopathy. *Journal of Research in Personality, 36*(6), 556–563. Furnham, A., Richards, S. C., & Paulhus, D. L. (2013, March). The dark triad of personality: A 10 year review. *Social and Personality Psychology Compass, 7*(3), 199–216.

76. O'Reilly III, C. A., Doerr, B., & Chatman, J. A. (2018, June). "See You in Court": How CEO narcissism increases firms' vulnerability to lawsuits. *Leadership Quarterly, 29*(3), 365–378.

77. Stavchuk, K. (2019, November 4). *Narcissistic CEOs weaken collaboration and integrity.* Insights by Stanford Business. https://www.gsb.stanford.edu/insights/narcissistic-ceos-weaken-collaboration-integrity

78. Tokarev, A., Phillips, A. R., Hughes, D. J., & Irwing, P. (2017, October). Leader dark traits, workplace bullying, and employee depression: Exploring mediation and the role of the dark core. *Journal of Abnormal Psychology, 126*(7), 911–920.

79. Rachman, G. (2014, July 21). The Kremlin's Machiavelli has led Russia to disaster. *Financial Times.* https://www.ft.com/content/cc3ca75c-10c5-11e4-812b-00144feabdc0

80. Benner, E. (2017, March 3). Have we got Machiavelli all wrong? *The Guardian*. https://www.theguardian.com/books/2017/mar/03/have-we-got-machiavelli-all-wrong
81. Adobe. (2022). *Adobe fast facts*. https://www.adobe.com/about-adobe/fast-facts.html
82. Zaveri, P. (2021, April 28). *Here's how Adobe CEO Shantanu Narayen has used people-centric policies and a strategic mindset to lead the software giant*. https://www.businessinsider.com/adobe-ceo-shantanu-narayen-leadership-people-centric-policies-strategic-mindset-2021-3
83. Adobe CEO shows you how to surpass the status quo. (2019, July 25). *Investor's Business Daily*. https://www.investors.com/news/management/leaders-and-success/adobe-ceo-shows-you-surpass-status-quo/. Emphasis added.
84. Adobe Communications Team. (2021, October 15). My #AdobeLife: Michael Stoddart on the "magic" to creating a meaningful and fulfilling career. *Adobe Blog*. https://blog.adobe.com/en/publish/2021/10/15/michael-stoddart-magic-creating-meaningful-fulfilling-career
85. Adobe Life Team. (2021, December 20). Alberto De Caro on blending tech and people skills, and getting the support you need to take risks. *Adobe Blog*. https://blog.adobe.com/en/publish/2021/12/20/alberto-de-care-blending-tech-and-people-skills
86. Juran, K. (2018, September 10). "Adobe for All" comes to life. *Adobe Blog*. https://blog.adobe.com/en/publish/2018/09/10/adobe-for-all-comes-to-life
87. Juran, K. (2019, September 16). Empower every voice: Adobe for All summit 2019. *Adobe Blog*. https://blog.adobe.com/en/2019/09/16/empower-every-voice-adobe-for-all-summit-2019
88. In Action. (n.d.). *Adobe diversity and inclusion*. https://www.adobe.com/diversity/adobe-for-all-in-action.html
89. Adobe Corporate Communications. (2021, February 09). Adobe earns top accolade for its people centric approach to business. *Adobe Blog*. https://blog.adobe.com/en/publish/2021/02/09/forbes-award-americas-best-employers

CHAPTER 4

1. Statista Research Department. (2021, July 23). *Twitter: Number of employees 2020*. Statista. https://www.statista.com/statistics/272140/employees-of-twitter/. Macrotrends. (n.d.). *Twitter revenue 2011–2021: TWTR*. https://www.macrotrends.net/stocks/charts/TWTR/twitter/revenue
2. Statista Research Department. (2021, September 7). *Leading countries based on number of Twitter users as of July 2021*. Statista. https://www.statista.com/statistics/242606/number-of-active-twitter-users-in-selected-countries/
3. Nazar, J. (2013, October 8). *14 famous business pivots*. Forbes. https://www.forbes.com/sites/jasonnazar/2013/10/08/14-famous-business-pivots/#2a8e17415797
4. Ibid.
5. Carlson, N. (2011). *The real history of Twitter*. Business Insider. http://www.businessinsider.com/how-twitter-was-founded-2011-4
6. Ibid.
7. Glassdoor. (2021). *Twitter "company culture" reviews*. Glassdoor. https://www.glassdoor.com/Reviews/Twitter-company-culture-Reviews-EI_IE100569.0,7_KH8,23.htm
8. Nisen, M. (2014). *How Facebook and Twitter built the best employee trainingprograms in Silicon Valley*. Quartz. https://qz.com/185585/how-facebook-and-twitter-built-the-best-employee-training-programs-in-silicon-valley/
9. Paul, K. (2020, May 12). Twitter announces employees will be allowed to work from home "forever." *The Guardian*. https://www.theguardian.com/technology/2020/may/12/twitter-coronavirus-covid19-work-from-home
10. Nisen, M. (2014). *How Facebook and Twitter built the best employee training programs in Silicon Valley*. Quartz. https://qz.com/185585/how-facebook-and-twitter-built-the-best-employee-training-programs-in-silicon-valley/
11. Weingarten, G. (2007, April 8). Pearls before breakfast: Can one of the nation's great musicians cut through the fog of a D.C. rush hour? Let's find out. *Washington Post*. www.washingtonpost.com/wp-dyn/content/article/2007/04/04/AR2007040401721.html
12. Coren, S. (2013). Sensation and perception. In D. K. Freedheim & I. B. Weiner (Eds.), *Handbook of psychology: Vol. 1. History of psychology* (2nd ed., 100–128). Wiley. Kass, S., & Robbins, B. D. (2016). Sensation and perception. In R. Bargdill & R. Broomé (Eds.), *Humanistic contributions for psychology 101: Growth, choice, and responsibility* (pp. 25–41). University Professors Press. Zacks, J. M. (2020). Event perception and memory. *Annual Review of Psychology, 71*, 165–191.
13. Baker, H. (2021, June 29). A new type of optical illusion tricks the brain into seeing dazzling rays. *Live Science*. https://www.livescience.com/scintillating-starburst-illusion.html
14. Hubble Team. (2022, May 6). *The official list of every company's back-to-office strategy*. Hubble. https://hubblehq.com/blog/famous-companies-workplace-strategies
15. Mervosh, S. (2019, July 11). It's easy to hate selfies. But can they also be a force for good? *New York Times*. https://www.nytimes.com/2019/07/11/style/selfies-instagram.html
16. Ibid.
17. Haden, J. (2012, August 10). *Why what kind of car you drive matters*. Indian Nursing Council. www.inc.com/jeff-haden/small-business-owners-does-it-matter-what-you-drive.html
18. Levin, K. (1936). *Principles of topological psychology* (F. Heider & G. M. Heider, Trans.). McGraw-Hill.
19. Zenger, J., & Folkman, J. (2019, February 5). The 3 elements of trust. *Harvard Business Review, 87*(2), 1–2. https://hbr.org/2019/02/the-3-elements-of-trust?utm_medium=email&utm_source=newsletter_daily&utm_campaign=mtod&referral=00203
20. Devos, T. (2014). Stereotypes and intergroup attitudes. In F. T. L. Leong, L. Comas-Díaz, G. C. Nagayama Hall, V. C. McLoyd, & J. E. Trimble (Eds.), *APA handbook of multicultural psychology: Vol. 1. Theory and Research* (pp. 341–360). American Psychological Association. He, J., Kang, S. K., Tse, K., & Toh, S. M. (2019). Stereotypes at work: Occupational stereotypes predict race and gender segregation in the workforce. *Journal of Vocational Behavior, 115*, 103318.
21. Soule, S. A., Drabkin, D., & Nishiura Mackenzie, L. (2019, June 24). The stereotypes in MBA case studies.

Harvard Business Review. https://hbr.org/2019/06/the-stereotypes-in-mba-case-studies

22. Ibid.

23. Ibid.

24. Lamy, D., Leber, A. B., & Egeth, H. E. (2013). Selective attention. In A. F. Healy, R. W. Proctor, & I. B. Weiner (Eds.), *Handbook of psychology: Vol. 4. Experimental psychology* (2nd ed., pp. 267–294). Wiley.

25. Simons, D. (2010, March 10). *Selective attentiontest* [Video]. https://www.youtube.com/watch?v=vJG698U2Mvo

26. Simons, D. (2010, March 13). *The "door" study* [Video]. https://www.youtube.com/watch?v=FWSxSQsspiQ

27. Gabrieli, G., Lee, A., Setoh, P., & Esposito, G. (2021). An analysis of the generalizability and stability of the halo effect during the COVID-19 pandemic outbreak. *Frontiers in Psychology, 12*, 547. Lammers, W. J., Davis, S., Davidson, O., & Hogue, K. (2016, Spring). Impact of positive, negative, and no personality descriptors on the attractiveness halo effect. *Psi Chi Journal of Psychological Research, 21*(1), 29–34.

28. Parrett, M. (2015). Beauty and the feast: Examining the effect of beauty on earnings using restaurant tipping data. *Journal of Economic Psychology, 49*, 34–46.

29. Nahari, G., & Ben-Shakhar, G. (2013, March). Primacy effect in credibility judgements: The vulnerability of verbal cues to biased interpretations. *Applied Cognitive Psychology, 27*(2), 247–255. Sullivan, J. (2019). The primacy effect in impression formation: Some replications and extensions. *Social Psychological and Personality Science, 10*(4), 432–439.

30. Greenwald, R. (2021, January 5). Matchmaker's advice on how to make a great first impression at work. *Harvard Business Review.* https://hbr.org/2021/01/a-matchmakers-advice-on-how-to-make-a-great-first-impression-at-work

31. Postman, L., & Bruner, J. S. (1952). Hypothesis and the principle of closure: The effect of frequency and recency. *Journal of Psychology: Interdisciplinary and Applied, 33*, 113–125. Plonsky, O., & Erev, I. (2017, March). Learning in settings with partial feedback and the wavy recency effect of rare events. *Cognitive Psychology, 93*, 18–43. Jiménez, L., Gallego, D., Agra, O., Lorda, M. J., & Méndez, C.. (2021). Proportion of conflict, contingency learning, and recency effects in a Stroop task. *Quarterly Journal of Experimental Psychology, 75*(8), 1528–1540. https://doi.org/10.1177/17470218211056813

32. Knight, R. (2020, June 15). How to do performance reviews—remotely. *Harvard Business Review.* https://hbr.org/2020/06/how-to-do-performance-reviews-remotely

33. Preston, M. G. (1936). Contrast effects and the psychometric function. *American Journal of Psychology, 48*, 625–631. Kopelman, M. D. (1975, November). The contrast effect in the selection interview. *British Journal of Educational Psychology, 45*(3), 333–336. Boillaud, E., & Molina, G. (2015, April). Are judgments a form of data clustering? Reexamining contrast effects with the k-means algorithm. *Journal of Experimental Psychology: Human Perception and Performance, 41*(2), 415–430. Cartaud, A, Lenglin, V., & Coello, Y. (2022). Contrast effect of emotional context on interpersonal distance with neutral social stimuli. *Cognition, 218*, 104913.

34. Wexley, K. N., Yukl, G. A., Kovacs, S. Z., & Sanders, R. E. (1972). Importance of contrast effects in employment interviews. *Journal of Applied Psychology, 56*(1), 45. Lubbe, D., & Nitsche, A. (2019). Reducing assimilation and contrast effects on selection interview ratings using behaviorally anchored rating scales. *International Journal of Selection and Assessment, 27*(1), 43–53.

35. Thomsen, A. (1941). Psychological projection and the election: A simple class experiment. *Journal of Psychology: Interdisciplinary and Applied, 11*, 115–117. Chang, V. T., Overall, N. C., Madden, H., & Low, R. S. (2018, February 1). Expressive suppression tendencies, projection bias in memory of negative emotions, and well-being. *Emotion, 18*(7), 925.

36. Everyday Health. (2017, November 15). *Psychological projection: Dealing with undesirable emotions.* www.everydayhealth.com.https://www.everydayhealth.com/emotional-health/psychological-projection-dealing-with-undesirable-emotions/

37. Clark, J. L., & Green, M. C. (2017, August 30). Self-fulfilling prophecies: Perceived reality of online interaction drives expected outcomes of online communication. *Personality and Individual Differences, 133*, 73–76. Jussim, L. (2017, March 22). Accuracy, bias, self-fulfilling prophecies, and scientific self-correction. *Behavioral and Brain Sciences, 40*, e18. Madon, S., Jussim, L., Guyll, M., Nofziger, H., Salib, E. R., Willard, J., & Scherr, K. C. (2018). The accumulation of stereotype-based self-fulfilling prophecies. *Journal of Personality and Social Psychology, 115*(5), 825.

38. Whitehead, S. (2019, December 5). *Pygmalion effect and burnout: When employees are pushed too hard.* Panmore Institute. http://panmore.com/pygmalion-effect-and-burnout-when-employees-are-pushed-too-hard

39. Bourdage, J. S., Wiltshire, J., & Lee, K. (2015, March). Personality and workplace impression management: Correlates and implications. *Journal of Applied Psychology, 100*(2), 537–546. Maher, L. P., Gallagher, V. C., Rossi, A. M., Ferris, G. R., & Perrewé, P. L. (2018). Political skill and will as predictors of impression management frequency and style: A three-study investigation. *Journal of Vocational Behavior, 107*, 276–294.

40. *Keeping up appearances: Influencers' role as social actors.* (2019, June 13). Medium. https://medium.com/@admin_97/keeping-up-appearances-influencers-acting-as-social-actors-b03c33b78df0

41. Ibid.

42. Bande, B., Jaramillo, F., Fernández-Ferrín, P., & Varela, J. A. (2019). Salesperson coping with work-family conflict: The joint effects of ingratiation and self-promotion. *Journal of Business Research, 95*, 143–155. Long, D. M. (2021). Tacticality, authenticity, or both? The ethical paradox of actor ingratiation and target trust reactions. *Journal of Business Ethics, 168*(4), 847–860.

43. Sun, H., Guo, H., Wang, K., Sun, L., & Wang, L. (2021). Upward ingratiation outside the workplace and supervisor's human resource decisions: Moderating effect of Zhongyong thinking. *Frontiers in Psychology, 12*, 1753.

44. Dweck, C. S. (2018, March). Reflections on the legacy of attribution theory. *Motivation Science, 4*(1), 17–18. Martinko, M. J., Douglas, S. C., & Harvey, P. (2006). Attribution theory in industrial and organizational psychology: A review. In G. P. Hodgkinson & J. K. Ford (Eds.), *International review of industrial and organizational psychology 2006* (Vol. 21., pp. 127–187). Wiley. Hewett, R., Shantz, A., Mundy, J., & Alfes, K. (2018). Attribution theories in human resource management research: A review and research agenda. *The International Journal of Human Resource Management, 29*(1), 87–126.

45. Harvey, P., Madison, K., Martinko, M., Crook, T. R., & Crook, T. A. (2014, May). Attribution theory in the organizational sciences: The road traveled and the path ahead. *Academy of Management Perspectives, 28*(2), 128–146. Mehlman, R. C., & Snyder, C. R. (1985, October). Excuse theory: A test of the self-protective role of attributions. *Journal of Personality and Social Psychology, 49*(4), 994–1001.

46. Heath, D. (2010, June 9). The fundamental attribution error: It's the situation, not the person. *Fast Company.* https://www.fastcompany.com/1657515/fundamental-attribution-error-its-situation-not-person

47. Harvey, J. H., & McGlynn, R. P. (1982, August). Matching words to phenomena: The case of the fundamental attribution error. *Journal of Personality and Social Psychology, 43*(2), 345–346. Ross, L. D., Amabile, T. M., & Steinmetz, J. L. (1977, July). Social roles, social control, and biases in social-perception processes. *Journal of Personality and Social Psychology, 35*(7), 485–494. Jouffre, S., & Croizet, J.-C. (2016, August). Empowering and legitimizing the fundamental attribution error: Power and legitimization exacerbate the translation of role-constrained behaviors into ability differences. *European Journal of Social Psychology, 46*(5), 621–631.

48. Knight, R. (2021, May 14). When you're stuck working with a slacker. *Harvard Business Review.* https://hbr.org/2021/05/when-youre-stuck-working-with-a-slacker

49. Larson, J. R., Jr. (1977, September). Evidence for a self-serving bias in the attribution of causality. *Journal of Personality, 45*(3), 430–441. Arkin, R. M., Gabrenya, W. K., Jr., Appelman, A. S., & Cochran, S. T. (1979, January). Self-presentation, self-monitoring, and the self-serving bias in causal attribution. *Personality and Social Psychology Bulletin, 5*(1), 73–76. Lee-Bates, B., Billing, D. C., Caputi, P., Carstairs, G. L., Linnane, D., & Middleton, K. (2017, September). The application of subjective job task analysis techniques in physically demanding occupations: Evidence for the presence of self-serving bias. *Ergonomics, 60*(9), 1240–1249.

50. Ruhl, C. (2021, April 19). *Self-serving bias: Definition and examples.* Simple Psychology. https://www.simplypsychology.org/self-serving-bias.html

51. See, for example, Allport, F. H. (1955). Perception and theories of learning: The behavior theory approach. In F. H. Allport (Ed.), *Theories of perception and the concept of structure: A review and critical analysis with an introduction to a dynamic-structural theory of behavior* (pp. 437–466). Wiley. Bernacki, M. L., Crompton, H., & Greene, J. A. (2020). Towards convergence of mobile and psychological theories of learning. *Contemporary Educational Psychology, 60,* 101828.

52. Robson, D. (2017, August 28). *The amazing fertility of the older mind.* BBC. https://www.bbc.com/future/article/20170828-the-amazing-fertility-of-the-older-mind

53. Clark, R. E. (2004, October). The classical origins of Pavlov's conditioning. *Integrative Physiological and Behavioral Science, 39*(4), 279–294.

54. Davey, G., & Cullen, C. (1988). Human operant conditioning and behavior modification. Wiley.

55. Thorndike, E. L. (1927). The law of effect. *American Journal of Psychology, 39,* 212–222.

56. Skinner, B. F. (1936). The effect on the amount of conditioning of an interval of time before reinforcement. *Journal of General Psychology, 14,* 279–295. Michael, S., Gallagher, J. J., Calvin, A. D., Hanley, C., McConnell, J. V., & McGuigan, F. J. (1961). An overview of stimulus-response reinforcement theory. In *Psychology* (pp. 321–329). Allyn & Bacon.

57. Luthans, F., & Martinko, M. J. (1981). Organizational behavior modification: A way to bridge the gap between academic research and real world application. *Journal of Organizational Behavior Management, 3*(3), 33–50. Stajkovic, A. D., & Luthans, F. (1997, October). A meta-analysis of the effects of organizational behavior modification on task performance, 1975–95. *Academy of Management Journal, 40*(5), 1122–1149.

58. Kohll, A. (2018, August 14). *How to build a positive company culture.* Forbes. https://www.forbes.com/sites/alankohll/2018/08/14/how-to-build-a-positive-company-culture/?sh=12b39c8b49b5

59. Wexley, K. N., & Nemeroff, W. F. (1975, August). Effectiveness of positive reinforcement and goal setting as methods of management development. *Journal of Applied Psychology, 60*(4), 446–450. Chastain, A. N., Tarbox, J., Meshes, E., & Wang, Y. (2022, February 11). A pilot study: Evaluating the effects of defusion on choice making under negative and positive reinforcement contingencies. *Psychological Record,* 1–15.

60. Huhlman, H. (2017, October 16). It's science, baby! Proving the power of positive reinforcement at work. *Entrepreneur.* https://www.entrepreneur.com/article/302489

61. Cherry, K. (2021, April 15). *How negative reinforcement works.* Verywell Mind. https://www.verywellmind.com/what-is-negative-reinforcement-2795410

62. Burger, R. (2009, March 11). The marvelous benefits of positive and negative reinforcement. *Selah Independent.*

63. Asadullah, A. B. M., Juhdi, N. B., Islam, M. N., Ahmed, A. A. A., & Abdullah, A. B. M. (2019). The effect of reinforcement and punishment on employee performance. *ABC Journal of Advanced Research, 8*(2), 47–58. McConnell, J. V. (1990, December). Negative reinforcement and positive punishment. *Teaching of Psychology, 17*(4), 247–249.

64. Ibid.

65. Chan, C. K. J., & Harris, J. A. (August 2017). Extinction of Pavlovian conditioning: The influence of trial number and reinforcement history. *Behavioural Processes, 141*(Pt. 1), 19–25. Kunnavatana, S. S., Bloom, S. E., Samaha, A. L., Slocum, T. A., & Clay, C. J. (2018, Spring). Manipulating parameters of reinforcement to reduce problem behavior without extinction. *Journal of Applied Behavior Analysis, 51*(2), 283–302.

66. Lundin, R. W. (1961). Schedules of reinforcement. In *Personality: An experimental approach* (pp. 76–101). MacMillan.

67. Ibid.

68. Crossman, E. K. (1991). Schedules of reinforcement. In W. Ishaq (Ed.), *Human behavior in today's world* (pp. 133–138). Praeger. Okouchi, H. (2010, Winter). An exploration of remote history effects in humans: II. The effects under fixed-interval, variable-interval, and fixed-ratio schedules. *Psychological Record, 60*(1), 27–42.

69. Ibid.

70. Ibid.

71. Ibid.

72. Bandura, A. (1977). *Social learning theory.* Prentice-Hall. Bandura, A. (1991, December). Social cognitive theory of self-regulation. *Organizational Behavior and Human Decision Processes, 50*(2), 248–287. Bandura, A. (2012). Social cognitive theory. In A. W. Kruglanski, E. T. Higgins, & P. A. M. Van Lange (Eds.), *Handbook of theories of social psychology* (Vol. 1., pp. 349–373). SAGE.

73. Bandura, A. (1997). *Self-efficacy: The exercise of control.* W. H. Freeman/Times Books/Henry Holt. Bandura, A. (2013). The role of self-efficacy in goal-based motivation. In E. A. Locke & G. P. Latham (Eds.), *New developments in goal setting and task performance* (pp. 147–157). Routledge.

74. Laws, S. (n.d.). Want to compete in the big leagues with Amazon and Google? Take these risks. *Inc.* https://www.inc.com/partners-in-leadership/want-to-compete-in-big-leagues-with-amazon-google-take-these-risks.html

75. Tu, M., & Li, M. (2021, May 12). What great mentorship looks like in a hybrid workplace. *Harvard Business Review.* https://hbr.org/2021/05/what-great-mentorship-looks-like-in-a-hybrid-workplace

76. Bandura, A., & Adams, N. E. (1977, December). Analysis of self-efficacy theory of behavioral change. *Cognitive Therapy and Research, 1*(4), 287–310. Bandura, A., Reese, L., & Adams, N. E. (1982, July). Microanalysis of action and fear arousal as a function of differential levels of perceived self-efficacy. *Journal of Personality and Social Psychology, 43*(1), 5–21.

77. Vancouver, J. B., Thompson, C. M, Tischner, E, C., & Putka, D. J. (2002, June). Two studies examining the negative effect of self-efficacy on performance. *Journal of Applied Psychology, 87*(3), 506–516.

78. Ibid.

79. Gielnik, M. M., Bledow, R., & Stark, M. S. (2020). A dynamic account of self-efficacy in entrepreneurship. *Journal of Applied Psychology, 105*(5), 487.

80. Bandura, A. (1999). Social cognitive theory of personality. In *Handbook of personality: Theory and research* (2nd ed., 154–196). Guilford Press. Hoover, J. D., Giambatista, R. C., & Belkin, L. Y. (2012, December). Eyes on, hands on: Vicarious observational learning as an enhancement of direct experience. *Academy of Management Learning and Education, 11*(4), 591–608.

81. Bandura, A. (1999). Social cognitive theory of personality. In *Handbook of personality: Theory and research* (2nd ed., pp. 154–196). Guilford Press. Bandura, A. (1991, December). Social cognitive theory of self-regulation. *Organizational Behavior and Human Decision Processes, 50*(2), 248–287.

82. McAllister, C., Steffensen, D. J., Perrewé, P. L., Brooks, C. D., & Wang, G. (2020, May 21). How to cope with that "always-on" feeling. *Harvard Business Review.* https://hbr.org/2020/05/how-to-cope-with-that-always-on-feeling

83. Bandura, A. (1989, September). Human agency in social cognitive theory. *American Psychologist, 44*(9), 1175–1184. Wood, R., & Bandura, A. (1989, July). Social cognitive theory of organizational management. *Academy of Management Review, 14*(3), 361–384.

84. Hale, J. (2019, May 7). *More than 500 hours of content are now being uploaded to YouTube every minute.* Tubefilter. https://www.tubefilter.com/2019/05/07/number-hours-video-uploaded-to-youtube-per-minute/

85. Barnett, J. (2021, April 23). *Catch&Release raises $14 M in series a funding! Read our exclusive Q&A with founder Analisa Goodin.* GingerBread Capital. https://gingerbreadcap.com/catchrelease-analisa-goodin-interview/

86. San Francisco Egotist. (2018, August 6). *Egotist briefs: Analisa Goodin of Catch&Release.* https://www.thesfegotist.com/editorial/2018/08/06/egotist-briefs-analisa-goodin-of-catch release/

87. Thomas, J. (2021, October–November). 100 women of impact. *Entrepreneur, 49*(7), 46.

88. Miaskiewicz, G. (Host). (2021, September 15). Analisa Goodin, founder & CEO of Catch&Release [Audio podcast episode]. In *The Startup Foundations.* Capbase. https://www.spreaker.com/user/12940214/analisa-goodin-founder-ceo-of-catch-rele

89. Catch&Release. (2021). *Catch&Release.* https://www.catchandrelease.com

90. Goodin, A. (2020, November 10). *Why found content is now a permanent part of the creative mix.* Ad Age. https://adage.com/article/catchandrelease/why-found-content-now-permanent-part-creative-mix/2292951

91. Downing, S. (2018, November 15). Here's why this S.F. tech startup founder hires people with restaurant experience. *San Francisco Business Times.* https://www.bizjournals.com/sanfrancisco/news/2018/11/15/licensing-content-from-internet-catch-release.html

CHAPTER 5

1. Fundable. (n.d.). *Under Armour startup story.* https://www.fundable.com/learn/startup-stories/under-armour

2. Under Armour. (2021, February 10). *Under Armour reports fourth quarter and full year 2020 results.* UA Newsroom. https://about.underarmour.com/Q4FY2020EARNINGS

3. Fundable. (n.d.). *Under Armour startup story.* https://www.fundable.com/learn/startup-stories/under-armour

4. Ibid.

5. Bhattarai, A. (2017, October 31). Under Armour's terrible year just got worse. *The Washington Post.* https://www.washingtonpost.com/news/business/wp/2017/10/31/under-armours-terrible-year-just-got-worse/

6. Wilen, H. (2020, September 9). Under Armour laying off 600 employees due to COVID-19 impact. *Baltimore Business Journal.* https://www.bizjournals.com/baltimore/news/2020/09/08/u

nder-armour-laying-off-another-600-employees.html

7. Under Armour. (n.d.). *Welcome to the home of the best. Bring your A-game here.* http://www.underarmour.jobs/why-choose-us/our-history/

8. Unger, M. (2013, August). A look inside Under Armour. *Baltimore.* http://www.baltimoremagazine.net/2013/8/1/a-look-inside-under-armour

9. Schneider-Levy, B. (2016, May 11). *Under Armour employees share Kevin Plank's best advice & company perks.* Footwear News. http://footwearnews.com/2016/focus/uncategorized/under-armour-employees-share-kevin-planks-best-advice-220213/

10. Schneider-Levy, B. (2016, May 11). *Under Armour employees share Kevin Plank's best advice & company perks.* Footwear News. http://footwearnews.com/2016/focus/uncategorized/under-armour-employees-share-kevin-planks-best-advice-220213/

11. Knowledge at Wharton Staff. (2011, January 5). Under Armour's Kevin Plank: Creating "the biggest, baddest brand on the planet." *Knowledge at Wharton.* https://knowledge.wharton.upenn.edu/article/under-armours-kevin-plank-creating-the-biggest-baddest-brand-on-the-planet/

12. Augustine, A. A., & Larsen, R. J. (2015). Personality, affect, and affect regulation. In M. Mario, P. R. Shaver, M. Cooper, & R. J. Larsen. (Eds.), *APA handbook of personality and social psychology: Personality processes and individual differences* (Vol. 4, pp. 147–165). American Psychological Association. George, J. M. (1996). Trait and state affect. In K. R. Murphy (Ed.), *Individual differences and behavior in organizations* (p. 145). Jossey-Bass. Yang, L.-Q., Cropanzano, R., Daus, C. S., & Martínez-Tur, V. (Eds.). (2020). *The Cambridge handbook of workplace affect.* Cambridge University Press.

13. Charles, S. T., & Robinette, J. W. (2015). Emotion and emotion regulation. In P. A. Lichtenberg, B. T. Mast, B. D. Carpenter, & J. Loebach Wetherell (Eds.), *APA handbook of clinical geropsychology: Vol. 1. History and status of the field and perspectives on aging* (pp. 235–258). American Psychological Association. Diener, E., Thapa, S., & Tay, L. (2020). Positive emotions at work. *Annual Review of Organizational Psychology and Organizational Behavior, 7,* 451–477. Frijda, N. H. (1993). Moods, emotion episodes, and emotions. In M. Lewis & J. M. Haviland (Eds.), *Handbook of emotions* (pp. 381–403). Guilford Press.

14. Ong, A. D., & Zautra, A. J. (2015). Intraindividual variability in mood and mood regulation in adulthood. In M. Diehl, K. Hooker, & M. J. Sliwinski (Eds.), *Handbook of intraindividual variability across the life span* (pp. 198–215). Routledge. Mazur-Socha, Z., & Przepiórka, A. (2021). Affective correlates of negative mood regulation expectancies: A systematic review and meta-analysis. *Journal of Research in Personality, 92,* 104098. Guterman, Y., Kleifeld, I., & Vegmister, R. (2015). Just think! Mood regulation effects of cognitive activity. In L. Zysberg & S. Raz (Eds.), *Emotional intelligence: Current evidence from psychophysiological, educational and organizational perspectives* (pp. 57–70). Nova Science.

15. Lang, A., & Ewoldsen, D. R. (2015). The measurement of positive and negative affect in media research. In K. Doveling, C. von Scheve, & E. A. Konijn (Eds.), *The Routledge handbook of emotions and mass media* (pp. 79–98). Routledge. Nikolaev, B., Shir, N., & Wiklund, J. (2020). Dispositional positive and negative affect and self-employment transitions: The mediating role of job satisfaction. *Entrepreneurship Theory and Practice, 44*(3), 451–474. Rice, F., Davidovich, S., & Dunsmuir, S. (2017). Emotion regulation and depression: Maintaining equilibrium between positive and negative affect. In C. A. Essau, S. S. LeBlanc, & T. H. Ollendick (Eds.), *Emotion regulation and psychopathology in children and adolescents* (pp. 171–195). Oxford University Press.

16. Kinni, T. (2021, May 13). All the feels: Why it pays to notice emotions in the workplace. *Insights.* https://www.gsb.stanford.edu/insights/all-feels-why-it-pays-notice-emotions-workplace

17. Ibid.

18. Barsade, S. G., Coutifaris, C. G. V., & Pillemer, J. (2018). Emotional contagion in organizational life. *Research in Organizational Behavior, 38,* 137–151. Tee, E. Y. J. (2015, June 23). The emotional link: Leadership and the role of implicit and explicit emotional contagion processes across multiple organizational levels. *Leadership Quarterly, 26*(4), 654–670.

19. Barsade, S. (2020, March 26). The contagion we can control. *Harvard Business Review.* https://hbr.org/2020/03/the-contagion-we-can-control

20. Ibid.

21. Ibid.

22. Ibid.

23. Gabriel, A. S., Daniels, M. A., Diefendorff, J. M., & Greguras, G. J. (2015, May). Emotional labor actors: A latent profile analysis of emotional labor strategies. *Journal of Applied Psychology, 100*(3), 863–879. Ashforth, B. E., & Humphrey, R. H. (1993, January). Emotional labor in service roles: The influence of identity. *Academy of Management Review, 18*(1), 88–115. Hochschild, A. R. (1983). *The managed heart: Commercialization of human feeling.* University of California Press.

24. Gabriel, A. S., Koopman, J., Rosen, C. C., Arnold, J. D., & Hochwarter, W. (2020, February 19). Don't just put on a happy face at work. *Harvard Business Review.* https://hbr.org/2020/02/dont-just-put-on-a-happy-face-at-work

25. Ibid.

26. Côté, S. (2005, July). A social interaction model of the effects of emotion regulation on work strain. *Academy of Management Review, 30*(3), 509–530. Grandey, A. A. (2003, February). When "the show must go on": Surface acting and deep acting as determinants of emotional exhaustion and peer-rated service delivery. *Academy of Management Journal, 46*(1), 86–96. Nesher Shoshan, H., & Venz, L. (2022). Daily deep acting toward coworkers: An examination of day-specific antecedents and consequences. *Journal of Organizational Behavior, 43*(1), 112–124. Xanthopoulou, D., Bakker, A. B., Oerlemans, W. G. M., & Koszucka, M. (2017, November 27). Need for recovery after emotional labor: Differential effects of daily deep and surface acting. *Journal of Organizational Behavior, 39*(4), 481–494.

27. Paraskevi, S. C., & Ashforth, B. E. (2015, January). Revisiting the debate on the relationship between display rules and performance: Considering the explicitness of display rules. *Journal of Applied Psychology, 100*(1), 249–261. Mastracci, S., & Adams, I. T. (2021). Fitter, happier: Display rules in policing. *Journal of Police and Criminal Psychology, 36*(3), 592–602.

28. Cropanzano, R., Weiss, H. M., & Elias, S. M. (2004). The impact of display

rules and emotional labor on psychological well-being at work. In P. L. Perrewé & D. C. Ganster (Eds.), *Emotional and physiological processes and positive intervention strategies* (Vol. 3, pp. 45–89). JAI Press.

29. Côté, S. (2005, July). A social interaction model of the effects of emotion regulation on work strain. *Academy of Management Review, 30*(3), 509–530. Kenworthy, J., Fay, C., Frame, M., & Petree, R. (2014, February). A meta-analytic review of the relationship between emotional dissonance and emotional exhaustion. *Journal of Applied Social Psychology, 44*(2), 94–105. O'Brien, E., & Linehan, C. (2019). Problematizing the authentic self in conceptualizations of emotional dissonance. *Human Relations, 72*(9), 1530–1556.

30. Vignoli, M., Mazzetti, G., Converso, D., & Guglielmi, D. (2021). How workers' emotional dissonance explains the association between customers' relations, burnout and health in an Italian supermarket chain. *La Medicina del Lavoro, 112*(3), 200.

31. Martin Braunstein, L., Gross, J. J., & Ochsner, K. N. (2017, October). Explicit and implicit emotion regulation: A multi-level framework. *Social Cognitive and Affective Neuroscience, 12*(10), 1545–1557. Gross, J. J., & Thompson, R. A. (2007). Emotion regulation: Conceptual foundations. In J. J. Gross (Ed.), *Handbook of emotion regulation* (pp. 3–24). Guilford Press. McRae, K., & Gross, J. J. (2020). Emotion regulation. *Emotion, 20*(1), 1.

32. Appleton, A. A., Loucks, E. B., Buka, S. L., & Kubzansky, L. D. (2014, October). Divergent associations of antecedent- and response-focused emotion regulation strategies with midlife cardiovascular disease risk. *Annals of Behavioral Medicine, 48*(2), 246–255. Eldesouky, L., & English, T. (2019). Regulating for a reason: Emotion regulation goals are linked to spontaneous strategy use. *Journal of Personality, 87*(5), 948–961. Gross, J. J. (1998, January). Antecedent- and response-focused emotion regulation: Divergent consequences for experience, expression, and physiology. *Journal of Personality and Social Psychology, 74*(1), 224–237.

33. Ibid.

34. Molinsky, A. (2015, April 20). Emotional intelligence doesn't translate across borders. *Harvard Business Review.* https://hbr.org/2015/04/emotional-intelligence-doesnt-translate-across-borders

35. Salovey, P., & Mayer, J. D. (1989). Emotional intelligence. *Imagination, Cognition and Personality, 9*(3), 185–211. Joseph, D. L., Jin, J., Newman, D. A., & O'Boyle, E. H. (2015, March). Why does self-reported emotional intelligence predict job performance? A meta-analytic investigation of mixed EI. *Journal of Applied Psychology, 100*(2), 298–342. Mattingly, V., & Kraiger, K. (2019). Can emotional intelligence be trained? A meta-analytical investigation. *Human Resource Management Review, 29*(2), 140–155.

36. Goleman, D. (2020, December 22). What people (still) get wrong about emotional intelligence. *Harvard Business Review.* https://hbr.org/2020/12/what-people-still-get-wrong-about-emotional-intelligence

37. Jack, K. (2020, October 31). *Why hiring managers seek people with high levels of emotional intelligence.* Forbes. https://www.forbes.com/sites/jackkelly/2020/10/31/why-hiring-managers-seek-people-with-high-levels-of-emotional-intelligence/?sh=840feaecb478

38. Elliott, D. (2021, June 1). *6 things to know about the future of skills and workplace learning.* World Economic Forum. https://www.weforum.org/agenda/2021/06/workplace-skills-learning-linkedin-report/

39. Cumello, J. (2020, November 20). How to hire for emotional intelligence—a practical guide in the age of COVID-19. *Fast Company.* https://www.fastcompany.com/90578776/how-to-hire-for-emotional-intelligence-a-practical-guide-in-the-age-of-covid-19

40. Goleman, D. (1996). *Emotional intelligence: Why it can matter more than IQ.* Bloomsbury. Goleman, D., Boyatzis, R. E., & McKee, A. (2013). *Primal leadership: Unleashing the power of emotional intelligence.* Harvard Business Press.

41. See, for example, Harms, P. D., & Credé, M. (2010, June). Remaining issues in emotional intelligence research: Construct overlap, method artifacts, and lack of incremental validity. *Industrial and Organizational Psychology: Perspectives on Science and Practice, 3*(2), 154–158. Joseph, D. L., Jin, J., Newman, D. A., & O'Boyle, E. H. (2015). Why does self-reported emotional intelligence predict job performance? A meta-analytic investigation of mixed EI. *Journal of Applied Psychology, 100*(2), 298. Murphy, K. M. (2006). *A critique of emotional intelligence: What are the problems and how can they be fixed?* Erlbaum.

42. Emre, M. (2021, April 12). The repressive politics of emotional intelligence. *The New Yorker.* https://www.newyorker.com/magazine/2021/04/19/the-repressive-politics-of-emotional-intelligence

43. Cherry, K. (2020, May 25). *Utilizing emotional intelligence in the workplace.* Verywell Mind. https://www.verywellmind.com/utilizing-emotional-intelligence-in-the-workplace-4164713

44. Carmeli, A. (2003). The relationship between emotional intelligence and work attitudes, behavior and outcomes: An examination among senior managers. *Journal of Managerial Psychology, 18*(8), 788–813.

45. Allport, G. W. (1935). Attitudes. In C. Murchison (Ed.), *A handbook of social psychology* (pp. 798–844). Clark University Press. Bem, D. J. (1970). *Beliefs, attitudes, and human affairs.* Brooks/Cole. McVittie, C., & McKinlay, A. (2017). Attitudes and attributions. In B. Gough (Ed.), *The Palgrave handbook of critical social psychology* (pp. 269–289). Palgrave Macmillan.

46. Ajzen, I., & Fishbein, M. (2005). The influence of attitudes on behavior. In A. D. Albarracin, B. T. Johnson, & M. P. Zanna (Eds.), *The handbook of attitudes* (pp. 173–221). Erlbaum. Ajzen, I., & Fishbein, M. (1972, January). Attitudes and normative beliefs as factors influencing behavioral intentions. *Journal of Personality and Social Psychology, 21*(1), 1–9. Ajzen, I. (1991, December). The theory of planned behavior. *Organizational Behavior and Human Decision Processes, 50*(2), 179–211.

47. Chang, E. H., Milkman, K. L., Chugh, D., & Akinola, M. (2019). Diversity thresholds: How social norms, visibility, and scrutiny relate to group composition. *Academy of Management Journal, 62*(1), 144–171. Legros, S., & Cislaghi, B. (2020). Mapping the social-norms literature: An overview of reviews. *Perspectives on Psychological Science, 15*(1), 62–80.

48. Festinger, L. (1957). *A theory of cognitive dissonance.* Stanford University Press. Morvan, C., & O'Connor, A.

(2017). *An analysis of Leon Festinger's* A Theory of Cognitive Dissonance. Routledge.

49. Eggerth, D. E. (2015). Job satisfaction, job performance, and success. In P. J. Hartung, M. Savickas, & W. B. Walsh (Eds.), *APA handbook of career intervention: Applications* (Vol. 2, pp. 453–463). American Psychological Association. Judge, T. A., Zhang, S. C., & Glerum, D. R. (2020). Job satisfaction. In V. I. Sessa & N. A. Bowling (Eds.), *Essentials of job attitudes and other workplace psychological constructs* (pp. 207–241). Routledge.
50. Allen, T. (2021, April 7). The pandemic is changing employee benefits. *Harvard Business Review.* https://hbr.org/2021/04/the-pandemic-is-changing-employee-benefits
51. Company profile: Bev. (n.d.). *Inc.* https://www.inc.com/profile/bev
52. Byrne, Z. S. (2015). Understanding employee engagement: Theory, research, and practice. Routledge. Mone, E. M., & London, M. (2018). Employee engagement through effective performance management: A practical guide for managers (2nd ed). Routledge.
53. Harter, J. (2020, October 16). *U.S. employee engagement reverts back to pre-COVID-19 levels.* Gallup. https://www.gallup.com/workplace/321965/employee-engagement-reverts-back-pre-covid-levels.aspx
54. White, A. (2022, February 17). *8 employee engagement statistics you need to know in 2022.* HRCloud. https://www.hrcloud.com/blog/8-employee-engagement-statistics-you-need-to-know-in-2021
55. Stein, D., Hobson, N., Jachimowicz, J. M., & Whillans, A. (2021, October 13). How companies can improve employee engagement right now. *Harvard Business Review.* https://hbr.org/2021/10/how-companies-can-improve-employee-engagement-right-now
56. Al-Jabari, B., & Ghazzawi, I. (2019). Organizational commitment: A review of the conceptual and empirical literature and a research agenda. *International Leadership Journal, 11*(1), 78–119.
57. Meyer, J. P., & Allen, N. J. (1991). A three-component conceptualization of organizational commitment. *Human Resource Management Review, 1*(1), 61–89.
58. Knotts, K. G., & Houghton, J. D. (2021). You can't make me! The role of self-leadership in enhancing organizational commitment and work engagement. *Leadership and Organization Development Journal, 42*(5), 748–762.
59. Organ, D. W. (1988). *Organizational citizenship behavior: The good soldier syndrome.* Lexington Books. Smith, C. A., Organ, D. W., & Near, J. P. (2016). Organizational citizenship behavior: Its nature and antecedents. In G. J. Boyle, J. G. O'Gorman, & G. J. Fogarty (Eds.), *Work and organisational psychology: Research methodology; assessment and selection; organisational change and development; human resource and performance management; emerging trends: innovation/globalisation/technology* (pp. 129–144). SAGE.
60. Cook, J. (2021, March 8). *Six ways to go the extra mile for your customers.* Forbes. https://www.forbes.com/sites/jodiecook/2021/03/08/six-ways-to-go-the-extra-mile-for-your-customers/?sh=2580ab085fbc
61. Carpenter, N. C., Whitman, D. S., & Amrhein, R. (2021). Unit-level counterproductive work behavior (CWB): A conceptual review and quantitative summary. *Journal of Management, 47*(6), 1498–1527. Ones, D. S., & Dilchert, S. (2013). Counterproductive work behaviors: Concepts, measurement, and nomological network. In K. F. Geisinger, B. A. Bracken, J. F. Carlson, J.-I. C. Hansen, N. R. Kuncel, S. P. Reise, & M. C. Rodriguez (Eds.), *APA handbook of testing and assessment in psychology: Vol. 1. Test theory and testing and assessment in industrial and organizational psychology* (pp. 643–659). American Psychological Association.
62. Activision Blizzard reportedly fires 20 employees following harassment claims. (2021, October 19). *The Guardian.* https://www.theguardian.com/us-news/2021/oct/19/activision-blizzard-reportedly-fires-employees-harassment-claims
63. Vilas Boas, A. A., & Morin, E. M. (2016). Work-related stress, psychological well-being, and work engagement: Effects and relation to quality of working life. In A. M. Rossi, J. A. Meurs & P. L. Perrewé (Eds.), *Stress and quality of working life: Interpersonal and occupation-based stress* (pp. 109–129). Information Age Publishing. Yang, J. (2017). Understanding work stress. In S. Wadhwa (Ed.), *Stress in the modern world: Understanding science and society* (pp. 175–185). Greenwood.
64. Lui, J. (2021, June 15). *U.S. workers are among the most stressed in the world, new Gallup report finds.* CNBC. https://www.cnbc.com/2021/06/15/gallup-us-workers-are-among-the-most-stressed-in-the-world.html
65. Milenkovic, M. (2021, April 9). *42 worrying workplace stress statistics.* American Institute of Stress. https://www.stress.org/42-worrying-workplace-stress-statistics-2
66. Abbas, M., & Raja, U. (2018, April 2). Challenge-hindrance stressors and job outcomes: The moderating role of conscientiousness. *Journal of Business and Psychology, 34*(2), 189–201. Lepine, J. A., Podsakoff, N. P., & Lepine, M. A. (2005, October). A meta-analytic test of the challenge stressor—Hindrance stressor framework: An explanation for inconsistent relationships among stressors and performance. *Academy of Management Journal, 48*(5), 764–775.
67. Prem, R., Ohly, S., Kubicek, B., & Korunka, C. (2017, January). Thriving on challenge stressors? Exploring time pressure and learning demands as antecedents of thriving at work. *Journal of Organizational Behavior, 38*(1), 108–123. https://www.ncbi.nlm.nih.gov/pmc/articles/PMC5244684/
68. HR Revolution Middle-East Magazine. (2017, January 22). *Challenge stressors versus hindrance stressors, and resources to overcome stressors.* HR Revolution. http://www.hrrevolution.me/challenge-stressors-versus-hindrance-stressors-and-resources-to-overcome-stressors/
69. Cao, X., Masood, A., Luqman, A., & Ali, A. (2018, August). Excessive use of mobile social networking sites and poor academic performance: Antecedents and consequences from stressor-strain-outcome perspective. *Computers in Human Behavior, 85*, 163–174. Cheung, F., & Tang, C. (2010). The influence of emotional dissonance on subjective health and job satisfaction: Testing the stress-strain-outcome model. *Journal of Applied Social Psychology, 40*(12), 3192–3217.

70. Sonnentag, S., & Fritz, C. (2015). Recovery from job stress: The stressor-detachment model as an integrative framework. *Journal of Organizational Behavior, 36*(Suppl. 1), S72–S103.

71. Nelson, D. L., & Simmons, B. L. (2011). Savoring eustress while coping with distress: The holistic model of stress. In J. C. Quick & L. E. Tetrick (Eds.), *Handbook of occupational health psychology* (2nd ed., pp. 55–74). American Psychological Association. Shen, Y., Wang, S., Chen, J., & Wu, J. (2020). Development and validation of a Chinese version of the eustress-distress psychological response scale. *Social Behavior and Personality: An International Journal, 48*(8), 1–10.

72. Ibid.

73. Perrewé, P. L., Rosen, C. C., & Maslach, C. (2012). Organizational politics and stress: The development of a process model. In G. R. Ferris & D. C. Treadway (Eds.), *Politics in organizations: Theory and research considerations* (pp. 213–255). Routledge.

74. Morin, C. M., & Carrier, J. (2021). The acute effects of the COVID-19 pandemic on insomnia and psychological symptoms. *Sleep Medicine, 77*, 346.

75. Cowen, T. (2021, October 25). *America's national mood disorder.* Bloomberg. https://www.bloomberg.com/opinion/articles/2021-10-25/america-s-negative-politics-are-creating-a-national-mood-disorder

76. Campbell, M., & Gavett, G. (2021, February 10). What COVID-19 has done to our well-being, in 12 charts. *Harvard Business Review.* https://hbr.org/2021/02/what-covid-19-has-done-to-our-well-being-in-12-charts

77. Lazarus, R. S. (2006). Emotions and interpersonal relationships: Toward a person-centered conceptualization of emotions and coping. *Journal of Personality, 74*(1), 9–46. Teixeira, R. J., Applebaum, A. J., Bhatia, S., & Brandão, T. (2018). The impact of coping strategies of cancer caregivers on psychophysiological outcomes: An integrative review. *Psychology Research and Behavior Management, 11*, 207.

78. Ibid.

79. Bihary, M. (2021, January 11). 7 ways to de-stress when you can't go outside. *Harvard Business Review.* https://hbr.org/2021/01/7-ways-to-de-stress-when-you-cant-go-outside

80. Curtin, M. (2017, May 30). Neuroscience says listening to this song reduces anxiety by up to 65 percent. *Inc.* https://www.inc.com/melanie-curtin/neuroscience-says-listening-to-this-one-song-reduces-anxiety-by-up-to-65-percent.html

81. American Psychological Association. (2020, May). *Stress in the time of COVID-19* (Vol. 1). https://www.apa.org/news/press/releases/stress/2020/stress-in-america-covid.pdf

82. Luthans, F., Youssef, C. M., & Avolio, B. J. (2007). *Psychological capital: Developing the human competitive edge* (Vol. 198). Oxford University Press.

83. Maykrantz, S. A., Nobiling, B. D., Oxarart, R. A., Langlinais, L. A., & Houghton, J. D. (2021). Coping with the crisis: The effects of psychological capital and coping behaviors on perceived stress. *International Journal of Workplace Health Management, 14*(6), 650–665.

84. Jones, P., & Drummond, P. (2022, February 2). Construction and evaluation of a mindfulness-based quality of life and well-being program (MQW) in a randomized trial. *Current Psychology*, 1–22.

85. Meister, J. (2021, August 4). *The future of work is employee well-being.* Forbes. https://www.forbes.com/sites/jeannemeister/2021/08/04/the-future-of-work-is-worker-well-being/?sh=75af5094aed0

86. Ibid.

87. Ibid.

88. Ibid.

89. Ibid.

90. Ibid.

91. Ibid.

92. Ibid.

93. Ibid.

94. Comparably. (2020, October 12). *Happiest employees 2020.* https://www.comparably.com/news/happiest-employees-2020/

95. Chacko, E. (2020, July 27). *Eric Yuan's leadership lessons for building lasting enterprise value.* Entrepreneur & Innovation Exchange. https://eiexchange.com/content/eric-yuans-leadership-lessons-for-building-lasting-enterprise-va

96. Liu, J. (2020, November 3). *Zoom has the happiest employees of 2020—here's why.* CNBC Make It. https://www.cnbc.com/2020/11/03/zoom-has-the-happiest-employees-of-2020heres-why.html

97. Subotovsky, S. (n.d.). *The secrets of Zoom's success.* Emergence Capital. https://www.emcap.com/thoughts/CEO-Eric-Yuan-on-the-secrets-of-zooms-success/

98. Feifer, J. (2020, December). Zoom into the future. *Entrepreneur, 48*(7), 58.

99. Zoom: A best place to work in 2021! (2021, January 22). *Zoom Blog.* https://blog.zoom.us/zoom-best-place-to-work-2021/

100. Krigsman, M. (Host). (2018, December 17). Customer experience with Eric Yuan CEO Zoom Video Communications (No. 321) [Video podcast episode]. In *CXOTalk*. https://www.youtube.com/watch?v=-6bSx6g_eW0

101. Yuan, E. (2019, September 11). How to be an empathetic leader [Video presentation]. https://www.youtube.com/watch?v=xeZEixpzqpo

102. Entrepreneur. (2021, April 21). *13 leadership lessons from Zoom founder and CEO Eric Yuan.* https://www.entrepreneur.com/article/368550

CHAPTER 6

1. Investopedia. (n.d.). *A look at Coca-Cola's advertising expenses (KO, PEP).* http://www.investopedia.com/articles/markets/081315/look-cocacolas-advertising-expenses.asp

2. Rovell, D. (2011). *AriZona's Arnold Palmer brand aiming to top Snapple.* CNBC. http://www.cnbc.com/id/45614646

3. Fulton, W. (2016). *Why AriZona iced tea is cheaper than water.* Thrillist. https://www.thrillist.com/drink/nation/arizona-iced-tea-price-don-vultaggio-interview

4. Rossen, J. (2016, November 16). *Why is AriZona Iced Tea cheaper than water?* Mental Floss. http://mentalfloss.com/article/88735/why-arizona-iced-tea-cheaper-water

5. Fulton, W. (2016). *Why AriZona iced tea is cheaper than water.* Thrillist. https://www.thrillist.com/drink/nation/arizona-iced-tea-price-don-vultaggio-interview

6. Rossen, J. (2016, November 16). *Why is AriZona iced tea cheaper than water?* Mental Floss. http://mentalfloss.com/article/88735/why-arizona-iced-tea-cheaper-water

7. Ibid.

8. Fulton, W. (2016). *Why AriZona iced tea is cheaper than water.* Thrillist. https://www.thrillist.com/drink/nation/arizona-iced-tea-price-don-vultaggio-interview

9. DeVon, C. (2022, October 13). *AriZona Iced Tea CEO vows to keep the 99-cent price tag "for as long as we can."* CNBC. https://www.cnbc.com/2022/10/13/arizona-iced-tea-ceo-vows-to-keep-99-cent-price-tag.html

10. Fulton, W. (2016). *Why AriZona iced tea is cheaper than water.* Thrillist. https://www.thrillist.com/drink/nation/arizona-iced-tea-price-don-vultaggio-interview

11. Rossen, J. (2016, November 16). *Why is AriZona iced tea cheaper than water?* Mental Floss. http://mentalfloss.com/article/88735/why-arizona-iced-tea-cheaper-water

12. Forbes Business Council. (2021, June 28). *12 Ways to find what motivates your employees.* Forbes. https://www.forbes.com/sites/forbesbusinesscouncil/2021/06/28/12-ways-to-find-what-motivates-your-employees/?sh=2dbe1fcf78cf

13. Refer to the following for an overview of work motivation theory: Grant, A. M., & Shin, J. (2012). Work motivation: Directing, energizing, and maintaining effort (and research). In R. M. Ryan (Ed.), *Oxford handbook of motivation* (pp. 505–519). Oxford University Press; Kanfer, R. (2012). Work motivation: Theory, practice, and future directions. In S. W. J. Kozlowski (Ed.), *The Oxford handbook of organizational psychology* (Vol. 1, pp. 455–495). Oxford University Press; Kanfer, R., Frese, M., & Johnson, R. E. (2017, March). Motivation related to work: A century of progress. *Journal of Applied Psychology, 102*(3), 338–355.

14. Kanfer, R. (1990). Motivation theory and industrial and organizational psychology. In M. D. Dunnette (Ed.), *Handbook of industrial and organizational psychology* (Vol. 1., 2nd ed., pp. 75–130). Consulting Psychologists Press.

15. Kanfer, R., Frese, M., & Johnson, R.E. (2017, March). Motivation related to work: A century of progress. *Journal of Applied Psychology, 102*(3), 338–355.

16. Maslow, A. H. (1943, July). A theory of human motivation. *Psychological Review, 50*(4), 370–396.

17. Mahmoud, W. A., & Bridwell, L. G. (1976, April). Maslow reconsidered: A review of research on the need, hierarchy theory. *Organizational Behavior and Human Performance, 15*(2), 212–240. Harrigan, W. J., & Commons, M. L. (2015, April). Replacing Maslow's needs hierarchy with an account based on stage and value. *Behavioral Development Bulletin, 20*(1), 24–31.

18. Ibid.

19. Alderfer, C. P. (1969). An empirical test of a new theory of human needs. *Organizational Behavior and Human Performance, 4*(2), 142–175. Shin, H.-J., & Kim, J.-I. (2019). Meaning of happiness based on ERG theory in middle-aged Korean women. *Korean Journal of Women Health Nursing, 25*(3), 315–328. Schneider, B., & Alderfer, C. P. (1973, December). Three studies of measures of need satisfaction in organizations. *Administrative Science Quarterly, 18*(4), 489–505.

20. Herzberg, F., Mausner, B., & Snyderman, B. B. (1959). *The motivation to work* (2nd ed.). Wiley. Herzberg, F. (2003, January). One more time: How do you motivate employees? *Harvard Business Review, 81*(1), 87–96. Zhang, X., Jinpeng, X., & Khan, F. (2020). The influence of social media on employee's knowledge sharing motivation: A two-factor theory perspective. *SAGE Open, 10*(3), 2158244020942495.

21. Ibid.

22. Leadership-Central.com. (n.d.). *Two factor theory: Herzberg's motivation theory.* http://www.leadership-central.com/two-factor-theory.html#axzz3YDaoZUtX

23. King, N. (1970, July). Clarification and evaluation of the two-factor theory of job satisfaction. *Psychological Bulletin, 74*(1), 18–31. Wall, T. D., & Stephenson, G. M. (1970, September). Herzberg's two-factor theory of job attitudes: A critical evaluation and some fresh evidence. *Industrial Relations Journal, 1*(3), 41–65. Furnham, A., Eracleous, A., & Chamorro-Premuzic, T. (2009). Personality, motivation and job satisfaction: Hertzberg meets the big five. *Journal of Managerial Psychology, 24*(8),765–779. Holmberg, C., Caro, J., & Sobis, I. (2018). Job satisfaction among Swedish mental health nursing personnel: Revisiting the two-factor theory. *International Journal of Mental Health Nursing, 27*(2), 581–592.

24. McClelland, D. C. (1961). *The achieving society.* Van Nostrand. McClelland, D. C. (1975). *Power: The inner experience.* Irvington. Harrell, A. M., & Stahl, M. J. (1981, April). A behavioral decision theory approach for measuring McClelland's trichotomy of needs. *Journal of Applied Psychology,66*(2), 242–247. Liu, Y.-S., & Arendt, S. W. (2016, June). Development and validation of a work motive measurement scale. *International Journal of Contemporary Hospitality Management,28*(4),700–716.

25. Zalis, S. (2021, May 25). *Black female entrepreneurs are launching more businesses than ever: Here's what they need to help them mature.* Forbes. https://www.forbes.com/sites/shelleyzalis/2021/05/25/black-female-entrepreneurs-are-launching-more-businesses-than-ever-heres-what-they-need-to-help-them-mature/?sh=fac90376bc0c

26. Kohler, L. (2021, March 29). *Does money really mitigate burnout?* Forbes. https://www.forbes.com/sites/lindsaykohler/2021/03/29/does-money-really-mitigate-burnout/?sh=520e60821a0f

27. Gerdeman, Dina, G. (2019, January 28). Forget cash, here are better ways to motivate employees. *Harvard Business School Working Knowledge.* https://hbswk.hbs.edu/item/forget-cash-here-are-better-ways-to-motivate-employees

28. Perkbox. (n.d.). *Employee recognition guide: 16 employee recognition examples that show appreciation.* https://www.perkbox.com/uk/guide/employee-recognition/examples

29. Rynes, S. L., Gerhart, B., & Parks, L. (2005, February). Personnel psychology: Performance evaluation and pay for performance. *Annual Review of Psychology, 56*(1), 571–600.

30. Pink, D. H. (2009). *Drive: The surprising truth about what motivates us.* Riverhead Books.

31. Ariely, D., Gneezy, U., Loewenstein, G., & Mazar, N. (2009, April). Large stakes and big mistakes. *Review of Economic Studies, 76*(2), 451–469.

32. Latham, G. P., & Locke, E. A. (1979, September). Goal setting—a motivational technique that works. *Organizational Dynamics, 8*(2), 68–80. Locke, E. A., & Latham, G. P. (2002, September). Building a practically useful theory of goal setting and task motivation: A 35-year odyssey. *American Psychologist, 57*(9), 705–717. Locke, E. A., & Latham, G. P. (1990). *A theory of goal setting and task performance.* Prentice Hall. Epton, T., Currie, S., & Armitage, C. J. (2017, December). Unique effects of setting goals on behavior change: Systematic review and meta-analysis. *Journal of Consulting and Clinical Psychology, 85*(12), 1182–1198.

33. Gregory, J. B., & Levy, P. E. (2015). How feedback and goals drive behavior: Control theory. In J. B. Gregory & P. Levy (Eds.), *Using feedback in organizational consulting* (pp. 21–30). American Psychological Association. Clayton, M., & Nesnidol, S. (2017, April). Reducing electricity use on campus: The use of prompts, feedback, and goal setting to decrease excessive classroom lighting. *Journal of Organizational Behavior Management,37*(2), 196–206. Neubert, M. J. (1998). The value of feedback and goal setting over goal setting alone and potential moderators of this effect: A meta-analysis. *Human Performance,11*(4), 321–335.

34. Locke, E. A., & Latham, G. P. (1990). *A theory of goal setting and task performance.* Prentice Hall. Latham, G. P., & Baldes, J. J. (1975, February). The "practical significance" of Locke's theory of goal setting. *Journal of Applied Psychology, 60*(1), 122–124. Kleingeld, A., van Mierlo, H., & Arends, L. (2011). The effect of goal setting on group performance: A meta-analysis. *Journal of Applied Psychology, 96*(6), 1289–1304.

35. Ibid.

36. *25 entrepreneurs explain the best way to get out of one's comfort zone.* (n.d.). CBNation. https://rescue.ceoblognation.com/2021/11/15/25-entrepreneurs-explain-the-best-ways-to-get-out-of-ones-comfort-zone/

37. Locke, E. A., Latham, G. P., & Erez, M. (1988, January 1). The determinants of goal commitment. *Academy of Management Review,13*(1), 23–39. Swaim, J., & Henley, A. (2017, February). The use of influence tactics and outcome valence on goal commitment for assigned student team projects. *Journal of Management Education, 41*(1), 118–145.

38. Pira, A. (2020, January 16). *Why it's important for companies to celebrate success.* Forbes Books. https://forbesbooks.com/why-its-important-for-companies-to-celebrate-success/

39. Clear, J. (n.d.). *The Goldilocks rule: How to stay motivated in life and business.* https://jamesclear.com/goldilocks-rule

40. Erez, M. (1977, October). Feedback: A necessary condition for the goal setting–performance relationship. *Journal of Applied Psychology,62*(5), 624–627. Kim, J. S., & Hamner, W. C. (1976, February). Effect of performance feedback and goal setting on productivity and satisfaction in an organizational setting. *Journal of Applied Psychology,61*(1), 48–57. Wack, S. R., Crosland, K. A., & Miltenberger, R. G. (2014, Spring). Using goal setting and feedback to increase weekly running distance. *Journal of Applied Behavior Analysis,47*(1),181–185.

41. Forbes Coaches Council. (2021, May 27). *How to encourage candid employee feedback: 14 tips for CEOs.* Forbes. https://www.forbes.com/sites/forbescoachescouncil/2021/05/27/how-to-encourage-candid-employee-feedback-14-tips-for-ceos/?sh=34c1c792407c

42. Latham, G. P., & Seijts, G. H. (1999, July). The effects of proximal and distal goals on performance on a moderately complex task. *Journal of Organizational Behavior, 20*(4), 421–429. Latham, G. P., & Locke, E. A. (2007). New developments in and directions for goal-setting research. *European Psychologist,12*(4), 290–300. Ford, R. C. (2017, May). Combining performance, learning, and behavioral goals to match job with person: Three steps to enhance employee performance with goal setting. *Business Horizons, 60*(3), 345–352.

43. Adams, J. S. (1963, November). Towards an understanding of inequity. *Journal of Abnormal and Social Psychology, 67*(5), 422–436. Polk, D. M. (2011). Evaluating fairness: Critical assessment of equity theory. In D. Chadee (Ed.), *Theories in social psychology* (pp. 163–190). Wiley-Blackwell. Ryan, J. C. (2016, May). Old knowledge for new impacts: Equity theory and workforce nationalization. *Journal of Business Research, 69*(5), 1587–1592.

44. Greenberg, J. (1989, March). Cognitive reevaluation of outcomes in response to underpayment inequity. *Academy of Management Journal,32*(1), 174–184.

45. Thibaut, J. (1950). An experimental study of the cohesiveness of underprivileged groups. *Human Relations,3*, 251–278.

46. Colquitt, J. A., Conlon, D. E., Wesson, M. J., Porter, C. O., & Ng, K. Y. (2001, June). Justice at the millennium: A meta-analytic review of 25 years of organizational justice research. *Journal of Applied Psychology, 86*(3), 425–445. Greenberg, J., & Colquitt, J. A. (2005). *Handbook of organizational justice.* Erlbaum. Graso, M., Camps, J., Strah, N., & Brebels, L. (2020). Organizational justice enactment: An agent-focused review and path forward. *Journal of Vocational Behavior, 116*, 103296.

47. Wong, K. (2020, September 22). *9 tips for building trust in the workplace.* Achievers. https://www.achievers.com/blog/building-trust-workplace/

48. UN Women. (2020, September 14). *Explainer: Everything you need to know about pushing for equal pay.* https://www.unwomen.org/en/news/stories/2020/9/explainer-everything-you-need-to-know-about-equal-pay

49. Fleischman, E. (2015, August 4). The dangers of playing favorites at work. *Fortune.* http://fortune.com/2015/08/04/favoritism-careers-leadership/

50. Wiles, R. (2017, April 20). *U-Haul's Shoen is ASU's executive of the year.* AZCentral. https://www.azcentral.com/story/money/business/2017/04/20/u-haul-s-shoen-asus-executive-year/100622936/

51. Konrad, A. (2021, November 1). *VC firm 11.2 capital raises $101 million to back more "deep tech" companies like ginkgo bioworks and hinge health.* Forbes. https://www.forbes.com/sites/alexkonrad/2021/11/01/112-capital-raises-101-million-to-back-deep-tech-like-ginkgo-bioworks/?sh=6e2be3222916

52. Knight, R. (2020, April 20). How to talk to your team when the future is uncertain. *Harvard Business Review.* https://hbr.org/2020/04/how-to-talk-to-your-team-when-the-future-is-uncertain

53. Greenberg, J. (1990, October). Employee theft as a reaction to underpayment inequity: The hidden

cost of pay cuts. *Journal of Applied Psychology, 75*(5), 561–568.

54. Vroom, V. H. (1964). *Work and motivation*. Wiley. Matsui, T., & Terai, T. (1975, April). A cross-cultural study of the validity of the expectancy theory of work motivation. *Journal of Applied Psychology, 60*(2), 263–265. Barba-Sánchez, V., & Atienza-Sahuquillo, C. (2017, December). Entrepreneurial motivation and self-employment: Evidence from expectancy theory. *International Entrepreneurship and Management Journal, 13*(4), 1097–1115.
55. Ellingson, J. E., & McFarland, L. A. (2011, September). Understanding faking behavior through the lens of motivation: An application of VIE theory. *Human Performance, 24*(4), 322–337.
56. Georgiadis, C. (2021, January 28). *Women of the C-suite: Maxeme Tuchman of Caribu on the five things you need to succeed as a senior executive.* Medium. https://medium.com/authority-magazine/women-of-the-c-suite-maxeme-tuchman-of-caribu-on-the-five-things-you-need-to-succeed-as-a-senior-9ad909ed5457
57. Weiner, R. (n.d.). *Cuba virtual Jewish history tour.* Jewish Virtual Library. https://www.jewishvirtuallibrary.org/cuba-virtual-jewish-history-tour
58. Thomas, J. (2021, October–November). 100 women of impact. *Entrepreneur.*
59. Kriese, E. (2020, October 15). Maxeme Tuchman drew from her "past lives" to create Caribu. *The Keyword.* https://blog.google/outreach-initiatives/diversity/caribu-pop-up-magazine/
60. Caribu. (n.d.). *Caribu: Playtime is calling.* https://caribu.com/team/
61. Rebel One. (2020, June 10). Founder series—Maxeme Tuchman, CEO + Co-Founder, Caribu.com—RBL1 Live [Video interview]. https://www.youtube.com/watch?v=u9blxpjRCOQ
62. Harvard Business School Alumni. (2020, May 20). *Keeping families connected.* https://www.alumni.hbs.edu/stories/Pages/story-bulletin.aspx?num=7368
63. Georgiadis, C. (2021, January 28). *Women of the C-suite: Maxeme Tuchman of Caribu on the five things you need to succeed as a senior executive.* Medium. https://medium.com/authority-magazine/women-of-the-c-suite-maxeme-tuchman-of-caribu-on-the-five-things-you-need-to-succeed-as-a-senior-9ad909ed5457
64. Thomas, J. (2021, October–November). 100 women of impact. *Entrepreneur.*
65. Rebel One. (2020, June 10). Founder series—Maxeme Tuchman, CEO + Co-Founder, Caribu.com—RBL1 Live [Video interview]. https://www.youtube.com/watch?v=u9blxpjRCOQ
66. Georgiadis, C. (2021, January 28). *Women of the C-suite: Maxeme Tuchman of Caribu on the five things you need to succeed as a senior executive.* Medium. https://medium.com/authority-magazine/women-of-the-c-suite-maxeme-tuchman-of-caribu-on-the-five-things-you-need-to-succeed-as-a-senior-9ad909ed5457

CHAPTER 7

1. America's most loved workplaces 2021. (2021). *Newsweek.* https://www.newsweek.com/americas-most-loved-workplaces-2021
2. Spotify. (2022, February 2). *Spotify technology S.A. announces financial results for fourth quarter 2021.* https://investors.spotify.com/financials/press-release-details/2022/Spotify-Technology-S.A.-Announces-Financial-Results-for-Fourth-Quarter-2021/default.aspx
3. Carbonara, P. (2021, October 22). Spotify is America's most loved workplace. *Newsweek*. https://www.newsweek.com/2021/10/29/spotify-americas-most-loved-workplace-1639982.html
4. Tingvall, J. B. (2017, January 16). People growth = company growth. *Spotify HR Blog.* https://hrblog.spotify.com/2017/01/16/people-growth-company-growth/
5. Hedman, A. (2019, June 13). Show me the incentive! *Spotify HR Blog.* https://hrblog.spotify.com/2019/06/13/show-me-the-incentive/
6. Aubrey, S. (2021, October 10). IVF on us: Spotify leads the way with family benefits for Australian staff. *Sydney Morning Herald*. https://www.smh.com.au/lifestyle/life-and-relationships/ivf-on-us-spotify-leads-the-way-with-family-benefits-for-australian-staff-20211004-p58x54.html
7. Spotify. (2022). *Being here / Life at Spotify.* https://www.lifeatspotify.com/being-here
8. FertilityIQ. (2021). *2021 FertilityIQ workplace index*. https://www.fertilityiq.com/topics/fertilityiq-data-and-notes/fertilityiq-workplace-index
9. Ryan, R. M., & Deci, E. L. (2020). Self-determination theory and the facilitation of intrinsic motivation, social development, and well-being. *American Psychologist, 55*(1), 68. Ryan, R. M., & Deci, E. L. (2020). Intrinsic and extrinsic motivation from a self-determination theory perspective: Definitions, theory, practices, and future directions. *Contemporary Educational Psychology, 61*, 101860.
10. Marinoff, E. (2022, March 22). *Why intrinsic motivation is so powerful (and how to find it).* Lifehack. https://www.lifehack.org/839224/internal-motivation
11. Deci, E. L. (1975). *Intrinsic motivation*. Plenum. Hagger, M. S., Koch, S., & Chatzisarantis, N. L. D. (2015, January). The effect of causality orientations and positive competence-enhancing feedback on intrinsic motivation: A test of additive and interactive effects. *Personality and Individual Differences,72*, 107–111.
12. Locke, E. A., & Schattke, K. (2019). Intrinsic and extrinsic motivation: Time for expansion and clarification. *Motivation Science, 5*(4), 277. Vallerand, R. J., & Ratelle, C. F. (2002). Intrinsic and extrinsic motivation: A hierarchical model. *Handbook of Self-Determination Research, 128*, 37–63.
13. Heather, R. (2020, June 10). *5 Simple ways to make boring tasks more engaging for employees.* CEO Hangout. https://ceohangout.com/ways-make-tasks-engaging-for-employees/
14. Ibid.
15. Deci, E. L., Koestner, R., & Ryan, R. M. (1999). A meta-analytic review of experiments examining the effects of extrinsic rewards on intrinsic motivation. *Psychological Bulletin, 125*(6), 627. Malik, M. A. R., Choi, J. N., & Butt, A. N. (2019). Distinct effects of intrinsic motivation and extrinsic rewards on radical and incremental creativity: The moderating role of goal orientations. *Journal of Organizational Behavior, 40*(9–10), 1013–1026.
16. Deci, E. L. (1975). *Intrinsic motivation.* Plenum. Deci, E. L. (1972, October). The effects of contingent and

noncontingent rewards and controls on intrinsic motivation. *Organizational Behavior and Human Performance, 8*(2), 217–229. Deci, E. L., & Koestner, R. (1999, November). The undermining effect is a reality after all. *Psychological Bulletin, 125*(6), 692. Pritchard, R. D., Campbell, K. M., & Campbell, D. J. (1977, February). Effects of extrinsic financial rewards on intrinsic motivation. *Journal of Applied Psychology, 62*(1), 9–15. Olafsen, A. H., Halvari, H., Forest, J., & Deci, E. L. (2015, March 24). Show them the money? The role of pay, managerial need support, and justice in a self-determination theory model of intrinsic work motivation. *Scandinavian Journal of Psychology, 56*, 447–457.

17. De Meulenaere, K., Boone, C., & Buyl, T. (2015, January). What is the impact of seniority-based pay on labor productivity? *Academy of Management Annual Meeting Proceedings, 2015*(1), 1.

18. Yamazaki, M., & Hirata, N. (2020, July 16). *With shift toward merit-based pay, Japan's Hitachi to drop old ways.* Reuters. https://www.reuters.com/article/us-hitachi-pay-idUSKCN24H3CW

19. Mitchell, R., Schuster, L., & Jin, H. S. (2020). Gamification and the impact of extrinsic motivation on needs satisfaction: Making work fun? *Journal of Business Research, 106*, 323–330.

20. Pierson, D. A., Koziara, K. S., & Johannesson, R. E. (1983, Winter). Equal pay for jobs of comparable worth: A quantified job content approach. *Public Personnel Management, 12*(4), 445. Singh, M., Pandey, J., Sohani, S. S., Jha, J., & Varkkey, B. (2018, April). Job points model: An open source tool to determine the comparable worth of jobs. *Indian Journal of Industrial Relations, 53*(4), 711–716. Patten, T. H., Jr. *Fair pay: The managerial challenge of comparable job worth and job evaluation.* Jossey-Bass. Gittleman, M., & Pierce, B. (2011, January). Inter-industry wage differentials, job content and unobserved ability. *Industrial and Labor Relations Review, 64*(2), 356–374.

21. Ibid.

22. Mitra, A., Gupta, N., & Shaw, J. D. (2011). A comparative examination of traditional and skill-based pay plans. *Journal of Managerial Psychology, 26*(4), 278–296. Murray, B., & Gerhart, B. (2000). Skill-based pay and skill seeking. *Human Resource Management Review, 10*(3), 271–287.Léné, A. (2014, September). Skill-based pay in practice: An interactional justice perspective. *European Journal of Training and Development, 38*(7), 628–641. Richard, J., & Kang, E. (2018). Culture, competencies and compensation: A framework for pay for performance incentives. *American Journal of Management, 18*(4), 33–48.

23. Karcher, I. (2019). *Why more companies are turning to skill-based compensation programs.* Aon. https://humancapital.aon.com/insights/articles/2019/why-more-companies-are-turning-to-skill-based-compensation-programs

24. Vander Ark, T. (2021, June 29). *The rise of skills-based hiring and what it means for education.* Forbes. https://www.forbes.com/sites/tomvanderark/2021/06/29/the-rise-of-skills-based-hiring-and-what-it-means-for-education/?sh=15fd44594fa7

25. Boachie-Mensah, F., & Dogbe, O. D. (2011, December). Performance-based pay as a motivational tool for achieving organisational performance: An exploratory case study. *International Journal of Business and Management, 6*(12), 270–285. Wang, T., Thornhill, S., & Zhao, B. (2018, July). Pay-for-performance, employee participation, and SME performance. *Journal of Small Business Management, 56*(3), 412–434.

26. Fallon, N. (2021, November 19). What is a merit pay increase? *Business News Daily.* https://www.businessnewsdaily.com/16303-merit-pay-increase.html

27. Ibid.

28. Kelly, J. (2021, September 8). *Companies are paying $100,000 sign-on bonuses to attract workers.* Forbes. https://www.forbes.com/sites/jackkelly/2021/09/08/companies-are-paying-100000-sign-on-bonuses-to-attract-workers/?sh=74a01ccf3b9f

29. Ogbonnaya, C., Daniels, K., & Nielsen, K. (2017, January). Does contingent pay encourage positive employee attitudes and intensify work? *Human Resource Management Journal, 27*(1), 94–112.

30. Brooks, C. (2017, January 25). Performance-based pay won't motivate employees as much as you think. *Business News Daily.* https://www.businessnewsdaily.com/9712-performance-based-pay.html

31. Arthur, J. B., & Kim, D-O. (2005, September). Gainsharing and knowledge sharing: The effects of labour–management co-operation. *International Journal of Human Resource Management, 16*(9), 1564–1582. Benson, G. S., & Lawler, E. E., III. (2016). Employee involvement: Research foundations. In M. J. Grawitch & D. W. Ballard (Eds.), *The psychologically healthy workplace: Building a win-win environment for organizations and employees* (pp. 13–33). American Psychological Association.

32. Wallerich, P. (2021, October 4). *Example of successful voluntary gain-sharing plan in a most popular Parisian restaurant: Bouillon Chartier (EN).* CR&M. https://conseilremuneration.fr/example-of-successful-voluntary-gain-sharing-plan-in-a-most-popular-parisian-restaurant-bouillon-chartier-en/?lang=en

33. Florkowski, G. W. (1987, October). The organizational impact of profit sharing. *Academy of Management Review, 12*(4), 622–636. Magnan, M., & St-Onge, S. (2005, June). The impact of profit sharing on the performance of financial services firms. *Journal of Management Studies, 42*(4), 761–791. Lee, J. H., Kubo, Y., Fujiwara, T., Septiana, R. M., Riyanto, S., & Iwasa, Y. (2018, July). Profit sharing as a management strategy for a state-owned teak plantation at high risk for illegal logging. *Ecological Economics, 149*, 140–148.

34. Ettling, J. (1990, August). Winning and losing with ESOPs: The design of effective employee stock ownership plans. *Academy of Management Best Papers Proceedings, 1990*, 269–273. Parrish, S., & PeConga, G. (2015, March). Incentive strategies for employee stock ownership plan-owned companies. *Journal of Financial Service Professionals, 69*(2), 31–33. Bergstein, W. M., & Williams, W. (2013, April). The benefits of employee stock ownership plans. *CPA Journal, 83*(4), 54–57.

35. Cassell, W., Jr. (2021, July 27). *6 Successful companies that are employee-owned.* Investopedia. https://www.investopedia.com/articles/insights/051316/6-successful-companies-are-employeeowned.asp

36. Blasi, J., Kruse, D. L., & Conway, M. (2019, May 30). *Sharing profits and*

ownership with workers not only makes them happier, it benefits the bottom line too. The Conversation. https://theconversation.com/sharing-profits-and-ownership-with-workers-not-only-make-them-happier-it-benefits-the-bottom-line-too-111803

37. Mangla, I. S. (2016, December 9). *Researchers have identified the types of intelligence that make aging workers valuable.Quartz*. https://qz.com/857430/researchers-have-identified-the-types-of-intelligence-that-make-aging-workers-valuable/

38. Ibid.

39. Twenge, J. M., Campbell, S. M., Hoffman, B. J., & Lance, C. E. (2010, September). Generational differences in work values: Leisure and extrinsic values increasing, social and intrinsic values decreasing. *Journal of Management, 36*(5), 1117–1142.

40. Stieg, C. (2021, January 14). *How the pandemic killed your motivation, and 6 simple ways to get it back, according to science*. CNBC. https://www.cnbc.com/2021/01/14/research-how-to-find-motivation-for-work-exercise-and-other-goals.html

41. Ibid.

42. Johns, G., Lin, X. J., & Yongqing, F. (1992, December). Mediating and moderating effects in job design. *Journal of Management, 18*(4), 657. Kempner, T., & Wild, R. (1973, February). Job design and productivity. *Journal of Management Studies, 10*(1), 62–81. Daniels, K., Gedikli, C., Watson, D., Semkina, A., & Vaughn, O. (2017, September). Job design, employment practices and well-being: A systematic review of intervention studies. *Ergonomics, 60*(9), 1177–1196. Cullinane, S.-J., Bosak, J., Flood, P. C., & Demerouti, E. (2014, November). Job design under lean manufacturing and the quality of working life: A job demands and resources perspective. *International Journal of Human Resource Management, 25*(21), 2996–3015.

43. Chung, K. H., & Ross, M. F. (1977, January). Differences in motivational properties between job enlargement and job enrichment. *Academy of Management Review, 2*(1), 113–122. Bishop, R. C., & Hill, J. W. (1971, June). Effects of job enlargement and job change on contiguous but nonmanipulated jobs as a function of workers' status. *Journal of Applied Psychology, 55*(3), 175–181. Dewi, T. R., Pramanik, P. D., & Haryono, J. (2022). Job enlargement on employees' motivation: A case study in a hotel during COVID-19 pandemic. In M. Rahmanita (Ed.), *Current issues in tourism, gastronomy, and tourist destination research* (pp. 274–279). Routledge. Berdicchia, D., Nicolli, F., & Masino, G. (2016). Job enlargement, job crafting and the moderating role of self-competence. *Journal of Managerial Psychology, 31*(2), 318–330.

44. Campion, M. A., Cheraskin, L., & Stevens, M. J. (1994, December). Career-related antecedents and outcomes of job rotation. *Academy of Management Journal, 37*(6), 1518–1542. Jeon, I. S., Jeong, B. Y., & Jeong, J. H. (2016, October). Preferred 11 different job rotation types in automotive company and their effects on productivity, quality and musculoskeletal disorders: Comparison between subjective and actual scores by workers' age. *Ergonomics, 59*(10), 1318–1326. Ravikumar, B., Mohan, K., & Ram, V. S. (2020). The influence of job rotation practices on employee performance, mediation effect of human factor and motivation. *International Journal of Management and Humanities, 4*(6). https://www.ijmh.org/wp-content/uploads/papers/v4i6/F0579024620.pdf

45. Stein, D., Hobson, N., Jachimowicz, J. M., & Whillans, A. (2021, October 13). How companies can improve employee engagement right now. *Harvard Business Review*. https://hbr.org/2021/10/how-companies-can-improve-employee-engagement-right-now

46. Chung, K. H., & Ross, M. F. (1977, January). Differences in motivational properties between job enlargement and job enrichment. *Academy of Management Review, 2*(1), 113–122. Tumi, N. S., Hasan, A. N., & Khalid, J. (2022). Impact of compensation, job enrichment and enlargement, and training on employee motivation. *Business Perspectives and Research, 10*(1), 121–139.

47. Hackman, J. R., & Oldham, G. R. (1980). *Work redesign*. Addison-Wesley. Hackman, J. R., & Oldham, G. R. (1976, August). Motivation through the design of work: Test of a theory. *Organizational Behavior and Human Performance, 16*(2), 250–279. Blanz, M. (2017, January). Employees' job satisfaction: A test of the job characteristics model among social work practitioners. *Journal of Evidence-Informed Social Work, 14*(1), 35–50.

48. Uzialko, A. (2021, November 9). Autonomy keeps employees happy, study finds. *Business News Daily*. https://www.businessnewsdaily.com/75-autonomy-keeps-employees-happy-study-finds.html

49. Brandon, E. M. (2021, December 14). 40% of U.S. produce is wasted. This vertical farming startup is fighting to change that. *Fast Company*. https://www.fastcompany.com/90705741/40-of-produce-is-wasted-this-farming-startup-is-fighting-to-change-that

50. Schmidt, C. (2021, August 20). *How employee feedback has evolved and where it's headed next*. Forbes. https://www.forbes.com/sites/forbeshumanresourcescouncil/2021/08/20/how-employee-feedback-has-evolved-and-where-its-headed-next/?sh=7e063cf9bb52

51. Spreitzer, G. M. (1995, October). Psychological empowerment in the workplace: Dimensions, measurement and validation. *Academy of Management Journal, 38*(5), 1442–1465. Spreitzer, G. M., Kizilos, M. A., & Nason, S. W. (1997, December 15). A dimensional analysis of the relationship between psychological empowerment and effectiveness, satisfaction, and strain. *Journal of Management, 23*(5), 679. Dust, S. B., Resick, C. J., Margolis, J. A., Mawritz, M. B., & Greenbaum, R. L. (2018, February 12). Ethical leadership and employee success: Examining the roles of psychological empowerment and emotional exhaustion. *Leadership Quarterly, 29*(5), 570–583.

52. Ibid.

53. Zhou Koval, C., vanDellen, M. R., Fitzsimons, G. M., & Ranby, K. W. (2015, May). The burden of responsibility: Interpersonal costs of high self-control. *Journal of Personality and Social Psychology, 108*(5), 750–766.

54. Spreitzer, G. M. (1995, October). Psychological, empowerment in the workplace: Dimensions, measurement and validation. *Academy of Management Journal, 38*(5), 1442–1465. Spreitzer, G. M., Kizilos, M. A., & Nason, S. W. (1997, December 15). A dimensional analysis of the relationship between psychological

empowerment and effectiveness, satisfaction, and strain. *Journal of Management, 23*(5), 679. Dust, S. B., Resick, C. J., Margolis, J. A., Mawritz, M. B., & Greenbaum, R. L. (2018, February 12). Ethical leadership and employee success: Examining the roles of psychological empowerment and emotional exhaustion. *Leadership Quarterly, 29*(5), 570–583.

55. Ibid.

56. Cherry, K. (2021, March 15). *Self-determination theory and motivation.* Verywell Mind. https://www.verywellmind.com/what-is-self-determination-theory-2795387

57. Spreitzer, G. M. (1995, October). Psychological empowerment in the workplace: Dimensions, measurement and validation. *Academy of Management Journal, 38*(5), 1442–1465. Spreitzer, G. M., Kizilos, M. A., & Nason, S. W. (1997, December 15). A dimensional analysis of the relationship between psychological empowerment and effectiveness, satisfaction, and strain. *Journal of Management, 23*(5), 679. Dust, S. B., Resick, C. J., Margolis, J. A., Mawritz, M. B., & Greenbaum, R. L. (2018, February 12). Ethical leadership and employee success: Examining the roles of psychological empowerment and emotional exhaustion. *Leadership Quarterly, 29*(5), 570–583.

58. Top 20 female entrepreneurs to look out for in 2021. (2021, June 19). *Entrepreneurs Herald.* https://www.entrepreneursherald.com/blog/top-20-female-entrepreneurs-to-look-out-for-in-2021

59. Baumeister, R. F., & Vohs, K. D. (2002). The pursuit of meaningfulness in life. *Handbook of Positive Psychology, 1*, 608-618.

60. Nikolova, M., & Cnossen, F. (2020, April 8). What makes a job meaningful? *Up Front.* https://www.brookings.edu/blog/up-front/2020/04/08/what-makes-a-job-meaningful/

61. Payscale. (n.d.). *The most meaningful jobs.* https://www.payscale.com/data-packages/most-and-least-meaningful-jobs/most-meaningful-jobs

62. Zucker, R. (2021, July 27). Breaking free from a "9 to 5" culture. *Harvard Business Review.* https://hbr.org/2021/07/breaking-free-from-a-9-to-5-culture

63. Pink, D. H. (2001). *Free agent nation: The future of working for yourself.* Warner Business Books. Pfeffer, J. (2006, October). Why free agents don't feel free. *Business 2.0, 7*(9), 78.

64. Stahl, A. (2021, January 7). *7 fast-growing industries for freelancers.* Forbes. https://www.forbes.com/sites/ashleystahl/2021/01/07/7-fast-growing-industries-for-freelancers/?sh=db1fbef5fef8

65. Hicks, W. D., & Klimoski, R. J. (1981, June). The impact of flextime on employee attitudes. *Academy of Management Journal, 24*(2), 333–341. Spieler, I., Scheibe, S., Stamov-Roßnagel, C., & Kappas, A. (2017, January). Help or hindrance? Day-level relationships between flextime use, work-nonwork boundaries, and affective well-being. *Journal of Applied Psychology, 102*(1), 67–87.

66. Arbon, C. A., Facer, R. L., II, & Wadsworth, L. L. (2012, Fall). Compressed workweeks—Strategies for successful implementation. *Public Personnel Management, 41*(3), 389–405. Baltes, B. B., Briggs, T. E., Huff, J. W., Wright, J. A., & Neuman, G. A. (1999, August). Flexible and compressed workweek schedules: A meta-analysis of their effects on work-related criteria. *Journal of Applied Psychology, 84*(4), 496–513. Hyatt, E., & Coslor, E. (2018, March). Compressed lives: How "flexible" are employer-imposed compressed work schedules? *Personnel Review, 47*(2), 278–293.

67. Daniels, L. (2016). The person's relating to others at work questionnaire (PROWQ): A modified version of the PROQ applied to job sharing at senior levels in the workplace. In A. Kalaitzaki, J. Birtchnell, & M. Newberry (Eds.), *Relating theory—Clinical and forensic applications* (pp. 123–135). Palgrave Macmillan. Williamson, S., Cooper, R., & Baird, M. (2015). Job-sharing among teachers: Positive, negative (and unintended) consequences. *Economic and Labour Relations Review, 26*(3), 448–464.

68. Diab, A. (2016, March 30). 5 Flexible work strategies and the companies that use them. *Fast Company.* https://www.fastcompany.com/3058344/5-flexible-work-strategies-and-the-companies-who-use-them

69. Golden, T. D. (2004, August). Unraveling telecommuting and satisfaction: Towards a relational view. *Academy of Management Proceedings, 2004*, F1–F6. Allen, T. D., Golden, T. D., & Shockley, K. M. (2015, October). How effective is telecommuting? Assessing the status of our scientific findings. *Psychological Science in the Public Interest, 16*(2), 40–68.

70. Guyot, K., & Sawhill, I. V. (2020, April 6). Telecommuting will likely continue long after the pandemic. *Up Front.* https://www.brookings.edu/blog/up-front/2020/04/06/telecommuting-will-likely-continue-long-after-the-pandemic/

71. Wilson, A. (2020, April 29). *11 companies that have adopted unlimited holidays (and what they found).* Workstars. https://www.workstars.com/recognition-and-engagement-blog/2020/04/29/11-companies-that-have-adopted-unlimited-holidays-and-what-they-found/#Roku

72. Gately, B. (n.d.). We tried unlimited holiday for three years. Here's everything that went wrong. *The Workspace.* https://www.charliehr.com/blog/we-tried-unlimited-holiday-heres-everything-that-went-wrong/#comment-4507807547

73. Sephora. (n.d.). *About us.* https://www.sephora.com/beauty/about-us

74. Hakikat, E. (2019, July 11). *Sephora's 5-stage strategy for improving the employee and customer experience.* Inside HR. https://www.insidehr.com.au/sephora-strategy-improving-employee-customer-experience/

75. Hopp, D. (2022, February 23). *14 weird (but true) facts about Sephora. Byrdie.* https://www.byrdie.com/sephora-facts

76. Smith, K. (2019, March 5). *Culture + engagement: How Sephora leverages the intrinsic link to drive purpose and inclusion.* [Keynote]. Qualtrics X4. https://www.qualtrics.com/events/x4-ex-breakthrough-sessions/culture-engagement-how-sephora-leverages-the-intrinsic-link-to-drive-purpose-and-inclusion/

77. Arps, B. (2017, May 5). *11 secrets Sephora employees don't tell you.* Business Insider. https://www.businessinsider.com/heres-what-sephora-employees-dont-tell-you-2017-5

78. Douglas, E. (2020, October 27). Sephora's VP HR: "We belong to something beautiful." *HRD America.* https://www.hcamag.com/us/news/profiles/sephoras-vp-hr-we-belong-to-something-beautiful/237328

CHAPTER 8

1. HQCA Focus. (2021, March 30). *Patients who left without being seen (LWBS) by an emergency department doctor.* https://focus.hqca.ca/emergencydepartments/patients-who-left-without-being-seen-lwbs-by-an-emergency-department-doctor/
2. Thomas Jefferson University Hospital. (n.d.). *Improving ED flow through the UMLN II.* http://www.hpoe.org/Case_Studies/ThomasJEffersonUniversityHospital_EDFlow_UMLNII.pdf. Jefferson Health. (n.d.). *About us.* https://hospitals.jefferson.edu/about-us.html
3. Love, D. B. (2016, May 2). *Thomas Jefferson University Hospital.* Elite Learning. https://www.elitelearning.com/resource-center/nursing/thomas-jefferson-university-hospital/
4. Pecci, A. (n.d.). Lighting the way: Thomas Jefferson University Hospital Emergency Department earns 2017 lantern award. *ENA Connection.* https://www.enaconnection-digital.org/enaconnection/june_2018/MobilePagedArticle.action?articleId=1396562#articleId1396562
5. ER inspector. (2019, September 19). *Thomas Jefferson University Hospital.* https://projects.propublica.org/emergency/hospital/390174
6. Love, D. B. (2016, May 2). *Thomas Jefferson University Hospital.* Elite Learning. https://www.elitelearning.com/resource-center/nursing/thomas-jefferson-university-hospital/
7. Ibid.
8. Ibid.
9. Leonard, K. (2018). *Elements of teamwork in the workplace.* Chron. http://smallbusiness.chron.com/elements-teamwork-workplace-692.html
10. Goodman, P. (2018). *15 advantages of teamwork in the workplace.* ToughNickel. https://toughnickel.com/business/15-Advantages-of-teamwork-in-the-workplace
11. Love, D. B. (2016, May 2). *Thomas Jefferson University Hospital.* Elite Learning. https://www.elitelearning.com/resource-center/nursing/thomas-jefferson-university-hospital/
12. Ibid.
13. For an overview of teams in organizations, see Kozlowski, S. W. J., & Bell, B. S. (2013). Work groups and teams in organizations. In D. K. Freedheim & I. B. Weiner (Eds.), Handbook of psychology: *Vol. 12.* Industrial and organizational psychology (2nd ed., pp. 412–469). Wiley; Croitoru, N., & Salas, E. (2020). Work teams in organizations. In L. L. Koppes (Eds.), *Historical perspectives in industrial and organizational psychology* (p. 249). Routledge.
14. Vergne, J.-P. (2020). Decentralized vs. distributed organization: Blockchain, machine learning and the future of the digital platform. *Organization Theory.* https://doi.org/10.1177/2631787720977052. Seidel, M.-D. L. (2018). Questioning centralized organizations in a time of distributed trust. *Journal of Management Inquiry, 27*(1), 40–44.
15. Katzenbach, J. R., & Smith, D. K. (2005, July). The discipline of teams. Harvard Business Review, *83*(7/8), 162–171. Stewart, G. L., Manz, C. C., & Sims, H. P. (1999). Team work and group dynamics. Wiley.
16. Ibid.
17. Thomson, S. (2015, December 9). *Google's surprising discovery about effective teams.* World Economic Forum. https://www.weforum.org/agenda/2015/12/googles-surprising-discovery-about-effective-teams/
18. Newman, A., Donohue, R., & Eva, N. (2017, September). Psychological safety: A systematic review of the literature. Human Resource Management Review, *27*(3), 521–535.
19. Forbes Business Council. (2020, December 7). *15 ways to promote psychological safety at work.* Forbes. https://www.forbes.com/sites/forbesbusinesscouncil/2020/12/07/15-ways-to-promote-psychological-safety-at-work/?sh=6fc4b2923b27
20. Clark, N. F. (2018, January 19). *How to build the amazing team of your dreams.* Forbes. https://www.forbes.com/sites/womensmedia/2018/01/19/how-to-build-the-amazing-team-of-your-dreams/2/#2d5de1593a5e
21. Karpis, P. (2019, May 30). *3 strategies for building an effective team.* Forbes. https://www.forbes.com/sites/paulinaguditch/2019/05/30/3-strategies-for-building-an-effective-team/?sh=4dc2e6b63898
22. Ibid.
23. Bonebright, D. A. (2010, February). Forty years of storming: A historical review of Tuckman's model of small group development. Human Resource Development International, *13*(1), 111–120. Tuckman, B. W. (1965, June). Developmental sequence in small groups. Psychological Bulletin, *63*(6), 384–399. Tuckman, B. W., & Jensen, M. A. C. (1977, December). Stages of small-group development revisited. Group and Organization Studies, *2*(4): 419–427. Hildebrandt, A., & Marr, J. (2020). Nick Saban–A case study for recruitment methods and application of Tuckman's model of team development. *Global Journal of Business Pedagogy, 4*(1), 214.
24. Gersick, C. J. G. (1988). Time and transition in work teams: Toward a new model of group development. Academy of Management Journal, *31*(1), 9–41. Gersick, C. J. G. (1991, January). Revolutionary change theories: A multilevel exploration of the punctuated equilibrium paradigm. Academy of Management Review, *16*(1), 10–36. Gersick, C. (2020). Reflections on revolutionary change. *Journal of Change Management, 20*(1), 7–23.
25. Celani, A., & Tasa, K. (2010, August). We're all in this together: Examining associations between collectivistic group norms, collective efficacy, and team performance. Academy of Management Annual Meeting Proceedings, pp. 1–6. Chatman, J. A., & Flynn, F. J. (2001, October). The influence of demographic heterogeneity on the emergence and consequences of cooperative norms in work teams. Academy of Management Journal, *44*(5), 956–974. De Jong, B. A., & Bijlsma-Frankema, K. M. (2009, August). When and how does norm-based peer control affect the performance of self-managing teams? Academy of Management Annual Meeting Proceedings, pp. 1–6. Gavac, S., Murrar, S., & Brauer, M. (2017). Group perception and social norms. In Social psychology: How other people influence our thoughts and actions (pp. 333–359). Greenwood Press/ABC-CLIO. Taggar, S., & Ellis, R. (2007, April). The role of leaders in shaping formal team norms. Leadership Quarterly, *18*(2), 105–120.
26. Karten, N. (2012, October 17). *How team norms can boost team effectiveness.* TechWell. https://www.techwell.com/techwell-insights/2012/10/how-team-norms-can-boost-team-effectiveness

27. Hunterwalk. (2016, September 3). *Google finds that successful teams are about norms not just smarts.* https://hunterwalk.com/2016/09/03/google-finds-that-successful-teams-are-about-norms-not-just-smarts/

28. Beal, D. J., Cohen, R. R., Burke, M. J., & McLendon, C. L. (2003, December). Cohesion and performance in groups: A meta-analytic clarification of construct relations. Journal of Applied Psychology, *88*(6), 989–1004. Carron, A. V., Eys, M. A., & Burke, S. M. (2007). Team cohesion: Nature, correlates, and development. In D. Lavallee & S. Jowett (Eds.), Social psychology in sport (pp. 91–101). Human Kinetics. Cruwys, T., Gaffney, A. M., & Skipper, Y. (2017). Uncertainty in transition: The influence of group cohesion on learning. In B. Bizumic, K. I. Mavor, & M. J. Platow (Eds.), Self and social identity in educational contexts (pp. 193–208). Routledge.

29. Your project needs a charter. Here's what that means. (2016, November 3). Harvard Business Review. https://hbr.org/2016/11/your-project-needs-a-charter-heres-what-that-means

30. Stagl, K. C., Burke, C. S., Salas, E., & Pierce, L. (2006). Team adaptation: Realizing team synergy. In C. S. Burke, E. Salas, & L. G. Pierce (Eds.), Understanding adaptability: A prerequisite for effective performance within complex environments (pp. 117–141). Elsevier. van Knippenberg, D., Nishii, L. H., & Dwertmann, D. J. G. (2020). Synergy from diversity: Managing team diversity to enhance performance. *Behavioral Science and Policy, 6*(1), 75–92.

31. Personal interview with Derrick Hall, president and CEO of the Arizona Diamondbacks (April 22, 2017).

32. Felps, W., Mitchell, T. R., & Byington, E. (2006, January). How, when, and why bad apples spoil the barrel: Negative group members and dysfunctional groups. Research in Organizational Behavior, *27*, 175–222.

33. Barrick, M. R., Stewart, G. L., Neubert, M. J., & Mount, M. K. (1998, June). Relating member ability and personality to work-team processes and team effectiveness. Journal of Applied Psychology, *83*(3), 377–391.

34. Miner, F. C. (1984, February). Group versus individual decision making: An investigation of performance measures, decision strategies, and process losses/gains. Organizational Behavior and Human Performance, *33*(1), 112–124. Steiner, I. D. (1966). Models for inferring relationships between group size and potential group productivity. Behavioral Science, *11*(4), 273–283. Mejias, R. J. (2007, February). The interaction of process losses, process gains, and meeting satisfaction within technology-supported environments. Small Group Research, *38*(1), 156–194. Feitosa, J., & Salas, E. (2021). Today's virtual teams: Adapting lessons learned to the pandemic context. *Organizational Dynamics, 50*(1), 100777.

35. Ibid.

36. Karau, S. J., & Williams, K. D. (1993). Social loafing: A meta-analytic review and theoretical integration. *Journal of Personality and Social Psychology, 65*(4), 681. Alyahya, M. A., Elshaer, I. A., & Sobaih, A. E. E. (2021). The impact of job insecurity and distributive injustice post COVID-19 on social loafing behavior among hotel workers: Mediating role of turnover intention. *International Journal of Environmental Research and Public Health, 19*(1), 411.

37. Chamorro-Premuzic, T. (2015, March 25). Why group brainstorming is a waste of time. Harvard Business Review. https://hbr.org/2015/03/why-group-brainstorming-is-a-waste-of-time

38. Wu, J., Mei, W., Liu, L., & Ugrin, J. C. (2020). The bright and dark sides of social cyberloafing: Effects on employee mental health in China. *Journal of Business Research, 112*, 56–64. Tandon, A., Kaur, P., Ruparel, N., Ul Islam, J., & Dhir, A. (2021). Cyberloafing and cyberslacking in the workplace: Systematic literature review of past achievements and future promises. *Internet Research, 32*(1), 55–89.

39. Stokel-Walker, C. (2020, February 7). *Cyberloafing: The line between rejuvenating and wasting time.* BBC. https://www.bbc.com/worklife/article/20200206-cyberloafing-the-line-between-rejuvenating-and-wasting-time

40. Ibid.

41. Ibid.

42. Glassman, J., Prosch, M., & Shao, B. (2015). To monitor or not to monitor: Effectiveness of a cyberloafing countermeasure. Information and Management, *52*(2), 170–182.

43. Asch, S. E. (1951). Effects of group pressure upon the modification and distortion of judgments. In H. S. Guetzkow (Ed.), *Groups, leadership and men: Research in human relations* (pp. 177–190). Carnegie Press.

44. Wise, S. (2014, October). Can a team have too much cohesion? The dark side to network density. *European Management Journal, 32*(5), 703–711.

45. Zakrzewski, C. (2016, March 13). The key to getting workers to stop wasting time online. Wall Street Journal. https://www.wsj.com/articles/the-key-to-getting-workers-to-stop-wasting-time-online-1457921545

46. Steinmetz, J., & Pfattheicher, S. (2017, October). Beyond social facilitation: A review of the far-reaching effects of social attention. Social Cognition, *35*(5), 585–599. Williamson, E. G. (1926). Allport's experiments in "social facilitation." Psychological Monographs, *35*(2), 138–143.

47. Kirkman, B. L., Rosen, B., Tesluk, P. E., & Gibson, C. B. (2004, April). The impact of team empowerment on virtual team performance: The moderating role of face-to-face interaction. Academy of Management Journal, *47*(2), 175–192. Malhotra, A., Majchrzak, A., & Rosen, B. (2007, February). Leading virtual teams. Academy of Management Perspectives, *21*(1), 60–70. Montoya-Weiss, M. M., Massey, A. P., & Song, M. (2001, December). Getting it together: Temporal coordination and conflict management in global virtual teams. Academy of Management Journal, *44*(6), 1251–1262. Feitosa, J., & Salas, E. (2021). Today's virtual teams: Adapting lessons learned to the pandemic context. *Organizational Dynamics, 50*(1), 100777.

48. Babu, S. (2021, November 11). *2021 remote work statistics.* Small Business Trends. https://smallbiztrends.com/2021/11/remote-work-statistics.html

49. Steinhorst, C. (2020, October 30). *6 tactics to create high performing virtual teams during shutdown.* Forbes. https://www.forbes.com/sites/curtsteinhorst/2020/10/30/6-tactics-to-create-high-performing-virtual-teams-during-shutdown/?sh=53882d334b04

50. Senior, K. (2019, April 30). *5 successful virtual teams & why they work.* Business2Community. https://www.business2community.com/strategy/5-suc

cessful-virtual-teams-why-they-work-02196454

51. Magpili, N. C., & Pazos, P. (2018, February). Self-managing team performance: A systematic review of multilevel input factors. Small Group Research, *49*(1), 3–33. Neck, C. P., Connerley, M. L., & Manz, C. C. (1997). Toward a continuum of self-managing team development. In M. M. Beyerlein & D. A. Johnson (Eds.), Advances in interdisciplinary studies of work teams (vol. 4, pp. 193–216). Elsevier Science/JAI Press.
52. Stewart, H. (2019, August 27). *16 companies that don't have managers.* Happy. https://www.happy.co.uk/blogs/16-companies-that-don-t-have-managers/
53. Blakeman, C. (2014, July 22). Companies without managers do better by every metric. Inc. https://www.inc.com/chuck-blakeman/companies-without-managers-do-better-by-every-metric.html
54. deLeon, L. (2001, Winter). Accountability for individuating behaviors in self-managing teams. Organization Development Journal, *19*(4), 7–19. Langfred, C. W. (2007, August). The downside of self-management: A longitudinal study of the effects of conflict on trust, autonomy, and task interdependence in self-managing teams. Academy of Management Journal, *50*(4), 885–900.
55. Rosenfield, S., Newell, M., Zwolski, S., Jr., & Benishek, L. E. (2018, May). Evaluating problem-solving teams in K–12 schools: Do they work? American Psychologist, *73*(4), 407–419. Scott, J. T. (Ed.). (2005). Chapter 10: Managing teams and work groups. In Concise handbook of management: A practitioner's approach (pp. 79–84). Routledge.
56. Reynolds, A., & Lewis, D. (2017, March 30). Teams solve problems faster when they're more cognitively diverse. Harvard Business Review. https://hbr.org/2017/03/teams-solve-problems-faster-when-theyre-more-cognitively-diverse
57. Aime, F., Humphrey, S., Derue, D. S., & Paul, J. B. (2014, April). The riddle of heterarchy: Power transitions in cross-functional teams. Academy of Management Journal, *57*(2), 327–352. Boroș, S., van Gorp, L., Cardoen, B., & Boute, R. (2017, March). Breaking silos: A field experiment on relational conflict management in cross-functional teams. Group Decision and Negotiation, *26*(2), 327–356.
58. Organ, C., & Bottorff, C. (2021, December 17). *What are cross-functional teams? Everything you need to know.* Forbes. https://www.forbes.com/advisor/business/cross-functional-teams/
59. Taras, V., Baack, D., Caprar, D., Jiménez, A., & Froese, F. (2021, June 9). Research: How cultural differences can impact global teams. *Harvard Business Review.* https://hbr.org/2021/06/research-how-cultural-differences-can-impact-global-teams
60. Taras, V., Baack, D., Caprar, D., Dow, D., Froese, F., Jimenez, A., & Magnusson, P. (2019, December). Diverse effects of diversity: Disaggregating effects of diversity in global virtual teams. *Journal of International Management, 25*(4), 100689. https://doi.org/10.1016/j.intman.2019.100689
61. Ibid.
62. Ibid.
63. SHRM. (2015, November 30). *Understanding workplace cultures globally.* https://www.shrm.org/resourcesandtools/tools-and-samples/toolkits/pages/understandingworkplaceculturesglobally.aspx
64. Bennett, M. J., & Hammer, M. (2017). A developmental model of intercultural sensitivity. In Y. Kim (Ed.), *The international encyclopedia of intercultural communication* (vol. 1, issue 10). Wiley. Hernandez, F., & Kose, B. W. (2012, July). The developmental model of intercultural sensitivity: A tool for understanding principals' cultural competence. *Education and Urban Society, 44*(4), 512–530.
65. Chin, T., Meng, J., Wang, S., Shi, Y., & Zhang, J. (2022, January). Cross-cultural metacognition as a prior for humanitarian knowledge: When cultures collide in global health emergencies. *Journal of Knowledge Management, 26*(1), 88–101. Chua, R. Y. J., Morris, M. W., & Mor, S. (2012, July). Collaborating across cultures: Cultural metacognition and affect-based trust in creative collaboration. *Organizational Behavior and Human Decision Processes, 118*(2), 116–131. Mor, S., Morris, M., & Joh, J. (2013, September). Identifying and training adaptive cross-cultural management skills: The crucial role of cultural metacognition. *Academy of Management Learning & Education, 12*(3), 453–475.
66. Wood, L. (2021, October 1). *Global cross-cultural training market poised to grow by $1.46 billion during 2021–2025—ResearchAndMarkets.com.* Business Wire. https://www.businesswire.com/news/home/20211001005606/en/Global-Cross-Cultural-Training-Market-Poised-to-Grow-by-1.46-Billion-During-2021-2025---ResearchAndMarkets.com
67. See, for example, Hackman, J. R. (1987). The design of work teams. In J. W. Lorsch (Ed.), Handbook of organizational behavior (pp. 315–342). Prentice Hall; Ilgen, D. R., Hollenbeck, J. R., Johnson, M., & Jundt, D. (2005, February). Teams in organizations: From input-process-output models to IMOI models. Annual Review of Psychology, *56*(1), 517–543; McGrath, J. E. (1964). Social psychology: A brief introduction. Rinehart and Winston; Stock, R. M. (2014, May). How should customers be integrated for effective interorganizational NPD teams? An input-process-output perspective. Journal of Product Innovation Management, *31*(3), 535–551.
68. Stewart, G. L., Manz, C. C., & Sims, H. P. (1999). Team work and group dynamics. Wiley. Thompson, J. D. (1967). Organizations in action: Social science bases of administrative theory. McGraw-Hill.
69. Daft, R. L. (2015). Organization theory and design. Cengage.
70. Chakravarty, A. K. (2014). Supply chain transformation: Evolving with emerging business paradigms. Springer.
71. Daft, R. L. (2015). Organization theory and design. Cengage.
72. Potter, J. (2020, April 27). *The ideal team size at work may be smaller than you think.* Forbes. https://www.forbes.com/sites/jaimepotter/2020/04/27/the-ideal-team-size-at-work-may-be-smaller-than-you-think/?sh=7552094f630a
73. Ibid.
74. Barry, B., & Stewart, G. L. (1997, February). Composition, process, and performance in self-managed groups: The role of personality. Journal of Applied Psychology, *82*(1), 62–78.
75. Peeters, M. A. G., Van Tuijl, H. F. J. M., Rutte, C. G., & Reymen, I. M. M. J.

(2006, August). Personality and team performance: A meta-analysis. European Journal of Personality, *20*(5), 377–396.

76. Schneider, B. (1987, September). The people make the place. Personnel Psychology, *40*(3), 437–453. Schneider, B., Goldstein, H. W., & Smith, D. B. (1995, Winter). The ASA framework: An update. Personnel Psychology, *48*(4), 747–773.
77. Bretz, R. D., Jr., Ash, R. A., & Dreher, G. F. (1989, September). Do people make the place? An examination of the attraction-selection-attrition hypothesis. Personnel Psychology, *42*(3), 561–581. Butler, B. S., Bateman, P. J., Gray, P. H., & Diamant, E. I. (2014, September). An attraction-selection-attrition theory of online community size and resilience. MIS Quarterly, *38*(3), 699–728. Ployhart, R. E., Weekley, J. A., & Baughman, K. (2006, August). The structure and function of human capital emergence: A multilevel examination of the attraction-selection-attrition model. Academy of Management Journal, *49*(4), 661–677. Schneider, B., Smith, D. B., & Paul, M. C. (2001). P-E fit and the attraction-selection-attrition model of organizational functioning: Introduction and overview. In H. Thierry, M. Erez, & U. Kleinbeck (Eds.), Work motivation in the context of a globalizing economy (pp. 231–246). Erlbaum.
78. Landry, L. (2020, March 5). *Why managers should involve their team in the decision-making process.* Harvard Business School Online. https://online.hbs.edu/blog/post/team-decision-making
79. Ibid.
80. Gregersen, H. (2018, March). Better brainstorming. Harvard Business Review, *96*(2), 64–71. Litchfield, R. C. (2008, July). Brainstorming reconsidered: A goal-based view. Academy of Management Review, *33*(3), 649–668. Taylor, D. W., Berry, P. C., & Block, C. H. (1958, June). Does group participation when using brainstorming facilitate or inhibit creative thinking? Administrative Science Quarterly, *3*(1), 23–47.
81. Markman, A. (2017, May 18). Your team is brainstorming all wrong. Harvard Business Review. https://hbr.org/2017/05/your-team-is-brainstorming-all-wrong
82. Ibid.
83. Lafargue, V. (2016, June 20). How to brainstorm like a Googler. Fast Company. https://www.fastcompany.com/3061059/how-to-brainstorm-like-a-googler
84. Nichols, M. (2021, January 27). *Three ways digital brainstorming can be better than in-person.* Forbes. https://www.forbes.com/sites/forbesbusinesscouncil/2021/01/27/three-ways-digital-brainstorming-can-be-better-than-in-person/?sh=72e6f73a6219
85. Delbecq, A. L., & Van de Ven, A. H. (1971, July/August). A group process model for problem identification and program planning. Journal of Applied Behavioral Science, *7*(4), 466–491. Foth, T., Efstathiou, N., Vanderspank-Wright, B., Ufholz, L.-A., Dütthorn, N., Zimansky, M., & Humphrey-Murto, S. (2016, August). The use of Delphi and nominal group technique in nursing education: A review. International Journal of Nursing Studies, *60*, 112–120. Van de Ven, A. H., & Delbecq, A. L. (1974, December). The effectiveness of nominal, Delphi, and interacting group decision making processes. Academy of Management Journal, *17*(4), 605–621.
86. Ibid.
87. For detailed discussions of groupthink, see Janis, I. L. (1971, November). Groupthink. Psychology Today, *5*(6), 43–46, 74–76. Janis, I. L. (1972). Victims of groupthink: A psychological study of foreign-policy decisions and fiascoes. Houghton Mifflin. Janis, I. L. (1982). Groupthink: Psychological studies of policy decisions and fiascoes. Houghton Mifflin. DiPierro, K., Lee, H., Pain, K. J., Durning, S. J., & Choi, J. J. (2022). Groupthink among health professional teams in patient care: A scoping review. *Medical Teacher, 44*(3), 309–318.
88. Walker, P. (2021, October 11). Cummings right about "false groupthink," says Covid inquiry chair. *The Guardian.* https://www.theguardian.com/world/2021/oct/12/cummings-right-about-false-groupthink-says-covid-inquiry-chair
89. Mitchell, A., Gottfried, J., Kiley, J., & Matsa, K. E. (2014, October 21). *Political polarization & media habits.* Pew Research Center. http://www.journalism.org/2014/10/21/political-polarization-media-habits/
90. Leetaru, K. (2017, December 18). *Why 2017 was the year of the filter bubble?* Forbes. https://www.forbes.com/sites/kalevleetaru/2017/12/18/why-was-2017-the-year-of-the-filter-bubble/#2bf17d3f746b
91. Schkade, D., Sunstein, C. R., & Hastie, R. (2007, June). What happened on deliberation day? California Law Review, *95*(3), 915–940.
92. Blanding, M. (2021, February 8). *The power of groupthink: Study shows why ideas spread in social networks.* BerkeleyHaas. https://newsroom.haas.berkeley.edu/research/the-power-of-groupthink-study-shows-how-easy-it-is-to-influence-social-networks/
93. PepsiCo. (2022). *About the company.* https://www.pepsico.com/about/about-the-company
94. Stringer, H. (2019, September 1). A psychologist at PepsiCo. *Monitor on Psychology, 50*(8), 62.
95. Bigalke, T. (2022, March 29). *5 ways to feel confident using your voice at work.* PepsiCo. https://www.pepsico.com/news/story/5-ways-to-feel-confident-using-your-voice-at-work
96. Daugherty, C. (2021, September 28). 6 ways to step out of your comfort zone. PepsiCo. https://www.pepsico.com/news/story/6-ways-to-step-out-of-your-comfort-zone

CHAPTER 9

1. Arizona State University. (2022). *Facts at a glance: Fall 2021—Metropolitan campuses.* https://uoia.asu.edu/sites/default/files/asu_facts_at_a_glance_-_fall_2021_0.pdf
2. Ibid.
3. Arizona State University. (n.d.). *Plan: Mission statement.* University Office of Evaluation and Educational Effectiveness. https://uoeee.asu.edu/plan-mission-statement
4. Arizona State University. (2014). *ASU ranked among top schools for veterans.* https://asunow.asu.edu/content/asu-ranked-among-top-schools-veterans
5. Arizona State University. (2021, February 5). *ASU climbs to sixth in national research rankings.* ASU News. https://news.asu.edu/20210205-discoveries-asu-climbs-sixth-national-research-rankings
6. Most innovative schools National universities. (n.d.). *U.S. News.* https://w

ww.usnews.com/best-colleges/rankings/national-universities/innovative

7. Arizona State University. (n.d.). *Guiding an innovative, transformative new American university.* http://www.asu.edu/admin/

8. Arizona State University. (2016, September 13). *ASU selected nation's most innovative school for second straight year.* https://asunow.asu.edu/20160912-asu-news-asu-selected-nations-most-innovative-school-second-straight-year

9. Arizona State University. (n.d.). *Starbucks College Achievement Plan.* https://starbucks.asu.edu/

10. Arizona State University. (2016). *Global engagement: Addressing global water crisis with 33 Buckets.* https://starbucks.asu.edu/

11. For overviews, see Fischhoff, B., & Broomell, S. B. (2020). Judgment and decision making. *Annual Review of Psychology, 71,* 331–355; Koopman, P. L., Broekhuijsen, J. W., & Wierdsma, A. F. M. (1998). Complex decision-making in organizations. In P. J. D. Drenth, H. Thierry, & C. Johannes Wolff (Eds.), *Handbook of work and organizational psychology: Organizational psychology* (pp. 357–386). Psychology Press/Erlbaum.

12. Simon, H. A. (1960). *The new science of management decision.* Harper & Brothers. Osmani, J. (2016, March). Group decision-making: Factors that affect group effectiveness. *Academic Journal of Business, Administration, Law & Social Sciences, 2*(1), 23–38.

13. Kannan, P. V. (2021, April 2). *How the pandemic has changed customer service.* Forbes. https://www.forbes.com/sites/forbesbusinesscouncil/2021/04/02/how-the-pandemic-has-changed-customer-service/?sh=77ff32ff2374

14. Thomas, L. (2020, April 27). *Curbside pickup at retail stores surges 208% during coronavirus pandemic.* CNBC. https://www.cnbc.com/2020/04/27/coronavirus-curbside-pickup-at-retail-stores-surges-208percent.html

15. Wickramasinghe, S. (2022, February 19). *15 biggest cybersecurity attacks in 2021.* Privacy Affairs. https://www.privacyaffairs.com/cybersecurity-attacks-in-2021/

16. Foss, N. J., & Weber, L. (2016, January). Moving opportunism to the back seat: Bounded rationality, costly conflict, and hierarchical forms. *Academy of Management Review, 41*(1), 61–79. Lorkowski, J., & Kreinovich, V. (2018). *Bounded rationality in decision making under uncertainty: Towards optimal granularity.* Springer.

17. Ibid.

18. Baumol, W. J. (2004). On rational satisficing. In M. Augier, H. A. Simon, & J. G. March (Eds.), *Models of a man: Essays in memory of Herbert A. Simon* (pp. 57–66). MIT Press. Janis, I. L., & Mann, L. (1996). Satisficing. In J. Billsberry (Ed.), *The effective manager: Perspectives and illustrations* (pp. 157–159). SAGE. Luan, M., Fu, L., & Li, H. (2018, January 15). Do maximizers maximize for others? Self-other decision-making differences in maximizing and satisficing. *Personality and Individual Differences, 121,* 52–56.

19. Hodgkinson, G., & Sadler-Smith, E. (2018). The dynamics of intuition and analysis in managerial and organizational decision making. *Academy of Management Perspectives, 32*(4), 473–492. Julmi, C. (2019). When rational decision-making becomes irrational: A critical assessment and re-conceptualization of intuition effectiveness. *Business Research, 12*(1), 291–314.

20. Dearborn, George V. N. (1916, November). Intuition. *Psychological Review, 23*(6), 465–483. Isenman, L. (2013, Winter). Understanding unconscious intelligence and intuition: "Blink" and beyond. *Perspectives in Biology and Medicine, 56*(1), 148–166.

21. Browne, S. J. (2021, October 2). 4 ways trusting your intuition is a superpower. *Forbes.* https://www.forbes.com/sites/womensmedia/2021/10/02/4-ways-trusting-your-intuition-is-a-superpower/?sh=1cd8efc2c8e6

22. Gigerenzer, G., Hertwig, R., & Pachur, T. (2011). *Heuristics: The foundations of adaptive behavior.* Oxford University Press. Martí, R., Pardalos, P. M., & Resende, M. G. C. (Eds.). (2018). *Handbook of heuristics.* Springer.

23. Chen, C.-S., Cheng, J.-C., Lin, F.-C., & Peng, C.-L. (2017). The role of house money effect and availability heuristic in investor behavior. *Management Decision, 55*(8), 1598–1612. Schwarz, N., & Vaughn, L. N. (2002). The availability heuristic revisited: Ease of recall and content of recall as distinct sources of information. In D. Griffin, D. Kahneman, & T. Gilovich (Eds.), *Heuristics and biases: The psychology of intuitive judgment* (pp. 103–119). Cambridge University Press.

24. Mass, H. (2013, July 8). The odds are 11 million to 1 that you'll die in a plane crash. *The Week.* http://theweek.com/article/index/246552/the-odds-are-11-million-to-1-that-youll-die-in-a-plane-crash

25. Kahneman, D. (2011). *Thinking, fast and slow.* Farrar, Straus and Giroux.

26. Epley, N., & Gilovich, T. (2006, April). The anchoring-and-adjustment heuristic: Why the adjustments are insufficient. *Psychological Science, 17*(4), 311–318. Henrizi, P., Himmelsbach, D., & Hunziker, S. (2021). Anchoring and adjustment effects on audit judgments: Experimental evidence from Switzerland. *Journal of Applied Accounting Research,22*(4), 598–621.

27. Dumm, R., Eckles, D., Nyce, C., & Volkman-Wise, J. (2017, September). Demand for windstorm insurance coverage and the representative heuristic. *Geneva Risk and Insurance Review, 42*(2), 117–139. Nilsson, H., Juslin, P., & Olsson, H. (2008, June). Exemplars in the mist: The cognitive substrate of the representativeness heuristic. *Scandinavian Journal of Psychology, 49*(3), 201–212.

28. Cherry, K. (2021, April 10). *What is the representativeness heuristic?* Verywell Mind. https://www.verywellmind.com/representativeness-heuristic-2795805

29. Stasser, G., & Titus, W. (1987, July). Effects of information load and percentage of shared information on the dissemination of unshared information during group discussion. *Journal of Personality and Social Psychology, 53*(1), 81–93. Palley, A. B., & Soll, J. B. (2019). Extracting the wisdom of crowds when information is shared. *Management Science, 65*(5), 2291–2309.

30. Green, D. W. (1990). Confirmation bias, problem-solving and cognitive models. In J. P. Caverni, J. M. Fabre, & M. Gonzalez (Eds.), *Cognitive biases* (pp. 553–562). North-Holland. Winking, J. (2018, January 17). Exploring the great schism in the social sciences: Confirmation bias and the interpretation of results relating to biological influences on human behavior and psychology. *Evolutionary Psychology, 16*(1). https://journals.sagepub.com/doi/10.1177/1474704917752691

31. Ciampaglia, G. L., & Menczer, F. (2018, June 21). Biases make people vulnerable to misinformation spread by social media. *Scientific American*. https://www.scientificamerican.com/article/biases-make-people-vulnerable-to-misinformation-spread-by-social-media/https://www.scientificamerican.com/article/biases-make-people-vulnerable-to-misinformation-spread-by-social-media/#

32. Buontempo, G., & Brockner, J. (2008, January). Emotional intelligence and the ease of recall judgment bias: The mediating effect of private self-focused attention. *Journal of Applied Social Psychology, 38*(1), 159–172. Weingarten, E., & Hutchinson, J. W. (2018, March). Does ease mediate the ease-of-retrieval effect? A meta-analysis. *Psychological Bulletin, 144*(3), 227–283.

33. Bhattacharya, C., & Jasper, J. D. (2018, April 15). Degree of handedness: A unique individual differences factor for predicting and understanding hindsight bias. *Personality and Individual Differences, 125*, 97–101. Hoffrage, U., Hertwig, R., & Gigerenzer, G. (2011). Hindsight bias: A by-product of knowledge updating? In G. Gigerenzer, R. Hertwig, & T. Pachur (Eds.), *Heuristics: The foundations of adaptive behavior* (pp. 223–241). Oxford University Press. Hoffrage, U., & Hertwig, R. (1999). Hindsight bias: A price worth paying for fast and frugal memory. In G. Gigerenzer, P. M. Todd, & ABC Research Group (Eds.), *Simple heuristics that make us smart* (pp. 191–208). Oxford University Press.

34. Chang, V. T., Overall, N. C., Madden, H., & Low, R. S. T. (2018, February 1). Expressive suppression tendencies, projection bias in memory of negative emotions, and well-being. *Emotion, 18*(7), 925–941. Krueger, J. I., & Acevedo, M. (2005). Social projection and the psychology of choice. In M. D. Alicke, D. A. Dunning, & J. Krueger (Eds.), *The self in social judgment* (pp. 17–41). Psychology Press.

35. Kalmanovich-Cohen, H., Pearsall, M. J., & Siegel Christian, J. (2018, April 5). The effects of leadership change on team escalation of commitment. *Leadership Quarterly, 29*(5), 597–608. Staw, B. M. (1997). The escalation of commitment: An update and appraisal. In S. Zur (Ed.), *Organizational decision making* (pp. 191–215). Cambridge University Press.

36. Emich, K. J., & Pyone, J. S. (2018, February 2). Let it go: Positive affect attenuates sunk cost bias by enhancing cognitive flexibility. *Journal of Consumer Psychology, 28*(4), 578–596. Hsuchi, T., & Wallsten, T. S. (2011, August). A query theory account of the effect of memory retrieval on the sunk cost bias. *Psychonomic Bulletin and Review, 18*(4), 767–773.

37. Steele-Johnson, D., & Kalinoski, Z. T. (2014, January). Error framing effects on performance: Cognitive, motivational, and affective pathways. *Journal of Psychology: Interdisciplinary and Applied, 148*(1), 93–111. Enslin, Z., Hall. J. H., & du Toit, E. (in press). The susceptibility of management accountants to framing bias. *Meditari Accountancy Research*.

38. Perera, A. (2021, June 10). *Framing effect.* Simply Psychology. https://www.simplypsychology.org/framing-effect.html

39. Kappel, M. (2018, April 4). *How to encourage employee involvement in decision making.* Forbes. https://www.forbes.com/sites/mikekappel/2018/04/04/how-to-encourage-employee-involvement-in-decision-making/?sh=3cccbc06561c

40. For overviews of creativity in organizations, see Martin, L., & Wilson, N. (Eds.). (2018). *The Palgrave handbook of creativity at work*. Palgrave Macmillan; Kaufman, J. C., & Sternberg, R. J. (Eds.). (2019). *The Cambridge handbook of creativity* (2nd ed.). Cambridge University Press; van Knippenberg, D., & Hirst, G. (2015). A cross-level perspective on creativity at work: Person-in-situation interactions. In C. E. Shalley, J. Zhou, & M. A. Hitt (Eds.), *The Oxford handbook of creativity, innovation, and entrepreneurship* (pp. 225–244). Oxford University Press; Zhou, J., & Hoever, I. J. (2014). Research on workplace creativity: A review and redirection. *Annual Review of Organizational Psychology and Organizational Behavior, 1*, 333–359.

41. For overviews of innovation in organizations, see Anthony, S. D. (2012, January). *The little black book of innovation: How it works, how to do it* (p. 1). *Harvard Business School Press Books*. Neiva, E. R., Mendonça, H., Ferreira, M. C., & Francischeto, L. L. (2017). Innovation in organizations: Main research results and their practical implications. In C. V. Torres, E. R. Neiva, & H. Mendonça (Eds.), *Organizational psychology and evidence-based management: What science says about practice* (pp. 157–185). Springer; Poole, M. S., & Van de Ven, A. (Eds.). (2021). *The Oxford handbook of organizational change and innovation*. Oxford University Press.

42. The 10 most innovative small and mighty companies of 2021. (2021, March 9). *Fast Company*. https://www.fastcompany.com/90600295/small-mighty-most-innovative-companies-2021

43. Kretchmer, H. (2020, June 26). *From dining pods to see-through masks: 6 ways innovations are helping in the pandemic.* World Economic Forum. https://www.weforum.org/agenda/2020/06/inventions-coronavirus-covid19-innovation/

44. Amabile, T. A. (1983, August). The social psychology of creativity: A componential conceptualization. *Journal of Personality and Social Psychology, 45*(2), 357–376. Amabile, T. A. (1998, September). How to kill creativity. *Harvard Business Review, 76*(5), 76–87.

45. Ibid.

46. Ibid.

47. Ibid.

48. Ibid.

49. Alavi, S. H., & Farzam, F. (2019). Surveying the validity characteristics of organizational creativity scale in sport. *Journal of Sport Management and Motor Behavior, 15*(30), 275–287. DiLiello, T. C., & Houghton, J. D. (2008, March). Creative potential and practised creativity: Identifying untapped creativity in organizations. *Creativity and Innovation Management, 17*(1), 37–46.

50. Naiman, L. (2018, February 2). *The secret to finding creative solutions from legendary designers*. Creativity at Work. https://www.creativityatwork.com/do-designers-really-have-a-formula-for-creativity/

51. Amabile, T. M., Conti, R., Coon, H., Lazenby, J., & Herron, M. (1996, October). Assessing the work environment for creativity. *Academy of Management Journal, 39*(5), 1154–1184. DiLiello, T. C., Houghton, J. D., & Dawley, D. (2011, March). Narrowing the creativity gap: The moderating effects of perceived support for creativity. *Journal of Psychology: Interdisciplinary and Applied, 145*(3),

151–172. Zhang, L., Bu, Q., & Wee, S. (2016, November). Effect of perceived organizational support on employee creativity: Moderating role of job stressors. *International Journal of Stress Management, 23*(4), 400–417.

52. Wigert, B., & Robison, J. (2018, December 19). *Fostering creativity at work: Do your managers push or crush innovation?* Gallup. https://www.gallup.com/workplace/245498/fostering-creativity-work-managers-push-crush-innovation.aspx
53. DiLiello, T. C., Houghton, J. D., & Dawley, D. (2011). Narrowing the creativity gap: The moderating effects of perceived support for creativity. *Journal of Psychology, 145*(3), 151–172.
54. Ibid.
55. Jarvenpaa, S. L., & Välikangas, L. (2020). Advanced technology and end-time in organizations: A doomsday for collaborative creativity? *Academy of Management Perspectives, 34*(4), 566–584.
56. Amabile, T. M., Conti, R., Coon, H., Lazenby, J., & Herron. H. (1996). Assessing the work environment for creativity. *Academy of Management Journal, 39*(5), 1154–1184. DiLiello, T. C., Houghton, J. D., & Dawley, D. (2011). Narrowing the creativity gap: The moderating effects of perceived support for creativity. *Journal of Psychology, 145*(3), 151–172.
57. Ibid.
58. Ibid.
59. Farooq, M. (2021, July 8). *9 companies that let your creative side run wild.* Firsthand. https://firsthand.co/blogs/job-search/companies-that-let-your-creative-side-run-wild
60. Love Money. (2021, February 24). *World-changing inventions for 2021 and beyond.* https://www.lovemoney.com/gallerylist/97646/worldchanging-inventions-for-2021-and-beyond
61. Spirer, A. (2020, September 15). *Bridget Levine of Frenchie: "Rise above the imitators by focusing on your brand and not anyone else's."* Medium. https://medium.com/authority-magazine/bridget-levine-of-frenchie-bulldog-be-there-to-lead-the-team-and-show-compassion-they-are-not-4ffacd0b743
62. Daisyme, P. (2020, November 9). 3 innovation strategies for solving "impossible" problems. *Entrepreneur.* https://www.entrepreneur.com/article/358900
63. Knight, K. E. (1967, October). A descriptive model of the intra-firm innovation process. *Journal of Business, 40*(4), 478–496.
64. Baar, S. (2017, January 16). *The 3 types of innovation: Product, process, & business model.* Differential. https://differential.com/insights/the3typesofinnovation/
65. Knight, K. E. (1967, October). A descriptive model of the intra-firm innovation process. *Journal of Business, 40*(4), 478–496.
66. Vermum, F. (2021, June 22). *The first running shoe made from data. Adidas disruptive innovation that changes the shoe game.* Sport and Sustainability International. https://www.sportsustainability.org/news-events/future-shoe
67. Knight, K. E. (1967, October). A descriptive model of the intra-firm innovation process. *Journal of Business, 40*(4), 478–496.
68. Thomas, L. (2021, March 10). *COVID changed how we think of offices. Now companies want their spaces to work as hard as they do.* CNBC. https://www.cnbc.com/2021/03/10/1-year-into-covid-employers-rethink-offices-and-function-matters-most.html
69. Knight, K. E. (1967, October). A descriptive model of the intra-firm innovation process. *Journal of Business, 40*(4), 478–496.
70. Yakowicz, W. (2022, January 27). 6 Effective ways to change your employees' behavior. *Inc.* https://www.inc.com/will-yakowicz/6-ways-you-can-influence-employee-behavior.html
71. Knight, K. E. (1967, October). A descriptive model of the intra-firm innovation process. *Journal of Business, 40*(4), 478–496.
72. Hong, J., Hou, B., Zhu, K., & Marinova, D. (2018, April). Exploratory innovation, exploitative innovation and employee creativity. *Chinese Management Studies, 12*(2), 268–286.
73. Ogburn, W. F. (1957). Cultural lag as theory. *Sociology and Social Research, 41*, 167–174. Langan, D., Schott, N., Wykes, T., Szeto, J., Kolpin, S., Lopez, C., & Smith, N. (2016, January). Students' use of personal technologies in the university classroom: Analysing the perceptions of the digital generation. *Technology, Pedagogy and Education, 25*(1), 101–117.
74. Phelan, D. (2019, November 1). *Google buys Fitbit for $2.1 billion: Here's what it means.* Forbes. https://www.forbes.com/sites/davidphelan/2019/11/01/google-buys-fitbit-for-21-billion-heres-what-it-means/?sh=79465e4d732f
75. McDonald's. (n.d.). *Our history: Ray Kroc & the McDonald's brothers.* https://www.mcdonalds.com/us/en-us/about-us/our-history.html
76. McDonald's. (n.d.). *Franchising overview.* https://corporate.mcdonalds.com/corpmcd/franchising-overview.html
77. Gregory, L. (2017, February 5). *McDonald's operations management, 10 decisions, productivity.* Panmore Institute. http://panmore.com/mcdonalds-operations-management-10-decisions-areas-productivity
78. Ibid.
79. McDonald's. (n.d.). *Our history: Ray Kroc & the McDonald's brothers.* https://www.mcdonalds.com/us/en-us/about-us/our-history.html
80. Gregory, L. (2017, February 5). *McDonald's operations management, 10 decisions, productivity.* Panmore Institute. http://panmore.com/mcdonalds-operations-management-10-decisions-areas-productivity
81. McDonald's. (n.d.). *Brand introduction: McDonald's philosophy and history.* https://m.mcdonalds.co.kr/eng/story/intro/brandhistory.do
82. Bailey, R. (2020, March 30). *How has McDonald's been so successful for so long?* https://www.franchisedirect.com/information/markettrendsfactsaboutfranchising/thesuccessofmcdonalds/8/1111/

CHAPTER 10

1. IBM Archives. (n.d.). *A culture of think.* http://www-03.ibm.com/ibm/history/ibm100/us/en/icons/think_culture/
2. Braswell, S. (2014). From IBM to Google, the birth of company culture. *USA Today.* https://www.usatoday.com/story/money/business/2014/11/22/ozy-ibm-google-company-culture/19345427/
3. IBM Archives. (n.d.). *A culture of think.* http://www-03.ibm.com/ibm/history/ibm100/us/en/icons/think_culture/

4. Forbes. (n.d.). *IBM*. https://www.forbes.com/companies/ibm/?sh=44fea9c39c45

5. IBM. (2001, June 11). *Q: Have any IBM employees ever won the Nobel Prize?* https://www.ibm.com/ibm/history/reference/faq_0000000511.html

6. Alsop, T. (2021, March 12). *IBM revenue 2020*. Statista. https://www.statista.com/statistics/265003/ibms-revenue-since-1999/

7. IBM. (n.d.). *Corporate responsibility at IBM*. https://www.ibm.com/ibm/responsibility/supplychain.shtml

8. King, R. (2011). *IBM: Corporate culture stands in way of enterprise analytics adoption*. ZDNet. http://www.zdnet.com/article/ibm-corporate-culture-stands-in-way-of-enterprise-analytics-adoption/

9. Henley Business Review. (2013, January 21). *Imperilled business machines: The rise and fall and rise of IBM*. https://henleybusinessreview.wordpress.com/tag/restructuring/

10. Ibid.

11. Ibid.

12. IBM. (n.d.). *Supply chain social responsibility*. http://www-3.ibm.com/procurement/proweb.nsf/contentdocsbytitle/United+States~Supply+chain+social+responsibility

13. IBM. (n.d.). *Corporate responsibility at IBM*. https://www.ibm.com/ibm/responsibility/supplychain.shtml

14. For a detailed overviews of ethics in business organizations, see Collins, D., & Kanashiro, P. (2022). *Business ethics* (3rd ed.). SAGE; Johnson, C. E. (2022). *Organizational ethics: A practical approach* (5th ed.). SAGE.

15. Makrygiannis, K. (2020, June 26). *Global businesses divided on implications of COVID-19 crisis for company ethics*. EY.com. https://www.ey.com/en_gl/news/2020/06/global-businesses-divided-on-implications-of-covid-19-crisis-for-company-ethics

16. Ibid.

17. Di Miceli da Silveira, A. (2013, July). The Enron scandal a decade later: Lessons learned? *Homo Oeconomicus, 30*(3), 315–347. Petrick, J. A., & Scherer, R. F. (2003, Spring). The Enron scandal and the neglect of management integrity capacity. *Mid-American Journal of Business, 18*(1), 37–49.

18. Egan, M. (2021, January 15). *Wells Fargo can't seem to escape its troubled past*. CNN. https://edition.cnn.com/2021/01/15/investing/wells-fargo-bank-earnings-scandal/index.html

19. Piper, K. (2020, October 15). *The case for taking AI seriously as a threat to humanity*. Vox. https://www.vox.com/future-perfect/2018/12/21/18126576/ai-artificial-intelligence-machine-learning-safety-alignment

20. Blackman, R. (2020, October 15). A practical guide to building ethical AI. *Harvard Business Review*. https://hbr.org/2020/10/a-practical-guide-to-building-ethical-ai

21. Ibid.

22. See, for example, Linehan, C., & O'Brien, E. (2017, April 8). From telltale signs to irreconcilable struggles: The value of emotion in exploring the ethical dilemmas of human resource professionals. *Journal of Business Ethics, 141*(4), 763–777.

23. Nelson, J. S. (2020, June 3). *5 ethical challenges during COVID-19 that businesses need to meet*. Ethical Systems. https://www.ethicalsystems.org/5-ethical-challenges-during-covid-19-that-businesses-need-to-meet/

24. Smith, I. H., & Kouchaki, M. (2021, November/December). Building an ethical company. *Harvard Business Review*. https://hbr.org/2021/11/building-an-ethical-company

25. Gustafson, A. (2013, Fall). In defense of a utilitarian business ethic. *Business and Society Review, 118*(3), 325–360. Schumann, P. L. (2001, Summer). A moral principles framework for human resource management ethics. *Human Resource Management Review, 11*(1/2), 93. Vearrier, L., & Henderson, C. M. (2021). Utilitarian principlism as a framework for crisis healthcare ethics. *HEC Forum, 33*(1), 45–60.

26. Ibid.

27. Ibid.

28. Bazerman, M. H. (2020, September/October). A new model for ethical leadership. *Harvard Business Review*. https://hbr.org/2020/09/a-new-model-for-ethical-leadership

29. Ibid.

30. Johnson, C. E. (2022). *Organizational ethics: A practical approach* (5th ed.). SAGE.

31. BBC. (2022, January 4). *Elizabeth Holmes: Theranos founder convicted of fraud*. https://www.bbc.com/news/world-us-canada-59734254

32. Johnson, C. E. (2022). *Organizational ethics: A practical approach* (5th ed.). SAGE.

33. Kohlberg, L., & Hersh, R. H. (1977, April). Moral development: A review of the theory. *Theory Into Practice, 16*(2), 53–59.

34. Kohlberg, L. (1963). The development of children's orientations toward a moral order: I. Sequence in the development of moral thought. *Vita Humana, 6*(1–2), 11–33.

35. Heyman, G. D., & Lee, K. (2012). Moral development: Revisiting Kohlberg's stages. In *Developmental psychology: Revisiting the classic studies* (pp. 164–175). SAGE.

36. Josephson Institute. (n.d.). *About Josephson Institute*. http://josephsoninstitute.org/about/

37. CHARACTER COUNTS! (n.d.) *The six pillars of character*. https://charactercounts.org/character-counts-overview/six-pillars/

38. https://charactercounts.org/

39. Ibid.

40. Ibid.

41. CHARACTER COUNTS! (n.d.) *The six pillars of character*. https://charactercounts.org/character-counts-overview/six-pillars/

42. Josephson, M. S., & Hanson, W. (1992). *Making ethical decisions*. Josephson Institute of Ethics.

43. Clark, C. (2021, June 23). *Powerful people are less likely to be understanding when mistakes are made*. Science Daily. https://www.sciencedaily.com/releases/2021/06/210623194032.htm

44. Keltner, D. (2017, October 13). Sex, power, and the systems that enable men like Harvey Weinstein. *Harvard Business Review*. https://hbr.org/2017/10/sex-power-and-the-systems-that-enable-men-like-harvey-weinstein

45. Frank, D., & Kalev, A. (2020, May/June). Why sexual harassment programs backfire. *Harvard Business Review*. https://hbr.org/2020/05/why-sexual-harassment-programs-backfire

46. Rosenblatt, J. (2021, May 23). *Theranos CEO's lavish lifestyle ruled fair*

game for trial. BNN Bloomberg. https://www.bnnbloomberg.ca/theranos-ceo-s-lavish-lifestyle-ruled-fair-game-for-trial-1.1607610#:~:text=%E2%80%8BTheranos%20Inc.,alleged%20fraud%2C%20a%20judge%20ruled

47. Hess, A. J. (2021, September 15). *In 2020, top CEOs earned 351 times more than the typical worker.* CNBC. https://www.cnbc.com/2021/09/15/in-2020-top-ceos-earned-351-times-more-than-the-typical-worker.html

48. Langley, M., & Benioff, M. (2019, October 15). How salesforce closed the pay gap between men and women. *Wired.* https://www.wired.com/story/how-salesforce-closed-pay-gap-between-men-women/

49. Elkind, E. (2021, January 13). *Americans trust CEOs more than their own government, survey finds.* CBS News. https://www.cbsnews.com/news/edelman-trust-barometer-2021-ceo-government/

50. Jiang, Z. (2019, November 14). Why withholding information at work won't give you an advantage. *Harvard Business Review.* https://hbr.org/2019/11/why-withholding-information-at-work-wont-give-you-an-advantage

51. Johanson, M. (2021, August 8). *Research shows that we look more favourably on those whom we see more often. What does that mean for managers in newly hybrid setups?* BBC. https://www.bbc.com/worklife/article/20210804-hybrid-work-how-proximity-bias-can-lead-to-favouritism

52. Ibid.

53. Steinbauer, R., Renn, R. W., Taylor, R. R., & Njoroge, P. K. (2014). Ethical leadership and followers' moral judgment: The role of followers' perceived accountability and self-leadership. *Journal of Business Ethics, 120*(3), 381–392.

54. Popomaronis, T. (2020, August 20). These 11 famously disgraced CEOs have entered the reputation hall of shame. *Entrepreneur.* https://www.entrepreneur.com/slideshow/354739

55. Devi, A. (2020). 10 best companies in customer service & what you can learn from them. *Happy Fox.* https://blog.happyfox.com/10-best-companies-customer-service/#Publix

56. Sunil, P. (2021, May 28). *Most overworked cities in the world 2021: Hong Kong, Singapore and Bangkok top rankings.* Human Resources Online. https://www.humanresourcesonline.net/most-overworked-cities-in-the-world-2021-hong-kong-singapore-and-bangkok-top-rankings

57. Meikle, K. (2019, February). *How does overworking affect physical and mental health?* Passport Health. https://www.passporthealthusa.com/employer-solutions/blog/2019-2-overworking-affect-physical-and-mental-health/

58. Jacobs, E. (2021, December). The future of work. *Financial Times.* https://www.ft.com/content/7202c5d4-fbc9-4ad7-93c2-cb05e6b582e9

59. Goldhill, O. (2016, February 21). *Neuroscientists have found a basis for the "I was just following orders" excuse. Quartz.* https://qz.com/621274/neuroscientists-have-found-a-basis-for-the-i-was-just-following-orders-excuse/

60. Todd, S. (2020, January 24). *The secret to dealing with cynics at work.* Quartz. https://qz.com/work/1790859/how-to-deal-with-cynical-coworkers/

61. Ibid.

62. Ibid.

63. Northern Arizona University. (2016, April 16). *Employees with supportive managers may be less cynical of workplace, but may not feel more loyal to company.* Phys.org. https://phys.org/news/2016-04-employees-cynical-workplace-loyal-company.html

64. Scott, K. A., & Zweig, D. (2016). Understanding and mitigating cynicism in the workplace. *Journal of Managerial Psychology, 31*(2), 552–569.

65. Northern Arizona University. (2016, April 16). *Employees with supportive managers may be less cynical of workplace, but may not feel more loyal to company.* Phys.org. https://phys.org/news/2016-04-employees-cynical-workplace-loyal-company.html

66. Garner, J. T. (2013, February 4). How to communicate dissent at work. *Harvard Business Review.* https://hbr.org/2013/02/how-to-communicate-dissent-at

67. Market Insider. (2019, May 20). *Research finds majority of employees fearful of sharing ideas, opinions & concerns at work.* https://markets.businessinsider.com/news/stocks/research-finds-majority-of-employees-fearful-of-sharing-ideas-opinions-concerns-at-work-1028213831

68. Blair, B. A., & Bligh, M. C. (2018). Looking for leadership in all the wrong places: The impact of culture on proactive followership and follower dissent. *Journal of Social Issues, 74*(1), 129–143.

69. Wheeler, M. (2014, February 17). *Asiana airlines: "Sorry, Captain. You're wrong."* LinkedIn. https://www.linkedin.com/pulse/20140217220032-266437464-asiana-airlines-sorry-captain-you-re-wrong/

70. Market Insider. (2019, May 20). *Research finds majority of employees fearful of sharing ideas, opinions & concerns at work.* https://markets.businessinsider.com/news/stocks/research-finds-majority-of-employees-fearful-of-sharing-ideas-opinions-concerns-at-work-1028213831

71. Brykman, K., & Raver, J. (2021, February 25). *Why employees hesitate to speak up at work—and how to encourage them.* The Conversation. https://theconversation.com/why-employees-hesitate-to-speak-up-at-work-and-how-to-encourage-them-154357

72. Banerjee, K. (2021, October 20). *5 tips on how to deliver bad news in the workplace.* Workest by Zenefits. https://www.zenefits.com/workest/5-tips-on-how-to-deliver-bad-news-in-the-workplace/

73. Harris, W. (2020, May 29). *4 Examples of brands giving tough news during COVID-19.* Campaign Monitor. https://www.campaignmonitor.com/blog/email-marketing/brands-giving-tough-news-during-covid-19/

74. For an overview of corporate social responsibility, see Argenti, P. A. (2016). *Corporate responsibility.* SAGE.

75. Pope, R. (2021, October 14). *Recent study reveals more than a third of global consumers are willing to pay more for sustainability as demand grows for environmentally-friendly alternatives.* Business Wire. https://www.businesswire.com/news/home/20211014005090/en/Recent-Study-Reveals-More-Than-a-Third-of-Global-Consumers-Are-Willing-to-Pay-More-for-Sustainability-as-Demand-Grows-for-Environmentally-Friendly-Alternatives

76. Kileba, J. (2018, December 16). Return on ethics (ROE): Does your organisation pay attention to this? *Fifth Estate.* https://www.capitalfm.co.ke/eblog/return-on-ethics-roe-d

oes-your-organisation-pay-attention-to-this/

77. Mariano, K. (2019, July 11). ROE (return on ethics): Positive marketing can boost sales and customer loyalty. *Travel Daily*. https://www.traveldailymedia.com/roe-return-on-ethics-positive-marketing-can-boost-sales-and-customer-loyalty/

78. Carroll, A. B. (1991). The pyramid of corporate social responsibility: Toward the moral management of organizational stakeholders. *Business Horizons, 34*(4), 39–48. Carroll, A. B. (2016). Carroll's pyramid of CSR: Taking another look. *International Journal of Corporate Social Responsibility, 1*(1), 1–8.

79. Thompson, R. (2020, January 3). *Airbnb offers free emergency housing for people displaced by Australian bushfires*. Mashable. https://mashable.com/article/airbnb-australia-bushfire-accommodation

80. Bird, J. (2021, September 29). *OpenText survey shows increase in demand for ethically sourced goods*. OpenText. https://www.opentext.com/about/press-releases?id=5188A6174DE447FCAC930758694BBCB9

81. Holden, E. (2020, May 27). US lets corporations delay paying environmental fines amid pandemic. *The Guardian*. https://www.theguardian.com/environment/2020/may/27/epa-corporation-environmental-fines-decision

82. Visser, W. (2006). Revisiting Carroll's CSR. *Corporate Citizenship in Developing Countries: New Partnership Perspectives,29*.

83. Forbes. (n.d.). *Eve Kekeh*. https://www.forbes.com/profile/eve-kekeh/?list=30under30-europe-social-entrepreneurs&sh=20d8139d1d30

84. Morgan, B. (2021, October 26). *20 companies that use their profits for social good*. Forbes. https://www.forbes.com/sites/blakemorgan/2021/10/26/20-companies-that-use-their-profits-for-social-good/?sh=1711e2f711a8

85. Wong, K. (2020, August 3). *Core company values: 12 inspiring examples*. Achievers. https://www.achievers.com/blog/company-core-value-examples/

86. Cox, L. K. (2022, March 4). *27 mission and vision statement examples that will inspire your buyers*. HubSpot. https://blog.hubspot.com/marketing/inspiring-company-mission-statements

87. Resources for Employers. (n.d.). *Code of ethics policy*. https://resources.workable.com/professional-code-of-ethics-policy

88. Phartiyal, S., Ahmed, A., & Blanchard, B. (2021, February 9). *Apple supplier Wistron to restart India factory, still on probation*. Reuters. https://www.reuters.com/article/us-apple-india-wistron-idUSKBN2A90PU

89. Nieweler, A. (2021, January 4). *7 items to include in your company's code of ethics*. WhistleBlower Security. https://blog.whistleblowersecurity.com/blog/7-items-to-include-in-your-companys-code-of-ethics

90. Zheng, Y., Epitropaki, O., Graham, L., & Caveney, N. (2022). Ethical leadership and ethical voice: The mediating mechanisms of value internalization and integrity identity. *Journal of Management, 48*(4), 973–1002.

91. Sherman, L. (2017, March 13). *Why boards must step up to deter corporate scandals.Forbes*. https://www.forbes.com/sites/lensherman/2017/03/13/why-boards-must-step-up-to-deter-corporate-scandals/#3648248a1b79

92. Welch, K., & Stubben, S. (2020, January 14). Throw out your assumptions about whistleblowing. *Harvard Business Review*. https://hbr.org/2020/01/throw-out-your-assumptions-about-whistleblowing

93. Clark, D. (2020, February 27). *60 percent of "most ethical" companies have this in common*. Benefits Pro. https://www.benefitspro.com/2020/02/27/60-of-most-ethical-companies-have-chief-ethics-or-compliance-officers-412-94314/?slreturn=20220502102635

94. Smith, I. H., & Kouchaki, M. (2021, November/December). Building an ethical company. *Harvard Business Review*. https://hbr.org/2021/11/building-an-ethical-company

95. Ibid.

96. Ibid.

97. Ibid.

98. Ibid.

99. Sachs, A. (2007, April 19). The new world of crisis management. *Time*. http://content.time.com/time/magazine/article/0,9171,1612698,00.html

100. Smith, D. J. (2011, January 28). Jet Blue crisis management. *Marketplace of Life*. http://themarketplaceoflife.blogspot.com/2011/01/jet-blue-crisis-management.html

101. Business Insider. (2007). *JetBlue's week-long operational breakdown*. http://www.businessinsider.com/pr-disasters-crisis-management-2011-5#jetblues-week-long-operational-breakdown-2007-6

102. Ibid.

103. Bailey, J. (2007, February 19). JetBlue's C.E.O. is "mortified" after fliers are stranded. *New York Times*. https://www.nytimes.com/2007/02/19/business/19jetblue.html

104. Ibid.

105. Smith, D. J. (2011, January 28). Jet Blue crisis management. *Marketplace of Life*. http://themarketplaceoflife.blogspot.com/2011/01/jet-blue-crisis-management.html

106. Bailey, J. (2007, February 19). JetBlue's C.E.O. is "mortified" after fliers are stranded. *New York Times*. https://www.nytimes.com/2007/02/19/business/19jetblue.html

CHAPTER 11

1. Iqbal, M. (2022, January 11). Uber revenue and usage statistics (2022). *Business of Apps*. https://www.businessofapps.com/data/uber-statistics/

2. O'Connell, B. (2019, July 23). History of uber: Timeline and fact. *TheStreet*. https://www.thestreet.com/technology/history-of-uber-15028611

3. Isaac, M. (2017, February 22). Inside Uber's aggressive, unrestrained workplace culture. *New York Times*. https://www.nytimes.com/2017/02/22/technology/uber-workplace-culture.html?_r=1

4. Garvey, J. (2019, September 13). The workflow engine for HR. *PeopleGoal*. https://www.peoplegoal.com/blog/what-is-formal-and-informal-communication

5. Ibid.

6. Isaac, M. (2017, February 22). Inside Uber's aggressive, unrestrained workplace culture. *New York Times*. https://www.nytimes.com/2017/02/22/technology/uber-workplace-culture.html?_r=1

7. Ibid.

8. Garvey, J. (2019, September 13). The workflow engine for HR. *PeopleGoal.* https://www.peoplegoal.com/blog/what-is-formal-and-informal-communication

9. Smarp. (2020, July 14). How to tackle grapevine communication in the workplace. *The Employee Communications and Advocacy Blog.* https://blog.smarp.com/grapevine-communication-in-the-workplace

10. Ibid.

11. Griswold, A. (2017). Uber is designed so that for one employee to get ahead, another must fail. *Quartz.* https://qz.com/918582/uber-is-designed-so-that-for-one-employee-to-succeed-another-must-fail/

12. Bradt, G. (2017). Why Uber needs a mu sigma culture to survive. *Forbes.* https://www.forbes.com/sites/georgebradt/2017/06/10/why-uber-needs-a-mu-sigma-culture-to-survive/?sh=67736693315f

13. Feldman, B. (2017, June 5). Uber hires business-school academic Frances Frei to reshape the company. *Intelligencer.* http://nymag.com/selectall/2017/06/uber-hires-frances-frei-to-reshape-the-company.html

14. For an overview, see May, S., & Mumby, D. K. (2005). *Engaging organizational communication theory and research: Multiple perspective.* SAGE; Mumby, D. K., & Kuhn, T. R. (2018). *Organizational communication: A critical introduction (2e).* SAGE.

15. Berlo, D. K. (1960). *The process of communication.* Holt, Rinehart, & Winston; Shannon, C. E., & Weaver, W. (1949). *The mathematical theory of communication.* University of Illinois Press; Gillespie, D. J., & Schiffman, R. (2018). A critique of the Shannon–Weaver theory of communication and its implications for nursing. *Research and Theory for Nursing Practice,32*(2), 216–225.

16. Statista. *In response to COVID-19, what digital communication channels did your organization begin using for the first time or dramatically increase use of?* https://www.statista.com/statistics/1201336/covid-use-adoption-communication-channels/

17. Jercich, K. (2021, November 16). The biggest healthcare data breaches of 2021. *HealthcareITNews.com.* https://www.healthcareitnews.com/news/biggest-healthcare-data-breaches-2021

18. Shinkman, R. (2021, February 10). COVID-19 leads to explosion in cyberattacks, data breaches. *Healthcaredive.com.* https://www.healthcaredive.com/news/covid-19-leads-to-explosion-in-cyberattacks-data-breaches/594911/

19. Gifford, R. (2011). The role of nonverbal communication in interpersonal relations. In *Handbook of interpersonal psychology: Theory, research, assessment, and therapeutic interventions* (pp. 171–190). Wiley; Matsumoto, D., Hwang, H. C., & Frank, M. G. (2016). *APA handbook of nonverbal communication.* American Psychological Association.

20. Iman, R. (2020, February 25). The power of body language in the workplace. *Forbes.* https://www.forbes.com/sites/forbesbusinesscouncil/2020/02/25/the-power-of-body-language-in-the-workplace/?sh=45bc4ef1418e21; Noblio, B. (2020, June). *Coronavirus has stolen our most meaningful ways to connect.* CNN.com. https://edition.cnn.com/interactive/2020/06/world/coronavirus-body-language-wellness/

21. Noblio, B. (2020, June). Coronavirus has stolen our most meaningful ways to connect. *CNN.com.* https://edition.cnn.com/interactive/2020/06/world/coronavirus-body-language-wellness/

22. Ibid.

23. Ibid.

24. Johnson, A. M., & Lederer, A. L. (2005). The effect of communication frequency and channel richness on the convergence between chief executive and chief information officers. *Journal of Management Information Systems,22*(2), 227–252; Mirzaei, T., & Esmaeilzadeh, P. (2021). Engagement in online health communities: Channel expansion and social exchanges. *Information & Management, 58,* (1), 103404.

25. Button, K., & Rossera, F. (1990, December). Barriers to communication. *Annals of Regional Science,24*(4), 337; Chen, M.-H., & Agrawal, S. (2017, December). Do communication barriers in student teams impede creative behavior in the long run?—A time-lagged perspective. *Thinking Skills and Creativity,26,* 154–167.

26. Smith, C. (2021, September 23). Communication filters 'R' Us—But don't let them own us! *Making Business Matter.* https://www.makingbusinessmatter.co.uk/communication-filters/

27. Sweney, M., & Partridge, J. (2021, February 12). KPMG's Bill Michael resigns after telling staff to 'stop moaning'. *The Guardian.* https://www.theguardian.com/business/2021/feb/12/kpmg-bill-michael-resigns-after-telling-staff-to-stop-moaning

28. Goyeneche, R. (2020, July 23). How to stop information overload in its tracks. *Forbes.* https://www.forbes.com/sites/womensmedia/2020/07/23/how-to-stop-information-overload-in-its-tracks/?sh=31ef7f2d58e1

29. Ibid.

30. Ibid.

31. Hill, A. (2021, September 15). Generational conflict over climate crisis is a myth, UK study finds. *The Guardian.* https://www.theguardian.com/environment/2021/sep/15/generational-conflict-over-climate-crisis-is-a-myth-uk-study-finds

32. Ibid.

33. Innolect. *The costs of poor listening.* http://innolectinc.com/services-overview/the-cost-of-poor-listening/

34. Friston, K. J., Sajid, N., Quiroga-Martinez, D. R., Parr, T., Price, C. J., & Holmes, E. (2021). Active listening. *Hearing Research, 399,* 107998; Weger, H. Jr., Bell, G. C., & Robinson, M. C. (2014, January). The relative effectiveness of active listening in initial interactions. *International Journal of Listening,28*(1), 13–31.

35. Vozza, S. (2019, January 28). 6 reasons why you're a bad listener (and how to change it). *Fast Company.* https://www.fastcompany.com/90293558/6-reasons-why-youre-a-bad-listener-and-how-to-change-it

36. Drollinger, T., Comer, L. B., & Warrington, P. T. (2006, February). Development and validation of the active empathetic listening scale. *Psychology and Marketing, 23*(2), 161–180; Shrivastava, A. (2014, July). Active empathic listening as a tool for better communication. *International Journal of Marketing & Business Communication,3*(3/4), 13–18.

37. Butts, M. M., Becker, W. J., & Boswell, W. R. (2015). Hot buttons and time sinks: The effects of electronic communication during nonwork time on emotions and work-nonwork conflict. *Academy of Management Journal, 58*(3), 763–788.

38. Brodsky, A., & Barsade, S. (2016, January). Advancing research on interpersonal communication: Communicating in all directions. *Academy of Management Annual Meeting Proceedings, 2016*(1), 1; Lunenburg, F. C. (2010). Formal communication channels: Upward, downward, horizontal, and external. *Focus on Colleges, Universities, and Schools, 4*(1), 1–7; Roberts, K. H., & O'Reilly, C. A. (1974, June). Measuring organizational communication. *Journal of Applied Psychology, 59*(3), 321–326.

39. Martic, K. (n.d.). 10 ways to foster upward communication in the workplace. *Haiilo.* https://haiilo.com/blog/10-ways-to-foster-upward-communication-in-the-workplace/

40. Song, X., Shi, W., Ma, Y., & Yang, C. (2015, October 15). Impact of informal networks on opinion dynamics in hierarchically formal organization. *Physica A, 436*, 916–924; Horak, S., Afiouni, F., Bian, Y., Ledeneva, A., Muratbekova-Touron, M., & Fey, C. F. (2020). Informal networks: Dark sides, bright sides, and unexplored dimensions. *Management and Organization Review,16*(3), 511–542.

41. Davis, K. (1953, September). Management communication and the grapevine. *Harvard Business Review,31*(5), 43–49; Baerjee, P., & Singh, S. (2015, June). Managers' perspectives on the effects of online grapevine communication: A qualitative inquiry. *Qualitative Report,20*(6), 765–779; Kast, G. (2019). Grapevine communication in communication centers: The needs and effects. *Communication Center Journal, 5*(1), 181–183.

42. Dores Cruz, T. D., Nieper, A. S., Testori, M., Martinescu, E., & Beersma, B. (2021). An integrative definition and framework to study gossip. *Group & Organization Management, 46*(2), 252–285; Drapkin, J. (2005, November). The dirty little secret about gossip. *Psychology Today,38*(6), 54–60; Foster, E. K., & Rosnow, R. L. (2006). Gossip and network relationships. In D. C. Kirkpatrick, S. Duck, & M. K. Foley (Eds.), *Relating difficulty: The processes of constructing and managing difficult interaction* (pp. 161–180). Erlbaum.

43. Dolev, D., & Malki, D. (1996). The Transis approach to high availability cluster communication. *Communications of the ACM, 39*(4), 64–70; Kudratilloev, N. A., & Akhmedov, B. A. (2021). Application of communication-cluster technologies in pedagogical institutions: Interactive methods of processing graphic data. *Scientific Progress, 1*(5), 191–198.

44. Mishra, J. (1990). Managing the grapevine. *Public Personnel Management, 19*(2), 213–228.

45. Keith, K. D. (2018). Ethnocentrism: Our window on the world. In K. D. Keith (Ed.), *Culture across the curriculum: A psychology teacher's handbook* (pp. 391–406). Cambridge University Press.

46. "I have said School of the South; because in reality, our north is the South. There must not be north, for us, except in opposition to our South. Therefore we now turn the map upside down, and then we have a true idea of our position, and not as the rest of the world wishes. The point of America, from now on, forever, insistently points to the South, our north." (Joaquín Torres García, *Constructive Universalism*, BS AS, *Poseidon*, 1941).

47. Hall, E. T. (1976). *Beyond culture.* Anchor; Jeong, J. Y., & Crompton, J. L. (2018, February). Do subjects from high and low context cultures attribute different meanings to tourism services with 9-ending prices? *Tourism Management,64*, 110–118; Kittler, M. G., Rygl, D., & Mackinnon, A. (2011, April). Beyond culture or beyond control? Reviewing the use of hall's high-/low-context concept. *International Journal of Cross Cultural Management,11*(1), 63–82.

48. Meyer, E. (2017, July-August). Being the boss in Brussels, Boston, and Beijing. *Harvard Business Review.* https://hbr.org/2017/07/being-the-boss-in-brussels-boston-and-beijing

49. Ferraro, G. P., & Briody, E. K. (2012). *The cultural dimensions of global business* (7th ed.) Pearson

50. Ibid.

51. Ibid.

52. Adams, S. (2020, May 16). The best commencement speeches Of 2020. *Forbes.* https://www.forbes.com/sites/susanadams/2020/05/16/the-best-commencement-speeches-of-2020/?sh=a05b5e773f09

53. Toegel, G., & Barsoux, J.-L. (2016, June 8). 3 situations where cross-cultural communication breaks down. *Harvard Business Review.* https://hbr.org/2016/06/3-situations-where-cross-cultural-communication-breaks-down

54. Stagecoach Group. (n.d.). *Current operations.* https://www.stagecoachgroup.com/about/our-companies/current-operations.aspx

55. Blink. (n.d.). *Blink hero: Ricky Sickelmore, stagecoach.* https://joinblink.com/intelligence/blink-hero-ricky-sickelmore-stagecoach/

56. Blink. (n.d.). *Transport case study.* https://joinblink.com/resources/case-studies/transport

57. Middleton, W. (2017, November 6). *Customer-centered transformation drives results.* KPMG LLP. https://assets.kpmg/content/dam/kpmg/uk/pdf/2017/11/ceo-evolution-stagecoach-group.pdf

58. Wordsworth, N. (2019, June 18). Stagecoach and Blink win 2 international awards for digital workplace. *Rail Insider.* https://railinsider.co.uk/2019/06/18/stagecoach-and-blink-win-2-international-awards-for-digital-workplace/

59. Affini. (n.d.). *Stagecoach replaces legacy analogue radio system with new DMR.* https://www.affini.co.uk/portfolio/stagecoach-replaces-legacy-analogue-radio-system-with-new-dmr/

CHAPTER 12

1. Linden, A. D. (2015, November 29). Those great American creations: Thanksgiving and football. *Sport in American History.* https://ussporthistory.com/2015/11/26/those-great-american-creations-thanksgiving-and-football/

2. Klein, C. (2014, September 4). The birth of the national football league. *History.com.* https://www.history.com/news/the-birth-of-the-national-football-league

3. Ibid.

4. NFL. (2019). NFL 100. *NFL.com.* https://www.nfl.com/100/original-towns/

5. A&E Television Networks. (2018, May 11). Super bowl history. *History.com.* https://www.history.com/topics/sports/super-bowl-history

6. Nadar, M. (2021, November 20). 10 most profitable sports leagues in the world. *Sportsunfold.* https://www.sportsunfold.com/10-most-profitable-sports-leagues-in-the-world/

7. Levy, D. (2017, October 3). NFL ratings: DID 200 million people really watch games in 2011? *Bleacher Report*. https://bleacherreport.com/articles/1013086-nfl-ratings-did-200-million-people-really-watch-games-in-2011
8. NFL. (2021, September 9). Ranking the NFL's biggest contracts for 2021. *NFL.com*. https://www.nfl.com/photos/ranking-the-nfl-s-biggest-contracts-for-2021
9. McGinnis, H. (2011, February 12). NFL lockout for dummies: Explaining the NFL labor dispute in Layman's terms. *NFL Lockout for Dummies*. https://bleacherreport.com/articles/606091-nfl-lockout-for-dummies-explaining-the-nfl-labor-dispute-in-laymans-terms
10. Ibid.
11. Ibid.
12. For detailed overviews of organizational trust definitions and research, see De Jong, B. A., Kroon, D. P., & Schilke, O. (2017). The future of organizational trust research: A content-analytic synthesis of scholarly recommendations and review of recent developments. In P. A. M. Van Lange & B. Rockenbach (Eds.), *Trust in social dilemmas* (pp. 173–194). Oxford University Press; García, A. B., Pender, E., & Elgoibar, P. (2016). The state of art: Trust and conflict management in organizational industrial relations. In L. Munduate, M. Euwema, & P. Elgoibar (Eds.), *Building trust and constructive conflict management in organizations* (pp. 29–51). Springer; Schilke, O., Reimann, M., & Cook, K. S. (2021). Trust in social relations. *Annual Review of Sociology,47*, 239–259.
13. Ranker. (2021). *The most trustworthy celebrities in the world*. https://www.ranker.com/list/most-trustworthy-celebrities/celebrity-listshttps://www.ranker.com/list/most-trustworthy-celebrities/celebrity-lists
14. Newcomb, A. (2020, December 16). From scandals to retirement, these CEOs made waves in 2020. *NBC NEWs.com*. https://www.nbcnews.com/business/business-news/scandals-retirement-these-ceos-made-waves-2020-n1251386
15. Thompson, B. (2021, November 29). Public trust in scientists rose during the Covid-19 pandemic. *Wellcome*. https://wellcome.org/news/public-trust-scientists-rose-during-covid-19-pandemic
16. John, M. (2021, January 13). Public trust crumbles under COVID-19, fake news-survey. *Reuters*. https://www.reuters.com/business/media-telecom/reuters-next-public-trust-crumbles-under-covid-19-fake-news-survey-2021-01-13/
17. Ibid.
18. Choi, B. K., Moon, H. K., & Nae, E. Y. (2014, September). Cognition- and affect-based trust and feedback-seeking behavior: The roles of value, cost, and goal orientations. *Journal of Psychology, 148*(5), 603–620; Mayer, R. C., Davis. J. H., & Schoorman F. D. (1995, July). An integrative model of organizational trust. *Academy of Management Review, 20*(3), 709–734; McAllister, D. J. (1995, February). Affect- and cognition-based trust as foundations for interpersonal cooperation in organizations. *Academy of Management Journal, 38*(1), 24–59; Han, S., Harold, C, M., & Cheong, M. (2019). Examining why employee proactive personality influences empowering leadership: The roles of cognition- and affect-based trust. *Journal of Occupational and Organizational Psychology, 92*(2), 352–383.
19. Zak, P. J. (2017, January-February). The neuroscience of trust. *Harvard Business Review*. https://hbr.org/2017/01/the-neuroscience-of-trust#:~:text=Compared%20with%20people%20at%20low,lives%2C%2040%25%20less%20burnout
20. Choi, B. K., Moon, H. K., & Nae, E. Y. (2014, September). Cognition- and affect-based trust and feedback-seeking behavior: The roles of value, cost, and goal orientations. *Journal of Psychology, 148*(5), 603–620; Mayer, R. C., Davis, J. H., & Schoorman, F. D. (1995, July). An integrative model of organizational trust. *Academy of Management Review, 20*(3), 709–734; McAllister, D. J. (1995, February). Affect- and cognition-based trust as foundations for interpersonal cooperation in organizations. *Academy of Management Journal, 38*(1), 24–59; Han, S., Harold, C. M., & Cheong, M. (2019). Examining why employee proactive personality influences empowering leadership: The roles of cognition-and affect-based trust. *Journal of Occupational and Organizational Psychology, 92*(2), 352–383.
21. Frei, F. X., & Morriss, A. (2020, May-June). Begin with trust. *Harvard Business Review*, https://hbr.org/2020/05/begin-with-trust
22. Ibid.
23. Ibid.
24. Ibid.
25. Ibid.
26. Ibid.
27. Guest, D. E. (2016). Trust and the role of the psychological contract in contemporary employment relations. In *Building trust and constructive conflict management in organizations* (pp. 137–149). Springer; Rousseau, D. M. (2011). The individual–organization relationship: The psychological contract. In S. E. Zedeck (Ed.), *APA Handbook of industrial and organizational psychology, Vol 3: Maintaining, expanding, and contracting the organization* (pp. 191–220). American Psychological Association; Soares, M. E., & Mosquera. P. (2019). Fostering work engagement: The role of the psychological contract. *Journal of Business Research, 101*, 469–476.
28. Delgado-Márquez, B. L., Belitski. M., & Delgado-Márquez, L. (2013). The role of individuals' social networks density on their transfers of trust behaviors and expectations: A Social capital approach. In D. Gefen (Ed.), *Psychology of trust: New research* (pp. 305–324). Nova Science; Wang, F., She, J., Ohyama, Y., Jiang, W., Min, G., Wang, G., & Wu, M. (2021). Maximizing positive influence in competitive social networks: A trust-based solution. *Information Sciences, 546*, 559–572.
29. Colquitt, J. A., Scott, B. A., & LePine, J. A. (2007). Trust, trustworthiness, and trust propensity: A meta-analytic test of their unique relationships with risk taking and job performance. *Journal of Applied Psychology, 92*(4), 909; Tomlinson, E. C., Schnackenberg, A. K., Dawley, D., & Ash, S. R. (2020). Revisiting the trustworthiness–trust relationship: Exploring the differential predictors of cognition- and affect-based trust. *Journal of Organizational Behavior, 41*(6), 535–550.
30. Bezek, I. (2021, December 15). 7 Struggling CEOs that have fallen from favor in 2021. *Investorplace*. https://investorplace.com/2021/12/7-str

uggling-ceos-that-have-fallen-from-favor-in-2021/

31. For an overview see Elgoibar, P., Euwema, M., & Munduate, L. (2016). *Building trust and constructive conflict management in organizations*. Springer; Roche, W. K., Teague, P., & Colvin, A. J. S., (2016). *The oxford handbook of conflict management in organizations*. Oxford University Press.

32. Walsh, S. (2021, October 20). Netflix's Ted Sarandos admits he "Screwed Up" Dave Chappelle response. *Vanity Fair*. https://www.vanityfair.com/hollywood/2021/10/netflixs-ted-sarandos-admits-he-screwed-up-dave-chappelle-response

33. Lovric, D., & Chamorro-Premuzic, T. (2018, June 28). Too much team harmony can kill creativity. *Harvard Business Review*. https://hbr.org/2018/06/too-much-team-harmony-can-kill-creativity

34. Ibid.

35. Ibid.

36. Amason, A. C. (1996, February). Distinguishing the effects of functional and dysfunctional conflict on strategic decision making: Resolving a paradox for top management teams. *Academy of Management Journal, 39*(1), 123–148; Bobot, L. (2011, January). Functional and dysfunctional conflicts in retailer-supplier relationships. *International Journal of Retail & Distribution Management, 39*(1), 25–50; John-Eke, E. C., & Akintokunbo, O. O. (2020). Conflict management as a tool for increasing organizational effectiveness: A review of literature. *International Journal of Academic Research in Business and Social Sciences, 10*(5), 299–311.

37. Ibid.

38. Jehn, K. A. (1997, September). A qualitative analysis of conflict types and dimensions in organizational groups. *Administrative Science Quarterly, 42*(3), 530–557; Marineau, J. E., Hood, A. C., & Labianca, G. J. (2017, August 22). Multiplex conflict: Examining the effects of overlapping task and relationship conflict on advice seeking in organizations. *Journal of Business and Psychology, 33, 595–610.*

39. Pondy, L. R. (1967, September). Organizational conflict: Concepts and models. *Administrative Science Quarterly, 12*(2), 296–320; Parvaresh-Masoud, M., Cheraghi, M. A., & Imanipour, M. (2021). Workplace interpersonal conflict in prehospital emergency: Concept analysis. *Journal of Education and Health Promotion, 10*, 347.

40. U.S. Department of Labor. (n.d.). *Workplace violence*. https://www.osha.gov/SLTC/workplaceviolence/

41. Chang, W.-L., & Lee, C-Y. (2013, November). Virtual team E-leadership: The effects of leadership style and conflict management mode on the online learning performance of students in a business-planning course. *British Journal of Educational Technology, 44*(6), 986–999; Kilmann, R. H., & Kenneth W. Thomas. (1975, December). Interpersonal conflict-handling behavior as reflections of Jungian personality dimensions. *Psychological Reports, 37*(3 Pt 1), 971–980; Min, J., Iqbal, S., Shafique Khan, M. A., Akhtar, S., Anwar, F., & Qalati, S. A. (2020). Impact of supervisory behavior on sustainable employee performance: Mediation of conflict management strategies using PLS-SEM. *PLoS One, 15*(9), e0236650.

42. De Dreu, C. K. W., & Weingart, L. R. (2003, August). Task versus relationship conflict, team performance, and team member satisfaction: A meta-analysis. *Journal of Applied Psychology, 88*(4), 741–749; de Wit, F. R. C., Greer, L. L., & Jehn, K. A. (2012, March). The Paradox of intragroup conflict: A meta-analysis. *Journal of Applied Psychology, 97*(2), 360–390.

43. De Wit, F. R. C., Jehn, K. A., & Scheepers, D. (2013, November). Task conflict, information processing, and decision-making: The damaging effect of relationship conflict. *Organizational Behavior and Human Decision Processes, 122*(2), 177–189.

44. For overviews, see Dreu, C. K. W., Hillie Aaldering, D., & Saygi, Ö. (2015). Conflict and Negotiation within and between Groups. In M. Mikulincer, P. R. Shaver, John F. Dovidio, & J. A. Simpson (Eds.), *APA Handbook of personality and social psychology, Volume 2: Group processes*, (pp. 151–176). American Psychological Association; Thompson, L. L., Wang, J., & Gunia, B. C. (2013). Negotiation. In J. M. Levine (Ed.), *Group processes*, (pp. 55–84), Psychology Press; Filzmoser, M., Vetschera, R., & Koeszegi, S. T. (2021). Negotiation processes: Empirical insights. *Handbook of Group Decision and Negotiation*, 61–79.

45. The negotiation process explained here is based on information contained in Lewicki, R. J., Weiss, S. E., & Lewin, D. (1992, May). Models of conflict, negotiation and third party intervention: A review and synthesis. *Journal of Organizational Behavior, 13*(3), 209–252.

46. Emotional triggers: How emotions affect your negotiating ability. (2018, April 26). www.pon.harvard.edu.https://www.pon.harvard.edu/daily/negotiation-skills-daily/how-emotions-affect-your-talks/

47. Quast, L. (2016, August 8). 10 Tips to help you win every negotiation. *Forbes*. https://www.forbes.com/sites/lisaquast/2016/08/08/10-tips-to-help-you-win-every-negotiation/#35c9bc4436d0

48. Angoff, S. E. (1961, January). Impartial opinion and constructive criticism of mediators, mediation agencies and conciliators. *Labor Law Journal, 12*(1), 67; Lewicki, R. J., Weiss, S. E., & Lewin, D. (2021). Models of conflict, negotiation and third party intervention. *Journal of Organizational Behavior, 13*(3), 209–252; Ross, W. H., & Conlon, D. E. (2000, April). Hybrid forms of third-party dispute resolution: Theoretical implications of combining mediation and arbitration. *Academy of Management Review, 25*(2), 416–427; Ibsen, C. L. (2021). Conciliation, mediation and arbitration in collective bargaining in Western Europe: In search of control. *European Journal of Industrial Relations, 27*(1), 23–39.

49. Gorman, T. (2012, January 18). The arbitration process. *Baseball Prospectus*. www.baseballprospectus.com/article.php?articleid=15864; What is baseball arbitration? (2021, March 11). *The Stadium Reviews*. https://thestadiumreviews.com/blogs/info/what-is-baseball-arbitration/

50. Lewicki, R. J., Weiss, S. E., & Lewin, D. (2021). Models of conflict, negotiation and third party intervention. *Journal of Organizational Behavior, 13*(3), 209–252; Bolkan, S., & Goodboy, A. K. Negotiating in distributive bargaining scenarios: The effect of

sharing one's alternative. *Communication Studies,72*(4), 720–733.

51. Fisher, R. (1982, February). Getting to yes. *Management Review,71*(2), 16–21; Elgoibar, P., Medina, F. J., Euwema, M. C., & Munduate, L. (2021). Increasing integrative negotiation in European organizations through trustworthiness and trust. *Frontiers in Psychology,12*, 2180.
52. Ibid.
53. Kristi, H. (2013, April 24) How to negotiate a higher salary. *Forbes Woman*. www.forbes.com/sites/work-in-progress/2013/04/24/how-to-negotiate-a-higher-salary/
54. Fisher, R. & Ury, W. (1983). What if they are more powerful? (Develop your BATNA—best alternative to a negotiated agreement). In B. Patton (Ed.), *Getting to Yes* (pp. 101–111). Berkely Law; Pinkley, R. L., Conlon, D. E., Sawyer, J. E., Sleesman, Vandewalle, D. J., & Kuenzi, M. (2019). The power of phantom alternatives in negotiation: How what could be haunts what is. *Organizational Behavior and Human Decision Processes, 151*, 34–48.
55. Sebenius, J. K. (2005). Negotiation analysis: A characterization and review. In M. H. Bazerman (Ed.), *Negotiation, decision making and conflict management* (Vols. 1–3, pp. 18–41). Edward Elgar; Jingjing, Y., Zhang, Z.-X., & Liu, L. A. (2020). When there is no ZOPA: Mental fatigue, integrative complexity, and creative agreement in negotiations. *Negotiation and Conflict Management Research*. Advance online publication.
56. California Association of Winegrape Growers. (n.d.). *California Winegrape Industry*. https://www.cawg.org/Wine 1/About/Industry/Shared_Content/About/Industry.aspx?hkey=d993db02-bd40-49dd-94fb-6a94ca89fe5a
57. Romano, A. (2020, October 8). A vintage lost? *Wine Spectator*. https://www.winespectator.com/articles/a-vintage-lost-napa-and-sonoma-vintners-say-2020s-fire-and-smoke-has-ruined-much-of-their-harvest
58. Williams, L. (2017, November 3). Understanding smoke taint. *Wine Spectator*. https://www.winespectator.com/articles/understanding-smoke-taint-in-wine
59. Allied Grape Growers. (2016). *What is Allied Grape Growers?* http://www.alliedgrapegrowers.org/aboutus.php
60. Downey Brand, L. L. P. (2021, July 7). *A Legal Analysis: 2020 Winegrape Rejections*. Allied Grape Growers. http://www.alliedgrapegrowers.org/pdfs/Legal%20Analysis%20-%202020%20Winegrape%20Rejections.pdf
61. Fish, T. (2020, October 1). We'll make it even better: A Q&A with Meadowood co-owner Bill Harlan. *Wine Spectator*. https://www.winespectator.com/articles/we-ll-make-it-even-better-a-q-a-with-meadowood-owner-bill-harlan
62. Shonk, K. (2021, January 11). *10 notable negotiations of 2020*. Program on Negotiation—Harvard Law School. https://www.pon.harvard.edu/daily/10-notable-negotiations-of-2020

CHAPTER 13

1. Marketplace. (n.d.). *Procter & Gamble Corporate History*. https://www.marketplace.org/2008/05/20/procter-gamble-corporate-history
2. Horowitz, A. (2011). How Procter & Gamble became the maker of everything you buy for your house. *Business Insider*. http://www.businessinsider.com/protor-gamble-makes-everything-2011-2
3. P&G. (n.d.). *P&G announces fourth quarter and fiscal year 2021 results*. https://pginvestor.com/financial-reporting/press-releases/news-details/2021/PG-Announces-Fourth-Quarter-and-Fiscal-Year-2021-Results/default.aspx
4. Macrotrends. (n.d.). *Procter & Gamble: Number of employees 2010-2021: PG*. https://www.macrotrends.net/stocks/charts/PG/procter-gamble/number-of-employees
5. Abrams, R. (2014, August 1). Procter & Gamble to streamline offerings, dropping up to 100 Brands. *New York Times*. https://www.nytimes.com/2014/08/02/business/procter-gamble-to-drop-up-to-100-brands.html
6. Reeder, J. (2017, September 6). Innovation isn't a 'hobby' for P&G or greater Cincinnati. *The Enquirer*. https://www.sec.gov/Archives/edgar/data/80424/000119312517277911/d454837ddefa14a1.pdf
7. Horowitz, A. (2011). How Procter & Gamble became the maker of everything you buy for your house. *Business Insider*. http://www.businessinsider.com/protor-gamble-makes-everything-2011-2
8. P&G. (n.d.). *Transforming the gold standard of clinical trials with home as clinics*. https://us.pg.com/blogs/home-as-clinics/
9. P&G. (n.d.). *Awards and recognition*. https://us.pg.com/awards-and-recognition/
10. For an overview of leadership research see one or more of the following: B. R. Bass. (2008). *The Bass handbook of leadership: Theory, research, and managerial applications* (4th ed.) Free Press; Carnton, A. M. (2022). The science of leadership: A theoretical model and research agenda. *Annual Review of Organizational Psychology and Organizational Behavior, 9*, 6.1–6.33; R. J. House, & Aditya, R. N. (1997 Special Issue 1997). The social scientific study of leadership: Quo Vadis? *Journal of Management, 23*(3), 409; A. G. Jago. (1982, March). Leadership: Perspectives in theory and research. *Management Science, 28*(3), 315–336.
11. Mukherjee, R. B., & Krish, A. (2021). Experience: Post-pandemic reset. *TATA Consultancy Services*. https://www.tcs.com/what-we-do/services/cloud/microsoft/white-paper/post-pandemic-rese
12. Corbett, H. (2020, June 30). How companies are supporting working parents in the COVID economy. *Forbes*. https://www.forbes.com/sites/hollycorbett/2020/07/30/how-companies-are-supporting-working-parents-in-the-covid-economy/?sh=5a1908c8328f
13. Bashin, M. (2018, March 20). Four lessons from Indra Nooyi's inspirational journey. *Technovationchallenge.org*. https://technovationchallenge.org/2018/03/20/four-lessons-indra-nooyis-inspirational-journey/
14. See for example Foti, R. J., & Hauenstein, N. M. A. (2007, March). Pattern and variable approaches in leadership emergence and effectiveness. *Journal of Applied Psychology, 92*(2), 347–355; Kwok, N., Hanig, S., Brown, D. J., & Shen, W. (2018, April 28). How leader role identity influences the process of leader emergence: A social network analysis. *The Leadership Quarterly, 29*(6), 648–662.
15. Elmes, J. (2016, February 4). Business schools "Must Challenge Leader Stereotypes." *Times Higher Education*. https://www.timeshighereducation.com/news/business-schools-must-challenge-leader-stereotypes; for an historical perspective on stereotyping see Taylor,

E., Guy-Walls, P., Wilkerson, P., & Addae, R. (2019). The historical perspectives of stereotypes on African-American males. *Journal of Human Rights and Social Work, 4*(3), 213–225.

16. Robinson, B. (2021, June 12). New research identifies essential leadership skills for resilient and effective team members. *Forbes*. https://www.forbes.com/sites/bryanrobinson/2021/06/12/new-research-identifies-essential-leadership-skills-for-resilient-and-effective-team-members/?sh=74ffecc62dce
17. Ibid.
18. See, for instance, Neubert, M J., & Taggar, S. (2004, April). Pathways to informal leadership: The moderating role of gender on the relationship of individual differences and team member network centrality to informal leadership emergence. *Leadership Quarterly, 15*(2), 175–194; Pan, J., P., Liu, S., Ma, B., & Qu, Z. (2018, May 10). How does proactive personality promote creativity? A multilevel examination of the interplay between formal and informal leadership. *Journal of Occupational and Organizational Psychology, 91*(4), 852–874.
19. Pidgeon, E. (2021, July 5). These are the top CEOs for 2021. *CEO Magazine*. https://www.theceomagazine.com/business/management-leadership/top-ceos-2021/
20. Kearney, P. J. (2017, August 23). 5 Tips for teacher leaders. *Huffington Post*. https://www.huffingtonpost.com/entry/five-tips-for-teacher-leaders_us_599dd57ae4b0b87d38cbe701
21. Chiu, C.-Y. (Chad), Nahrgang, J. D., Bartram, A., Wang, J., & Tesluk, P. (2021, September 27). Research: Informal leadership comes at a cost. *Harvard Business Review*. https://hbr.org/2021/09/research-informal-leadership-comes-at-a-cost
22. Chiu, C.-Y. (Chad), Balkundi, P., & Weinberg, F. J. (2017, April). When managers become leaders: The role of manager network centralities, social power, and followers' perception of leadership. *The Leadership Quarterly, 28*(2), 334–348; Clemens, J. K. (1994, June). Leaders versus managers: The case of captain Vere. *Journal of Leadership Studies, 1*(3), 117–128; Watkins, M. D. (2012, June). How managers become leaders. *Harvard Business Review, 90*(6), 64–72; Zaleznik, A. (1977, May). Managers and leaders: Are they different? *Harvard Business Review, 55*(3), 67–78.
23. Martic, K. (2022). Leadership vs. Management: The 5 main differences. *Haiilo*. https://haiilo.com/blog/leadership-vs-management/
24. Manz, C. C., & Sims, H. P. Jr. (1991). Superleadership: Beyond the myth of heroic leadership. *Organizational Dynamics, 19*(4), 18–35; Pearce, C. L., Sims, H. P. Jr., Cox, J. F. Ball, G., Schnell, E., Smith, K. A., & Trevino, L. (2003). Transactors, transformers and beyond: A multi-method development of a theoretical typology of leadership. *Journal of Management Development, 22*(4), 273–307.
25. McCandless, K. (2022, May 18). Pros and Cons of transactional leadership. *The Ascent*. https://www.fool.com/the-ascent/small-business/human-resources/articles/transactional-leadership/
26. Ates, N. Y., Tarakci, M., Porck, J. P., Van Knippenberg, D., & Groenen, P. (2019, February 28). Why visionary leadership fails. *Harvard Business Review*. https://hbr.org/2019/02/why-visionary-leadership-fails
27. Manz & Sims, "SuperLeadership"; Manz, C., & Sims, H. P. Jr. (2001). *The new superleadership: Leading others to lead themselves*. Berrett-Koehler; Pearce, C. L., & Sims, H. P. Jr. (2002, June). Vertical versus shared leadership as predictors of the effectiveness of change management teams: An examination of aversive, directive, transactional, transformational, and empowering leader behaviors. *Group Dynamics: Theory, Research, and Practice, 6*(2), 172–197.
28. Ibid.
29. Forbes Business Council. (2021, October 12). 15 Ways to empower your employees. *Forbes*. https://www.forbes.com/sites/forbesbusinesscouncil/2021/10/12/15-ways-to-empower-your-employees/?sh=281f51da30c8
30. See, for example, Jenkins, W. O. (1947, January). A review of leadership studies with particular reference to military problems. *Psychological Bulletin, 44*(1), 54–79; Stogdill, R. M. (1948). Personal factors associated with leadership: A survey of the literature. *Journal of Psychology: Interdisciplinary and Applied, 25*, 35–71; Wyatt, M., & Silvester, J. (2018, February 14). Do voters get it right? A test of the ascription-actuality trait theory of leadership with political elites. *The Leadership Quarterly, 29*(5), 609–621.
31. Colbert, A. E., Judge, T. A., Choi, D., & Wang, G. (2012, August). Assessing the trait theory of leadership using self and observer ratings of personality: The mediating role of contributions to group success. *Leadership Quarterly, 23*(4), 670–685; Derue, D. S., Nahrgang, J. D., Wellman, N., & Humphrey, S. E. (2011). Trait and behavioral theories of leadership: An integration and meta-analytic test of their relative validity. *Personnel Psychology, 64*(1), 7–52; Penney, S. A., Kelloway, E. K., & O'Keefe, D. (2015). Trait theories of leadership. In I. O'Boyle, D. Murray & P. Cummins (Eds.), *Leadership in sport* (pp. 19–33). Routledge/Taylor & Francis Group.
32. Kirkpatrick, S. A., & Locke, E. A. (1991, May). Leadership: Do traits matter? *Academy of Management Executive, 5*(2), 48–60; Zaccaro, S. J. (2007, January). Trait-Based perspectives of leadership. *American Psychologist, 62*(1), 6–16.
33. Hemphill, J. K., & Coons, A. E. (1957). *Leader behavior: Its description and measurement* (Research Monograph No. 88). Ohio State University, Bureau of Business Research; Tremblay, M., Gaudet, M.-C., & Parent-Rocheleau, X. (2018). Good things are not eternal: How consideration leadership and initiating structure influence the dynamic nature of organizational justice and extra-role behaviors at the collective level. *Journal of Leadership & Organizational Studies, 25*(2), 211–232.
34. Cartwright, D., & Zander, A. (1960). *Group dynamics research and theory (2nd ed.)*. Row, Peterson; Katz, D., & Kahn, R. L. (1951). Human organization and worker motivation. In *Industrial productivity*, Industrial Relations Research Association; Likert, R. (1961). *New patterns of management*. McGraw-Hill.
35. Blake, R. R., & Mouton. J. S. (1964). *The managerial grid*. Gulf.
36. See, for example, Danelo Barbour, J. (2013). Contingency management and situational leadership theories. In B. J. Irby, G. H. Brown, R. LaraAiecio, & S. A. Jackson (Eds.), *The Handbook of educational theories* (pp. 917–921). IAP Information Age; Hughes, R. L.,

Ginnett, R. C., & Curphy, G. J. (1998). Contingency theories of leadership. In G. R. Hickman (Ed.), *Leading Organizations: Perspectives for a new era* (pp. 141–157). SAGE; Fiedler, F. E. (1964). A contingency model of leadership effectiveness. In L. Berkowitz (Ed.), *Advances in experimental social psychology* (Vol. 1, pp. 149–190). Academic Press; Fiedler, F. E. (1967). *A theory of leadership effectiveness*. McGraw-Hill.

37. Hersey, P., & Blanchard, K. H. (1969). *Management of organizational behavior: Utilizing human resources*. Prentice Hall; Blanchard, K. H., Zigarmi, D., & Nelson, R. B. (1993, November). Situational leadership® after 25 years: A retrospective. *Journal of Leadership Studies, 1*(1), 21–36; Luo, H., & Liu, S. (2014). Effect of situational leadership and employee readiness match on organizational citizenship behavior in China. *Social Behavior and Personality, 42*(10), 1725–1732; Tortorella, G., & Fogliatto, F. (2017). Implementation of lean manufacturing and situational leadership styles: An empirical study. *Leadership & Organization Development Journal, 38*(7), 946–968.

38. House, R. J. (1971, September). A path goal theory of leader effectiveness. *Administrative Science Quarterly, 16*(3), 321–339; House, R. J. (Fall 1996). Path-Goal theory of leadership: Lessons, legacy, and a reformulated theory. *Leadership Quarterly*, 323; House, R. J., & Mitchell, T. R. (2007). Path-Goal theory of leadership. In R. P. Vecchio (Ed.), *Leadership: Understanding the dynamics of power and influence in organizations* (2nd ed., pp. 241–254). University of Notre Dame Press; Bickle, J. T. (2017, October). Developing remote training consultants as leaders-dialogic/network application of path-goal leadership theory in leadership development. *Performance Improvement, 56*(9), 32–39.

39. Kerr, S., & Jermier, J. M. (1978, December). Substitutes for leadership: Their meaning and measurement. *Organizational Behavior and Human Performance, 22*(3), 375–403; Nübold, A., Muck, P. M., & Maier. G. W. (2013, February). A new substitute for leadership? followers' state core self-evaluations. *Leadership Quarterly, 24*(1), 29–44; Velez, M. J., & Neves. P. (2017, July). The relationship between abusive supervision, distributive justice and job satisfaction: A substitutes for leadership approach. *European Review of Applied Psychology/Revue Européenne De Psychologie Appliquée, 67*(4), 187–198.

40. Gill, L. (2019, October 16). Three myths about self-managing organisations, debunked. *Medium.com*. https://medium.com/culturati/three-myths-and-misconceptions-about-self-managing-organisations-2f23c298c79b

41. Dansereau, F., Graen, G., & Haga, W. J. (1975, February). A vertical dyad linkage approach to leadership within formal organizations: A longitudinal investigation of the role making process. *Organizational Behavior and Human Performance, 13*(1), 46–78; Gerstner, C. R., & Day, D. V. (1997, December). Meta-Analytic review of leader-member exchange theory: Correlates and construct issues. *Journal of Applied Psychology, 82*(6), 827–844; Seo, J. (Jamie), Nahrgang, J. D., Carter, M. Z., & Hom, P. W. (2018, May). Not all differentiation is the same: Examining the moderating effects of leader-member exchange (LMX) configurations. *Journal of Applied Psychology, 103*(5), 478–495.

42. Miller, K. (2022). 21 Famous transformational leadership examples. *Future of Working*. https://futureofworking.com/21-famous-transformational-leadership-examples/

43. Bass, B. M. (1985). *Leadership and performance beyond expectations*. Free Press; Avolio, B. J., & Bass, B. M. (1988). Transformational leadership, charisma, and beyond. In J. G. Hunt (Ed.), *Emerging leadership vistas* (pp. 29–49). Lexington Books.

44. Bass, *Leadership and Performance beyond Expectations;* Hinkin, T. R., & Schriesheim, C. A. (2008, November). An examination of 'Nonleadership': From Laissez-Faire leadership to leader reward omission and punishment omission. *Journal of Applied Psychology, 93*(6), 1234–1248; Robert, V., & Vandenberghe, C. (2021). Laissez-faire leadership and affective commitment: The roles of leader-member exchange and subordinate relational self-concept. *Journal of Business and Psychology, 36*(4), 533–551.

45. Colvin, G. (2016, December 14). Warren Buffett's very ordinary management. *Fortune*. http://fortune.com/2016/12/14/warren-buffetts-very-ordinary-management/

46. Conger, J. A., & Kanungo, R. N. (1987). Toward a behavioral theory of charismatic leadership in organizational settings. *Academy of Management Review, 12*(4), 637–647; Conger, J. A. (Summer 99 1999). Charismatic and transformational leadership in organizations: An insider's perspective on these developing streams of research. *Leadership Quarterly, 10*(2), 145; Sy, T., Horton, C., & Riggio, R. (2018, January 3). Charismatic leadership: Eliciting and channeling follower emotions. *The Leadership Quarterly, 29*(1), 58–69.

47. Conger, J. A. (1990, September). The dark side of leadership. *Organizational Dynamics, 19*(2), 44–55; Howell, J. M. (1988). Two faces of Charisma: Socialized and personalized leadership in organizations. In J. A. Conger & R. N. Kanungo (Eds.), *Charismatic leadership: The elusive factor in organizational effectiveness* (pp. 213–236). Jossey-Bass.

48. Andersson, T. (2018). Followership: An important social resource for organizational resilience. In S. Tengblad & M. Oudhuis (Eds.), *The resilience framework: Organizing for sustained viability* (pp. 147–162). Springer Science + Business Media; Carsten, M. K., Uhl-Bien, M., West, B. J., Patera, J. L., & McGregor, R. (2010, June). Exploring social constructions of followership: A qualitative study. *Leadership Quarterly, 21*(3), 543–562.

49. See, for example, Hogg, M. A. (2004). Social categorization, depersonalization, and group behavior. In M. B. Brewer & M. Hewstone (Eds.), *Self and social identity* (pp. 203–231). Blackwell.

50. Foti, R. J., Hansbrough, T. K., Epitropaki, O., & Coyle, P. T. (2017, April). Dynamic viewpoints on implicit leadership and followership theories: Approaches, findings, and future directions. *The Leadership Quarterly, 28*(2), 261–267; Lord, R. G. L., Epitropaki, O., Foti, R. J., & Hansbrough, T. K. (2020). Implicit leadership theories, implicit followership theories, and dynamic processing of leadership information. *Annual Review of Organizational Psychology and Organizational Behavior, 7*, 49–74.

51. Foti, R. J., Fraser, S. L., & Lord, R. G. (1982, June). Effect of leadership labels and prototypes on perceptions of political leaders. *Journal of Applied Psychology, 67*(3), 326–333; Harkiolakis, N., Halkias, D., & Komodromos,

M. (2017, June). A historical view of leadership prototypes: Looking backward to move forward. *International Leadership Journal, 9*(2), 3–16; Ubaka, A., Lu, X., & Gutierrez, L. (2020). Is White always the standard? Using replication to extend what we know about leadership prototypes. In S. Taneja (Ed.), *Academy of Management Proceedings,2020*(1) 17502. Academy of Management.

52. Junker, N. M., Stegmann, S., Braun, S., & Van Dick, R. (2016). The ideal and the counter-ideal follower—advancing implicit followership theories. *Leadership & Organization Development Journal, 37*(8), 1205–1222; Lord, R. G., Epitropaki, O., Foti, R. T., & Hansbrough, T. K. (2020). Implicit leadership theories, implicit followership theories, and dynamic processing of leadership information. *Annual Review of Organizational Psychology and Organizational Behavior, 7*, 49–74.

53. Cheong, M., Yammarino, F. J., Dionne, S. D., Spain, S. M., & Chou-Yu, T. (2019). A review of the effectiveness of empowering leadership. *The Leadership Quarterly, 30*(1), 34–58; Vecchio, R. P., Justin, J. E., & Pearce, C. L. (2010, June). Empowering leadership: An examination of mediating mechanisms within a hierarchical structure. *Leadership Quarterly, 21*(3), 530–542; Lee, A., Willis, S., & Tian, A. W. (2018). Empowering leadership: A meta-analytic examination of incremental contribution, mediation, and moderation. *Journal of Organizational Behavior, 39*(3), 306–325; Zhang, S., Ke, X., Xiao-Hua., Wang, F., & Liu, J. (2018, April 18). Empowering Leadership and employee creativity: A dual-mechanism perspective. *Journal of Occupational and Organizational Psychology, 91*(4), 896–916.

54. Moran, M. (2020, December 20). 5 ways to create an empowered workplace in 2021. *Fast Company*. https://www.fastcompany.com/90587922/5-ways-to-create-an-empowered-workplace-in-2021

55. Segal, E. (2020, December 7). How to lead by example in a crisis. *Forbes*. https://www.forbes.com/sites/edwardsegal/2020/12/07/how-to-lead-by-example-in-crisis-situations/?sh=1f12a8d113fa

56. Schultz, J. (2021, January 21). What is coaching in the workplace and why is it important? *PositivePsychology.com*. https://positivepsychology.com/workplace-coaching/

57. Boogaard, K. (n.d.). 21 Companies who value big ideas. *The Muse*. https://www.themuse.com/advice/21-companies-who-value-big-ideas

58. Hallam, S. (2021, December 16). The 100 most transparent tech companies of 2021. *The Org*. https://theorg.com/insights/the-100-most-transparent-tech-companies-of-2021

59. Brower, T. (2021, September 19). Empathy is the most important leadership skill according to research. *Forbes*. https://www.forbes.com/sites/tracybrower/2021/09/19/empathy-is-the-most-important-leadership-skill-according-to-research/?sh=20e837123dc5

60. Drescher, M. A., Korsgaard, M. A., Welpe, I. M., Picot, A., & Wigand, R. T. (2014, April 14). The dynamics of shared leadership: Building trust and enhancing performance. *Journal of Applied Psychology, 99*(5),771–783; Pearce, C. L., & Manz, C. C. (2005, May). The new silver bullets of leadership: The importance of self- and shared leadership in knowledge work. *Organizational Dynamics, 34*(2), 130–140; Pearce, C. L. (2004, February). The future of leadership: Combining vertical and shared leadership to transform knowledge work. *Academy of Management Executive, 18*(1), 47–57; Zhu, J., Liao, Z., Yam, K. C., & Johnson. R. E. (2018, June 8). Shared leadership: A state-of-the-art review and future research agenda. *Journal of Organizational Behavior, 39*(7), 834–852; Liang, B. J., Van Knippenberg, D., & Gu, Q. (2021). A cross-level model of shared leadership, meaning, and individual creativity. *Journal of Organizational Behavior, 42*(1), 68–83.

61. Sanfilippo, M. (2021, December 1). Shared leadership: How modern businesses run themselves. *Business News Daily*. https://www.businessnewsdaily.com/135-shared-leadership-social-media-fuel-business-growth.html

62. Kearney, E., Shemla, M., van Knippenberg. D., & Scholz, F. A. (2019). A paradox perspective on the interactive effects of visionary and empowering leadership. *Organizational Behavior and Human Decision Processes, 155*, 20–30.

63. Manz, C. C. (1986, July). Self-Leadership: Toward an expanded theory of self-influence processes in organizations. *Academy of Management Review, 11*(3), 585–600; Stewart, G. L., Courtright, S. H., & Manz, C. C. (2011, January). Self-Leadership: A multilevel review. *Journal of Management, 37*(1), 185–222; Knotts, K., Houghton, J. D., Pearce, C. L., Chen, H., Stewart, G. L., & Manz, C. C. (2022). Leading from the inside out: A meta-analysis of how, when, and why self-leadership affects individual outcomes. *European Journal of Work and Organizational Psychology, 31*(2), 273–291; Harari, M. B., Williams, E. A., Castro, S. L., & Brant, K. K. (2021). Self-leadership: A meta-analysis of over two decades of research. *Journal of Occupational and Organizational Psychology, 94*(4), 890–923.

64. Blanchard, K. (2014, February 6). Three ways to be an effective self-leader: You can't lead others if you can't lead yourself, and you can't lead yourself without the right tools. *Fast Company*. www.fastcompany.com/3026046/leadership-now/3-ways-to-be-an-effective-self-leader

65. Neck, C. P., & Houghton, J. D. (2006). Two decades of self-leadership theory and research: Past developments, present trends, and future possibilities. *Journal of Managerial Psychology, 21*(4), 270–295.

66. Ibid.

67. Ibid.

68. Ibid.; Neck, C. P., & Manz, C. C. (1992, December). Thought self-leadership: The influence of self-talk and mental imagery on performance. *Journal of Organizational Behavior, 13*(7), 681–699.

69. Gallo, C. (2016, May 24). 3 Daily habits of peak performers, according to Michael Phelps' coach. *Forbes*. https://www.forbes.com/sites/carminegallo/2016/05/24/3-daily-habits-of-peak-performers-according-to-michael-phelps-coach/#2264c0dd102c

70. McGuire, J. (n.d.). *The case for values based leadership: Maximizing people and profitability* (White paper). Corporate Education Group. www.corpedgroup.com/resources/ml/ValuesBasedLeadership.asp

71. Gardner, W. L., Cogliser, C. C., Davism, K. M., & Dickens, M. P. (2011, December). Authentic leadership: A review of the literature and research agenda. *Leadership Quarterly, 22*(6), 1120–1145; Walumbwa, F. O., Avolio,

B. J., Gardner, W. L., Wernsing, T. S., & Peterson, S. J. (2008, February). Authentic leadership: Development and validation of a theory-based measure. *Journal of Management, 34*(1), 89–126; Sadani, Y. M., & Glenn Rowe, W. (2018, May 2). A reconceptualization of authentic leadership: Leader legitimation via follower-centered assessment of the moral dimension. *The Leadership Quarterly, 29*(6), 623–636.

72. Cashman, K. (2003). *Awakening the leader within: A story of transformation*. Wiley; George, B. (2007). *True North: Discover your authentic leadership*. Jossey-Bass.

73. Peus, C., Wesche, J. S., Streicher, B., Braun, S., & Frey, D. (2012, May). Authentic leadership: An empirical test of its antecedents, consequences, and mediating mechanisms. *Journal of Business Ethics, 107*(3), 331–348; Walumbwa et al. "Authentic leadership"; Clapp-Smith, R., Vogelgesang, G. R., & Avey, J. B. (2009, February). Authentic leadership and positive psychological capital: The mediating role of trust at the group level of analysis. *Journal of Leadership and Organizational Studies, 15*(3), 227–240.

74. Gallo, C. (2020, March 21). Marriott's CEO demonstrates truly authentic leadership in a remarkably emotional video. *Forbes*. https://www.forbes.com/sites/carminegallo/2020/03/21/marriotts-ceo-demonstrates-truly-authentic-leadership-in-a-remarkably-emotional-video/?sh=3015f3151654

75. Fry, L. W. (2003, December). Toward a theory of spiritual leadership. *Leadership Quarterly, 14*(6), 693–727; Fry, L. W. (2013). Spiritual leadership and faith and spirituality in the workplace. In J. Neal (Ed.), *Handbook of faith and spirituality in the workplace: Emerging research and practice* (pp. 697–704). Springer Science + Business Media; Yang, F., Y., Liu, J., Wang, Z., & Zhang, Y. (2017, October 13). Feeling energized: A multilevel model of spiritual leadership, leader integrity, relational energy, and job performance. *Journal of Business Ethics, 158, 983–997.*

76. Fry, L. W., Hannah, S. T., Noel, M., & Walumbwa, F. O. (2011, April). Impact of spiritual leadership on unit performance. *Leadership Quarterly, 22*(2), 259–270; Sapta, K. S. I., Rustiarini, N. W., Kusuma, I. G. A. E. T., & Astakoni, I. M. P. (2021). Spiritual leadership and organizational commitment: The mediation role of workplace spirituality. *Cogent Business & Management, 8*(1), 1966865.

77. Greenleaf, R. K. (1970). *The servant as leader*. Robert Greenleaf Center; Eva, N., Robin. M., Sendjaya, S., Van Dierendonck, D., & Liden, R. C. (2019). Servant leadership: A systematic review and call for future research. *The Leadership Quarterly, 30*(1), 111–132; Neubert, M. J., Kacmar, K. M., Carlson, D. S., Chonko, L. B., & Roberts, J. A. (2008, November). Regulatory focus as a mediator of the influence of initiating structure and servant leadership on employee behavior. *Journal of Applied Psychology, 93*(6), 1220–1233.

78. Percy, S. (2020, July 15). How servant leaders boost profits and employee morale. *Forbes*. https://www.forbes.com/sites/sallypercy/2020/07/15/how-servant-leaders-boost-profits-and-employee-morale/?sh=1e1a856a4b05

79. TalentMap. (n.d.). *How servant leadership wins the hearts and minds of employees*. https://talentmap.com/how-servant-leadership-wins-the-hearts-and-minds-of-employees/

80. Brown, M. E., & Treviño, L. K. (2006, December). Ethical leadership: A review and future directions. *Leadership Quarterly, 17*(6), 595–616; Brown, M. E., Treviño, L. K., & Harrison, D. A (2005, July). Ethical leadership: A social learning perspective for construct development and testing. *Organizational Behavior and Human Decision Processes, 97*(2), 117–134; Mostafa, A. M. S. (2018, May 10). Ethical leadership and organizational citizenship behaviours: The moderating role of organizational identification. *European Journal of Work and Organizational Psychology, 27*(4), 441–449.

81. Reiss, R. (2017, September 11). Top CEOs place high value on corporate ethics and social responsibility to drive business. *Forbes*. https://www.forbes.com/sites/robertreiss/2017/09/11/top-ceos-place-high-value-on-corporate-ethics-and-social-responsibility-to-drive-business/?sh=394f91c24473

82. Salih, A. M. (2020). *Cross-Cultural leadership: Being effective in an era of globalization, digital transformation and disruptive innovation*. Routledge.

83. Logemann, R. (2021, January 14). Remote work might force us to be better Cross-Cultural managers. *Forbes*. https://www.forbes.com/sites/forbesbusinesscouncil/2021/01/14/remote-work-might-force-us-to-be-better-cross-cultural-managers/?sh=41d1b4946bac

84. Team Ansa. (2021, May 6). Managing distributed teams: How to lead with cross-cultural empathy. *Ansa Blog*. https://blog.asana.com/2021/05/distributed-teams-cross-cultural-leadership/

85. Chhokar, J. S., Brodbeck, F. C., & House, R. J. (2008). *Culture and leadership across the world: The GLOBE book of in-depth studies of 25 societies*. Erlbaum; Gabrenya W. K. Jr., & Smith, P. B. (2015). Project GLOBE for scientists and practitioners: drawing clarity from controversy. In J. L. Wildman & R. L. Griffith (Eds.), *Leading global teams: Translating multidisciplinary science to practice* (pp. 33–65). Springer Science + Business Media; Javidan, M., Dorfman, P. W., De Luque, M. S., & House, R. J. (2006, February). In the eye of the beholder: Cross cultural lessons in leadership from project GLOBE. *Academy of Management Perspectives, 20*(1), 67–90; Pagda, Z., Bayraktar, S., & Jimenez, A. (2021). Exploring culture and leadership after 23 years: A replication of GLOBE project in Turkey. *Journal of International Management, 27*(1), 100822.

86. Ibid.

87. Ibid.

88. U.N. Women. (2022, September). *Facts and figures: Women's leadership and political participation*. https://www.unwomen.org/en/what-we-do/leadership-and-political-participation/facts-and-figures

89. Bucholz, K. (2022, March 10). How has the number of female CEOs in Fortune 500 companies changed over the last 20 years? *World Economic Forum*. https://www.weforum.org/agenda/2022/03/ceos-fortune-500-companies-female/#:~:text=2022%20is%20seeing%20a%20new,and%20only%207%20in%202002

90. Chamorro-Premuzic, T. (2021, March 7). If women are better leaders, then why are they not in charge? *Forbes*. https://www.forbes.com/sites/tomaspremuzic/2021/03/07/if-women-are-better-leaders-then-why-are-they-not-in-charge/?sh=3697bcdc6c88

91. Fairchild, C. (2014, July 8). Women CEOs in the Fortune 1000: By the Numbers. *Fortune*. http://fortune.com/2014/07/08/women-ceos-fortune-500-1000/

92. For an overview see Eagly, A. H., & Carli, L. L. (2004). Women and Men as Leaders. In J. Antonakis, A. T. Cianciolo, & R. J. Sternberg (Eds.), *The nature of leadership* (pp. 279–301). SAGE.

93. Eagly, A. H., Johannesen-Schmidt, M. C., & van Engen, M. L. (2003, July). Transformational, transactional, and laissez-faire leadership styles: A meta-analysis comparing women and men. *Psychological Bulletin, 129*(4), 569–591; Eagly, A. H., & Johnson. B. T. (1990, September). Gender and leadership style: A meta-analysis. *Psychological Bulletin, 108*(2), 233.

94. Eagly, A. H., & Carli, L. L. (2007, September). Women and the labyrinth of leadership. *Harvard Business Review, 85*(9), 63–71.

95. Konish, L. (2022, March 2). Biden pushes for paid family leave in State of the Union address. *CNBC.com*. https://www.cnbc.com/2022/03/02/biden-touts-paid-family-leave-in-state-of-the-union-address.html

96. *Is Paid Leave Available to Mothers and Fathers of Infants?* (2018). http://worldpolicycenter.org/policies/is-paid-leave-available-to-mothers-and-fathers-of-infants

97. Perraudin, F. (2019, August 4). Men less likely than women to cite impact of parental leave on career. *The Guardian*. https://www.theguardian.com/lifeandstyle/2019/aug/04/men-women-parental-leave-impact-career

98. Hoobler, J. M., Wayne, S. J., & Lemmon, G. (2009, October). Bosses' perceptions of family-work conflict and women's promotability: Glass ceiling effects. *Academy of Management Journal, 52*(5), 939–957.

99. Phillips, T. (2022, March 17). PlayStation gender discrimination lawsuit grows, as eight more women share experiences. *Eurogamer.net*. https://www.eurogamer.net/playstation-gender-discrimination-lawsuit-grows

100. Eagly & Carli. "Women and the Labyrinth of Leadership."

101. Siddiqui, F. (2021, December 14). Six Tesla workers file additional lawsuits alleging sexual harassment. *Washington Post*. https://www.washingtonpost.com/technology/2021/12/14/tesla-sexual-harassment/

102. Marchant, N. (2021, March 8). 5 ways to improve gender equality in the workplace. *World Economic Forum*. https://www.weforum.org/agenda/2021/03/gender-equality-in-the-workplace-ways-to-improve/

103. Ibid.

104. Ibid.

105. Tamny, J. (2016, July 4). The story of Chobani is about much more than yogurt. *Forbes*. https://www.forbes.com/sites/johntamny/2016/07/04/the-story-of-chobani-is-about-much-more-than-yogurt/?sh=2e3530056646

106. Doering, C. (2021, November 17). Chobani reveals surging sales as it moves closer to IPO. *Food Dive*. https://www.fooddive.com/news/chobani-reveals-surging-sales-as-it-moves-closer-to-ipo/610221/

107. Henry, P. (2017, February 18). Why some startups succeed (and why most Fail). *Entrepreneur*. https://www.entrepreneur.com/article/288769

108. Gelles, D. (2018, August 24). Hamdi Ulukaya of Chobani talks Greek yogurt and the American dream. *New York Times*. https://www.nytimes.com/2018/08/24/business/hamdi-ulukaya-chobani-corner-office.html

109. Fortune Editors. (2022, February 16). For Chobani's CEO, leadership means putting your people first. *Fortune*. https://fortune.com/2022/02/16/chobani-ceo-hamdi-ulukaya-leadership-next/

110. Ulukaya, H. (2016, March 31). Chobani founder: Higher wages important to our success. *CNN Money*. https://money.cnn.com/2016/03/31/news/economy/chobani-minimum-wage/index.html

111. Tarantino, O. (2017, December 5). 16 Things you don't know about Chobani yogurt. *Eat This, Not That!* https://www.eatthis.com/chobani/

112. Ulukaya, H. (2016, March 31). Chobani founder: Higher wages important to our success. *CNN Money*. https://money.cnn.com/2016/03/31/news/economy/chobani-minimum-wage/index.html

113. Sekulich, T. (2017, December 30). The model CEO: How Hamdi Ulukaya is forging new paths in the Chobani boardroom. *Tharawat Magazine*. https://www.tharawat-magazine.com/grow/chobani-ulukaya/

CHAPTER 14

1. Yahoo Finance. (n.d.). *NextEra Energy, Inc. (NEE)*. https://finance.yahoo.com/quote/NEE/

2. Forbes. (n.d.). *NextEra Energy | 2021 Fortune 500*. https://fortune.com/company/nextera-energy/fortune500/

3. NextEra Energy. (2017). *Investing in America's energy infrastructure sustainably and responsibly*. http://www.nexteraenergy.com/pdf/profile.pdf

4. Ibid.

5. NextEra Energy. (n.d.). *Our leadership*. http://www.nexteraenergy.com/company/bios.shtml

6. NextEra Energy. (n.d.). *NextEra Energy Careers | Benefits*. https://jobs.nexteraenergy.com/content/Benefits/?locale=en_US

7. Ibid.

8. NextEra Energy Inc. (n.d.). *August 2021 Investor Presentation*. https://www.investor.nexteraenergy.com/~/media/Files/N/NEE-IR/news-and-events/events-and-presentations/2021/08-10-21/August%202021%20Investor%20Presentation_vF.pdf

9. McKenzie, B. (n.d.). Bribery and corruption—FSA tells investment banks to improve procedures. *Lexology*. http://www.lexology.com/library/detail.aspx?g=ce18fc3a-e86a-4101-869b-b1d76043f136

10. Macrotrends. (n.d.). *NextEra Energy Revenue 2010–2021 | NEE*. https://www.macrotrends.net/stocks/charts/NEE/nextera-energy/revenue

11. Brass, D. J., & Krackhardt, D. M. (2012). Power, politics, and social networks in organizations. In D. C. Treadway & G. R. Ferris *(Eds.), Politics in organizations: Theory and research considerations* (pp. 355–375). Routledge/Taylor & Francis Group; Dundon, T., Lucio, M. M., Hughes, E., Howcroft, D., Keizer, A., & Walden, R. (2020). *Power, politics and influence at work*. Manchester University Press.

12. Keltner, D. (2007, December 1). The power paradox. *Greater Good*. http://greatergood.berkeley.edu/article/item/power_paradox

13. Ibid.

14. French, J. R. P., Raven, B. H. (Eds.). (1959). *The bases of social power.* Institute for Social Research; Wood, J. K. (2013). Fight the power: Comparing and evaluating two measures of french and Raven's (1959) Bases of social power. *Current Research in Social Psychology, 21, PsycINFO,* EBSCO*host.*

15. Shour, E. (2013). How to retain employees: 15 Practical takeaways from 6 case studies. *Best Practice in Human Resources.* X. https://bestpracticeinhr.com/?s=How+to+retain+employees%3A+15+Practical+takeaways+from+6+case+studies

16. Silkoset, R. (2020, December 18). Covid-19: The dysfunctional effect of coercive power to control the pandemic. *BI Business Review.* https://www.bi.edu/research/business-review/articles/2020/12/covid-19-the-dysfunctional-effect-of-coercive-power-to-control-the-pandemic/

17. Yukl, G., & Falbe, C. M. (1990, April). Influence tactics and objectives in upward, downward, and lateral influence attempts. *Journal of Applied Psychology, 75*(2),132–140; Kipnis, D., Schmidt, S. M., & Wilkinson, I. (1980, August). Intraorganizational influence tactics: Explorations in getting one's way. *Journal of Applied Psychology,65*(4), 440–452.

18. Young Entrepreneur Council. (2022, March 15). 8 Strategies for becoming a more persuasive leader. *Inc.* https://www.inc.com/magazine/202203/brit-morse/2022-regionals-qwick-jamie-baxter-chris-loeffler-staff-retention.html

19. Kim, L. (2016, November 18). 33 Traits of the most inspiring leaders. *Inc.* https://www.inc.com/larry-kim/33-characteristics-of-super-inspiring-leaders.html

20. Yukl, G., Y., Kim, H., & Falbe, C. M. (1996). Antecedents of influence outcomes. *Journal of Applied Psychology, 81*(3), 309.

21. Fontein, D. (2021, November 10). Accelerate decision-making by involving employees. *Thought Exchange.* https://thoughtexchange.com/blog/employee-involvement-decision-making/

22. Keeves, G., Westphal, J., & McDonald, M. (2017, January 20). Office politics: When managers flatter the CEO, but undermine him with journalists. *LSE Business Review.* http://blogs.lse.ac.uk/businessreview/2017/01/20/office-politics-when-managers-flatter-the-ceo-but-undermine-him-with-journalists/

23. Klotz, A. C., He, W., Yam, K. C., Bolino, M. C., Wei, W., & Houston III, L. (2018). Good actors but bad apples: Deviant consequences of daily impression management at work. *Journal of Applied Psychology, 103*(10), 1145.

24. Jiang, Z. (Joe). (2019, November 14). Why withholding information at work won't give you an advantage. *Harvard Business Review.* https://hbr.org/2019/11/why-withholding-information-at-work-wont-give-you-an-advantage

25. Ibid.

26. Detert, J. R., & Burris, E. R. (2016, January/February). Can your employees really speak freely? *Harvard Business Review.* https://hbr.org/2016/01/can-your-employees-really-speak-freely

27. Valentine, R. (2019, December 5). Ex-Razer employees accuse CEO of abusive behavior. *Gamesindustry.biz.* https://www.gamesindustry.biz/articles/2019-12-05-ex-razer-employees-accuse-ceo-of-abusive-behavior

28. Falbe, C. M., & Yukl, G. (1992, August). Consequences for managers of using single influence tactics and combinations of tactics. *Academy of Management Journal, 35*(3), 638–652; Rhodes, J. E., & Rhodes, L. G. (2017, May). Managing up: Using influence & collaboration. *Professional Safety, 62*(5), 30–31.

29. Ralston, D. A., Gustafson, D. J., Cheung, F. M., & Terpstra, R. H. (1993, June). Differences in managerial values: A study of U.S., Hong Kong and PRC managers. *Journal of International Business Studies,24*(2), 249–275.

30. Yukl, G., Fu, P. P., & McDonald, R. (2003, January). Cross-cultural differences in perceived effectiveness of influence tactics for initiating or resisting change. *Applied Psychology: An International Review, 52*(1), 68–82.

31. Sun, S., & Chen, H. (2017). Is political behavior a viable coping strategy to perceived organizational politics? Unveiling the underlying resource dynamics. *Journal of Applied Psychology, 102*(10), 1471.

32. Ferris, G. R., Ellen III, B. P., McAllister, C. P., & Maher, L. P. (2019). Reorganizing organizational politics research: A review of the literature and identification of future research directions. *Annual Review of Organizational Psychology and Organizational Behavior, 6*, 299–323; Landells, E. M., & Albrecht, S. M. (2017, February). The positives and negatives of organizational politics: A qualitative study. *Journal of Business And Psychology, 32*(1), 41–58; Hochwarter, W. A., Rosen, C. C., Jordan, S. L., Ferris, G. R., Ejaz, A., & Maher, L. P. (2020). Perceptions of organizational politics research: past, present, and future. *Journal of Management, 46*(6), 879–907.

33. Postma, N. (2021, July 14). You can't sit out office politics. *Harvard Business Review.* 2021. https://hbr.org/2021/07/you-cant-sit-out-office-politics

34. Chang, C.-H., Rosen, C. C., & Levy, P. E. (2009, August). The relationship between perceptions of organizational politics and employee attitudes, strain, and behavior: A meta-analytic examination. *Academy of Management Journal, 52*(4), 779–801; Ejaz, A., & Lacaze, D. (2016, January). Organizational politics and work outcomes: A moderated mediation model. *Academy Of Management Annual Meeting Proceedings,2016*(1), 1; Ferris, G. R., Frink, D. D., Galang, M. C., Zhou, J., & Howard, J. L. (1996, February). Perceptions of organizational politics: prediction, stress-related implications, and outcomes. *Human Relations, 49*(2), 233–266.

35. Ferris, G. R., Treadway, D. C., Brouer, R. L., & Munyon, T. P. (2012). Political skill in the organizational sciences. In D. C. Treadway & G. R. Ferris (Eds.), *Politics in organizations: Theory and research considerations* (pp. 487–528). Routledge/Taylor & Francis Group; Rosen, C. C., & Perrewé, P. L. *Power, politics, and political skill in job stress.* Emerald Group.

36. Jarrett, M. (2017, April 24). The 4 types of organizational politics. *Harvard Business Review.* https://hbr.org/2017/04/the-4-types-of-organizational-politics

37. Ferris, G. R., Russ, G. S., & Fandt, P. M. (1989). Politics in organizations. In R. A. Giacalone & P. Rosenfeld *(Eds.), Impression management in the organization* (pp. 143–170). Erlbaum; Munyon, T. P., Summers, J. K., Thompson, K. M., & Ferris, G. R. (Spring 2015). Political skill and work outcomes: A theoretical extension, meta-analytic investigation, and agenda for the

future. *Personnel Psychology, 68*(1), 143–184.

38. Postma, N. (2021, July 14). You can't sit out office politics. *Harvard Business Review.* https://hbr.org/2021/07/you-cant-sit-out-office-politics
39. Parker, C. P., Dipboye, R. L., & Jackson, S. L. (1995, December). Perceptions of organizational politics: An investigation of antecedents and consequences. *Journal of Management, 21*(5), 891–912; Sultan, S., Kanwal, F., & Gul, S. Factors of perceived organizational politics: An analysis of what contributes the most? *Pakistan Journal of Commerce & Social Sciences,9*(3), 999–1011.
40. Olya, G. (2021, March 15). 25 Companies laying off the most people thanks to coronavirus. *GoBankingRates.com.* https://www.gobankingrates.com/money/jobs/companies-laying-off-people-thanks-coronavirus/
41. Postma, N. (2021, July 14). You can't sit out office politics. *Harvard Business Review.* 2021. https://hbr.org/2021/07/you-cant-sit-out-office-politics
42. Warren, D. I. (1968). Power, visibility, and conformity in formal organizations. *American Sociological Review, 33*(6), 951–970; Lewis, P., & Simpson, R. (2012, June). Kanter revisited: Gender, power and (In)visibility. *International Journal of Management Reviews, 14*(2), 141–158; Leonardi, P. M., & Treem, J. W. (2020). Behavioral visibility: A new paradigm for organization studies in the age of digitization, digitalization, and datafication. *Organization Studies, 41*(12), 1601–1625.
43. Jarrett. The 4 types of organizational politics.
44. Francis, T., & Hoefel, F. (2018, November 12). *'True gen': Generation Z and its implications for companies.* McKinsey & Company. https://www.mckinsey.com/industries/consumer-packaged-goods/our-insights/true-gen-generation-z-and-its-implications-for-companies
45. Jhaveri, D. P. (2020, January 20). TikTok is full of Sephora and Chipotle employees spilling secrets. That can get complicated. *Vox.* https://www.vox.com/the-goods/2020/1/20/21059143/tiktok-sephora-chipotle-panera-starbucks
46. Starbucks. (2012, October 15*). Starbucks social media guidelines for Canada and U.S. partners.* https://globalassets.starbucks.com/assets/f945dbfa51904618982409e9c09c58b6.pdf
47. Gupta, B. (2022, January 13). Starbucks employees are begging you to answer this customer service question. *Mashed.* https://www.mashed.com/732914/starbucks-employees-are-begging-you-to-answer-this-customer-service-question/
48. Schultz, H., & Gordon, J. (2011). *Onward: How Starbucks fought for its life without losing its soul.* Rodale.
49. Starbucks. (2019). *Company Profile.* https://stories.starbucks.com/press/2019/company-profile/

CHAPTER 15

1. REI Co-op. (n.d.). *REI History: It started with an ice axe.* https://www.rei.com/blog/camp/rei-history-it-started-with-an-ice-axe
2. Whittaker. J. (n.d.). *About.* http://jimwhittaker.com/jim-whittaker
3. Purposeful Connections. (2016, July 14). *REI'S #Optoutside—10 critical insights for authentic and powerful purpose creation.* https://www.carolconeonpurpose.com/post/rei-s-optoutside-10-critical-insights-for-authentic-and-powerful-purpose-creation
4. REI Co-op. (n.d.). *Who we are.* https://www.rei.com/blog/camp/rei-history-it-started-with-an-ice-axe
5. Michelson, M. (2015, September 25). *REI co-op brand gets an overhaul.* https://www.rei.com/blog/camp/rei-co-op-brand-gets-an-overhaul
6. Scheiber, N. (2022, March 2). REI workers in New York vote to unionize. *New York Times.* https://www.nytimes.com/2022/03/02/business/rei-union-new-york.html
7. Vorhauser-Smith, S. (2013, August 14). How the best places to work are nailing employee engagement. *Forbes.* https://www.forbes.com/sites/sylviavorhausersmith/2013/08/14/how-the-best-places-to-work-are-nailing-employee-engagement/?sh=1387c5c15cc7
8. Fortune. (n.d.). *100 best companies to work for.* https://fortune.com/best-companies/search/
9. Boué, K. (2015, September 29). Yay for corporate culture. *Outdoor Industry Association.* https://outdoorindustry.org/article/yay-for-corporate-culture/
10. Purposeful Connections. (2016, July 14). *REI'S #Optoutside—10 critical insights for authentic and powerful purpose creation.* https://www.carolconeonpurpose.com/post/rei-s-optoutside-10-critical-insights-for-authentic-and-powerful-purpose-creation
11. Silicon Bayou News. (2016, September 7). *How REI, Southwest and Whole Foods built company cultures that drive their success, and so can you.* http://siliconbayounews.com/2016/09/07/rei-southwest-whole-foods-built-company-cultures-drive-success-can/
12. REI Co-op. (n.d.). *#OptOutside.* https://www.rei.com/opt-outside
13. For overviews of organizational culture see Ehrhart, M. G., Schneider, B., & Macey, W. H. (2014). *Organizational climate and culture: An introduction to theory, research, and practice.* Routledge/Taylor & Francis Group; Fleming, M., & Guldenmund, F. (2015). Organizational culture. In D. A. Boehm-Davis, F. T. Durso, & J. D. Lee (Eds.), *APA handbook of human systems integration* (pp. 589–604). American Psychological Association; Ostroff, C., Kinicki, A. J., & Muhammad, R. S. (2013). Organizational culture and climate. In N. W. Schmitt, S. Highhouse, & I. B. Weiner (Eds.), *Handbook of psychology, Vol. 12: Industrial and organizational psychology* (2nd ed., pp. 643–676). Wiley; Elsbach, K. D., & Stigliani, I. (2018). Design thinking and organizational culture: A review and framework for future research. *Journal of Management, 44*(6), 2274–2306.
14. Castrillon, C. (2021, December 29). Why 2022 is the year of workplace culture. *Forbes.* https://www.forbes.com/sites/carolinecastrillon/2021/12/29/why-2022-is-the-year-of-workplace-culture/?sh=331294c91bbb
15. Feiner, L. (2022, January 11). Facebook drops 36 spots on Glassdoor's annual best places to work list after a year of PR crises. *CNBC.com.* https://www.cnbc.com/2022/01/11/facebook-owner-meta-falls-on-glassdoor-annual-best-places-to-work-list.html
16. Schein, E. H. (1990, February). Organizational culture. *American Psychologist, 45*(2), 109–119.
17. Ibid.
18. Reiss, R. (2020, July 15). Top CEOs agree that culture is the key before,

during and after crisis. *Forbes*. https://www.forbes.com/sites/robertreiss/2020/07/15/top-ceos-agree-that-culture-is-the-key-before-during-and-after-crisis/?sh=ba547582cb2c

19. Hartnell, C. A., Ou, A. Y., & Kinicki, A. (2011, July). Organizational culture and organizational effectiveness: A meta-analytic investigation of the competing values framework's theoretical suppositions. *Journal of Applied Psychology, 96*(4), 677–694; Tong, Y. K., & Arvey, R. D. (2015). Managing complexity via the competing values framework. *Journal of Management Development, 34*(6), 653–673; Quinn, R. E., St Clair, L. S., Faerman, S. R., Thompson, M. P., & McGrath, M. R. (2020). *Becoming a master manager: A competing values approach*. Wiley.
20. Devi, A. (2021). 10 best companies in customer service & what you can learn from them. *Happy Fox*. https://blog.happyfox.com/10-best-companies-customer-service/
21. Down, R. (2019, February 21). Clan culture: pros and cons. *BreatheHR.com*. https://www.breathehr.com/en-gb/blog/topic/company-culture/clan-culture-the-pros-and-cons#:~:text=When%20applied%20to%20company%20culture,peers%20and%20employees'%20needs%20first
22. Goodall, O. (2019, May 23). There are four types of company culture. Do you know yours? *Real Business*. https://realbusiness.co.uk/four-types-of-company-culture
23. Fivecoat, D. (n.d.). 4 types of corporate culture. *TFCG*. https://www.thefivecoatconsultinggroup.com/the-coronavirus-crisis/four-types-corporate-culture
24. Hartnell, C. A., Ou, A. Y., & Kinicki, A. (2011, July). Organizational culture and organizational effectiveness: A meta-analytic investigation of the competing values framework's theoretical suppositions. *Journal of Applied Psychology, 96*(4), 677–694; Quinn, R. E., & Rohrbaugh, J. (1983, March). A spatial model of effectiveness criteria: Towards a competing values approach to organizational analysis. *Management Science, 29*(3), 363–377.
25. Hofstede, G. (1998, January). Identifying organizational subcultures: An empirical approach. *Journal of Management Studies, 35*(1), 1–12; Martin, J., & Siehl, C. (1983, September). Organizational culture and counterculture: An uneasy symbiosis. *Organizational Dynamics, 12*(2), 52–64.
26. Fortune. (2020). *Radio flyer*. https://fortune.com/best-workplaces-giving-back/2016/radio-flyer-inc/
27. Hofstede. "Identifying Organizational Subcultures"; Martin and Siehl. "Organizational Culture and Counterculture."
28. Emerson, T. (2018, June 11). How to manage subcultures in your organization. *Workforce.com*. https://workforce.com/news/how-to-manage-subcultures-organization
29. Ibid.
30. Denison, D. R. (1984, September). Bringing corporate culture to the bottom line. *Organizational Dynamics, 13*(2), 5–22; Saffold III, G. S. (1988, October). Culture traits, strength, and organizational performance: Moving beyond "Strong" culture. *Academy of Management Review, 13*(4), 546–558; Kotter, J. P. (2008). *Corporate culture and performance*. Simon and Schuster; Pandu, A., & Kamaraj, S. (2016, April). Correlates of organizational culture and social responsibility: An empirical study of college teachers. *Journal of Organisation & Human Behaviour, 5*(2), 14–22.
31. Laker, B. (2021, April 23). Culture is a company's single most powerful advantage. Here's why. *Forbes*. https://www.forbes.com/sites/benjaminlaker/2021/04/23/culture-is-a-companys-single-most-powerful-advantage-heres-why/?sh=14930cc4679e
32. Ibid.
33. Sull, D., Sull, C., & Zweig, B. (2022, January 11). Toxic culture is driving the great resignation. *MIT Sloan Management Review*. https://sloanreview.mit.edu/article/toxic-culture-is-driving-the-great-resignation/#:~:text=A%20toxic%20corporate%20culture%20is%20the%20single%20best%20predictor%20of,of%20culture%20that%20predicts%20attrition
34. Janis, I. L. (1973, September). Groupthink and group dynamics: A social psychological analysis of defective policy decisions. *Policy Studies Journal, 2*(1), 19–25; Sunstein, C., & Hastie, R. (2015, January). Wiser: Getting beyond groupthink to make groups smarter. *Harvard Business School Press Books*.
35. Schein, E. H. (1990, February). Organizational culture. *American Psychologist, 45*(2), 109–119; Schneider, B., Ehrhart, M. G., & Macey, W. H. (2011). Perspectives on organizational climate and culture. In S. Zedeck (Ed.), *APA handbook of industrial and organizational psychology, Vol 1: Building and developing the organization* (pp. 373–414). American Psychological Association.
36. Choy, E. (2020, February 9). Why is leadership storytelling so powerful? *Forbes*. https://www.forbes.com/sites/estherchoy/2020/02/09/why-is-leadership-storytelling-so-powerful/?sh=1c2688d02e46
37. Pollack, S. (2020, February 6). Work dress code: What it says about your business. *Workest by Zenefits*. https://www.zenefits.com/workest/work-dress-code-what-it-says-about-your-business/
38. Razzetti, G. (2020, February 10). How to use team rituals to boost your culture. *Fearless Culture*. https://www.fearlessculture.design/blog-posts/how-to-use-team-rituals-to-boost-your-culture
39. Coleman, C. 5 powerful ways rituals improve corporate culture. *Culture Wise*. https://culturewise.com/blog/corporate-culture-rituals/
40. CARROTS. (2020, September). 6 proven tips to recognize remote employees during COVID-19. https://www.carrots.ph/blog/recognizeremoteworkers
41. Karch, M. (2018, May 19). Odd Google Jargon terms. *Lifewire*. https://www.lifewire.com/google-jargon-terms-1616202
42. Silicon Valley lingo separates the insiders from the outsiders. (2021, March 30). *The Economist*. https://www.economist.com/prospero/2021/03/30/silicon-valley-lingo-separates-the-insiders-from-the-outsiders
43. Schein. "Organizational Culture."
44. Ibid.
45. Ramalingam, B., Nabarro, D., Oqubay, A., Carnall, D. R., & Wild, L. (2020, September 11). 5 principles to guide adaptive leadership. *Harvard Business Review*. https://hbr.org/2020/09/5-principles-to-guide-adaptive-leadership
46. Schein. "Organizational Culture."

47. Ellwood, B. (2022, January 11). Supervisors who cultivate a sense of shared identity at work have employees who are less likely to burn out. *PsyPost.org*. https://www.psypost.org/2022/01/supervisors-who-cultivate-a-sense-of-shared-identity-at-work-have-employees-who-are-less-likely-to-burn-out-62344

48. Schein. "Organizational Culture."

49. Arnold, P., & Kruzan, T. (2012, May). Organizational culture roadblocks and shortcuts for leveraging diversity: Part 1. *Profiles in Diversity, 14*(3), 71.

50. Flockett, A. (n.d.). Worst company for gender diversity in the boardroom. *Startups Magazine*. https://startupsmagazine.co.uk/article-zoom-identified-worst-company-gender-diversity-boardroom

51. Schein, "Organizational Culture"; Schraeder, M., & Self, D. R. (2003). Enhancing the success of mergers and acquisitions: An organizational culture perspective. *Management Decision, 41*(5), 511–522; Dewan, A. (2016, September). Organizational culture & human resource management: A scenario in the case of mergers & acquisitions. *Amity Global HRM Review, 6*, 62–65.

52. Bligh, M. C. (2006, November). Surviving post-merger "Culture Clash": Can cultural leadership lessen the casualties? *Leadership, 2*(4), 395–426; Van den Steen, E. (2010, October). Culture clash: The costs and benefits of homogeneity. *Management Science, 56*(10), 1718–1738; Milligan, S. (2014, August). Culture Clash! *HR Magazine, 59*(8), 18–24.

53. Kapner, S. (2021, December 23). Tiffany's new French owner brings a makeover—and a culture clash. *Wall Street Journal*. https://www.wsj.com/articles/tiffanys-new-french-owner-brings-a-makeoverand-a-culture-clash-11640264191

54. Parent, J. D., & Lovelace, K. J. (2018). Employee engagement, positive organizational culture and individual adaptability. *On the Horizon*; Rinke, W. J. (1998, November). How to build a positive organizational culture. *Food Management, 33*(11), 17.

55. Raouna, K. (2021, July 29). 10 startups with the best company culture in 2022. *Proof Hub*. https://blog.proofhub.com/10-startups-with-the-best-company-culture-in-2021-e0ec395b5d22

56. Goffee, R., & Jones, G. (1998). *The character of a corporation*. Harper Collins.

57. Peart, N. (2020, December 14). Meet The Best Company Workplace Culture Awards 2020—according to comparably. *Forbes*. https://www.forbes.com/sites/nataliapeart/2020/12/14/best-company-workplace-culture-awards-2020/?sh=1005f56934d3

58. Goffee & Jones, *The character of a corporation.*

59. Baker, M. (2021, November 10). Two years into the pandemic, organizational culture is more important than ever. *Gartner*. https://www.gartner.com/en/articles/two-years-into-the-pandemic-organizational-culture-is-more-important-than-ever

60. Goffee & Jones, *The character of a corporation.*

61. Glassdoor Team. (2021, July 7). What it's really like to work at Netflix in the wake of Wall Street Journal Exposé. *Glassdoor.com*. https://www.glassdoor.com/blog/Netflix-wall-street-journal/

62. Goffee & Jones, *The character of a corporation.*

63. Ruiz-Palomino, P., Martínez-Cañas, R., & Fontrodona, J. (2013, August). Ethical culture and employee outcomes: The mediating role of person-organization fit. *Journal of Business Ethics, 116*(1), 173–188; Meinert, D. (2014, April). Creating an ethical culture. *HR, 59*(4), 22–27; Ullah, I., Hameed, R. M., Kayani, N. Z., & Fazal, Y. (2022). CEO ethical leadership and corporate social responsibility: Examining the mediating role of organizational ethical culture and intellectual capital. *Journal of Management & Organization, 28*(1), 99–119.

64. KAO. (2020, February 26). Kao makes the world's most ethical companies® list for 14 straight years. https://www.kao.com/global/en/news/sustainability/2020/20200226-001/

65. Dolan, S. L. (2015, October). Values, spirituality and organizational culture. *Developing Leaders, 21*, 22–27; Fawcett, S. E., Brau, J. C., Rhoads, G. K., Whitlark, D., & Fawcett, A. M. (2008, March). Spirituality and organizational culture: Cultivating the ABCs of an inspiring workplace. *International Journal of Public Administration, 31*(4), 420–438.

66. See, for example, Case, P., & Gosling, J. (2010, December). The spiritual organization: Critical reflections on the instrumentality of workplace spirituality. *Journal of Management, Spirituality and Religion, 7*(4), 257–282.

67. Douglas, E. (2020, September 11). "Cult or culture?": What is workplace spirituality? *HRD*. https://www.hcamag.com/us/news/general/cult-or-culture-what-is-workplace-spirituality/233340#_edn4

68. Tan, B.-S. (2019). In search of the link between organizational culture and performance: A review from the conclusion validity perspective. *Leadership & Organization Development Journal, 40*(3), 356–368.

69. Hofstede, G. (1984). *Culture's consequences: International differences in work-related values* (Vol. 5). SAGE; Hofstede, G. (2011). Dimensionalizing cultures: The Hofstede model in context. *Online Readings in Psychology and Culture, 2*(1), 2307–0919; Hofstede, G. (1980). Culture and organizations. *International Studies of Management and Organization, 10*(4), 15–41; Hofstede, G. (Summer 1983). National cultures in four dimensions. *International Studies of Management and Organization, 13*(1/2), 46–74; Taras, V., Kirkman, B. L., & Steel, P. (2010, May). Examining the impact of culture's consequences: A three-decade, multilevel, meta-analytic review of Hofstede's cultural value dimensions. *Journal of Applied Psychology, 95*(3), 405–439.

70. McSweeney, B. (2002). Hofstede's model of national cultural differences and their consequences: A triumph of faith—a failure of analysis. *Human Relations, 55*(1), 89–118; Hofstede, G. (2002). Dimensions do not exist: A reply to Brendan McSweeney. *Human Relations, 55*(11), 1355–1361; Minkov, M., & Kaasa, A. (2020). A test of Hofstede's model of culture following his own approach. *Cross Cultural & Strategic Management, 28*(2), 384–406.

71. Brock, D. M., & Siscovick, I. C. (2007). Global integration and local responsiveness in multinational subsidiaries: Some strategy, structure, and human resource contingencies. *Asia Pacific Journal of Human Resources, 45*(3), 353–373; Rosenzweig, P. M. (2006). The dual logics behind international human resource

management: Pressures for global integration and local responsiveness. In G. K. Stahl & I. Björkman (Eds.), *Handbook of research in international human resource management* (pp. 36–48). Edward Elgar; Gaur, A. S., Ma, H., & Ge, B. (2019). MNC strategy, knowledge transfer context, and knowledge flow in MNEs. *Journal of Knowledge Management, 23*(9), 1885–1900.

72. Bartlett, C. A., & Ghoshal, S. (2002). *Managing across borders: The transnational solution* (2nd ed.). Harvard Business School Press; Wang, P. (2020). Research on enterprise human resource standardization management in the new era. *Population, Resources & Environmental Economics, 1*(1), 15–17; Wurm, B., & Mendling, J. (2020). A theoretical model for business process standardization. In *International conference on business process management* (pp. 281–296). Springer.

73. Evans, P., Pucik, V., & Barsoux, J.-L. (2002). *The global challenge: Frameworks for international human resource management.* McGraw-Hill; Ouyang, C., Liu, M., Chen, Y., Li, J., & Qin, W. (2019). Overcoming liabilities of origin: Human resource management localization of Chinese multinational corporations in developed markets. *Human Resource Management, 58*(5), 543–561; Song, S. (2020). Actualization of growth potential in international joint ventures: The moderating effects of localization strategies. *Journal of World Business, 55*(2), 101024.

74. Guzzo, R. A. (1996). The expatriate employee. In C. L. Cooper & D. M. Rousseau (Eds.), *Trends in organizational behavior* (Vol. 3, pp. 123–137). Wiley; Lee, Y., & Larwood, L. (1983, December). The socialization of expatriate managers in multinational firms. *Academy of Management Journal, 26*(4), 657–665; Tung, R. L. (1988). *The new expatriates: Managing human resources abroad.* Ballinger/Harper & Row; Guo, Y., Rammal, H. G., & Pereira, V. (2021). Am I "In or Out"? A social identity approach to studying expatriates' social networks and adjustment in a host country context. *Journal of Business Research, 136*, 558–566.

75. Dore, K. (2021, May 18). The top reason why Americans abroad want to dump their U.S. citizenship. *CNBC.com.* https://www.cnbc.com/2021/05/18/the-top-reason-why-americans-abroad-want-to-dump-their-citizenship.html

76. Derr, C. B., Jones, C., & Toomey, E. L. (Fall 1988). Managing high-potential employees: Current practices in thirty-three U.S. Corporations. *Human Resource Management, 27*(3), 273–290; Finkelstein, L. M., Costanza, D. P., & Goodwin, G. F. (2018). Do your high potentials have potential? The impact of individual differences and designation on leader success. *Personnel Psychology, 71*(1), 3–22.

77. Feldman, D. C., & Tompson, H. B. (Winter 1992). Entry shock, culture shock: Socializing the new breed of global managers. *Human Resource Management, 31*(4), 345–362; Ward, C., Bochner, S., & Furnham, A. (2001). *The psychology of culture shock* (2nd ed.). Routledge; Simanjuntak, D., & Fitriana, R. (2020). Culture shock, adaptation, and self-concept of tourism human resources in welcoming the new normal era. *Society, 8*(2), 403–418.

78. Mendenhall, M. E., & Stahl, G. K. (2000). Expatriate training and development: Where do we go from here? *Human Resource Management, 39*(2–3), 251–265; Romero, E. J. (2002). The effect of expatriate training on expatriate effectiveness. *Journal of Management Research, 2*(2), 73–78; Haile, S., & White, D. (2019). Expatriate failure is a common challenge for multinational corporations: Turn expatriate failure to expatriate success. *International Journal of Business & Public Administration, 16*(1), 27–40.

79. Winkelman, M. (1994, November). Cultural shock and adaptation. *Journal of Counseling and Development, 73*(2), 121–126; Simanjuntak, D., & Fitriana, R. (2020). Culture shock, adaptation, and self-concept of tourism human resources in welcoming the new normal era. *Society, 8*(2), 403–418.

80. Zabetian, F. (2021, June 10). Connecting abroad: The cultural etiquette of international business. *Forbes.* https://www.forbes.com/sites/forbestechcouncil/2021/06/10/connecting-abroad-the-cultural-etiquette-of-international-business/?sh=4a6807fd2050

81. Hays, R. D. (1971, Fall). Ascribed behavioral determinants of success-failure among U.S. expatriate managers. *Journal of International Business Studies, 2*(2), 40–46; Tung, R. L. (1987, May). Expatriate assignments: Enhancing success and minimizing failure. *Academy of Management Executive, 1*(2), 117–125; Haile, S., & White, D. (2019). Expatriate failure is a common challenge for multinational corporations: Turn expatriate failure to expatriate success. *International Journal of Business & Public Administration, 16*(1), 27–40.

82. Tung, R. L. (1987, May). Expatriate assignments: Enhancing success and minimizing failure. *Academy of Management Executive, 1*(2), 117–125; Gupta, R., Banerjee, P., & Gaur, J. (2012, October). Exploring the role of the spouse in expatriate failure: A grounded theory-based investigation of expatriate' spouse adjustment issues from India. *International Journal of Human Resource Management, 23*(17), 3559–3577; Dang, Q. T., Rammal, H. G., & Michailova, S. (2021). Expatriates' families: A systematic literature review and research agenda. *Human Resource Management Review, 32*(4), 100877.

83. Driscoll, I. (2014, October 21). Expat's dilemma: Out of sight—and mind? *BBC.* www.bbc.com/capital/story/20141020-expat-woes-out-of-sight-and-mind

84. Schachter, H. (2014, March 23). Key steps to change corporate culture. *Globe and Mail.* www.theglobeandmail.com/report-on-business/careers/management/key-steps-to-change-corporate-culture/article17557724/

85. Schein, E. (Summer 1983). The role of the founder in creating organizational culture. *Organizational Dynamics, 12*(1), 13–28; Hambrick, D. C., & Mason, P. A. (1984, April). Upper echelons: The organization as a reflection of its top managers. *Academy of Management Review, 9*(2), 193–206; Baykal, E. (2022). Family firms and the effects of organizational culture on their innovation. In Information Resources Management Association (Ed.), *Research anthology on strategies for maintaining successful family firms* (pp. 1082–1102). IGI Global.

86. Onderick-Harvey, E. (2018, May 18). 5 behaviors of leaders who embrace change. *Harvard Business Review.* https://hbr.org/2018/05/5-behaviors-of-leaders-who-embrace-change

87. O'Reilly III, C. A., Chatman, J., & Caldwell, D. F. (September 1991). People and organizational culture:

A profile comparison approach to assessing person-organization fit. *Academy of Management Journal, 34*(3), 487–516; Swider, B. W., Zimmerman, R. D., & Barrick, M. R. (2015). Searching for the right fit: Development of applicant person-organization fit perceptions during the recruitment process. *Journal of Applied Psychology, 100*(3), 880–893.

88. McCord, P. (2018, January–February). How to hire. *Harvard Business Review.* https://hbr.org/2018/01/how-to-hire
89. Cranmer, G. A., Goldman, Z. W., & Booth-Butterfield, M. (2017, January). The mediated relationship between received support and job satisfaction: An Initial application of socialization resources theory. *Western Journal of Communication, 81*(1), 64–86; Kammeyer-Mueller, J., Wanberg, C., Rubenstein, A., & Zhaoli, S. (2013, August). Support, undermining, and newcomer socialization: Fitting in during the first 90 days. *Academy of Management Journal, 56*(4), 1104–1124; Chao, G. T., O'Leary-Kelly, A. M., Wolf, S., Klein, H. J., & Gardner, P. D. (1994, October). Organizational socialization: Its content and consequences. *Journal of Applied Psychology, 79*(5), 730–743.
90. Ashforth, B. E., Saks, A. M., & Lee, R. T. (July 1998). Socialization and newcomer adjustment: The role of organizational context. *Human Relations, 51*(7), 897–926; Ashforth, B. E., Sluss, D. M., & Harrison, S. H. (2007). Socialization in organizational contexts. *International Review of Industrial and Organizational Psychology 2007, 22*, 1–70. Wiley.
91. Dust, S. (2021, March 3). These are the hidden challenges of onboarding in a remote environment. *Fast Company.* https://www.fastcompany.com/90609859/the-hidden-challenges-of-onboarding-in-a-remote-environment
92. Durlauf, S. N., & Young, H. P. (Eds.) (2004). *Social dynamics* (Vol. 4). MIT Press; Farmer, T. W., Talbott, B., Dawes, M., Huber, H. B., Brooks, D. S., & Powers, E. E. (2018). Social dynamics management: What is it and why is it important for intervention? *Journal of Emotional and Behavioral Disorders,26*(1), 3–10.
93. Maryville University. (n.d.). *4 things to know about group dynamics in the workplace.* https://online.maryville.edu/blog/4-things-to-know-about-group-dynamics-in-the-workplace/
94. Klinghoffer, D., Young, C., & Haspas, D. (2019, June 6). "Every new employee needs an onboarding 'Buddy.'" *Harvard Business Review.* https://hbr.org/2019/06/every-new-employee-needs-an-onboarding-buddy
95. Feldman, D. C. (1976, September). A contingency theory of socialization. *Administrative Science Quarterly, 21*(3), 433–452; Feldman, D. C. (1976, September). A practical program for employee socialization. *Organizational Dynamics, 5*(2), 64–80; Feldman, D. C., & O'Neill, O. A. (2014). The role of socialization, orientation, and training programs in transmitting culture and climate and enhancing performance. In K. M. Barbera (Ed.), *The Oxford handbook of organizational climate and culture* (pp. 44–64). Oxford University Press.
96. Shah, D. (2016, February 10). Why company culture is crucial. *Entrepreneurial thought leaders.* Speech presented at Stanford University eCorner Speaker Series, Stanford, CA.
97. Halligan, B. (Interviewee). (2020, October 19). HubSpot's startup to scale-up journey. *Jungle Ventures Founders Assembly.* https://www.youtube.com/watch?v=VO2vxg2lEmo
98. Shah, D. (2021). The HubSpot culture code [slide deck]. https://network.hubspot.com/slides/the-hubspot-culture-code-1f8v20t3a?_ga=2.107892929.2134150291.1645652940-227011939.1645652940 (Original work published 2013).
99. Shah, HubSpot CTO and Founder. (n.d.). *HubSpot.* https://www.hubspot.com/company/management/dharmesh-shah
100. Shah, D. (2021, May 20). Culture is a product you build for your people. *OnStartups.* https://www.onstartups.com/culture-is-product
101. *HubSpot Careers / Awards.* (2022). https://www.hubspot.com/careers/awards

CHAPTER 16

1. Macrotrends. (n.d.). *Alphabet: Number of Employees 2010-2021 / GOOG.* https://www.macrotrends.net/stocks/charts/GOOG/alphabet/number-of-employees
2. Google. (n.d.). *Our Offices.* https://about.google/locations/?region=north-america&office=mountain-view; Goodwin, D. (2022, February 2). Google Q4 search ad revenue: $43.3 billion. *Search Engine Land.* https://searchengineland.com/google-q4-2021-earnings-379735
3. Eatough, E. (2021, June 7). 20 best job benefits and the companies that offer them. *BetterUp.* https://www.betterup.com/blog/best-job-benefits
4. Carlson, N. (2014, January 10). A Google programmer 'blew off' a $500,000 salary at a startup—because he's already making $3 million every year. *Insider.* https://www.businessinsider.com/a-google-programmer-blew-off-a-500000-salary-at-startup-because-hes-already-making-3-million-every-year-2014-1
5. Filfilan, K. (2017, May 22). How Google rewards employees by paying unfairly. *Change Board.* https://www.changeboard.com/article-details/15204/how-google-rewards-employees-by-paying-unfairly/
6. Feloni, R. (2015, April 11). Inside Google's policy to "pay unfairly"—why 2 people in the same role can earn dramatically different amounts. *Insider.* https://www.businessinsider.com/google-policy-to-pay-unfairly-2015-4
7. Filfilan, K. (2017, May 22). How Google rewards employees by paying unfairly.
8. The Economic Times. (2017, February 16). *You might want to work for Google after seeing these photos.* https://economictimes.indiatimes.com/work-career/you-might-want-to-work-for-google-after-seeing-these-photos/untitled-36-jpg/slideshow/57187317.cms
9. Stewart, J. B. (2013, March 15). Looking for a lesson in Google's perks. *New York Times.* https://www.nytimes.com/2013/03/16/business/at-google-a-place-to-work-and-play.html
10. Yarow, J. (2015, August). Google just announced a massive overhaul of its business structure. *Business Insider.* http://www.businessinsider.com/google-new-operating-structure-2015-8
11. Boris, V. (2020, April 8). How leaders at all levels are taking on change management. *Harvard Business Publishing Corporate Learning.* https://w

ww.harvardbusiness.org/how-leaders-at-all-levels-are-taking-on-change-management/

12. Elias, J. (2020, November 18). Alphabet CFO explains how Google fixed a dip in productivity during the early days of the COVID-19 pandemic. *CNBC.com*. https://www.cnbc.com/2020/11/18/how-google-improved-employee-productivity-during-covid-19-pandemic.html

13. For an overview of change management see Deszca, G., Ingols, C., & Cawsey, T. F. (2020). *Organizational Change—An Action-Oriented Toolkit (4e)*. SAGE; Raina, R. (2020). *Change management and organizational development*. SAGE.

14. Higgs, M., & Rowland, D. (2005). All changes great and small: Exploring approaches to change and its leadership. *Journal of Change Management*, *5*(2), 121–151.

15. Ashkenas, R. (2013, April 16). Change management needs to change: Interaction. *Harvard Business Review*.

https://hbr.org/2013/04/change-management-needs-to-cha

16. Layne, R. (2021, February 10). Has #MeToo changed how Hollywood hires? *Harvard Business School Working Knowledge*. https://hbswk.hbs.edu/item/has-metoo-changed-how-hollywood-hires

17. The DADA syndrome is an adaptation of the Kübler-Ross death and dying model to the context of organizational change as outlined in the following sources: Morano, R. A. (1977, November). How to manage change to reduce stress. *Management Review,66*(11), 21; Rashford, N. S., & Coghan, D. (1996). Phases and levels of organisational change. In J. Billsberry (Ed.), *The effective manager: Perspectives and illustrations* (pp. 119–130). SAGE. Zell, D. (2003, March). Organizational changes as a process of death, dying and rebirth. *Journal of Applied Behavioral Science,39*(1), 73–96.

18. Lewin, K. (1947). Frontiers in group dynamics: Concept, method and reality in social science: social equilibria and social change. *Human Relations,1*, 5–41; Burnes, B. (2004, September). Kurt Lewin and the planned approach to change: A Re-appraisal. *Journal of Management Studies,41*(6), 977–1002; Bakari, H., Hunjra, A. I., & Niazi, G. H. S. (2017, April). How does authentic leadership influence planned organizational change? The role of employees' perceptions: Integration of theory of planned behavior and Lewin's three step model. *Journal of Change Management,17*(2), 155–187.

19. Salzmann, K. (2022, March 30). No mention of 'boys' and 'girls' allowed in Disney parks. *Washington Free Beacon*. https://freebeacon.com/culture/gender-banned-from-disney-parks/

20. Miller, J. R. (2022, March 30). Disney exec vows more gay characters amid huge inclusivity push. *New York Post*. https://nypost.com/2022/03/30/disney-executive-wants-more-lgbtqia-minority-character/

21. Lewin, K. (1951). *Field theory in social science: Selected theoretical papers* (D. Cartwright, Ed.). Harpers; Burnes, Kurt Lewin and the Planned Approach to Change.; Ennis, G. (2017, October). What does it take to change this? *Supervision,78*(10), 15–18.

22. Maxwell, P. D. (2005). Resistance to change and change management. In N. Borkowski & K. A. Meese, *Organizational behavior in health care* (pp. 379–411). Jones and Bartlett; Nelson-Brantley, H. V., & Ford, D. J. (2017, April). Leading change: A concept analysis. *Journal of Advanced Nursing,73*(4), 834–846.

23. Guerra, J. (2021, June 4). 11 Brands that Support the LGBTQ+ community all year round. *In Style*. https://www.instyle.com/fashion/clothing/brands-supporting-lgbtq

24. Raguso, J. (2019, November 6). 3 major companies that are crushing the podcast game. *Msmdesignz.com*. https://www.msmdesignz.com/blog/3-major-companies-that-are-crushing-the-podcast-game/

25. MacLellan, L. (2022, February 21). For some workers, there's a whole life unfolding in the metaverse. *Quartz at Work*. https://qz.com/work/2126161/three-ways-the-metaverse-could-change-future-of-work/

26. Ranjan, N. (2021, February 4). How the pandemic has impacted customer expectations. *Forbes*. https://www.forbes.com/sites/forbesbusinesscouncil/2021/02/04/how-the-pandemic-has-impacted-customer-expectations/?sh=5ed1c9903185

27. Martins, A. (2022, February 1). Most consumers want sustainable products and packaging. *Business News Daily*. https://www.businessnewsdaily.com/15087-consumers-want-sustainable-products.html

28. interObservers. (2021, February 2). *The 15 most eco friendly & sustainable companies*. https://interobservers.com/eco-friendly-products/

29. Segal, E. (2022, March 1). The growing dangers and risks companies face if they do not cut ties with Russia. *Forbes*. https://www.forbes.com/sites/edwardsegal/2022/03/01/the-growing-dangers-and-risks-companies-face-if-they-do-not-cut-ties-with-russia/?sh=6356e6ef2f4c

30. Kelly, J. (2021, October 1). Baby boomers are leaving the workforce to live their best lives in a silver tsunami "great retirement" trend. *Forbes*. https://www.forbes.com/sites/jackkelly/2021/10/01/baby-boomers-are-leaving-the-workforce-to-live-their-best-lives-in-a-silver-tsunami-great-retirement-trend/?sh=3ff8a9d1260b

31. Boitnott, J. (2016, February 9). How the baby boomers' exit will affect the way you do business. *Inc*. https://www.inc.com/john-boitnott/how-to-bridge-the-talent-gap-as-baby-boomers-leave-your-company.html

32. Daniel, T. A. (2003, Summer). Tools for building a positive employee relations environment. *Employment Relations Today,30*(2), 51–64; Positive employee relations key to defeating corporate campaigns. *Management Report for Nonunion Organizations,33*(3), 7–8.

33. Doyle, K. (2021, July 14). Sonia Syngal on leading gap Inc. through the Pandemic. *Insights by Stanford Business*. https://www.gsb.stanford.edu/insights/sonia-syngal-leading-gap-inc-through-pandemic

34. Levitsky, A. (2020, August 11). Mozilla Corp. restructures, lays off 250 employees. *Silicon Valley Business Journal*. https://www.bizjournals.com/sanjose/news/2020/08/11/mozilla-restructures-lays-off-250.html

35. Antoncic, B., & Hisrich, R. D. (2001). Intrapreneurship: Construct refinement and cross-cultural validation. *Journal of Business Venturing, 16*(5), 495–527; Antoncic, B., & Hisrich, R. D. (2003). Clarifying the intrapreneurship concept. *Journal of Small Business and Enterprise Development, 10*(1), 7–24; Blanka, C. (2019). An individual-level perspective on

intrapreneurship: A review and ways forward. *Review of Managerial Science, 13*(5), 919–961.

36. Chamorro-Premuzic, T. (2020, March 26). Why you should become an "Intrapreneur." *Harvard Business Review.* https://hbr.org/2020/03/why-you-should-become-an-intrapreneur

37. Swart, C. (November 19, 2021). Intrapreneurship: How to foster an entrepreneurial culture. *Investec.* https://www.investec.com/en_gb/focus/innovation/intrapreneurship-the-importance-of-fostering-entrepreneurship-at-work.html

38. Deeb, G. (2016, February 18). Big companies must embrace intrapreneurship to survive. *Fortune.* https://www.forbes.com/sites/georgedeeb/2016/02/18/big-companies-must-embrace-intrapreneurship-to-survive/#73caeaa348ab

39. Alas, R. (2015). Resistance to institutional and organizational change: An individual perspective. In *Change management and the human factor: Advances, challenges and contradictions in organizational development* (pp. 153–165). Springer; Amarantou, V., Kazakopoulou, S., Chatzoudes, D., & Chatzoglou, P. (2018). Resistance to change: An empirical investigation of its antecedents. *Journal of Organizational Change Management, 31*(2), 426–450; Kotter, J. P., & Schlesinger, L. A. (1979, March). Choosing strategies for change. *Harvard Business Review, 57*(2), 106–114.

40. Kogan, V. (2020, June 15). Three tips for managing resistance to change. *Forbes.* https://www.forbes.com/sites/forbescoachescouncil/2020/06/15/three-tips-for-managing-resistance-to-change/?sh=6a3673dc642b

41. Torben, R. (2011, May 23). Top 12 reasons why people resist change. www.torbenrick.eu.https://www.torbenrick.eu/blog/change-management/12-reasons-why-people-resist-change/; Creasy, T. (2022, March 31). Understanding why people resist change. *Prosci.* https://blog.prosci.com/understanding-why-people-resist-change

42. Kotter, J. P. (2012, October). Leading change, with a new preface by the author. *Harvard Business School Press Books*; Kang, S. P., Chen, Y., Svihla, V., Gallup, A., Ferris, K., & Datye, A. K. (2022). Guiding change in higher education: An emergent, iterative application of Kotter's change model. *Studies in Higher Education, 47*(2), 270–289.

43. Youngblood, S. A., DeNisi, A. S., Molleston, J. L., & Mobley, W. H. (1984, September). The impact of work environment, instrumentality beliefs, perceived labor union image, and subjective norms on union voting intentions. *Academy of Management Journal, 27*(3), 576–590; Mulder, C. P. (2013, January). Unions' resistance to capital and the potential for class transformation. *Rethinking Marxism, 25*(1), 114–120.

44. Alas, Resistance to institutional and organizational change; Kotter & Schlesinger, "Choosing Strategies for Change."

45. Troyani, L. (2107, May 25). 3 Examples of organizational change done right. *Tiny Pulse.* https://www.tinypulse.com/blog/3-examples-of-organizational-change-and-why-they-got-it-right

46. Southern, M. (2022, May 6). Employee voice in the workplace [Ultimate Guide]. *Oak Engage.* https://www.oak.com/blog/employee-voice/

47. Nisen, M. (2014, May 19). Threatening to fire workers doesn't make them more productive. *Quartz.* https://qz.com/210884/threatening-to-fire-workers-doesnt-make-them-more-productive/

48. Joseph, J., & Gaba, V. (2020). Organizational structure, information processing, and decision-making: A retrospective and road map for research. *Academy of Management Annals, 14*(1), 267–302; Peiró, J. M. (1987). Organizational structure. In P. J. D. Drenth (Ed.), *Advances in organizational psychology: An international review* (pp. 191–206). SAGE.; Bourgeois III, L. J., McAllister, D. W., & Mitchell, T. R. (1978, September). The effects of different organizational environments upon decisions about organizational structure. *Academy of Management Journal, 21*(3), 508–514.

49. Smithson, N. (2018, September 8). Burger King's organizational structure analysis. *Panmore Institute.* http://panmore.com/burger-king-organizational-structure-analysis

50. Lombardo, J. (2019, February 15). Walmart: Organizational structure & organizational culture. *Panmore Institute.* http://panmore.com/walmart-organizational-structure-organizational-culture

51. Schoenherr-Wustl, N. (2019, July 15). Self-managed teams come with a serious warning. *Futurity.* https://www.futurity.org/self-managed-teams-pay-inequity-2104662-2/

52. Mayer, P. (2019, February 14). Starbucks Coffee's organizational structure & its characteristics. *Panmore Institute.* http://panmore.com/starbucks-coffee-company-organizational-structure

53. Zara, C. (2020, October 12). What's happening at Disney? Major changes underway as company doubles down on streaming. *Fast Company.* https://www.fastcompany.com/90563430/whats-happening-at-disney-major-changes-underway-as-company-doubles-down-on-streaming

54. Shepard, J. M. (1969, February). Functional specialization and work attitudes. *Industrial Relations, 8*(2), 185–194; Adiharja, H. S., & Hendarsjah, H. (2020). Analysis of the relationship between personal competencies and individual work performance with job specialization, formalization, and centralization as moderators. *The Asian Journal of Technology Management, 13*(3), 243–256.

55. Ugoani, J. (2021). Understanding the relationship between departmentalization and management performance: First Bank's exemplary model. *International Journal of Environmental Planning and Management, 7*(2), 59–71; Price, J. L. (Winter 1968). The impact of departmentalization on interoccupational cooperation. *Human Organization, 27*(4), 362; Yeh, D., & Jing-Hwa, J. (2002, January). An empirical study of the influence of departmentalization and organizational position on software maintenance. *Journal of Software Maintenance and Evolution: Research and Practice, 14*(1), 65–82.

56. Davis, S. M. (1974, Fall). Two models of organization: Unity of command versus balance of power. *Sloan Management Review, 16*(1), 29–40; Fayol, H. (1949). *General and industrial management* (C. Storrs, Trans.). Sir Isaac Pitman & Sons; Wren, D. A., Bedeian, A. G., & Breeze, J. D. (2002, October). The foundations of Henri Fayol's

administrative theory. *Management Decision,40*(9), 906; Segrest, S. L., Andrews, M. C., Geiger, S. W., Marlin, D., Martinez, P. G., Perrewe, P. L., & Ferris, G. R. (2020). Leapfrogging at work: Influencing higher levels in the chain of command. *Personnel Review, 49*(8), 1769–1786.

57. Wong, C. A., Elliott-Miller, P., Laschinger, H., Cuddihy, M., Meyer, R. M., Keatings, M., Burnett, C., & Szudy, N. (2015, March). Examining the relationships between span of control and manager job and unit performance outcomes. *Journal of Nursing Management,23*(2), 156–168; Entwisle, D. R., & Walton, J. (1961, March). Observations on the span of control. *Administrative Science Quarterly,5*(4), 522–533; Ouchi, W. G., & Dowling, J. B. (1974, September). Defining the span of control. *Administrative Science Quarterly,19*(3), 357–365; Udell, J. G. (1967, December). An empirical test of hypotheses relating to span of control. *Administrative Science Quarterly,12*(3), 420–439; Urwick, L. F. (1956, May). The manager's span of control. *Harvard Business Review,34*(3), 39–47; Urwick, L. F. (1974, June). V. A. Graicunas and the span of control. *Academy of Management Journal,17*(2), 349–354.

58. Steemit. (2017). *What is span of control? And how to use it Google and KFC, and similarities between them.* https://steemit.com/google/@mamunjm/what-is-span-of-control-and-how-to-use-it-google-and-kfc-and-similarities-between-them

59. Real, K., Fay, L., Isaacs, K., Carll-White, A., & Schadler, A. (2018). Using systems theory to examine patient and nurse structures, processes, and outcomes in centralized and decentralized units. *HERD: Health Environments Research & Design Journal, 11*(3), 22–37; Fayol, *General and Industrial Management*; Wren et al., The foundations of Henri Fayol's administrative theory.; Zábojník, J. (2002, January). Centralized and decentralized decision making in organizations. *Journal of Labor Economics,20*(1), 1.

60. See, for example, Fong, K. H., & Snape, E. d. (2015, January). Empowering leadership, psychological empowerment and employee outcomes: Testing a multi-level mediating model. *British Journal of Management,26*(1), 126–138; Frazier, M. L., & Fainshmidt, S. (2012, December). Voice climate, work outcomes, and the mediating role of psychological empowerment: A multilevel examination. *Group and Organization Management,37*(6), 691–715; Choi, I. (2020). Moving beyond mandates: organizational learning culture, empowerment, and performance. *International Journal of Public Administration, 43*(8), 724–735.

61. Courtright, J. A., Fairhurst, G. T., & Rogers, L. E. (1989, December). Interaction patterns in organic and mechanistic system. *Academy of Management Journal,32*(4), 773–802; Gillen, D. J., & Carroll, S. J. (1985, November). Relationship of managerial ability to unit effectiveness in more organic versus more mechanistic departments. *Journal of Management Studies,22*(6), 668–676; Zanzi, A. (1987, March). How organic is your organization? Determinants of organic/mechanistic tendencies in a public accounting firm. *Journal of Management Studies,24*(2), 125–142; Dust, S. B., Resick, C. J., & Mawritz, M. B. (2014, April). Transformational leadership, psychological empowerment, and the moderating role of mechanistic-organic contexts. *Journal of Organizational Behavior,35*(3), 413–433.

62. Ibid.

63. Podsakoff, P. M., Williams, L. J., & Todor, W. D. (1986, December). Effects of organizational formalization on alienation among professionals and nonprofessionals. *Academy of Management Journal,29*(4), 820–831; Peters, G. (1988, September). Organisation as social relationship, formalisation, and standardisation: A Weberian approach to concept formation. *International Sociology,3*(3), 267–282; Mattes, J. (2014, June). Formalisation and flexibilisation in organisations—dynamic and selective approaches in corporate innovation processes. *European Management Journal,32*(3), 475–486; Fischer, R., Ferreira, M. C., Van Meurs, N., Gok, K., Jiang, D.-Y., Fontaine, J. R. J., Harb, C., Cieciuch, J., Achoui, M., Mendoza, M. S. D., Hassan, A., Achmadi, D., Mogaji, A. A., & Abubakar, A. (2019). Does organizational formalization facilitate voice and helping organizational citizenship behaviors? It depends on (national) uncertainty norms. *Journal of International Business Studies, 50*(1), 125–134.

64. Hatch, M. (2022, January 25). 6 strict rules Elon Musk makes his employees follow. *Your Tango.* https://www.yourtango.com/news/rules-elon-musk-employees-follow

65. Kerr, S., & Jermier, J. M. (1978). Substitutes for leadership: Their meaning and measurement. *Organizational Behavior and Human Performance, 22*(3), 375–403.

66. Eva, N., Sendjaya, S., Prajogo, D., & Madison, K. (2021). Does organizational structure render leadership unnecessary? Configurations of formalization and centralization as a substitute and neutralizer of servant leadership. *Journal of Business Research, 129*, 43–56.

67. Toren, N. (1976, July). Bureaucracy and professionalism: A reconsideration of Weber's thesis. *Academy of Management Review,1*(3), 36–46; Spicer, M. W. (2015, January). Public administration in a disenchanted world: Reflections on Max Weber's value pluralism and his views on politics and bureaucracy. *Administration & Society,47*(1), 24–43; Kanter, R. M. (2019). The future of bureaucracy and hierarchy in organizational theory: A report from the field. In P. Bourdieu & J. S. Coleman (Eds.), *Social theory for a changing society* (pp. 63–93). Routledge; Walton, E. J. (2005, April). The persistence of bureaucracy: A meta-analysis of Weber's model of bureaucratic control. *Organization Studies,26*(4), 569–600; Weiss, R. M. (1983, April). Weber on bureaucracy: Management consultant or political theorist? *Academy of Management Review,8*(2), 242–248.

68. Concepts presented in the following discussion are taken in part from these sources: Anand, N., & Daft, R. L. (2007, November). What is the right organization design? *Organizational Dynamics,36*(4), 329–344; Duncan, R. (1979, Winter). What is the right organization structure? Decision tree analysis provides the answer. *Organizational Dynamics,7*(3), 59–80; Galbraith, J. R. (1973). *Designing complex organizations.* Addison-Wesley; Galbraith, J. R. (1977). *Organization design.* Addison-Wesley; Galbraith, J. R. (1971, February). Matrix organization designs. *Business Horizons,14*(1), 29.

69. *Pesico.com.* https://www.pepsico.com/about/about-the-company

70. Joyce, W. F. (1986). Matrix organization: A social experiment. *Academy of Management Journal, 29*(3), 536–561; Sytch, M., Wohlgezogen, F., & Zajac, E. J. (2018). Collaborative by design? How matrix organizations see/do alliances. *Organization Science,29*(6), 1130–1148.

71. Roff, R. (2002, November). Ending the frustration: Engineering people plan engages employees to help bring order, add value to the workplace. *Boeing Frontiers.* https://www.boeing.com/news/frontiers/archive/2002/november/i_ca1.html

72. Bartunek, J. M., & Woodman, R. W. (2012). Organizational development. In K. S. Cameron, & G. M. Spreitzer (Eds.) *The oxford handbook of positive organizational scholarship* (pp. 727–736). Oxford University Press; Frank, D. E. P., Tokarski, K. O., & Gong, J. (2015). *Change management and the human factor: Advances, challenges and contradictions in organizational development*. Springer; Huffington, C., Cole, C, & Brunning, H. (2018). *A manual of organizational development: The psychology of change*. Routledge.

73. For an overview of OD process models see McLean, G. L. (2006). *Organization development: Principles, processes, practices.* Berrett-Koehler.

74. For reviews of differing types of OD interventions see Frank, F., & Brown, L. D. (1974, February). Organization development. *Annual Review of Psychology,25*(1), 313; Neuman, G. A., Edwards, J. E., & Raju, N. S. (1989, September). Organizational development interventions: A meta-analysis of their effects on satisfaction and other attitudes. *Personnel Psychology,42*(3), 461–489; Coghlan, D., & Shani, A. B. R. (2013). Organizational-development research interventions: Perspectives from action research and collaborative management research. In H. S. Leonard, R. L. Arthur, M. Freedman, & J. Passmore (Eds.), *The Wiley-Blackwell handbook of the psychology of leadership, change, and organizational development* (pp. 443–460). Wiley-Blackwell.

75. Margulies, N., Wright, P. L., & Scholl, R. W. (1977, December). Organization development techniques: Their impact on change. *Group and Organization Studies,2*(4), 428–448; Kiel, J. M. (2016, October). Using organizational development for electronic medical record transformation. *The Health Care Manager,35*(4), 305–311.

76. BasuMallick, C. (2021, March 11). 4 Companies that have nailed their employee recognition strategy. *Toolbox HR.* https://www.toolbox.com/hr/employee-recognition/articles/employee-recognition-strategy-e xamples/

77. Beer, M. (2021, December 14). To change your company's culture, don't start by trying to change the culture. *Harvard Business School Working Knowledge.* https://hbswk.hbs.edu/item/to-change-your-companys-culture-dont-start-by-trying-to-change-the-culture

78. Zappos. *Holacracy and self-organization.* https://www.zapposinsights.com/about/holacracy

79. Margulies et al., "Organization Development Techniques."

80. Partida, D. (2021, April 27). The top 6 ways AI is improving business productivity. *Techopedia.com.* https://www.techopedia.com/the-top-6-ways-ai-is-improving-business-productivity-in-2021/2/34505

81. Emery, F. (1993). Characteristics of socio-technical systems. In B. Trist (Ed.), *The social engagement of social science: A Tavistock anthology, Volume 2: The socio-technical perspective* (pp. 157–186). University of Pennsylvania Press; van Eijnatten F. M. (1998). Developments in socio-technical systems design (STSD). In *Handbook of work and organizational psychology Volume 4: Organizational psychology* (2nd ed., pp. 61–88). Psychology Press/Erlbaum (UK)/Taylor & Francis.; Hughes, H. P. N., Clegg, C. W., Bolton, L. E., & Machon, L. C. (2017, October). Systems scenarios: A tool for facilitating the socio-technical design of work systems. *Ergonomics,60*(10), 1319–1335.

82. Hammer, L. & Zimmerman, K. L. (2011). Quality of work life. In S. Zedeck (Ed.), *APA handbook of industrial and organizational psychology. Vol 3: Maintaining, expanding, and contracting the organization* (pp. 399–431). American Psychological Association; Kocman, A. & Weber, G. (2018, January). Job satisfaction, quality of work life and work motivation in employees with intellectual disability: A systematic review. *Journal of Applied Research in Intellectual Disabilities,31*(1), 1–22.

83. Wilson, A. (2020, March 12). 10 businesses that have mastered work/life balance. *Workstars.com.* https://www.workstars.com/recognition-and-engagement-blog/2020/03/12/10-businesses-that-have-mastered-work-life-balance/

84. Lomranz, J. Lakin, M., & Schiffman, H. (1973, June) A three-valued typology for sensitivity training and encounter groups. *Human Relations,26*(3), 339; Nikels, H. J., Mims, G. A., & Mims, M. J. (2007, June). Allies against hate: A school-based diversity sensitivity training experience. *Journal for Specialists in Group Work, 32*(2), 126–138; Thurman, D. (2021). The cultural lives of sensitivity training. *American Quarterly,73*(2), 285–309.

85. NASCAR requires Kyle Busch to take sensitivity training. (2021, November 1). *NASCAR.com.* https://m.nascar.com/news-media/2021/11/01/nascar-requires-kyle-busch-to-take-sensitivity-training/

86. Jason, L. A., Ferone, L., & Anderegg, T. (Summer 1979). Evaluating ecological, behavioral, and process consultation interventions. *Journal of School Psychology,17*(2), 103–115; Lipshitz, R. & Sherwood, J. J. (1978, October). The effectiveness of third-party processes consultation as a function of the consultant's prestige and style of intervention. *Journal of Applied Behavioral Science, 14*(4), 493–509; Lalonde, C., & Adler, C. (2015). Information asymmetry in process consultation: An empirical research on leader-client/consultant relationship in healthcare organizations. *Leadership & Organization Development Journal, 36*(2), 177–211; Kwon, K., Lee, J. Y., Park, J. G., & Zaballero, A.G. (2020). Process consultation within and across cultures. *The Journal of Applied Behavioral Science, 56*(3), 322–346.

87. Beauchamp, M. R., McEwan, D., & Waldhauser, K. J. (2017, August). Team building: Conceptual, methodological, and applied considerations. *Current Opinion in Psychology,16*, 114–117; Dyer, W. G., Dyer Jr., W.

G., & Dyer, J. H. (2007). *Team building: Proven strategies for improving team performance, 4e*. Jossey-Bass; Murrell, K., & Valsan, E. H. (1985). A team-building workshop as an OD intervention in Egypt. *Leadership and Organization Development Journal, 6*(2), 11–16.

88. Randolph, W. A., & Posner, B. Z. (1982, September). The effects of an intergroup development OD intervention as conditioned by the life cycle state of organizations: A laboratory experiment. *Group and Organization Studies, 7*(3), 335–352; Killen, M.,, Hitti, A., & Mulvey, K. L. (2015). Social development and intergroup relations. In M. Mikulincer, P. R. Shaver., E. Borgida., & J. A. Bargh (Eds.), *APA handbook of personality and social psychology.Vol. 2: Group processes* (pp. 177–201). American Psychological Association.

89. The Editors of Encyclopaedia Britannica. (2018). General electric: American corporation. *Encyclopaedia Britannica*. https://www.britannica.com/topic/General-Electric

90. Immelt, J. R. (2017, September-October). How I remade GE. *Harvard Business Review*, 2017 Issue. https://hbr.org/2017/09/inside-ges-transformation

91. Hansen, S. (2022, January 24). The rise and fall of General Electric (GE). *Investopedia*. https://www.investopedia.com/insights/rise-and-fall-ge/

92. Immelt, How I remade GE.

93. Ibid.

94. Ibid.

95. Hartzell, S. (2021, August 13). Lewin's 3-stage model of change: Unfreezing, changing & refreezing. *Study.com*. https://study.com/academy/lesson/lewins-3-stage-model-of-change-unfreezing-changing-refreezing.html

96. The Week Staff. (2015, April 18). The end of GE Capital. *The Week*. https://theweek.com/articles/550122/end-ge-capital

97. General Electric. (n.d.). *GE Surpassed $5 billion in research & development*. https://www.ge.com/news/press-releases/ge-surpassed-5-billion-research-development

98. General Electric. (n.d.). *GE Locations Directory / GE Countries*. https://www.ge.com/directory

99. Randewich, N., & Scott, A. (2018, June 19). General Electric loses place in Elite Dow Jones industrial average. *Reuters*. https://www.reuters.com/article/us-walgreens-boots-ge/general-electric-loses-place-in-elite-dow-jones-industrial-average-idUSKBN1JF359

100. Clough, R., & Kochkodin, B. (2018, February 23). GE cuts $2.4 billion from biggest pension deficit on S&P 500. *Bloomberg*. https://www.bloomberg.com/news/articles/2018-02-23/general-electric-cuts-2-4-billion-off-s-p-worst-pension-deficit

NAME INDEX

SUBJECT INDEX